GEARRFAR FÍNEÁIL AR DHAOINE A BHFUIL
LEABHAIR THAR TÉARMA ACU
FINES WILL BE CHARGED ON OVERDUE BOOKS

AR AIS FAOIN DÁTA DATE DUE	AR AIS FAOIN DÁTA DATE DUE
16 MAR 1995	2 0 DEC 2011
2 6 JAN 2005	
9/11/06	
24/4/75	
02 MAR 2009	
17 FEB 2010	
0 2 MAR 2009	
0 2 JUN 2011	

The Heroic Process
Form, Function and Fantasy in Folk Epic

The Proceedings of the International Folk Epic Conference
University College Dublin
2 – 6 September 1985

Edited by

BO ALMQVIST
SÉAMAS Ó CATHÁIN
PÁDRAIG Ó HÉALAÍ

THE GLENDALE PRESS

First published 1987 by

The Glendale Press
18 Sharavogue
Glenageary Rd. Upper
Dun Laoghaire
Co. Dublin
Ireland

ISBN 0 907606 45 8

This edition is limited to seven hundred and fifty copies

Jacket illustration: Brush drawing *The Taín*, Louis le Brocquy
Jacket design: David L. Murphy

Typeset by Print Prep, Dublin

CONTENTS

iii

PREFACE

These Proceedings of the International Folk Epic Conference, organized by the Department of Irish Folklore and held at University College Dublin from 2 — 6 September 1985, contain most of the papers delivered on that occasion. The Conference was held in commemoration of both the one hundred and fiftieth anniversary of the publication of the Finnish folk epic, *Kalevala* (1835-1985) and of the fiftieth anniversary of the commencement of systematic and large-scale folklore collecting in Ireland with the establishment in 1935 of the Irish Folklore Commission — later the Department of Irish Folklore.

It has not been possible to include here the comments of the distinguished band of official *rapporteurs* to the Conference — Professor Michael Branch of the University of London, Professor Anna-Leena Siikala of Helsinki University, Dr Ruth Finnegan of the Open University, United Kingdom, and Dr Donald Archie MacDonald of the University of Edinburgh. However, their contributions and the commentaries provided by other Conference speakers and delegates have been incorporated to some extent in the revised form of the papers printed here.

The publication of this book marks the end of a process begun nearly four years ago when Michael Branch, Director of the School of East European and Slavonic Studies at the University of London and himself a scholar in the field of Finnish and Fenno-Ugric studies, paid a visit to the Department of Irish Folklore at University College Dublin. The seed sown on that occasion has grown into this large volume.

Though the Finnish and Irish achievement was honoured in the holding of the International Folk Epic Conference and this achievement is again highlighted — in more permanent fashion — by the appearance of these Proceedings, the range of the papers delivered extends far beyond Finland and Ireland — and even beyond the Fenno-Ugric or Celtic worlds.

The editing and proof-reading of this volume has been beset with many difficulties due to the variety of languages and subject matter involved in the articles. We have received expert assistance from various colleagues in solving particular problems; our special thanks are due to David Evans, Kevin O'Nolan and David Wasserstein. Nevertheless, there are bound to be faults and failings for which we accept full responsibility. We would wish to emphasize, however, that inconsistencies may be only apparent, due to the divergences between Old and Modern Irish forms or to differences in Irish and Scottish Gaelic terminology. In our capacity as editors, we especially appreciate the excellent co-operation with the many authors as well as the efficiency of the Glendale Press and its printers and typesetter.

Finally, our special thanks are due to the Folklore of Ireland Society and to the Ministry of Education, Helsinki, for material help without which publication would not have been possible.

Baile Átha Cliath agus Gaillimh   *Lá Fhéile Bríde*

BO ALMQVIST   SÉAMAS Ó CATHÁIN   PÁDRAIG Ó HÉALAÍ

Pages 1-264 also published in *Béaloideas*, Vols. 54-5, 1986-7.

PLACENAMES, ETYMOLOGY, AND THE STRUCTURE OF *FIANAIGECHT**

ROLF BAUMGARTEN
(Dublin Institute for Advanced Studies)

In the literary critic's mind onomastics will not figure prominently as a *Hilfswissenschaft*. For medieval Irish literature, however, the consideration of proper names (and placenames in particular) as functional elements is of unusual interest. Placenames may be considered in the following contexts: itineraries and catalogues of names, symbolism, etymology, and the provenance of a story. My main concern here is with etymology. This includes eponymic aetiology; the terms 'etymology', and 'etymologizing' will be used throughout in a sense to be explained presently.

One must bear in mind that the medieval study of language and proper names is epistemologically different from modern linguistics and onomastics. Yet even E.R. Curtius, in an appendix to his work *European Literature and the Latin Middle Ages* (London 1953), entitled 'Etymology as a category of thought' failed to do justice to etymology as a branch of medieval science. In fact, constant modern abuse and ridicule directed towards its results, has prevented its appreciation. It is unfortunate that it shares its name with a branch of modern historical and comparative linguistics. The foundations of medieval philosophical etymology are described, e.g. by Isidore in his *Etymologiae* I, xxix (for the details of which I refer to a paper in the Medieval Academy of Ireland journal, *Peritia* 2 (1983) 225-8). This early seventh-century work by the bishop of Seville had an immediate and lasting influence

*I am grateful to Tomás Ó Cathasaigh and to Liam Breatnach for helpful criticism.

1

on the Irish scholarly scene.[1] The key sentence there is *Omnis enim rei inspectio etymologia cognita planior est*. In other words, etymology serves the knowledge of things through the comprehension of language. The underlying philosophy is aptly expressed in an Old Irish gloss on Psalm 15, in the Milan codex (or rather, a gloss on a Latin commentary): Ml. 37a14 *Is fó dobertar inna anman fonna inni fordingrat*, 'the names are given in accordance with the qualities they signify'.[2] The methodology is not defined in any detail. In the typical Irish glossary entry (and I will deal with etymologizing in literature in a moment), the lemma is usually a nominal (including proper names and epithets), whose 'meaning' (*vis*) is explained (with or without a quotation) using linguistic forms which are both phonetically and semantically suitable, either by direct 'derivation' and 'equation', or through an intermediate stage of adapting the lemma, or after the resolution of the lemma into components.[3] Furthermore, medieval etymology does not aim at unique solutions, so that we may find several different explanations closely following on each other.

Early Irish scholars married paronomasia (punning) and folk etymology, with medieval scientific etymology, and developed it into a fine art.[4] One could say that they became more Isidorean than Isidore himself. They seemingly did not accept Isidore's *caveat* that some words and names cannot be etymoligized. Etymologizing of proper names permeates all

---

1 See J.N. Hillgarth, 'Ireland and Spain in the seventh century', *Peritia* 3 (1984), 1-16.

2 *Thesaurus Palaeohibernicus*, ed. Wh. Stokes and J. Strachan, Cambridge 1901-3, Vol. 1, 94.

3 The very term for 'etymology' in early Irish (or for one of its procedures) is, I suggest, the result of etymology: *bélrae n-etarscartha* lit. 'language of separation', looks like a loan-translation of *etymologia*, viz. *bélrae* representing *-logia*; and *etymo(n)*, etymologized through Greek τέμνω 'to cut', represented by *etarscarad*, 'cutting'.

4 It was labelled by Osborn Bergin in his 1938 Rhŷs lecture as the 'pseudo-science of etymology' ('The native Irish grammarian', *Proceedings of the British Academy* 24 (1938), 205); he adds (p. 206): 'It resulted in an enormous waste of time and energy in futile speculation'.

genres of (especially earlier) medieval Irish literature.[5] It occurs in a variety of functions and realizations. Formally, literary etymologizing is either implicit, or (through narrator's intrusion) introduced by *.i.*, and/or formally concluded by *is de atá X*, 'therefore there is X', which alternates with *is de asber(a)r X*, 'therefore X is so called'; or, even, framed by question and conclusion.

In the following, I shall discuss first of all two instances of literary etymologizing, both of which are, functionally, constituent parts of the narrative progression — while formally, the first is implicit, and the second explicit, viz. (i) the name of Finn's son *Oisín*, and (ii) the name of the Otherworld people, *aes síde*. After that I shall discuss two instances where etymologies of several different placenames are interwoven for another literary purpose; I shall call this 'creative etymologizing': (iii) the first half of the tale *Bruiden Átha hÍ*, and (iv) one of the versions of the Death of Finn.

Before we go on to the examples, let me briefly mention some collections of etymologies made during the eleventh and twelfth centuries, viz. the *Dindsenchas*,[6] i.e. placename explanations, overtly didactic, in verse with prose abstracts; *Cóir Anmann*,[7] a handbook of heterogeneous personal name and epithet explanations; and *Acallam na Senórach*,[8] a

---

5 It is worthwhile quoting the cynical comment by John B. Arthurs, who, taking his cue from a line-cheville in (cf. fn. 6) *MDs* 3, 460.23 (*ní rosmairn mesce 'malle*), says about these etymologies: 'With all this one might well accept a poet's assertion that "strong drink hath not confounded" these things, i.e. that it hath clarified them for him' ('The Legends of Place-Names', *Ulster Folklife* [1] (1955), 39).

6 E. Gwynn, ed., *The Metrical Dindsenchas*, 5 Vols., Dublin 1903-35 (*R.I.A. Todd Lecture Series*, Vols. 8-12) [abbrev.: *MDs*]. — Wh. Stokes, ed., 'The prose tales in the Rennes *Dindsenchas*', *Revue Celtique* 15 (1894) 272-336, 418-84; 16 (1895) 31-83, 135-67, 269-312 [abbrev.: *Ds*]. — Ch. Bowen, 'A Historical Inventory of the *Dindsenchas*', *Studia Celtica* 10-11 (1975-6), 113-37.

7 Wh. Stokes, ed., '*Cóir Anmann* (Fitness of names)', in *Irische Texte*, Vol. 3, Part 2, Leipzig 1897, 285-444.

8 Wh. Stokes., ed., *Acallamh na Senórach*, in *Irische Texte*, Vol. 4, Part 1, Leipzig 1900 [abbrev.: *AS*], — Nessa Ní Shéaghdha, ed., *Agallamh na Seanórach*, 3 Vols., Baile Átha Cliath 1942-5 (*Leabhair ó Láimhsgríbhnibh*, Vols. 7, 10, 15) [abbrev.: *AS²*].

Rahmenerzählung of a meeting of St Patrick with survivors of Finn's Fian, who, during a circuit of Ireland, tell Patrick and his scribe tales and episodes which provide Fenian explanations of the placenames en route.

(i) *Oisín*

On a margin in the Book of Leinster (twelfth century) are extant two quatrains on the mothers of two of the Fenian heroes, viz. Diarmait ua Duibne and Oisín. They occur in association with the *Dindsenchas* poem 'Áth Liac Find cid dia tá', 'Ford of the Stone of Finn', (*LL* 21821ff; cf. note 14):

1. Mathair Diarmata on Daíl	'The daughter of Currech mac Cathaír[9]
ingen Churrig meic Cathaír,	was the mother of Diarmait from the river Dael,
is Blaı Derg din Banbai braiss	And Blaı Derg from great Banba
mathair Ossıne amnaiss.	was the mother of strong Oisın(e).'[10]

Blaí's name elsewhere[11] is *Bla ingen (in) Deirg Dianscothaig*, i.e. her father's name (a fosterbrother of Caílte's) is *Derg Dianscothach*. Thus, we either read *Blai De[i]rg*, lit. 'Blai of Derg', short for 'daughter of Derg', or we take (as I have done) *Derg* as an *ad hoc* epithet of her own, which, at the same time, hints at her father's name ('the Red'), and is a

---

9. Her name is *Cochrann* in the Rawlinson genealogies of the Lagin (M.A. O'Brien, ed., *Corpus Genealogiarum Hiberniae*, Dublin 1962, 121a32): *Cuirrech mac Cathaír, díbad a chland ar non habuit nisi unus filius Slechtaire qui cecidit la Find 7 una filia id est Cochrann máthair Diarmata meic Duib m. Duibne 7rl.* — *Currech* will be discussed below in the context of *Bruiden Átha hÍ*; for *Slechtaire* cf. note 47.

10. *Oisíne/oisíne* are variants of the more usual *Oisín/oisín* (cf. K. Meyer, *Fianaigecht*, Dublin 1910 (*R.I.A. Todd Lecture Series*, Vol. 16), xviii, note 3).

11. *AS* 50: *dochuaidh Oisín co Sídh Ochta Cleitigh, bhail a raibhe a mháthair .i. Bla inghean Deirc Dhianscothaig; Banshenchus* (ed. M.C. Dobbs, *Revue Celtique* 48 (1931), 214): *Bla ingen in Deirg Dianscothaig, mathair Oisin m. Find*.

suitable epithet of a deer in the shape of which she appears in the next quatrain.[12]

2. Ticed i rricht eilte [i̧lle]　　'She used to come hither in
　　　　　　　　　　　　　　　　　the shape of a deer
　　hi comdáil na díbergge　　　to meet the warrior band,
　　co ndernad ossine de　　　　So　that　thereof　a　fawn
　　　　　　　　　　　　　　　　　(*oisin(e)*) was begotten
　　ri Blaı nDeirgg i rricht　　　on Blaı Derg while she was in
　　eilte.　　　　　　　　　　　　the shape of a deer.'

In the first line, instead of my additional *ille* (with elision of the initial vowel), K. Meyer[13] supplied *Ticed [Blaí] i rricht eilte* to account for the missing syllable, but this results in an imperfect end-rhyme. Unlike Meyer and the editors of the Book of Leinster diplomatic edition,[14] who took *oisín* here to be the proper name, I take it to be an appellative (to be spelt with a lower case initial), because this is etymologizing at work: it explains the name of her son *Oisín* from the fact that, when Blaí conceived in the shape of a deer, she conceived a fawn (*oisín*); the possible formal conclusion, viz. 'this is why her son is called *Oisín*', does not occur here. The father is not mentioned, but he is everywhere else said to be Finn, i.e. the leader of a *díberg* or *fian*.[15]

12　I shall not discuss here T.F. O'Rahilly's notion of *Derg* being a name for the ancestor-deity among the Lagin (v. *Early Irish History and Mythology*, Dublin 1957, 126, note 2).

13　*Op. cit.*, xxvi.

14.　See *The Book of Leinster*, ed. R.I. Best & M.A. O'Brien, Vol. 3, Dublin 1957, 729. [This diplomatic edition of the manuscript will be referred to by *LL*, with line-number.]

15　See K. McCone, '*Aided Cheltchair Maic Uthechair*: Hounds, Heroes and Hospitallers in Early Irish Myth and Story', *Ériu* 35 (1984), 1-30. The daughter of Derg is the main actor in the 'Ballad of the mantle', where she brings her chastity-testing cloak to test the Fian's women, including Finn's then wife Maighean (or Maighinis). She identifies herself to Finn's company (quatrain 20, v. L. Chr. Stern, 'Die gaelische Ballade vom Mantel in Macgregors Liederbuche', *Zeitschrift für celtische Philologie* 1 (1897), 294-326; this quatrain is not found in the *Duanaire Finn* version of the ballad, *La da raibh Fionn ag ol*, v. G. Murphy, ed., *Duanaire Finn*, Part II, London 1933 (Irish Texts Society, Vol. 28), 330). The quatrain reads

(ii) *Aes síde*

From the point of view of etymology, the mythological tale *Echtra Conli*, 'Conle's faring forth to the Otherworld', is of unusual interest in more than one way. It functions (in its extant form) as an explanation of the name of Conle's brother *Art Oenfer*, 'Art the Lone', who is alone after Conle's departure. It has, in one version, an 'extraneous etymological frame', i.e. its etymologizing function rests on information supplied in the frame, though it lacks relevance for the embedded *echtra* proper.[16]

Within the tale there is an etymology of *aes síde*, 'people of the Otherworld', as given by the Otherworld woman in the course of introducing herself and her place of origin. It is explicit and in direct speech.

Caínchomracc lenn cen debuith. Síd már i táam[17] *conid de suidiu nonn-ainmnigther 'áess síde'.*[18]

I translate:
'There is fair play in our land without strife. We live in great peace (*síd*); therefore we are called *aes síde*.'
Only Thurneysen understood this rightly,[19] in my opinion. It

(in Classical Modern Irish spelling by G. Murphy, *Duanaire Finn*, Part III, Dublin 1953 (Irish Texts Society, Vol. 34), 160): *Tabhraidh mo bhrat domh, a mhná, / 's mé inghean an Deirg ghránna, / nocha dhearnas*[-*sa*] *do locht / acht feis re Fionn faobharnocht*, 'Give me my cloak, o woman, I am the daughter of the hateful Dearg. To have slept with Fionn of the unsheathed weapons is the only fault I have committed.' This is another reference to the liaison of Bla(i) with Finn implied in the above etymologizing quatrain on Oisín's mother. (See also T.P. Cross, 'The Gaelic "Ballad of the Mantle" ', *Modern Philology* 16 (1918-9), 153-62.)

16 I am at variance with J. Carney as regards the analysis of this tale ('The Deeper Level of Early Irish Literature', *Capuchin Annual* 1969, 160-71).

17 For the idiom with the preposition *i*, cf. e.g. *Bai sidhe hi cocadh fri Find* (L.-Chr. Stern, 'Le manuscript irlandais de Leide', *Revue Celtique* 13 (1892), 7).

18 J. Pokorny, 'Conle's abenteuerliche Fahrt', *Zeitschrift für celtische Philologie* 17 (1928), 193-205, § 1.

19 See *Zeitschrift für vergleichende Sprachforschung* 28 (1887), 292:
    — See also T. Ó Cathasaigh, 'The Semantics of *Síd*', *Éigse* 17 (1977-8), 137ff.

etymologizes *aes síde*, 'people of the Otherworld', through the homonym *síd*, 'peace', on account of there being great peace there.

The following are two instances of literary etymology of a more complex nature, where several etymologies are interwoven to provide the substance and structure of the tale, as well as certain intertextural features,[20] the phenomenon for which I proposed above the term 'creative etymologizing'.

(iii) *'Bruiden Átha hÍ'*

The Fenian tale entitled *Bruiden Átha hÍ*, 'The Hostel at Áth hÍ', is clearly Old Irish, linguistically (with the exception of those innovations which arose in the course of transmission) and stylistically. K. Meyer first edited it in 1893 from the R.I.A. manuscript[21] (later, in *Fianaigecht*, xix, he revised his original dating to the ninth century); V. Hull based his edition[22] on the Yellow Book of Lecan (=YBL) and dated the composition to the eighth century. I hesitate to subscribe to the latter dating, e.g. because of the occurrence of *ro*-preterites in narrative. In the following first half (approximately) of the tale I have introduced slight changes in the text (using both Mss, i.e. T.C.D. YBL 212a8 (= col. 951) and R.I.A. D iv 2, fo. 88 (66) m), that will make it more easily readable, without trying to reconstruct it to Old Irish.

> Bruiden Átha hÍ inso sís.
>
> Fecht do Find hua Baíscne i Cinn Chuirrig. Baí-sium cen mnaí fri ré cian. Luid-sium didiu dochum na Siúire co n-accae in n-ingin mbachlaig oc Dún Iascaig oc folcad a

---

20　See Anne Heinrichs, ' "Intertexture" and its functions in early written sagas . . .', *Scandinavian Studies* 48 (1976), 127-45. She says (127): 'A feature, then, is "intertextural" when it, as one part of a text, points directly to another part of the text that appears sooner or later . . . The text to come may be anticipated by the audience beforehand, or it may come as a revelation when it occurs, the author allowing a connection to appear only then.' [Tomás Ó Cathasaigh kindly provided me with a copy of this paper.]

21　'Two Tales about Finn', *Revue Celtique* 14 (1893), 241-9.

22　'Two Tales about Find', *Speculum* 16 (1941), 322-33.

cinn. Bodamair a hainm-side. Conda tuc (laiss) co mboí ina
farrad.

Currech Lifi do Laignib dia tá Ráith Churrig, is é ro
marb a chomalta-som .i. Dub hua Duibne dia rabae Diarmait
macc Duib maic Duibne. Luid Find didiu fecht n-aill do
thetarracht allae for Currech. Doluid Currech siar co tallad
a cenn dia mnaí-sium .i. do Bodamair conda ruc lais sair.
Doluid didiu Find ina diaid-sium co ruc a chenn de-sium.

Is de atá Cenn Currig. Is de ro cét
Currech Lifi cona lí ní cach rí dia rodamair,
rucad uad a chenn i céin cosa sliab ós Bodamair.

Mac máthar do Fothad Canainne in Currech sin. Boí-
sium didiu for écill Finn co ndernsat córai. Co nderna Find
coirm do Fothad. Ro cuired iarum don chormaim. Asbert
Fothad: 'Is geis dam-sa ól corma conid fri haigthi bána
adlústar.' — 'Ní hurusa didiu a n-í-sin. Atá cáin Cormaic i
nÉre co cenn secht mbliadnae nad rubthar guin duini,' ol
Find, 'acht cena atát rudilsi gona duini ar ind (?) .i. Slige
Midluachra, Áth Fir Diad, Áth Cliath, Belach nGabráin,
Áth Noa, Cnámchaill, Conachlad, Dá Chích Anann for
Luachair Dedad.' Luid iarum Find corici Dá Chích Anann
do tharrachtain gona duini.

'Tiagam,' ol Téit[e] ingen Macniad, siur Fothaid Canainne . . .

'The following is the tale of the Hostel at Áth hÍ.

Once Finn ua Baíscne was at Cenn Currig. He was without a woman for a long time. So he went to the river Siúir
and saw a young peasant woman washing her head at Dún
Iascaig. Bodamair was her name. And he took her (with
him), and she stayed with him.

Currech of Life of the Leinstermen, from whom there is
Ráth Churrig, had killed his fosterbrother Dub ua Duibne,
from whom came to be Diarmait mac Duib maic Duibne.
So Finn went on another occasion on a raid over there
after [or to the detriment of] Currech.[23] Currech, for his

23 Dub was Finn's foster-brother as well as the father of a member of
    his Fian. Finn's location at this occasion is uncertain, though it

part, went west to cut his wife Bodamair's head off, and he took it with him to the east.[24] So Finn went after him and took his head off. Therefrom there is Cenn Currig. Of this was sung:

Currech of Life with his splendour, it was not just any king to whom he yielded. His head was carried far from him to the mountain above Bodamair.[25]

The said Currech had the same mother as Fothad Canainne. So the latter was lying in wait for Finn until they made peace. And Finn prepared a feast for Fothad. He was then invited to the feast.[26] Fothad said: "It is a *geis* of mine to partake in a feast, unless it is partaken in the company of cut-off heads."

"That is not easy to arrange. There is the *cáin* of Cormac

must have been considerably further north than Dún Iascaig, even if we don't take 'west' and 'east' of the following sentence literally in the modern geographical sense.

24 The use of infixed -*da*- for masculine or neuter in the singular is rare in Old Irish.

25 The name occurs as *Bodamair/Badamair* and as *Bodammair/Badammair* (with non-lenited *m*). For the latter see e.g. 'Conall Corc and the Corco Luigde' (ed. K. Meyer, *Anecdota from Irish Manuscripts*, Vol. 3, Halle 1910), 62.27: *Is de Feidlimthig mac Tigernaich. Ba rí Muman. Ni luid hi Caisel, acht classa Bodumbir lais,* (cf. V. Hull, *Proceedings of the Modern Language Association of America* 42 (1947), 905). In our case the name has a lenited *m*, as shown by the rhyme with -*rodamair* (3 sg. *ro*-pret. of *daimid*); the possible variant -*radamair* would take *Badamair* as its rhyme.

26 I assume that there was an early simple verb *cuirithir* 'fetches, invites' (cf. Modern Irish *cuireadh* 'invitation') which formed its perfect with *ro* (as our form *ro cuired*), similar to the compound *do-cuirethar* 'invites' beside *do-cuirethar* 'puts, throws' (suppletive perfect passive *do-ralad*), as postulated by R. Thurneysen, *A Grammar of Old Irish*, Dublin 1946, § 762; see also H. Pedersen, *Vergleichende Grammatik der keltischen Sprachen*, Vol. 2, Göttingen 1913, 498. D. Greene's comment on the relevant forms in *Orgain Denna Ríg* (v. *Fingal Rónáin, and Other Stories*, Dublin 1955, 68): '*do-cuirethar* (the finite forms here have *ro*- substituted for *do*-) "invites" ' is not convincing.

in Ireland for seven years which prevents manslaying,"[27] said Finn, "but there is permissible manslaying beyond the edge [of the territory],[28] viz. Slige Midluachra, Áth Fir Diad, Áth Cliath, Belach nGabráin, Áth Noa, Cnámchaill, Conachlad, Dá Chích Anann in Luachair Dedad." Then Finn went to Dá Chích Anann in search of manslaying.

"Let us go," said Téite, daughter of Macnia and sister of Fothad Canainne . . .'

The second half of the tale describes, with some interesting dramatic dialogue, how Finn unwittingly kills Fothad's sister and her companion, who were on their way to Finn's feast for Fothad. This, tragically, brings about the perpetuation of the enmity with Fothad, the termination of which Finn was about to celebrate.

27 The *cáin* of a king is the integrity of the system, based on the king's *fírinne* 'righteousness', and the observation of his *gesa* 'prohibitions'. The period of seven years is unusual if it refers to the interval between two *feis Temrach*, at which the *cáin* would be reaffirmed, as 'The Irish ordeals' § 55 takes it (ed. Wh. Stokes, in *Irische Texte*, Vol. 3, Part 1, Leipzig 1891); cf. the following note. I shall propose a different interpretation of this phrase below.

28 For *ar ind*, the Mss read *ar F*ind (YBL), *ar Fi*[*n*]*d* (D iv 2), 'said Finn', as in the preceding line. 'The Irish ordeals' (cf. the preceding note), which uses this passage, and which reports (though not as speech) *acht cena . . . Anann* almost verbatim, reads *acht cheana badar rudilsi gona duine ann .i. . . .*; it adds 'If it were in one of these places that any man avenged his wrong no retaliation was made upon him'. P. Ó Riain does not deal with this aspect in his paper 'Boundary Association in Early Irish Society', *Studia Celtica* 7 (1972), 12-29. The list of names (I mentioned in the beginning itineraries and catalogues amongst the contexts of appraisal of proper names in literature), which here suspends the action, calls for closer investigation elsewhere. It lists (stereotyped) frontier-names, as is already apparent from the generics *slige, áth, belach*. It is highly charged 'semantically', thus creating a suitable atmosphere for the ensuing killing: *Áth Fir Diad*, where Cú Chulainn kills Fer Diad in *Táin Bó Cuailgne*; *Áth Cliath* may be (unless the list can be shown to be otherwise geographically ordered) *Áth Cliath Medraige*, the grave of the seven sons of Ailill Ólom in *Cath Maige Mucrama* (and *Orgain Átha Cliath* of the tale-lists [cf. the following note] may be an alternative title); *Cnámchaill* translates as 'The Wood of the Bones'; etc.

Concerning the title *Bruiden Átha hÍ* (the age of which is uncertain), I am not sure whether *bruiden* here is intended to mean 'hall', or 'hostile encounter (in a hall)'. In the meaning 'hall', *bruiden* is, in the earlier period, followed by the name of the proprietor.[29] In *Acallam na Senórach* there are two references to a *bruiden* (*bruigen*), 'a hostile encounter', between Fothad and Finn. The first occurs in the story of *Tulach in Trír*,[30] 'The Hill of the Three', where three daughters of the king of Scotland die of grief for their three Fenian lovers of twenty years standing, who were killed in Leinster in a *bruiden* between Finn and [Fathad Canann] mac Mic Con maic Maicnia[d].[31] The text adds 'and the poets give no numbers of the losses of the Fianna and of the people of Fathad Canann there.' (3397-8). The second occurs in the story of *Cnoc in Eoluis*[32], 'The Hill of Knowledge'. There Finn's druid, while auguring from the clouds, sees the place where a *bruiden* will be brought about by Fathad Canann mac Meic Con mheic Mhaicniadh. Above it he sees three threatening clouds (*nél(l) glan, nél(l) glas*, and *nél(l) derg*), an augury of slaughter and destruction (reminiscent of the bloody prophecy preceding the march in *Táin Bó Cuailgne*).[33] Our

---

29 For the five or six royal *bruidne* (banqueting-halls) of early Irish tradition, see T.F. O'Rahilly, *op. cit.*, 121ff. There are no titles beginning with *Bruiden* in the Middle Irish tale-lists (v. P. Mac Cana, *The Learned Tales of Medieval Ireland*, Dublin 1980); there are several *Togail bruidne* ... Of the latter, *Togail Bruidne Da Derga* and *Togail Bruidne Da Choca* are entitled *Bruiden* ... in some manuscripts of Modern Irish provenance. For the development of the meaning of *bruiden*, see (most recently) Mac Cana, *op. cit.*, 97 with note 77.

30 *AS* 3383, cf. *AS*[2] 2, 153.6.

31 I shall explain the reversal of Fothad's ascendants here and in the following instance, which are based on the misunderstanding of a rhetorical passage in *Bruiden Átha hÍ*, when editing the whole of the latter text elsewhere. (By way of etymological antonomasia, *Mac Con* is referred to as *cana(nn)* 'whelp', as in his grandson Fothad *Cana(i)nn(e)*'s by-name.)

32 *AS* 7577, cf. *AS*[2] 1, 156.5.

33 Cf. *AS* 7587 (*Atciu nél glan ... Atciu néll glas ...*) *Néll derg nach deirgi crú glan / atciu ann ara n-uachtar / mad cath budh fatha feirgi / dath na fala foirdheirgi*, with *Táin Bó Cúailnge, Recension I* (ed. C. O'Rahilly, Dublin 1976), 50, reading *Atchíu forderg, atchíu rúad*.

tale does not contain a description of such an encounter however. It concludes with *Ro baí olc imon cormaim iar sin co n-ar[r]alad ár fénnide nÉrenn eturru iarum. Ro baí didiu cechtar n-aí for éicill a chéili ón uair sin amach céin ro bátar i mbethaid .i. Find 7 Fothad Canaindi*, 'There was evil on account of the ale-feast after that, and the slaughter between them of the Fian-members of Ireland was continued. From then on Finn and Fothad Canainne were lying in wait for each other as long as they lived.' There is no single major encounter referred to here, but rather the resumption of an ongoing feud; the same phrase, *for éicill*, as before the peace bid is used (cf. *Boí-sium didiu for écill Finn co ndernsat córai* above). It is possible that the verbal form *co n-ar[r]alad (ár)* (from *ar-cuirethar*, 'increases, prolongs') was early misunderstood as *co ralad (ár)*, 'and (a slaughter) was made' (the verbs *-cuirethar*, *fo-ceird*, etc., are frequently used with *ár*, etc.),[34] or that it was taken to be from *ar-áili*, 'causes, brings about'.[35] This then generated, through misunderstanding, the two references in the *Acallam* to a specific major encounter, as well as a title *Bruiden Átha hÍ* (of uncertain date). There is a title *Orgain Átha hÍ* in the Middle Irish tale-lists (it could be translated as 'The slaughter at Áth hÍ'); but we cannot know what tale this refers to.[36]

When analysing the above half-tale, its first section (to the end of the verse) has the appearance of an eponymic aetiology of *Cenn Currig*. The place is mentioned at the beginning, and there is what I have called 'formal conclusion to etymologizing' (preceding the confirmatory verse), *Is de atá Cenn Cuirrig*, 'Therefrom there is *Cenn Currig*'. When reduced to the prerequisites for the second section, the content of the first section is the slaying by Finn of a pérson called *Currech*.[37]

---

34   Cf. *Scéla Mucce Meic Dathó* (ed. R. Thurneysen, Dublin 1935), 5: *co-ralta ár fer nÉrenn impe*.

35   Hull (329 note 4) thinks that *conaralad* (the other Ms reads *con-ararad*) is actually a scribal corruption of *con-ralad* [sic], 'the perfective form of *cuiridir*', 'through confusion with *ar-áli* "instigates"', the pret. pass. 3rd sing. of which would be *-arálad*'.

36   See Mac Cana, *op. cit.*, 46 and 61.

37   The second section is formally connected to the first through *in Currech sin* 'the said Currech'.

Before we can attempt a deeper appreciation of the structure of the first section and of the author's technique, some
information has to be filled in concerning the three proper
names *Cenn Currig*, *Currech Lifi*, and *Bodamair*. Their
medieval etymologies will be seen to be the focal points of
the analysis.

Cenn Currig is a hill by the river Siúir in Munster, near
Cahir (south of Cashel) at the eastern end of the Galtee
Mountains. The etymology of *Cenn Currig* in the tale represents a common type, where, in double-barrelled names, the
second element is explained as a personal name. In this
particular case, the generic first element is *cenn* which means
'head, peak, headland'. The name is explained as 'the head of
[the person called] Currech', viz. the cut-off head, or the
resting place of the cut-off head. The person is called in full
Currech Lifi do Laignib, 'Currech of the plain of Life of the
Leinstermen' (see below). *Bodamair* is a place (see the verse)
below the hill *Cenn Currig*. As regards the author's technique
in this case, I shall argue that *Bodamair* as the name of the
woman whom Finn meets by the river, is a silent conversion
of the placename into its eponym. Similarly (though it
represents an unusual pattern), the person *Currech Lifi*,
'Currech of the plain of Life', results from the implicit conversion of placename + placename into (eponymous) personal
name + placename.[38]

The double placename *Currech Lifi* denotes the Marsh of
(the plain of) Life (the Curragh of Kildare). It occurs as such
in, e.g. the Old Irish address to Aed Dub mac Colmán,[39] *in
Currech Liphi do thír?*, 'is the Curragh of Life your land?'.
It occurs as *Currech*, with the attribute *cona lí*, in the Old
Irish poem in praise of Brigit, 'Slán seiss a Brigit co mbúaid'.[40]
The distich in question reads: *marid Currech cona lí / ní mair
nach rí ro boí for*, 'the splendid Curragh remains, none of the

38 *Life* (not originally feminine) was first the name of a plain in Co.
    Kildare. Through *abann Lifi* (: *mag Lifi*) it became the name of
    the river Liffey ('Anna Livia'). *Life* was etymologized through a
    woman called *Life* (v. *MDs* 2.60; *Ds*, no. 12).
39 See K. Meyer, ed., 'Aed Dub mac Colmáin, Bishop-Abbot of Kil-
    dare', *Zeitschrift für celtische Philologie* 9 (1913), 458-60.
40 K. Meyer, ed., *Hail Brigit*, Halle/Dublin 1912, §12.

kings remains that ruled over it' (the same verb is used for the place and the person). In our tale, the same attribute occurs with the personage *Currech Lifi*, viz. *Currech Lifi cona lí* (though it must be pointed out that *lí* occurs elsewhere in verse in collocation with *Life*).

Concerning the author's procedure, we also see that the personage *Currech* from Life in Leinster, himself the product of etymologizing, is used to etymologize the name *Cenn Currig* in Munster. The fact that the latter place is in a different tribal area, reflects the free-ranging movements of the Fian.

I now paraphrase the sequence of this section of the tale, with some comment as to the author's procedure. Finn is at *Cenn Currig* [the tale can be said to start ominously, because elsewhere *cenn*-names are explained through cut-off heads]. He meets a woman by the name of *Bodamair* [at the end of the section *Bodamair* occurs as a placename in the very area]. He goes to avenge his foster-brother Dub, the father of a member of his Fian, on Currech [the eponymic origin of *Currech* is not explicitly referred to in the tale]. Currech, for his part, goes to kill Bodamair, which leads to Finn, in revenge, killing Currech and cutting his head off. The head of *Currech* is taken to the hill above the place *Bodamair*, which is named *Cenn Currig* after the killer of *Bodamair*.

We see how the author has etymologized three placenames, not as an end in itself, but in order to correlate and interweave their explanations for the creation of this section of the tale and of two of its actors.

I suggested above that the reference to the *bruiden* in *Acallam na Senórach* originated in a misunderstood phrase of our tale. Furthermore, the verse of our tale is used as the first quatrain of a *Dindsenchas* poem (*MDs* 3, 234, *LL* 25720; no prose in *LL*), to which five quatrains are added (with a *dúnad* after the third, fourth, and sixth). The placename to be explained, *Cenn Currig* in Munster, is not specifically mentioned in this form in the poem which starts *Currech Life* . . . , itself originally a Leinster placename, the Curragh of Kildare (see above). Thus, E. Gwynn entitled the poem 'Currech Life' and placed it in Leinster (*MDs* 5, 18 and 31; but see *MDs* 3, 519). In *AS*[2] 2, 43.11, there is a shift of emphasis as primarily the name of the Curragh of Kildare is explained through Finn's killing of Currech there. In AS^2 3, 90.4 (verse), there is a reference, also ultimately based on misunderstanding, to *Cuirreach Bodhamhrach*, intended for 'The Curragh of Bodhamhair'; similarly in the prose, *ibid.* 84: *ro-ghluais-[s]iomh roimhe and soin cona mhuinntir ina choimhideacht 7 ina chomhleanmhain cco Sídh Ochta Cleitigh, 7 acc tocht re taobh Churraigh Bodhamhrach at-chí an ccuirr . . .* , 'Then, together with his people he headed towards Síd Ochta Cleittig [the *síd* at the side of Clettech on the Boyne], and while travelling along the Curragh of Bodamair he sees a crane . . .' The prose *Dindsenchas* (e.g. *Ds*, no. 49) misrepresents most of the tale. And finally, the change of the ancestry of Fothad in *AS* was attributed (note 31 above) to the misunderstanding of a rhetorical passage in the tale not printed here.

It will be noticed that our tale is very similar to Old Irish tales of the Ulster Cycle or the Cycles of the Kings, in language, style, motifs, topography, etymologizing, narrator's intrusion, use of dialogue, rhetorics, etc. The same applies to its companion tale *Tucait fhaghbála in fesa do Finn inso ocus marbad Cú(i)lduib.*[41] Another, shorter, Old Irish version of the latter, viz. how Finn kills Cúldub and obtains *imbas forosnai* (a type of divination), is part of an example given in a legal context (Ms T.C.D. H 3 18; *Corpus Iuris Hibernici*, ed. D.A. Binchy, Dublin 1978, 879.23).[42] These tales presuppose the existence at the time of other related ones, among other things because of the number of actors and persons introduced without comment, whose status would have been known (thematically or incidentally) from those other contexts, e.g. Fothad Cana(i)nn(e),[43] Diarmait, Oisín, Cúldub, Caílte

41. See Hull, *op. cit.*, 329.
42 K. Meyer, ed. 'Finn and the Man in the Tree', *Revue Celtique* 25 (1904), 344-9. Similarly, *Echtra Fergusa Maic Leti* of the Ulster Cycle is extant as a 'leading case' in the same legal commentary (v. D.A. Binchy, ed. 'The Saga of Fergus Mac Léti', *Ériu* 16 (1952), 33-48).
43 The tale referrred to in the tale-lists by *Serc Caillige Bérre do Fhothud Chana(i)nd(e)* (Mac Cana, *op. cit.*, 48 and 58) is not extant; its age remains uncertain. Cf. from the (twelfth-century) *Bansenchas* poem 'Ádam óenathair na ndóene' by Gilla Mo Dutu, The Book of Lecan, Facsimiles in collotype of Irish manuscripts II (Dublin 1937) fo. 210ra44 (cf. *LL* 16919f) *Cailleach Berre bind*

(Finn's sister's son), or Téite (daughter of Macnia and mother
of Goll mac Morna, according to later sources). Obviously,
the above tales (as well as one or two others, also capriciously,
not systematically, modernized from Old Irish exemplars in
the manuscript tradition; v. K. Meyer, *Fianaigecht*, xvii ff,
and G. Murphy, *Duanaire Finn*, Part III, lv, ff.) were written
down not later than the early tenth century, though they are
extant only in fifteenth- and sixteenth-century manuscripts.
We may well ask why so few tales of an Old Irish 'Fenian
Cycle' (? 'Cycles') survived? It will be necessary here to refer
to both the nature of early Irish tradition (there are no such
tales in the extant pre-Norman codices) and the vagaries of
Irish manuscript tradition in general (there are, as already
mentioned, a few tales extant in much later manuscripts that
ultimately derive from lost Old Irish exemplars). And why
are such tales not listed in the Middle Irish lists of tales in
any number (as far as we can see)? The answer to both questions may lie in the consideration of the functions of the
earliest Irish tales. The Fenian tales (though otherwise equal
to other Old Irish learned tales) were not of societal relevance,
i.e. they had no tribal[44] historical, genealogical, or religious
function.[45] This, possibly, explains their absence (their fate
is shared by lyric poetry) from the extant type of pre-Norman
codices and from the tale-lists. They were treated as equal in
other learned functions, e.g. as illustrations in legal (see above)
or lexicographical[46] contexts.

The main actors of the early Fenian tales became attached

---

buan builig / bean Fothaid Chanand na cet, 'the long-lived, merry
Caillech Bérri of the sweet-sounding name was the wife of Fothad
Canann of the many warriors'.

44 The Fian are said to be *éclann* 'kinless', or *díthir* 'landless' (v. Meyer,
op. cit. [1910], ix). Relationship of Fenian persons is often described through females. — On the 'national' level, Finn was not
accepted into *In lebar gabála*.

45 D. Ó Corráin has recently begun a critical evaluation of early Irish
literature in terms of historical intention and achievement; v. 'Irish
Origin Legends and Genealogy: Recurrent Aetiologies', in *History
and Heroic Tale. A Symposium*, ed. T. Nyberg, etc., Odense Uni-
versitets forlag 1985, 51-96 (see esp. 56, 72, 85).

46 See K. Meyer, ed. 'Find and the jester Lomnae' (in *op. cit.* [1910],
xix), a tale preserved in Cormac's Glossary, s.v. *Orc tréith*.

to, or synchronized with, personages of historical importance. Currech was made a son of Catháir Már (as in quatrain 1 of example (i) above).[47] Finn was attached to Cormac mac Airt. There is an instance of synchronization in *Bruiden Átha hÍ* above, viz. *Atá cáin Chormaic i nÉre co cenn secht mbliadnae nad rubthar guin duini*, 'There is the *cáin* of Cormac in Ireland for seven years which prevents manslaying.' This passage, to the end of the name-list, was taken into the 'Irish ordeals' (v. note 28). I suggest, however, that our tale had originally *caínchomrac*, 'fair play, peace' (the term we saw in example (ii) of *Echtra Conli* above), so that the synchronization was of an uncertain later date. (The two phrases, *cáin chormaic* and *caínchomrac*, were of course, palaeographically and in speech, very similar.) The motif of seven years' peace occurs in a similar way, e.g. at the end of *Táin Bó Cúailnge, Rec. I* (ed. C. O'Rahilly) 4156: *Secht mblíadna iar sin ní roibi guin duine eturru i nnÉrind*, 'For seven years after that no one was killed between them in Ireland.'[48]

Before going on to example (iv), the Death of Finn, I want to discuss briefly a different matter. At the outset, I mentioned 'itineraries and catalogues of names' amongst the contexts of appraisal of proper names in literature. They are common in early Irish literature, but their forms and functions have not been investigated. We met with one in *Bruiden Átha hÍ*, where I suggested (note 28) that amongst its functions are the suspension or slowing down of a line of events with dramatic effect and the creation of a particular atmosphere. Below on p. 19 is an itinerary from *Acallam na Senórach*, with its counterpart from the post-Norman recension of c. two

---

47 See the passage from the Leinster genealogies quoted in note 9 above. He does not yet appear as a son of Catháir in the *Timna Chatháir Máir* (v. M. Dillon, ed., *Lebor na Cert*, Dublin 1962, Appendix A). – Slechtaire, the only son of Currech in the genealogies, figures in the *dindsenchas* of *Tipra Sengarmna* (*MDs* 3, 242; *Ds*, no. 52), where he and his mother *Sengarman* are killed when trying to avenge Currech.

48 For the motif of the seven-year kingship see [of Bres] *Cath Maige Tuired* (ed. E.A. Gray, 1982, Irish Texts Society, Vol. 52, 180; [of Lugaid Mac Con] *Cath Maige Mucrama* (ed. M. O Daly, 1975, Irish Texts Society, Vol. 50, 296); [of Ailill Ólom] *ibid.*, 374.

centuries later. (Italic single letters mark departures from the
editors' texts as regard capital or lower-case spelling.) Of the
many interesting features arising from this itinerary and from
the comparison of its two recensions, I shall briefly mention
three, and discuss a fourth in more detail.

(a) At no. (11), *Tír Maine* (: *Uí Maine*) is probably a case
of interchange of generics (rather than of omission of generic
preceded by, and dependent on, certain other terms; see
below). I do not think (with Stokes) that *breicthír* of *AS* is
a proper name. Meaning 'checkered land', it points to the
implicit etymology of *Tír Maine* as *tír muine*, 'land of
thicket(s), or brake(s)'. AS^2 (re-)converts this into the common type of etymology, where the second element is (taken
as) the eponymic, with patronymic (or more) added; its
retention of *breic-* may indicate appreciation of the etymology
as in the earlier recension. Amongst other examples of the
latter in the itinerary is (7) *Loch Gréine ingine Finn*. Since
we are dealing with a linguistic/literary device, it is irrelevant
that the ancestry in *Tír Maine mheic Eachdhach Fir Dá
Ghiall* corresponds to genealogical records, while in *Loch
Gréine ingine Finn* the patronymic represents the tendency
to etymologize (or replace and etymologize) placenames
through (invented) Fenian persons and matters.

(b) In no. (5) *Sliabh Echtge inghine Nuadha Aircetláim*,
the patronymics differ in *AS* and AS^2, the latter agreeing
with *Dindsenchas*. This represents the maximal forms (in
such context) of the Irish name for the Aughty Mountains
(between counties Clare and Galway). The minimal form is
(6) *Echtghe*. There are two types of shortening of basically
double-barrelled placenames. The most common is the conditioned omission of the generic after certain governing
nominals, e.g. *cath Muccrama, cath Roth, Find Fáil, sluag
senAilbe, rí Guill*. The other is the omission of the generic
(mainly) in adverbial phrases, the type *i nEchtghe*, or *i nÉtur*
(: *Benn Étair*). A rare sub-group of the latter is represented
by *a hÍtha* (: *Mag (n)Ítha*, etymologized through a personage
Íth), further conventionalized, without attention to inflection.

(c) In (5) *Sliabh Echtge, AS^2* inserts, as part of the general,
typical embellishment, the attribute *adhuathmhar* between

Itinerary from *Acallamh na Senórach*

AS 1008	AS² 1, 82.23
Do gluais Pátraic cona muinntir 7 táncatar rompa anes	Ro ghluaiseadar ó Mhuimhneachuibh ann sin . . . Is eadh conoir inar ghabhsat, .i.
1 tre medhan Muman 7 } a Mairtine moir Muman andes 7 do 2 do Luimnech nU*lad* 7 } Loimenach U*lad Fr*	i Mairtine meadhónaigh Mumhon,
3 i *f*idh na cuan re n-abar Creatalach 7	do *f*hiodh na ccuan ris a ráitear an Chreatshalach,
4 a Sliabh Uighi in Rígh 7	do Shliabh Oidhe an Rí áit a ttorchair Criamhthann mac fearchonta Fiodhaigh,
5 a Sliabh Echtge inghine Nuadha Aircetlaim 7	do Shliabh n-adhuathmhar nEchtghe inghine Ursgaithighe bean Fhearghusa Iuscca mheic Ruidhe rua[i]dh arm-ghlaisi . . . ,
6 do Chuaille Cepáin a nEchtghe airm a torchair Cepán mac Morna 7	do Chuaille chían-oirrdheirc Cheapáin áit a ttorchair Ceapán mac Mórna an mílidh 7
7 do Loch na Bó Girre risa n-abar Loch Gréine ingine Finn 7	do Loch na Bó Giorra ris a ráitear Loch nGréine inghine Finn ag na fileadhaibh,
8	do *m*hagh Mín meic Iúghoine ris a ráitear Mínmhagh,
9	do Fhiodh mbláith ard-chaoin mBreasail,
10	do hSuca sruth-linntigh,
11 a *m*breicthir re n-abar Tír Maine isin tan-so 7	do *b*hreicThír Maine mheic Eachdhach Fir Dá Ghíall 7
12 do *l*och linnghaeth re n-abar Loch Cróine [isin tan-sa *Fr*].	do chúan Locha leathon-ghuirm Linnghaoith fris a n-aborthar Loch caomh-áluinn Cróine an ionbhaidh si.

the two elements of the name. This adjective alliterates with
the second element, and is in grammatical congruence with
the first (in verse such adjectives can be in congruence with
either element according to the metrical requirements). The
pattern is A- b- B-, or, more elaborate still, (12) (*do chúan*)
Locha leathon-ghuirm Linnghaoith, A- a-(b-) A-(b-). In (9)
do Fhiodh mbláith ard-chaoin mBreasail, the redactor probably got it wrong, since *ard-chaoin* does not obey the pattern.

(d) Stage (2) of the itinerary is *do Luimnech nUlad*.
Luimnech was the name for Limerick and the upper Shannon
estuary (in the south-west of Ireland). While this is certainly
en route between the Mairtine, around Emly, and the wood
of Cratloe (west of Limerick in Co. Clare) [no. (3) of the
itinerary], the additional *nUl-*, as it is abbreviated in the
manuscript, is puzzling. It can hardly be for anything but
nUlad, 'of the Ulstermen' (in the north of Ireland). Stokes
suggested tentatively (p. 370), with reference to *Dindsenchas*,
that *Luimnech* may be miswritten for *Luibnech*. The *Dindsenchas*[49] connects this place, which has not been identified,
with the raid of the Ulstermen into Munster, described in the
tale *Mesca Ulad*, another title of which (or of a version of
which) is *Boethréim Ulad*.[50] The latter title is reflected in a
line cheville of the *Dindsenchas* poem: *borb in baeth-réim*, 'it
was a wild mad journey'. The poem begins (*MDs* 4, 220) *Sund
ro coscrad in chétach / ba cruthach in caem-étach / ... Tri
coícait luban ...* [my translation] 'Here the "cétach" was
destroyed, it was a well-cut beautiful garment ... It had 150
tassels ...' The 'cétach' was a wonderful mantle belonging
to Crimthann, said to be worth 100 (*cét*), an etymology of
cétach, cumals. The name *Luibnech* is etymologized on
account of the mantle of the 'tassels' (*luban*, pl. *luibne*, adj.
luibnech) having been destroyed there. This episode is not in
Mesca Ulad / Boethréim Ulad, as we have it. The collocation
Luibnech Ulad is not known to occur elsewhere. I have little
doubt that the addition of *Ulad* to *Luibnech* (presuming all
the time that Stokes' emendation is correct) is a reference to
the adventure of the Ulstermen, based on information as in

49 *MDs* 4, 220, 435; *Ds*, no. 121.
50 See J.C. Watson, ed., *Mesca Ulad*, Dublin 1941, xiii.

the *Dindsenchas*[51] (or a version of the tale itself), a display of learning. The redactor of the later AS^2 omits this stage, though he otherwise enlarges the itinerary. In order to back up this explanation I give another similar instance, again from an *Acallam na Senórach* itinerary (*AS* 6045, not in AS^2) . . . *a leachMachaire Lí thes, 7 do corcaig Maigi* [? *maigi*] *Ulad siar, áit i rrabadur Ula*id *i llongport a forbaissi a Cathair na Claenratha dar' marbsatar Cú-rí mac Daire, 7 do Lathair Luingi sís, áit a mbidis longa Clainde Dedad* . . . , '. . . in Machaire Lí of the warriors in the south, and westwards to the marsh of Mag Ulad where the Ulstermen had camped when they besieged Cathair na Claenratha and killed Cú Roí mac Dáire, and down to Láthair Luinge where the ships of Clann Dedad used to be . . .' The *corcach Maigi Ulad*, 'the marsh of M. U.' (? is *M. U.* a proper name here) is situated, from internal evidence, in the western part of Machaire Lí, between Sliab Mis and Tráig Lí in Kerry. In this instance, the occurrence of *Ulad* in a Munster place(name) is actually explained in the text (*áit* . . . *mac Dáire*). The reference is to the place of the encampment of the Ulstermen at their siege at Cathair na Claenratha (= Cathair Con Roí) when Cú Chulainn killed Cú Roí.[52]

The problems encountered in the above itinerary alone (and it matters not in this context whether some of my suggestions might be wrong) suffice to show the necessity of defining the medieval placename (and proper name in general) in view of differing surface forms, and of carrying out a great amount of intratextual work before placenames can be abstracted, in view of their use in etymologizing, intertextural (cf. note 20), and stylistic functions in texts.

(iv) *Death of Finn*
I now return to a discussion of one more instance of

---

51   There is also the *dindsenchas* of *Luimnech* 'Limerick' (*MDs* 3, 270; *Ds*, no. 57 [not in *LL*]), beside that of *Luibnech*. It is possible that the author of *AS* chose or mistook the latter for an alternative of the former.

52   See R. Thurneysen, 'Die Sage von CuRoi', *Zeitschrift für celtische Philologie* 9 (1913), 189-234; *Id.*, *Die irische Helden- und Königsage*, Halle 1921, 429ff.

creative literary etymologizing of the type seen in *Bruiden Átha hÍ* above. K. Meyer assembled, from several fragments and references, one of the versions of the Death of Finn.[53] As in the case of heroes of other cycles, Finn here meets his death after violating a *geis* (a prohibition). The *geis* was to drink out of a horn (Irish *adarc*). He violates his *geis* when drinking from a well at a place called 'The Horns of Iuchna' (*Adarca Iuchna*). An analysis of the tale shows the focal points to be two placenames which carry most of the features of the tale. I give the implicit explanations of these placenames (as I understand them), before I paraphrase the tale in its likely sequence. The placenames are *Adarca Iuchna* and **Léimm Finn*. *Adarca Iuchna* is, as I said, (understood as) 'The Horns of Iuchna', the second element taken to be an eponym. The text here has *Iuchba*, but elsewhere the name is *Iuchna* (see also the variant *Adarca bó Iuchna*).[54] If *Iuchna* here refers to the daughter of Goll mac Morna, the name carries a reference to Finn's traditional enemy Goll. In a *Duanaire Finn* poem (which has a reference to a different version of the Death of Finn), Finn is said to have fallen *tre inghin Ghuill*, 'through the daughter of Goll', i.e. 'through the plotting of the daughter of Goll'.[55] **Léimm Finn*, (understood as) 'The Leap of Finn', does not in this form occur in the text. Finn is said to be going to *a léimm*, 'his leap'. This, however, presupposes a placename **Léimm Finn* (cf. *Léimm Con Culainn*), which is etymologized through him, and then (as frequently elsewhere),[56] the eponym replaced by the pronoun in this unambiguous context.

53 'The Death of Finn Mac Cumaill', *Zeitschrift für celtische Philologie* 1 (1897), 462-5; Murphy, *op. cit.* (1953), xli.

54 Meyer supplied the name *Adarca Iuchba* from a different deathtale of Finn, in order to understand the opening of his second fragment. While elsewhere (*AS, Dindsenchas*) *Iuchna* is a male personage in the explanation of *Adarca* (*bó*) *Iuchna*, we find *Iuchna Ardmór ingen Ghuill meic Morna* acting in 'The chase of Síd na mBan and the death of Finn' (Meyer, *op. cit.* [1910], 68.26).

55 See E. Mac Neill, ed., *Duanaire Finn*, Part I, Irish Texts Society, Vol. 7, London 1907, 48 (poem 19.5). Murphy, *op. cit.* (1953), 43.

56 E.g. *Lebor na hUidre* (ed. R.I. Best and O. Bergin, Dublin 1929), 8996 ('Fled Bricrend') *Eircid co Budi mac mBain for se coa áth*

The tale probably ran as follows: One day, when the Fian-members are deserting him because of his old age, Finn decides to test his running and leaping, and to go to 'His Leap' (*a léimm*) on the river Boyne. It was a *geis* of his to drink out of a horn (*adarc*). Disregarding it would mean the end of his life, as his then wife Smirnat (or Smirgat), daughter of Fothad Canainne, had revealed to him. This is why he used to drink from cups. On the way to 'His Leap', Finn takes a drink from a well at a place called *Adarca Iuchna* ('The Horns of Iuchna'). A woman reminds him of the violation of his *geis*, which he acknowledges as a foreboding of his death. He leaps and dies between two rocks at 'His Leap' . . .

Again, we see the author interweaving elements derived from, or correlated to, the explanations of different place-names when creating this tale, viz. Finn's *geis* and its viola-tion, and the presence of the woman, at *Adarca Iuchna*; and his leap and death at **Léimm Finn*.

I hope I have succeeded in bringing to light, within the limits of this short paper, some aspects of the extraordinary awareness in earlier medieval Ireland of the possible meanings of proper names, what I have called 'etymologizing', and its structural, intertextual, and aesthetic functions in literature. There is little hope, however, that these functions and features can ever be entirely recovered and appreciated. Since we are dealing with a linguistic/literary device, consideration of ono-mastic reality in the modern sense is irrelevant, viz. whether a place was named after a person or matter, or a story was invented to account for the name. There are at least three different levels of etymology in literature to be distinguished:

(1) incidental or additive etymology, as, e.g., in *Bruiden Átha hÍ* above, *Cuirrech Lifi do Laignib dia tá Ráith Cuirrig, is é* . . .

(2) constituent etymology, as, e.g., the explanation of Oisín's name in example (i) above;

['Áth Budi']; or *AS* 2680 *Tech Moling meic Ḟaelain meic Ḟeradaig Ḟind, uingi d' ór ó nech ar a thech 'na chill* (which *AS²* 2, 91.5 does not appreciate). See also J. Carney, *Studies in Irish Literature and History*, Dublin 1955, 67, note 1.

(3) creative etymology, the use of the explanation(s) of one or more names in the creation of a tale.

Formally, etymology is either implicit or explicit (as always in incidental etymology); the narrator's formal conclusion of etymology within the earlier tales is common. We saw how certain early etymologies failed to be appreciated already to some extent in the *Dindsenchas* and the *Acallam na Senórach* (themselves storehouses of etymology), most clearly, however, in the post-Norman *Agallamh* (AS^2). I am aware of the fact that more detailed analyses are required to provide a fuller understanding of etymology, linguistic and literary, in this sense. All in all, however, I should say (with an adaptation of the words of Curtius, referred to at the start of this paper) that in earlier medieval Ireland 'Etymology was a category of thought and of literary creation'.

ORAL AND LITERARY FENIAN TALES

ALAN BRUFORD
(University of Edinburgh)

The Fenian cycle ranked as a national epic for both Irish and Scottish Gaels long before James Macpherson tried to construct a fake epic in English prose for the Scottish Highlanders out of elements of some of the ballads. It is hardly necessary to illustrate this with such evidence as the use of the cycle's name, *fiannaíocht*, to cover all heroic storytelling in Ireland, or accounts of Scottish countrymen doffing their bonnets out of respect for the subject-matter of the ballads they were going to chant. The Ulster cycle, which is older and which seems to us to include far more of truly heroic tone, was treated up to the middle of the last century and later, among traditional reciters, as a mere adjunct whose relationship to the matter of Fionn and the Fianna was little understood but known to be subsidiary. Only scholarly research has re-established the primacy of the matter of Cú Chulainn; oral tradition knows nothing about it.

In form, however, the Fenian cycle is nothing like a single epic or even a consistent cycle of poems. Except that it is confined to one language, this 'matter of Ireland' would be more diverse, confused and contradictory even than the Arthurian 'matter of Britain'. It seems as though every member of the poetic caste from the twelfth century to the eighteenth must have tried his hand at composing either a ballad (or two!) or a prose tale about the Fenians, and where he had heard nothing he could use to fill in a gap — a name, a line of descent, the cause of a dispute — each one felt free to invent, or at any rate to adapt something for himself. Thus there are at least half a dozen contradictory accounts of Fionn mac Cumhaill's own descent, not to mention his relationship to major supporting characters such as Caoilte and Mac Lughach,[1] and characters who in earlier tales are his adversaries turn up in later tales as friends or followers, like Aillén[2] or the Fatha Conán, one of the Fenians in late romances, who seems to derive from the hostile supernatural figure Fothad Canainne.

It is necessary in considering the history of the cycle to define not merely the two categories of narrative in my title, but three: first, written narrative, composed more or less on to paper, though not therefore designed necessarily for solitary silent reading;[3] second, literary narrative, composed by professional *seanchaithe*, historians and storytellers, or poets, but passed on generally though not exclusively in oral forms; and third, folk narrative, told by storytellers or sung by singers with no formal training, which might derive mainly or only in small part from written or literary sources. The distinction is seldom made as clear as it should be. It should be added that all three forms could be varied at will by the transmitter to some degree, for the scribes of Early Modern Irish manuscripts took pleasure in substituting words or phrases from other exemplars, other stories or poems, or their own heads for those in their exemplar.[4] A few Irish scribes of the eighteenth century went so far as to write new sequels to stories they had copied, as well as composing new romances on the traditional pattern.[5] Others seem to have taken complete folktales from oral tradition and recast them to a varying extent in literary language,[6] though with one

1 E. MacNeill, *Duanaire Finn* I, Irish Texts Society (= ITS) Vol. 7, London 1908, xxxii, lii-lviii; G. Murphy, *Duanaire Finn* III, ITS Vol. 43, Dublin 1953, lix, lxxvii, 206, etc.

2 Murphy, *op. cit.*, 197-8.

3 A. Bruford, *Gaelic Folk-Tales and Mediaeval Romances*, Dublin 1969 (= *Béaloideas* 34), 45-7, 55-61.

4 *Ibid.*, 48.

5 *Ibid.*, 50-1.

6 *Ibid.*, 51, 123, 127-9, 136-7, 140-3.

exception[7] it seems that the earlier romancers may have borrowed names, ideas and motifs from folk as well as literary oral tradition, but not whole plots of stories.

The Fenian lays belong to the second class: they were composed in the literary syllabic metres of the later Middle Ages, though perhaps not to the standards required of poets of the first rank, and some of them were probably not written down until they were recorded from oral tradition in the past two centuries. We know that bardic praise-poetry of this period was designed primarily to be learned and chanted publicly by a professional reciter (*reacaire*), not normally its composer, and might or might not then be written down in a manuscript book of poems (*duanaire*) by a scribe, to preserve it for future generations in case it died out in the more highly valued oral tradition. The same scheme of values no doubt applied to narrative ballads, but since their subject-matter was of less ephemeral interest than eulogies of contemporary chieftains, the manuscripts were less necessary.

Prose tales are different: as I have argued elsewhere,[8] they are too ornate and academic in their language, and their descriptive set-pieces or 'runs' are too varied to have been designed to be learned completely by heart by some sort of *reacaire*, or to be either prompt-book or written record of an improvised performance. Like romances of chivalry in other parts of late medieval Europe, they were probably composed in writing and designed to be read aloud. Manuscript copies of some prose tales circulated throughout the Gaelic-speaking area from Co. Cork to the Hebrides in the seventeenth century, and were still being copied and used for reading aloud to attentive audiences in the farm kitchens of Munster little over a century ago. Since the hearers of such a reading might take away with them the gist of the story and even a good part of its wording if they had the sort of oral memory well attested in recent Gaelic storytellers, the written heroic romances came to circulate alongside international folktales in oral tradition, and inventive narrators freely combined

7 *Eachtra Iollainn Airmdheirg* from AT 301, *ibid.*, 84-5.
8 Bruford, *op. cit.*, 46-7.

elements from both to make new stories.[9]

I have written already[10] of the development in oral tradition of Fenian tales which can be traced to written originals: here I want to consider some of those oral tales where some literary influence is detectable but existing manuscripts cannot provide the only sources. First, however, let us look further at the meaning and atmosphere of the cycle as a whole.

It has generally been argued that the Fenian cycle contains more 'popular' elements than the Ulster cycle, and lays less emphasis on the values of a warrior aristocracy. Some writers, like the late Gerard Murphy, have gone on to suggest that modern folktales may often preserve the original forms of stories which were later made into romances by literary men. For instance, Murphy found it hard to believe that the extraordinarily popular motif of the Fenians being invited to a magic dwelling in which they stick to their seats until released by someone bringing a magic solvent could derive from the single late mediaeval romance *An Bhruidhean Chaorthuinn*, 'The Rowantree Hall'. But the relationships between Gaelic romances and folktales provide plenty of examples of such inventions spreading with remarkable speed,[11] and the fact that this motif was known to every storyteller in Gaelic Ireland at the beginning of this century, and brought into practically any Fenian hero tale where it could be fitted in, simply means that it was a good story. It is surely more significant that as in the romance, the heroes are nearly always the literary Fianna, the rescuer is often named as Diarmaid, the remedy he brings is usually the blood of specified persons or animals, and the comic character for whom the remedy runs out so that he has to be pulled free by main force, leaving the skin of his bottom sticking to the seat, is generally named as Conán. Murphy's argument that this part of the story survives in folktales but not in the manuscripts because 'the rump was not so freely spoken of in the halls of the gentry' suggests an anachronistic picture of the Irish aristocracy of the fifteenth century, who seem to

9 *Ibid.*, 55 ff. and *passim*.
10 *Ibid.*, 106-33.
11 *Ibid.*, 14-6, 242-3 and *passim*.

have changed wives almost as often as bed-linen[12] and were not likely to be prudes: as I have pointed out[13] the manuscripts have no inhibitions about mentioning Conán's arse, but Murphy must have been relying on Patrick Pearse's published edition, which omits the relevant phrase in deference to the sensibilities of his own time. It could be added that the 'Fionn agus Lorcan' oral type which Murphy seems to suggest as the original setting for the motif[14] is recognisable in at least one version from Scotland,[15] and does not include this motif — which is far less popular in Scottish oral tradition than in Irish — though a similar introduction with an invitation to a funeral leads to a quite different motif.[16]

But though Murphy's ideas about the relationship between romance and folktale were sometimes wrong, many of the points he made about the earlier traditions lying behind the literary Fenian cycle must be treated with respect. It can be taken as established, for instance, that the name of Fionn himself derives from the Celtic god or divine hero celebrated in such placenames of Roman times as Vindobona, now Vienna.[17] It does not follow, however, that his character in the mediaeval cycle or the plots of the stories have any basis in pagan Irish mythology. Identifying gods can be fun, but it seldom has useful results. Take this argument: Fionn, according to several accounts a descendant of the god Nuadu, is

12 K. Nicholls, *Gaelic and Gaelicised Ireland in the Middle Ages*, Dublin 1972, 73-4.

13 Bruford, *op. cit.*, 3-4.

14 Murphy, *op. cit.*, xxiv-xxxiii.

15 The last episode added to Lachlann MacNeill's extended version of 'Leigheas Coise Céin' (Bruford, *op. cit.*, 240) — from Islay, the part of Gaelic Scotland with the closest connections to Ireland.

16 More precisely the hero (Gormshuil, from *Leigheas Coise Céin*, replacing Fionn) is persuaded to engage a new servant when the helper corresponding to Lorcán leaves him, whose only wages are to be that Gormshuil must watch his grave the night he dies. He drops dead as soon as they get home, and Gormshuil watching in the old church is assailed by a 'swelling hag' such as appears in a Scottish local legend derived from the end of AT 303 (Bruford, 'Scottish Gaelic Witch Stories', *Scottish Studies* 11 [1967], 18-9) and saved by his helper summoned with a whistle.

17 Murphy, *op. cit.*, lxxxiv; P. Mac Cana, *Celtic Mythology*, London 1970, 110.

clearly equivalent in some sense to the Welsh Gwynn son of Nudd, who is called king of the otherworld (Annwn) and in folklore leads the Wild Hunt or hounds of Annwn.[18] But the equivalent to Gwynn as ruler of the underworld and leader of the Wild Hunt in Ireland is the ancestor deity Donn, and Donn is a name given to Fionn's follower Diarmaid, or in later tales to his father: it has therefore been suggested that Diarmaid is simply an avatar of Donn.[19] But if Diarmaid and Fionn are aspects of the same divine figure, what is Fionn doing when he allows his wife Gráinne to elope with his *alter ego* Diarmaid, and then sets off in hot pursuit of himself and ultimately causes his own death? This sort of identification seldom clarifies anything.[20]

In fact Fionn, whatever his origins, is regularly presented in the literature as a mortal man, if an unusually long-lived one — or at least with a long prime to his life: in most of the stories he is an active warrior alongside his own grandson Oscar — and endowed with a limited clairvoyant ability if he chews his famous thumb, but a champion of mortals a g a i n s t those people of the otherworld who as a body include the surviving traditions of the pagan Irish pantheon. (For convenience I will describe these otherworld people, *Tuatha Dé Danann, aes síde*, more recently *síobhraigh, sidhichean* and the like, hereafter as fairies, though this does not carry with it any implications of sweetness, quaintness or diminutive size, only magical power and danger.) It has been pointed out often enough how Fionn and the Fenians spend much of their time fighting either against fairy opponents or overseas invaders who may be human, supernatural or as often as not a blend of the two. In view of the consistently dual treatment of the Gaelic otherworld as an overseas 'land of youth' and an underground realm there is no need to see any significant

---

18 Mac Cana, *loc. cit.*; I. Foster, Appendix G to Murphy, *op. cit.*, 198-204. See Máire MacNeill, *The Festival of Lughnasa*, Oxford 1962, 203-4, for Donn as rider in the sky as well as leader of the Fairy Host in recent belief.

19 Mac Cana, *op. cit.*, 113.

20 If Fionn is really a god of the dead, though, it would explain the tradition of his smell of death mentioned by Dáithí Ó hÓgáin in his paper below.

difference in kind between the two sorts of attackers, though later concepts of the overseas invader were certainly influenced by the reality of the Vikings. It has not, I think, been pointed out how closely the main situations in these tales reflect those in modern fairy legends, themselves localised relics of an earlier mythology which have continued to be believed and to terrify country people of all ages until recent times. Leaving aside those tales which represent the Fenians as giants, usually comic giants — partly because Daithí Ó hÓgáin deals with them at some length, (see below p. 211 ff.) and partly because they mainly represent a burlesque stratum of tradition which, like most origin legends in developed societies, was rarely taken entirely seriously — the most frequent themes in prose and verse are (1) battles with fairies or invaders; (2) 'helper-tales', in which a mysterious person with magical powers helps the Fenians against other hostile beings; (3) the abduction of a woman by a fairy or foreigner; (4) the appearance of another sort of mysterious stranger who either makes fools of the Fenians, or lures them to a world overseas or in (5) a *bruidhean*, a fairy dwelling where they are imprisoned and threatened with death; (6) the Fenians may also, like Cú Chulainn, be enlisted by one band of fairies to fight another. Direct battles are not appropriate to the small-scale encounters of modern fairy legend, and helpful fairies, though they appear in local legend, are more typical of international *Märchen*; but the other situations are closely paralleled in the legends. The abducted woman, usually but not always rescued from the fairy host, is a theme almost as important as the infant changeling in local tradition; tales of leprechauns, uruisgs and other solitary fairies making fools of mortals abound, and the way the Fenians are carried overseas by the Giolla Deacair's horse is the same way in which children may be carried into a loch by a water-horse, unable to get off its back; the man enticed to join the dance in a fairy hill, or the woman kept there and forced to bake for the fairies, is in very much the same position as the Fenians in a *bruidhean*; and there are plenty of tales of young men carried off by the fairy host, not to fight battles for them, but to take their part in a hurling or shinty match.

The mortal characters in fairy legends are essentially

ordinary people, neighbours or ancestors of those who tell about them, and the role of the Fenians in the more literary tales is very similar. Far from being giants with superhuman strength, they are threatened by outside forces and win with difficulty (or there would be no story worth telling). They enjoy the simple life of hunters — though I will be qualifying this phrase shortly — because they are not courtiers but paid soldiers: very well paid by some later accounts in terms of the dues they claimed in land, game rights, and other tribute of a feudal nature almost up to *jus primae noctis*.[21] They are regularly represented as being in conflict with the king they serve, Cormac mac Airt, and the end of the cycle comes when Cormac's son Cairbre Lifechair tries to withdraw some of their rights and is killed in battle by the mutinous Fenians. In some ways Fionn is more like Robin Hood than King Arthur, though he is closer to the earliest concept of Arthur as a war-leader who is not a king, and the aristocratic Gaels would have had no truck with Robin's idea of robbing the rich to feed the poor. Nevertheless Fionn, as an independent and disaffected army leader, belonging according to some gene-alogists to a vassal tribe — I doubt if we have any right to brush off MacNeill's contention on this point as cavalierly as Murphy tried to do[22] — represents an opposition to the aristocracy such as in practice hardly ever existed in early Ireland, save perhaps for a very few successful clerics of low birth. In this sense at least the Fenian cycle is more popular: its heroes are not all kings' sons such as hold the centre of the stage in practically all other later Gaelic hero tales.[23]

But despite undercurrents of rebellion the Fenians are consistently represented as an army defending Ireland as a whole on behalf of the king of all Ireland. This too has very little to do with history: no major battle in Irish history, even Clontarf, has not involved Irishmen fighting on both sides.

21 Many tales mention these and they are cited as the cause of the Battle of Gabhair which put an end to the Fenians, but it is difficult to find an accessible version in print: I can now refer to J.F. Nagy, *The Wisdom of the Outlaw*, Berkeley 1985, 53-4. See also Cecile O'Rahilly, ed., *Cath Finntrágha*, Dublin 1962, 24.

22 Murphy, *op. cit.*, 212.

23 Bruford, *op. cit.* (1969), 23.

But it has a lot to do with the creation of the concept of an Irish nation. Fionn has certain tribal links in early sources with Leinster and possibly Meath, but his followers and their adventures are connected with every province of Ireland, though perhaps less with Ulster, which already had its own older, more aristocratic matter for stories.[24] From quite early in the Middle Irish period the Fenians are shown in the service of the king of Tara, Cormac, the legendary culture hero of the Uí Néill dynasties.[25] It is surely significant that the burgeoning of Fenian matter, both in the form of written prose and of literary ballads which may have taken centuries to reach the written page, coincides with the period from the tenth century to the twelfth when the doctrine that the king of Tara had regularly been high-king of Ireland was being developed by historians, and a *de facto* high-kingship of Ireland was from time to time briefly established by various provincial kings.[26] Fianna of the various provinces are mentioned occasionally, but Fionn's men are regularly called *Fianna Éireann*, (or *Fianna Fáil*!), 'Fenians of Ireland', not Fenians of Tara.

The first stimulus to the idea of Irish nationhood came no doubt from the Viking raids of the ninth and tenth centuries, but the exaggeration of the Norse threat in *Cogadh Gaedhel re Gallaibh*, 'The War between Gaels and Vikings', is merely designed to glorify Brian Bóramha and his dynasty, and hardly reflects the attitudes of eleventh-century Ireland where most Norsemen were merchants rather than warriors. One of the few real Norse names used for invaders in the cycle, Maghnus, comes from the campaign of Magnus Barelegs at the end of that century, but as many of the Fenians' attackers come from more or less fictitious kingdoms such as Sorcha or Ioruaidh as from the definitely Scandinavian Lochlann. It

24 Even the Ulster cycle includes episodes set in all the provinces, though since Connacht and next to it Cú Roi's West Munster are most prominent, it makes all the more sense for the rival cycle to centre on Leinster and Tara.

25 For this view of Cormac see T. Ó Cathasaigh, *The Heroic Biography of Cormac mac Airt*, Dublin 1977.

26 Murphy, *op. cit.*, lx-lxi; F.J. Byrne, *The Rise of the Uí Néill and the High-Kingship of Ireland*, O'Donnell Lecture XIII, Dublin 1969.

seems likely that the second wave of *Gaill* to hit Ireland, the
Norman invasion, really precipitated the consciousness of
nationhood: the realisation that the Gaels as a race were
threatened was the ideal stimulus to produce a national epic.
By the later Middle Ages even the enemies in many earlier
tales, the fairies, join the Fenians to fight off the invading
'King of the World' in the romance *Cath Finntrágha*, 'The
Battle of Ventry';[27] the Tuatha Dé Danann were after all
Irish fairies, and despite the historians' depiction of them
as a race defeated by the ancestors of the Gaels, there may
well have been a lingering belief in them as Ireland's former
gods.

The shape and feel of the cycle are generally agreed to have
been established about the time of the coming of the Normans
in *Agallamh na Senórach* (conventionally rendered 'The Colloquy of the Ancients', but it is seldom that pompous: 'The
Old Fogeys' Ramblings' might be nearer the mark). Older
traditions there certainly were, but it is hard to believe that
much of the setting and atmosphere of literary or indeed any
fiannaíocht as we know it goes back far beyond the *Agallamh*.
It surely established the convention that the tales were told
by the aged Fenians, Oisín and Caoilte, who had seen them
all happen,[28] to St Patrick himself, who significantly keeps

27 C. O'Rahilly, *op. cit.*, 11-3, 48-50. Scottish oral tradition may
    localise the scenes of events, but normally unlike Macpherson
    acknowledges Ireland as the Fenians' home ground; it was probably
    the Normanisation of the Scottish crown under the sons of Malcolm
    Canmore which provoked Scottish Gaels to revert to thinking of
    Ireland as the 'Old Country', and this has never been lost. The hero
    of a Scottish Gaelic folktale is far more likely to be son of the king
    of Ireland (*mac Rìgh Éireann*) than son of the king of Scotland.
    But some may think of the Fenians as Scottish: the late Donald
    Sinclair, Tiree, thought that Goll was different from the rest
    because he was an Irishman (School of Scottish Studies (SA) tape
    SA 1968/26 B8).
28 The implied rules of evidence, so to speak, prefer an eye-witness
    account written down from dictation (oral transmission was
    not regarded as accurate) and so the *Táin* is dictated by Fergus mac
    Róich raised from his grave (R. Thurneysen, *Die Irische Helden-
    und Königsage*, Halle 1921, 252-67). The historians set the scene
    of the Ulster cycle too long before writing to allow the heroes to
    survive, so one has to be revived by 'fasting against him'.

on calling on his scribe Brocán to write them down;[29] both
the eye-witness account and the written record gave authority
to a story at this date. We will come back to Patrick and his
books later. But the *Agallamh* is also a turning-point for the
whole ethos of the cycle, if only because its author tried to
fit together the disparate traditions about the Fenians he
knew. The pastoral element, the praise of nature and the
chase, is something quite foreign to earlier heroic literature:
if Cú Chulainn sees a strange bird he tries to kill it, rather
than writing poems about it. The *Agallamh* incorporates
pastoral poems which seem to come from what has been
called 'hermit poetry', praising the beauty and peace of nature
and living creatures in a way more appropriate for contem-
plative clerics than active warriors or even hunters. It is not
the first source to put such poems into the mouths of the
Fianna,[30] but from then on the pastoral element crops up,
though sporadically, in the prose as well. It may indeed be
worth suggesting that it was the attribution of nature poetry
to the Fenians which allowed Scottish hunters and game-
keepers like Domhnall mac Fhionnlaigh nan Dàn or Duncan
Bàn Macintyre to write about the peaceful joys of the deer-
forest in the same vein, which has fewer reflections in modern
Irish verse.

What sort of hunters were the Fenians? The early fragmentary references may give a picture of solitary trappers going
out on their own to bring in game and skins for their own
use — Fionn and his son 'Oiséne' meet at the latter's solitary
camp-fire and fail to recognise each other[31] — but in the
later romances and ballads, convention seems to demand the
full paraphernalia of an Irish royal hunt, with hounds and
beaters rousing the game from the coverts and driving it past
huntsmen who sit in their butts or hunting-mounds (*dumha*

29 S.H. O'Grady, *Silva Gadelica*, London 1892, I, 107, 113, 117,
    222, etc.
30 See K.H. Jackson, *Studies in Early Celtic Nature Poetry*, Cambridge
    1935, 41-4, 172-5: Jackson argues that these earlier, mostly seasonal
    poems, as well as later Fenian lore, have a different character from
    the ascetic hermit poems.
31 Murphy, *op. cit.*, lv, quoting K. Meyer, *Fianaigecht*, Dublin 1910,
    24 ff.

seilge),[32] just waiting for deer and other animals to come by and be shot or speared. This betrays the pastoral fallacy: with all that racket going on you would not have much chance to stop and listen to a blackbird singing. Nor is this the pleasure of simple country folk: each of the Fenians is represented as keeping a pair of hounds of his own,[33] and with the pay of extra huntsmen and beaters, it would be a costly and aristo-cratic form of sport, much like the more solitary deerstalking which is taken as the ideal pursuit for a gentleman in later Scottish Gaelic verse. In fact it is just what off-duty soldiers might do, like tiger-hunting in India, and fits well with the representation of the Fenians as a standing army.

The standing army is another anachronism. From the thirteenth century on some mediaeval Irish chieftains kept small bands of mercenaries, mostly Hebridean galloglasses to fight their wars for them,[34] but they were unpopular as an imposition on the tenants who had to pay their quartering (*buannacht*) and appear in an unfavourable light generally in literature: I have argued elsewhere that the word *amhus*, 'mercenary', has gone steadily downhill since the author of *Eachtra Chonaill Ghulban* depicted one band as coarse, ferocious creatures who speedily became ogres when the episode was used by folk narrators.[35] A substantial national standing army of patriotic Irishmen is quite another matter, and such a thing never really existed. It would be tempting to see the whole idea as an extrapolation backwards from the legend of the sleeping warriors who one day will awake to save the country in her hour of need, save that the Fenians are better known in this role in Scotland than in Ireland. Even if as I have suggested the nationalism is a secondary addition, there is still no evidence for substantial bands of wandering 'hunter-warriors' in early Christian Ireland. It is

32 O'Grady, *op. cit.*, 258-9, 306, illustrate the pattern.
33 Murphy, *op. cit.*, civ, and poems cited there: Murphy's modern parallels mention 'small farmers' and 'townsmen' keeping harriers, not poor countrymen, and the deerhounds of the Fenians would surely have been larger and finer dogs.
34 Nicholls, *op. cit.*, 87-90.
35 Bruford, *op. cit.* (1969), 15; cf. Murphy, *op. cit.*, 177, n. 4.

difficult to fit the idea into the network of tribal territories
with all action initiated by some member of the hierarchy of
over-kings and under-kings which seems to constitute the
historians' official concept of the period, though it could
have some basis in the period of conquest, conflict and
migration before the coming of Christianity and reliable
annals, when large war-bands from Ireland raided Britain,
settled in Scotland and conquered half of Ulster for the Uí
Néill. This is after all where the early historians chose to set
the cycle; but no doubt Zimmer's theory of Norse origin is
right to the extent that the arrival of wandering war-bands
of Vikings in the ninth century reminded the Irish that
such things could exist.[36] Perhaps the Fenians are a combination of a memory of a former age like this, a euhemerised
version of the Wild Hunt or the fairy host, and — by all means
— Joseph Nagy's concept of a fossilised adolescent peer-
group, boy scouts who like Peter Pan won't grow up and
leave the camp-fire to live in houses (see Nagy below, p.
161 ff). But certainly what has been made out of these
elements is a fictional construct, made to tell stories about,
with no more basis in fact than the vast company of wandering bards which inflicted itself on the historical king Guaire
in the story of the finding of the *Táin*.

This fictional patriotic army remains paradoxically disaffected and even downright rebellious to its king Cormac,[37]
and torn by internal dissension which ranges from bickering
to blood-feud, since Fionn's first lieutenant Goll is also his
father's killer by some accounts. Conflict is necessary to a
good epic and even the nostalgia of the *Agallamh* is tempered
with a little tragedy, but the theme of the elopement of
Diarmaid and Gráinne would really have provided all that was
needed: it sets even Oisín against his own father Fionn, and

---

36 *Zeitschrift für deutsches Altertum* 35 (1891), 1 ff. and 252 ff.
37 Not only are Fenians regularly reported as the killers of Cairbre
    Lifechar, king of Ireland, in the battle of Gabhair, but a Scottish
    ballad (J.F. Campbell, *Leabhar na Feinne*, London 1872, 141-2)
    has his father Cormac being killed by them in a dispute over a
    woman with Oisean. On the other hand Kennedy's prose (*ibid.*,
    185) takes Cairbre to be a usurper of Cormac's throne, not his heir.

leads to the final unconnected tragedy just as surely as the
affair of Lancelot and Guinevere leads to the death of Arthur.
The internal conflict is more stressed in literary than folk
narratives; so indeed is the constant tension with the king.
The Fenians are not outlaws, but above and beyond the law,
powerful enough to unseat the king who pays them and
often out of his reach. This is perhaps an alternative reaction
to the same situation which produced the nationalism: the
Fianna are the army of Ireland, but the only king claiming to
rule all Ireland that the late mediaeval writers knew was the
king of England, and Cormac is treated with as much loyalty
as they felt to him. In fact the Hiberno-Norman barons of
the fifteenth century often were as independent of the Crown
as the Fenians, so this is not entirely wish-fulfilment, but
there is an obvious change of attitude from the Ulster tales
where the idea of high-kingship is either ignored or treated as
elective. Folktales tend to simplify the situation by calling
Fionn himself a king.

One other feature which belongs firmly to the literary side
of the cycle is characterisation. This is mostly pretty elemen-
tary — comedy of humours rather than comedy of manners
— and only a few characters are established: the *jeune premier*
Oscar, Diarmaid the great lover, Conán the sarcastic and
savage (who tends to degenerate in later tales into a boastful
buffoon), Caoilte the swift and playful, Fionn the ageing
leader with prophetic powers. Goll, developed in some ballads
as an alternative hero, has his smouldering feud with Fionn
but little individual character, and even Oisín, perhaps a bit
more thoughtful than most as a poet, has no very distinct
personality before his arguments with St Patrick. There is
enough there, however, to add interest to the dialogue or a
comic interlude between battles, and individual authors could
assign traits of personality as well as special skills to established
or invented names when they wanted more. Most seem to
have been content with by-play between Conán and Diarmaid
for light relief, and this has carried over into the oral tradition,
which deals with the characters in its own way but does not,
I think, add to their number.

So what elements in Fenian folktales are really folk
elements? Some can be recognised by the way they distort

the heroic/pastoral ambience of the literary tales. Fionn as a comic giant pretending to be his own baby in a cradle and biting the finger of a visiting giant clearly belongs to a different world, and I know of no evidence for the story before the eighteenth century: the first instance seems to be from Scotland, though the story has hardly been known there since, and the collector felt that it had been made up to discredit the ancient heroes.[38] The fact that either the giant in the cradle or his visitor may alternatively be named as Cú Chulainn — originally the small young hero *par excellence* — shows how little the story has to do with Fenian or any other literature.

Other elements may have arisen in folk tradition because Gaelic society and attitudes have changed since the Middle Ages. Diarmaid's *ball seirce*, the magic love spot which makes any woman who sees it fall in love with him, is not in the romance (cf. Ó hÓgáin below, p. 227 ff.) or any of the older tradition because it is not needed. In Old Irish tales, possibly founded on pagan myth, though not uninfluenced by monastic distrust of the daughters of Eve, a woman often takes the initiative in an elopement with the assurance of a conquering goddess: Deirdre in the older version of her story, *Longes mac n-Uislenn*, forces Naoise to carry her off from her husband-to-be by threatening to shame him, and Gráinne uses magic and the same sort of blackmail to make Diarmaid take her in the same way. Modern storytellers are not conditioned to accept this sort of behaviour or to put any blame on a woman — unless she is a witch or a supernatural hag — so they introduce the magical motif to absolve Gráinne of blame. The idea has reached Scotland as well as Ireland, but as part of this story at least I do not think it can be very old. The same cannot be said of the alternative end to the story, where Diarmaid is not simply killed by the boar of Benbulben, as in the romance, but kills it first and only gets his death-wound from a venomous bristle that runs into his foot when Fionn asks him to measure the body with his bare feet. Apart from the memories of Achilles and Adonis that it stirs, the

38 *Ibid.*, 7.

episode survives in folk memory mainly on the periphery, in Scotland and Co. Cork, whereas the more straightforward account in the romance seems to have taken over in between. But in any case this is hardly a folk motif, since it features prominently in the ballad form of the story, 'Laoidh Dhiarmaid', which is now known mainly from Scotland but may have been composed by a poet who used the literary metres about the same time as the surviving prose romance – and Scotland and Co. Cork also preserve most of the folktales that reflect written originals most closely. The motif functions to increase Diarmaid's status, making him almost invulnerable and only to be killed by a treacherous trick, and if he is originally a god it may well be part of the original story, dropped by the romancer because there is nothing very heroic about it.

Another social element in Irish and a few Scottish folktales is the exploitation of the obligations connected with death and funerals, important in all Celtic societies but particularly in the small communities of the recent Gaeltachts. An invitation to a funeral was a particularly binding social obligation, so in the Lorcán story mentioned above it is used to entice the Fenians into the *bruidhean*: in the Scottish parallel the invitation is actually to watch the grave the night after the funeral. Similarly in an episode found in versions of 'Céadach' and other tales when the hero has killed one monster the least he can do is to honour its dying request to take the news of its death to another creature, which of course instantly attacks him to avenge its friend, and, when he kills it, in its turn makes a similar dying request.

This story of Céadach is one where it is very hard to tell literary from folk elements. Hundreds of versions have been recorded in Ireland, and a fair number in Scotland: next to the *Bruidhean Chaorthainn*, or rather its central motif of sticking to the seats, it is probably the most popular of all Fenian tales. It cannot possibly have spread from the late Munster Ms version of which only four texts survive, which in any case is evidently a written-down version of the folktale with a perfunctory end, and some would-be literary touches added by the scribe.[39] On the other hand there are

39 Bruford, *op. cit.* (1969), 123-6.

fuller folk versions from both Ireland and Scotland with elements that seem too complex for pure folktale. For instance the story often begins with a scene in which Céadach, the hero, wins a bride who follows him rather than a rival suitor: he joins the Fenians to escape from this rival who nonetheless catches up and kills him towards the end of the story. It is not typical of folktale construction to have such a character waiting in the wings throughout the greater part of the story, and the Munster Ms and a few other versions leave out this introduction and have Céadach killed by an unknown assailant. This structure and the hero's constant name, among other features, suggest an earlier literary origin, very possibly a lost written romance, which need not be much older than the sixteenth century in order to have succeeded in generating an oral story which is now of such popularity.[40] To the literary references from the fifteenth to the early nineteenth century to a Céadach as one of the Fenians which I have collected in my book[41] I can add a mention of him as a fallen Fenian in a poem in *Duanaire Finn* which Murphy dated as thirteenth-century,[42] though he is given a conventional epithet, *fear go n-aoibh*, 'happy man' or 'handsome man', which gives no indication of his history.

The end of the Céadach story seems certainly more like folktale than literary romance: after a shape-changing battle in mid-air — a possible mediaeval element if, as in some folk versions, both rivals first met as students of magic with Manannán — the two opponents kill each other, but Céadach is resurrected often by his wife copying the actions of birds she watches. This is a commonplace of international *Märchen*; alternatives are a borrowing of the *Bruidhean Chaorthuinn* cure with blood, or a confusion with another common resurrection motif, the 'Everlasting Fight', which could be closest to the literary original if any.[43] Still, it is hard to avoid won-

40 *Ibid.*, 126-7.
41 *Ibid.*, 123.
42 MacNeill, *op. cit.*, 48 (lay XIX, verse 14); Murphy, *op. cit.*, 42.
43 Bruford, *op. cit.* (1969), 126 and note 27. The motif of resurrection by copying animals is said by Stith Thompson (*Motif-Index of Folk Literature*, Copenhagen 1955-8, motif B. 512) to be most usual of serpents, but birds are not uncommon in Gaelic variants as far as I know.

dering why in a whole group of versions the way to resurrect
the hero is shown by birds, he and his rival kill each other in
mid-air in bird form, and the rival's name is Londubh, 'Blackbird'. It is possible that this complex of bird symbols was
prompted by the coincidence of the mid-air fight and the
resemblance of Céadach's name to *céirseach*, a bird often
associated with the *londubh*[44] in poetry and lore; there is
even a name not unlike Londubh which could have been used
for this character in the original romance, if there was one.[45]
But the blackbird in Fenian lore has in any case a meaning
which seems to go beyond the tuneful songster of the grove
in nature-poetry, though of course this aspect of the bird is
noticed too.

It is probably a red herring, this blackbird, but it is curious
how its name keeps on cropping up in Fenian lore. It is
natural enough that a character called Fionn, 'fair', tends to
have opponents called Dubh, 'black': one of the earliest of all
references to a character called Find who was a hunter and
warrior is in the Latin verse text of the puzzle-tale still told
in Gaelic about Fionn and Dubhan, in a ninth-century Continental Ms,[46] and his opponent there is called Dub — though
they are no more than personified black and white counters
there. But the *lon* element on its own is used for opponents
and monsters too — 'a dreadful beast called Lun' in a Fenian
folktale collected in the last century,[47] or the blackbird whose
shank is bigger than a deer's leg which Oisín catches in the
story of his last hunt: we will return to this presently, but
here it is worth noting that there is a ghost word in Scottish
Gaelic dictionaries, *lon*, 'elk' (extended by Forbes to cover

---

44 Bruford, *op. cit.* (1969), 124-5 and n. 12; but *céirseach* is feminine
    and means either a female blackbird or a thrush, associated with
    the blackbird in the manner of Robin Redbreast and Jenny Wren.
45 An Dubhlaoch, one of the main opponents of Céadach in the late
    romance *Eachtra na gCuradh* (ed. Meadhbh Ní Chléirigh, Baile Átha
    Cliath 1941) — but the name is roughly equivalent to 'the Black
    Knight', as conventional a villain-name as you can get.
46 G. Murphy, 'The Puzzle of the Thirty Counters', *Béaloideas* 12
    (1942), 23-8.
47 Murphy, *op. cit.* (1953), xix.

moose and buffalo),[48] which seems to derive solely from the lexicographers' refusal to believe in this blackbird bigger than a modern deer — so the word had to mean something else, why not the extinct elk whose bones were sometimes dug up in the bogs? One can see their point — w h y a blackbird? If it were just for the incongruity, like the hunted wren which needs to be brought back in a wagon in French ritual and Anglo-Scots song,[49] why not a wren, which is smaller and has undoubted mythical significance as 'King of the Birds' and midwinter sacrifice? Perhaps it had to be something that was not taboo at other times — but were small birds like blackbirds fair game in early Ireland, or does our present distaste for Italian thrush-hunters (like that for French horse-butchers) have deep roots? In any case there is greater incongruity in the name of Fionn's sword, Mac an Luin, which the lexicographer seems to accept as meaning 'son of the blackbird'.[50] The ballad of the Smithy, 'Duan na Ceardaich', explains that it was made by a supernatural blacksmith named Lon mac Lìobhainn in Scottish versions, Lon mac Líomhtha in *Duanaire Finn*.[51] Except in the *Duanaire* the ballad is known almost exclusively from Scottish oral tradition, where it has remained enormously popular especially as a chant for New Year guisers going round the houses,[52] but its plot has been collected as a prose story in

---

48 A.R. Forbes, *Gaelic Names of Beasts . . . etc.*, Edinburgh 1905, 13, 70, 158: see also *ibid.*, 246, for a saying in which the blackbird is again strangely masterful, 'supposed by some to refer to either the Roman or Scandinavian invader.'

49 E.A. Armstrong, *The Folklore of Birds*, London 1958, 147-9.

50 Royal Irish Academy, *Contributions to a Dictionary of the Irish Language*, s.v. '1 lon'. The quantity seems to rule out the similar *lúin*, 'lance', associated with Celtchar and other heroes.

51 No. XXXVI. Mac Líomhtha, 'Son of Whetting', is an appropriate name for a sword-smith, and it may well be that the Scottish name has been assimilated to placenames such as Loch Leven (Lìobhainn).

52 At least in the Uists, where most versions have been collected recently. Is it a coincidence that the ballad was used at the time of year traditional for wren hunts?

Ireland and the Isle of Man;[53] it is in a literary metre and
dated by Murphy c.1400 on its language[54] — this is literary
tradition of some antiquity. Why call a rather ogre-like blacksmith 'blackbird'? Or, as O'Rahilly turned the *bolg* of the Fir
Bolg from a bag into a lightning-god,[55] should we look for a
second meaning for *lon*?

I have illustrated the dangers of the name game already,
and before I find myself suggesting that blackbirds are a
'multiform' of wrens, I had better leave this game for someone else to finish if they dare. Time also forbids me going
into some other anomalous prose tales, such as *Bodach an
Chóta Lachtna*, 'The Churl in the Drab Coat', where the late
Irish Ms version is paralleled by Scottish folktales which
put Murchadh son of Brian in place of Fionn and seem to
have links with another late Irish manuscript tale, seemingly
made out of a folktale, *Giolla an Fhiugha*, 'The Servant with
the Billhook'.[56] Ignorance forbids me to meddle with the
Fenian lays, and I want to end by considering two points in
folktales at the beginning and end of the whole cycle.

The stories of Fionn's birth and young days have been dealt
with by others (see Ó hÓgáin, Nagy below), and I want to
consider only one element in them where oral tradition has
more to say than the literature, the story of how Fionn got
his 'thumb of knowledge', which he had only to chew or lay
below his upper teeth — folktale tellers make much more of a
meal of it than literary texts[57] — for clairvoyant insight. (I
can remember no account which specifies w h i c h thumb it is:
the stories of its origin suggest the right, if Fionn was right-
handed, but it is an odd ambiguity.) I am not concerned with

53 Murphy, *op. cit.* (1953), 86-7 lists prose versions from Ireland and
    one in very corrupt verse from Co. Donegal (*Gaelic Journal* 11,
    137-8); for the Manx version see A.W. Moore, *The Folk-Lore of
    the Isle of Man*, Douglas 1891, 27-9 (from Train's collection: King
    Olave Goddardson replaces Fionn and Caoilte).
54 *Op. cit.* (1953), 85.
55 T.F. O'Rahilly, *Early Irish History and Mythology*, Dublin 1946,
    43-57.
56 Bruford, *op. cit.* (1969), 129, 142-3.
57 *Ibid.*, 219 and n. 27.

what is generally seen as an older explanation, in which the thumb was caught in the closing door of a fairy dwelling,[58] but with the story still popular in oral tradition that he got the power by being the first to taste a salmon he was cooking for someone else, because he used the relevant thumb to press down a blister that rose on the fish's skin and then put it in his mouth to cool it.[59] This is obviously a variant of an international tale, which though it has been catalogued as AT 673, 'The White Serpent's Flesh' in the *Types of the Folktale* is a legend rather than a *Märchen*.[60] The standard European type in which the hero acquires magic or healing powers from being first to taste the flesh of a snake he is cooking for his master is certainly known in Scotland if not Ireland, told of St Fillan (Faolan), Michael Scot and the founder of the Beaton family of physicians among others.[61] Another version is associated in the Icelandic *Vǫlsunga saga* with Sigurd, the

---

58 Murphy, *op. cit* (1953), 55. The accidental nature of the gift is in keeping with modern fairy legend again.

59 The blister does not appear in *Macgnímartha Find* (ed. K. Meyer, *Revue Celtique* 5 (1881-3), 195-204) but is stressed in many folk versions: the power may be seen as residing in the juice of the cooked fish rather than its skin, as Norse parallels mention the blood of the dragon's heart. The healing power of a drink from Fionn's hands mentioned in *Tóruigheacht Dhiarmada agus Ghráinne* (ed. Neasa Ní Shéaghdha, ITS 48, Dublin 1967, 90, 1. 1575) is ascribed there to his handling of the (whole?) salmon: compare the healing gift in the international folktale.

60 It is not clear which of the versions listed by S. Ó Súilleabháin and R.Th. Christiansen, *The Types of the Irish Folktale*, FF Communications 188, Helsinki 1963 under AT 673 are versions of the Fionn tale, which of the other tradition noted in the heading told of Carroll O'Daly, or whether any mention the snake. Since Scottish versions may set the snake incident in another country Ireland's lack of snakes would not prevent the tale being told. Investigation proves in fact that some of the versions listed are in fact mere accounts of Fionn's thumb of knowledge, with no description of how he got it: the three references to *Béaloideas* 7 are all of this sort.

61 D.A. MacDonald and A. Bruford, *Scottish Traditional Tales*, Edinburgh 1974, 96-7; W. Grant Stewart, *The Popular Superstitions and Festive Amusements of the Highlanders of Scotland* (new ed. London 1851), 53-6; J.F. Campbell, *Popular Tales of the West Highlands*, new ed., London 1890-3, Vol. 2, 377-83.

Volsung, who slew the dragon Fáfnir and roasted its heart for his adviser Regin the smith, but burned his fingers on it, licked them, and was at once able to understand the birds which were talking of Regin's plans to kill him. The saga itself is no earlier than the fourteenth century, but the incident is depicted on two Manx crosses of the late tenth or early eleventh centuries.[62] The roasting of the heart alone merely reflects the size of the dragon, depicted on another Manx cross simply as a huge snake. Snakes are long-established symbols of knowledge and especially healing in Europe, but unknown in Ireland: salmon, especially Boyne salmon as in *Macgnímartha Finn*, 'The Boyhood Deeds of Finn', were symbols of knowledge and poetic or prophetic inspiration in Ireland, and would be obvious substitutes for the snake. But these arguments work equally well in the other direction, and the Irish story might possibly be archetype for the European legend.

One development in folk tradition may throw some light on the relationship between the Fionn and Sigurd stories. The knowledge acquired by the taster of the white snake is generally a gift of healing or clairvoyance which lasts for life but has no immediate application, and is normally available without a recapitulation of putting the burnt finger in the mouth (though some Scottish versions borrow this detail from Fionn). For Sigurd and for Fionn in most of the folktales, however, the knowledge immediately tells them that the man who set them to cook heart or salmon and who intended to taste it first is an enemy. Regin is plotting to kill Sigurd — he is in fact the dragon's brother — and the man who caught Fionn's salmon and set him to cook it is either planning to

62 P.M.C. Kermode, *Manx Crosses*, London 1907, 170-7. In discussion of this paper by Rory McTurk and H.R.E. Davidson it was pointed out that this episode is also told in the Eddic lay Fáfnismál (prose following strophe 31 and strophes 32 ff.; H. Kuhn, ed., *Edda*, Heidelberg 1962, 186-8. These references are older than the saga probably, but not now agreed to be older than the crosses. Kermode's dating of these (*op. cit.* 179-80) is a century later than that given in the text, which follows A.M. Cubbon's booklet *The Art of the Manx Crosses*, Douglas 1971, 26-9.

kill Fionn, or in most Scottish and perhaps a few Irish versions Fionn is bound to kill him, for he is the man who killed Fionn's father Cumhall.[63] In the *Macgnímartha* he is a druid who like the doctor in the serpent tales wants the knowledge for himself, but accepts quietly that he is not fated to have it and bestows his own name upon Fionn. In oral versions of the tale of Fionn's youthful deeds there is a revenge element which rounds off the story much more satisfactorily, and in some versions Fionn finds out by his newly acquired powers where his father's sword, with which he was killed, is hidden, and kills the killer with it.[64] It is not impossible for loose ends to be tied up in this way in the course of oral transmission:[65] the resemblance to the Sigurd motif, however, must raise the question whether this oral tradition may not represent an older if not the oldest form of the episode.

A curiously primitive element in these Scottish versions has only come to my notice since I started to write this paper. Modern storytellers refer to the catcher of the salmon (or more often trout) who had killed Cumhall as Arca Dubh, 'Black Arca', and this name or something very close to it[66] appears in most of the Scottish versions that give him a name, back to one written in Mull in 1803. Another black opponent for Fionn is no surprise, but the word *arca* is not to be found

---

63. J.F. Campbell, *op. cit.* (1890-3), 352-3; *op. cit.* (1872), 37-8; J.G. Campbell, *The Fians. Waifs and Strays of Celtic Tradition* 4, London 1891, 20 and 26; A. MacLellan, *Stories from South Uist*, trans. J.L. Campbell, London 1961, 8-9; *Scottish Studies* 1 (1957), 205-10; IFC Ms 1029, 296-305 (Barra); at least eight other storytellers from S. Uist, Barra, Vatersay and Tiree have recorded versions with this element for the School of Scottish Studies.

64. The sword (sometimes named as Mac a' Luin) appears in a majority of the recordings, the manuscript and published versions cited except J.F. Campbell, *op. cit.* (1890) (killing and finding sword not connected?) and the two in *The Fians* (fisher killed with his own rod; torn asunder). Cf. *Béaloideas* 3 (1931-2), 187-95, where Fionn kills the giant who has his father's sword, though Goll is named as Cumhall's killer.

65. Bruford, *op. cit.* (1969), 236-7.

66. Forca in J.F. Campbell, *op. cit.* (1872); Arcan in J.F. Campbell, *op. cit.* (1890-3, Vol. 2); Arcai in J.G. Campbell, *op. cit.*; Arca or Arcaidh in all modern versions cited in n. 63.

in dictionaries, and I was driven to wonder whether there could be a connection with *erc* or *orc*, poetic names for a salmon. However my colleague D.A. MacDonald tells me that in Uist *arca* is a word still used for the vagina of a cow or other large animal, and the late Donald Alasdair Johnson, a remarkable South Uist storyteller, once recorded an explanation for the name which in other cases he only hinted at.[67] Arca Dubh had been expelled from the Fenians for bestiality with a cow, which was killed and its vulva put round his neck as a collar and a visible sign of the name he bore ever after. This may be merely a folk etymology for a name which could not be explained, but it may be an ancient element which other storytellers have suppressed at least when they have told the story to outsiders. Narrators are more willing to admit a strong sexual element which is certainly present in the killing of Cumhall by Arca Dubh in revenge: Cumhall is killed, perhaps can only be killed, in bed as soon as he has consummated his marriage with the king of Lochlann's daughter, and thus begotten Fionn who is eventually to avenge him.[68] The symbolism of his death in that situation by his own sword in the hands of someone whose name means Black Vulva and who was hidden under the bed during the lovemaking could certainly be exploited by any Freudian, and the death of that killer by the same sword in the hands of the son who has acquired new potency from a fish (substituting for a snake?) fits the pattern almost as well.

The very last act of the cycle has no known literary prototype. This is the story of Oisín's last hunt, known in Scotland often by the proverbial phrase *Oisean an Déidh na Féinne*, 'Ossian After the Fenians [had Vanished]'; more prosaically referred to as 'Oisín and Patrick's Housekeeper' by Murphy

---

67 In the first recording he would not name the crime, later when he knew the fieldworkers better he was fairly explicit about the punishment, but only to an Italian student who could not understand him did he state plainly that Arca Dubh was 'making a bull of himself on the cow' (*a' dèanamh tarbh dhe fhéin air a' bhoin*).

68 So in printed Scottish versions in note 63 except *Leabhar na Feinne*; not very clear in *The Fians*, 24, different *ibid.*, 16.

in Ireland.[69] The situation is that established by the literary *Agallamh*, that Oisín (in this tale alone, without Caoilte) has survived his companions by many years and tells his story to St Patrick. A few Scottish versions provide an explanation rather different both from the well-known account in Micheál Cuimín's eighteenth-century lay of his visit with the beautiful Niamh to Tír na nÓg, 'The Land of the [Ever-]Young', or the Irish folktales in which he is otherwise tempted to Tír na hÓige, 'The Land of Youth'. Unlike Murphy,[70] I am prepared to believe that Cuimín first simplified the *Agallamh*'s vague account of Oisín and Caoilte spending unspecified numbers of years in various fairy hills in Ireland into a visit to an overseas otherworld. Of the elements he used, the fairy woman who invites a mortal to the overseas 'Earthly Paradise' is a literary motif no doubt with pagan antecedents which recurs from the Old Irish 'Voyage of Bran' onwards, and the idea that time passes more quickly in the otherworld is also in *Immram Brain* — at least the prose narration, which is not as remarkably early as the verse passages may be[71] — and still recurs in folk legend, though the 'Rip Van Winkle' type telling of a man caught up in a fairy dance, very widely known over the past century in Scotland, has parallels in Wales but seemingly none

---

69 Murphy, *op. cit.* (1953), xix-xx, with list of versions; S. Ó Súill-eabháin, *A Handbook of Irish Folklore*, Dublin 1942, 593, No. 19, for summary; J.F. Campbell, *op. cit.* (1890-3), 2, 113-20 (versions from Barra, Sutherland and Argyll, referred to below as B, S, A); *op. cit.* (1872), 38-9 (Mull, 1803: 'M'); J.G. Campbell, *op. cit.*, 82-4 (Tiree? 'T'); *Tocher* 29 (1978), 292-301 (Sutherland/Ross, 'R'). Unpublished Scottish versions include Campbell of Islay Ms XVI, 147 (summary from Mull) and recordings in the School of Scottish Studies from Tiree, Arisaig, South Uist (2), and four more from Sutherland or Ross-shire travellers; some of these are cited below.

70 Murphy, *op. cit.* (1953), xxii-iii.

71 G. Murphy, *Early Irish Lyrics*, Oxford 1956, 216, accepts an early eighth- or even seventh-century date for the verses in *Immram Brain*, which imply the story of the invitation. Tales like *Serglige Con Culainn*, the last of the types paralleled by fairy legends listed above, where the mortal is invited to help the otherworld host, have a distinct theme, but this may be involved in some traditions of Oisín.

in Ireland.[72] Cuimín may also have been inspired to some extent by the tales of dream visits to Heaven and Hell composed by Irish clerics in the Dark Ages and later,[73] which owe something to the pagan stories of a summons to the otherworld, or a Gaelic version of the related international folktale type AT 470, 'Friends in Life and Death'. In some Scottish versions of this a cleric is summoned to the otherworld by a skull he has spoken to and after visions of punishments there returns to earth to find that a hundred years or more have passed in what seemed an afternoon. Like Oisín he is warned not to dismount from his horse except on a special mat, but when he forgets the prohibition and touches the earth he does not only become an old man but crumbles into dust.[74] In Scotland the story is known in this form but never told of Oisean; in Ireland the ending is told of Oisín, whose entry into the otherworld may however be rather different from either AT 470 or Cuimín's lay.[75] It is still

---

72 See A. Bruford, 'Legends Long Since Localised...', *Scottish Studies* 24 (1980), 54-5.

73 St J.D. Seymour, *Irish Visions of the Other-World*, London 1930: the passing of time in such visions naturally tends to follow the reverse principle, that a long journey is over in one night.

74 C. Maclean, 'A' Ministear agus an Claban', *Scottish Studies* 1 (1957), 65-9, is the only Scottish Gaelic version I can cite complete with this ending. However, two other travellers with the same surname as the Alasdair Stewart who recorded the tale for Calum have recorded versions in Lowland Scots with this end, and a similar story with little account of otherworld punishments was popular in Shetland (C. Maclean, *Shetland Folk Book* III, 65-7; A. Bruford, *The Green Man of Knowledge* . . ., Aberdeen 1982, 68-71).

75 Oisín's journey to the Otherworld is listed by Ó Súilleabháin and Christiansen, *op. cit.* as AT 470*, 'The Hero Visits the Land of the Immortals', but I have not seen any version of the skull type with a similar end from Ireland, where it is one of the less common international religious tales, possibly because the native type has taken over. Oisín is led into the Otherworld by a deer he chases, a bird that steals his ring (see n. 78 below), or even carried there on a funeral bier in versions printed in early numbers of *Béaloideas* (1 [1927-8], 219; 2 [1929-30], 254 [1933-4], 191) but not simply invited by a beautiful fairy woman as in the lay. One Scottish account, J.G. Campbell, *op. cit.*, 80, says that Oisean was s e n t to Tìr na h-Oige.

quite possible that Cuimín first adapted the international type to explain Oisín's longevity, but that folktale tellers have sometimes rejected his too literary introduction; on the other hand he may have added this introduction to an existing folk tradition about Oisín. In either case there is no question of the tradition being very ancient, because it depends on the idea of Oisín's survival established by the *Agallamh*, and though that has reached Scotland this explanation has not. Indeed there is no reason in oral tradition why the Fenians and St Patrick should not have been near-contemporaries; only a literary person who knew there were six generations between Cormac and Laoghaire in the genealogies or two hundred years between them in the pseudo-historical annals would find any difficulty in making Oisín survive to Patrick's time.

Most Scottish versions of the tale in fact do not bother to explain Oisean's longevity, but simply represent him as an aged man living in the house of Patrick, who is often represented as married to Oisean's daughter! (Even in Catholic areas of Scotland St Patrick has travelled less well than the Fenians: he may be represented as having the tithes (*càin*) of all Ireland, but Campbell of Islay's translation of him into 'Peter Mac Alpin' probably shows how little knowledge of him the average Argyll Gael in his day would have had.[76]) A version of the story recorded from two Sutherland travellers called Alasdair Stewart, Aili Dall or Blind Sandy and his nephew known as Brian,[77] does however explain Oisean's long life by the gift of a magic ring from the fairy wife he once had. She is nothing like Cuimín's Niamh, but belongs to a well-established group of fairy wives who impose conditions on their husbands and leave them when these are broken.[78] Oisean was visited by her in the form of a crow

---

76 J.F. Campbell, *op. cit.* (1872), 38, summarising the book-burning story below as heard 'over and over again, in Scotland'. *Pàdruig* is almost always Englished as Peter if it is the name of a Scottish Gael, and Mac Alpin is not far from St Patrick's traditional patronymic *mac Calpruinn*, son of Calpurnius.

77 SA 1958/73 A11; SA 1958/72 A13-B1 and Linguistic Survey Tape 965 (=R).

78 See T.F. O'Rahilly, *Gadelica* I (1913), 282; Bruford, *op. cit.* (1969), 134-5.

and broke her enchantment by spending a night with her, but
he is not to mention in what form he first saw her. He is
enraged when she sells a puppy he wanted to keep and calls
her 'you black crow' (*o, fheannag dhubh*), on which she flies
off in that form, but gives him the ring and tells him he will
live as long as he keeps it on his finger. At the end Oisean's
attendant is washing the old man in a stream and takes the
ring off his finger: a crow carries it off and Oisean goes home
— after killing the attendant — and dies.[79] The story may
well have a long history, for a rather garbled version of it is
in the Mull manuscript of 1803 mentioned above,[80] and is
quite as well in tune with Gaelic fairy traditions as the
invitation to Tír na nÓg which it replaces in Scotland.

The story that follows in Scottish versions serves to
explain why today's Fenian lore seems so fragmentary and
confused: Campbell of Islay calls it an allegory of the Ossianic
controversy.[81] Once more the written text is taken as the
authority. Patrick himself has been writing down Oisean's
tales, but he cannot believe them all — in the tradition of the
flyting dialogues which introduce some of the ballads. When
the fine haunch of a deer that the saint shows his father-in-

---

79 This is 'Brian's' version (R), learned from his grandmother, and
seems slightly more appropriate to this tale than the variant told
by Aili Dall and his daughter Mary (SA 1957/48 B2) who agree in
making the woman appear as an ugly woman, who becomes beautiful after a night with Oisean — a motif told of fairy or divine figures
in Gaelic lore too often to need a parallel cited — and only turns
into a raven (which later steals the ring) when he reproaches her
with her former ugliness.

80 M (see note 69): a raven steals the ring, which keeps Oisín from
dying or going blind, and the blind old man finds it again when his
grandson, Patrick's son, lets him fall over a cliff — presumably to
get rid of the old nuisance! — after the blackbird hunt. In a story
from Co. Sligo, *Béaloideas* 2 (1929-30), 254, a bird steals the ring
which preserves Oisín from hunger, to make him follow it to his
fairy mother's home in Tír na hÓige. It may be relevant that a
'Ring of Youth', *Fáinne na hÓige*, often appears in Irish tales both
as a magic object and a princess's name.

81 J.F. Campbell, *op. cit.* (1890-3), 2, 118 — 'Oisian, MacPherson, Dr
Smith, and their party, fused into "Ossian", Dr Johnson, and his
followers, condensed into "Padraig!" '.

law provokes the response that Oisean has seen a blackbird's leg bigger than that, Patrick flies in a rage and throws the books of the old man's lies in the fire: his daughter rescues them, but much has been lost for ever.[82] Whoever made up this story was no ignorant peasant: he may not have been literate, but he knew that Fenian lore was in books (manuscripts rather than print, since the story was certainly well established before 1800) and had discussed it enough with his contemporaries to know there were gaps and discrepancies in the stories. It is not usually stated that Oisean was a giant himself, though he may still have been very strong,[83] but perhaps he had shrunk along with the rest of the world. At any rate the proof of his veracity recalls Conan Doyle's 'Lost World' of dinosaurs — I wonder if Doyle knew of it? — though perhaps the real meaning of the tale is that it is bad manners to accuse a storyteller of exaggerating, and Patrick is in effect taught a lesson like 'the man who had no story'.[84]

The Irish versions of the story are more in the burlesque giant-tale tradition: they emphasise Oisín's enormous appetite, though even Scottish versions mention how he 'had to wear a

82 This seems the most logical, and is R's account, except that the girl seems to be Patrick's daughter rather than Oisean's; but most versions in fact choose one of two different options — (1) Oisean himself burns the books and his daughter saves some (B; Angus MacLellan, S. Uist, SA 1963/13 B2); or (2) Patrick burns them but later repents (and saves some, Aili Dall; too late, T; Mrs Peggy MacDonald, Angus MacLellan's sister, SA 1959/58 B1). In M, the earliest version, there is another twist which those concerned with saving family papers may find the most likely of all — Oisean's daughter throws her father's tales in the fire, and the others can only save a little.

83 S, contributed in English, calls Oisean 'the last of the giants' (and no other name) which suggests that someone telling the story in English translated *Féinn* as 'giants'; references to him as a giant in A, summarised next, may be due to Campbell himself. Oisean's strength is most stressed in T and the modern Tiree version told by Donald Sinclair (SA 1960/70 A, SA 1958/2/6) where he lifts a stone sixteen builders could not.

84 Listed by Ó Súilleabháin and Christiansen, *op. cit.*, as AT 2412B: a man with no story to tell has strange, usually horrific experiences soon after and is told at the end 'now you have a story'.

hunger-belt' or had his belly pinned together with skewers.[85]
St Patrick's housekeeper (he is clearly thought of in terms of
the parish priest) thinks she is generous in offering the hero a
quarter of an ox, the butter of a whole churning, and an out-
size oatcake for each meal. The blackbird's leg is to be bigger
than the beef, a rowan berry than the lump of butter, an ivy
leaf than the bannock[86] — a contrast of wild nature and the
farm rather than a comparison of foods. But what follows is
clearly the same story: finding the leaf and berry is peculiar
to the Irish variant and appeasing Oisean's hunger in the field
with venison[87] to the Scottish. Otherwise the same elements
are there: the boy to help the (often blind) old hero, the
special dog to kill the game, the hole in the ground and the
whistle or horn (*Barra-Buadh*) blown to summon big and
then yet bigger game, and the dog which has to be killed
through its gaping mouth before it turns its blood-lust on

85 Belt, M, S; skewers, B, T; in the latter he asks for the 16 men's food
    to do their work.
86 Based on Ó Súilleabháin, *op. cit.*, and versions this may follow —
    Béaloideas 2 (1929-30), 65-7, 256-7; *ibid.* 5 (1915), 292-3; also
    Choice Notes from 'Notes and Queries', *Folklore*, London 1859,
    103-4, from Co. Clare; J. Curtin, *Myths and Folklore of Ireland*,
    Boston 1890, 337-42. Rather garbled in P. Kennedy's *Legendary
    Fictions of the Irish Celts*, London 1866, 240-2, where a lark's leg
    is bigger than a shoulder of mutton and 'the berry of the wild ash
    ... as large as a sheep' — surely a mistranslation. In Scotland S and
    a Wester Ross traveller's recording (SA 1957/26-27, which turns
    Patrick into a cattle-reiver!) speak of beef rather than venison, as in
    the Irish versions.
87 The deer may just allow Oisean to let out his belt (one or more are
    cooked, usually boiled in a cauldron but sometimes (R, S) roasted
    on a camp fire) but the meal may also renew his youth (M), or
    restore his sight and hearing (T, R). In T he apparently vanishes
    into the woods and is never seen again: his grandson brings back
    the bone. But in R the boy (here just a servant) tastes the meat
    first and leaves a mark on Oisean's eye — an echo of Fionn and the
    salmon at the other end of the cycle? In A it is worse and he remains
    blind, but 'if he had eaten all he could have recovered his sight'.
    In M he would have been as good as new if the boy had not taken
    some, and seems to be blind until he finds his ring; in S and B he
    evidently stays blind, and in the latter he is angry with the boy for
    eating three of the nine stags.

the hunters.[88] The Irish details are more logical — the hound is chosen for its grip as a puppy and the horn found buried in the pit summons the great blackbird which the hound kills — the Scottish more mysterious — the hound is a survivor of the Fenians, itself sometimes found buried under a clump of rushes, with a name that recalls the blackbird's yellow bill;[89] the hole may be dug to protect the boy's ears from the ear-splitting whistle;[90] and the dog kills the deer it summons to feed Oisean, while the blackbird is found and killed later, usually with an arrow.[91] But there is enough in common to create a strong presumption that the story was known, in some form, whether 'folk', oral literary or even written, before

88 In Scotland Oisean kills it by putting a hand down its throat (B, M) with which he takes out its liver and lungs (T); in Ireland he throws a metal ball or stone down its throat usually. Both methods are common in Gaelic tales, and the second at least derives ultimately from Cú Chulainn's killing of the hound which gave him his name.

89 Biorach-Mac-Buidheag M, Biorach mac Buidheig T, Mac Buidheig B, (phonetically) 'cue baie mac kill e buiach' A, Biorach a' Bhuidheag R: *biorach*, 'sharp', is in three and *buidhe*, 'yellow' in all. Note that Fionn's own hound is called Bran mac Buidheag in a version of the boyhood deeds (J.F. Campbell, *op. cit.* [1890-3], 3, 351-3). The dog is found under a clump of rushes — A, R; Oisean wishes for the worst dog of the Fenians — M, B, T — and knows it has come when he feels its weight lying on his legs — M, B.

90 In Irish versions the *Barra-Buadh* or some sort of horn or whistle is buried in the pit; in M it is Fionn's cauldron that is dug up to cook the deer, in B and T likewise a cauldron is dug up; but in R after digging up the dog, and in A 'firelocks and spades' as well, the boy has to dig a hole and put his head in it while Oisean whistles (A) or shouts loudly (R). M also makes him shout, but T and B like Irish versions give him an instrument to whistle on — a whistle from his pocket in B, the blackbird's bone itself in T, where the boy is told to put his fingers in his ears.

91 Blackbird killed with an arrow in S (where three flights of birds of increasing size replace the different sizes of deer, so this is like the Irish versions) by Oisean's hand guided by the boy; later, by Oisean after he has recovered his sight in R; by the boy (with a firelock?) in A. In the other versions Oisean simply finds a blackbird chick in a hole in a rock (B), or just pulls out the leg-bone from the hole (M, T). In some Scottish versions the boy, not here a relative but a

the links between the two countries were broken in the seventeenth century. It has the character of a folktale, but it manages to incorporate a good deal of magic and mystery beside the burlesque, and it would have no meaning without the literary cycle to which it supplies the final chapter.

The different classes of tradition are inextricably inter-woven, and this is surely one way in which *fiannaíocht* and a great deal of other Gaelic storytelling is quite different from that of most other parts of Europe.

servant, is killed to prevent him telling of the mysteries he has seen, by Oisean before he gets home (B), after he has lost his ring (R), or apparently by the rest of the household next day (A): perhaps he is also killed because of the power he has got from eat-ing the deer. In B, as in T, the servant is one of the Fenians' atten-dants, wished for along with the dog, with a 'red' name (Mac na Ruaghadh, Tòn Ruadh!).

HEROES AND ANCESTORS

WILLIAM GILLIES
(University of Edinburgh)

I hope the by-way which I explore in the present paper will not prove too rough and overgrown, especially for non-Celtic readers, and that it will eventually lead through to more familiar ground, and prompt thoughts on some wider questions regarding the status of characters in literary cycles. I naturally also hope that I shall not be found to have led us up a *cul-de-sac*.

I should start by explaining the nature of the question which has been puzzling me, and which I shall attempt to answer, or at least to articulate, in what follows. I have been interested for some years in the Campbells, that widely ramified Gaelic clan whose sphere of influence radiated outwards from Argyll — the old 'coastland of the Gaels' of Dalriada — and whose chiefs were styled Earls (later Dukes) of Argyll. My researches on the Campbells led me into an investigation of their self-image in the political sphere, and of the ways in which that image was reflected in their literature and traditions. The story is a complex and — to me at least — a compelling one, and I have touched on some facets of it in a paper presented to the Gaelic Society of Inverness.[1] During the course of these researches I have become increasingly conscious of the oddness of the Campbell claim to descent

---

1 Published as 'Some Aspects of Campbell History' in *Transactions of the Gaelic Society of Inverness*, 50 (1976-8), 256-95.

from Diarmaid Ua Duibhne, the Fenian warrior celebrated most famously in the heroic-romantic tale *Tóruigheacht Dhiarmada agus Ghráinne* and in the ballad on his death. Amongst the various non-historical figures claimed as ancestors by the major Gaelic families — and there are several classes of these — Diarmaid Ua Duibhne appeared unusual, to say the least. Even in the context of the Campbells' uncommonly complex genealogical claims it seemed to involve a different class of personage from the sorts which are customarily invoked to enhance or extend the upper reaches of Highland family trees. It is this apparent oddity which I wish to investigate in what follows.

Historically speaking, the Campbells emerge from relative obscurity to become a force in Gaelic politics in the fourteenth century, i.e. in the period following the Wars of Independence, in which their support for the Bruce cause had been consistent and well-judged. The influence of the House of Argyll grew rapidly thereafter, both through wide territorial acquisitions in the southern Highlands and by establishing a presence at the Scottish court, which led in time to preferment and high office. Thus in the fifteenth and sixteenth centuries the Earls of Argyll played a double role. On the one hand they were courtiers of the Kings of Scots, playing a leading part in national politics and on occasion acting as agents of the Crown against other Highland clans; but at the same time they were also participating fully in Highland (i.e. Gaelic) politics, as can be inferred (for example) from the pattern of intermarriage between daughters of the Campbell Earls and the sons of the other leading northern Irish families.[2]

In the Gaelic world such a rise to prominence carried with it genealogical implications. One simply could not operate at the levels to which the Campbells aspired without a

2 In the absence of a full and authoritative treatment of the history of the Campbells, see the anonymous *Clan Campbell: House of Argyll*, Glasgow 1871; A. McKerral, *The Clan Campbell*, Edinburgh 1953; C.M. MacDonald, *The History of Argyll*, Glasgow n.d.; and 'Ane Accompt of the Genealogie of the Campbells', in *Highland Papers*, Vol. 2, ed. J.R.N. MacPhail (Scottish History Society, Second Series, Vol. 12), Edinburgh 1916, 69-111.

decent-sounding pedigree. The courtesy and diplomacy of bardic verse, which was a necessary corollary to greatness, demanded reference to one's ancestors. It was part of the business of the *filí* or professional court poets to know everybody's pedigrees; and by the time that such considerations seriously affected the Campbells the genealogies of the longer-established leading families had long been woven into a more or less unified structure placing them in relationship to one another and tracing each back to the Deluge and beyond. Moreover, given the intensely political basis of genealogy it was necessary for the genealogists to be prepared to make certain adjustments to their schemes from time to time, to take account of the waxing or waning fortunes of particular families in real life.[3]

The Campbells are an excellent illustration of the last point. By the seventeenth century their own *seanchaithe* had provided them with their 'official' pedigree back to Adam: but there is evidence for divergence of scholastic opinion as to how to derive them from the patriarch; and also for earlier, and by then officially discarded versions of the Campbell pedigree.[4] And when in the seventeenth century these Gaelic versions were conflated by antiquarians with accounts designed to cater for Lowland sensibilities (in particular by providing a Norman pedigree) the result is an even more extraordinary hotch-potch. In the treatise entitled *Ane Accompt of the Genealogie of the Campbells*,[5] which best reflects this fusion of the old, professional Gaelic lore with more popular Gaelic and Lowland antiquarian strands of tradition, we find a brave attempt to synthesize all these different categories into a unified sequence. I shall not here attempt to unravel its complexities, the major elements of which have been elegantly explicated by David Sellar in his article 'The Earliest Camp-

---

3 See in general D. Sellar, 'Highland Family Origins — Pedigree Making and Pedigree Faking', in *The Middle Ages in the Highlands*, ed. Loraine Maclean of Dochgarroch, Inverness 1981, 103-16; at the comparative level cf. D.P. Henige, *The Chronology of Oral Tradition*, Oxford 1974, chapter 1.

4 Cf. Gillies, *op. cit.*, 293 (n. 40); I hope to expand this summary elsewhere.

5 See note 2.

bells — Norman, Briton or Gael?':[6] However, it may help to give some idea of the alternative lines of derivation on offer if we consider the following quatrain from a sub-bardic poem in the Turner Manuscript, where the poet feels able to address his Campbell patron as

Bretannach don bhuidhinn bhonnghloin,	'(You are) a Briton of the bright-footed company,
Eirionnach fial o chlar chuinn,	a generous Irishman from the plain of Conn,
Spainneach do rug buaidh ar bhannaibh,	a Spaniard who was victorious over armies,
Francach fad chul clannach cruinn.	a Frenchman in respect of your luxuriant, well-groomed hair.'

Here, I take it, 'Briton' refers to descent from King Arthur (the line favoured by the Campbell *fili*), 'Irishman' to Diarmaid Ua Duibhne (to whom we shall return directly), 'Spaniard' to the Milesian pseudo-history, and 'Frenchman' to the supposed Norman pedigree of the Campbells.[7] A brief sample of *Ane Accompt* will serve to indicate the quality of its author's sources and the ground rules he observed.

Diarmid odhuine (from whom the Campbells are called Siol dhiarmid (id est the seed of Diarmid) was a great and eminent person in Ireland and very honorablie mentioned in the Irish traditionell antiquities as a person of great couradge and strength and very amiable to be looked upon, he had to his wife Grain, daughter to Cornig [*sic*] mc Airt vic Chuinn Cheudchathchich and so she was great grand child to Conn Ceudchataith so called because he fought ane hundered battells; whereby the Campbells are descended of the noble race of the O'Neills. This Dhiarmid odhuibhne had a son called Dhuine deudgheal (that is whyte toothed) who had to his son Gillocolum or Malcolm oduibhn, which Malcom oduibhn having gone to Normandie in ffrance, took in mariage the heretrix of

6 *Scottish Studies*, 17 (1973), 109-25.
7 Cf. Gillies, *op. cit.*, 278-9.

Beochamps (that is to say Campus bellus or pleasant field) being sister daughter to William the Conqueror . . .[8]

When we recall the context of these seventeenth-century sources it is easy enough to understand what has happened: familiarity with the timescale of European history made their authors uncomfortably aware of the yawning chasm between the earliest recorded Campbells (in the thirteenth century) and the early historic or prehistoric setting into which Arthur and the Milesian pseudo-history were conventionally placed. They set about filling the gap with doubly unhistorical 'ancestors' — Diarmaid Ua Duibhne (and a whole series of further Diarmaids) amongst them.

Now if this were all that lay behind the occurrence of Diarmaid Ua Duibhne in the ancestry of the Campbells I should have no right to be making a fuss about him here: it would simply be a matter for students of the specialised subject of pedigree-making and pedigree-faking. But this is far from being the case; for more detailed investigation of the development of the Campbell genealogy shows that the Fenian descent was not the product of the learned Gaelic tradition — the *seanchaithe* and *filí* — but actually had to fight its way in, only becoming respectable in the seventeenth century when the professional Gaelic *literati* were dying away. I have suggested elsewhere that the latter's sense of genealogical propriety would have provided sufficient reason to exclude a Fenian derivation: in other words, belief in the descent from Diarmaid must have been non-learned, at least in the first instance.[9]

In fact there is plenty of evidence to show that Diarmaid's esteem as progenitor of the Campbells sprang from a widespread p o p u l a r belief, both in Campbell parts of the Highlands and elsewhere; the associated assumption, that he was a 'real' person, is equally well attested. A good source of evidence for these points is the testimony collected in the Highland Society of Scotland's *Report on the Authenticity of the Poems of Ossian*, whose conclusion was that its enquiry had

8 Ed. MacPhail (see note 2), p. 79.
9 Gillies, *op. cit.*, 280; see further below.

tended to show 'the universal traditionary belief of the existence of Fingal and his heroes'.[10] I shall quote now from one especially relevant piece of testimony, that of Hugh MacDonald of Kilpheder in South Uist.[11] (It was taken down in Gaelic from MacDonald's dictation in 1800; the translation was made for purposes of including the testimony in the *Report*.) MacDonald, whose views are important since he was an unlettered (though not uncultured) man, has this to say:

> The names of men, and of clans and tribes, either prior to Oisean or coeval with him, which we can all mention, prove that the Féinne inhabited our Highlands and Isles; and we have genealogies of some of the heroes whom he [= Oisean] celebrated.

Here we have, I presume, a reference to Diarmaid as ancestor of the Campbells. MacDonald then proceeds, obviously thinking of some of the dolmens or natural features said by popular tradition to have been set up by the Fenians, to suggest that such edifices are:

> . . . monuments of the good name and ingenuity of Ossian's heroes. These evince that they possessed arts that enabled them to perform works, of which their degenerate descendants cannot comprehend the method, nor even conceive the possibility, of execution.

Here we have the opposite of the 'progress' theory, with a vengeance; more important for present purposes we have a witness who is prepared to take the authenticity of the Fenian heroes as being beyond question, whatever other adjustments have to be made. As he says in his conclusion:

> The farther back we trace the traditions, and the more accurately we enquire into the characters to which they allude, our convictions become the stronger that they can neither be fictitious nor imaginary.

The strength of the particular link between Diarmaid and the Campbells is emphasized by J.F. Campbell of Islay in his

10 Ed. H. Mackenzie, Edinburgh 1805; see p. 79.
11 *Ibid.*, Appendix, pp. 48-52.

Popular Tales of the West Highlands. [12] It is also attested by many allusions in the literature, in 'clan history' and in oral traditions of or about the *Sìol Dhiarmaid* or *Sliochd Dhiarmaid* over the last century and a half. Moreover, it is underpinned by toponymic traditions in various parts of the Highlands, especially in connection with the death of Diarmaid. [13] The following especially striking example is derived from the Rev. Alexander Pope's collection of heroic ballads (collected around 1739 in Reay), where it is said *à propos* of his version of 'Bàs Dhiarmaid', that it was 'in esteem among a tribe of Campbells, who live in Caithness, and would derive their pedigree from that Hero'. [14] He goes on:

> There is an old fellow in this parish that very gravely takes off his bonnet as often as he sings Duan Dearmot. I was extremely fond to try if the case was so, and getting him to my house I gave him a bottle of ale, and begged the favour of him to sing Duan Dearmot; after some nicety he told me that to oblige his parish minister he would do so, but to my surprise he took off his bonnet. I caused him stop, and would put on his bonnet: he made some excuses, however, as soon as he began, he took off his bonnet. I rose and put it on. At last he was like to swear most horribly, he would sing none, unless I allowed him to be uncovered; I gave him his freedom, and so he sung with great spirit. I then asked him his reason; he told me it was out of regard to the memory of that Hero. I asked him if he thought that the spirit of that Hero was present; he said not; but he thought it well became them who descended from him to honour his memory.

To resume, the Campbell traditions present us with a claim to descend, not from some discreetly distanced Norman or Norwegian or Irish ruler, but from someone whom we might have been inclined to discount as a possible progenitor, think-

---

12 Second edition, London 1890-3, Vol.3, 60, cf. 63, 70.
13 See N. Ross, *Heroic Poetry from the Book of the Dean of Lismore*, Edinburgh 1939, 221-3.
14 Printed by J.F. Campbell, *Leabhar na Feinne*, London 1872, 218, from which the following quotation is taken.

ing of him either as a patently fictitious, literary character with no business to be stepping outside the circumscribed world of heroic-romantic tale and ballad, or as one of a group of beings with supernatural attributes and of gigantic size who once inhabited the country we live in but belong to a different Age (or on a different ontological plane, or whatever) from ourselves.

Of course, if we were to widen the terms of the enquiry by glancing at the comparative evidence, these grounds for rejecting Diarmaid might begin to look a little less watertight. There are plenty of examples, both ancient and modern, from literate and non-literate societies, of people's accepting literary, mythological and such-like categories of beings as the ancestors of living families.[15] Indeed the labours of the Irish synthetic historians are cited by comparativists, alongside evidence from the other Celtic languages, as an outstanding example of the euhemeristic and other processes involved.

Moreover, when we look a little more closely at the Gaelic evidence bearing on the Fenians, there are positive signs of the sort of development which might have led to their becoming unexceptionable ancestors in other circumstances. Well before the Campbells achieved their latter-day prominence, Fionn and his warrior band had been assigned a time-scale and given a part to play within the later prehistoric (i.e. pre-Christian) phase of Irish pseudo-history. In these 'historical' sources at least there is no sign that Fionn and the Fian were meant to be regarded as magically endowed giants: Fionn was simply the leader of the palace guard. At the very close of the classical period of Irish literature Geoffrey Keating felt it necessary to make this point explicitly and forcefully:

> . . . tar ceann gur scríobhadh iomad d'fhinnscéalaibh filidheachta ar Fhionn agus ar an bhFéin . . . is dearbh gur scríobhadh staire fírinneacha inchreidthe orra. Agus is dearbh fós nach raibhe ainmhéid 'n-a bpearsanaibh acht

---

15 See, for example, Henige, *op. cit.*, 7, 48-9; D.P. Henige, *Oral Historiography*, London 1982, 100.

mar an druing do mhair ré n-a linn féin; agus ní raibhe
ionnta acht buannadha do ríoghaibh Éireann ré cosnamh
agus ré caomhna na críche dhóibh, amhail bhíd caiptine
agus saighdiuiridhe ag gach rígh aniú ré cosnamh a chríche
féin.

'Although many imaginative romances have been written
about Fionn and the Fian . . . still it is certain that true
credible accounts of them were also written. And it is also
certain that their bodies were not abnormally large, but
only like those of their contemporaries; and they were
nothing more than hired warriors of the Kings of Ireland,
to defend and protect the country for them, as every king
now has captains and soldiers to defend his own domin-
ions'.[16]

Testimony to the same effect comes from the translator of
the *Book of Common Order of the Church of Scotland*, John
Carswell, who shows us that he makes no distinction between
the characters of the Fenian cycle and those of the other
cycles of early Irish literature — the mythological, Ulster, and
'historical' cycles. To the reforming Superintendent of Argyll
they are all unfit subjects for Christians to dwell upon:

> . . . eachtradha dímhaoineacha buaidheartha brēgacha
> saoghalta, do cumadh ar Thuathaibh Dé Dhanond, agas ar
> Mhacaibh Mīleadh, agus ar na curadhaibh, agas [ar] Fhind
> mhac Cumhaill gona Fhianaibh, agas ar mhórān eile nach
> āirbhim agas nach indisim andso . . .

> '. . . vain hurtful lying wordly tales composed about
> the Tuatha Dé Danann, and about the Sons of Milesius,
> and about the heroes and Fionn mac Cumhaill with his
> warriors, and about many others whom I do not recount
> or mention here . . .'[17]

16 G. Keating, *History of Ireland*, ed. D. Comyn and P.S. Dinneen,
    Vol. 2, London 1908 (= Irish Texts Society, Vol. 8), pp. 326-7.
    The rationalist line taken here by Keating is essentially the same as
    that of Hugh MacDonald, Kilpheder (above).
17 *Foirm na nUrrnuidheadh*, ed. R.L. Thomson, Edinburgh 1970,
    11, 179. The book originally appeared in 1567.

Again, it can be seen that the learned Gaelic tradition has provided Diarmaid Ua Duibhne with some of the accreditation he would need if he were ever to become wanted as an ancestor. Just as befell some of the heroes of the Ulster cycle, an antiquarian sense of decency provided Diarmaid (and Fionn) with pedigrees, and did so soon enough for these to be included in the main early genealogical collections.[18] Yet the fact remains that, amongst the learned *filí* who acted as brokers of such genealogical material, there were no 'takers' for Fenian pedigrees. As I have indicated, even the Campbell bardic verse (i.e. that composed by the MacEwen *seanchaithe* of the Earls of Argyll or by other *filí* during their tenure of that official position) shows a studied ignorance of any descent from Diarmaid. One must assume, I think, that despite evidence for learned — perhaps antiquarian would be a better word — attention to the figures of Fenian heroes, any such 'euhemerising' tendency did not reach the critical degree of acceptance to provide a platform for further development, either because it started too late or because it was subject to inhibiting factors. Possible examples of the latter might include the relative lateness of the Fenians' episode in the synchronic history — all the desirable affiliation points occurring many generations before their time; or distaste for their all too flourishing literary and popular personalities, including such difficulties as the fact that their legends cast them in the role of subordinates (as the King's guard), whereas bardic convention cultivated the notion of autonomous rule as a prerequisite for poetic support, and genealogists were likewise concerned solely with those who enjoyed or aspired to dominion and rule.

Similarly, if one goes beyond the rarefied circles of the learned, one could argue that scribes who headed poems 'Fionn sang this' or 'Oisín sang this', must have had at least qualified feelings of trust in the *quondam* existence of the

18 See M.A. O'Brien, *Corpus Genealogiarum Hiberniae*, Vol. 1, Dublin 1962, 22, 99 (Find); 45 (Diarmait). Cf. also, for family ties attributed to Diarmaid in the ballads, *Duanaire Finn*, ed. E. Mac Neill and G. Murphy, London 1908-53 (Irish Texts Society, Vol. 7, 28, 43), Nos. XVIII, XLII, XLIII, LXV.

author they had just credited.[19] I presume, moreover, that
those texts which dwell upon Fionn's endurance of the
torments which pre-Christian figures were obliged to suffer
in hell argue at least the possibility of a belief in the his-
toricity of Fionn.[20] And if we set aside Diarmaid in Campbell
territories for a moment there is ample testimony to popular
assumptions that the Fenians had lived, all over the Gaelic
world.[21] Yet at this level too, why is it that nobody, except
in Argyll, seems to have seen fit to link his (or anybody else's)
family with the Fenians? It is considerably easier to come
across seal-folk or people related to the fairies! While it is
always difficult to predict how members of other cultures,
and perhaps especially popular cultures, would have responded to questions one cannot put to them, I suspect that,
insofar as these things were articulated, the Fenians would
have been regarded as coming to an end with Oisein/Oisín
(if not before); that a sense of differentness of kind would
have been fundamental, bolstered by awareness of their
superhuman qualities and stature, which was commemorated
all around by their toponymic memorials; and that a sharing
or communal attitude towards them would have tended to
prevent any exclusive appropriating of one of them as one's
'own'. That is to say, even if Fionn's hunting-knoll or the ben
of the great boar-hunt were firmly located in one's own

19 One is, however, mindful of the self-distancing comments of the
scribe of the Book of Leinster *Táin: Sed ego qui scripsi hanc his-
toriam aut verius fabulam quibusdam fidem in hac historia aut
fabula non accommodo. Quaedam enim ibi sunt praestigia demonum,
quaedam autem figmenta poetica, quaedam similia vero, quaedam
non, quaedam ad deflectationem stultorum.* 'But I who have
written this story, or rather this fable, give no credence to the
various incidents related in it. For some things in it are the decep-
tions of demons, others poetic figments; some are probable, some
improbable; while still others are intended for the delectation of
fools.' See *Táin Bó Cúalnge from the Book of Leinster*, ed. Cecile
O'Rahilly, Dublin 1967, 136, 272.
20 See Murphy, *Duanaire Finn*, Part III (1953), cii-ciii.
21 See, e.g., Keating, *op. cit.*, Vol. 2, 326, 348, etc. I am not concerned here with the precise q u a l i t y of the belief, which would
obviously vary.

locality, one would be aware that the Fenians wandered free and had equally valid ties with other parts besides.

Furthermore, I suppose, it could be suggested that an attested tendency for originally distinct cycles to become confused in the later stages of the tradition, together with the existence of certain literary characters who were known to have real posterity, could combine to make the sort of development under discussion an occasional possibility. It is true that in some late sources Fenian characters rub shoulders with characters originally belonging to the mythological cycle or of other provenance. And it is true that some literary-traditional figures can be associated with historical families for the good reason that they are basically historical people whose stories have seemed worth telling and who have subsequently 'taken off' as literary characters. Examples would include Muireadhach Albanach Ó Dálaigh, the eponymous ancestor of the Mac Vurich family of poets to the Lords of the Isles; Gerald fitz-Maurice, Third Earl of Desmond (the Gearóid Iarla of tradition); and Murchadh, son of Brian Bóramha, in whose case we have heroic-romantic tales and ballads of the sort usually associated with the Fenians.[22] Yet it has to be said that the more 'literary' such a personage becomes, the less relevant are matters of 'real-life' biographical detail, including questions of posterity: how important, for instance, would the family life, or indeed the ancestry, of Murchadh mac Briain have been to the audience of a story about him told in the Scottish Highlands in the nineteenth century?[23] Moreover, and perhaps even more telling, the process of 'heroisation' appears to be a one-way one: the facts about an individual are drawn out into the currents of genre, and that is that. If we are to regard the case of Diarmaid Ua Duibhne and the Campbells as a counter-example to this principle we must recognise that a strong counterpull would be needed to 'de-heroise' him.

If general considerations provide no obvious lines along which to explain our case we should ask whether it contains any special features, i.e. special circumstances associated with

22 See Murphy, *op. cit.* (1953), 194-7.
23 Campbell, *op. cit.* (1860-3), Vol. 2, 209-31.

Diarmaid (as opposed to other popular heroes) or the Campbells (as opposed to other clans) or some other specific factor. As will readily be understood, no certainties are to be expected; yet I believe there are some curious and possibly significant features, which I should like to mention in conclusion. I group these according to the differing elements which contribute to the case, and describe them for what they are worth; it may be that severally or collectively they have helped to tip the scales in favour of what can now be seen as a decidedly unusual case.

In the first place the name Duibhne would seem to be relevant in any event, at least in a supporting role. *Ua Duibhne* or *Mac Uí Dhuibhne* is one of the usual ways of describing or naming the literary Diarmaid.[24] One Duibhne was also an eponym of the Campbells, giving rise to the patronymic *Mac Uí Dhuibhne*, the collective *Duibhnich*, and so on. I agree with Sellar in regarding this Duibhne as historical, perhaps the earliest historical character in the Campbell pedigree.[25] Now the name is in fact a very rare one, and it seems plausible to speculate that 'Mac Uí Dhuibhne' (or similar) applied to the Campbell chief, or 'Clann Uí Dhuibhne' applied to his people could have helped to create the presumption of identity with Diarmaid Ua Duibhne, and assisted the latter to enter the Campbell pedigree. This might be the more likely to happen in that, some time after the thirteenth century, a new patronymic came into use, the Campbell chiefs thence being styled 'Mac Cailein', after Cailein Mór (*ob.* c. 1296). This had the effect of pushing the earlier eponym, Duibhne, into a sort of limbo; his name would be preserved, thanks to the collective 'Duibhnich',[26] but the reasons for commemorating him must have faded as Cailein Mór over-

---

24 Murphy, *op. cit.* (1953), xlvii, etc.
25 Sellar, *op. cit.*, 111-2.
26 The form 'Guimhnich', which is more usual in later Scottish Gaelic tradition, must have been abstracted from a form with lenition — *Uí Dhuibhne* or *Mac Uí Dhuibhne* — at a time when Duibhne was no longer a clearly remembered *persona*.

took him as the key ancestor, namely the founder of the latest phase in the family's fortunes.[27]

Connection with a boar may have counted in the same way. It will be recalled that the Diarmaid of story and ballad generally meets his end by treading on the venomous bristles of the great boar he has killed.[28] At the same time, a boar has been the heraldic symbol of the Campbells for some considerable time, and it is worth asking whether this could have acted as a catalyst, along with the coincidence of the name Duibhne.[29] Admittedly there is some uncertainty as to the precise antiquity of the boar as a Campbell symbol, and one cannot exclude the possibility that it was attributed to them after and because of the importation of Diarmaid into their pedigree. But references to the *torc*, 'boar', of the Campbells are fairly widespread in Scottish Gaelic poetry (including satiric allusions to 'pigs' in a derogatory sense); and the explanation of *Ane Accompt*, which derives the heraldic boar from one killed in France by the early fifteenth-century Duncan Campbell, may either be factually correct, or a Normanising reflex of a genuine Campbell tradition predating the equation of Diarmaid with Ua Duibhne.[30]

If we turn now to the Campbells as a clan — or, to be more precise, an individually ambitious but relatively closely-knit group of families — there may have been reasons to make them particularly liable to attract genealogical 'gatecrashers', and, having attracted them, to grant them admittance. Two such possibilities have occurred to me. In the first place I am intrigued by the correlation claimed between 'genealogical fever' and the emergence of 'upstarts' and 'parvenus'[31] in the context of Sellar's persuasive suggestion that the Campbells were newcomers to Argyll sometime shortly before they appear on record there, being originally a British family perhaps based in the Lennox.[32] To put this more concretely,

---

27 See Henige, *op. cit.* (1974), 27, 66 for the psychology of these developments.
28 See Ross, *op. cit.*, 221-3.
29 See MacDonald, *op. cit.*, 202.
30 *Highland Papers*, Vol. 2, 95.
31 Henige, *op. cit.* (1974), 6.
32 Sellar, *op. cit.*, 119-21.

if the Campbells were strangers, even foreigners (in origin at least), settling in the heartland of Gaeldom amongst well-established Gaelic families at a time when political fortunes were waxing and waning all around them, might they not have been that little bit more prone than the next clan to seek links with the established (i.e. Gaelic) order where they could find them, or to accepting such suggestions if they were made by others for them? (I fancy that 'Oh, you must be . . .' and 'Oh, they must be . . .' may very often be prior to 'Oh, we must be . . .' in circumstances like this.) On a slightly different tack, could it be that the 'British' and 'kingly' obsessions of the learned tradition failed to answer the needs of families who found themselves settling in almost colonial situations in widely differing parts of the Highlands as Campbell influence spread, and left the way open for more homespun deductions to take place?

I have also wondered whether there was anything peculiar to Diarmaid himself. While I have not been able to identify any consistent patterns in Fenian tradition to lend support to this notion I have noted comparative discussion of the 'hunter or warrior of . . . outstanding ability . . . [the man of] prowess and charismatic personality' as a type of the 'outsider' or 'interloper' who is one of the prime building blocks for constructing genealogy in oral tradition.[33] This fits the Fenians to a tee. Admittedly, it would fit Fionn (and perhaps some of the others) as well as Diarmaid; but one could argue that Diarmaid combined charisma — *par excellence* — with the advantage of not being the fully specified leader of the group, and not being compromised by some of the negative or unpleasant attributes sometimes associated with Fionn.[34]

Finally one may ask whether there was anything in the Scottish (as opposed to the Irish) Gaelic tradition, either in the way Scottish Gaels regarded their *fiannaíocht* or in their attitude towards their genealogy, that might have helped to provide the spark we are trying to account for. I believe there are some valid and interesting distinctions to be made between

33 Henige, *op. cit.* (1974), 34.
34 See, for example, the remarks of Dáithí Ó hÓgáin below.

Scotland and Ireland in both these contexts. As regards the
fiannaíocht, why is it, for instance, that the death of Diarmaid
is commemorated by so many Ben Gulbans throughout
Gaelic Scotland?[35] And on the genealogical side we should
bear in mind that the Campbells' physical proximity to the
Lowlands, their holding of lands there, and their involvement
in Lowland Scottish politics must have brought them into
contact with a different set of preconceptions, priorities and
fixations about genealogical *desiderata*. It may be that this
area too would repay further study than has been possible
so far, and could supply some condition of (say) 'inter-
cultural instability' which might make genealogical novelties
or aberrations more likely to occur.[36]

Perhaps one or more of the above lines of questioning has
bearing on the question of Diarmaid Ua Duibhne and the
Campbells, or perhaps the lesson is rather that the unexpected
can happen and has happened here. At all events I hope that
our exploration of one corner of the Gaelic tradition, although
finally inconclusive, will have offered some food for thought
both to those familiar with the material and to those to whom
it is *terra incognita*. Despite the identification of certain
general or universal-looking principles at work in the Gaelic
material, we should bear in mind that the scatter of mythological, historical, literary, etc., categories subject to those
principles will be specific to a given culture and a given time,
as will questions of emphasis and mobility between categories.
Seeking parallels from outside Gaelic culture may hence not
be a legitimate objective; and we should certainly not expect
to be able to produce them. Nevertheless, I should like to
conclude by citing an example from Ancient Greek literature
which seems to me to share some suggestive features with
ours. The origin legends of the Theran colony of Cyrene in

35 Compare W.J. Watson, *The Celtic Place-names of Scotland*, Edin-
    burgh 1926, 208. The forthcoming edition of the ballads in the
    Book of the Dean of Lismore by Dr D.E.M. Meek will be impor-
    tant in this context.
36 Forthcoming works on the Beatons and, as I understand, 'MS
    1467' by Dr J.W.M. Bannerman promise much-needed illumination
    in this area.

North Africa, as told by Herodotus and Pindar, offer us a choice between what would in Irish terms be 'historical cycle' and 'mythological cycle' accounts; but the roughly contemporary local Cyrenaean poet Eugammon sought to 'connect the Kyrenaian dynasty with the epic world' by the expedient of postulating a son of Odysseus and Penelope.[37] I wonder what Pindar and Herodotus would have thought of this, just as I wonder what the Campbell *seanchaithe* made of Diarmaid Ua Duibhne.

37 Further parallels offering quite close correspondences with the Gaelic scenario will be found in Chapter 6 of Professor A.H. Norris' forthcoming work *The Arab Conquest of the Western Sahara*, proofs of which he has kindly allowed me to see.

FIANAIGECHT IN THE PRE-NORMAN PERIOD

PROINSIAS MAC CANA
(Dublin Institute for Advanced Studies)

One of the things one notices about literatures born of mythologies is that personal names may be either all-important or unimportant, depending on the particular perspective from which we view the textual context at any given time. I have referred elsewhere to the urge towards variant reproduction which is a feature of insular Celtic oral tradition and to the inner dynamism of the mythic themes and structures that enables them to generate variant reflexes in response to changes in social or political circumstance or to regional appropriateness. Themes and motifs are transferred freely from one character to another, so that, for example, the same or similar experiences may be ascribed to several different Arthurian heroes, the same expedition to the otherworld is attributed variously to Arthur, Pryderi and Brân, and a number of episodes in the Ulster cycle have their reflexes in the stories of Fionn and the *fiana*. Thus while the underlying thematic structures are relatively stable, the names are highly variable, as if belonging to the accidents rather than to the essentials of traditional narrative. And yet, on the other hand, we are all familiar with the mythological assumption that the name is in a very large sense the person: *der Name deckt sich mit dem Wesen und ist die Offenbarung des Wesens;*[1]

---

1 W. Schulze, (*Kuhns*) *Zeitschrift f. vergl. Sprachf.* 40 (1907), 411 n. 1.

that to change one's name is to change one's role and even one's very being (as in certain rites of initiation); and that to know the name (or, indeed, the names) of a deity is to have access to him and to exercise a certain control over or claim upon his favours.

This dual perception of the significance of names has its analogue in the differing views of two Celtic scholars who have concerned themselves with the *fianaigecht* and the name and *persona* of Fionn mac Cumhaill. For A.G. van Hamel *Fionn* is a simple epithet devoid of any deeper significance:

> His name means 'White' and would suit anybody, like Dub, 'Black', or Derg, 'Red'. We have no right to identify Finn, because of his name, with the Welsh divinity, Gwynn ab Nudd' (*Gwynn* being the linguistic cognate of Old Irish *Finn*).[2]

For Gerard Murphy, however, Finn's name supplements other contextual evidence that he was originally a god: Gaulish inscriptions preserve the related deity-name *Vindonnus* (Celtic *Vindonnos*) and the placename constituent *Vindo-*, which, analogy suggests, probably also referred to a deity, while Welsh has of course the god Gwynn ap Nudd.[3] In fact Fionn's divine origins are now generally accepted, and his name, however precisely it be etymologized, seems in the Irish and Celtic consciousness to have combined the notion of brightness and illumination with that of the discovering of knowledge, both of which figure largely in the stories of Fionn. (The relevant detail on the etymology and semantics of *finn* are set out clearly in Dr Joseph Nagy's recent book on the Finn cycle,[4] a well-informed and sensitive interpretation of the mythological import of the whole corpus.)

I have mentioned the phenomenon of variant reproduction by which versions of a given theme or episode are assigned to different and perhaps quite unrelated heroes. The converse of

---

2 *Aspects of Celtic Mythology*, Rhŷs Mem. Lect., Brit. Acad., 1934, 26 f.

3 G. Murphy, *Duanaire Finn*, Part III, Dublin 1953, lxxxi ff.

4 J.F. Nagy, *The Wisdom of the Outlaw*, Berkeley 1985; see index s.v. *Finn*, and especially p. 236.

this is the case in which thematic analogy, especially where it occurs in a consistent pattern, seems to indicate not simple narrative transference from one distinct character to another but rather the virtual identity of the several characters involved. Once the process is observed in action it is susceptible of considerable theoretical extension, as for example in the work of T.F. O'Rahilly, whose formidable scholarly ingenuity almost succeeded in reducing the gallery of Irish gods to a simple binary system of two opposing deities who bear different names in different contexts. Whatever of O'Rahilly's general conclusion — which few scholars would accept without substantial caveats and qualifications — the assumption on which it is based, namely that the same deity could be known under several names, is well attested by the internal evidence of Irish literature as well as by Celtic epigraphy, and this led Gerard Murphy (as well as O'Rahilly, though much more tentatively) to suggest that 'Fionn was another name for the god Lugh, just as "Ruad Rofessae" and "Echaid Ollathir" were names for the Daghdha.'[5] There is, as he demonstrates, a striking parallelism between the mythologies of the two heroes — for example, Fionn is repeatedly brought into conflict with enemies who appear to be supernatural and may be typified as one-eyed and 'burners', just as the god Lugh fought and slew the demonic Balor 'just as he was about to burn up Ireland with his evil eye' — and the *rapprochement* of the two characters receives some onomastic support from the fact that the two names are conjoined in the compound Findlug (i.e. Fionn-Lugh), which is attested in a variety of texts, including what Murphy terms 'the mythical portion of the genealogies'.

By Kuno Meyer's definition (which is accurate if not exhaustive), a *fian* was 'a larger or smaller band of roving warriors, who had joined for the purpose of making war on their own account', and to become a member of such a band was termed *dul for fíanas* (*fénidecht*).[6] Clearly then, in so far as the practice of *fénidecht* was a historical phenomenon, there could have been many such bands, most of which would

5 *Op. cit.*, lxxxiv ff.
6 K. Meyer, *Fianaigecht*, Dublin 1910, ix.

have left little or no trace in the extant records, and this is in fact the position reflected vestigially in the literature. We read of a number of different *fiana*, each normally designated from the name of its leader (Meyer, *op. cit.*, xiii), some historical, some wholly mythological, it would seem. There is for instance reference to the *fiana* of Fothad Canainne, a figure still trailing behind him the remnants of a complex mythology. One of the triad of brothers, he is described as 'a leader of *fiana* among the men of Connacht' (though generally connected with Leinster), he is associated with fire and represented as an opponent of Fionn, and his inferential divinity is confirmed by the soubriquet Cáindia, 'fair god'. He was the hero of two elopement or love tales included in the archetype of the Middle Irish tale-lists and therefore probably extant in or before the tenth century. One of these, *Serc Caillige Bérre do Fhothud Chanainne*, 'The Love of Fothad Canainne for the Hag of Beare' (or *vice versa*), brings our hero into contact with the most enduring and most universal of all the epiphanies of the Irish earth-goddess, and one would give a lot to know the outcome, but unfortunately the tale seems to have perished. The other, *Aithed mná Ailella re Fothad Canann*, 'The Elopement of Ailill's wife with Fothad Canainne', survives in several summary versions, the oldest of which, according to its editor, Vernam Hull, has some linguistic features as old as the *prima manus* of the Würzburg glosses and therefore reflects an archetype of the first half of the eighth century or still earlier. That he was, like Fionn, something of a mythical *coureur* is borne out by a reference in the Rennes *dinnshenchas* to an amorous adventure of his with the eponym (Lethderg) of the placename Carraic Lethdeirg.[7]

Fothad is given several different pedigrees in the historical literature, one of which makes him son of Maicnia son of Lugaid.[8] But, as Gerard Murphy has pointed out (as well as O'Rahilly), a comparison of the various sources makes it clear beyond doubt that Maicnia, Lugaid, Mac Con (who is

7 *Revue Celtique* 16 (1895), 43.
8 T.F. O'Rahilly, *Early Irish History and Mythology*, Dublin 1946, 11.

often given as the father of Lugaid), and the god Lug are all
secondary variants of a single divine character.[9] Given the
substantial equivalence of Lug and Fionn and also the fact
that Fothad Canainne is evidently one of the forms (together
with Goll, Aed, and Balor) assumed by the constant opponent
of the hero represented by Fionn and Lug, there cannot be
any doubt about the close interrelationship between the
principal leaders of *fiana* on the mythico-ideological level.
Fionn is brought into close association with Mac Con in at
least two texts: he fights on Mac Con's side in the battle of
Cenn Abrat and kills the old *fénnid* Ferchess in revenge for
the death of Mac Con; in the latter instance Fionn is described
as Mac Con's *fénnid*, which here seems to mean his *fian*-
leader.[10] O'Rahilly goes so far as to conclude that the *fian* of
Lugaid mac Con (*aliter* Mac Con) was 'the forerunner of the
fian of Finn', which may in a certain sense be true, but requires
so many qualifications as to be almost meaningless.

That stories about Mac Con's *fian* were current in the
second half of the seventh century is suggested by a brief
passage in Tírechán's 'Memoir of St Patrick' in the *Book of
Armagh* which purports to record the words of a giant whom
Patrick has raised from the grave:

> *Ego sum macc maicc Cais maic Glais qui fui subulcus
> rig Lugir rig Hirotae. Iugulavit me fian maicc (maicc) Con
> in regno Coirpri Niothfer anno .c. usque hodié.*

> 'I am the son of Cas son of Glas, and I was swineherd
> of king Lugar king of Hirōt. The *fian* of Mac Con slew me
> in the reign of Coirpre Nia Fer one hundred years to to-
> day.'[11]

I have also drawn attention elsewhere to the *dinnshenchas*
of Sliab Bladma which, it seems to me, probably preserves a
variant of the story alluded to by Tírechán: here another
Mac Con kills Bregmael, the smith of Cuirche mac Snithe,

9 Murphy, *op. cit.*, 205, 447.
10 O. Bergin *et al.*, eds., *Anecdota from Irish Manuscripts* ii, Dublin
    1908, 76; K. Meyer, *op. cit.*, 38.
11 J. Gwynn, ed., *The Book of Armagh*, Dublin and London 1913,
    27; W. Stokes, ed., *The Tripartite Life of Patrick*, London 1887,
    Vol. 2, 324.

king of Medraige and Herot (which placename corresponds to
Tírechán's *Hirota*), as well as Bregmael's herd (*buachaill*).[12]
But the web is still more complex. In the poem 'Étsid in
senchas sluagach',[13] to which O'Rahilly gave the title 'Imthechta' Clainne Tuirill' and which Thurneysen dated not
earlier than the eleventh century we are told that Lug sent the
three sons of Tuirill abroad, in expiation for their crime in killing his father Ethliu, to seek a number of wondrous objects,
one of which was the magic hound of the 'royal smith' (gen.
ríggobonn) of Irua(i)d. This marvellous hound which was
brought into the possession of Lug next turns up in a Fionn-
ballad of the twelfth century, 'Dám thrír táncatar i-lle';[14]
it is said to have belonged to the king of Irua(i)th and is
brought to Fionn and the *fian* by three strange warriors from
overseas. Another version of the tale as associated with Fionn
is included in *Acallam na Senórach*, 'The Colloquy with the
Ancients', the great collection of *fianaighecht* compiled probably towards the end of the twelfth century.

The author of the Fionn ballad explicitly links his narrative with 'Imthechta Clainne Tuirill', but a comparison of
the two texts suggests that there is little reason to think that
either has been borrowed or adapted directly from the other.
It seems more likely that this is another instance of the parallelism between Fionn and Lug, in which case it is not unlikely
that two analogous tales involving three supernatural brothers
and a magic hound with Lug and with Fionn were already
current before the eleventh and twelfth centuries. The role
of the smith of Iruaith tends to support this. He is killed by
Mac Con together with the herdsman (*subulcus, buachaill*) of

12 E. Gwynn, ed., *The Metrical Dindshenchas*, Part II, Dublin 1906,
    54; *Revue Celtique* 15 (1894), 31; P. Mac Cana, *Proceedings
    of the International Congress of Celtic Studies 1959*, Dublin 1962,
    88-93.
13 Ed., Thurneysen, *Zeitschrift f. celt. Phil.* 12 (1810), 239 ff. It is a
    forerunner of the fourteenth-century tale *Oidheadh Chloinne
    Tuireann*.
14 L. Chr. Stern, ed., *Festschrift Whitley Stokes*, Leipzig 1900, 8-
    12; see *Zeitschrift f. celt. Phil.* 3 (1901), 433 f. for a later copy
    from the *Book of Lismore*.

the king of Iruaith,[15] and his is the magic hound brought to Mac Con and to Fionn. He seems in fact to have been a familiar figure in certain areas of medieval tradition dealing with the otherworld or with the supernatural peoples of Ireland (which is much the same thing): in the tale of the First Battle of Mag Tuired, where he is called Aengaba na hIruaithe (with *aengaba* the near equivalent of the *ríoggobae* of 'Imthechta Clainne Tuirill'), he has quite an important part as one of the chiefs of the Tuatha Dé Danann,[16] but, perhaps even more significantly in the present context, he is doubtless one and the same mythical character as Lon mac Líomhtha in the well-known Fionn ballad, who puts the Fiana under *geasa* to pursue him in a race to his smithy and as reward presents them with charmed weapons. He describes himself as 'teacher of smiths to the king of Lochlainn in Bergen', but in fact the race ends not in Lochlainn (Norway) but in the Cave of Corann (i.e. in the hill of Keshcorran in Sligo).[17]

With regard to the name Iruaith, which crops up in various forms from Tírechán onwards, I have suggested that it was the name of a place in south Connacht, which, like other places in Ireland, was the focus of traditions of supernatural phenomena; that it was, or came to be, used as a name for the otherworld and consequently was sometimes thought of as being overseas; and that finally it became a synonym for Lochlainn in its dual reference to the Otherworld and Norway. I have also suggested that the well-known tale of the battle of Mag Muccrama, in which Mac Con slew Art mac Cuinn, king of Ireland, may have been located in south Connacht because Mac Con was already known as the hero of the events which led to the death of the royal swineherd and/or smith of Iruaith.

But, it may be asked, what particular relevance has all this

---

15 I adopt here for convenience a standardized form of this place-name; cf. my discussion of the several variants, *loc. cit.*

16 *Ériu* 8 (1916), 34, 36 (see n. 1), etc.

17 E. MacNeill, ed., *Duanaire Finn* Part I, London 1908; G. Murphy, ed., *Duanaire Finn* Part II, London 1933, poem XXXVI; R.Th. Christiansen, *The Vikings and the Viking Wars in Irish and Gaelic Tradition*, Oslo 1931, 197-215, 413. Murphy dates this ballad c. 1400, *op. cit.* (1953), 85.

for the development of the Fionn cycle? For one thing it helps to confirm what we can otherwise infer: that there was a prolific tradition of *fianaigecht* during the pre-Norman period which was recorded only casually and sparsely — and often belatedly — in the surviving texts. And it also exemplifies the way in which the traditions of Fionn and Lug so often run in parallel and sometimes converge and intertwine.

But the analogy between Fionn and Lug, though striking, is not total. The main discrepancies have been marked out clearly by Gerard Murphy:

Fionn, however, as we have seen, is consistently represented as a warrior-hunter-poet-prophet. Lugh, on the other hand, though poetry is among the crafts of which he is master, is never represented as being primarily a hunter or a prophet, but rather as being simultaneously the possessor of crafts such as carpentry, smith-craft, harping and leechcraft. Both difference and resemblance could be explained on the hypothesis that Fionn was the god worshipped in the place of Lugh by some tribe, or group of tribes, who did not worship Lugh.[18]

Here we are in the realm of informed speculation, or extrapolation, and well beyond the limits of demonstration, yet it seems to me that Murphy is on firmer ground in seeking to explain the differences between Fionn and Lug in terms of function or regional distribution than is O'Rahilly in viewing it in terms of chronological priority within Irish tradition. It is fairly well established from the study of Celto-Roman epigraphy and iconography on the Continent and in Britain that a given principal deity's repertoire of functions and attributes could vary considerably by extension, contraction or shifting of emphasis when he was venerated under one or other of his by-names and in regional concentrations of his cult; the very fact that a deity is constantly defined in a particular region or context by an epithet or soubriquet which becomes an autonomous name is in itself clear evidence of an altered perspective: in other words, the deity has developed something of a new 'personality' or 'image' under his new label. There is there-

18 *Op. cit.* (1953), lxxxv.

fore no reason to suppose that the related mythological complexes of Fionn and Lug did not coexist since the earliest
period of Irish tradition, and even earlier still in common
Celtic tradition.

For Lug (as represented by the god Lug rather than by the
fian-leader [Lugaid] Mac Con) the antiquity of the complex is
attested by the remarkable correspondence between it and
what we know of Celtic *Lugus/Mercurius from Classical and
Celto-Roman documents. Similarly, in the case of Fionn the
remarkable analogies between his myth and that of king Arthur
of Britain are such that both must be presumed to derive
from a common insular Celtic tradition. (The Welsh lore
about Gwynn ap Nudd seems to corroborate this and even
to suggest that the British and Irish peers bore the same name,
though this need not be an absolute and exclusive inference.)
From our point of view one of the main differences between
the cycles of (Lugaid) Mac Con and Fionn within the period
encompassed by the written literature, say from the early
seventh century onwards, is that the Fionn cycle was in the
ascendant as a comprehensive expression of *fianaigecht*,
expanding and diversifying and assimilating to itself the
traditions of the other *fiana* and their leaders, whereas the
cycle of (Lugaid) Mac Con did not develop as a reflex of
fianaigecht but as part of a very different and in many ways
contrasting genre: the learned corpus of political 'history'
and the 'histories' of the kings who formed it. As James
Carney has written of the tale of the battle of Mag Muccrama
in which Mac Con defeated and killed Art mac Cuinn:

> It belongs rather to a *genre* that one might call 'political
> scripture', a mixture of genuine history with symbolic
> fiction: its function is to propagandise rather than to
> entertain.[19]

The remarkable thing is, however, that the written record
of what must have been a vital and prolific literature about
Fionn and his *fian* remains quite sparse and sketchy until the
eleventh century. The surviving texts from these early centuries
were catalogued by Kuno Meyer in 1910, and his inventory
was later revised by Gerard Murphy.[20] It is a very modest

19 M. Dillon, ed., *Irish Sagas*, Dublin 1959, 159.
20 Meyer, *op. cit.*, xvi f; Murphy, *op. cit.* (1953), lv ff.

corpus, yet it does encompass all the essential elements of
Fionn's mythico-literary profile. He is a hunter, and as such
he lives much of the time in the woods and other uncultivated
parts of the country; he is a warrior, a seer and a verse-maker,
and he practises *imbas forosnai* and *teinm laída*, two of the
three divinatory rites used by the poet-seers, the *filid*, to attain
mantic illumination; he is a wooer of women — 'in every up-
land and in every forest that Fionn frequented there would
be a particular woman for him'[21] — and he is, with good
reason, jealous of his exclusive rights over those women allied
with him. He is credited with a number of lyric/nature poems
dating from this early period, but the attribution to him is
probably secondary in all or most instances and it is not easy
to say when he and his companions came to be typically
associated with the composition of nature lyrics.

Already in the tenth century Fionn and the *fian* were
being brought within the ambit of Cormac mac Airt, king of
Tara and legendary lawgiver (I tend to agree with Gerard
Murphy that this special connection is an innovation in the
Fionn-tradition), and in the eleventh century, to quote
Murphy, 'Fionn was probably definitely placed in the pseudo-
historical scheme.' This is reflected in the considerable number
of references to Fionn in works of learned *senchas* as well as
in poems of the *dinnshenchas* belonging to the eleventh century. In this as in other areas of literary activity the eleventh
century was the lead-in to an extraordinary spate of redaction
and compilation which conserved much earlier tradition in a
numerous variety of adaptations and re-creations. The culmination of this activity with regard to the *fianaighecht* was the
rapid expansion of the specialized genre of the Fionn ballad
and the composition of the *Acallam*, a frame-tale comprising
over two hundred stories and anecdotes told in a pleasant
prose interspersed with countless passages of lyric and quasi-
historical verse. As with so much else in Irish learning and
literature this period was a turning point for the Fionn cycle,
at least in the written tradition, a time when inherited material
was assiduously revised and new norms accorded acceptance

21 *Cormac's Glossary*, s.v. *orc tréith*, printed separately by Meyer,
   op. cit., lvii.

or consciously devised.[22] It is therefore a convenient lower limit for this survey of the early evolution of *fianaigecht*.

T.F. O'Rahilly has noted that there is evidence in the literature of several versions of the Fionn legend in the medieval period,[23] a Leinster version, a Munster version and perhaps a Midland version, and yet, as it happens, some of the earliest references to *fianaighecht* come from the north-east, from the broad hinterland of the monastery of Bangor on Belfast Lough, which was evidently the centre of a phase of sustained learned and literary activity during the seventh and part of the eighth century. In so far as the literature is concerned this activity has become closely associated with the manuscript known as *Cín Dromma Snechta*, 'The Book of Druim Snechta', which, to judge by its title, was compiled at the otherwise little-known monastery of Drumsnat in Co. Monaghan.

This manuscript has not survived, but on the basis of the linguistic character of texts said to derive from it Rudolf Thurneysen assigned it to the first half of the eighth century, and, whether or not we accept his dating, the fact remains that the language of a number of the *Cín Dromma Snechta* texts is unquestionably very early and that some of them relate clearly to the literary and historical context of east Ulster in the seventh century. One of these texts, *Immram Brain*, 'The Voyage of Bran', a poetic account of Bran's journey to the otherworld, has a section dealing with the extraordinary birth and the career of a certain Mongán son of Fiachna,[24] and he is also the focus of four short tales which were evidently included in *Cín Dromma Snechta*. Mongán was a historical figure, the son of the king of Dál nAraidi, and he flourished in the early seventh century (*ob.* 625 *Annals of Ulster*), but he had also a mythological aspect, perhaps through assimilation to an otherworld namesake, and enjoyed easy commerce with the supernatural inhabitants of the *síd* (as did the members of Fionn's *fian*).

---

22 Cf. G. Murphy's comment on the way in which *Acallam na Senórach* 'fixed' Fionn's literary background for the future, *op. cit.* (1953), lxi.

23 *Op. cit.*, 275.

24 K. Meyer and A. Nutt, eds., *The Voyage of Bran*, Vol. I, London 1895, 24-9; A.G. van Hamel, ed. *Immrama*, Dublin 1941, 16 f.

One of the four anecdotes tells more explicitly the story of Mongán's birth outlined in *Immram Brain*: while his father Fiachna was in northern Britain (Albe) aiding his friend Aedán mac Gabráin king of Scottish Dál Riada in warfare against the Saxons, the god Manannán approached his wife at home and persuaded her to lie with him in order to protect her husband from certain death and thereby to conceive a famous son.[25] Unlike most of the other well-known instances of the divine father motif, in this case the god informed the mortal father of the arrangement and then saved his life, and Fiachna acquiesced in the one and was duly grateful for the other.

The verses in *Immram Brain* speak of Mongán's great valour (a feature that goes unnoticed in the four anecdotes) and describe him as a champion among warriors (*fénnidi*). The word *fénnid* is not infrequently used in the general sense of warrior, but other indications of Mongán's involvement with *fianaigecht* suggest that it may here have the more precise meaning 'members of *fiana*'. The notice of Mongán's death in the *Annals of Tigernach* states that he was killed by a stone thrown by Artur son of Bicor Pretēne 'the Briton' (?)[26] and quotes a quatrain by the poet Becc Boirche attributing his death to the warriors of Cantire (*Cenn Tíre*) in Scotland. This corresponds to the reference by the tenth-century Cinaed ua hArtacáin in his poem on the deaths of famous heroes, where he records that 'Mongán who was the diadem of every troop fell by the *fian* of Cantire'.[27]

Significantly the other half of the quatrain in which this occurs is concerned with the death of Fionn, for a close connection between the two characters emerges dramatically in another of the four *Cín Dromma Snechta* anecdotes.[28] When the *fili* Forgoll stated that Fothad Airgdech (brother of Fothad Canainne) was slain at Dubthair in Leinster, Mongán promptly contradicted him and for this *lèse-majesté* was threatened with the full rigour of the poet's deadly satire.

---

25   Meyer and Nutt, *op. cit.*, 42-5.
26   But cf. K. Marstrander, *Revue Celtique* 36 (1915), 354, n.1.
27   Ed. W. Stokes, *Revue Celtique* 23 (1902), 310 f., 322, 328.
28   Meyer and Nutt, *op. cit.*, 45 ff., 49 ff.

But rescue was at hand. Caílte mac Rónáin, who was one of the prominent members of the *fian* and a foster-son of Fionn, came from the otherworld, travelling on foot (he was renowned among the *fiana* for his fleetness of foot), from the far south-west, where one of the traditional locations of the otherworld lay off the coast, to the royal court of Dál nAraidi in the north-east. Moreover, Mongán was able through his own mantic perception to follow the course of his journey throughout the length of Ireland. When he arrived Caílte vindicated Mongán's stand: he described how Fionn and his followers had come from Scotland and given battle to Fothad Airgdech on the Ollarbae (the Larne river), how he himself had slain him with a cast of his spear and how they had buried him with his precious ornaments. When they went to the place indicated, everything was as he had said and there was an ogam inscription to verify the manner of Fothad's death.

But the most intriguing point of all in this little narrative is that Caílte when recalling the battle of Ollarbae spoke to Mongán as if he had been present there and inadvertently addressed him as Fionn. Mongán hurriedly brushed this aside, but the final sentence of the text underlines it saying: 'Mongán, however, was Fionn, though he would not let it be told.'

This little tale is as important for what it implies as for what it reveals directly. It takes for granted an easy familiarity on the part of readers or hearers with the general content of *fian* lore and links it with the contemporary cultural environment of east Ulster. The battle of Ollarbae was one of the 'two fatal battles of the *fian*', and it was the losses sustained by the *fian* there and at the battle of Gabra that brought about its final dissolution.[29] Its name crops up frequently in Fionn texts down to the modern period, but what is of particular interest to us here is that there would seem to have been a relatively developed tradition about it already at the time when the *Cín Dromma Snechta* text was composed, and that this early record of it is based entirely on the alleged relationship between Mongán mac Fiachna and

29 Cf. W. Stokes, ed., *Acallam na Senórach, Irische Texte*, Fourth Series, Vol. 1, Leipzig 1900, ll. 1095-1144.

Fionn. Indeed if we accept the identification of the two characters with all its logical implications, we must regard Mongán not merely as the avatar or reincarnation of Fionn but also as the living repository of his legend.

Similarly when the author/redactor of the *Cín Dromma Snechta* tale identified Mongán with Fionn and represented him as being much more knowledgeable than the *filid* were about the 'history' and exploits of the *fian*, he must have been fully aware of the inferences which could be drawn from it regarding the currency and status of *fianaigecht* in the early seventh century.

There are many reasons why the cultural climate in east Ulster in the seventh century should have been particularly favourable to the development of the Fionn tales: the emergence of a more liberal, personal and eclectic view of literature (than that conventionalized by the *filid*) among men of quality and learning; the geographical position of the area and the political and ecclesiastical affiliations deriving from it which made it a meeting-place for Irish and northern British thought and tradition; the deep interest of Irish *littérateurs* in the intimate relations between secular and supernatural (as personified in the Janus character of Mongán and exemplified most consistently in the Fionn cycle), an interest which in the intellectual hinterland of Bangor seems to have been combined with a certain imaginative, lyric expressionistic interpretation such as we find in the verse of *Immram Brain* or the prose of *Echtrae Conlai*. In short, east Ulster in the seventh century was the focus of a remarkable phase of literary activity which handled traditional materials in a free, fresh and sometimes innovational style unconstrained by the *filid*'s rigid hierarchy of socio-literary values.

We have no means of knowing from strictly contemporary evidence what stage in its development the Fionn cycle had reached by this time, but for the author(s) of the cluster of anecdota about Mongán it had already acquired much of its later identity — the laconic reference to Caílte and to Ollarbae indicate this — and there is at least one item of evidence which may represent the early seventh century as a time in which *fian*-lore was actively cultivated. In the *Liber Hymnorum* version of the preface to *Amra Choluim Chille* it is

stated that the *filid*, when threatened with banishment by
king Aed mac Ainmirech, were maintained for three years
by the king of Ulster (apparently Mael Coba son of Fiachna
mac Demmáin) and that it was during their stay in Ulster
they 'set about composing *fian*-stories (v. 11 *sgéla fēne,
Egerton Ms 1782, scela fénned, Yellow Book of Lecan*) of
their own invention; and things did not happen at all as they
related, but it was in order to impose them on the uncouth
people among whom they were then living that eloquent
filid invented these lying fictions.'[30]

One cannot of course be certain what exactly these 'lying
fictions' were that were being invented in the first half of
the seventh century (Mael Coba's *obit* is at 647 in the *Annals
of Ulster*): if *fian/fénnidi* refers here to the Ulster heroes
they may relate to the early elaboration of the Ulster cycle
in writing, but if it follows more normal usage then they are
more likely to mean the *fian*-lore and perhaps also other
tales of similar style and temper. For example, the title
rígfhéinnid is accorded Maeluma mac Baetáin, one of the
royal dynasty of Ailech, who was active in the early seventh
century and went, like Mongán's father, to assist Aedán mac
Gabráin in his warfare against the Anglo-Saxons, and who
seems to have become a legendary figure soon after his own
time, not only in Ireland but also in Britain. The references
to him suggest a *fian*-leader rather than a conventional
battle-leader.

One of his exploits, perhaps that in which he slew the
brother of Ethelfrid king of Northumberland, was the subject
of a story which has been lost but which is recorded in a
medieval tale-list under the title *Echtra Maíle Uma maic
Baítáin*, 'The Adventure of Maíl Uma son of Baítán'; despite
the fact that it occurs in only one (list A) of the two major
tale-lists I believe this to have been a relatively early tale. It
belongs with two other lost tales about northern heroes of
the late sixth and early seventh centuries: *Sluagad Fiachna
maic Baítáin co Dún nGuaire i Saxanaib*, 'The Hosting of
Fiachna son of Baítán to Dún Guaire in the Land of the

---

30   Cf. J.W. Bernard and R. Atkinson, eds., *Liber Hymnorum*, London
1898, Vol. 1, 162 ff.

Saxons' (A) and *Echtra Aedáin maic Gabráin*, 'The Adventure
of Aedán son of Gabrán' (A and B), and there is a good deal
of other evidence which indicates that there was at one time
a considerable body of narrative about important events and
outstanding personalities in eastern Ulster and northern
Britain/Scotland during what was a crucial and pivotal period
of history, both cultural and political, for both Ireland and
Britain. After all, it is not mere accident that the struggles of
the northern Britons against the Saxons (and among themselves) during this short period should have come to constitute the heroic age of the later British peoples, especially
the Welsh.

To judge by what remains of it this east-Ulster historical
literature had something of the freshness and immaturity of
a new creation that had not been adapted to the traditional
learned criteria for heroic narrative. It had a certain *naiveté*
and acceptance of magic which is reminiscent of popular or
folk storytelling, and it had some of the tendency to blur the
boundary between the secular and the supernatural which
characterizes the whole tradition of *fianaigecht*. But it proved
largely ephemeral: for the most part it has survived only in a
handful of tales and anecdotes and in scattered fragments and
references. In the seventh century, however, it was a living
literary force because its subject-matter had a living relevance,
an immediacy and excitement, for those *nua-litridi* who at
this very time were actively engaged in the creation of a new
written literature free of the constraints on form and subject-
matter which controlled the professional oral literature of the
filid. Perhaps the main reason why this Ulster-Scottish literary
complex failed to sustain its early vigour is that the focus of
literary activity, so far as the *literati* were concerned, subsequently shifted away from east Ulster, thereby depriving
the Ulster-Scottish cycle of its immediate relevance and of
the peculiar creative energy which brought it into being in
the first place. This may also help to explain why the oral
cycle of Fionn and the *fian*, after its promising appearance in
the Mongán legend, should have occurred so fleetingly in the
manuscript tradition of the next two or three centuries.

Yet another pivotal period for the history of *fianaigecht* was
the early and mid-ninth century, when the Viking raids on

Ireland were at their most wilful and destructive. Without exaggerating the Norse depredations it is clear that they affected the fortunes of many Irish monasteries — Bangor was one of them — as well as the pattern of emigration of monastic clerics and scholars to the Continent, but they probably impinged most profoundly in those early years on the emotions and the imagination of the population at large, unlearned and unsophisticated, for whom reports of these marauders from overseas were more reminiscent of otherworld beings than of the conventional raiding and plundering forays which were a familiar feature of Irish life. But given the nature of this influence it could only surface in the written literature after a considerable lapse of time — as it did in the event. There are some indications that already within the Viking period, or soon after, the Norsemen were being assimilated to the mythical people known as Fomoir(i) who irrupted periodically into the Irish world from the beginning of time, threatening the destruction of social order (as well as being assimilated, it must be said, to their divine opposites, the Tuatha Dé Danann), but it is only when we reach the twelfth century that we find the Lochlannaig — to give the Vikings the name by which they are generally known in heroic-romantic literature — established in the role of the Fomore as an accepted part of the furniture of *fianaigecht* story-telling. From then until our own day they have continued to play unendingly the same role of medieval space invaders invariably repulsed by the valour and magic resources of Fionn and his *fian*.[31]

But what later became a cliché of Fionn ballads and stories must have begun as a reaction to a phase of alternating psychic tension, disturbance and release among large sections of the community — it is well to remember that the monasteries which bore the brunt of the Viking raids in the ninth century had extensive holdings of land and large numbers of tenants (*manaig*) and other dependants who would have had rude experience or vivid reports of the alien warriors. This, I suggest, became part of the popular, sub-literary tradition and acted as a stimulus to the *fian*-lore which flourished within it and

31 *Procs. of the Intern. Congress of Celtic Studies, Dublin, 1959*, Dublin 1962, 94-9.

which, by reason of its characteristic themes and flexible structure, offered a particularly receptive context for this kind of folk rumour.

But, as we have noted already, the effect of these events did not become manifest for another two centuries or more, and the obvious question is why this should have been so, why indeed the whole Fionn cycle should have been so largely neglected in the written text from the seventh or eighth century to the eleventh or twelfth.

The explanation is to be sought, most likely, in the peculiar status of the *fiana* in relation to the rest of society. Though they and their function are recognized in native law and considered necessary for the good of the community,[32] this is nevertheless subject to the general reservations, both explicit and implicit, created by the fundamental ambivalence of their relationship to the main social institutions. Though the *fénnid* is acknowledged by society and resorted to when occasion requires it, normally he lives and acts outside society or on its periphery, relying on his own strength and enterprise for the support and protection which he can no longer expect from the solidarity of his kinsfolk and tribe. For to become a *fénnid* was to sever the connections with one's clan, divesting oneself of privileges and responsibilities alike. The *fénnidi* were often, as Meyer puts it, 'men expelled from their clan (*éclaind*), or landless men (*díthir*), sons of kings who quarrelled with their fathers, men proclaimed, or men who seized this means to avenge some private wrong by taking the law into their own hands.'[33] They may also originally — or ideally — have constituted an age-class, representing a formalized association between youth and military activity which is well attested in other societies, an association reflected in the familiar synonym of *fénnid: oac féne.*[34]

Even though it is often difficult to discriminate in the literature between elements that have to do with historical and mythical *fiana* respectively, it is clear that in both cases

32 Cf. K. Meyer, *op. cit.* (1910), ix and references cited there.
33 *Ibid.* Cf. K. Meyer, ed., *Tecosca Cormaic*, Dublin 1909, §31.10: *fénnid cách co trebad*, 'everyone is a *f*. until he takes up husbandry'.
34 Cf. A. Rees and B. Rees, *Celtic Heritage*, London 1961, 62 f.; K. McCone, *Ériu* 35 (1984), 29, 36 n. 12.

the *fiana* were thought of as quintessential outsiders, associated typically with the liminal areas of forest and wilderness, and owing first loyalty to the fraternity not to tribe or kingdom.

Where the Ulster hero gave allegiance to his king seated in his royal capital, the *féinnid* obeyed only the leader of his *fian*. Where the former had his own permanent fort, his own territory and his own retainers, the latter gives the impression of continual movement within a changing geography. Whereas the Ulster cycle concerned itself with organized society, with the integrity of the political unit — kingdom or province — and the guarding of territorial boundaries, the *fianaigecht* belonged in a world where places were important, even sacred, but political boundaries were ill-defined or irrelevant.

In all of this *fiana* and *fianaigecht* are the antithesis of the Ulster heroes and the Ulster cycle, and the ideology — or rather the spirit — which informs them runs almost wholly counter to the ideology which underpinned the conservative structure of a society in which cosmic collapse was equated with the decay of the distinctions of class and category, and which for that reason was carefully conserved and propagated by the *filid*, jurists, and other learned and privileged brethren of the native establishment. It is only to be expected, therefore, that the attitude of the learned establishment towards the *fiana* should have reflected some of the ambivalence that characterized the role of the *fiana* themselves in relation to the institutions and values of organized society. On the ideological level they were perceived as a mediating element between order and chaos, secular and supernatural, natural and cultivated, youth and maturity, feeling and thinking, while on the empirical level they catered for the maverick elements who found no compatible place, or sought none, within the settled community, offering an outlet for their energies while restraining their excesses. But they were independent and unpredictable and therefore a potential danger to the *status quo* — good reason why they should be treated with circumspection by the *filid* and their associates.

Conversely, the features which rendered *fiana* and *fianaigecht* suspect to the guardians of society would have commended them to the people at large. There is clear testimony that *fian*-lore was widely current among the common people from

the eleventh century onwards, and there is a strong presumption that it had flourished long before then in popular
storytelling. This might seem to lend some weight to the
theory proposed by Eoin Mac Neill to the effect that the
Fionn cycle originated among the indigenous peoples who
inhabited Ireland before the Celts and whose descendants
constituted the *aithech-thuatha* or subject-peoples of early
historical times,[35] though, as Marie-Louise Sjoestedt has
pointed out, Mac Neill's theory does not take account of the
fact that myths comparable to those of the *fiana* are found in
the Germanic world.[36] In any event the concept of *fianaigecht*
and the reality must have seemed particularly congenial to
those peoples who probably formed the bulk of the population
and who were excluded from full partnership with the
dominant Celtic tribes for as long as ethnic distinctions were
clearly fixed in the amber of learned memory.

I have already referred to the difficulty of distinguishing,
where necessary, between mythical and historical *fianaigecht*,
between, as it were, the ideal and the real. For example
there is considerable emphasis in certain written accounts
of the *fiana* on their *esprit de corps* and on the trials and
precepts which regulated their admission to the brother-
hood and their conduct thereafter, but it may not have been
all that easy for the innocent bystander caught up in their
activities, especially if propertied, to perceive and appreciate
the difference between them and less ethical marauders.
Marie-Louise Sjoestedt is on doubtful ground when she
claims that the *fénnid* 'is never represented as a brigand';
certainly he turns up at times in very doubtful company.
Richard Sharpe has shown the importance accorded in early
Irish literature to those organized bands of brigands who
frequently go by the name of *díbergaig*, 'marauders, free-
booters, bandits', *Dictionary of the Irish Language* (DIL) in
Irish and *laici* in Latin.[37] Ecclesiastical writers, to whom

35   MacNeill, *op. cit.*, xxiv.
36   M. Dillon, trans., *Gods and Heroes of the Celts*, London 1949, 87.
37   R. Sharpe, 'Hiberno-Latin *laicus*, Irish *láech* and the Devil's Men',
     Ériu 30 (1979), 74 ff.

they were particularly abhorrent, view their practice of *díberg* as a continuation of paganism and themselves as the agents of the Devil. They picture them as organized in groups (often of nine) and bound by some form of ritual allegiance involving an oath (*uotum mali*) and insignia (*signa diabolica*),[38] and in 'The Old Irish Table of Penitential Commutations' *díberg* is included among the sins for which there can be no remission of penance.[39] In fact the attitude of the Church to these medieval 'flying columns' is summed up fairly by the DIL s.v. *díberg* when it says that 'Those engaged in "díberg" seem in early times to have been regarded as outside the pale of Christianity and in league with evil powers'. As Kim McCone suggests, this may explain why the existence of the *díbergaig* is generally ignored and only occasionally grudgingly acknowledged in the legal tracts.[40]

But if the *díbergaig* have had, no doubt deservedly, a much poorer press than the *fiana*, the fact remains that the demarcation between them is sometimes less definite than the composers of *Acallam na Senórach* or the Fionn lays would have cared to admit. The author of the somewhat puritanical *Apgitir Chrábaid*, 'The Alphabet of Piety' (eighth century?) took a more jaundiced view of *fiannas*, the activities of *fiana*, as he listed its four effects on mankind: 'It contracts territories; it increases enmity; it cuts off life; it lengthens torments',[41] though admittedly his may be a biassed testimony, and it is more than balanced by an item in *Immacallam in dá Thuarad*, 'The Colloquy of the two Sages' (*c.* 900?) which includes the 'extinction of *fiannas* among the signs of approaching social catastrophe'.[42] But even in secular *fian*-literature the special status of the *fiana* is sometimes blurred by associ-

---

38 Sharpe, *op. cit.*, 82 ff.; cf. also C. Plummer, *Vitae Sanctorum Hiberniae*, Oxford 1910, Vol. 1, cii n. 1; Vol. 2, 384 s.v. *uotum malum*.

39 Ed. D.A. Binchy, *Ériu* 19 (1962), 58 f., §5. Cf. O'Mulconry's Glossary §309: *díberg . . . ní la laochacht ad-rímter . . . ar ní bí i coir laochachtae diúltad Dé ⁊ giallnae demuin*, 'Díberg is not accounted as of the heroic profession, for it is not part of the proper behaviour of the hero to reject God and serve the Devil.'

40 *Ériu* 35 (1984), 28 f.

41 Ed. V. Hull, *Celtica* 8 (1968), 72 f., §25.

42 Ed. W. Stokes, *Revue Celtique* 26 (1905), 46 f., §235.

ation with more nondescript categories. According to a text which may be of the eleventh century 'Fionn mac Cumhaill was chief of the household to Cormac and head of his exiles and mercenaries and of the rest of his soldiery (*7 cech ceithirne archena)*.[43] In *Macgnímartha Find*, 'Fionn's Boyhood Deeds', Fiacail mac Codna is described as a *foglaid*, 'reaver, plunderer' in §7, and in §23 Fiacail mac Conchinn, whom I take to be essentially the same character, is described as a *féinid*.[44]

More importantly, the story of *Togail Bruidne Da Derga* which hinges upon the conflict between Conaire's kingship and the brigandage (*díberg*) of his foster-brothers, uses the terms *fían*, *fénnid* and *fíanlag* as if they were almost synonymous with *díberg* (in the sense 'band of reavers') and *díbergach* (e.g. ll. 620-4).[45] The problem would appear to be that, while *fían* and *díberg* shared the same semantic field,

43 Printed by L. Chr. Stern, *Zeitschrift f. celt. Phil.* 1 (1897), 472; cited by Murphy, *op. cit.* (1953), xli.

44 Ed. K. Meyer, *Revue Celtique* 5 (1881-3), 197 ff. On the essential identity of the two Fiacails see also O'Rahilly, *op. cit.*, 554 s.n. *Fiacclach*.

45 A rather similar scenario occurs in the *Vita Gildae* ascribed to Caradoc of Llancarfan (ed. H. Williams, *Gildas*, Cymmrodorion Record Series, III, 1899, pp. 401-5). Arthur was the king of all Britain and a close friend of Gildas, but the saint's twenty-three brothers resisted his authority, especially the eldest of them, Hueil, who 'submitted to no king, not even to Arthur' and who persistently provoked and harrassed his rightful ruler: 'He would often swoop down from Scotland, set up conflagrations, and carry off spoils with victory and renown. In consequence, the king of all Britain, on hearing that the high-spirited youth had done such things and was doing similar things, pursued the victorious and excellent youth, who, as the inhabitants used to assert and hope, was destined to become king. In the hostile pursuit and council of war held in the island of Minau [i.e. Man], he killed the young plunderer [*praedatorem*].' Gildas was in Ireland at the time, but when he returned to Britain a large assembly of clerics and laity met him to arrange with Arthur the atonement for the killing. Gildas, however, gave him the kiss of forgiveness and his blessing, and Arthur did penance for his transgression and made amends, as best he could, until the end of his life.

Clearly the role of Hueil and his brothers is very close to that of Conaire's foster-brothers, the sons of Donn Désa, and their British

the former had a wider denotational and connotational range: when the *fiana* were good, they were very, very good, but when they were bad, they were *díbergaig* — more or less. In *Tochmarc Ailbe* this distinction seems to be rationalized discreetly in terms of allegiance to the 'high-king'. *Féinnidi* and *díbergaig* and *foglaidi* are included among all the worthy kinds of people invited to king Cormac's feast, and the *díbergaig* and the *fiana* are placed together at the feast and served together with the same foods. It is also stated that during the time Fionn was banished from Cormac's court and separated from the *fian* because of Gráinne, 'all the men of Ireland who were estranged from the king and engaged in free-booting activities (*for dimfeirg on rí*) would gather into Fionn's household, until such time as they should be reconciled with Cormac'.[46] This would suggest that, in the wake of the regularization of the Fian's position as Cormac's army in the learned doctrine of the tenth and subsequent centuries, *fiannas* was identified with the *fénnid*'s activity in the service of the king, *díberg* with his activity as a freelance without the constraints and responsibilities attaching to the king's patronage.

What emerges from all this is that the *fiana* — both myth and reality — had to be treated with some caution by the learned establishment comprising the Church as well as the *filid*. Both had good reasons for wishing to insulate the *status quo* from the threat of sudden unregulated change over which they had no control. Despite their original and still underlying conflict of interests, they had, at least by the seventh century, achieved an effective form of coexistence and collaboration which was to bring them closer and closer together in the course of the following centuries. And the closer they

allies — they were all *díbergaig* — and Conaire's bond of affection for his dissident foster-brothers is matched by Arthur's deep friendship with Gildas. The setting of the theme and its elaboration are very different in *Togail Bruidne Da Derga* and the *Vita Gildae*, but, allowing for this, the central motif of the 'mortal' embarrassment of the well-intentioned king by his close friends is virtually the same in both cases.

46 Ed. R. Thurneysen, *Zeitschrift f. celt. Phil.* 13 (1921), 260 §6, 254 §1.

were together the less likely were the monastic redactors to accord a high priority to the writing of *fian*-lore.

The solution for this martial free enterprise was the same as that often applied to modern economic free enterprise: nationalization. There is much in van Hamel's interpretation of Irish, and Celtic, religion which I find unacceptable, but I find myself almost in total agreement with him when he says that the 'essential identity of Fenian and Arthurian legend shows that the religion of the land, and its expression in the form of paradigmatic hero-tales, continues a deeply rooted Celtic tradition'.[47] In prehistoric times Fionn and Athur (however he was then named) were evidently pictured as the opponents of external demonic powers in what was basically a myth of cosmic conflict between the forces of destruction and chaos and the defenders of the cosmic precinct, here particularized as Ireland in the one case and Britain in the other. Essentially, of course, this concept was metaphysical and ideological, not part of *Realpolitik*, but the value of myths is that they can be applied to actual historical problems and crises, and so the Arthur myth was localized in sixth-century Britain and his mythic enemies identified with the all too actual threat posed by the Saxon invasions.

Ireland was spared serious foreign intervention until the Norse incursions began at the end of the eighth century, but when it came it produced a similar reflex assimilation of myth to history (and history to myth). The Norsemen were equated to the Fomoire, and this provided an occasion for assigning a quasi-historical role as protector of the national territory to Fionn and his *fian* (I say quasi-historical because the Lochlannaig of the romantic-heroic literature are far removed from the *Geinti* or the *Gaill* of the annals). D.A. Binchy has said of the Norse invasions that, while it would be anachronistic to claim that they created a common sentiment of Irish nationality, 'they did evoke that sense of "otherness" which lies at the basis of nationalism', and even though I cannot accept his formulation of the phenomenon without some qualification, there can be little doubt that the events of the ninth century brought about a certain politiciza-

47   As n. 2 *supra*, p. 30 f.

tion of the cultural concept of nationality which coincided neatly with the (partial) historicization of the role of the *fiana* as the protectors of the land of Ireland. Moreover, this development more or less coincided in time with the propagation of the doctrine of the 'high-kingship' by which learned historians of the establishment sought to impose on behalf of the Uí Néill dynasty the notion that the king of Tara was of right the over-king of all Ireland; from the tenth century what has been described as a political fiction – the 'high-kingship' – had become virtually a historical fact. This was all part of a sequence of profound socio-political, cultural and religious change which extended from about the tenth century to the end of the twelfth, and one small element in this sequence of change was the nationalization of the *fiana*.

By fixing them securely to the 'high-kingship', specifically to that of Cormac mac Airt dated notionally in the third century A.D., the 'pseudo-historians' pretended to draw the *fiana* in from their characteristic habitat on the margins of society and to establish them in close *rapport* with its central institutions. No doubt the change belonged more to theory than to reality, but it was a genuine recognition of the popularity and widening acceptance of *fianaigecht*. It is a well-attested fact – attested for example in the sixteenth and seventeenth century in Ireland – that in times of socio-cultural upheaval, or even of rapid unplanned change, popular or sub-learned genres and strata of literature can surface and win general acceptance once the crust of learned orthodoxy is broken. The *fianaigecht* seems to be an instance of this: the great expansion in the writing of *fianaigecht* belongs to the eleventh and twelfth centuries, which suggests that its graph began to rise some time before that, and I think one can safely conclude therefore that the linking of Fionn with Cormac mac Airt in the tenth century is the first admission of its rising status.

TWENTIETH-CENTURY RECORDINGS OF SCOTTISH GAELIC HEROIC BALLADS

JOHN MacINNES
(University of Edinburgh)

The ballads[1] that we call Fenian or Ossianic make their first appearance in literature in Ireland in the twelfth century. Some eight hundred years later a number of these heroic ballads or lays (as well as a couple of ballads on non-Fenian themes) still survive in the repertoire of traditional singers in Gaelic Scotland. Over the past thirty-five years the ballads and their melodies have been fairly exhaustively recorded by some members[2] of the staff of the University of Edinburgh's School of Scottish Studies, and are preserved in the School's archives. Eventually all of these will be published on disc and cassette in the School of Scottish Studies series 'Scottish Tradition', under the general editorship of Dr Peter Cooke. The second disc in the series, *Music from the Western Isles*, contains a Fenian ballad 'Latha dh'an Fhinn am Beinn Iongnaidh', 'A day when the Fenians were in the Mountain of Marvels', sung by a notable singer from South Uist, the late Mrs Archie MacDonald.

I shall give below[3] a representative sample of the ballads

1 'Ballad' and 'lay' are used interchangeably throughout.
2 Notably C.I. Maclean and D.A. MacDonald. Ballads were recorded from the Forties onwards by Dr and Mrs J.L. Campbell, the pioneers of wire and tape-recording of Gaelic song.
3 For reasons of space alone, it has not proved possible to provide transcriptions of these examples.

in our archives. I do not intend, however, to comment in detail on each individual item nor, with one or two exceptions, to discuss the textual relationships of our recorded versions with those to be found in earlier collections. Questions of time apart, the fact is that the main interest and value of the recordings lie in the music and in the performance of individual singers. From a purely literary point of view, even our most complete texts add little of interest to what we can find in print; whereas earlier transcriptions of the music of the ballads are much rarer and apparently less accurate or more difficult to interpret. This makes these melodies from the living tradition of unique value but I am not competent to deal with problems of musicology.

Certainly the texts in general are of great interest from both historical and anthropological points of view, showing what did survive and in what form they are preserved. How full or how fragmentary are they? How pure or how corrupt is the transmission? Why did they survive in some communities and not in others? There are also some questions that, I fear, can never be answered now. For instance, when we are dealing with what we call a corrupt text, what did the singers themselves make of it? While the main lines of the narrative may be clear enough, there are frequently obscure words and phrases upon which the singers might have provided their own gloss, whether their personal interpretation would have solved any literary cruces for us or not. This applies particularly to recordings made in the early 1950s by singers who are now dead.

In view of all these things, I shall on the whole confine my remarks to a sketch of the background — the specifically Scottish cultural setting — for although this is a literary inheritance in which Scots and Irish Gaels share, the differing historical circumstance of the two countries tended to produce, as one might predict, certain divergent features. Indeed, the most obvious of these is the survival in Scottish Gaelic oral tradition of the heroic lay as a sung form — whereas in Ireland the practice of singing the ballads has now apparently come to an end.

Now if the Fenian ballads appear as early as the twelfth century in literary form, the fact that oral versions exist at all in a living tradition at the present time is undeniably a remarkable instance of cultural continuity and survival. Yet, whatever may be true of the melodies, so far as textual transmission goes, this is true only in a broad, general sense.

None of the ballads in the archives, some of which appear to be purely Scottish compositions, can be traced to such remote origins. On the whole, the later medieval period is probably as early as we can go.

Duain na Féinne(adh), the 'poems of the Fenian-band', is the commonest term now in circulation for the Fenian lays. Fionn and his warriors are not known collectively in colloquial Gaelic as *Fian(n)a* but as *Féinn*, *Fèinn* or *Finn*, depending on dialect: with the article *An Fhéinn*, etc. An individual member is *Fiantaiche*; the plural *Na Fiantaichean* is to be heard side by side with *An Fhéinn*. In some areas *fiantaiche* denotes a wild, uncouth person, more commonly applied to a male than a female, but the feminine *ban-fhiantaiche* is also known. In some of the strict Presbyterian communities *fiantaiche* may have the connotation of 'anti-ecclesiastical' or be applied to non-churchgoing members of that society. Indeed, in certain contexts *fiantaiche* can quite happily be translated as 'heathen' or even 'pagan'. This is no doubt connected with the debates in which Oisein is made the opponent of St Patrick; but the ascetic evangelicalism of relatively modern times clearly plays a major part in this particular semantic development. All over the Gaelic-speaking area, the phrase *cothrom na Féinne(adh)* — the chance of a fair fight, traditionally offered by the Fenians to their opponents in battle — is still used in the sense of 'fair play'. But not everyone who uses that phrase is aware of the historical or linguistic connections with *fiantaiche*.

There is no Gaelic word for 'ballad' in the sense of 'narrative poem'. A heroic lay may be *dàn*, *duan* or *laoidh*.[4] More precisely, in present day usage, these three terms are used in titles by which singers and listeners alike identify a ballad, e.g. 'Dàn na h-Inghinne', 'Duan na Ceardaich', 'Laoidh

---

4 *Rann*, 'verse', may be used occasionally; *rann* is sometimes applied to any composition which is fairly short and not sung.

a' Choin Duibh'. Using 'poem' as a convenient term for the moment, these are respectively 'The Poem of the Maiden', 'The Poem of the Smithy' and 'The Poem of the Black Hound'. Occasionally òran, the unmarked term in modern spoken Gaelic for song-poem, has also been used, to judge from titles in collections. The one ballad from the Isle of Skye in our archives, recorded by myself in 1953, was known to the reciter, Donald Robertson, as 'Oran-mór na Féinne'. He could trace it back in his family to the middle of the nineteenth century but there was no melody for it. The term 'òran-mór', where it exists in genuine oral tradition, does not seem to denote any particular verse structure — in contrast to ceòl-mór and port-mór in piping. Of the examples I know, two are choral refrain compositions (of the waulking-song type). The phrase is qualitative, with an aura of dignity, even grandness.

Of the other terms, dàn is not now used in the ordinary registers of spoken Gaelic. Duan ranges from 'song, rhymed composition, ditty' to 'recitation'; like iorram, 'rowing-song', it is extended to mean 'harping on, being excessively repetitious', etc. Specifically it is used of certain compositions: Christmas carols, Hogmanay rhymes, and other miscellaneous poems, recited not sung.

In some respects the most interesting term is laoidh. Hector Maclean, who was one of J.F. Campbell's fellow-workers, has a note: 'Laoidh, lay, ode, lyric; it differs from dàn a poem, in being more melodious and capable of being sung. It narrates rapidly a few events ending tragically, almost invariably the death of a hero'.[5] As to the last, Maclean no doubt had in mind the Fenian 'Laoidh Dhiarmaid' and the non-Fenian 'Laoidh Fhraoich': these two heroes, Diarmad and Fraoch, both die tragically.

Most modern tradition-bearers imply that all the ballads were at least 'capable of being sung'; where they were not, it was because the melody had been lost in transmission. None the less, it may be the case that some ballads were

5 J.F. Campbell, *Popular Tales of the West Highlands*, London 1892, Vol. 3, 87.

always recited rather than sung.[6] One of my best informants, the late Domhnall Chaluim Bàin (Donald Sinclair) of Tiree certainly thought that this might be so. He also endorsed, without any prompting by me, the judgement expressed by Hector Maclean to the effect that *laoidh* was 'more melodious'.

I may add that in everyday Gaelic usage, the generic sense of *laoidh* is 'hymn, spiritual song'. There is no doubt a continuity of meaning here from early times: the word was used *inter alia* in the sense of a 'poem as medium for legal, historical, religious and didactive lore.' But our easy acceptance in Gaelic of the use of *laoidh* in sacred and secular contexts alike is surely striking.

Fionn and his men were regarded as historical characters. They were also accorded what practically amounted to a religious veneration. It is told traditionally that one of the nineteenth-century collectors, the Rev. Dr John MacDonald of Ferintosh, a minister of the Free Church of Scotland, once asked an old man in Kintail whether he believed in the historical existence of the *Féinn*. The man apparently was shocked that the minister should even ask such a question and retorted: 'Do I believe in Christ!' Modern scholars' theories that Fionn originally belonged more to the realm of mythology than of history were anticipated by Dr Alexander MacBain. On one occasion he is said to have roused an audience of Gaelic speakers in Glasgow to intense anger by expressing these ideas. To such people, Fionn and Gráinne had virtually the status of Biblical characters; in that respect not so different in popular imagination from Adam and Eve, who, of course, were regarded as historical characters also. People who would never deny the truth of the Scriptures believed equally strongly in the Gaelic messianic tradition that puts Fionn, lying in Tom na h-Iubhraich, near Inverness, in the role of Sleeping Warrior who will one day reappear to restore the Gaels of Scotland to their former greatness. They also had the evidence of placenames to remind them of the

6   Rev. Alexander Pope in a letter dated 15 November 1763 says 'that the g r e a t e s t   n u m b e r of them have particular tunes to which they are sung.' [My emphasis.] See *Highland Society of Scotland's Report on Ossian*, Edinburgh 1805, 52-5. Quotation on p. 54.

names and exploits of these gigantic warriors of song and legend. Not surprisingly a very substantial body of Fenian folktales has been recorded direct from the storytellers by the collectors of the School of Scottish Studies. From the wealth of textual material in collections of the past, taken down from the mouths of the people, we know that the ballads too were immensely popular.

Viewed against that background, then, what is curious is not so much that the ballads have survived into the twentieth century but rather that so few of them should have survived. Discounting variants, re-recordings, and odd fragments, and counting titles only, the total of s u n g ballads in the School's collection amounts to no more than half-a-dozen, to which we can add the two non-Fenian heroic lays. There are, however, in addition to that, genuine oral versions without melodies, as already indicated, and there are others in manuscript which may be genuine enough texts but have come from printed sources.

In terms of contemporary Gaelic oral culture Fenian tales and heroic ballads alike (Fenian or not) are now little more than curiosities but the quantitative difference is none the less striking. Progressive anglicisation, the devastation of the Clearances, emigration in general, changes in literary fashion: all these are well-known contributory factors in the over-all decline. But perhaps because the ballad-singers were specialists in a more demanding craft, they were fewer in number from the beginning.

Nevertheless, most of Gaelic Scotland is represented in the early manuscript collections. Galloway alone, in the extreme south-west of the country, where Gaelic survived until 1700 or later, is blank. Since Manx Gaelic ballads are mentioned in the eighteenth century, we may assume that the seanachies and singers of Galloway knew them too.

Setting aside the *Book of the Dean of Lismore*,[7] substantial collecting begins about 1739 with the work of the Rev. Alexander Pope — Alasdair Pàp, as he was still remembered in Sutherland in my boyhood — minister of the parish of Reay in Caithness. Before 1760 the Rev. James Maclagan in Perth-

7 Discussed in D. Meek's paper below, p. 131 ff.

shire had made 'a good collection'; Rev. Donald MacNicol, an Argyll minister, was a contemporary collector; and the work continued well into the nineteenth century, with Presbyterian clergymen prominent throughout.[8] With one or two exceptions, these were ministers of the Established Church of Scotland, whose attitudes towards the secular arts were markedly different from those of the equally Gaelic Evangelicals of the nineteenth century, most of whom severed themselves from the Established Church at the Disruption of 1846. This has some relevance to the distribution of ballads in the twentieth century.

The areas from which our recordings come are as follows: on the Scottish mainland, Sutherland and Ross-shire; in the Islands, Skye, Mull, Tiree, North and South Uist, Benbecula, and Barra.

The bulk of our recordings — in fact, all the 'titles' alluded to above, given in more or less close variants by a number of singers — come from the Catholic communities of Benbecula, South Uist and Barra, in the Outer Hebrides. From the same communities we also have manuscript versions of texts without melodies. The other areas I have named are each represented by one singer only: these are Presbyterian communities. The breakdown for the latter is as follows: on the mainland of Scotland, one from Lairg in the South of Sutherland; one from Lochalsh, four from Kintail: both on the western coast of Ross-shire; in the Islands, one from Mull, four from Tiree: both in the Southern Hebrides; one from the Isle of Skye (without melody). I shall have some further comments to make on these later.

This distribution does not reflect simply a religious divide in Gaelic culture. Distance from centres of anglicising influence has clearly played a crucial part for there are no ballads to be found now, nor within the last thirty-five years, in the Roman Catholic communities of mainland Scotland. Nevertheless, religion has played its own part. Beginning towards the end of the eighteenth century, and continuing into the twentieth century, a popular movement of radical dissent developed within Gaelic Presbyterianism. It was essentially

8   See J.F. Campbell, *Leabhar na Feinne*, London 1872.

a form of recluse religion practised in, and attempting to
dominate, open society; the great majority of its converts
came to regard the arts as *vanitas vanitatis*. Fenian ballads
may have become a special target because of their 'heathenish'
associations: symbols, as it were, of a competing faith. Certainly other types of song (e.g. waulking-songs) continued to
flourish in the heartland of Evangelical Presbyterianism. But
even as early as 1763 the Rev. Alexander Pope notes that
'many of them [the ballads] are lost, partly owing to our
clergy, who were declared enemies to these poems . . .'[9]

I want now to make some comments on a number of
individual ballads. The first, 'Duan na Ceardaich', is confined
to the North Uist to Barra group of islands. Throughout that
area it was, within the period of the School's collecting work,
and for a considerable length of time before that, the best
known of all lays. This is largely due to the fact that it was
put to use as one of the *Duain Challainn*,[10] the Hogmanay
Rhymes recited by bands of guisers during their circuit of
the township. So far as I know, it is the only example of a
heroic lay in that repertoire. It was sometimes sung by the
guisers; this, too, is unusual, if not unique: *Duain Challainn*
were normally recited or declaimed.

The oldest literary version is in the seventeenth century
Irish anthology *Duanaire Finn*,[11] the editor dates it to about
1400. The ballad recounts how Fionn and some of his warriors
had weapons forged for them by Lon mac Líomhtha, the
supernatural smith, and how Caoilte got his name.

The argument of the ballad, as set out by the editor of
Duanaire Finn, runs thus:

---

9   Pope, *loc. cit.* Pope was writing in an area — the Whig 'Mackay's
    Country' (*Dùthaich Mhic Aoidh*) — where Evangelicalism was
    already an established tradition. Even there, however, Evangelical
    ministers such as the Rev. Murdoch MacDonald of Durness were
    patrons of the Gaelic arts.

10 See A. Carmichael, *Carmina Gadelica*, Vol. 1, Edinburgh 1928,
    126 ff.

11 G. Murphy, ed., *Duanaire Finn*, Part II, Irish Texts Society Vol. 28,
    London 1933. 'Argument of the Poem': p. vii; text and translation:
    p. 2 ff.

Eight of the Fiana, including Fionn and Daolghus, find themselves on Sliabh Luachra [in Kerry]. A monstrous warrior approaches them. He says that he is Lon, chief smith of Norway, and that he has come to race the Fiana. Thereupon he leaps from them. The eight Fian warriors follow him. Lon takes them from Kerry by Limerick through Clare, Galway and Roscommon to the hill of Keshcorran [in South East Sligo]. Lon enters the cave of Keshcoran. In the cave is a smithy with smiths at work. Lon sets about making a sword. Daolghus assists him. Daolghus grows warm till his face glows like a lighted coal. The smiths present ask who this man can be, using the compound adjective *Caoilte* 'slender and hot' to describe him. Fionn fixing on the adjective decides that Daolghus shall be for ever known as Caoilte. Lon offers the Fian hospitality and presents them with spears and swords, the names of which are given. At sun-rise next morning the Fian, having slept soundly, find themselves once more on Sliabh Luachra,

The phrase 'chief smith of Norway' requires elucidation. *Lochlann*, translated 'Norway' above, and in many contexts in modern Gaelic meaning just that, is in earlier, medieval Gaelic a fabulous land which later came to be associated with the Vikings and their homeland. But in other contexts, as here, it remains 'the wonderland of Norway, hovering between geography and romance', as one scholar neatly puts it. In Lochlann there is 'one fixed point', *Beirbhe*, translated Bergen.[12]

In order to show something of the relationship between the literary ballad of c.1400 and the oral versions still current in Scotland, I shall quote the English translation given in *Duanaire Finn* and then translate the oral version,[13] paraphrasing where a detailed commentary would otherwise be

12 R. Th. Christiansen, *The Vikings and the Viking Wars in Irish and Gaelic Tradition*, Oslo 1931, 416 and 421.
13 For other translations from current or recent oral tradition, see Margaret Fay Shaw (Mrs J.L. Campbell), *Folksong and Folklore of South Uist*, Oxford 1977, 31; J.L. Campbell, *Stories from South Uist* (told by Angus Maclellan), London 1961, 17-9.

required. I take the *Duanaire Finn* text to be the original of the oral versions: comparison of the Gaelic texts leave little doubt that they are ultimately derived from it.

1 Write it, Brogán, a writing, in truly pleasant wise speech, something of the adventures of the son of Cumhall who endured many hard trials.

2 Let us listen to what Oisín says in very mild most pure speech; I have not heard from the valiant troop a tale it were more fitting to write.

3 Tell, son of the prince, in clear voice of little falsehood: recount for us sweetly and gently the true tales of the Fian.

4 Tell us, without omitting it (let it be no heedless answer), why the breaker up of combats was called Caoilte.

5 We arrive one day on Luachair Deadhadh; our company was eight brave men, seven of us about the high king: dear was that noble and gentle warlike band.

6 I and Daolghus and Diarmaid, three who obtained roasting in hunting booth, the three sons of the One Craftsman of Beare, Fionn himself and Mac Lughach.

7 We were but a short while on the hill (long will that tale be remembered) till there came to us on the fair-sodden plain a hugely tall warrior with a single foot.

8 Wonderful was the appearance of the warrior: we take up arms on seeing him: he had three arms swinging: his face was the colour of coal.

9 One foot supported him on the mountain as he approached us from peak to peak: he had one eye in his forehead, and his gaze was on the son of Cumhall.

10 One leap sufficed to carry him over each fair-sodden wild glen. Hardly did the edge of his garment reach over his buttocks.

11 He wore a shirt of twisted waxed thread, a gray tunic and a red mantle and a great jet-black waxed hooded

cloak of deerskin on the upper portion of his body.

12 His big straight dark-blue foot was more than each warrior's hand could hold: longer than the shaft of each spear was the distance from his knee to his ankle.

13 A headgear for the same cloak was about his head, which had the appearance of (?) coal. The shadow of his hand and his gloom were sufficient danger for us.

14 When he had come upon the hill, having approached us, he said, 'May the gods bless thee, son of Cumhall.'

15 'May they bless thee too (?)', said Fionn the warrior; 'Who art thou, single man whom I know not? Tell us thy true name, O man with the skin garment.'

16 'Lon son of Líomhtha is the name I have been given; I have mastered the nature of every craft; it is I who am teacher of smiths to the king of Lochlann in Bergen.

17 'Líomhthach the young, daughter of Bolcán, she had no ill fortune in her children: no object of pity is the man who won my mother, who bore me and my other brother.

18 'To seek an even race I have come to you from Bergen: they say that you are swift, O people skilled in craft:

19 'A *geas* and the pangs of a woman in travail (?) be upon you, ye leaders in every strait, if the eight of you do not follow me to the door of my smithy.'

20 He leaps from us like a spring wind going over mountain tops. We followed him forthwith, a few of the nobles of the Fian.

21 By the side of Luachair Deadhaidh, past the gate of Bealach Luimnigh, over Sliabh Oidhidh, over Eachtghe, we go in four bands.

22 The smith formed one of those bands: everyone was far behind him; he had a big advantage over Daolghus: Fionn came after them unaccompanied.

23 Diarmaid and Mac Lughach were three hills' length behind them: I and the three sons of the Craftsman formed a brave band of four.

24 Through Magh Maoin, through Magh Maine did we go (they were far from us after our journey), into great Magh Meadhbha across Áth Bearbha, over Mucais:

25 Close by the grave of Fraoch son of Fiodhach (it was no easy going), over Gleann Cuilt and over Cruachain: there Daolghus quickened his pace.

26 From Magh Luirg down to Seaghais, indeed, we catch up on one another: the smith and Daolghus went from us into the bare hill of Ceann Sléibhe.

27 We come right up to the Cave of Corann: 'He has gone before us,' said Daolghus: 'Wait awhile, smith: thou shalt not go in alone.'

28 They go together into the cavern, Fionn pressing upon them manfully: they found bellows a-blowing: they found earth and a forge,

29 Anvils and sledgehammers being smitten and a swift strong blast of flame, seven swords too stretched out in straight and lovely masses (?).

30 Lon himself said, beseeching them (?), to the grim and mighty gathering, 'This alone is my portion of the weapons yet unmade.'

31 He put a tongs into the hearth and lifted a stone with four ridges: the smith and Daolghus carried out some keen and nimble hammering.

32 The smith had two great sledgehammers and a strong graysided tongs: he had three hands attending to his tools: Daolghus responded well.

33 They make a hard sharp sparkling blade of good success (?) in striking: for a hilt's length it lacked two edges, a fair gray shoot of steel.

34 Daolghus grew warm beside the forge (stout were his combats): redder than glowing coal was his complexion after the work.

35 The smiths, who were full rough and surly, said, 'Who is the slender warm man without weakness who is stretching the bar of steel?'

36 Fionn, who made every problem easy, said answering them, 'That shall be his name always: Daolghus shall be called Caoilte.'

37 There you have the manner of his naming (Good were his valour and his deeds). Caoilte who was not wont to refuse, it is fitting to write his tidings.

38 'Let the soldiery who have come to us be attended to', said Lon the strong: 'Let a rich bed-chamber be made ready which will befit the son of Cumhall.

39 'Give them to keep, to each man the price of his journey, to do battle and combat, a spear and a blue blade of true fierceness.

40 'Leave stedfast Fionn to me: I shall give him a pair for battle, a straight spear, a very straight spear, and a truly lovely long sword.'

41 They give us the charmed weapons thereupon when they had been made, seven swords and nine spears from which came many wounds out of harsh fierceness.

42 Mac an Luin was the name of Cumhall's sword which caused the flesh of men to suffer: Diarmaid of the poems had the Drithlinn: the Créchtach was Caoilte's hard blade.

43 Fead and Fí and Fosgadh (many victories have they won me), these were the swords of the Craftsman's three sons (they broke up many hard situations).

44 Here in my hand is Gearr na gColann which used to be girt on me in fights: Mac Lughach had the Échtach: he was happy as he went to victory.

45 Good was our dark-brown clothing and our music of brown-plumaged hooded birds: at rising time next day we had had sufficient sleep.

46 When the sun rose next day on pure Sliabh Luachra our long swords were good and our thick strong spears.

47 It is hard that there should be a complete end to the fairhaired truly pure host: O white-penned writer of Patrick, woe for him who has attained the days when men write about them.

And now the translation of the oral version:

On a day when the Féinn were on Luachair Leodhair, four young men (warriors) in the company: myself and Osgar and Daorghlas, and Fionn himself, the son of Cumhall.

We saw coming from the mountains a tall dark, one-legged man with a cloak of dark-grey skin and an apron of the same dress.

Fionn spoke there on the mountainside to him as he was passing them, 'To what land is your journey, man with the skin cloak?'

'Lon son of Lìobhann is my name — if you are bent on hearing my story — I was for a time tending goats for the King of Lochlann in Gailbhinn.

I am of the line of MacAsgaill's daughter who was good in charge of children: happy the woman who was mother to me and my other brother.

If you mean to attend at the smithy, then I bind you to go to a dark glen at the west of the world far from its door.'

'Smith, where is your smithy: would we be the better for seeing it?

'If I could help it, you would not be the better for seeing it — why should you be?'

Then they set off on their journey, [through] the Province of Luimneach; they reached the green Knoll of Dreathaibh and there divided into four companies.

One band was the Smith's, another was the band of Daorghlas, another was the band of Dearg mac Dreathaibh; Fionn was the last, he was by himself.

The Smith took but one stride to cross each wild glen: we

could scarcely see a corner of his cloak on his buttocks.

'Open, open!' said the Smith, 'Don't shut the door before me,' said Daorghlas. 'I would not leave you in the doorway of my smithy, all alone in a perilous place!'

There they got bellows for blowing, there they got gear for the smithy; then there came four smiths: repulsive, misshapen men.

Four arms on each smith; tools for gripping, tongs of iron; the smith who attended them spoke: no less well did Daorghlas answer.

It was Daorghlas who was heating the forge (the man who stays standing): redder than oak charcoal was his face from the fruit of his labour.

Then one of the smiths spoke, fearfully and angrily: 'The right hand of that thin one who has no fear in him has ruined my steel anvil.'

Fionn spoke, he was there beside them, for it was he who was holding the tongs: 'Daorghlas being called "Caoilte" — that will make it a widespread name!'

They got there beaten out the straight, bright swords — a band fully armed with the magic swords of the green.

'Fead' and 'Faoidh' and 'Eigheach' and 'Conalach son of the Smithy'; the twelve swords of Diarmaid — many a man they killed.

I had 'Geard na Colann', useful in time of battle; 'Mac a' Luin' in the hand of the son of Cumhall, it never left unsevered a shred of mortal flesh.

Do you remember the day of the tongue in the smithy of the Clan of MacLiobhann? Tonight I lament my condition after counting the company.

It is interesting to note what changes have occurred in the course of transmission. First, the oral version omits the preamble (four quatrains), the coda (one quatrain), and any reference not only to St Patrick's scribe Brogán but also to Oisín, though the latter is of course known as the poet of the

Féinn in Gaelic Scotland. Second, practically the entire litany of Irish placenames is dropped: this is natural enough. Of those that remain *Luachair Deadhadh* becomes *Luachair Leodhain, Leothaid* (gen. of *leathad* 'slope') and *Leothair*. For *Eachtghe* the oral lay substitutes either *Breitheamh* or *Dreathaibh. Bealach Luimnigh*, the 'Pass of Luimneach' (Limerick), however, is discernible in the phrase which has been transcribed hitherto as *buidheann choige(amh) luimneach* and translated as 'five bands'. The word for a 'fifth' (i.e. a province) of Ireland appears elsewhere in Scots Gaelic e.g. *Coigeamh Mhumha na h-Eireann*, the Province of Munster; earlier versions of our lay have *Air Choige Mhumha* and *Mar chuige mugha na luimedheirg* in the corresponding quatrain. *Lochlann* remains but *Beirbhe*, Bergen, becomes *Gailbhinn* (Galway) here; although *Beirbhe* remains in earlier variants. It is found also in the poetry of Mairi Nighean Alasdair Ruaidh.[14] Third, the names of the swords are little changed: even within the group of very close variants on which the translation is based, we get *Geur nan Calg* as an alternative to *Geard na Colann*: 'Sharp of Swords' and 'Guard of Body' respectively. *Fasgadh* appears in an earlier printed version.

Finally, two diverting corruptions. *Ollamh gabhonn*, 'teacher of smiths' becomes *uallach ghabhar*, 'tending goats': the correspondence is clear, visually and aurally, even if the option taken is not. It is, presumably, a recent change: earlier variants from oral tradition keep the original sense. Similarly, *na teangann*, 'of the tongue' is *na teannruith*, 'of the hard running', in earlier variants.

The ballad in oral tradition has been stripped down to the essential narrative. Just enough is kept to preserve the weird, surrealistic atmosphere: the vivid description of the Supernatural Smith and his helpers is unimpaired; at the same time, the scene in the smithy is naturalistic in its detail: Caoilte red in the face from blowing the bellows; Fionn standing up because he has to hold the red-hot iron on the anvil with the great pincers. The warriors of the *Féinn* are brought into a familiar, everyday setting.

14　See J. Carmichael Watson, *Gaelic Songs of Mary MacLeod*, London 1934, 125: 'This is perhaps the only name of a place in Scandinavia which survives in modern Scottish Gaelic . . .'

The next ballad is 'Duan na Muilgheartaich/Muirgheartaich' (the name exists in a number of variants), the lay that tells of the monstrous, one-eyed hag (a small minority of earlier versions make her a male) who comes across the sea to fight the *Féinn*. It is now known only in South Uist and Barra though it once had a wide distribution. The name is still remembered in Tiree and no doubt elsewhere.

The Muilgheartach, to construct a composite picture, is a horrible apparition: bald, red, thick-maned; her forehead is dark-grey, charcoal coloured, her teeth red and slanting; she is one-eyed and the darting glance of her eye is keener than a winter star. The great bristles of her head are like withered brushwood covered with hoarfrost. She carries a rusty sword, etc. etc.

She is associated with the Ocean Smith; when she is killed by the *Féinn*, the Smith informs the High King, his father; this king in some variants is the King of Lochlann and, in related stories, the Muilgheartach his (foster-)mother.

She herself is first seen 'coming on the tops of the waves'; she attacks the *Féinn* 'like the sea against the stones of a shingle beach'; after her death, the king swears that he will kick the sea into storm, lift it from its walls of waves and drag the land with curved crooks out of the ocean.

Nineteenth-century collectors and scholars, apparently in line with theories then current concerning Nature gods and Nature myths, explained the Muilgheartach as a personification of the sea.

The Rev. J.G. Campbell of Tiree, a noted collector and interpreter of Gaelic oral tradition, calls her 'the ocean itself in the flesh.'[15] Donald Sinclair, son of one of Campbell's informants, told me that his father, Calum Bàn, a fisherman, would glance out when the sea looked threatening and remark, *Tha droch coltas air a' Mhuilgheartaich an diugh*, 'The Muilgheartach has a bad appearance today.'

This raises the interesting question: is the idea of 'the ocean itself in the flesh' a concept of native Gaelic tradition? Or did the learned minister of Tiree impart the notion to Calum Bàn?

15 J.G. Campbell, *The Fians*, London 1891, 131.

At all events, the Muilgheartach is always closely connected with the sea. The same scholars and collectors interpreted her name as a compound of *muir*, 'sea' and *iar*, 'west' or *ear*, 'east', with an adjectival suffix. The name may contain *muir* (with the not uncommon l/r interchange); the rest of the proposed etymology is not possible.

R. Th. Christiansen is inclined to think that, while

> . . . as she appears in the ballads she seems to belong to Gaelic tradition . . . [she has a] parallel in certain old stories of gigantic females living in the Northern seas . . . there are accounts in old Norse sources, as in more recent tradition, of beings that seem to bear a resemblance to the Muireartach. The márgygr of the Speculum regale belongs to this class, she was seen on the Greenland coast, was of tremendous size, and had thick heavy hair which fell all around her head and neck. She was web-footed and used to appear before great storms. [16]

Christiansen's suggestion of a Norse origin makes good sense and better sense if we regard *márgygr* as a slip for *margýgr*, 'sea-ogress'. Neither *Muirgheartach* nor any of its variant forms, however, can be derived directly from *margýgr*. It may be instructive to consider the Lowlands Scots *Gyrecarlin(g)*, 'an ogress', etc., whose name is Norse (*gýgr* and *kerling* woman) but many of those attributes are those of the *Cailleach*, the great Hag of Gaelic tradition, associated with wild weather, the wilderness, the deer, etc. The *Gyrecarlin* appears to be a composite figure; the *Muilgheartach* may be likewise. Her name, also, to extend these speculations, may be a contamination product of Norse and Gaelic elements. In this connection, the personal name Muircheartach can hardly be irrelevant. [17]

16 Christiansen, *op. cit.*, 412.
17 The Irish Muircheartach who was killed in 943, fighting against the Norsemen, had the nickname *na gcochull gcraiceann*, 'of the skin coverings'; an appellation also given to characters of romance and folklore, among them the Supernatural Smith. In a waulking-song the phrase *A Mhuilgheartach nan cochull craicinn* is used abusively and taken by singers to refer to the *Muilgheartach* of the ballad. Cf. J.L. Campbell and F. Collinson, *Hebridean Folk-*

The next ballad is 'Laoidh Dhiarmaid', 'The Lay of Diarmad' (the name is usually inflected *Diarmad*, gen. *Diarmaid* in Scots Gaelic). Once widely distributed, it has been recorded as a sung ballad only in South Uist and Barra, and in Kintail. I myself heard a part of it recited in Skye in my boyhood; Domhnall Chaluim Bàin in Tiree knew of it; and snatches of it are still quoted here and there throughout the Highlands and Islands.

The oldest literary version is in the *Book of the Dean of Lismore*. The following details are taken from Neill Ross, *Heroic Poetry from the Book of the Dean of Lismore*:

> Fionn has never forgiven his sister's son Diarmaid (the classical Gaelic and Irish form)... for eloping with Fionn's unloving wife, Gráinne... A formal reconciliation has been made, but Fionn is bent on revenge... Fionn prevailed on Diarmaid to go to hunt the venomous magic boar and is himself unscathed. Disappointed at this, Fionn asks Diarmaid to measure and remeasure the boar. The venomous bristles pierce Diarmaid's sole and he dies...
>
> In Scotland, the scene of the boar-hunt and Diarmaid's death is located in Sutherland, in Kintail, in Brae Lochaber, in Knapdale, in Skye, in Tiree, and most firmly in Perthshire... This poem, which is not found in Ireland, we are probably safe in regarding as not only purely Scottish, but of Perthshire origin.[18]

Nowadays the lay is invariably known as 'Laoidh Dhiarmaid': the first line of verse 3 in the Dean's book is *Eisdidh beag madh ail Libh Laoidh*, 'Listen a little, if you would have a lay'; our sung versions begin at that line. In earlier collections, *Dàn, Duan, Cumha*, 'Elegy, Lament', and *Bàs*, 'Death', all appear in the title. The Rev. Alexander Pope has a celebrated account of the singing of this lay:

songs, Vol. 2, Oxford 1977, 128 and 237. The Irish 'Laoidh na Mná Móire thar lear', 'The Lay of the Giantess who comes from across the sea', is relevant also.

18 N. Ross, *Heroic Poetry from the Book of the Dean of Lismore*, Scottish Gaelic Texts Society Vol. 3, Edinburgh 1939, 221-2.

There is an excellent poem, called Duan Dearmot, it
is an elegy on the death of that warrior, and breathes the
sublime very much. This poem is in esteem among a tribe
of Campbells that live in this country [the parish of Reay
in Caithness], and would derive their pedigree from that
hero . . . There is an old fellow in this parish that very
gravely takes off his bonnet as often as he sings Duan
Dearmot: I was extremely fond to try if the case was so,
and getting him to my house I gave him a bottle of ale,
and begged the favour of him to sing Duan Dearmot; after
some nicety, he told me that to oblige his parish minister
he would do so, but to my surprise he took off his bonnet.
I caused him stop, and would put on his bonnet; he made
some excuses; however as soon as he began, he took off his
bonnet, I rose and put it on; he took it off, I put it on. At
last he was like to swear most horribly he would sing none,
unless I allowed him to be uncovered; I gave him his freedom, and so he sung with great spirit. I asked him the
reason; he told me it was out of regard to the memory of
that hero. I asked him if he thought that the spirit of that
hero was present; he said not; but he thought it well
became them who descended from him to honour his
memory . . . [19]

Of the ballads in general Pope observes:

The greatest number are called Duans . . . others have
different names, but the Duans are generally set to some
tunes d i f f e r e n t   f r o m   t h e   r e s t . (My emphasis.)

In view of the use of *Laoidh* in this ballad, does Pope's
comment have any connection with Hector MacLean's remark,
quoted above, that *laoidh* is 'more melodious' than *dàn*?
Since Pope says that the 'greatest number are called Duans',
it seems unlikely; but there may be something here to be
investigated.

'Laoidh a' Choin Duibh', 'The Lay of the Black Hound', is
my next example. It is known in Benbecula, South Uist, and
Lochalsh — the last, however, a mere fragment recorded from

19 Pope, *loc. cit.*

the late Mary Stewart, a member of a family of 'travelling-folk'.

The ballad tells of the fight between Bran, Fionn's famous hound, and the Black Hound, belonging to a stranger. The Black Hound kills a hundred and fifty (the numbers vary) of the hounds of the *Féinn* before Fionn looses Bran, who kills the Black Hound. 'Laoidh a' Choin Duibh' is one of a group of ballads that exists in another verse form. I shall comment on these later, taking them together.

The next ballad, 'Laoidh Chaoilte', 'The Lay of Caoilte', appears on the School of Scottish Studies disc *Music from the Western Isles* under the title 'Latha dh'an Fhinn am Beinn Iongnaidh'. This is actually the first line of the lay, which is also known as 'Caoilte and the Giant', etc. Here is the English translation which is given in the booklet that accompanies the disc:

A day when the Fenians were in the Mountain of Marvels / All of the Fenians, the fierce men / They sent Caoilte, because of his swiftness / Ahead of them to act as guide. / They saw a house far off / With its two doors open / A lovely maid stood on its floor / And a big fire burning steadily / She gave me, as it seemed to me, / Two-thirds of her food and two-thirds of her attire. / Who loomed over me obscuring the light / In the rough doorway but a great giant. / 'Keep well clear of me / It wasn't you I came for / But for a sweetheart I had long ago / A honey-sweet girl with beguiling eyes / Seven years have I waited for her / And today I have met you to your misfortune.' / He cast with all his venom / The great spear that was in his hand. / I made a sudden, stabbing cast / And struck his five heads off his neck. / I rested my elbow on the ground / And my wounds bled heavily.

We now come to two non-Fenian heroic ballads, the first of which is 'Laoidh Fhraoich', 'The Lay of Fraoch'. It has been recorded in Skye, South Uist, Tiree, and Mull. To this may be added a version made up of a text (without melody) from Skye and a tune from South Uist.

This distribution suggests a popularity which tradition

corroborates. The scene of the ballad's events is localised in three places: Rannoch, in Perthshire; Loch Awe-side in Argyll; the island of Mull. The oldest literary version, ascribed to an author whose name has been variously interpreted, is in the *Book of the Dean of Lismore*. Ross dates it to the fourteenth century, summarises the story, and gives a brief account of its relationship with the early Irish tale *Táin Bó Fraích*:

> Fraoch son of Fiodhach and of the fairy Be Fhionn, a prince of Connacht and the fairest of the men of Ireland and Scotland, comes to the house of Ailill and Meadhbh, king and queen of Connacht, to woo their daughter Fionnabhair. He refuses, however, to pay such a bride-price as they ask. To prevent his carrying off Fionnabhair, Ailill plans his death. He gets him to swim in a pool in which is a deadly monster. By asking him to fetch a rowan branch from the far side of the pool, Ailill keeps Fraoch in the water until the monster seizes him. With a knife thrown to him by Fionnabhair, Fraoch, though wounded, slays the monster ... [Fraoch] is removed by fairies and shortly healed ... in the end Fionnabhair is betrothed to him ...
>
> In the poem it is Meadhbh, who in anger at Fraoch's refusal to be her lover, compasses Fraoch's death. She sends him to fetch magic rowans guarded by a monster in the loch at the root of the tree. With the knife thrown by Fionnabhair he fights the beast, but as he kills it he dies himself ...[20]

I do not intend to comment on this further as the whole question of the relationship of ballad to tale, etc. has been meticulously examined by Dr Meek.[21]

'Laoidh Fhraoich', as all the singers call it, appears also, in earlier collections, as 'Duan' or 'Bàs Fhraoich'. This last is the title in the collection made by Jerome Stone (1727-56). In 1756, the year of his death, Stone contributed an English poem of 20 ten-line stanzas, entitled 'Albin and the Daughter

20 Ross, *op. cit.*, 250-1.
21 D. Meek, 'Táin Bó Fráich and other "Fráech" Texts', *Cambridge Medieval Celtic Studies* 7 (1984), 1-37; 8 (1984), 65-85.

of Mey', to the *Scots Magazine*. It purports to be a translation of 'The Death of Fraoch'; in reality it is no more than loosely based on the original Gaelic ballad. A stanza from the middle of the poem gives an impression of the style:

> Amidst Lochney, at distance from the shore,
> On a green island, grew a stately tree,
> With precious fruit each season cover'd o'er,
> Delightful to the taste and fair to see:
> This fruit, more sweet than virgin honey found,
> Serv'd both alike for physic and for food:
> It cur'd diseases, heal'd the bleeding wound,
> And hunger's rage for three long days withstood,
> But precious things are purchas'd still with pain
> And thousands try'd to pluck it, but in vain.

The importance of this 'translation' is two-fold: first, it brought to the attention of a non-Gaelic public the existence of heroic ballads in the Gaelic language; and, secondly, it was known to James Macpherson and almost certainly encouraged him in his career as an author.[22] 'Laoidh Fhraoich', therefore, in addition to its interest within Gaelic tradition, has a significant place in Scottish literature generally — indeed, in the development of European Romanticism.

The second non-Fenian ballad is 'Am Bròn Binn', 'The Melodious Sorrow' or, as it is commonly translated, 'The Sweet Sorrow'. Our recordings come from the islands of Benbecula and South Uist, and from Lairg in Sutherland on the mainland. It has no literary origin and appears to be a purely Scots Gaelic composition.

The fullest versions (in earlier collections from oral tradition) tell how the King of Britain has Sir Balbha (variants Sior Falaich, Fios Falaich, etc.) sail across the ocean to seek a beautiful maiden he has seen in a dream. He finds her seated on a throne in a castle; the hostile 'Great Man' of the castle is lulled to sleep by the maiden's harp-music and song; Sir

22 See D.S. Thomson, 'Bogus Gaelic Literature c. 1750 c. 1820', *Trans. of the Gaelic Society of Glasgow* 5 (1958), 172-88; esp. 174-6.

Balbha beheads him with his own (the Great Man's) sword and sails off with the maiden.

In our sung versions this Great Man does not appear: it is Fios Fallach who is lulled to sleep and treacherously put to death by the maiden.

Instead of 'King of Britain' we may have (though not in our contemporary versions) *Rìgh Artair*, 'King Arthur'. The name Fios Falach, too, is Arthurian: it has been shown ultimately to derive from 'Sir Gawain' or variant forms of his name.

The most recent study of the Arthurian affinities of 'Am Bròn Binn' is to be found in a wide-ranging investigation of Arthurian material in Gaelic by Prof. Gillies.[23] This makes it unnecessary for me to comment further on this aspect, except to say it is the only ballad in current Gaelic tradition that may be called 'Arthurian'. The name, however, requires a word or two. 'The Melodious Sorrow', with its apparently romantic over-tones is, I think, unique in Gaelic oral tradition. While it is not inconceivable, given the background, that it is modelled on a title or phrase from the Romances, I believe we should consider an alternative possibility. The Arthurian Round Table — *Am Bord Cruinn* — appears in two earlier versions of our ballad. (It is known in other contexts also, oral and literary). *Bord Cruinn* and *Bròn Binn* stand in the same place — the end phrase — in the text. I suggest *Bròn Binn* is a garbling of *Bord Cruinn*.

Finally, I shall comment briefly on a number of fragments I recorded in the island of Tiree from the late Donald Sinclair — Domhnall Chaluim Bàin. In the course of my fieldwork with him, extending over ten years and more, I was able to elicit from him that he had heard heroic ballads in his boyhood. It is important to emphasise that he was not an active ballad singer and that by the time he consented to record these fragments, old age and infirmity had greatly affected his remarkable powers of intellect and memory. His best remem-

23 W. Gillies, 'Arthur in Gaelic Tradition Part I: Folktales and Ballads; Part II: Romances and Learned Lore', *Cambridge Medieval Celtic Studies* 2 (1981), 47-72; 3 (1982), 41-75.

bered ballad was 'Laoidh Fhraoich', of which he knew several
more verses than those recorded. He had heard and could recall
a verse or two of the ballad of Mànus (Magnus) King of Lochlann, the Death of Osgar, both Fenian ballads, and the non-
Fenian Death of Conlaoch the son of Cù Chulainn. He himself
did not know the name Conlaoch and, as he reconstructed
the story, it was Cù Chulainn who was slain by his own father.
By the time he made the recordings he had begun to jumble
these fragments in his memory.

A quite different problem arises with regard to the recordings from Kintail. The singer, the late James C.M. Campbell
was a noted concert artist who also knew a number of
traditional Gaelic songs. He probably heard Fenian lays in
Kintail in his boyhood but it is not clear to what extent both
words and melodies were affected by written sources. His
style of singing also is non-traditional.

The two ballads recorded from Mary Stewart in Lochalsh
and from Alasdair (Aili) Stewart in Sutherland might well
have come from Island tradition; both Stewarts belonged to
the travelling tinsmith class whose circuit included the Islands.

The majority of ballad singers in our archives are women.
One sometimes gets the impression even from genuine tradition
bearers that the preservation and transmission of heroic ballads
was something of a male preserve. But obviously this was not
the case. Both men and women were singers and reciters of
lays. James Cumming tells of Christina Sutherland and
Isabella MacKay (Iseabail Bhàn) in the parish of Reay in
Caithness sitting up a whole winter night reciting poems of
every description, each in turn and sometimes together repeating them. When under twelve years she [Christina] would
sooner commit to memory a long Duan than most if not any
of her acquaintances who were come to maturity. She would
go three miles and more to hear a poem not previously recited
in her hearing. Christina Sutherland's two brothers also
'excelled as reciters'.[24]

Christina was born in 1775. Twelve years earlier, Rev.
Alexander Pope discusses a ballad which 'some old women

24   Cited by J.F. Campbell, *op. cit.* (1872), xxxii.

repeat with great spirit'. This testimony takes us back into
the seventeenth century. Pope also has this to say about the
singers (though not specifically women) and ballad melodies:

> The music is soft and simple; but when these airs are
> sung by two or three or more good voices, they are far
> from disagreeable.[25]

I have no evidence from the Gaelic communities of the
present that ballads in their 'normal' verse form (but see
below) were sung by several singers together. Perhaps something of this kind, however, is implied in the Rev. Donald
Macleod of Glenelg's letter of 1764 where he states that the
'Highlanders, at their festivals and other public meeting,
acted the poems of Ossian'.[26] When Donald Robertson in
Skye recited his version of 'Dàn na h-Inghinne' he inserted
Esan, 'he' and *Ise*, 'she' before each verse of the dialogue
between Fionn and the Maiden in that lay. Debate poems,
such as 'Caraid is Namhaid an Uisge-bheatha', 'Friend and
Enemy of Whisky', were 'acted' as a dialogue in North Uist
until about the end of the last century: something of the
same kind, then, might have been done with ballads.

At any rate, singing by several voices could have an important implication. A number of lays are constructed with
repeated couplets: the second couplet of the quatrain being
repeated to form the first couplet of the next quatrain. This
is characteristic of one category of songs that are said to have
been choral;[27] moreover, this is a category that is very strongly
associated with women and the compositions of women
poets. There are indeed compositions of male authorship
within it but so close is the connection of the form with
women's poetry that one song, obviously of male authorship,
has been fitted out with a circumstantially detailed account
of how it was really composed by a woman.

25 Pope, *loc. cit.*
26 *Report on Ossian*, p. 29. Cf. J. Logan, *The Scottish Gael*, Edinburgh
    1976 (Reprint; first published 1831), 247.
27 See J. MacInnes, 'The Choral Tradition in Scottish Gaelic Songs',
    Trans. of the Gaelic Society of Inverness 46 (1969-70), 44-65.

Occasionally such choral songs, sung in quatrains with repeated couplets, may be found in close variants in the waulking-song tradition.[28] The latter has preserved songs once used for other communal tasks and furthermore has attracted to it a number of songs, usually lyrical songs that belong, loosely speaking, to the choral tradition of which waulking-songs are now the central strand. A few ballads have also been drawn into the corpus of waulking-songs. One of these, 'Latha bha an Ridire ag òl', 'One day when the knight was drinking' appears only in the form of a waulking-song, complete with a normal chorus of vocables such as we get with these work-songs. The versions we have recorded introduce the 'Black Hound', and Bran, no doubt from 'Laoidh a' Choin Duibh' ('The Lay of the Black Hound', mentioned above). One fragmentary printed version of 'Latha bha an Ridire ag òl' prefixes a couplet from 'Laoidh Fhraoich'.[29] Frances Tolmie remarks:

> Several narrative songs, such as 'The Melodious Sorrow', or 'Dream of the King of Britain' and 'The Lay of the Black Dog' ... were sung to the same air with similar refrain.[30]

In Frances Tolmie's collection there are two songs on the death of Diarmad. The first, without a vocable refrain, is recognisably a variant of 'Laoidh Dhiarmaid', 'The Lay of Diarmad', and is so titled. The other, in waulking-song form, with vocables, is given the title of 'Cumha Dhiarmaid', and is really another song rather than a variant of the *Laoidh*. Finally, in a number of collections, Oisein's song to his mother appears with vocable refrains: it seems to have been sung only in that form, not in quatrains. It does not follow,

---

28 See *Scottish Tradition 3. Waulking songs from Barra* (Disc TNGM III and accompanying booklet); Cf. J.L. Campbell and F. Collinson, *Hebridean Folksongs* Vol. 3, Oxford 1981, 40-5; p. 235 ff.

29 K.C. Craig, *Orain Luaidh Mairi nighean Alasdair*, Glasgow 1949, 46.

30 *Journal of the Folk-song Society* No. 16 (part 3 of Vol. 4: 1911), 254. (Usually referred to as The Tolmie Collection). For 'Group III — Ancient Heroic Lays', see pp. 245-54.

however, that ballads which were sung with vocable refrains
were necessarily or exclusively used as waulking-songs or
work-songs of any kind. There were other choral refrain songs
that were preserved and transmitted outside the work-song
culture.

How are we to interpret all this? The evidence is exiguous
and perhaps insufficient to lead to any certain conclusion;
all the possible interpretations will contain an element of
speculation. I would suggest, somewhat tentatively, that
first the distinctive roles of men and women in preserving
and transmitting Fenian and other heroic lays is an old and
well-established tradition and that, secondly, this has left a
structural impress on the corpus of surviving ballads.

There are also differences, though not readily assignable
to male and female roles, in the traditional manner of singing
the ballads. The 'prosody' of traditional Gaelic singing, except
in the domain of work-song, clearly aims at maintaining a
conversational rhythm: as older singers used to insist, a song
should be 'told'. As a general observation, this applies not only
to the so-called 'syllabic' metres[31] but to other metrical forms

31 Demotic Gaelic versions of heroic lays do not observe, except
    accidentally, the strict syllabic count of literary originals. The
    same qualification applies, of course, to lays for which no literary
    originals exist; and the same is true of other forms of 'syllabic'
    versification in vernacular Scots Gaelic.
        Murphy argues that the syllabic verse of the literary ballads
    should be read 'in accordance with natural Irish word-stress'. Irish
    and Scots Gaelic are both 'stress-timed' languages (to use Pike's
    terminology) in which, by definition, stress pulses and hence
    the stressed syllables are isochronous. It therefore follows, if the
    'syllabic' verse is performed (spoken or sung) with a pattern of
    stressing identical with that of speech, that there are no syllabic
    metres in Gaelic. There is no *differentia*.
        MacNeill took the view that 'all syllables, in whatsoever position,
    and however lightly accented in modern pronunciation, must be
    regarded as equally accented'.
        The evidence from Scots Gaelic, on the whole, bears out Murphy's
    theory: the opposition of stressed versus unstressed syllables, as
    perceived by the native speaker, is maintained. This is not to say,
    however, that singing 'with speech-rhythm', or *quasi parlando*
    singing, always exhibits a stress-pattern i d e n t i c a l with that of
    speech.

as well. The technique, however, is not crudely mechanical for it allows subtle modifications of quantity (invariably preserving phonemic distinctions) while syllables that are unstressed in ordinary speech may be given a certain amount of stress.

In contrast to this, a few singers, all from South Uist, employ a different prosody in singing ballads. Certain unstressed syllables are here given a prominent stress, and in highly unusual, probably even unique, positions; as, for instance, when the second syllable of a dissyllabic word is stressed at the end of a line.[32] Such stressing does not occur even in waulking-songs. An example of this type of singing can be heard on the disc *Music from the Western Isles*, where Mrs Archie MacDonald sings 'Latha dh'an Fhinn am Beinn Iongnaidh'. In the notes to the ballad, I have drawn attention to this 'tendency to regularise the tempo, which may point to a break with tradition in the twentieth century'. This is a problem which demands rigorous examination by a Gaelic-speaking musicologist who has also an adequate training in linguistics. It is worth noting that although other Uist singers, older than Mrs Archie MacDonald, have a similar style, the singing of her aunt, Mrs Peggy MacDonald, shows a much closer observance of ordinary speech stress, while that of her mother, Mrs Marion Campbell, exhibits even more conspicuously the same characteristics as the daughter's. Yet mother and aunt were near each other in age – and both were born in the 1860s. A recent, important article by Mr Terence P. McCaughey[33] goes over this ground, examines the salient problems, and emphasises their implications for our claim that the survival of ballads in Scots Gaelic preserves a medieval style of performance.

Although most of the singers who contributed to the

For a summary of Murphy's and MacNeill's views, see Murphy, *op. cit.* (1953), xc-xcii.

32 It is conceivable that a stress such as that on the second syllable of *Éirinn* 'Ireland', might derive from *deibhidhe* metre. ('The words *sing: liking* are an example of this form of rime in English', Murphy, *loc. cit.*).

33 T.P. McCaughey, 'The performing of Dán', *Ériu* 35 (1984), 39-57.

archives of the School of Scottish Studies are now dead —
only Miss Penny Morrison of South Uist remains — over the
years a small number of men and women have interested
themselves sufficiently in the tradition to learn several ballads.
The Rev. William Matheson learnt the melody of 'Laoidh
Fhraoich' from Duncan MacDonald, South Uist, and com-
bined it with a text learnt from his uncle-by-marriage, Donald
Morrison, Skye.[34] Professor Neil MacCormick of Edinburgh
University learnt the same lay from his grand-uncle Capt.
Dugall MacCormick of Glasgow and Mull. Mrs Catriona Gar-
butt learnt 'Am Bròn Binn' from Mrs Kate MacCormick,
Benbecula; and Miss Ishabel T. MacDonald learnt 'Duan na
Ceardaich' from Mrs Archie MacDonald, South Uist.

By such means, the tradition of singing heroic lays in Gaelic
Scotland will continue for at least another generation.

34 Text, translation and transcription of melody in *Tocher* 35 (1981),
    292-7.

DEVELOPMENT AND DEGENERATION IN GAELIC BALLAD TEXTS*

DONALD E. MEEK

(University of Edinburgh)

Introductory

In this paper I propose to discuss a subject which brings together Scotland, Ireland and Scandinavia. One of the major themes of the narrative poems in that body of verse which we loosely describe as 'Gaelic ballads' is the Viking threat to the sovereignty of Ireland, and the efforts of the Fian warrior-bands to defend their land. The development and transmission of Gaelic ballads on the Vikings and related subjects were explored in the magisterial work of the Norwegian scholar, Reidar Th. Christiansen, whose book, *The Vikings and the Viking Wars in Irish and Gaelic Tradition*, was published in Oslo in 1931.[1] Professor Christiansen's book remains fundamental to our understanding of the Gaelic ballad tradition as a whole — and in the term 'Gaelic' I include both the Irish and Scottish Gaelic ramifications of that tradition. Professor Christiansen not only focused his attention on the portrayal of the Vikings in the Gaelic ballads, but he was also at pains to demonstrate that different versions of individual ballads existed, some distinctively Irish, some distinctively Scottish, and some distinguished by features of a thematic or stylistic

*This paper has been rewritten to include responses to the main points which were raised in discussion after it had been delivered. I am grateful to those who participated in the discussion, and particularly to Professor Pádraig Ó Fiannachta and Professor Joseph Falaky Nagy, the main discussants, for their helpful comments.

1 On the Viking theme in Gaelic ballads, see also P. Mac Cana, 'The Influence of the Vikings on Celtic Literature' in B. Ó Cuív, ed., *The Impact of the Scandinavian Invasions on the Celtic-speaking Peoples c. 800-1100 A.D.*, Dublin 1975, 78-118, and especially 94-7.

variety. In my discussion, I hope to examine the development of Gaelic ballad texts over the centuries with regard to a particular, and necessarily limited, body of poems. In doing so, I acknowledge the debt which I owe to Professor Christiansen, whose methodology has been my model in this complex and underworked field. My overall aim, however, will be different from his, since I shall not explore themes, but I shall attempt to describe tentatively, and in general terms, what sorts of development occur in ballad texts, and why these developments should take place.

Perhaps it would be helpful at this point to define what I mean by 'Gaelic ballads', and to give some account of their style and structure, since my paper is primarily concerned with stylistic and structural change. The term 'ballads' is used to cover a body of verse which is sometimes also known as 'lays', or specifically 'Fenian lays'. The words 'ballad' and 'lay' are, however, somewhat misleading — the former because it suggests that the poems in question are always narrative poems directly comparable with ballads in English and Scots, and the latter because it tends to make us think of nineteenth-century English romantic verse (as in Sir Walter Scott's 'Lay of the Last Minstrel'). The adjective 'Fenian' — which can be applied only to poems about Fionn mac Cumhaill and the Fiana — also carries political overtones in the modern Irish context.[2] The Gaelic terminology is not really very helpful either. What we term a 'ballad' would have been known to the Gaelic people of Ireland and Scotland as *laoi(dh)*, *dán*, or *duan*. Certainly in later tradition, these terms can be used interchangeably of the same poem, although there may once have been some degree of meaningful differentiation.[3]

Whatever term we use — and I myself intend to employ 'ballad' for the present — we are dealing with a type of verse which shows a great deal of thematic and stylistic variety. Within the Gaelic ballad corpus, we do indeed find a high

---

2 Cf. the approach to *Fianaigheacht* (Fian-lore) implicit in the introduction to N. O'Kearney, ed., 'The Battle of Gabhra' in *Transactions of the Ossianic Society* I (1853), 9-67.

3 See F. Collinson, *The Traditional and National Music of Scotland*, London 1966, 40, note 3.

proportion of narrative poems describing hunts, battles, combats, expeditions of one kind or another, and other types of heroic adventure; but we also encounter elegies and eulogies which focus our attention on the qualities of individual heroes, lyrics which describe or evoke the sights and sounds of nature with only passing reference to warrior deeds, and poems of debate in which a conversation between two individuals, commonly Oisín and St Patrick, is the main feature. In many poems, a dialogue between Oisín and Patrick provides the frame for the recounting of heroic exploits; Oisín, sometimes grudgingly, passes on his recollections of the Fiana to Patrick who has asked for a story. Besides employing a dialogue structure of this kind, individual ballads can combine elements of several of the verse-types which we have already identified within the corpus; a ballad narrating the death of a warrior (as, for example, 'The Death of Diarmaid') may consist of an account of the circumstances of the tragedy, interspersed with thumb-nail sketches of the surrounding countryside and rounded off with a brief or extended eulogy of the warrior. A single ballad may thus incorporate a number of different styles, with accompanying changes of mood and tempo.[4]

However varied they may be in their themes and styles, Gaelic ballads are generally concerned with the exploits and achievements of warriors. The warrior-bands, or Fiana, associated with Fionn mac Cumhaill are, of course, pre-eminent in

4 The principal editions and collections of ballads used in this paper are: (a) *Scottish*: N. Ross, ed., *Heroic Poetry from the Book of the Dean of Lismore*, Scottish Gaelic Texts Society Vol. 3, Edinburgh 1939 (referred to as HP^1); D.E. Meek, 'The Corpus of Heroic Verse in the Book of the Dean of Lismore', unpublished Ph.D. thesis, University of Glasgow 1982 (intended to replace the earlier edition by Ross, and therefore referred to as HP^2); J.F. Campbell, ed., *Leabhar na Feinne*, London 1872, reprinted Shannon 1972; (b) *Irish*: Charlotte Brooke, ed., *Reliques of Irish Poetry*, Dublin 1789; E. MacNeill, ed., *Duanaire Finn*, Part I, Irish Texts Society Vol. 7, London 1908; G. Murphy, ed., *Duanaire Finn*, Parts II-III, Irish Texts Society Vols. 28 and 43, London and Dublin 1933 and 1953; An Seabhac (Pádraig Ó Síochfhradha), ed., *Laoithe na Féinne*, Dublin 1941.

'The Death of Diarmaid' occurs as No. XI in HP^1, and No. XIII in HP^2.

the ballad corpus as it survives today, and as we see it from the twelfth century, when the ballads began to attain literary prominence; but we need to remember that ballads about the Ulster heroes survived, albeit in smaller number, in Irish and Scottish Gaelic tradition until relatively recently.[5] Indeed, narrative poems about Ulster heroes may once have enjoyed some degree of popularity, especially in the period before the Finn Cycle achieved its ascendancy. It is, I think, highly significant that our earliest 'clear forerunner of the popular type of ballad addressed to St Patrick by Oisín or Caoilte' involves Patrick and the great Ulster hero Cú Chulainn, and is to be dated to the tenth or eleventh century.[6] Heroes who owed their allegiance to other parts of Ireland may also have been commemorated in narrative verse. One of the most popular ballads in Scottish Gaelic tradition until the present day has been 'Laoidh Fhraoich', 'The Lay of Fraoch', which describes the killing of the Connacht hero Fraoch mac Fiodhaigh by a water-monster, and which was evidently composed in the Carnfree district of Co. Roscommon. 'Laoidh Fhraoich' bears a close but perplexing relationship to the early (eighth-century?) Irish prose-tale *Táin Bó Fraích*, 'The Driving of Fraoch's Cattle'.[7] However we define this relationship, it serves to remind us that ballads cannot always be studied in isolation from prose literature, and that prose and verse accounts of the same story can sometimes be found. The great compendium of prose and verse relating to the Fiana, *Acallam na Senórach*, 'The Colloquy with the Ancients', in all its recensions from the late twelfth century onwards, furnishes

---

5 See Campbell, *op. cit.*, 9-19; Brooke, *op. cit.*, 265-71. The ballad corpus in the *Book of the Dean of Lismore* contains one dialogue-ballad with Ulster characters (No. XVIII in HP^1, and No. XIX in HP^2), and two apologues with Ulster themes (No. XXIV in HP^1, and No. XXIII in HP^2; and No. XXVI in HP^1).

6 Mac Cana, *op. cit.*, 8; G. Murphy, *The Ossianic Lore and Romantic Tales of Medieval Ireland*, Dublin 1961, 21.

7 The earliest text of the ballad is in the *Book of the Dean of Lismore* (No. XXIX in HP^1, and No. XXVII in HP^2). See D.E. Meek, '*Táin Bó Fraích* and Other "Fráech" Texts: A Study in Thematic Relationships', Parts I-II, in *Cambridge Medieval Celtic Studies* 7 (Summer 1984), 1-37, and 8 (Winter 1984), 65-85.

ample evidence of that.[8] Some ballads may, in fact, require a prose 'introduction' to explain the background to their plot, or they may presume knowledge of a tale or group of tales. Other ballads are wholly self-contained in their story-line.

Besides their interest in heroes and their achievements, Gaelic ballads share common ground in their metrical form. The term 'ballad' might make us think that they were composed in stressed metres like the Scots ballads; they are, however, composed in loose forms (*óglachas*) of syllabic verse (*dán*).[9] Syllabic verse can be seen at its high point, in all its strictest glory, in bardic poetry. The composers of Gaelic ballads usually rested content with an imitation of the metre concerned, and they did not strive to satisfy the strict bardic requirements of rhyme and alliteration. Depending on the nature of the composition and the competence of the poet, there might be a certain heightening and ornamentation of metrical syle, but seldom to any noticeable degree of strictness. When a ballad is found to have an unusually strict metrical form, it is legitimate to suppose that it may not have begun its life as a ballad, but more probably as an apologue in a bardic poem, from which it has subsequently become detached.[10] The absence of metrical strait-jackets meant that ballads could employ a less specialised type of

---

8 W. Stokes and E. Windisch, eds., *Irische Texte mit Übersetzungen und Worterbuch*, Fourth Series, Vol. 1, Leipzig 1900, contains the earlier *Acallam*; a later version is in Nessa Ní Shéaghdha, ed., *Agallamh na Seanórach*, Parts I-III, Baile Átha Cliath 1942-5.

9 The most common metres in surviving texts are *deibhidhe* and forms of *rannaigheacht*, chiefly *rannaigheacht mhór* or *rannaigheacht bheag*. The corpus of 27 ballads edited in HP^2 from the *Book of the Dean of Lismore* has 16 in *rannaigheacht* metres (11 in *rannaigheacht mhór*), and 9 in *deibhidhe*; *Duanaire Finn*, with a total of 69 items, has about 41 in *deibhidhe*, and about 19 in *rannaigheacht* types (9 in *rannaigheacht mhór*). In the later tradition, *rannaigheacht* metres do appear to be the more common; cf. P.A. Breatnach, 'Irish Narrative Poetry after 1200 A.D.', in *Studia Hibernica* 22-3 (1982-3), 18.

10 This is certainly the case with the ballad describing the death of Conlaoch by his father Cú Chulainn, which began as an apologue in an elegy by Giolla Coluim mac an Ollaimh (No. XXIV in HP^1, and No. XXIII in HP^2).

vocabulary than bardic poems, and that the syntax of quatrains approximated more closely to what we today would regard as 'ordinary' speech. Not that ballads were free from set phrases and chevilles, from well-worn adjectives and modes of description — such conventions abound in the ballads — but the overall style of a ballad is much less esoteric, much less 'scholastic', than that of a finely wrought bardic poem. The original language of the majority of surviving ballads, composed in the period from c.1200 to c.1600, was Classical Common Gaelic, the shared literary language of Ireland and Scotland, but it often made concessions to vernacular speech in matters of morphology, rhyme, and lexis.[11]

It will be evident from these characteristics of the language and structure of the Gaelic ballad that, from a technical point of view, it was the poor relation of the bardic poem. Yet in its less esoteric nature lay much of the secret of its survival. When the bardic poem showed itself to be largely incapable of existing without the life-support system of the bardic schools, the ballad continued to breathe, and found a welcome home among the ordinary people of Gaelic Ireland and Gaelic Scotland, where the singing of ballads can still be heard on occasion.[12] Given the relaxed style of the ballad, and the longevity of the tradition, it is hardly surprising that texts have been subjected to processes of change across the centuries. Compared with the bardic poem, the ballad was adaptable — ready to change and to be changed in response to new linguistic, literary and social pressures. There were, of course, disadvantages in such adaptability, since ballad texts could all too easily become the victims of human misunderstanding, and even of human mischief.

The possibility of change within ballad texts was doubtless facilitated by the modes of their transmission. In Gaelic Scotland from at least the eighteenth century, the ballads can be

11 Cf. Murphy, *Duanaire Finn*, *op. cit.* (1953), cvii-cxxi.
12 The custom of singing or chanting the ballads has lingered longer in Scotland than in Ireland. See Collinson, *op. cit.*, 41-8, for examples of tunes. In his paper below 'Twentieth-century Recordings of Scottish Gaelic Heroic Ballads', Dr John MacInnes has presented specimens from the archives of the School of Scottish Studies, Edinburgh.

seen to exist primarily in an oral context, and the majority
of collections made in the Scottish Highlands and Islands
from that date contain material which had been orally transmitted.[13] In Ireland too, the ballads were propagated by word
of mouth in the same period, but, as Professor Christiansen
has pointed out, Ireland had a much stronger tradition of
manuscript compilation,[14] and many small poem-books
devoted solely to ballads are preserved in such institutions
as the Royal Irish Academy.[15] These reflect what was virtually
a scribal cottage-industry which was avidly pursued in the
later eighteenth century, and the earlier nineteenth century,
by scribes like Mícheál Óg Ó Longáin of Co. Cork.[16] The
poem-books produced by the Ó Longáin family show very
fine penmanship, and are sometimes decorated with illu-
minated initials. More typical of the general tradition are the
less ornate poem-books, their texts more roughly written and
their pages well thumbed by continual use. In comparing the
body of ballads extant in Scotland in this later period with
that found in Ireland, I am struck — as Christiansen was[17] —
by the greater amount of variation found in the Scottish
material. It seems likely that the wide-spread availability of
manuscripts in Ireland had the effect of stabilising textual
development. Nevertheless, the Irish manuscript versions show
considerable variety of readings. Although Irish poem-books
did cross to Scotland in this period, they did so only in small
numbers, and there is no evidence that they exerted a deter-
minative influence on the Scottish tradition.[18]

13 Christiansen, *op. cit.*, 47-61.
14 *Ibid.*, 47.
15 There are also manuscripts of 'mixed' type sometimes containing
    prose and verse with some ballads; examples are Royal Irish Academy
    manuscripts 23 M 6, 23 C 9, and 23 C 15.
16 W. Gillies, 'An Irish Manuscript in Scotland', in *Scottish Gaelic
    Studies* 13, Part I (1978), 127-9.
17 Cf. Christiansen's comments on the Scottish Gaelic versions of
    'Teanntachd Mhór na Féinne', *op. cit.*, 109.
18 Examples of Irish poem-books in Scotland include two items col-
    lected by Peter Turner, and now in the National Library of Scotland
    (Mss 72.2.4 and 72.2.5). Cf. the circumstances of the manuscript
    discussed by Gillies, *op. cit.*

Before 1700, of course, Ireland and Scotland possessed a vital scribal tradition, and ballads are found in major manuscript compilations in both countries. The principal Scottish manuscript containing ballad texts is the *Book of the Dean of Lismore*, compiled between 1512 and 1542 by Perthshire scribes, most notably James MacGregor, Dean of Lismore, and his brother Duncan, who have preserved some twenty-seven complete ballads and several fragments and stray quatrains. [19] Sixty-nine ballad texts are found in the Irish manuscript *Duanaire Finn*, compiled in Ostend (Belgium) about 1627 by Aodh Ó Dochartaigh for his patron, the Irish soldier of fortune Captain Sorley MacDonnell of Antrim. [20] *Duanaire Finn*, 'The Poem-book of Fionn' is devoted exclusively to ballads about Fionn and the Fiana, unlike the *Book of the Dean of Lismore* which contains ballads about the Ulster heroes, as well as other verse types (bardic, courtly, satiric etc.). The format of the *Duanaire* strongly suggests that its contents are derived from manuscript compilations of the type represented by the later poem-books. [21] The practice of recording ballads in manuscript is further attested in the recensions of *Acallam na Senórach*, [22] and in the specimens contained in the *Book of Leinster*, compiled before 1160. [23] The writing down of Gaelic ballads has, therefore, a long history, but we need to remember that both oral and written methods of transmission are likely to have been of importance from the beginning, and that changes could be introduced to the texts in either medium. The movement of the texts from written to oral transmission, and *vice versa*, may also have contributed to textual development.

19 See note 4.
20 *Ibid*.
21 The key to the compilation of *Duanaire Finn* lies in the final section. At the conclusion of No. LVI, the scribe signals the end of his current batch of material. He then continues with No. LVII ('A Oisín as fada do shúan . . .'), a poem which normally heads up the later Irish poem-books devoted to Fian ballads. I hope to discuss this further elsewhere.
22 The later *Acallam* edited by Ní Shéaghdha, *op. cit.*, is particularly rich in this respect.
23 R.I. Best and M.A. O'Brien, eds., *The Book of Leinster*, Vol. 3, Dublin 1957, 663; Vol. 4, Dublin 1965, 994-1005.

My own research hitherto has concentrated on the corpus of ballads in the *Book of the Dean of Lismore*. Besides trying to elucidate the texts as they stand in this manuscript, I have been concerned to establish the relationship of the Dean's texts to those in other Scottish and Irish collections. I have also tried to gain some understanding of the development, across the centuries, of the ballad texts represented in this source. In so doing, I have become acutely conscious of the profusion of variant versions of individual ballads which exist in Ireland and Scotland; consequently, I cannot claim to have done more than scratch the surface of my present topic.[24] I would emphasise also that my main concern to date has been with the evidence provided by written texts, and that much remains to be discovered about such matters as the live performance of ballads, which no doubt had a considerable bearing on textual development.[25]

Scribal Presentation of Ballad Texts in the *Book of the Dean of Lismore*

The *Book of the Dean of Lismore* presents many problems to an editor. The majority of these are caused by its orthography, which is based on that of Middle Scots,[26] although it does occasionally appear to preserve traces of what we would regard as 'conventional' Gaelic orthography. Its scribes also write in secretary hand, rather than Gaelic script (*corralitir*), so that the manuscript appears outlandish and impenetrable to scholars who are more familiar with 'normal' Gaelic documents.

A further distinctive feature of the *Book of the Dean* is the degree to which its scribes have introduced changes to the original drafts of their texts. These changes are particularly marked in the ballad texts in the manuscript. Some changes can readily be seen to be the result of scribal errors and misunderstandings, but the majority clearly derive from variant

24 See note 4.
25 An important recent contribution to this area of study is T.P. McCaughey, 'The Performing of Dán', in *Ériu* 35 (1984), 39-57.
26 For a discussion of the background to, and possible significance of, this orthography, see D.E. Meek, 'Gàidhlig is Gaylick anns an Meadhon Aoisean' (forthcoming).

versions of the ballad texts which evidently became available to the scribes after they had written their first drafts. No less than eight of the ballad texts contain alterations of this kind; these extend from the alteration of individual words to the provision of variant line readings, variant quatrains, and even additional quatrains. When the scribes alter words, lines and quatrains, they usually cancel their first readings, and write the alternative readings in superscript; additional quatrains are generally written in the lower margins, with caret marks to indicate where they should be inserted in the sequence of verses in the first draft. The cancellation of earlier readings makes it improbable that the scribes were aiming to produce a *variorum* edition of their texts, and it is equally unlikely that they were aware of 'variant readings' as an integral part of the tradition. My impression is that they were really conflating their versions on a 'last past the post' principle; that is to say, if they had written their first draft and then found a variant version, they incorporated the divergent features of the second version into their first draft, possibly in the belief that the second version was better because it was bigger, or because it was more recently to hand.[27]

The *Book of the Dean* thus contains evidence of great significance for our understanding of the development of Gaelic ballad texts. It indicates that ballad texts were by no means 'fixed', even within what can be called in broad terms 'the classical period', and the scribes' deletions and alterations provide a vivid picture of textual variation which is normally obscured by the immaculate presentation of such sources as *Duanaire Finn*.

The Composition and 'Authorship' of Ballads

The textual developments which are attested in the *Book of the Dean of Lismore* raise many questions, but the most

---

27 It is to be noted that the editorial principles of HP^1 do not allow the scribes' emendations to be displayed in the edited texts or apparatus, and it would seem that such emendations are seldom recognised. HP^2 aims to provide a diplomatic transcription and restoration of the texts as they stand in the manuscript, with a full discussion of the emendations.

important question relates to the composition of ballad texts, and the processes by which such poems come into existence. If textual variation is in evidence in certain ballad texts by the sixteenth century, when did such development begin? Is it a sign of degeneration, and an indication that, by the end of the Middle Ages, unscrupulous tradition-bearers were meddling with hitherto unaltered texts? Or should we suppose that the ballad tradition allowed for an extended process of composition whereby a number of poets across the centuries could 'add their bit' to a developing text? As the recorders of ballad texts have generally not been as helpful as the scribes of the *Book of the Dean* in showing the process of conflation, how much of this process has occurred without any signs which are detectable by us today? What, indeed, had happened to the texts of ballads in the *Book of the Dean of Lismore* long before they came to be written in that manuscript?

One ballad text in the *Book of the Dean* points up these questions very forcefully. This is the ballad known as 'Caoilte and the Animals' (No. IX in HP^1 and HP^2). Of all the ballad texts which have been emended by the scribes subsequent to the writing of the first draft, this one shows the greatest flurry of scribal activity; emendation extends from the alteration of prepositions to the substitution of alternative lines and quatrains (see Table 1). In the case of this text, too, we have the good fortune to possess two versions which are earlier than that in the *Book of the Dean*, as well as one which is later. The versions earlier than that found in the *Book of the Dean* are that represented by a few quatrains found in the earlier *Acallam na Senórach* of c.1175, and the one contained in the later (thirteenth- or fourteenth-century) recension of the *Acallam*, a well-developed version;[28] the version which is later than the one included in the *Book of the Dean* is in *Duanaire Finn* (No. VII). The *Book of the Dean* version is by far the longest extant version, with 72 quatrains; that in the later *Acallam* has 55 quatrains, while the text in *Duanaire Finn* has a mere 29 quatrains.

The later *Acallam* provides a prose introduction to the ballad and explains the circumstances of its plot. Fionn plans

28   Ní Shéaghdha, *op. cit.*, Part III, 72-83.

treachery against Cormac mac Airt, but he is foiled, and Cormac puts him in prison. The ballad relates how Caoilte mac Rónáin, the fastest man in the Fian, goes to Tara to free Fionn. After some unprofitable pranks, he makes a bargain with Cormac whereby he will achieve Fionn's release. Caoilte is to fetch a couple of all the wild animals in Ireland, and the special feature of this ballad is the long catalogue of animal pairs (mainly birds) and places where they have been captured. This catalogue is, however, absent from the quatrains in the earlier *Acallam*; one of these refers to Caoilte's capturing of the wild animals, while the others mention his feats of running. A brief passage in the *Acallam* makes it clear that the story of Fionn's release by means of Caoilte's 'odd drove' was known at this stage, but the quatrains have not yet been brought together in a sequence relating specifically to this adventure.[29] In the later *Acallam* version, on the other hand, the disparate quatrains of the earlier text are found among the introductory quatrains describing Caoilte's pranks, and there is a catalogue of 19 quatrains. In the *Book of the Dean* text, which is closely related to that of the later *Acallam*, the catalogue contains 23 quatrains. By contrast, the *Duanaire Finn* text has a catalogue of only 5 quatrains, one of which is peculiar to the *Duanaire*. My impression is that we are dealing here with a ballad which has been a 'growing concern' from the twelfth century to the end of the fifteenth century, and that the catalogue of animals and placenames was its main growth-point. The text in the *Book of the Dean* may well show the catalogue approaching its fullest extent. Yet, at the same time as it may have encouraged textual expansion, the catalogue was capable of being reduced without harming the overall plot of the poem, and it is probably some such process of reduction or atrophy which is reflected in the very brief version in the *Duanaire* text, which is a century later than that in the *Book of the Dean*. Besides the catalogue, there are other ways in which this ballad appears to have grown. For instance, the *Book of the Dean* and the later *Acallam* versions both contain a piece of *dindshenchas*, 'lore

29 Stokes and Windisch, *op. cit.*, 103, ll. 3614-5; 136, ll. 4976-8, 205, ll. 7367-78.

of famous places' concerning Bodhamair which was evidently not integral to the story of the ballad, but which may have been attracted to it because of the placename interest of the catalogue.[30] The episodic nature of the ballad also allowed for the introduction of incidents which extended the story, as in the quatrains (unique to the *Book of the Dean*) which describe Caoilte's frustrations with the two houses given to him to accommodate the animals when he arrived at Tara.[31]

The key to the development which I believe took place in the ballad about Caoilte and the animals lies in its episodic and highly formulaic style. The catalogue of animal pairs consists of a long string of verses, of which almost every line begins with the numeral 'two' and concludes with a placename. It would not be difficult to imitate such quatrains or to add episodes which emphasised the hardships faced by Caoilte. With a couple of other ballads in the *Book of the Dean*, I suspect that a somewhat similar process has occurred, to a greater or lesser degree. For example, there is a little ballad at the beginning of the collection (No. I in *HP*[1] and *HP*[2]) which commemorates the graves of five of the Fian warriors — Oisín's in the north, Diarmaid's in the south, Osgar's in the east, Caoilte's in the west, and Conán's below the speaker's feet. Conán Maol was, of course, the unpeaceable man of the Fian — *aoinfhear bu mhór grúig is gráin*, 'an individual of great surliness and loathing', as he is called in this text — and it is a trifle strange to see his memory being preserved in this poem about more attractive heroes. You will notice, however, that the location of his grave is not a compass point, and this, together with a metrical detail involving the *dúnadh* (the formal 'closing' device) of the poem,[32] makes

30 The *dindshenchas* relating to Bodhamair is discussed below by Rolf Baumgarten in his paper 'Placenames and the Structure of *Fianaigecht*', cf. pp. 1-24.

31 These occur as qq. 63-7 in *HP*[1], and qq. 62-6 in *HP*[2].

32 A *dúnadh* is formed by repeating the opening word or letters of a poem at its very end (i.e. as its last word or letters). In this case, the poem opens with 'Atá...' and '...atá' is repeated at the end of q. 4. The verse about Conán follows, and it is also closed with '...atá'. It is therefore possible that the poem originally ended at q. 4.

me suspect that the verse describing Conán's grave was a later addition to the text, perhaps intended to 'cock a snook' at the earlier verses. In later Irish versions of this poem, the text usually includes a further verse on Mac Lughach which is similar to that on Conán, and the poem is recast as a dialogue between Oisín and Patrick, with a suitable alteration to the first verse to allow the resurrection of Oisín![33] In this poem, too, a fair degree of formulaic structure is evident, with each quatrain beginning with the words *Atá fán tulaigh so* ... 'Beneath this mound lies . . .'

Besides the possibility that individual quatrains could be added to a ballad text by employing the formulaic pattern of existing verses, we need also to envisage the probability that the tradition allowed for the development of formulaic verse units which could be used at appropriate points in different ballads. One of the most intriguing poems in the *Book of the Dean* is a ballad describing a quest by nine Fian warriors, seemingly for a cultic dog of some kind (No. XIV in *HP*[1], and No. XVI in *HP*[2]). In the course of their search, the warriors encounter forces of Cat-heads and Dog-heads whom they defeat by unfurling their banners during the conflict. Nine quatrains are devoted to the unfurling of the banners, beginning with Fionn's *Dealbh Ghréine*, 'Image of Sun', and all attest the same formulaic structure, opening with the words *Do thógamar* ... 'We raised . . .' followed by the name of a banner. In later tradition, particularly in Gaelic Scotland, these 'banner quatrains' are usually found as ornaments in ballads which narrate encounters with the Vikings, and a close study of the banner names does tend to suggest that this may have been their original context.[34] In the poem in the *Book of the Dean*, they seem rather out of place, and it is interest-

---

33 An Seabhac, *op. cit.*, 286-7. The poem is usually found in the later collections (as here) as the second part of a composite piece entitled 'Taisce na bhFiann', 'The Treasure of the Fians' which begins *Atá fa thonnaibh na dtonn* . . . . The similarity in structure and theme (concealment of treasures or warriors under sea or land) has brought the two items together.

34 D.E. Meek, 'The Banners of the Fian in Gaelic Ballad Tradition', in *Cambridge Medieval Celtic Studies* 11 (Summer 1986), 29-69.

ing to note that the greater part of the poem consists of formulaic sequences.[35]

In the light of such evidence, then, I would suggest that we should not regard the textual emendations which appear in the *Book of the Dean of Lismore* as a peculiar feature of this manuscript, or as a sign of late maltreatment of the ballad tradition. More probably, these emendations reflect a continuing process of adjustment which has a very long history. This process demands that we envisage 'authorship' as a rather loose concept which allowed for the growth and development of texts beyond their 'original' form. This 'original' form may well have been the work of a single author, but the normal practice of ascribing the composition of ballads to legendary figures such as Oisín or Caoilte obscures the identity of the first poet, and allows for the adjustment of a text by any number of later 'poets'. Interestingly, five ballads in the *Book of the Dean of Lismore* are ascribed to non-legendary 'authors' — Giolla Coluim mac an Ollaimh, Ailéin mac Ruaidhrí (two ballads), An Caoch ó Chluain (?), and a certain Ó Floinn.[36] Only in the case of Giolla Coluim mac an Ollaimh can we be reasonably certain of having identified the original author, but the text of the poem as found in the *Book of the Dean*

---

35 These sequences are (a) a placename sequence, describing the quest throughout Ireland (qq. 2-8); (b) a spear-casting sequence (qq. 11-3); (c) a roll-call sequence (qq. 15-7); and (d) the banner sequence (qq. 19-27). I suspect that the poem is a pastiche of earlier formulaic units.

36 The attributions are as follows: 'The Death of Conlaoch' (No. XXIV in HP^1, and No. XXIII in HP^2) to Giolla Coluim mac an Ollaimh; 'The Death of Diarmaid' (No. XI in HP^1, and No. XIII in HP^2) and 'The Death of Oscar' (No. XXIII in HP^1, and No. XXII in HP^2) to Ailéin mac Ruaidhrí; 'The Lay of Fraoch' (No. XXIX in HP^1, and No. XXVII in HP^2) to An Caoch ó Chluain (?); and a short comic piece (No. XVIII in HP^1, and No. XVII in HP^2) to Ó Floinn (HP^1 misreads the manuscript ascription). We know nothing so far about Ailéin mac Ruaidhrí (a Clanranald name?) or Ó Floinn. On the difficulties in the identification of An Caoch ó Chluain (?), see Meek, *op. cit.* (1984), 36-7.

attests alterations which have been made since the time of original composition.[37]

While it seems reasonable to suppose that ballad texts are often the work of more than one author, we need to guard against seeing such a process as uncontrolled and haphazard. I do not think that we should regard every reciter of a ballad as a poet or potential poet.[38] Ballad texts can usually be classified in families according to their distinctive features — and this would not be possible if the texts were being adjusted *ad lib*. Some families may be distinguished by what seem to be regional characteristics. Also, within the classical period (i.e. until about 1600), adjustments were made in accordance with the metrical and stylistic requirements of the tradition, and often in such a way that the alterations are difficult to detect. After 1600, however, texts are altered with much less sensitivity to their individuality, theme or general shape. While such changes can be accommodated under the general heading of textual development, they could be regarded as 'degenerative' in relation to the norms of ballad composition in the classical tradition. In the *Book of the Dean of Lismore* we find adjustments which, for the most part, fall clearly within the classical type, but there are some which appear to foreshadow the developments usually found in eighteenth- and nineteenth-century ballad versions. We shall look at both kinds of alteration as we find them in this manuscript.

37 For Giolla Coluim mac an Ollaimh, see W.J. Watson, *Scottish Verse from the Book of the Dean of Lismore*, Scottish Gaelic Text Society Vol. 1, Edinburgh 1837, reprinted 1978, 275. His *floruit* was c.1490. Alterations to the piece include its detaching from its original context (for which see *ibid.*, 277-8), the development of line variants, and the re-ordering of certain quatrains.

38 More detailed studies will probably find grounds for distinguishing between relatively minor alterations which could be made by a scribe or reciter (e.g., dialectal modifications), and more significant changes which have perhaps been made by an 'adjuster' (or school of 'adjusters'). For later texts, it will also be in order to consider such factors as poor memorisation of text, misunderstanding of words, phrases and lines, confusion of poems etc., and the levels at which these occur.

Visible Adjustments to Ballad Texts in the *Book of the Dean of Lismore*

Having considered some of the developments which probably occurred in certain ballad texts before they came to be written in the *Book of the Dean of Lismore*, we may now focus our attention on the alterations which the scribes have made to the first drafts of several of their poems. These can be classified most conveniently in three categories, with specific examples. It should be noted that the examples in the first category are not exhaustive, but are intended to illustrate general principles.

Type A. This involves the adjustment of words, phrases and whole lines within individual quatrains, and is the most common kind of change found in the texts. The text of 'Caoilte and the Animals' has been extensively altered in this way, and Table 1 provides a sample of the emendations which have been made. The original manuscript form of a line is given in Column (2), and the form of the adjusted line, based on the superscript readings, is given in Column (3). The corresponding line from the text in *Agallamh na Seanórach* (i.e. the later *Acallam*) is given in Column (1) for comparative purposes.

There is, in fact, no single explanation which accounts for the changes which are attested. On a linguistic level, there is little to choose between the original readings and the superscripts in terms of comprehensibility; the meaning of no line is demonstrably clarified by the superscripts, although it is possible that in q. 21 a, the superscript *ris a bean*, 'which I touch' is more transparent than *fa-dear*, 'which causes it', a conspicuously older verb-form.[39] With regard to morphology, there is no consistent modernisation of forms, although *fa-*

---

39 For *fa-dear* ($<$ *fo-fera*, with 3 sg. n. infixed pronoun), see *Dictionary of the Irish Language*, Compact Edition, Dublin 1983, 317, s.v. *fo-fera*, II. The use of *fa-dear(a)* in this way is well attested into the Early Modern period, and its meaning need not have been obscure even in the late Middle Ages. The superscript *ris a bean* as written gives an extra syllable to the line (beyond the requisite seven), although it may have been treated as *ris bean* in recitation (perhaps from earlier *ré mbean*?).

dear is altered in q. 21 a, and an analytic verb-form is substituted for a synthetic form in q. 26 c. Syntax also remains much the same in the superscripts as in the original readings. In q. 29 b, the superscript readings evidently have the effect of changing a negative statement into a positive one, with no change of meaning in the line. It is, indeed, noticeable that, in spite of the numerous alterations, the lines retain their original meanings throughout. This may well indicate that, to a certain extent, the reproduction of ballad lines was based on 'sense-units' which allowed for some amount of verbal variety.[40] It is apparent from the present sample that alterations are least liable to occur at the ends of lines, since line-endings are held in check by rhyme, particularly in this instance where the metre is *deibhidhe* with two end-rhyming couplets in each quatrain.[41]

The forms of animal names and placenames in the sample are of some interest. In q. 41 a, the forms *adharclōg* and

---

The only other hypermetric line in the sample from the *Book of the Dean* is the emended form of q. 26 b. This can be restored by reading *bheó* (sg.) for *bheótha* (pl., manuscript *woada*). This adjective was possibily meant to emphasise that the animals were to be alive, not dead, when caught, but the urge to insert it probably arose from the loss of a syllable in *lānamhuin* (*Agallamh*, q. 24 b). The original *Book of the Dean* reading compensates for this by means of the trisyllabic form *fiadhamhna*. The reduction of *lánamh-ain* to *lánmhain* or *lámhnain* with metathesis probably reflects dialectal variation; cf. the form *lánúin* in Connacht and Donegal (P.S. Dinneen, *Foclóir Gaedhilge agus Béarla*, Dublin 1927, s.v. *lánamha*).

40   Such variety is found in other types of Gaelic verse, and raises problems for editors. See the comments of William Gillies in his Review of C. Ó Baoill, ed., *Bàrdachd Shìlis na Ceapaich* (*Poems and Songs by Sìleas MacDonald*) in *Scottish Studies* 18 (1974), 143-8, and especially 146-7. In *HP*[2] no attempt will be made to create a synthetic text on the basis of these variations, which I would regard as having roughly equal weight; the edited text will be based, as far as possible, on the scribes' first draft, and their emendations will be discussed fully in the apparatus. I believe it would be dangerous to attempt the reconstruction of an 'original' text for a poem such as the one presently being discussed.

41   This does not, of course, mean that the end-rhymes could not be altered if required.

Caoilte and the Animals' – Ballad IX in the Book of the Dean of Lismore
A Selection of Variant Readings

(1) Agallamh na Seanórach		(2) Book of the Dean – Original Readings		(3) Book of the Dean – Superscripts
13 c	isin oidhche thall tré ghoid	15 c	anns an oidhche thall go beacht	an oidhche sin domh go beacht
18 b	tan ba háil dúinn aimhleas	20 b	mar a b'áil liom [a] aimhleas	do bu bhladh é do m'aimhleas
19 a	Iongnadh leam a ttuccais damh	21 a	Ioghnadh liom an ní fa-dear	Ioghnadh liom an ní ris a bean
20 d	cuibhdhe d'aird-rí airfideadh	22 d	bu chuibhdhe ól nō oirfide	cuir-sa th'úidh air oirfide
21 b	adubhart-sa re Corbmac	24 b	a d'fheóraich an sin Cormac	a d'fhiafruigh mis', dhe Chormac
24 a	Dā bhfaghthá, a Chaoilte, réd lá	26 a	Dā dtugtha thugam ré lá	Dā bhfaghtha tú dhomh ré lá
b	lánamhuin gacha fiadha	b	lámhnain gacha fiadhamhna,	lámhnain bheótha de gach fiadhán,
c	do-bhéruinn h'oide dhuit de	c	d'fhosglainn duit t'oid[e] air	do gheobhadh tú th'oid[e] air
d	go madh cuibhdhe ar ccomhmaoine.	d	gus an gcomha [a] c[h]umail.	go ceart comha [a]c[h]unbháil.
		29 a	Gluaisim róm thoir ō Theamhraigh,	Gluaisim turus ō Theamhraigh,
		b	nochar thriall fhir gan mheanmain	fá turus fir go meamna
28 c	is dā dhobhrán iar soin	32 c	is ii dhobhrán Iardomhain	is ii dhobhrán o shoin amach
30 d	dá smólach Leitre Lonn-gharcc	34 b	ii smeórach Leitre Lonnghairg	ii smeórach Leitre Lomaird
33 d	dhā ghealbhoinn na Seanainne	37 d	ii ghealbhann na Seanaibhle	ii gheal-eán* na Seanaibhle
39 b	dhā fhaidhírclín Leana hÚair	41 a	ii adharclóig an Léana Uair	ii adharcán Léana Fuaire
a	dhá chreabhoir ón cCoillidh Ruaidh	b	ii chreodhar on C[h]oillidh Ruaidh	ii chriodhar Craoibh[e] Ruaidhe

*Perhaps we should read *ghealán* (manuscript *zallane*).

Note: Variable words and phrases are shown in italics.

adharcán are dialectal variants of *adhaircín*, 'lapwing'; compare *faidhirclín* in the *Agallamh* text.[42] It is probable that *creodhar* and *criodhar* in q. 41 b, and *creabhoir* in the *Agallamh* text, are similarly explicable.[43] It is thus likely that some changes in the wording and word-forms of the ballad are due to the movement of the text from one dialect area to another. Such movement may also account for the variety in place-name forms in q. 34 b and q. 37 d (as compared with that in q. 33 d of the *Agallamh* text). In q. 32 c, the original *Book of the Dean* reading appears to preserve a placename which has been lost in the superscript, and is not attested in the *Agallamh* line.[44]

With regard to the relationship between the line-forms in the *Book of the Dean* and those in the *Agallamh* text, it is evident that the latter shares more common ground with the original *Book of the Dean* readings than with the superscript versions. In this way, the superscript readings in the *Book of the Dean* can be seen to derive from a version (or perhaps versions) of the poem which has (or have) drifted farther from the common ancestor-test which evidently underlies the *Agallamh* version and the original version in the *Book of the Dean*.[45]

42 Dinneen, *op. cit.*, 42.

43 *Ibid.*, s.v. *creabhar*.

44 The manuscript form of *Iardomhain* is *ear don*, and it seems likely that we should interpret this as a placename, although the *dobhráin* ('otters') are said in the next line to come ō *Charaidh dhonnbháin Dhobhair* ('from fair-brown Carrick Dover'). *Iardomhan* ('Western World') would seem to refer originally to a general area, and its significance may have been obscure to later transmitters of the poem, so that it was altered as in the *Agallamh* text and the superscript in the *Book of the Dean*. It may also have been felt to be redundant in view of the next line. Note that the *Agallamh* line lacks a syllable. On *Iardomhan*, see E. Hogan, *Onomasticon Goedelicum*, Dublin 1910, 452, s.v. *iardomon*, where a Scottish location is tentatively suggested. This does not suit the present context.

45 There are about 24 instances in which the original *Book of the Dean* readings are close to those in the *Agallamh*, and about 9 instances in which the superscript readings are close to the *Agallamh* reading.

It is perhaps worth noting that the detailed nature and extent of the emendations made to the text of this poem in the *Book of the Dean* would suggest that the scribes had access to manuscripts containing different versions of the ballad.

Type B. This category of emendation consists of the addition of further quatrains to the original manuscript draft of a poem, usually in the margins of the manuscript page. In contrast to the quatrains of Type C (below), the quatrains in this category cannot be said to come from another poem. They relate directly to the narrative structure of the poem to which they have been added.

Alterations of this kind are found in the *Book of the Dean* text of the ballad which is sometimes known as 'Eas Ruaidh' (No. XXI in *HP*[1], and No. XX in *HP*[2]). The ballad tells how a group of the Fian are at Eas Ruaidh (Assaroe, near Ballyshannon, Co. Donegal) when they see a large coracle bounding over the waves. The coracle contains a young lady of great size and beauty who discloses that she is fleeing from Mac Ríogh na Sorcha, 'The Son of the King of Sorcha', who wishes to marry her against her will. She asks for, and receives, the protection of Fionn. In due course, her pursuer arrives, and the Fian warriors engage in battle with him. He possesses great strength and puts up an immense fight against fifty of the Fian. Eventually he is slain by Goll mac Morna, and he is buried at Assaroe. The young lady remains with Fionn for a year.

The scribes have added five quatrains to their original text of this poem. These are appended at the foot of two pages in the manuscript,[46] and their positions in the sequence of the first draft are indicated by insertion marks. Of the five quatrains, four are found in similar positions almost invariably in later Scottish and Irish versions of the ballad, and one occurs only in Scottish versions (evidently in most of those which

---

46 These are manuscript pages 221 (one quatrain) and 222 (four quatrains).

have survived).[47] The prevalence of these quatrains in the later
versions might lead us to suppose that the first draft of the
poem in the *Book of the Dean* may have been based on a
defective source, and that at least four of the quatrains were
always part of this ballad. On the other hand, it is possible
that we are seeing textual development here, and that the
quatrains in question were composed at a later stage in the
life of the ballad. They may not have been in existence when
the first draft of the poem was written in the *Book of the
Dean of Lismore*, and we need to remember that the compilation of this manuscript took place over thirty years (or
more), so that there would be ample time for such development to occur after the writing of the first draft. It is, I
think, highly significant that all five quatrains may be called
'elaborative'. They do not add anything to the plot of the
poem, but they offer more descriptive detail, and they are all
concerned with the fight between the Fian warriors and the
invader.[48]

If the five quatrains are indeed the result of later composition, it is very interesting that four should occur so
regularly in the later Irish and Scottish versions of the poem.
These four may, in fact, go back to a single fairly influential
common source which was able to contribute to the development of the ballad in both Ireland and Scotland. The fifth
quatrain, which is found only in Scottish versions, may have
been added to the text in Scotland. A regional variation may
thus be reflected in the *Book of the Dean*, and the quatrain
may indicate that a distinctively Scottish version of the ballad
has begun to appear by this stage.

At the same time as the scribes have supplemented their
original draft of this poem, they have changed the position of
one of the quatrains in their first draft. In their revised text,
it is brought forward to a position which it usually occupies

---

47 For representative Irish versions, see Brooke, *op. cit.*, 288-93, and
    An Seabhac, *op. cit.*, 151-4; and for Scottish versions, see Camp-
    bell, *op. cit.*, 129-35.
48 The quatrains in HP^1 are 26 (found in the Scottish versions), 41,
    35, 37, and 39 (which are misplaced in the sequence of the edition);
    and in HP^2, 26, 32, 36, 38, 39.

in the later Irish and Scottish versions, and its new position is indicated by an insertion mark.[49] Other ballad texts in the *Book of the Dean* show minor alterations of this kind; for instance, in the ballad on the killing of Conlaoch by his father Cú Chulainn (No. XXIV in HP^1, and No. XXIII in HP^2), the scribes show that they wish to reverse the order of the third and fourth quatrains of their first draft. In this instance, however, the change takes the text away from the normal sequence of the quatrains in later versions, and the scribes may have been influenced by a version of the poem which is not available to us today.

Type C. This category also comprises quatrains which have been added to the original manuscript draft of a poem, but they are quatrains which may once have been part of another poem or another narrative. One such quatrain has been added to the *Book of the Dean* text of a ballad which describes a great hunt which was held by the Fian on Sliabh na mBan bhFionn (Slievenamon, a mountain in Co. Tipperary). This is No. V in HP^1 and HP^2. In the ballad, Oisín recounts to Patrick how the Fian warriors fared in the hunt. He rejoices in the splendid equipment of the warriors, the prowess of the hounds, and the extent of the prey, but he also refers to the slaughter of a large number of dogs by the boars which were roused in the course of the hunt. The hunters kill the boars, and this concludes what Oisín regards as the greatest hunt of the Fian. The poem is then formally 'closed' in the manuscript, but immediately after the *dúnadh* the scribes add the following quatrain:

Do b'iomadh laoch fuileach fiar	'Many a blood-stained warrior was lying toppled-over
air mullach shiar Sléibhe Crot,	on the western summit of Sliabh gCrot,
gan ach iall a choin 'na láimh	with only the leash of his hound in his hand

---

49 Q. 40 in HP^1, and q. 41 in HP^2. The scribes wish to move it to follow q. 35 in HP^1, and q. 34 in HP^2.

air an t-sliabh ō ár nan
dtorc.[50]

      there on the mountain after
      the slaughter caused by
      the boars.'

There is clear evidence that the scribes had indicated the position of this quatrain within their first draft, but the insertion mark cannot now be located.[51]

In the later versions of this poem, the 'Sliabh gCrot quatrain' is found only on the Scottish side. In Duncan Kennedy's First Collection, it occurs as the penultimate verse of the poem, where it takes the following form:

Biomad laoch fuileachdach fial,
Na sheasamh air sliabh Innse-crot,
Gu'n ach iall a choin na laimh,
'S e pilleadh o ár nan torc.[52]

The occurrence of this quatrain solely in Scottish tradition would suggest that it is a textual development which has taken place in Scotland, and it may well be true that its addition to the text of the Slievenamon ballad should be seen in this light. However, it is apparent that the quatrain preserves the name of a place which lies only a few miles west of Slievena-

50   The transliteration of this quatrain follows the editorial method of *HP*[2], which seeks to get as close as possible to the original manuscript text. The quatrain is not noted in *HP*[1].

51   The scribes place the letter *a* in the left-hand margin beside the quatrain, and presumably there was also an *a* inserted in the margin of the original draft, at the appropriate point.

52   The quatrain is reproduced from Campbell, *op. cit.*, 143-4. Some changes which are evident in the later form of the quatrain are worth noting. In line a, *fiar* becomes *fial* by *l/r* dissimilation. In line b, the first element in *Sléibhe Crot* is replaced by *Innse* (genitive sg. of *innis*, 'island'), and *sliabh* is substituted for *siar*, thus enabling it to accommodate the more common Scottish Gaelic sense of 'moor' rather than 'mountain'. A verbal construct is introduced to the line in the form *Na sheasamh*. Line c remains as in the earlier version. In line d, a verbal form *pilleadh* is also introduced. In both lines b and d, the verbal forms replace locational noun phrases, and their effect is to present the warriors as living rather than dead: 'Many a generous blood-shedding warrior was standing on the moor/upland of Innis-crot, with only the leash of his dog in his hand as he returned from the slaughter of the boars'.

mon itself. Sliabh gCrot is evidently to be equated with Mount Grud, on the northern edge of the Galtee Mountains, and on the southern side of the Glen of Aherlow.[53] We might therefore conclude that the quatrain has been added by a composer with a knowledge of the area, and that its aim is to extend the scope of the hunt.

The picture is rather more complex, since Sliabh gCrot is known as the focus of another hunt which is commemorated in a ballad called 'Seilg Sléibhe gCrot'. This ballad has survived only in Irish tradition. It relates how the Fian attend a feast given by Aonghas an Bhrogha, and after taunts about the capability of their dogs in a hunt, the Fian warriors depart. They prepare for a hunt on several mountains, including Sliabh gCrot, and Aonghas, as he has promised, sends a great herd of boars against them. The Fian dogs kill all the boars, and Bran kills the largest of the herd, which turns out to be Aonghas's son in disguise. The venom of the boars is such that the Fian lose ten hundred of their warriors.[54]

The 'Sliabh gCrot quatrain' does not correspond directly to any verse in the existing texts of 'Seilg Sléibhe gCrot', but it appears to refer to the general circumstances. The Slievenamon ballad mentions only the death of hounds by the boars, not the death of warriors, and it is possible that the 'Sliabh gCrot quatrain' belonged originally to another ballad which told much the same story about the hunt involving Aonghas's boars. The quatrain may have been attracted to the Slievenamon poem by the general similarity of theme and location in both items. The survival of this one quatrain may imply the atrophy of a larger text,[55] and it is significant that it has been preserved by becoming attached to another poem which was presumably more popular than the one to which it originally belonged. This pattern of development, involving the detaching of verses from their proper context and their attachment to other ballads, becomes very noticeable after 1600.

53 Hogan, *op. cit.*, 607, s.v. *sliab crott*.
54 An Seabhac, *op. cit.*, 113-7.
55 It may be relevant that Kennedy's text contains a further additional quatrain (q. 11) describing the prey killed by Bran; see Campbell, *op. cit.*, 143-4.

Post-Classical Ballad Versions

It has already been argued that the emendations which are
made to ballad texts in the *Book of the Dean of Lismore*
should be seen as part of a process of textual development
which antedates the *Book of the Dean*, and which is integral
to the ballad tradition. In the period after the compilation of
the *Book of the Dean of Lismore*, the texts continue to be
adjusted, and all three types of alteration which are found in
this manuscript are attested.

In the post-classical phase, however, changes take place in
the texts according to principles which differ somewhat from
those which are in force in the earlier period. While the *Book
of the Dean* contains many instances in which vernacular
forms have ousted classical forms in the language of the texts,
such alterations become more noticeable in the later period
as a knowledge of Classical Common Gaelic declines, and the
poems increasingly become the property of transmitters who
have little or no familiarity with the standards of the classical
composers.[56] With the decay and ultimate collapse of the
bardic schools, the knowledge and use of syllabic verse fell
into sharp decline, and it is not unusual to find verses in
stressed metre which have found their way into ballad texts.[57]
The urge to refashion, and particularly to amplify, the texts
becomes especially marked in the years after 1760, following
the publication of James ('Ossian') Macpherson's 'translations'.
While some ballad texts remain remarkably well preserved
until the second half of the nineteenth century or later, it is
more common to encounter versions which have been reshaped
in some way, occasionally grotesquely.

Before examining some of the adjustments characteristic
of the later tradition, we need to consider a development
which we may have glimpsed only fleetingly in the *Book of
the Dean of Lismore* when discussing alterations found in
Type C — namely the attenuation of ballad texts, and their

---

56 Cf. McCaughey, *op. cit.*, 48-9, 54-5. The extent of vernacular
    influence on the language of the ballads in the *Book of the Dean of
    Lismore* will be discussed in the published form of HP^2.

57 This is particularly noticeable in some of Duncan Kennedy's texts,
    for instance.

demise. This process of attentuation is attested, I think, in the case of the ballad about 'Caoilte and the Animals'. We noted that the version in *Duanaire Finn*, compiled a century or so after the *Book of the Dean of Lismore*, contains a mere 29 quatrains compared with 72 quatrains in the earlier text. The greatest reduction in the ballad appears to have taken place in the catalogue of animal pairs. This may reflect a change in taste on the part of Gaelic society after, say, 1550; or it may be that elaborate catalogues involving 'specialised' knowledge of this sort may have appealed much less to the audiences and transmitters who fostered the ballad texts in the post-classical period. This ballad does, in fact, disappear after 1627, and its demise may have been hastened by its unexciting story-line. Ballads which lack a strong, cohesive plot tend not to be well preserved in later tradition, and may suffer a severe reduction in size. For instance, the poems of debate between Oisín and Patrick which are found in very full versions in the *Book of the Dean of Lismore* (Nos. XIX and XX in HP^1, and Nos. X and XI in HP^2) are much shorter in their post-1700 forms, and tend to survive by attaching themselves to larger ballad texts, or by forming concatenations according to theme. While we can observe the attentuation and demise of ballad texts most clearly in the post-classical period, it seems likely that this process was normal even within the most creative phase of the tradition between 1200 and 1600, and that it extended also to well-turned narrative ballads which had become unacceptable for one reason or another.[58]

In the later tradition, we have several examples of ballads attested in the *Book of the Dean* which undergo some elaboration or expansion of text. These are usually narrative ballads, and the extent of elaboration varies. I suspect that one factor which influenced such modification was the relative popularity of the texts; some ballads which are known to have been popular have accumulated much additional detail and incident. In Ireland, the Slievenamon poem is preserved

---

58 The *Book of the Dean* contains six ballads which are not attested in later tradition. These may have dropped out of currency, or it may be that they are simply not recorded in existing manuscripts.

much as it stands in *Duanaire Finn* (No. LVIII), but in Scotland it develops another quatrain besides that about Sliabh gCrot.[59] In both countries, the poem about the Fian warriors' adventures at Eas Ruaidh does not develop much beyond the point represented by the emended text in the *Book of the Dean of Lismore*, but the popularity of this ballad may have encouraged the composition of other narrative poems about invaders who come to challenge the Fian. A more exuberant and uncontrolled type of textual expansion is attested in the case of another ballad which is found in the *Book of the Dean*, and also describes the appearance of an intriguing lady. This is the ballad known as 'The Girl with the Mantle' (No. VII in *HP*[1] and *HP*[2]), which evidently enjoyed great popularity in Ireland, and is frequently found in later Irish collections.[60] The version in the *Book of the Dean of Lismore* contains 21 quatrains, and the ballad is distinguished for its particularly deft articulation and spicy humour. The lady who comes to visit the Fian has a magic cloak which is able to test the faithfulness of the wives of the Fian warriors. Having boasted about their chastity, six of the Fian women are compelled to wear the mantle, with revealing results. Only the wife of Mac Reithe passes the test with any seemliness. The ribald mischief of the ballad appears to have appealed widely, and this appeal is probably reflected in the growth of the text. While the version in *Duanaire Finn* (No. LXV) has only 19 quatrains, nineteenth-century texts are regularly twice the length of the version in the *Book of the Dean of Lismore*,[61] and one late text extends to 130 quatrains![62]

59   See note 55.

60   This ballad is not represented in any collection made in Scotland after the *Book of the Dean*, although it is found in manuscripts of Irish provenance which have been brought into Scotland; see A. MacBain and J. Kennedy, eds., *Reliquiae Celticae*, Vol. 1, Inverness 1892, 116-8. For a recent discussion of the background to the poem, see W. Gillies, 'Arthur in Gaelic Tradition: Part I: Folktales and Ballads', in *Cambridge Medieval Celtic Studies* 2 (Winter 1981), 64-6.

61   See, for example, F.N. Robinson, 'A Variant of the Gaelic "Ballad of the Mantle"', in *Modern Philology* 1 (1903), 145-52, where a version with 46 quatrains is given.

62   An Seabhac, *op. cit.*, 81-92.

The expansion of the text is achieved by increasing the amount of dialogue between the warriors and their wives, and by repeating details of the testing process. The overall structure of the later versions preserves relatively few of the *deibhidhe* quatrains of the original poem, and metrical atrophy is much in evidence in the more recent verses.[63] The growth of this text is extreme, but not untypical of the changes which can occur in ballad versions in the post-classical period, and which, in this instance at least, can scarcely be said to improve the plot or structure of the earliest extant text of the poem.

Narrative ballads in later tradition can expand their texts not only by increasing and duplicating incidents, but by coming together to form conglomerate poems of considerable size. This tends to happen in the manner of the 'Sliabh gCrot quatrain' discussed above, with the confusion or assimilation of ballads on similar themes. In Irish ballad collections, for instance, a lengthy sequence entitled 'Tuarasgabháil Chatha Gabhra' ('The Account of the Battle of Gabhair') is commonly found.[64] This sequence tells the story of the last great battle of the Fian, in which they were cut down by Cairbre Lifeachair, and it is evident that it draws on, and synthesises, no less than four poems which are attested in the *Book of the Dean of Lismore* (Nos. XIX, XX, XXII and XXIII in *HP*[1], and Nos. X, XI, XXI and XXII in *HP*[2]).[65] There, the

---

63 The majority of additional verses in Robinson's edition (see note 61) are in a poor form of *rannaigheacht mhór* which tends to move towards regular stress in certain lines. Some of the earlier verses, originally in *deibhidhe*, are also being refashioned in this form of *rannaigheacht*. Cf. Breatnach, *op. cit.*, 18.

64 For discussion of the background to Gabhair, see D.E. Meek, 'Y Frwydr Olaf yn Nhraddodiad y "Fian" ', in *Ysgrifau Beirniadol* 13 (1985), 209-18.

65 See, for instance, O'Kearney, *op. cit.*, 68-133. The first pair of poems consists of an anti-clerical tirade by Oisín, and a debate between Oisín and Patrick; a promise by Oisín to provide stories about Gabhair in exchange for those about the Heavenly City (in the second poem) forms the link with the second pair, both of which are about the battle. The first of the Gabhair poems, spoken by Fearghus File, describes the bravery of Osgar in the manner of a

four poems are found in two pairs, with the pairs separated from one another. In the pairing of the poems in this manuscript, there may already be a feeling that poems on similar topics ought to be brought together, and that the separate items of narrative verse, so characteristic of the Finn Cycle, should somehow fit into a wider sequential frame. The attempt to form such a frame, as we see it in *Acallam na Senórach* in the twelfth century, or in the 'translations' of James Macpherson in the eighteenth, is possibly the greater manifestation of the urge to create, and to recreate, the tradition as exemplified in the ballads which we have discussed in this paper.

Conclusion

The treatment of ballad texts in the *Book of the Dean of Lismore* is of great importance to our understanding of the development of the Gaelic ballad tradition. The methodology of its scribes, untidy and perplexing as it may be, gives us a unique opportunity to observe the modification and growth of certain ballad texts at the close of the Middle Ages. What we observe to be happening by the mid-sixteenth century provides an insight into what took place before and after that date.

prose-tale 'run'; the second poem, which is much longer and more ambitious, gives details of his sufferings and heroism as he lies dying on the battlefield.

FENIAN HEROES AND THEIR RITES OF PASSAGE*

JOSEPH FALAKY NAGY
(University of California, Los Angeles)

In the study of Indo-European heroic traditions, scholars have tended to invest a good deal of energy in the search for the divine roots of the heroes on whom the traditions are centred. In the history of scholarship on the Fenian tales, however, this tendency to look for so-called 'mythological' resonances has created something of an impasse in the development of our understanding of this rich and long-lived tradition. The implicit and explicit distinctions that have been drawn between the supposedly archaic or mythological elements and the supposedly late or folk elements of *fiannaíocht* have acted in the main to thwart the posing of important questions about the significance of the Finn-tales as they have thrived down to recent times. Such artificially drawn distinctions, furthermore, have impeded scholarly appreciation of the thematic consistencies that mark the Fenian tradition from its earliest appearances in Old-Irish literature to stories collected from still-living informants. An unduly neglected observation, first enunciated by Marie-

*I am grateful to Alan Bruford, Angela Bourke, Michael Herity, Terence McCaughey and Dáithí Ó hÓgáin for their illuminating comments on this paper.

161

Louise Sjoestedt many years ago,[1] is that the Fenian cycle dwells on the theme of transformation or transition — that is, on the nature of passage between opposed states or categories. With the re-application and development of this observation, we can re-integrate the elements of the tradition previously dismantled by scholars in search of the archaic, as well as interpret these narratives within their historically evolving cultural context, instead of merely excavating them.

If we accept the conclusion arrived at by many folklorists that the central subject of heroic tale — if not of storytelling in general — is the process of social maturation, then the particular bent of the Fenian tradition as mentioned above may no longer seem particular. But it is the emphasis put by the tradition itself on the various modes of transition (not only that between childhood and adulthood) and the emphasis on the polarized structures within which these transitions take place — and out of which these same transitions can lead — it is these pervasive emphases in the stories about Finn and his band of men, the *fían*, that make the Fenian cycle distinctive within the Irish traditional narrative system and that, from a psychological point of view, help us to explain the fascination these stories have held for generation after generation of storytellers and their audiences. The adventures of Finn and his companions, dubbed by Sjoestedt 'heroes outside the tribe', are played out in zones beyond the civilized pale, or between the human and the supernatural pales. It is to this 'neither-world' that the *fénnidi* or hunter-warrior heroes

---

1   Marie-Louise Sjoestedt, *Gods and Heroes of the Celts*, trans. M. Dillon, London 1949, 81-91 (see also C. Ramnoux, 'The Finn Cycle: The Symbols of a Celtic Legend', *The Crane Bag* 2 [1978], 80-88 [repr. from *The Joyce Yearbook*, ed. Marie Jolas, Paris 1947. 'The *fíana* constitute a society independent of tribal society and resting on a basis, not of family or territory, but of initiation' (Sjoestedt, *op. cit.*, 90). More recent explorations of the 'liminality' of the Fenians and other Irish warrior-heroes are K. McCone's article '*Aided Cheltchair Maic Uthechair*: Hounds, Heroes and Hospitallers in Early Irish Myth and Story', *Ériu* 35 (1984), 1-30, and the author's *The Wisdom of the Outlaw: The Boyhood Deeds of Finn in Gaelic Narrative Tradition*, Berkeley and Los Angeles 1985.

featured in *fiannaíocht* gravitate: here they prove themselves, are accepted into the *fían*, and in most cases live out the rest of their heroic lives. Nowhere is this syndrome more overwhelmingly demonstrated than in the late medieval text *Cath Finntrágha*,[2] 'The Battle of Ventry', which features a seemingly unending succession of promising youths who venture forth to Ventry Bay to participate in a battle of cosmic proportions being waged by Finn and his *fían* against supernatural invaders from across the sea.

The passages achievable by means of the larger-than-life rituals of Fenian heroism depend upon the activities of fighting and hunting, the cornerstones of *fénnidecht* − that is, life in the *fían*. Let us recall that the words *fían* and *fénnid* derive from the Indo-European root that also gives us Latin *vēnāri*, 'to hunt', and English *win*.[3] In many cultures, hunting and warring in the wilderness constitute the designated vocation of the young male on the verge of manhood. For example, the youthful bachelor of the ancient Greek city-state (as described by Pierre Vidal-Naquet)[4] was in theory required to spend a certain amount of time in the outlands, living by means of hunting and raiding. The world of the young hunter-brigand, an adult in the making, is explored in a complex of Greek myths that includes the tales of Orion, Aktaion, Adonis, and Atalanta. The ideology behind this sub-mythology was summarized by Marcel Detienne thus:

> Situated at the intersection of the powers of life and the forces of death, the hunter's space constitutes at once that which is beyond the farmer's fields and their negation. Choice haunt of the powers of savagery, the domain open to the hunter belongs exclusively to the male sex ... Forbidden to girls and traversed by boys before they accede to the status of warriors and adults, the hunter's

---

2 Cecile O'Rahilly, ed., Medieval and Modern Irish Series (= MMIS) 20, Dublin 1962.

3 K. Meyer, *Fianaigecht*, RIA Todd Lecture Series (= RIA Todd Lect.) 16, Dublin 1910, vi; Sjoestedt, *op. cit.*, 82; *pace* H. Wagner, 'Beiträge zur vergleichenden Erforschung des Irischen', *Celtica* 11 (1976), 264-5.

4 *Le chasseur noir. Formes de pensée et formes de société dans le monde grec*, Paris 1981, 125-207.

terrain is not simply the negation of the farmer's fields and of the enclosed space of the home. It also constitutes a space outside of marriage that welcomes deviant forms of sexuality or those that are simply considered strange by the city-state ... As a liminal space where socially dominant sexual relations are as if suspended, the land of the hunt is open to the subversion of amorous pursuits, whatever their process or modality.[5]

Thus the initiand of Greek tradition, whatever missteps he seems to take, is ultimately hunting for his adulthood.

Our Irish evidence suggests a similar thrust to the institution of *fénnidecht*. According to an Old-Irish mirror for princes, the *Tecosca Cormaic*, 'Instructions of Cormac', everyone is a *fénnid* until he obtains a household (*fénnid cách co trebad*).[6] This adage is fleshed out elsewhere in medieval literature — for instance, in the story of how the druid Cathbad, while a *fénnid*, sired the great Ulster king Conchobar.[7] Cathbad's *fénnidecht* is terminated as soon as the father of the girl whom Cathbad has taken by force recognizes the *fénnid* as his son-in-law and grants him land. The rape of Conchobar's mother, committed in the setting of the wilderness, underscores an aberrant and dangerous sexuality associated with *fénnidecht* — a violation of sexual norms comparable to what we find in the world of the mythical Greek hunter. It is worth noting that in Highland legendry recorded not so long ago, the hunter's terrain is still the haunt of violent and sexual terrors, in the persons of the *glaistig* and other dangerous wild females sinisterly interested in hunters and their hunting.[8]

5 Mireille Muellner and L. Muellner, trans., *Dionysos Slain*, Baltimore and London 1979, 24-6. Another important recent study of hunting myths in Greek tradition is J. Fontenrose's *Orion: The Myth of the Hunter and the Huntress*, University of California Publications in Classical Studies 23, Berkeley 1981.

6 K. Meyer, ed. and trans., *The Instructions of King Cormac mac Airt*, RIA Todd Lect. 15, Dublin 1909, 46, §31.10.

7 K. Meyer, ed. and trans., 'Anecdota from the Stowe MS. no. 992', *Revue Celtique* (= *RC*) 6 (1883-5), 173-82; see also W. Stokes, ed. and trans., 'Tidings of Conchobar mac Nessa', *Ériu* 4 (1910), 22-3.

8 See J. MacDougall, coll. and G. Calder, ed., *Highland Fairy Legends*, Edinburgh 1910; repr. Ipswich 1978, 56-69, 75-6.

That the freedom theoretically enjoyed by hunters inevitably creates conflicts between the devotees of the hunt and members of society is illustrated picturesquely in a Hiberno-Latin poem preserved in the seventh-century *Hisperica Famina*:

> Once upon a time, leagues ago in the whirlpool of the years / When Phoeban dawn was flashing in the East, / a certain rampaging band of armed brigands / approached the outer boundaries of an enemy land. / At that time, while traversing the blue crests of the hills in hurried course, / they noticed among the groves a herd of bristly pigs. / Then a certain powerful chieftain with his iron lance / pierced the hairy flanks of a thick boar / and with skilful movement / twisted the broad neck from the corse dripping with gore. / Appointed men hewed a large olive tree with their swords, / struck the flintstone with hard metal, / made a fire with dry tinder, / and the fire-belching oven sent smoke through the leafy forest. / Then a square gridiron was made from crossed spits, / and they roasted the bristly flesh in the red flames / and attached the raw flesh to wooden stakes. / Purple drops of liquid gore fell among the sticks, / and the brigands tasted roasted morsels of the fleshy mass / and swilled the porky fodder down their throats. / Then the native inhabitants of that land / busily began to fortify the outer boundaries of their native soil, / lest a hostile attack prevail over their ancestral ploughfields. / And now traversing the familiar bypaths of their boundary-land, / they espied the aforesaid band of brigands among the oaks of the forest. / Then the leafy woodland resounded with the onrushing horde, / and instantly the audacious troop cried out / that no survivors of their force would escape from the cruel slaughter / before the savage claw of birds would bear them into the sky. / Next the raging leaders drew tight their battle lines / and turned their armed faces against the archers. / White stone is shot into the sky, / cruel darts penetrate alternately; / the aforesaid darts pierce meaty limbs, / and rivers of purple wind through fleshy flanks. / Enormous giants rush forward in battle / and sever round heads with their swords. / When the savage band

of robbers broke the attacking phalanx with the strength of their fighting, / they stripped the dead bodies of their clothing / and heartlessly rejoiced with terrible shouts. / Then retreating to their home soil on a backward course / the natives poured out a wealth of tales.[9]

We have here in effect a *fían*-tableau that corresponds to the portrait of *latrunculi* in the Irish saints' lives which was so artfully pieced together by Richard Sharpe.[10] Occasionally in these lives, as in the *Hisperica Famina* poem, the world of the hunter-brigands is evoked not only by scenes of extra-social violence but also by allusions to their particular lifestyle. Here is an example from *Adomnán's Life of Columba* in which we perhaps have a clue as to the culinary habits of the *fíana*:

> At another time, the saint came to the island of Hinba. And on that day he ordered that some indulgence in food should be allowed, even to the penitents. There was among the penitents there one Neman, Cather's son, who refused to take at the saint's bidding the proffered consolation. Him the saint addressed in these words: 'Neman, you do not accept an indulgence in diet that I and Baithene have granted. The time will come when in a wood, with thieves (*cum furacibus*), you will chew the flesh of a stolen mare.' And so afterwards, when he had returned to the world, this same man was discovered, according to the saint's word, in a forest pasture with thieves, consuming such flesh taken from a wooden griddle.[11]

It is within this cultural understanding of hunting and its exponents that we must view the stories about Finn and his *fían*. Whether or not this understanding was based upon ethnographic reality, and whether there actually were *fénnidi*, are questions we cannot answer now. But it is important to note

9 M.W. Herren, ed. and trans. *The Hisperica Famina. I. The A-Text*, Toronto 1974, 110-3.

10 'Hiberno-Latin *Laicus*, Irish *Láech* and The Devil's Men', *Ériu* 30 (1979), 75-92.

11 A. Orr Anderson and Marjorie Ogilvie Anderson, ed. and trans., *Adomnan's Life of Columba*, London 1961, 251-3 (I.21).

that the *fénnid* of the Fenian tradition is marked by a dramatic paradox. Finn, the leader of the *fían* and the conductor of its members' lives, is perennially engaged in the business of making men out of boys; ironically, but perhaps not inappropriately, Finn himself is a chronic youth playing the role of an adult (as in the boyhood deeds cycle), or, conversely, an aging adult attempting to relive his youth (as in the story of Diarmaid and Gráinne). For Finn and the other charter members of the *fían*, transitions are reversible. Perhaps for this reason, in the Fenian cycle we find outcast dwellers in the wilderness who despite their non-person status *vis-à-vis* society, evoke awe and are allowed to enter freely either of the worlds which flanks theirs: the world of Ireland ruled by a high-king, or the world of the *sídh*. The Cailte of the *Acallam na Senórach*, 'Colloquy with the Ancients', yearns for the old Fenian life and still attempts to live it, functioning as a reverse psychopomp who in some episodes can literarily revive the old memories.[12] Yet, despite this implicit rejection of the present and its conventions (a rejection that is made explicit in later strands of the tradition that emphasize Oisín over Cailte),[13] the old Fenian warrior, a representative of the narrative cycle that created him, is embraced by the representative of the new, Patrick, and welcomed in both human and supernatural households. Surely the conceit of Cailte and Oisín's living on into the Christian epoch is no mere convenient contrivance of a medieval anthologist eager to cast an acceptable frame for Fenian lore, but rather the natural development of a truth tested over and over again in Fenian narrative: that transition is transcendence, that to pass from one category into another gives the passenger at least the momentary chance to be freed from categorization altogether. Cailte and Oisín transcend time and are neither of the past nor of the present, just as they are neither old nor young in the conventional

12   The theme of the long-lived or revived hero is discussed in Nagy, 'Close Encounters of the Traditional Kind in Medieval Irish Literature', *Celtic Folklore and Christianity: Studies in Memory of William W. Heist*, ed. P.K. Ford, Santa Barbara and Los Angeles 1983, 129-49.
13   See Pádraig Ó Fiannachta's paper, 'The Development of the Debate between Patrick and Oisín' below.

senses of those terms. In this respect, they are like the narrative tradition itself, which in its seeming imperviousness to change obliterates the impression of the passage of time, and so it is not surprising that these two Irish Rip Van Winkles are emblematic within the *Acallam* not only of Fenian narrative lore but of lore in general. It is the transcendent aspect of transition that predominates in *fiannaíocht* as a whole, not just in the *Acallam*, which so spectacularly renders the Fenian tradition (and the lives of its two Fenian heroes) open-ended. Most Fenian heroes s t a y within the *fían* instead of completing their life-transitions, or they die while in the *fían*, thus achieving a kind of immortality through Fenian commemoration. If the tradition were to allow them to grow up — that is, leave the society of the *fían* and rejoin their r e a l societies — the tradition itself would disappear, and the magic of ever-continuing transition would vanish. Understandably, we hear far more about how heroes entered the *fían* and continually reaffirmed their membership in it through acts of valor and cunning, than about how they left it. But of course this unnatural retention leads to a contradiction, and the freedom of the *fían* occasionally gives way to a disquieting stability: in some texts, Finn is just another lord of another retinue and is even more oppressive than the masters of the real world. The Fenian tradition and the heroes that populate it attempt to maintain a delicate balance between fluidity and fixity; nothing and no one can be completed, but the resulting incompleteness must not become a restriction in itself.

The delicacy of the premise and the promise of the Fenian tradition is well expressed in a description of Fenian initiation tests which is preserved in a medieval text, *Áirem Muintiri Finn*, 'An Account of Finn's Band', and which was more or less incorporated by Keating into his famous account of the *fían* in the first Book of his *History of Ireland*.[14] I quote from O'Grady's edition of the *Áirem* (from Ms. Egerton 1782):

14 G. Keating, *Foras Feasa ar Éirinn: History of Ireland*, Vol. 2, ed. and trans. P.S. Dinneen, Irish Texts Society (= ITS) 9, London 1908, 332-4.

Ní gabtái fer díb so co mbo rífili dá leabar déc na filidhechta. ní gabtha fer díb fós co nderntái latharlog mór co roiched fillidh a uathróigi. ocus no chuirthe (*sic*) ann é ocus a sciath les ocus fad láime do chronn chuill. [ocus nó]nbar [lae]ch iar sin chuigi co nái sleguib leo ocus deich [n]imuiri atturru co ndibruigidís i nóinfecht é. ocus dá ngontai thairis sin é ní gabtai a bfianoigecht.

Ní gabtái fós fer díb so co nderntái fuiltfighi fair ocus go cuirthi trí feduib Erenn ina rith é co tigdísim uili ina diaid ar eiccill a gona. ocus ní bídh aturro acht in craeb do ega. dá rugta fair do gontai é ocus ní gabthai iar sin. da crithnaidhidís a airm ina láimh ní gabtai. dá tucad craeb isin choill ní dá fholt as a fhige ní mó no ghabtai. dá minaigedh crand crín fá a chois ní gabtái. mina lingedh tar crann bud comard r[e a] édan ocus mina cromad fó cradd bu[d coma]r[d] rena glún ní gabtai é. ocus mina tucad in dealg as a chois dá ingin gan toirm[esc] a retha uime ní gabtai a bfianaigecht é. ocus dá ndernadh sin uili fa do muir Finn é.[15]

15 S.H. O'Grady, ed. and trans., *Silva Gadelica*, London 1892, Vol. 1, 92-3. '... Not a man was taken until he were a prime poet versed in the twelve books of poesy. No man was taken till in the ground a large hole had been made (such as to reach the fold of his belt) and he put into it with his shield and a forearm's length of a hazel stick. Then must nine warriors, having nine spears, with a ten furrows' width betwixt them and him, assail him and in concert let fly at him. If past that guard of his he were hurt then, he was not received into Fianship. Not a man of them was taken till his hair had been interwoven into braids on him and he started at a run through Ireland's woods; while they, seeking to wound him, followed in his wake, there having been between him and them but one forest bough by way of interval at first. Should he be overtaken, he was wounded and not received into the Fianna after. If his weapons had quivered in his hand, he was not taken. Should a branch in the wood have disturbed anything of his hair out of its braiding, neither was he taken. If he had cracked a dry stick under his foot [as he ran] he was not accepted. Unless that [at his full speed] he had both jumped a stick level with his brow, and stooped to pass under one even with his knee, he was not taken. Also, unless without slackening his pace he could with his nail extract a thorn from his foot, he was not taken into Fianship; but if he performed all this he was of Finn's people.' (trans. O'Grady, *op. cit.*, Vol. 2, 100).

Of the various ways in which we could approach this fascinating passage, let us focus on three. Taken at their face value, these are rites of initiation, and as such they follow the procedure of such rituals as they have been analyzed by anthropologists.[16] Central to these Fenian tests is the principle of inversion: the future hunter, the *fían* initiate, is ritually transformed into game, forced to demonstrate mobility in the hunt and agility when trapped in a pit. Another characteristic of initiation ritual that is present in the Fenian tests is an insistence on precise performance even in small matters of detail: the candidate must see to it that the weapons he holds in his hands do not move at all, that not a single braid of hair is loosened, and that removing a thorn from his foot causes no delay. It is worth noting, however, that, unlike most real rites of passage, this Fenian exercise in the symbolism of locomotion appears to have no goal or termination, as if the *fían* initiate were to be pursued, and his pursuers were to chase him, forever. Thus the tradition presents us here with another emblem of the open-endedness of Fenian destiny: the end of the process of passage is virtually lost sight of, and the state of inbetweenness consequently receives codification as the *status quo* for the Fenian hero.

This analysis moves us onto a second level of interpretation. These Fenian rituals can also be viewed as non-narrative distillations of the narrative situations of racing and entrapment that pervade Fenian tales throughout their recorded history. In a popular variant of the story of how Finn received his name, a tale recorded in both medieval literature and oral tradition, the youthful hero's naming is a prelude to desperate pursuit: Finn is chased by his enemies but escapes

---

16 See A. van Gennep, *The Rites of Passage*, trans. Monika B. Vizedom and Gabrielle L. Caffee, Chicago 1960, and C. Lévi-Strauss, *The Naked Man. Introduction to a Science of Mythology (Mythologiques) 4*, trans. J. Weightman and Doreen Weightman, New York 1981, 667-75. Pádraig Ó Riain examines ritual reflexes in Irish literature (including this account of Fenian initiation and the tale of Mis, analyzed below) in his article 'A Study of the Irish Legend of the Wild Man', *Éigse* 14 (1982), 179-206.

from them unharmed.[17] We read in the invaluable twelfth-century text *Macgnímartha Finn*, 'The Boyhood Deeds of Finn', that the hero's being accepted into his mentor's *fían* is predicated upon his being able to keep up with the mentor during a spectacular race across Ireland. Finn's task is made all the more difficult by his determination to pick up leaden balls that the mentor drops in order to slow down his mercurial charge.[18] We are of course reminded of another mythical race, that of Atalanta and Melanion (or Hippomenes) in Greek tradition. For this savage huntress to pick up the golden apples dropped by her suitor in the course of their race is to enter the state of matrimony. Yet the marriage of Atalanta, in which the rules of god and man are shockingly violated, is after all a marriage of hunters, which in the eyes of society is no marriage at all. According to Apollodorus, the huntress and her hunter-bridegroom are transformed after their licentious honeymoon into lions (*Library* III.ix.2).[19] In all these narrative situations, as well as in the Fenian rites of passage, a manhunt in the wilderness does not lead prey or pursuer out of the forest; instead, it takes them even deeper into a realm that reflects society and its rules in a distorted way: this realm in Irish tradition is the world of Finn and his *fían*.

In the popular folktale commonly referred to as 'Finn and the Big Man', the famed swiftness and agility of the Fenians are put to use in the playing of games, in which the naive visiting giant is tricked into participating, to his ultimate detriment.[20] And so the tradition directs us to another aspect of the Fenian tests. They are not only rituals and meta- or

---

17   E. MacNeill, ed. and trans., *Duanaire Finn: The Book of the Lays of Fionn*, Part I, ITS 7, London 1908, 33-4; see also S. Ó Súilleabháin, *A Handbook of Irish Folklore*, Dublin 1942, 589.

18   Ed. and trans. K. Meyer, *RC* 5 (1882), 204.

19   Ed. and trans. J.G. Frazer, 2 vols. London 1921, Vol. I, 398-403. Other references to Atalanta in classical literature are noted by Frazer. I am indebted to Detienne's discussion of the ideological implications of this myth (*op. cit.*, 25-35, 40-52).

20   E.g. S. O'Sullivan, *The Folklore of Ireland*, New York 1974, 39; see Nagy, *op. cit.* (1985), 193-207, and Ó Súilleabháin, *op. cit.*, 590.

infra-narrative constructs; they are also games, Fenian recreations of their curious plight that are carried out in a spirit of deadly competition. There is in fact reference made in medieval Irish legal literature to a category of play known as *fianchluichi*, '*fian*-games', which are deemed most appropriate for youths and/or, presumably, those bereft of social rights and responsibilities, such as *fénnidi*.[21] It is unclear what precisely these *fian*-games are, but they are perhaps akin to the rough sports played by Finn in an episode of the *Boyhood Deeds* text in which he savagely trounces a group of boys he meets on the edge of settled territory. According to this account, it is Finn's defeated playmates who christen him.[22] Like the games played by members of the Ulster boy-troop with the young Cú Chulainn, another hero in another cycle,[23] the matches between Finn and the boys establish both identity and hierarchy. But in the Fenian tradition, the hierarchy generated and affirmed by such competition lies outside the ken of society proper. The *fian* initiate who emerges victorious from his race against pursuing *fénnidi* and is then received into the ranks of the hunting-party is expressing his alienation from society by engaging in these forbidden games.

The historian Keating, who incorporates this account of the Fenian rites of passage into his description of the life of Finn and his men, also includes a lengthy account of another set of Fenian activities,[24] seemingly more mundane than the momentous acts by which young man becomes Fenian hero. While this other set of activities may not seem on the surface to be either ritualistic or playful, it is, I suggest, as redolent of key Fenian themes as are the overt rites of passage we have just examined. The pit in which the *fénnid* is seasoned at the beginning of his career with a shower of spears, has its counterpart in the everyday life of the *fian*, as described by Keating.

21 D.A. Binchy, '*Mellbretha*', *Celtica* 8 (1968), 149-54.
22 K. Meyer, *op. cit.* (1882), 199-200. See also MacNeill, *op. cit.*, 33, and Ó Súilleabháin, *op. cit.*, 589.
23 Cecile O'Rahilly, ed. and trans., *Táin Bó Cúailnge: Recension I*, Dublin 1976, lines 418-56, 470-80.
24 Keating, *op. cit.*, 328.

In the course of a long day of hunting, which constituted their livelihood between Beltaine and Samhain, the Fenian warriors, according to Keating, would have only one meal. In the afternoon they sent their gillies with the spoils of the hunt to a hill near moorland. The servants so dispatched would build a fire on top of the hill and dig two pits in the moist earth, into which water would naturally seep. The gillies then heated granite rocks in the fire and piled them into the larger of the two pits, until the water in it boiled. The gillies then roasted some of the meat on spits near the fire, but the rest they tied into bundles and threw into the water of the pit, which was kept on a raging boil with the addition of more hot stones. Meanwhile, the Fenian heroes would arrive at the camp and, as part of this daily procedure, strip and wash themselves in the other pit: *ag buain allais díobh; agus ann sin ag suathadh a lúthach agus a gcuisleann, go gcuirdís amhlaidh sin a dtuirse dhíobh*,[25] 'removing the sweat from their bodies, and massaging their sinews and veins until they had thus relieved themselves of their fatigue.' After their lustrations, the Fenians enjoyed a meal including both roasted and boiled meat. At bedtime they erected their *fianbhotha*,[26] '*fian*-huts' and retired for the night, sleeping on beds made of tree-tips at the bottom, cotton-grass in the middle, and fresh rushes on top. These, Keating tells us, are known in old books as the three tickings of the *fían* (*trí coilceadha na Féine*),[27] and the cooking and washing pits of the *fénnidi* are what the peasantry call the *Fulachta Fian*.[28]

One of the earliest extant references to the *fulachta fían*,[29] burnt-out pits that mark the Irish landscape and continue to

25 *Ibid.*, ll. 5118-20.
26 *Ibid.*, l. 5122,
27 *Ibid.*, l. 5128.
28 *Ibid.*, l. 5113.
29 The archaeological evidence concerning *fulachta fían*, or *fulachta fia(dh)*, is reviewed in S. Ó Ríordáin's *Antiquities of the Irish Countryside*, fifth ed., revised R. de Valera, London and New York 1979, 84-8.

fascinate scholars of early Irish history,[30] adds a strange twist
to the scene painted for us by Keating. In the ninth- or tenth-
century compendium known as *Cormac's Glossary*, we find
the following entry under *esnad: ní nath acht is duchand,
ar ba hesnad ainm in chiuil dignitis na fianae um an bfulacht
fiansae*,[31] 'it is not a poem but a song [or "chant"], for the
name of the music that the *fiana* make around the cooking-
place (*fulacht*) of *fianas* ("*fían*-ship") is *esnad*.' Although the
author of this gloss does not specify the *fiana* or war-bands
who sing the *esnad*-song around the *fulacht* as being those of
Finn mac Cumaill, it is tempting, indeed reasonable, to connect the rugged scene the medieval glossator evokes to that
presented by Keating in the *Foras Feasa ar Éirinn* just para-
phrased. Let us recall that *Cormac's Glossary* does mention
Finn and his men elsewhere,[32] and that unspecific reference
to *fénnidi, fiana*, and *fianas* in medieval literature often
allude to the Fenian tradition, for the Fenian heroes and the
stories about them are emblematic of the life and ethos of
fiana in general.[33] Furthermore, the notion of the Fenian

30 Other references are listed in the Royal Irish Academy *Dictionary
    of the Irish Language* (= *DIL*), Dublin 1913-76, s.v. 1 *fulacht. Fol-
    ach fiann*, 'cache [?] of *fiana*' a term which appears in legal literature
    (*Corpus Iuris Hibernici* (ed. D.A. Binchy), Dublin 1978, Vol. 2,
    395.23; Vol. 3, 892.5; Vol. 4, 1322.1; Vol. 5, 1699.16), is perhaps in
    some cases a corruption of *fulacht fían(sa)* (Binchy, *op. cit.*, Vol. 5,
    1699.19, *fulucht fiannsa* — see *DIL*, sv. 1 *folach* [d]). Also worthy
    of investigation are the *fulacht na Morrígna*, 'cooking-place of
    the Morrígan' and its connection with the Fenian tradition: see
    K. Meyer, ed. and trans., *The Triads of Ireland*, RIA Todd Lect.
    13, Dublin 1906, 16; Nessa Ní Shéaghdha, ed., *Agallamh na Sean-
    órach*, Part II, Baile Átha Cliath 1942, 28-38; D. Hyde, ed. and
    trans., ' "The Cooking of the Great Queen" (*Fulacht na Mórrigna*)',
    Celtic Review 10 (1916), 335-50; D. Mackinnon, ed. and trans.,
    '*Fulacht na Morrigna*', *Celtic Review* 8 (1912), 74-6.
31 K. Meyer, ed., *Sanas Cormaic* (Yellow Book of Lecan version);
    O.J. Bergin *et al*, eds., *Anecdota from Irish Manuscripts*, Halle
    and Dublin 1912, Vol. 4, §562. Cf. the description of the *asnad
    fianso* in the Middle-Irish text *Tochmarc Ailbe*, 'The Wooing of
    Ailbe' edited by R. Thurneysen, *Zeitschrift für celtische Philologie*
    13 (1921), 262, ll. 11-2 (see P. Ó Riain's edition of *Cath Almaine*,
    MMIS 25, Dublin 1978, 49, note on *in dord fiansa*, l. 146).
32 Meyer, *op. cit.* (1912), §1018, 1084.
33 Nagy, *op. cit.* (1985), 41-79.

heroes as musicmakers is not alien to medieval tradition. Indeed, Finn and his men are well known for a peculiar sound that they make as a way of communicating with one another: the *dord fíansa*, 'hum of *fíanas*' or *dord fían*, 'hum of the *fíana*'. *Dord*, 'hum, murmur, low voice or sound', is cognate with Welsh *dwrdd*, 'noise, sound'. In many contexts Irish *dord* is used to describe natural sounds and/or animal noises,[34] but it also refers to a certain kind of human vocalizing, as in *dord fíansa*, the sound of which is said to make listeners fall asleep.[35] As noted by Hull, *andord* — which is *dord* with a negative or intensifying prefix — and *andorddán* (*andord* with a diminutive suffix) occur in various texts in conjunction with two other words signifying similar kinds of nonverbal singing or chanting: *sían* or *síanán*, and *esnad*.[36] For example, in the tale known as *Esnada Tige Buchet*, 'Songs of Buchet's House', the residents of the hospitaller Buchet's house are said to perform *a síanan 7 a n-andord 7 a n-esnam*.[37] Furthermore, the word *dord*, with which the Fenian sound is designated in tradition, is by itself semantically related to *esnad*. The *duchann* mentioned in *Cormac's Glossary* as the performance category to which *esnad* belongs, appears in the compound *muirduchann* 'sea-song' or 'mermaid', which has already been thoroughly examined by Charles Bowen.[38] The *locus classicus* for *muirduchann* is the dindshenchas tradition on Port Láirge.[39] This features the story of the drowning of Roth, who hears

34 *DIL*, s.v. *dord* and the verb *dordaid*.

35 G. Murphy, ed. and trans., *Duanaire Finn*, Part II, ITS 28, London 1933, 206, §8.

36 V. Hull, ed. and trans., *Longes Mac n-Uislenn: The Exile of the Sons of Uisliu*, New York 1949, 96, note on *a n-andord*, l. 101.

37 W. Stokes, ed. and trans. 'The Songs of Buchet's House', *RC* 25 (1904), 32, n. 2 (variant readings from the Bodleian MS. Rawlinson B. 512 and the Yellow Book of Lecan).

38 'Varia I. Notes on the Middle Irish word for "Mermaid" ', *Ériu* 29 (1978), 142-8.

39 W. Stokes, ed. and trans., 'The Rennes Dindshenchas', *RC* 15 (1894), 432-4; E. Gwynn, ed. and trans., *The Metrical Dindshenchas*, Vol. 3, RIA Todd Lect. 19, Dublin 1913, 190-3; W. Stokes, ed. and trans., 'The Bodleian Dinnshenchas', *Folklore* 3 (1892), 489-90.

what is referred as the *dord na murduchann*,[40] 'hum of the mermaid(s)', or 'hum of the sea-song(s)'. Thus both *esnad* and *duchann*, the words with which the glossator designates the *fíana*'s campfire boiling song, bring us back to *dord* and, I would suggest, the Fenian *dord* in particular.

Yet another way of bringing together the Cormac gloss on *esnad* and Keating's description of the *fulacht* is by way of comparison with the tale of the harper Dubh Ruis' wooing of the deranged woman Mis, which is preserved in an eighteenth-century text.[41] Discussed by Mac Cana and Partridge,[42] this narrative, characterized by its editor Ó Cuív as an Irish fore-runner of Freud,[43] offers us a sexually charged variant on Keating's idyllic scene of a Fenian afternoon. The girl Mis, driven insane by the loss of her father, becomes a fleet-footed cannibal in the wilderness. The musician Dubh Ruis sets out to capture her. He goes out into the wilderness with gold and silver as well as his instrument. At a certain spot he strips himself naked and, poised between two mounds of precious metals, plays his harp, producing music that, we are told elsewhere, was enchanting.[44] With this performance he lures Mis out of the wilderness. She asks questions about his harp, the gold, the silver, and finally the musician's exposed member. He invites her to sample his *crann clis*,[45] 'staff of play' = penis, and she does. In his postcoital hunger,

40 Stokes, *op. cit.* (1894), 433; *op. cit.* (1892), 490.
41 B. Ó Cuív, ed., 'The Romance of Mis and Dubh Ruis', *Celtica* 2 (1954), 325-33 (translated by D. Greene in *Great Irish Short Stories*, ed. V. Mercier, New York 1964, 32-6).
42 P. Mac Cana, 'Aspects of the Theme of King and Goddess in Irish Literature', *Études Celtiques* 7 (1956), 370-82; Angela Partridge, 'Wild Men and Wailing Women', *Éigse* 18 (1980-1), 25-37. See also J. Carney, *Studies in Irish Literature and History*, Dublin 1955, 162-4.
43 Ó Cuív, *op. cit.*, 327.
44 *Ibid.*, 325.
45 *Ibid.*, 330.69.

Dubh Ruis asks for some food. Mis runs off and catches a deer, which she brings back and wants to eat raw on the spot. But Dubh Ruis insists that the deer be cooked first, then eaten, and he constructs a *fulacht* along precisely the same lines as the *fulacht* described in Keating.[46] Having boiled the deermeat in the cooking-pit, the musical gourmet serves it to Mis and, after dinner, scrubs her with deer-fat in the warm broth left in the pit. *Chómshuaith snadhmanna a cuirp 7 a cnámha go huile . . . gur bhain srotháin allais aiste amhlaidh san*,[47] 'he rubbed the joints of her body and her bones entirely . . . so that he thus removed the stream of sweat from her.' The phrasing here is similar to that in Keating's description of the therapeutic bath the Fenian heroes enjoy.[48] Finally, Dubh Ruis tucks in Mis, now restored to her senses, on a bed made of the foliage of trees, cotton-grass, and fresh rushes: substances we encountered earlier as the tickings of the *fían*. After a few recuperative months in a makeshift dwelling (*both*)[49] constructed by Dubh Ruis, Mis is brought home and becomes the harper's wife.

Let us draw up an inventory of the parallels. In both Keating's description of the Fenians at rest and the recipe in narrative form for restoring a woman's senses, game is brought to a camp in the wilderness and cooked in a *fulacht*. The meal of the cooked meat is preceded or followed by stripping and a bath in a pit alongside the cooking-pit or in the cooking-pit itself. This washing brings about relaxation and renewal of the body, as well as a removal of the ardor, the sweat, of the day's hunting activities. Finally, rest is sought in a rustic bed consisting of fresh, soft, natural substances.

46 As noted in *ibid.*, 327, n. 4, and Ó Ríordáin, *op. cit.*, 87.
47 Ó Cuív, *op. cit.*, 331.116-9.
48 See above. *Agus do ghabhdaois timcheall an dara luig do luaidh-eamar thuas, ag folcadh a bhfolt agus ag nighe a mball agus ag buain allais díobh; agus ann sin ag suathadh a lúthach agus a gcuisleann, go gcuirdís amhlaidh sin a dtuirse dhíobh* (Keating, *op. cit.*, 328. 5116-20).
49 Ó Cuív, *op. cit.*, 331.125. Interestingly, the *fulacht* sites that have been excavated feature huts adjacent to the cooking-places – like the *fulachta* in Keating and the Mis text (Ó Ríordáin, *op. cit.*, 85-6, 88).

While these parallels can be drawn, we must establish a
rationale for drawing them. Why should we be comparing the
everyday life of *fénnidi* as described by Keating with this
dramatic event in the life of Mis in the first place? The latter
is a once-in-a-lifetime 'rite of passage' for a member of society
gone astray. The treatment of this bereaved woman resembles
other recorded Irish rituals that mark and/or effect transitions,
including the mantic *tarbfheis*, 'bull-feast',[50] and the bestial
Tirconnell inauguration ceremony described by Gerald of
Wales.[51] Indeed, if we accept Mac Cana's thesis that Mis
originally was a sovereignty figure and Dubh Ruis a royal
contender,[52] then we must conclude that their story involves
a pivotal passage for the male as well as the female protagonist.
The Fenian warriors' way of winding down the day, on the
other hand, is a part of their everyday cycle of activities. As I
stated earlier, the mythical life of Finn and his *fían* represents
a perpetual rite of passage, between nature and culture,
between this world and the otherworld, and between adoles-
cence and adulthood. Hence it is not surprising that what for
other narrative characters constitutes a turning point in life
should for the Fenian heroes become a mundane fact of their
chronically liminal life together. The same pattern of actions
— the hunting, the setting up of the *fulacht*, the washing, and
the making of a special rustic bed — constitutes an episode
in the myth of Mis but serves as a template for the myth of
the *fíana* as formulated by Keating.

The correspondence between the two texts, however, is
not complete. There is no sex for the Fenian heroes in the
afternoon, nor, in Keating's account, is any mention made
of musicmaking. But we do have the reference in *Cormac's
Glossary* to the Fenian *esnad* performed during the preparation of the *fulacht*. Therefore, Keating combined with the
medieval gloss gives us almost all the elements of the pattern

50 Eleanor Knott, ed., *Togail Bruidne Da Derga*, MMIS 8, Dublin
    1936, ll. 122-6; M. Dillon, ed., *Serglige Con Culainn*, MMIS 14,
    Dublin 1953, ll. 244-50.
51 J. O'Meara, trans., *The History and Topography of Ireland*, rev. ed.,
    Harmondsworth 1982, §102.
52 Mac Cana, *op. cit.*, 378-82.

that is fully realized in the tale of Mis. Conceivably, the
author of the latter text simply borrowed heavily from
Keating's history, recycling the description of the Fenian
fulacht and the bedding. This explanation would account for
the similarity between those two texts, but it would not
account for the complementarity that emerges between the
Keating description and the Cormac gloss when they are set
alongside the Mis text. I offer the alternative explanation
that a narrative and ritual pattern underlies all three texts:
a traditional pattern by no means limited to these three
examples.

In the Old-Irish telling of the Derdriu story known as the
Longes Mac n-Uislenn,[53] the three heroic sons of Uisliu are
said to have a special musical gift: when they perform *andord*,
cows give extra milk, and humans have their fill of peace and
musicmaking.[54] Noísiu is in fact busy at *andord* when Derdriu
first confronts him, and it is with the *andord* that he responds
to her proposition and summons his warrior brothers to ask
their advice as to whether or not he should elope with her.[55]
Later in the text, in the first of the two *reicni* that Derdriu
composes as an elegy for the dead sons of Uisliu, she refers
to the *andord* of Aindle[56] and the *sían* of the sons of Uisliu.[57]
She also reminisces poetically about the times when she
washed Noísiu by the fire (*folcud lim-sa dó 'con tein*)[58] and
about the wonderful meals she enjoyed when Noísiu prepared
the *fulocht* on what is termed in the poem the '*fían*-plain of
the forest' (*for feda fían-chlār*).[59] In the second *reicne*,
Derdriu refers to Noísiu's fame among the *fíana fer n-Alban*.[60]
This tragic tale of rites of passage gone awry presents a poignant contrast to the story of Dubh Ruis and Mis: in the story
of Derdriu, a male kind of music leads to a couple's union
through which they are exiled from society — the singing,

53 Hull, *op. cit.*
54 *Ibid.*, ll. 101-103.
55 *Ibid.*, ll. 100-1, 123-5.
56 *Ibid.*, l. 235.
57 *Ibid.*, l. 231.
58 *Ibid.*, l. 213.
59 *Ibid.*, ll. 220-1.
60 *Ibid.*, l. 284.

washing, and *fulacht* in the wilderness here represent distance
from rather than proximity to the cultural realm. In her
poem, the grief-stricken Derdriu contrasts these sylvan delights
with their social counterparts, in which now, because of the
death of Noísiu, she takes no delight. Mis, however, recognizes Dubh Ruis's harp-music and the cooking of meat as
cultural institutions, and she associates them with her deceased
father: it is likely with me, she says, that my father used to
cook his meat, and I know that it is better that way, and that
my way (raw) is worse.[61] Harp-music, sex, and the *fulacht*
bring Mis back to life and society and away from her morbid
obsession; Derdriu, haunted by the memory of the *andord*
and the *fulacht* made by her dead lover, finds in the end that
she has no choice but to depart from life.

Neither in the *esnad* entry in *Cormac's Glossary* nor in
Keating's description of the Fenians does sexual intercourse
occur around the Fenian *fulacht*, though it is central to the
fulacht experience as it happens in both the Mis and the
Derdriu tales. Of course we could say that the Fenian heroes
are all men, and therefore sex is inappropriate in this context,
or at least the idealizing Keating would refuse to mention it.
In the entry on *orc tréith* in *Cormac's Glossary*, we do learn
that Finn had a mistress handy near every forest and hill he
used to frequent, and that these women supplied and nourished
the *fían*.[62] But for the Fenian heroes — as for the male
hunters of Greek myth — women usually bring troublesome
transformations, and they do not really belong in the Fenian
world. Women then would be especially inappropriate in the
context of *echt*-Fenian activities such as the preparing of the
fulacht and the performance of the *dord fíansa*. It is probably more than just the familiar Fenian misogyny that
inspires Finn in the *Bruidhean Chaorthainn*, 'The Rowantree
Hall', to command his terrified companions not to face death
in the deceptive hostel like keening women (*mná caointe*),
but rather to strike up the *dord fíansa* and go out making

61 Ó Cuív, *op. cit.*, 329.56-8; 331.102-5 (*As cuimhin liom, ar sí,
    gur bruighte do bhíoch feoil agam athair, 7 atá fhios agam innis
    gurb amhlaidh as fear[r] í, 7 nach mar bhíoch sí agam-sa*).
62 Meyer, *op. cit.* (1912), § 1018.

music like men.[63] Ironically, and perhaps not accidentally, the Mis story is framed by feminine acts of mourning and keening: Mis goes mad after she mourns for her father too much, and the story serves as an introduction to an elegy supposedly composed by Mis after the death of her husband.[64] In the charming forest interlude, when Dubh Ruis woos and reforms Mis, there transpires a brief rehearsal of their later tragedy. Mis, awakening to find her lover gone, mistakenly thinks she has been abandoned and laments (*gabhas agā chaoine*)[65] with a lusty verse: *Ni hé an t-ór do chaoinim, an chruit bhinn, ná na heoin eadhbhair, / acht an crann clis do bhí aig Dubh Ruis mac Rághnaill*,[66] 'It is not the gold for which I keen, nor the melodious harp, nor his testicles — rather, I keen for the staff of play of Dubh Ruis mac Rághnaill.' The Derdriu tale as told in the *Longes Mac n-Uislenn* is similarly framed by female musical utterances that connote the absence or destruction of men: the text begins with Derdriu's fetal scream presaging bad times ahead for the Ulstermen,[67] and it ends with her *reicni* of lament discussed above. While the fate of Derdriu and Noísiu is not completely comparable to that of Dubh Ruis and Mis — the latter was not, as far as we know, responsible for her consort's death — it is worth noting that Dubh Ruis is (like Noísiu) the hero of an *aithed*, which is mentioned in medieval tale lists[68] — a lost story of elopement that (as suggested by Mac Cana) was probably cognate with the almost farcical but ultimately tragic tale we have been considering.[69]

Through the impact women have on men's lives in these non-Fenian narratives, male music, whether it be the non-

63 Ed. P. Mac Piarais, Dublin 1908, 17.
64 Ó Cuív, *op. cit.* 326; Partridge, *op. cit.*, 34.
65 Ó Cuív, *op. cit.*, 332.128.
66 *Ibid.*, 332.130-3.
67 Hull, *op. cit.*, ll. 6-79. The rarely attested verb used in the text to designate the sound made by the baby in the womb, *derdrethar /-derdrester* (*ibid.*, ll. 14, 51), is possibly related to the name Derdriu (*ibid.*, 73-2, note on *derdrethar*, l.14), though neither, at least according to Hull, is related to *dord* (*ibid.*).
68 P. Mac Cana, *The Learned Tales of Medieval Ireland*, Dublin 1980, 46, 57.
69 Mac Cana, *op. cit.* (1956), 281-2.

verbal vocalizing of *dord* or the sound of the harp, give way in time to *caoine*, women's own special kind of music. An important exception to this musical and sexual polarity is the *muirduchann*, the mermaid, who in the *dindshenchas* of Port Láirge already mentioned, entrances the hapless male Roth with her own *dord*, the *dord na murduchann*. Lulled into a sexual coma, Roth is torn to pieces and consumed by the monsters of the sea, including the bestial mermaid herself.[70] This account presents a grisly reversal of the process whereby Mis regained her social identity and Dubh Ruis gained a wife. In the hands — or in the voice — of this aquatic woman, the *dord* becomes a dangerous challenge to men and the cultural rules of eating. When performed by the Fenian heroes, however, the *dord* or *duchann* accompanies and perhaps even facilitates that archetypically cultural act, cooking.

In his massive survey of North and South American Indian mythology, *Mythologiques*,[71] the anthropologist Claude Lévi-Strauss demonstrates the universal mythopoeic tendency to integrate the culinary code with the acoustical code. In the several interlocked worlds of myth and ritual he explores, certain human-produced sounds are deemed definitely appropriate or inappropriate — even counterproductive — in certain situations of food-gathering, preparation, and consumption. The culinary and acoustical codes come together and sometimes clash in myth because, according to Lévi-Strauss, both cooking and music or noise-making are, on a symbolic level, techniques of mediation and alienation, means of decreasing and increasing the ideological 'space', as it were, between conceptual categories, such as culture and nature, this world and the otherworld, man and woman. This is the very space occupied in Gaelic tradition by those masters of passage, the Fenian heroes, and thus it is fitting that their rituals of initiation and affirmation are charged with the powerful symbols of the hunt, of cooking, and of music.

70 Gwynn, *op. cit.*, 192; Stokes, *op. cit.* (1894), 433; *op. cit.* (1892), 490.
71 J. Weightman and Doreen Weightman, trans., *The Raw and the Cooked, From Honey to Ashes, The Origin of Table Manners, The Naked Man*, New York 1969-81. Four vols.

THE DEVELOPMENT OF THE DEBATE BETWEEN PÁDRAIG AND OISÍN

PÁDRAIG Ó FIANNACHTA

(St Patrick's College, Maynooth)

In the context of the *Kalevala* the Fenian lay 'Agallamh Oisín agus Phádraig' is the lay most appropriately discussed. While it is true that the various Fenian lays were never properly woven into a unity yet occasionally in the later manuscripts a large number of them are given continuously within the framework of 'Agallamh Oisín agus Phádraig'. The arrangement is however sometimes inspired more by scribal convenience than by literary architectonics. The title 'Agallamh Oisín agus Phádraig' may echo to some extent the title of the great medieval work, *Acallam na Senórach*, or, as it is called in English, *The Colloquy with the Ancients*. The word *agallamh* means dialogue or conversation, but in the title of this paper the word 'debate' is used, partly in order to avoid all danger of confusion with the medieval text.

The late wholesale acceptance of the Fenian material in the literary tradition is frequently commented on. It is only very recently that we are arriving at a fuller understanding of the reasons for this. We owe this especially to the researches of Richard Sharpe and Kim McCone. In his perceptive article entitled 'Hiberno-Latin *laicus*, Irish *laech* and the Devil's Men',[1] Sharpe points out very clearly what the official

---

1 *Ériu* 30 (1979), 75-92.

church's attitude to the *díbheargach*, the *votivus mali crudelis*, the 'cruel man devoted to evil (?)'[2] was. It was one of extreme enmity and condemnation. Sharpe quotes with approval from the *Dictionary of the Irish Language* s.v. *díberg* (69.43-5): 'Those engaged in "díberg" seem in early times to have been regarded as outside the pale of Christianity and in league with evil powers'. He himself states that 'in Old Irish the meaning of *díberg*' is limited to this ritualised brigandage involving a *votum mali* and the wearing of *signa diabolica*.[3] The penances for associating with *díbheargaigh* were severe.[4]

Fian and *díberg* are distinguished in O'Mulconry's Glossary:

> Dibergg .i. di-bi-arg .i. ni la laochacht adrimt[h]er ut arg fiann, ar ní bí i cóir laochachtae diultad Dé agus giallnae Demuin.

> 'Dibergg .i. di-bi-arg *.i.e.* it is not with warrior status he is enumerated, because the denial of God and submission to the devil do not properly belong to warrior status.'[5]

This is a later distinction and is probably to be explained as a benign interpretation of the evidence, and parallels in some ways the change of meaning given to *laicus* and *laech*. McCone regards *díberga* and *fiana* as synonymous; he speaks of 'the warrior class or "second function" as a social institution which was apparently designated by the terms *díberg(a)* and *fían(a)*'.[6] *Togail Bruidne Da Derga* shows very clearly that the two terms are indeed interchangeable, e.g., §141 where Ingcél incites his companions to attack the hostel:

> 'Comérget súas, trá, a fiannu', for Ingcél, 'dochum in tigi.' Cota-érgat iarum la sodain na díbergaig dochum na Bruidne [7] fo-carthar a ndord n-impiu.

---

2 *Ibid.*, 92.
3 *Ibid.*, 83.
4 Cf. L. Bieler, *The Irish Penitentials*, Dublin 1963, 162, §§21, 22, 24, 25, 26.
5 W. Stokes and K. Meyer, *Archiv für Celtische Lexikographie*, Vol. 1, Halle 1898, 248, §309.
6 *Eriu* 35 (1984), 15.

' "Rise up, o *fianna*", said Ingcél, "and on to the house."
With that then the *díbergaig* march on to the Hostel and
made a murmur about it.'[7]

Recent scholarship shows convincingly that our early
literature, and writing of all kinds, originated in an ecclesiastical *milieu*; Liam Breatnach, Donnchadh Ó Corráin and
Aideen Breen, have proved conclusively in articles in the
most recent issue of *Peritia* that this is the case with the
Laws.[8] In a recent issue of *Léachtaí Cholm Cille*,[9] Donnchadh
Ó Corráin adds the *Corpus Genealogiarum* to the list of writings
which can be proved to have an ecclesiastical background.

A variety of aetiological stories explains how the church
and the *túath*, 'lay society', reached an accommodation in
the Laws. There are no such clearcut attempts at explaining
how Ulster hero tales (*rúraíocht*) became acceptable. It
may be that it was only later that this need was felt; the
tradition that the *Táin* was taken from Armagh in return for
the *Culmen* or the *Etymologiae* of Isodore of Seville and
that it was later recovered through the good offices of the
dead Fergus, and, according to some versions, through the
prayers and fastings of various saints, may constitute an
effort in this direction.

The explanation which is given for the acceptance of the
stories of the one-time execrated *fianna* is quite late and
occurs at the beginning of the great compilation already
referred to, namely, *Acallam na Senórach*. I quote from
Stokes:

Is ann sin do bhói Pátraic ac cantain na canóine coimdh-
eta, 7 ic etarmoladh in Dúilemhun 7 ic bendachadh na
rátha a roibhe Find mac Cumaill .i. Ráith Droma Deirc.
Ocus atconncatar na cléirigh dá n-indsaighi iatsum, 7 ro
ghabh gráin 7 egla iat roimh na feraibh móra cona conaibh
móra leo, uair nír lucht coimhré ná comhaimsire dóibh
iatt.

Is and sin do éirigh in t-éo flaithemhnais in t-uaithne

7 W. Stokes, ed., *Revue Celtique* 22 (1901), 313.
8 *Peritia* 3 (1984), 382-459.
9 *Léachtaí Cholm Cille* 16 (1986), 71-86.

airechais ₇ in t-aingil talmaide .i. Pátraic mac Alprainn .i. apstal na nGaoidhel, ₇ gabh*uis* in t-esríat do chrothad uisci choisrictha ar na feraibh móra, uair ro bhúi míle léighionn do dheamhnaibh uas a ceannaibh conuic in lá sin, ₇ dochuatar na demhna i cnocaibh ₇ i scalpaibh ₇ i n-imlibh na críche ₇ ind orba uatha ar cach leath; ₇ do šuidhedar na fir mhóra ina dheagaidh sin.[10]

O'Grady's fine translation goes thus:

Just then Patrick chanted the Lord's order of the canon and lauded the Creator, and pronounced benediction on the rath in which Finn mac Cumall had been: the rath of Drumderg. The clerics saw Caeilte and his band draw near them; and fear fell on them before the tall men with their huge wolf-dogs that accompanied them, for they were not people of one epoch or of one time with the clergy.

Then Heaven's distinguished one, that pillar of dignity and angel on earth: Calpurn's son Patrick, apostle of the Gael, rose and took the aspergillum to sprinkle holy water on the great men; floating over whom until that day there had been a thousand legions of demons. Into the hills and 'skalps', into the outer borders of the region of the country, the demons departed in all directions; after which the enormous men sat down.[11]

We have here an imaginative picture of the reconciliation of the Fianna and Christianity. The Fianna whose occupation was *gat ocus brat ocus guin daíne ocus díberg*,[12] 'theft and robbing and slaughter of men and rapine', and who wore the *signa diabolica*, are subjected to exorcism and admitted into the company of clerics, and not merely into the *túath*. The old order had indeed passed by the time of writing, that is probably the middle of the twelfth century. The Norse invasions in previous centuries no doubt helped to bring this about. The early Vikings were probably the Norse counterpart of the Irish Fianna, and were opposed most effectively

10 W. Stokes, ed., 'Acallamh na Senórach', *Irische Texte*, Series 4, Vol. 1, Leipzig 1900, 2-3, ll.58-71.
11 S.H. O'Grady, *Silva Gadelica*, Vol. 2, London 1892, 103.
12 Stokes, *op. cit.* (1901), 28.

by them. The stories and lays of the dreadful pagan feats of valour of the Fianna were duly censored and refined. Patrick himself is shown as most interested in their lore, but has qualms of conscience as can be seen from his remarks to Caeilte very early in their colloquy:

'Mun budh coll crábaidh, ocus mun bud maindnechnaige urnaighti, 7 mun bud tréigen acallma rígh nime 7 talman dúind, ro bo gairit linn t'acallaimsi, a óclaich.'

' "Were it not for us an impairing of the devout life, an occasion of neglecting prayer, and of deserting converse with God, we as we talked with thee, would feel the time pass quickly, o warrior." '[13]

Next morning, however, his conscience was set at rest:

Ocus do bhátur annsin co táinic maden arnamárach, ocus gabais Pátraic a eirredh uime, ocus táinic ar in faithchi amach, ocus trí fichit sacart, trí fichit sailmchétlaid 7 trí fichit naeimescub 'na farrad ac sílad creidmhe ocus crábaid sechnón Éirenn. Ocus doriachtadar a dhá aingel forcoiméta cum Pátraic ann sin .i. Aibelán ocus Solus-breathach, ocus fiafraighios díbh in budh móid le rígh nime ocus talman beith dósom ag éisdecht re scéla na Féinne. Frecrait na haingil dósom co comnart cubaidh: 'A anum a naeimchléirigh!' ar siat, 'ní mó iná trian a scél innisit na senlaeich út ar dáigh dermait 7 díchuimhne [orra]. Ocus scríbhthar [na scéla sin] letsa i támlorguibh filed ocus i mbriath[h]raibh olloman, ór budh gairdiugudh do dronguibh ocus do degdáinibh deridh aimsire éisdecht frisna scéluib sin.' Ocus do imt[h]igset na haingil [uada] iarsin.

'There they were until the morrow's morning came, when Patrick robed himself and emerged upon the green; together with his three score priests, three score psalmodists, and holy bishops three score as well, that with him disseminated faith and piety throughout Ireland. Patrick's two guardian angels came to him now: Aibelán and Solus-brethach, of whom he enquired whether in God's sight it were convenient for him to be listening to the stories of the Fianna. With equal emphasis, and concordantly, the angels answered him: "holy cleric, no more than a third part of their stories do those ancient warriors tell by reason of forgetfulness and lack of memory; but by thee be these stories written on tabular staffs of poets, and in ollave's words; for to the companies and nobles of the latter time to give ear to these stories will be for a pastime." Which said, the angels departed from him.'[14]

The circumstances, the large attendance of bishops and clerics, the robes etc. lend importance to the solemn occasion. The declaration must be regarded as of great import. Patrick is commanded to have the Fenian stories recorded for posterity. Incidentally it is said that these stories are to be the entertainment of the nobility for all time. Many other stories had been forgotten, we are told. This may be a reference to material unsuited for the records. It is clear that at this stage the Fianna have been romanticised. Tales and *seanchas* of cruel and dastardly behaviour were, we may presume, ignored or long forgotten. Nature poetry and other lyrical poetry may have been deliberately introduced to replace them. James Carney has shown that, most probably, 'Turus acam Dé hAíne' and 'Géisid cuan' in the *Acallam* itself had prior associations and were accommodated to the *Acallam* setting.[15]

When the angels departed from Patrick he straight away sent for Caeilte and his eight companions — *in nónbar óclaech do bí* — nine was a traditional *fian* number.

'In bfedubair cid fa tucad dom acallaim sib don chur so?' ar Pátraic. 'Ní fedumar immorro', ar Cáilte. 'Ar dáigh cu ro shléchtadh sibh do soiscéla rígh nime ocus talman .i. in fírDia forórda.' Is and sin tucad tonn baitsi Chíst tairsibh ac Pátraic, ag cinn baitse ocus creitme bhfer nEirenn.

'Patrick said: "know ye why ye are brought to confer with me?" "In sooth we know it not", they answered.

14 *Ibid.*, ll.290-302.
15 J. Carney and D. Greene, eds., *Celtic Studies. Essays in Memory of Angus Matheson*, London 1968, 22-32.

"To the end ye should make obeisance to the gospel of Heaven's and of Earth's king: the Very and most Glorious God". Then and there the waterwave of baptism was poured over them by the head of the baptism and belief of the men of Ireland.'[16]

The Fianna were now within the fold. Former tensions between the *fian* seem to have disappeared and memories thereof to go underground. The debate or contest between the Christian and the Fenian ideal did not surface in the literature for centuries. The earliest copy of 'Agallamh Oisín agus Pádraig' in an Irish manuscript is that in the *Duanaire Finn* manuscript, written by Aodh Ó Dochartaigh in Ostend in 1626-7. This is lay LVII in Gerard Murphy's edition.[17] In his notes to the poem he says as regards the date 'it is unlikely that the dialogue was composed before the sixteenth century'.[18] I would concur, though the evidence is slight and uncertain.

The poem as it stands in the *Duanaire* is simple and uncomplicated, and the loose *rannaigheacht* metre suits the laconic Patrick part very well. The lay opens with Patrick calling Oisín to pray to the sound of the bell for matins:

A Oisín as fada do shúan
    eiridh súas is éisd na sailm
ó thairnic do lúth is do rath
    do chuirtheá cath a ngleó garbh.

'Oisín, thy slumber is long:
    rise up and listen to the psalms,
now that your activity and prosperity are over,
    you used to do battle in fierce war.'   (1)

Oisín bemoans his plight:

16 Stokes, *op. cit.* (1900), ll.314-8; translation from O'Grady, *op. cit.*, 108.
17 G. Murphy, ed., *Duanaire Finn*, Part II (= Irish Text Society, Vol. 28), London 1933, 204-15.
18 G. Murphy, *Duanaire Finn*, Part III (= Irish Text Society, Vol. 43), Dublin 1953, 126.

Do tháirnic mo lúth is mo rath
  ó nach mairionn cath ag Fiond
i ccleircibh ní fhuil mo spéis
  nó ceol da n-éis ní binn liom.

'My activity and prosperity are over
  since Fionn no longer has a battalion.
After them I care not for clerics,
  nor is music sweet to me.'   (2)

Patrick boasts of the music of his clerics. Oisín retorts
with a rhapsodic praise of the music of nature so much loved
by Fionn to which he was once accustomed:

sgalgarnach luin Leitreach Laoi . . .
'the chatter of the blackbird of Leitir Laoí . . .'   (5c)

smólach guithbhinn Ghleanna in Sgáil . . .
'the sweet-voiced thrush of Gleann an Sgáil . . .'   (6a)

Da ghadar dhég do bhí ag Fionn . . .
'Fionn had twelve hounds . . .'   (7a)

shinntí gan locht in Dord Fian . . .
'the Dord Fian would be faultlessly sounded . . .'   (8b)

He also recalls Cnú Deireoil and his harp. Fionn is dead
Patrick harshly replies, and Oisín has one foot in the grave:
Oisín admits this but goes on immediately to praise Fionn's
generosity:

a ndeachaidh is na ffuil beó
  dob fearr fa ór Fionn na fFian,

'Fionn of the Fian was better as regards gold
  than all who have gone and all who are alive.'   (13cd)

He praises Fionn's valour *a nEirinn uill*, 'in great Ireland',
(14b) and abroad. He was victorious in Spain, in Lochlann
and in far away India:

on tsruth ar baisdeadh Críosd
  do theigh a chíos go Toigh in Duinn.

'his sway extended from the stream where Christ

was baptised to Teach an Duinn.'   (14cd)

Oisín's own plight is a sad one:

Mairg dhamh do hanadh dhá éis
    gan mo spéis a muirn no a cceól;
um damh críon d'aithle na slúagh,
    as damh is truagh a beith beó.

'Alas for me who have been left behind him.
    I have no care for merriment or music.
I am a worn out stag whose herds have left him.
    Woeful for me to be alive.'   (17)

He humbly begs Patrick to pray to God for Fionn and the
Fianna:

Sir a Patraic dhuinn ar do Dhia
    neamh d'Fionn na bFian is dá chloinn.

'Patrick, ask from your God, I pray you,
    that Fionn of the Fiana and his children reach heaven.'
                                            (20ab)

Patrick refuses because:

gurab é a mhian rena linn
    bheith a nglionn ag síansan sealg.

'for what he loved in his day
    was to be in a glen amid the clamour of the chase.'
                                          (21cd)

Oisín maintains that Patrick too would have yielded to
similar temptation, and would be equally generous to the
aos dána, 'poets'. Patrick asserts his loyalty to *Mac Dé Bhí*,
'the Son of the Living God' (23a), and boldly proclaims
Fionn to be in hell because of his generosity as well as other
misdeeds:

Gach ar pronn tú ⁊ Fionn d'ór
    olc do-chúaidh dhó ⁊ duit
ata sé a n-ifreann 'na gheall
    mar do-denadh feall ⁊ broid

'All the money you and Fionn bestowed

has ended badly for him and for you;
  he is in hell because of it;
    for he practised treachery and violence.'   (24)

Oisín refuses to believe this and proudly asserts that if
Fionn were in hell with Clanna Morna or Clanna Baoiscne
they would rescue him:

do-bheardaoís sin Fionn amach
  nó bhiadh in teach aca fén.

'they would carry Fionn out
  or else themselves would take possession of the house.'
                                                    (27cd)

Patrick flatly denies this:

Coig coigidh Eireann fa seach
  's na seacht ccatha boí san fFéin
ní tiubhraidís Fionn amach
  gér mhór a neart is a ttréin.

'The five separate provinces of Ireland
  and the seven battalions of the Fian
could not bring Fionn out,
  though their power and strength were great.'   (29)

Oisín seems to concede, but declares it a great injustice:

Créd do-rinne Fionn re Dia
  acht riar na cclíar is na sgol
is treas mór re bronnadh óir,
  is treas fós ré meadhair chon?

'What did Fionn do against God
  but attend to the learned and scholars,
now giving up much time to the bestowal of gold,
  another time to joyfully following hounds.'   (32)

But, says Patrick, all this left him without a thought for
God.
Oisín then wanders off to think of better days:

Atá sgél agam ar Fhionn
  ní raibh ionn acht sé fir dhég

gabhsam rí Sacsan na ffleadh
  is chuiriomar cath ar rígh Grég.

'I know a tale about Fionn;
  sixteen men only were there there:
we captured the festive king of England
  we went to war with the king of Greece.'   (34)

Then he thinks of the conquest of India, and the defeat
of Magnus son of the king of Lochlann.
  Patrick grows impatient; all this is past:

ní bhia is ní fhuil acht mar cheo.

'all those hosts of past time shall be, and already are, but
  mist.'   (37d)

Oisín has his parting shot:

A Pátraic na mbachall mbreac
  ní rachadh leat aithis Fhinn
nír ér sé duine fa ór
  ní thug a mbreig móid nó mionn.

'Patrick of the speckled croziers,
  you could not find fault with Fionn:
he never refused anyone as regards gold:
  he never perjured himself nor took false oath.'   (38)

Patrick concludes by advising Oisín to think of his approaching death:

tapair dot uaidh th'aire anos.

'turn your thoughts now to your tomb.'   (39d)

The -os here is a *dúnadh*, 'closure', a faint echo of *Ois-ín*
in the opening line of the poem.
  From this presentation it is clear that the ancient enmity
and tension between the *fian* and the church and *tuath*, 'lay
society', are more or less forgotten. What we have here are,
for the most part, the typical clerical attitudes to the soldier
or warrior life; added thereto are themes we find in the
anchoritic nature poetry and the Wild-man literature like that
dealing with Suibhne and Moling. The 'Agallamh' had sur-

faced, presumably, prior to the counter-Reformation, but clerical attitudes revealed in it are in line with counter-Reformation attitudes.

The simple uncomplicated 'Agallamh' as it first appeared soon developed and attracted other lays. Of the one hundred and one complete, and thirty four incomplete copies of the lay called 'Agallamh Oisín agus Phádraig' or its equivalent, and beginning *Oisín is fada do shuan* that I have noted in the printed catalogues of manuscripts in Ireland, England, and Wales, only seven are of the *Duanaire Finn* family. The earliest of these is by Liam Mac Cairteáin of the Blarney school, 1700-3. The one other Cork copy, written by T. Ó Fearghaile in 1800, was probably made from that. Two further copies come from the pen of Maurice O'Gorman. There is a fifth copy from Dublin in 1711 by Maurice Newby. The two remaining copies are from the north. The vast majority of texts are from the province of Munster, every county there being represented. From Leinster, Dublin and Kilkenny also provide copies. The Leinster county of Louth and the province of Ulster have very few — three expanded copies and the two copies of the shorter version. Gerard Murphy points out that the Scottish versions follow the shorter one; and adds that this fact 'makes it probable that the original form of the Dialogue is that given in *Duanaire Finn*'.[19]

I agree with Murphy here, but attention must be drawn to the debate enshrined in 'Laoi Chath Gabhra', published in *Transactions of the Ossianic Society*.[20] An earlier version of this appears in the *Book of the Dean of Lismore*, poem no. 87 in O'Rahilly's Index.[21] 'Laoi Chath Gabhra' became apparently an alternative basis for an omnibus version of the Fenian lays in Gaelic Scotland, though not to the same extent as the 'Agallamh' in Ireland.

The manuscript tradition of the 'Agallamh' is rich and

19 Murphy, *op. cit.* (1953), 125.
20 N. O'Kearney, ed., Vol. I (1853), 68-133.
21 *Scottish Gaelic Studies* 4 (1935), 35-54; edited by A. Cameron, *Reliquiae Celtica* 1 (1892), 10-9 and J.F. Campbell, *Leabhar na Feinne*, London 1872, 40-1.

varied. The very title varies; 'Agallamh Oisín and Phádraig' is the most common; it is also called 'comhagallamh', 'agallamh', 'agallmha', 'iomagallamh', 'crosántacht' and simply 'díospóireacht'. It is clearly meant for a popular audience. I feel many copies have something of the personal and individual quality of a living version of a folktale or folk song. They offer a great challenge therefore to the editor. The two possible approaches are well represented in the two best known editions, that of John O'Daly and that of An Seabhac.

The earlier edition by John O'Daly is in Vol. 4 of the *Transactions of the Ossianic Society* (1859), 1-63. The text is from 'a copy made in 1780 by a Laurence O'Foran who kept a village school at Killeen near Portlaw in the county of Waterford' (p. xxxi). Unfortunately I have not been able to find that manuscript, though another manuscript by the same scribe is in the library of the Royal Irish Academy (RIA 696). O'Daly apparently followed his exemplar faithfully, but omitted a final section because it was more or less identical with 'Laoi na Seilge' as printed in Charlotte Brooke's *Reliques of Irish Poetry* (Dublin 1789). Even as it stands O'Daly's text is quite long and runs to 175 quatrains. The vast majority, ninety three of the manuscripts of the complete texts, belong to a group of this kind. It is a fine lay. There are hints that it was performed in a drama-like fashion, the Oisín-parts in a bass key and those of Patrick in a tenor key.[22]

One may compare O'Daly's text with that in *Duanaire Finn*. Gerard Murphy used it to make some interesting emendations. It begins with almost the whole of the earlier lay, 34 quatrains of the 39 in a slightly more dramatic order and two new quatrains interspersed. It then takes off with Oisín celebrating in litanic praise the music of nature, with wonderful *dinnseanchas*, 'topographical', echoes,[23] e.g.:

Scaltarnach loin Leitreach Laoi
    tonn Rughraidhe ag buain re tráigh;
dordán an daimh ó Mháigh Mhaoin,
    búithre an laoigh ó Ghleann dhá Mháil.

22 Murphy, *op. cit.* (1954), 132.
23 Occasionally here the text is normalised and the translation emended.

'The warbling of the blackbird of Letter Lee,
    The wave of Rughraidhe lashing the shore;
The bellowing of the ox of Magh-maoin,
    And the lowing of the calf of Gleann-dha-mháil.'   (16.1)

Next he gives a description of the Fianna setting out on a
hunt, and names heroes and dogs:

Do bhí Luas ag Liagán Luaimneach
    is Dathchaoin ag Dáire duanach;
Léim ag Gobha Gaoithe an ghrinn,
    is Daol ag Caoilte mac Rónáin

'Liagán, the nimble, held Luadhas,
    And Dáire of the duans held Dathchaoin;
Gobha Gaoithe, the merry, held Léim,
    And Caoilte Mac Rónáin held Daol.'   (20.5)

Patrick is enthralled and does not intercept till Oisín breaks
down: the metre changes at times to loose *deibhí*:

A Phátraic, is truagh mise,
    am sheanóir go hatuirseach
gan réim, gan tapa, gan treoir
    ag triall chum aifrinn go haltóir.

'O Patrick, I am to be pitied,
    Being a broken-hearted old man;
Without sway, without agility, without vigor
    Going to mass at the altar.'   (22.3)

Gan deabhtha gan déanamh creach,
    gan imirt ar chleasaibh lúith;
gan dul ag suirghidh ná seilg
    dá cheird 'na raibh mo dhúil.

'Without conflicts, without taking of preys,
    Without exercising in feats;
Without going to woo or to the chase,
    Two amusements which I dearly loved.'   (22.5)

Patrick has to interfere at this point:

Sguir a sheanóir, léig dod bhaois,
  ní beag duit feasta a ndearrnaois;
smuain ar na piantaibh atá reomhad,
  d'imigh an Fhiann agus imtheochair.

'Cease, old man, let be thy folly,
  Enough for thee henceforth what thou hast already done:
Reflect on the pains that are before you,
  The Fenians are departed and thou shalt depart.'   (22.6)

Oisín retorts:

Má imthighim, a Phátraic, nár fhágthar thusa
  a fhir an chroidhe thoirmisgthe.

'If I depart, O Patrick, mayest thou not be left,
  O man of the ascetic heart.'   (22.7ab)

Then he wanders off to relate the adventure of the *colainn
gan cheann*, 'headless body'. Patrick hears him out and then
tells Oisín:

Is fearr fanamhain mar a taoi,
  ná bheith arís ina measc.

'Better to remain as thou art,
  Than to be again among them.'   (28.3cd)

Oisín disagrees and bemoans his lot:

Is mairg dom ghlac baisteadh riamh
  is olc do m'onóir dar liom;
air mbeith dham gan biadh, gan deoch,
  ag déanamh trosga is úrnaighthe.

'Alas! that I ever received baptism,
  It affects my honour, I perceive;
In being without food and drink,
  Whilst fasting and praying.'   (32.1)

A sharp exchange then takes place on the relative merits
of the Fenian fare and that now offered by Patrick. Then
Oisín asks in confidence:

an léigfear mo ghadhar nó mo chú
  liom go cúirt rígh na ngrás?

'Will my dog or my hound be let in
  With me, to the court of the king of grace?'   (36.1cd)

He is very disappointed when told this will not be allowed,
and rails against God and Patrick:

Dá mbiadh agamsa Conán
  fear mílabhartha na Féinne
do bhriseadh sé do cheann
  istigh i measc do chléire.

'Were Conan with me,
  The reviler of the Fenians;
He would break thy head,
  Within among thy clerics.'   (38.1)

Patrick tells him to have sense in his old age and not allow
his thoughts to dwell too long on the Fianna:

'Atá tú ar mearughadh i ndeire th' aoise,
  idir shlíghe dhíreach agus cham;
seachain slíghe cham na bpian
  is tiocfaidh aingil Dé faoid' cheann.

'Thou art astray at the close of thy life,
  Between the straight way and the crooked;
Shun the crooked path of pains
  And God's angels will come to meet you.'   (38.5)

Then follows a long skilfully arranged section where the
protagonists respond to one another in alternate quatrains,
Oisín flitting from incident to incident and distraction to
distraction and Patrick laying down his strict puritanical
code. When Patrick relaxes and alludes to the tenderness of
Christ, Oisín finds a chink in his armour:

mac rígh neimhe dhíbreas na huilc
  is mór a chion ar dhuine dhall.

'The Son of the king of heaven, who expels evil,
  Great is his love for a blind man.'   (46.2cd)

Oisín replies:

Más dall iad muintir Dé
   is gurab iad na daill is ansa leis;
is cosmhail nach gcuirfeadh an Fhiann,
   go teach na bpian dá sgrios.

'If the people of God are blind,
   And that the blind are they whom he loves best;
'Tis likely, he would not send the Fenians,
   To the house of pain to be exterminated.'   (46.3)

Patrick loses his patience and declares:

dob' fhearr Dia re haon uair
   na Fianna Éireann uile.

'God is better for one hour,
   Than all the Fians of Éire.'   (46.4)

Oisín retorts: Oscar would make *brúscar*, 'little bits' of
your *bachall*, 'crozier' if he were here; what a contest would
Oscar and God provide:

dá bhfaicfinnse mo mhac ar lár
   déarfainn gur fear láidir Dia.

'If I saw my son down,
   I would say that God was a strong man.'   (46.6cd)

He bursts forth into praise of the Fianna, their bravery,
their generosity, their loyalty. Patrick relents:

Oisín is binn liom do ghlór
   is beannacht fós le hanmain Fhinn.

'Oisín, sweet to me is thy voice,
   And a blessing furthermore, on the soul of Fionn.'
                                          (50.1ab)

By way of reconciliation he asks Oisín to relate the famous
'Seilg Shliabh na mBan bhFionn' to him (once again). Oisín
is not able to sustain his story for long, but Patrick continues
with his questioning, and invites such startling replies as:

Ní chanaimis an Fhiann gó
   is bréag linn níor samhladh riamh;

le fírinne is le neart ár lámh
   do thigmis slán as gach gliadh.

'We, the Fenians, never used to tell untruth,
   Falsehood was never attributed to us;
By truth and the might of our hands,
   We came safe out of every conflict.'   (52.2)

But all that is in the past for Oisín:

Ós anocht nach maireann an Fhiann
   nó Fionn fial na nduas;
do bhodhar siansán na salm
   is glór garbh na gclog mo chluas.

'As tonight the Fenians do not live,
   Or the hospitable Fionn of the gifts;
The loud chanting of the psalms,
   And the hoarse sound of the bells have deafened my
                                        hearing.' (54.3)

This rekindles the controversy and leads to the highpoint
of the debate. Patrick grows lyrical in praise of God:

Is é mo rígh-se dhealbhaigh neamh
   is é do bheir neart do laoch;
is é do chum an bith buan,
   is é do bheir bláth na gcraobh.

Is é do dhealbhaigh éasga is grian
   is é do bheir iasg ar linn;
is é do chruthaigh gort is féar
   ní hionann is éachta Fhinn.

'It is my king, who formed the heavens,
   It is he, who gives might to the warrior;
It is he, that created the universe,
   It is he, that gives the blossoms of the trees.

It is he, that made the moon and the sun,
   It is he, that brings fish into a lake;
It is he, that formed field and grass,
   Not like the deeds of Fionn.'   (54.7, 56.1)

In reply we have a re-statement of the Fenian ideal, a statement which is as heroic as anything in the *Táin* or the *Iliad*:

Ní ar chruthughadh gort ná féir
    thug mo rígh-se féin a dhúil;
ach ar choscairt corpa laoch,
    ar chosnamh críoch, is ar chur a chlú.

Ar shuirghidh ar imirt, ar sheilg,
    ar nochtadh meirge, a dtúis gleo;
ar imirt fithchille, is ar shnámh,
    is ar fheitheamh cháich i dtigh an óil.

' 'Twas not in forming fields and grass,
    That my king took delight;
But in mangling the bodies of heroes,
    In contesting kingdoms and spreading his fame.

In courting, playing and hunting,
    And unfolding his banner, in front of the fight,
In playing at chess and swimming,
    And in beholding all in the house of drinking.'   (56.2-3)

Then he challenges Patrick to say where God was when heroic feats were performed by the Fianna — when Dearg, and Maghnas Mór, and Tailc mac Treoin were overcome, as related in their lays. Patrick suggests a truce, but with a harsh reminder:

tuig go bhfuil Dia ar neamh na n-ord
    agus Fionn is a shlóite uile i bpéin.

'Understand that God dwells in heaven of the orders (of
    angels),
And Fionn and his hosts are all in pain.'   (58.7cd)

Oisín responds:

Ba mhór an náire sin do Dhia,
    gan glas na bpian do bhuain d'Fhionn;
Agus Dia féin dá mbiadh i mbruid
    go dtroidfeadh an flaith tar a cheann.

'Great would be the shame for God,
  Not to release Fionn, from the shackles;
For if God himself were in bonds,
  The chief would fight on his behalf.'   (60.1)

Patrick invites him to repent:

Buail d'ucht is doirt do dheór
  creid don té tá ós do chionn;
gidh gurb iongna leat a luadh,
  is é do rug buaidh ar Fhionn.

'Strike thy breast and shed thy tear,
  Believe in Him who is above;
Though thou art amazed at its being said,
  The chief would fight on his behalf.'   (60.7)

Oisín says he will weep indeed:

goilfeadsa go fras, ach ní fá Dhia
  acht faoi Fhionn na bhFiann gan bheith beo!

'I will cry my fill, but not for God,
  But for Fionn and the Fians not being alive.'   (62.2cd)

Patrick, perhaps to cheer him up, reverts again to his
request to tell of the great *seilg*, 'hunt', of Sliabh na mBan,
and off they both go, Patrick apparently being cast in the
role of the converted for the time being.

The O'Daly edition is fairly satisfactory and represents a
real version, though it would have been better if it had
included the final lay as well. The 'Agallamh' offered a framework for a unified presentation of the whole corpus of Ossianic
lays. This was availed of and the result is represented in
about seventeen surviving manuscripts. It may be possible to
establish a stemma for these, but what we really need is an
uncluttered edition from one of the more complete copies,
preferably, perhaps, that in British Library Additional 27946
from the pen of Eoghan Caomhánach of Co. Limerick and
dated 1821-8. This runs to 1196 quatrains and weaves together ten lays in addition to the original 'Agallamh' or
'exordium' as O'Grady calls it. The lays are: 'Seilg Shléibhe
na mBan bhFionn', 'Cath Chnoc an Áir', 'Laoi na Seilge',

'Meisce agus Rá na mBan (Laoi an Bhrait)', 'Seilg Sléibhe Fuaid', and 'Caoi Oisín i ndiaidh na Féinne'.

Eoghan Caomhánach adds a most interesting colophon (here quoted in slightly modernised spelling):

> Sin agat a léitheoir cheardúil ionann agus sé mhíle líne de imagallaimh Phádraig is Oisín, agus saoilim nach luaim bréag ar ndearbhadh dhuit gurab é tiomsú is folláine is dírí is ceirtfhírinní agus is iomláine coimhlíonadh dár tharla riamh oramsa cé gur léas an iomad; óir is fánach ní i gcoitinne nár casadh iomum, agus fós is fánach clochar ná coláiste in Éirinn nach bhfeaca mé a soláthair le mo linn, óir d'fhiosraíos iad uile. Gibé lochta atá air so ná tugaidh oilbhéim damhsa dá mbíthin, óir do scríobhas an tsuim-se ar an dtaobh istigh de na seacht laethibh is giorra san mbliain, mar is follas de réir an dáta, lá fhéile Thomáis 1828.

'Here you have ingenious reader the equivalent of 6000 lines of the 'Colloquy of Patrick and Ossian'; and I imagine that I utter no falsehood when I certify to you that it is a compilation the soundest, the most correct and thoroughly genuine, the most copiously complete, that (though I have read much) has ever come in my way. For, speaking generally, it is but some stray item of the kind that I have not met with; it is moreover but some odd academy or college in Ireland of which I have not in my time seen the collection, for I have visited them all. But whatever faults there be in this one, never revile me on their account; for this total I transcribed inside of the seventh shortest days in the year, as according to the date is evident. Festival of St. Thomas 1828.'[24]

Co. Limerick provides the earliest copies of this group. There are two copies by the same scribe, Séamas Ó Caoinleabháin, the earlier being O'Curry 31 and dated 1794-6; this runs to 1117 quatrains, but is missing the first 11 or so. The copy in RIA No. 506, is the longest of all; it is dated

24 S.H. O'Grady, *Catalogue of Irish Manuscripts in the British Museum*, Vol. 1, London 1926, 683-4.

1815-20 and runs to 1493 quatrains. This is headed 'Agallamh Oisín agus Phádraig agus Iomlán a nGníomhartha', 'The Debate between Oisín and Patrick and all their Deeds'.

Laoithe na Féinne edited by An Seabhac and published by the Folklore of Ireland Society in 1941, is a fine collection of lays, 64 in all. It begins with 'Agallamh Oisín agus Phádraig', and offers a version of the first variety of the long 'Agallamh', which runs to 270 quatrains. This is an edited version and represents no actual copy closely enough, though the text provided is interesting in its own right.

The 'Agallamh' in one or other of its guises was copied and recopied, especially in Munster, most of all from about 1775 to the time of the Great Famine, that is during the lifetime of Daniel O'Connell. It was chanted or sung at many firesides during the 1798 rebellion and the O'Connell agitations. I would consider the manuscript copies to have been in many cases memory aids to the singers. Dialect forms abound and show the oral element affecting the written text. For example, a tattered manuscript, B4 in the library of St Patrick's College, Maynooth, which arrived back in Ireland from Seattle through the kind offices of the Archbishop of Tuam, was written in Muskerry in 1815 and shows clear signs of the dialect of the area. It contained the omnibus 'Agallamh', but the first 300 quatrains or so are missing.

It seems that the oral recital or chanting of the Fenian lays in Ireland died out with the decay of the manuscript tradition. Even where the spoken language survived, the lays seem not to have done so. In Ireland, no Lönnrot appeared, unfortunately, but the urge to do what he did for Finland was there, and faint signs of movement in that direction are to be seen in the long 'Agallamh' which is best represented in manuscripts from West Limerick, and North Kerry, I might add. In conclusion I would like to quote from the interesting literary apologia that David Krause makes for 'the Hidden Oisín' in *Studia Hibernica* 6 (1966), 22-3:

> It is in their moments of over-statement and comic exaggeration that Oisín and Patrick become the more interesting for their frailties. This is quite a come-down for Ireland's great saint, and a similar descent for her

great Fenian hero, but it is a descent into human falli-
bility which appears to have made both characters more
accessible to the popular imagination. In the dual tone and
structure of these poems, at once epic and comic, the two
men have survived in Irish myth and folklore for at least
four and a half centuries.

MAGIC ATTRIBUTES OF THE HERO IN FENIAN LORE

DÁITHÍ Ó hÓGÁIN

(University College Dublin)

'Success and blessings to you! But where are the wise men and the storytellers of Ireland? Let that be written down in the mystic script of poets and in the words of the learned, so that everybody may bring home to his own country and land his report of what Caoilte and Oisín have told of their great deeds of valour and heroism and of the place-lore of Ireland.'[1]

These words are put into the mouth of the high-king of Ireland by that extraordinary text of the twelfth century entitled *Acallamh na Senórach*, 'The Colloquy with the Ancients'. In all, the text comprises about 90,000 words of interspersed prose and verse, and in it the author exploits the fancy that two of the Fianna warriors, Oisín the son of Fionn, and Caoilte the son of Rónán, survived the demise of the other great heroes and lived on until St Patrick's time.[2] They therefore were able to travel the country with the saint and his followers, relaying to them a great wealth of lore con-

---

1 W. Stokes, ed., *Acallamh na Senórach* = *Irish Texte* Fourth Series, Vol. 1, Leipzig 1900, 73.
2 The theme of a surviving ancient hero meeting St Patrick was already in existence before the *Acallamh* was written. In a text of the eleventh century, Cú Chulainn returns from the dead and recites to the saint a story of his adventures – R.I. Best and O.J.

cerning the lost epoch of the heroes and the places associated with them. It is evident that the author of the *Acallamh* wished to stabilise the lore of the Fianna by infusing a definite perspective into it, thereby reconciling it to his own learned and Christian culture. In this he was successful, for the *Acallamh* is in many ways a half-way house in the tradition of Fenian narrative. Behind it lies a whole series of stories which illustrate the mythical nature of Fionn and of his doings; following it is a more comprehensive, pseudo-historical, and, in a sense, romantic lore which presents the Fianna as a band of warriors who experienced many colourful adventures. This process was, of course, a general one which affected other types of heroic narrative in medieval Ireland; but in the case of the Fianna it was much intensified by the influence of the *Acallamh*.

Fionn Mac Cumhaill himself, it has been argued convincingly, was originally a deity,[3] and thus his portrayal has always been highly individualistic. A review of the earlier Fenian literature,[4] however, does not lead one to believe that the other leading heroes of the cycle were individualised to anything like the same extent. The names occur, they are actors in stories, but there is little surviving evidence of

Bergin, *Lebor na hUidre*, Dublin 1929, xxxiv, 278-87. For a twelfth-century poem of Oisín to Patrick, which may be independent of the *Acallamh*, see *Zeitschrift für celtische Philologie* 5 (1905), 180. The *Acallamh* was written about the year 1175, but the surviving texts of it are all incomplete. The earliest version is that edited by Stokes, *op. cit.* Another and quite distinct version is called 'An Agallamh Bheag', ['The Small Colloquy'], and part of this has been edited by D. de hÍde in *Lia Fáil* 1 (1926), 79-107. Finally, a recension — based on these two and dating from the fourteenth century — has been edited by Nessa Ní Shéaghdha (*Agallamh na Seanórach* Parts I-III, Baile Átha Cliath 1942-5). For a comparison of the texts and manuscripts, see these editions, as well as M. Dillon, *Stories from the Acallamh*, Dublin 1970.

3 See T.F. O'Rahilly, *Early Irish History and Mythology*, Dublin 1946, 271-81; G. Murphy, *Duanaire Finn* Part III, Dublin 1953, lxx-lxxxv.

4 Full lists down to the year 1400 are given in K. Meyer, *Fianaigecht*, Dublin 1910, xvi-xxxi; and Murphy, *op. cit.*, lv-lxx.

specific traits of character being ascribed to them.[5] The structure of the *Acallamh* on the other hand, demanded a fair amount of character portrayal of some of the leading heroes. Clearly the author utilised much material from earlier sources, but he did so selectively, tending to type-cast the characters according to the perspective on the tradition which he held and wished to promulgate. Thus his Oisín was the semi-primitive semi-contemplative old man, his Caoilte the messenger of the Fianna who through this office had obtained an amazing knowledge of the country's geography and topography, the Fianna in general were a rather robust nature-loving band with an attitude to events which was half-stoical and half-sentimental. The basic question is, of course, how apt and how true to pre-existing lore is this portrayal? This is a question which should not be confined to the *Acallamh*, but should be extended in both directions to cover the whole body of Fenian literature. In other words, were there other narratives of Fionn and his followers in existence down through the centuries which are not represented by the literature, and was there greater variety in those which are represented than we gauge from the literature?

Perhaps the most striking type of imagery concerning the Fianna in current lore is that which portrays them as having been giants, or at least as possessing colossal strength. With the general decline of Fenian lore in recent generations — particularly in the context of the replacement of the Irish language by English — this idea has proved to be the strongest survivor of all the lore. Many large rocks or boulders are still pointed out as having reached their present locations by way of being hurled as projectiles in a contest between Fionn Mac Cumhaill and a hostile giant.[6] It is clear that in such cases we

5 Their portrayal, with the exception of Fionn himself, is rather objective, with little attention to psychological analysis. To judge from the surviving texts, Oisín and Caoilte were (with Fionn) the best-known Fianna characters in the early period; so it appears that the author of the *Acallamh* was following sound precedents when choosing these two.

6 For references, see Murphy, *op. cit.*, xviii; C. Ó Cadhlaigh, *An Fhiannuidheacht*, Baile Átha Cliath 1947, 217; and Irish Folklore Collection (IFC) Catalogue at Department of Irish Folklore, University College Dublin (under the heading 'Fiannaíocht').

are dealing with ordinary aetiological giant-lore[7] being placed
in the context of the Fenian tradition, but it is reasonable to
enquire how far back does this process go. Is it purely an
example of degeneration, or is it based on some aspect of the
Fenian tradition which is native to it? Strictly speaking, the
hurling of rocks may not be a very ancient Fenian motif, but
there is plenty of evidence that the association of the Fianna
with large and commanding aspects of the landscape is long
and firmly established. We have several mountain-peaks around
the country known as *Suí Finn*, 'Fionn's Seat';[8] and a good
amount of similar attributions, such as a high plateau in Co.
Tipperary known as *Bord Fhinn*, 'Fionn's Table',[9] a group of
five standing stones in Co. Cavan known as 'Fionn Mac
Cumhaill's Fingers',[10] and a ring of rounded flags about nine
yards in diameter in Co. Wicklow known as 'Fionn's Griddle'.[11]

We have some sixteenth-century references to the gigantic
size of the Fianna in non-Gaelic documents[12] — these have a
false ring about them, but their falseness derives from satiric
exaggeration of an existing idea. One story, collected widely
from Gaelic-speaking areas of Ireland and Scotland, deals
directly with the idea. According to this, Oisín argues with
the housekeeper of St Patrick regarding the type of food he is
given to eat. He says that in the time of the Fianna he has seen
a blackbird's leg which was larger than the joint of meat she
is cooking, a berry larger than her butter, and an ivy-leaf
larger than her cake. To settle the question, he goes out into
a wood and returns with three such items — survivals also of

7   Motifs A901, A972, A984-A989 in S. Thompson, *Motif-Index of
    Folk-Literature*, Copenhagen 1955-8; Types 1000-1199 in A. Aarne
    and S. Thompson, *The Types of the Folktale*, Helsinki 1973. The
    latter source is referred to as AT, followed by type number,
    henceforth.
8   See E. Hogan, *Onomasticon Goedelicum*, Dublin 1910, 618;
    M. Comerford, *Kildare and Leighlin*, Vol. 2, Dublin 1884, 58.
9   IFC 54:376. See also Hogan, *op. cit.*, 119.
10 S.P. Ó Ríordáin, *Antiquities of the Irish Countryside*, London
    1965, 84.
11 P. Kennedy, *Legendary Fictions of the Irish Celts*, London 1866,
    186.
12 References in Murphy, *op. cit.*, xliii.

the lost epoch.[13] An episode in the *Acallamh* has certain resemblances to this. In this, Oisín goes to a well with a pail in which he catches eight salmon, with eight stalks of watercress and eight stalks of brooklime on top of them. He then goes and presents these to the high-king. All present are amazed, since each stalk is as wide as the king's knee.[14] It appears that the folk story was invented on the basis of this passage in the *Acallamh*,[15] and since it underlined the notion that the Fianna were of giant size it became very popular and spread widely.

The historian Seathrún Céitinn, writing around the year 1630, found it necessary to rebut the notion that Fionn Mac Cumhaill was a giant. 'It is plain', says Céitinn, 'that he was not of abnormal size as compared with his contemporaries.'[16] But Céitinn, through his very learnedness and preciseness, seems here to miss the point at issue. What the tradition was saying is that the Fianna were huge by comparison with the people whom Oisín and Caoilte encountered in Ireland at the time of St Patrick. This demonstrates for us what is the apparent source of the idea, which is the text of the *Acallamh* itself. For it is there repeatedly stated that the ancient heroes, Fianna and others, were of enormous size (the average envisaged having been about five times that of contemporary humans). [17] Thus, on the introduction into the text of Oisín and Caoilte, St Patrick and his followers are said to have been 'seized with dread and fear' before the big men, because — it is significantly stated, 'they were not of the same period and time as themselves'.[18] It is obvious from the whole tenor of the text that the author of the *Acallamh* was a learned man, and he would therefore share the prevalent antiquarian ideas of the time —

13 Lists of versions in *Béaloideas* 2 (1929-30), 68, 260; Murphy, *op. cit.*, xx; IFC Catalogue.

14 Stokes, *op. cit.*, 66-7.

15 It is possible, of course, that the folk story lies behind the *Acallamh* passage, but if so one would expect the *Acallamh* to reflect its plot more accurately. Murphy's suggestion re the history of the story (*op. cit.*, xxiii) seems unconvincing to the present writer.

16 P.S. Dinneen, *Foras Feasa ar Éirinn*, Vol. 2, London 1908, 330.

17 Stokes, *op. cit.*, 58-9, 62-3; de hÍde, *op. cit.*, 98.

18 Stokes, *op. cit.*, 3.

one of the most curious of which was that ancient peoples were very large in stature.[19] We may go further and speculate that the immediate source which suggested the idea to the author was the seventh-century Latin biography of St Patrick by Tíreachán, where the saint is said to have resuscitated a dead giant in order to baptise him. Those present, according to Tíreachán, were amazed at the massive size of the giant's grave.[20] This situation of awe recurs several times in the *Acallamh*, where huge mounds in different parts of the country are explained by Oisín and Caoilte as being the graves of dead Fianna heroes and heroines.[21] The selfsame explanation of mounds and tumuli is still popular in the lore of rural Ireland.[22]

Even where they are not understood to have been themselves giants, the Fianna are represented as being pitted against giants in a very popular stratum of late folk tradition. For example, a visiting giant in aggressive mood is bluffed by Fionn into departing without the single combat he sought. One story told all over Ireland has it that Fionn saw the giant approaching his house, and jumped into the cradle in the kitchen. When Fionn's wife explains to the giant that he is not at home, the visitor says he will wait and starts to play with the 'baby'. But the occupant of the cradle bites the visitor's finger off, and the agonised giant is informed by Fionn's wife that 'the children of the Fianna are born with teeth!' Fearing that the baby's father will be a horrific fighter,

---

19 The source of this idea appears to be the Old Testament mention (Genesis 6:4) of giants upon the earth in olden times, 'the mighty men of old, men of renown'. It is interesting to note that late tradition of King Arthur in Britain follows similar lines of development with regard to the landscape as the tradition of Fionn — see G. Ashe, *The Quest for Arthur's Britain*, London 1971, 149-54.

20 L. Bieler, *The Patrician Texts in the Book of Armagh*, Dublin 1979, 154. The story is repeated in the late ninth-century Irish biography of the saint in Irish — Kathleen Mulchrone, *Bethu Phátraic*, Dublin 1939, 76-7.

21 Stokes, *op. cit.*, 58-60, 62, 78.

22 Kennedy, *op. cit.*, 186; Daphne Pochin Mould, *Irish Pilgrimage*, New York 1957, 128; M. Seoighe, *Portrait of Limerick*, London 1982, 159; Ordnance Survey Letters, Co. Louth (1836), 53, 170; IFC Catalogue.

the giant beats a hasty retreat.[23] This story has a plot-structure which, in various guises, has been very popular in Ireland and elsewhere for a long time,[24] but its specific application to the Fenian context appears to have occurred quite late.[25] Another such trick for bluffing the giant has Fionn's wife tell him that the Fianna pass the time by flinging a huge boulder single-handed to and fro over the house without allowing it to touch the ground. In attempting the same feat, the giant nearly kills himself and withdraws from the area before a worse fortune might befall him![26] How such anecdotes came into the body of Fenian lore is readily explained, for conflict with other-world or extraordinary beings has been central to the tradition at all times.

Great heroes by their very nature possess gigantic strength and — as I have suggested — the *Acallamh* author found a motif which suited the notion in the phantasies of anti-quarianism. But the inflation of Fianna dimensions suited another and more logical purpose, for it helped to explain the time lapse between the ancient days of heroism and the new days of religion. If the physical size could be maximised, it accordingly meant that the life-span of the heroes could be maximised. So Oisín and Caoilte could be envisaged as bridging the great time-gap (about five ordinary lifetimes),[27] simply

23 References in *Béaloideas* 2 (1930), 227; Murphy, *op. cit.*, xvi; Type 1149 in S. Ó Súilleabháin and R.Th. Christiansen, *The Types of the Irish Folktale*, Helsinki 1967.

24 For other bluff stories in Irish tradition, see D. Ó hÓgáin, *An File*, Dublin 1982, 150-3, 433.

25 It is based on the international folktale AT 1149, 'Children Desire Ogre's Flesh', which plot was probably attracted by the ritual of chewing his thumb which was a specialty of Fionn (see notes 73 and 75 below).

26 S. O'Sullivan, *The Folklore of Ireland*, London 1974, 39; and IFC Catalogue. This anecdote derives from that of Fionn's mighty leap with a stone either on his hands or between his legs (see notes 28, 50 and 51 below), but the giant has been added.

27 The synchronisers of Irish history had, from the tenth century onwards, placed the heroic epoch of the Fianna in the reign of Cormac mac Airt, believed to have been the third century — see Murphy, *op. cit.*, xli, lix-lx; T. Ó Cathasaigh, *The Heroic Bio-graphy of Cormac mac Airt*, Dublin 1977, 24-6. This allowed for two hundred years to the time of Patrick.

because the Fianna lived gigantically long lives. Fionn, we are told in the *Acallamh*, lived to an age of two hundred and thirty years, and died only then from over-exerting himself at a mighty leap.[28] So, within that setting, it was advanced as credible, that Oisín and Caoilte could have survived into the time of St Patrick — a great and productive fancy which gave the *imprimatur* to the whole view of the Fianna as heroes with quite extraordinary attributes.

A side-effect of the process was to develop the aetiological sense in the Fenian lore. The two typical and spokesman-like survivors of the Fianna were at the centre of the stage when it mattered, that is at the beginning of the Christian era which was also the beginning of written Irish history.[29] So they represented the old order, that order which was seen as primeval, hence fundamental to the old world which Patrick was breaking into in order to change and refashion it. Accordingly, the introduction of the national saint into the corpus of Fenian lore had the effect of stressing and galvanising the aetiological aspects of it. The biographies of Patrick had long been a vehicle for the justification of the existing political and ecclesiastical structures of the country, and all of this was tied up with traditions of his itinerary and his association with particular places.[30] So, in the Fenian tradition, the taste for outdoor life and for topography was strengthened and developed by the adjunct of Patrician culture. But we should not over-stress this point, for it is likely that many such traits of the Fenian tradition predated the *Acallamh* by a long time. It is apparent that the landscape and the Fianna were associated together in a special way since the very earliest days of the lore — an indication, perhaps, of the mythical origin of Fionn himself.

28 Stokes, *op. cit.*, 72.
29 The author of the *Acallamh* would have been well aware that Christianity brought writing to Ireland, which factor accounts for the repeated commands he puts in Patrick's mouth to write down the lore.
30 See L. Bieler, *The Life and Legend of St Patrick*, Dublin 1948, 41-8; D. Ó hÓgáin, *The Hero in Irish Folk History*, Dublin 1985, 13-4, 323. A related motif occurs in the *Acallamh* (Stokes, *op. cit.*, 131-2).

In this regard an interesting example is furnished by the *fulachta Fiann* or 'cooking-pits of the Fianna', as they are commonly known. These are places where cooking was carried on by means of heated stones in ancient times.[31] Céitinn in the seventeenth century tells us how the Fianna, when out hunting, used to put water in pits in the yellow clay of the heath, place the meat in these, and then put heated stones on top of the meat to cook it: 'And these fires were so large that their sites are today in Ireland burnt to blackness, and these are now called Fulacht Fian by the peasantry.'[32] Open-air cooking is referred to by the term *fulachtadh* in the *Acallamh*, and Caoilte boasts in the same text of the many different types of meat and other food-stuffs which were brought to *fulacht Féinne* (the *fulacht*, i.e., cooking or cooking apparatus, of the Fenian band).[33] *Cormac's Glossary*, which was put together around the year 900 A.D., refers to a *fulacht fian* as a cooking-site of 'the fiana'.[34] This latter is the general term for warrior-hunters, which in a more restricted and definite sense signifies Fionn's band (the Fianna).[35] Obviously such warrior-hunters would cook their food in a rather spontaneous manner in the wilderness, but it is clear that the Fianna of Fionn Mac Cumhaill were traditionally seen as the typical actors in the role.[36] It may always have been so, and indeed the reference in *Cormac's Glossary* could be intended specifically for our Fianna. Roasting on a spit and broiling with stones in the forest occur as standard practice in eighth- and ninth-century Fenian

---

31 Ó Ríordáin, *op. cit.*, 43-5, 100.
32 Dinneen, *op. cit.*, 328.
33 Stokes, *op. cit.*, 21, 43-4, 74; de hÍde, *op. cit.*, 104-6.
34 K. Meyer, ed., *Sanas Cormaic* (i.e. *Anecdota from Irish Manuscripts* 4, Halle and Dublin 1912), 46. For further references, see *Contributions to a Dictionary of the Irish Language*, (DIL below), Royal Irish Academy 1913-75, s.v. *fulacht*.
35 DIL s.v. *fian*.
36 It appears as though much of the Fionn-lore was developed by such a warrior-hunter class. This might explain some general aspects of the tradition, e.g. its outdoor atmosphere, its populist nature, and the figure of Fionn as a more homely type of deity — see Murphy, *op. cit.*, ciii-cvi, xl-xliii; and also note 3 above.

texts.[37] For example an eighth-century description tells how Fionn met his son Oisín who had been missing for a year. Fionn had searched for him throughout Ireland, and eventually came on him as he was cooking a pig in the wilderness. Oisín did not at once recognise his father and reached for his weapons, but the situation was defused when both engaged in poetic conversation and all was made clear.[38] This is an interesting early example of an international folktale, AT 873, 'The Hero Discovers his Unknown Son', in Irish tradition.[39] But what interests us here is that the Fianna appear to have had a perennial association with outdoor cooking, and it is thus reasonable to assume that the modern folk explanation of ancient cooking-sites as relics of the Fianna is part of the basic aetiological impulse in the tradition.

Another aspect of the landscape commonly associated with Fenian lore is the dolmens — that is, prehistoric burial structures which entail a large rather flat rock raised on top of two or more other rocks.[40] The common name in Irish for a dolmen is 'leaba Dhiarmada agus Ghráinne', 'bed of Diarmaid and Gráinne' — imagery which recalls the famous Fenian romance which has the young woman, although betrothed to an ageing Fionn, eloping with the dashing young hero Diarmaid Ó Duibhne. During their flight from Fionn and his men, the folk say, the young lovers often slept on top of these dolmens, whose raised structures afforded a vantage point to fight off the foe if surprised.[41] This nomenclature has been used for centuries — Céitinn cites an example of it from his own time [42] — and there are certain references in the *Acallamh* which suggest that the author may have been aware of it. For

---

37   See Meyer, *op. cit.*, (1910), xviii-xx; Murphy, *op. cit.*, lv-lvii.
38   Meyer, *op. cit.*, (1910), 24-7.
39   Another version of this folktale — in a slightly later text — is the tragic account of Cú Chulainn killing his son Conlaí (A.G. van Hamel, *Compert Con Culainn and Other Stories*, Dublin 1956, 9-15).
40   Ó Ríordáin, *op. cit.* 57, 72-3, 84-5. For descriptions of many of these, see W.C. Borlase, *The Dolmens of Ireland*, 3 vols., London 1897.
41   See Murphy, *op. cit.*, xxxv; IFC Catalogue; and note 40 above.
42   Dinneen, *op. cit.*, 324-6.

instance, he describes the Fianna as raising three standing stones in order to place the bed of a sick man on them, and again gives the name of the gravestone under which Diarmaid was buried as 'Leaba Dhiarmada'.[43] It is at least clear that dolmens and perhaps other stone structures were already associated with the Fianna in medieval times – the implication being that they had been able to construct them due to their enormous strength.[44]

The earliest full version we have of the romance of Diarmaid and Gráinne dates from the fifteenth or sixteenth century,[45] but from references to the story we know that it was being told for hundreds of years before that. Details from it are mentioned in the *Acallamh*, and it appears in lists of stories told by learned men as early as the tenth century.[46] Scholars accept that it contains some archaic elements, even though the story itself can hardly be older than the ninth century.[47] Versions of the story have been collected from folk tradition all over Ireland and Gaelic Scotland,[48] and it appears to have been part of popular as well as learned culture at all times. It offers a good case-study for the change, development, and decay in the aesthetic quality of a story which has had large audiences for at least a millennium. For the moment, it is sufficient to point out that topographical details have helped to perpetuate its popularity and to colour the narrative. To illustrate this, we will quote in English translation part of a

43 Stokes, *op. cit.*, 33, 43.
44 Céitinn in the seventeenth century states that dolmens were called 'beds of the Fian' (Dinneen, *op. cit.*, 348). The ability to lift large rocks is attributed to the Fianna survivors in the *Acallamh* (Stokes, *op. cit.*, 63, 77-8, 111.)
45 Edited by Nessa Ní Shéaghdha, *Tóruidheacht Dhiarmada agus Ghráinne*, Dublin 1967.
46 References enumerated by Ní Shéaghdha, *ibid.*, x-xiv, 130-7; Murphy, *op. cit.*, xxxvi. The *Acallamh* reference in Stokes, *op. cit.*, 43. See also Máirín O'Daly in J. Carney and D. Greene, *Celtic Studies*, London 1968, 99-108.
47 For different theories on this question, see R.A. Breatnach in M. Dillon, *Irish Sagas*, Cork 1968, 135-47 and Murphy, *op. cit.*, xlvii.
48 Lists given by A. Bruford in *Gaelic Folk-Tales and Mediaeval Romances*, (= *Béaloideas* 34 [1966], Dublin 1969, 265-6. See also *ibid.*, 106-9; and Ní Shéaghdha, *op. cit.*, (1967), xviii-xxix.

version collected from the oral tradition of Co. Galway in
1936:

> Long ago in the time of the Fianna, Fionn Mac Cumhaill
> had a woman whose name was Gráinne. But Diarmaid Ó
> Duibhne had a love-spot which, if any woman saw, she
> would fall in love with him. Gráinne saw this spot, and
> they eloped together. They were followed by Fionn and
> his men, and they had to go on the run from place to
> place in order to avoid his vengeance. There is a place in
> Moynish called Diarmaid's Bed — above the beach — where
> they spent some time. After that they headed off down
> towards Oughterard. Coming to a river, Diarmaid decided
> to jump over it. There was a fairly large rock near the bank,
> and when he jumped he took the rock between his two
> ankles right over to the other side. Gráinne remarked,
> however, that he had leaped with the slope on the bank, so
> he leaped back over the river against the slope. But the rock
> is there still where he landed the first time, with a hole in
> the ground on either side of it where he left his footprints.
> And the place is named *Baile na Léime*, 'the Townland of
> the Leap' ever since . . .[49]

Diarmaid is portrayed in various literary sources as a great
leaper, but the specific motif which lies in the background
here is borrowed from the image of Fionn. An important text
states that Fionn died as a result of his exertions when, in his
old age, he jumped a river while carrying a large stone on his
palm. He did this at the instigation of a woman, who challenged him to repeat an earlier jump.[50] Accounts of this
magnificent, though fatal, feat of Fionn survived in oral
tradition until recent times, and various sites were pointed

49 IFC 159:479-82.
50 Maud Joynt, *Feis Tighe Chonáin*, Dublin 1936, 6, 43-5, i.e. from
    about the fifteenth century. From the tenth century onwards there
    are various incomplete accounts — *Zeitschrift für celtische Philo-
    logie* 1 (1896-7), 462-5; *ibid.*, II (1917), 44; Stokes, *op. cit.*, 72, 81.
    See also Meyer, *op. cit.*, (1910), xxii, xxv, and Murphy, *op. cit.*,
    xlii. For other characters to take on aspects of Fionn himself in
    the developing lore seems to be a general tendency — for one
    specific instance, see J.F. Nagy in *Celtica* 14 (1981), 8-14.

out as the place in question.[51] There are many other examples
of such mythological-type portrayal of the Fianna in later
folk tradition. For instance, it is said in Munster that Fionn,
reduced once by extreme penury to beachcombing for food,
put a curse on limpets — for which reason they are black in
colour ever since.[52] But particularly the origins of certain
social presuppositions are ascribed to Fionn. As one might
expect, these are typical of the values of traditional rural
society. For example, the ideal of self-sufficiency is encapsuled
in the Irish dictum: 'The greatest shame that ever came on
Fionn, a glass in his hand but nothing to put in it!'[53] The
ideal of co-operation is expressed in a Scottish maxim: 'Fionn
never abandoned a friend who stood at his right hand!'[54]
And the ideal of success in worldly affairs is expressed rather
bluntly in the quatrain: 'Four things to which Fionn gave his
hatred — a lean hound and a slow steed, a leader of a country
without shrewdness, and a man's wife who bears no children.'[55]

The late literary sources are somewhat more didactic. In
these Fionn and his men are stated to have been extraordinarily
generous, pure of heart, and true to their word. The folk
tradition, more earthy, does not expressly deny such moralistic
tenets, but it relishes narratives which often deny them in
practice. In avoiding this kind of abstraction, it has greater
honesty than the literature, which often contradicts its high-
sounding theories by portraying actions of the Fianna which

51 IFC 22:393, 54:5; N. O'Kearney, *Feis Tighe Chonáin Chinn-
    Shléibhe*, Dublin 1855, 131. In the *Journal of the Kilkenny
    Archaeological Society* 1 (1849-51), 361 a great leap is attributed
    to Fionn's rival, Goll.
52 P. Ó Laoghaire, *Sgeuluidheacht Chúige Mumhan*, Dublin 1895,
    18, 110; Máire Ní Chinnéide, ed., *Peig*, Dublin 1936, 105; *Béaloideas*
    5 (1935), 284, *ibid.*, 6 (1936), 29; IFC Catalogue. See also
    Murphy, *op. cit.*, xxi.
53 D. Hyde, *An Leath-Rann*, Dublin 1922, 68. See also *Irisleabhar
    na Gaedhilge* 4 (1889-93), 207; and *The Irish Press* 10/9/1940.
54 Hyde, *op. cit.*, (1922), 18.
55 *Irisleabhar na Gaedhilge* 16 (1906-7), 198.

are sordid enough.[56] But, as to curiosity regarding more
physical aspects of the great old heroic age, the folk tradition
sometimes deliberately amplifies the literary images. In the
literature, for instance, we have several long lists of names of
the Fianna's hunting-hounds.[57] Not satisfied with this, Cork
oral tradition furnishes us with the names of a dozen cats
which it claims Fionn had. This amusing enumeration goes
like this: 'Slender cat, old cat, fierce cat, excellent cat,
fat cat, morbid cat, striped cat, black cat, grey cat, wild cat,
yearling kitten, and malingerer!'[58] Cat-lovers will recognise
here a list of feline images which fairly describes the species.
It is almost as if Fionn is being made the patron of cats!

Mythologists have often pointed out that one of the oldest
themes regarding Fionn has him — in a classic pattern of Celtic
deities — contending with and defeating a one-eyed fiery
foe.[59] Thus, in the *Acallamh*, he first assumed leadership of
the Fianna from Goll (i.e., 'One-Eyed') by overcoming the
sprite Aillén, who set fire to the citadel of Tara every Hal-
loween night.[60] This is in fact a duplication of the one opposition functionary.[61] Redactors of such tradition in late
medieval times would tend to associate one-eyed otherworld
foes with the cyclops of Greek mythology, and with the giant
Polyphemus and his parallels in international folktales.[62]
The giant-like imagery already associated with the Fianna
would accelerate this process. At any rate, the type of giant-
lore currently found within the Fenian tradition was already
there in the fifteenth century, for, in a text dating from around

56 Good qualities of the Fianna — Stokes, *op. cit.*, 119-20 etc. For
    examples of idealisation of Fionn and his men in the later litera-
    ture, see Ó Cadhlaigh, *op. cit.*, 218-29. For treacherous traits in
    Fionn's character, see E. Mac Neill, *Duanaire Finn* Part I, London
    1908, xlix; Ó Cadhlaigh, *op. cit.*, 229-37.
57 Stokes, *op. cit.*, 146; P. Ó Siochfhradha, *Laoithe na Féinne*,
    Áth Cliath, 1941, 6, 67-9, 124.
58 *Béaloideas* 11 (1941), 61.
59 O'Rahilly, *op. cit.*, 72-4, 320; Murphy, *op. cit.*, lxviii-lxxv.
60 Stokes, *op. cit.*, 47-50.
61 See note 59 above.
62 See R. Graves, *The Greek Myths*, Vol. 2, Penguin Books, Har-
    mondsworth 1960, 355-7, 366 and AT 1137, 'The Ogre Blinded
    (Polyphemus)'.

that time, we have a version of a story which is widely disseminated in later lore. This tells how Fionn saves a child
from a giant who puts his gigantic hand into a house in order
to snatch the child away. Fionn achieves this victory due to
the assistance of some extraordinary helpers — a marvellous
hearer, a marvellous thief, a marvellous runner, etc.[63] It is in
fact a composite story, being a combination of the international folktale AT 513, 'The Skillful Companions',[64] and an
early Irish-Welsh motif (Hand-down-the-Chimney).[65] Some
scholars have suggested that the latter motif was part of the
Fenian lore from earliest times.[66] This is unlikely, but it
does seem to have been linked to Fionn because of the lore
in which he contends with phantoms and otherworld inhabitants of forts and raths. This would place the hero in an
original role of fighting against destructive forces of the underworld — a role for which tradition would naturally have to
equip him with extraordinary attributes.

Several literary narratives of the fifteenth and sixteenth
centuries describe how the Fianna are captured by hostile
magicians in a *bruíon* or palace, to escape from which they
must exert all their powers.[67] It is obvious that the *bruíon*
stories derive their central theme from the older literature,[68]
and some scholars incline towards the theory that such hostile
dwellings are an Irish version of the world of the dead.[69]
There are some indications that this might be so. One tale,

---

63   Joynt, *op. cit.*, 26-31. For list of folklore versions, see Type 513
     in Ó Súilleabháin and Christiansen, *op. cit.*
64   Some versions of this Fionn story are also related to AT 653,
     'The Four Skillful Brothers'.
65   Welsh version in R.L. Thomson, *Pwyll Pendeuic Dyuet*, Dublin
     1957, 17-20.
66   See Murphy, *op. cit.*, xiv-xvi.
67   Accounts of these narratives in Ó Cadhlaigh, *op. cit.*, 83-118; and
     Bruford, *op. cit.*, 115-8.
68   An early prototype for the situation is found in a twelfth-century
     story — *Revue Celtique* 7 (1886), 289-307; *ibid.* 13 (1892), 5-7.
     This tells of how Fionn, Oisín, and Caoilte find themselves in a
     sinister otherworld dwelling, the inhabitants of which they must
     fight. For dating and bibliography, see Meyer, *op. cit.*, (1910),
     xxiii, xxv; and Murphy, *op. cit.*, lx, 26-7.
69   References in Murphy, *ibid.*, xxxii-xxxiii.

for example, which was known in the tenth century but has
since been lost, told of an adventure which Fionn had in
'Dearc Fearna', which is an enormous prehistoric cavern in
Co. Kilkenny.[70] At any rate, the pitting of the Fianna against
powerful otherworld beings, against phantoms, monsters, and
giants, would entail the possession of prodigious strength
which — whether involving gigantic size or not — would allow
for the kind of feats which are arbitrarily attributed to them
in oral tradition. These feats include digging out valleys,
carrying bullocks under the arm, tearing up trees from their
roots and tearing large animals asunder in tug-of-wars with
giants.[71]

What has been said up to now amounts to this — that a
broad range of Fenian lore has been in existence for over a
thousand years, that the core of it has to do with aspects of
pre-Christian religion, that it has been 'historicised' into a
great heroic age, that this lore has been closely identified with
aspects of the landscape and tends to take on aetiological
perspectives, and that the popularity of the lore has never
waned. It has always remained a lively source of interest, and
has had the benefit of a sense of humour which has added to
its attraction without making it ridiculous. The question then
arises — were these various traits of the lore of sufficient
intensity to allow us to speak of the Fenian tradition as being
productively mythic in the Gaelic psyche? In other words,
could the leading characters in the lore be taken to embody
certain definite aspirations of the ordinary person?

70 This story *Echtra Fhind i nDerc Ferna* was apparently identical
    with *Uath Dercce Ferna*, also lost — see Meyer, *op. cit.*, (1910),
    xxiv. The same cavern occurs in a surviving poem of the period,
    in which it is the haunt of a monster — R.I. Best, O. Bergin, and
    M.A. O'Brien, *The Book of Leinster*, Vol. 1, Dublin 1954, 209.
    The cavern is now known as 'the Cave of Dunmore'. Hogan, *op.
    cit.*, 342, is incorrect when he doubts the identification, for
    native Irish speakers of the area called the Cave of Dunmore
    'Dearc Fhearna' — see J. Carrigan, *History of the Diocese of
    Ossory*, Dublin 1905, Vol. 3, 455, 459; and Carrigan Mss 29:157,
    48:23 (on microfilms p903-p904 in the National Library of
    Ireland). Townland names 'Coill Fhearna' and 'Áth Fhearna' are
    in the vicinity.
71 References in Murphy, *op. cit.*, xviii-xix.

We will begin with the personality who was always at the centre of the tradition, Fionn Mac Cumhaill himself. In early times, one of his most important images was that of a seer. Texts of the eighth and ninth centuries describe how he gained magical knowledge by chasing an otherworld being into a rath. The door was slammed on his thumb as he attempted to gain entry and, since the thumb was inside the rath for a while, it became possessed of knowledge.[72] So, when he wished to gain knowledge of past, present, and future, all Fionn need do ever after was to chew his thumb and his mind would be illumined.[73] We know from other sources that the chewing of flesh to gain knowledge was a ritual among poet-seers of ancient Ireland, and this has obviously coloured the imagery here.[74] The basic image in Fionn's case, however, may have been that of the child seer sucking his thumb and acquiring thereby the wisdom which pertains to poetry and prophecy.[75] So the motif of Fionn's thumb of knowledge seems to be of great antiquity. It is also one of the ideas concerning him that has had greatest vogue in oral tradition, it being a suitable mechanism to move the plot of all and every type of adventure narrative. A parallel idea developed from it

72 *Revue Celtique* 25 (1904), 344-6; *ibid.*, 14 (1893), 246; O'Rahilly, *op. cit.*, 328-9. These accounts are confusions of two distinct motifs, i.e. the otherworld drink and the thumb of knowledge — see O'Rahilly, *ibid.*, 326-9, and Ó hÓgáin, *op. cit.*, (1982), 211-5. Another example in a twelfth-century text — S.H. O'Grady, *Silva Gadelica*, London 1892, Vol. 1, 91.

73 See note 72 above, and *Revue Celtique* 5 (1881), 201.

74 References in O'Rahilly, *op. cit.*, 336-40; and Ó hÓgáin, *op. cit.*, (1982), 272-3, 441. The account (Meyer, *op. cit.* [1912], 64) states that a piece of meat used to be chewed and then laid behind the door as part of the ritual. Whether it is accurate or not, this account in time became confused with the independent tradition of Fionn's thumb. Two linguistic similarities could have helped the confusion of meat with thumb. First, the word used for the piece of meat is *mír*, 'portion', which resembles *mér*, 'finger' — referred to instead of thumb in *Revue Celtique* 25 (1904), 344-6. Secondly, the terms of measurement *mér*, 'finger' and *ordu* 'thumb' were commonly used in the sense of a piece or morsel of meat (see DIL).

75 The chewing would have derived from the ritual referred to in note 74 above. Placing of fingers in the mouth as a ritual is referred

in medieval times and is also evidenced by modern folk tradition — that of Fionn having a special tooth of knowledge, which is a natural transference from the thumb due to the process of chewing.[76]

This brings us to the question of the account of Fionn's youth, oral versions of which have been collected all over the Gaelic world and of which we have a literary redaction from the twelfth century.[77] From a study of the latter and of other references it is clear that this youth-biography of Fionn was in existence as a full narrative at an even earlier date. However, it can hardly predate the ninth century, as parts of it are influenced by the account of Cú Chulainn's youth which was compiled around that time.[78] At any rate, the youth-biography of Fionn, in both literature and folklore, contains an explanation of the thumb of knowledge which has been superimposed onto the earlier understandings of it. It is said that Fionn, at the age of seven, came to the river Boyne, where he met an elderly sage who had been for a long time seeking the salmon of knowledge which was in the river. Having finally caught the salmon, the sage ordered Fionn to

to in one very early Irish source — W. Stokes and J. Strachan, *Thesaurus Palaeohibernicus*, Vol. 2, Oxford 1901, 249. Engravings on an eighth-century cross-slab from Co. Donegal represent a man with his right thumb in his mouth — Françoise Henry, *La Sculpture Irlandaise*, Paris 1933, plate 16. These have been claimed to represent Fionn (Murphy, *op. cit.*, lxii). Thumb-sucking would be a natural trait of the archetypal child-hero. An interesting, though obviously unrelated, parallel is the child-portrayal of the ancient Egyptian god Horus — see Veronica Ions, *Egyptian Mythology*, London 1968, 72.

76   References in O'Rahilly, *op. cit.*, 334-6.
77   Lists of versions in S. Ó Duilearga, *Leabhar Sheáin Í Chonaill*, Baile Átha Cliath 1948, 427; R.Th. Christiansen, *The Vikings and the Viking Wars in Irish and Gaelic Tradition*, Oslo 1931, 20-5; Ó Súilleabháin and Christiansen, *op. cit.*, Type 673. The twelfth-century recension is published in *Revue Celtique* 5 (1881), 195-204. Other literary references in Mac Neill, *op. cit.*, 33-4, 36; Stokes, *op. cit.*, 47; Best and Bergin, *op. cit.*, 101-3; Joynt, *op. cit.*, 5. An in-depth study is J.F. Nagy, *The Wisdom of the Outlaw*, Berkeley 1985.
78   Cecile O'Rahilly, *Táin Bó Cúailnge, Recension 1*, Dublin 1976, 13-9.

cook it on a spit. Fionn burned his thumb by accident and put it into his mouth to relieve the pain. Thus he gets the first taste of the salmon and becomes a poet and prophet.[79] So we can see that, to the earlier tradition of Fionn's thumb, two other and distinct traditions have been added. One — widely attested in the early literature — is that the Boyne waters and the wonderful salmon therein are a source of mystical inspiration.[80] The other is comparable to an international motif B217.1.1. 'Animal languages learned from eating serpent'.[81] Some peculiar aspects of the Fionn-version, however, — namely the tasting by accident rather than deliberately, and the image of the burnt thumb — make it clear that it belongs to a special ecotype of an international folktale. There is obviously some connection between this motif and the story concerning Sigurd the Volsung in old Icelandic tradition.[82] It is very difficult to decide on the nature of this connection, but the most plausible theory is that the Irish or Scottish Gaels adopted and adapted the folktale from the Norse since they saw it as being suitable to the image of Fionn's mystical thumb. This would presumably have occurred when Norse influence on the Gaelic

79   Revue Celtique 5 (1881), 201.
80   References in T.F. O'Rahilly, op. cit., 318-23.
81   This motif also occurs in a widespread folktale AT 673 'The White Serpent's Flesh'.
82   For comparison and discussion of versions of the Sigurd story in medieval Norse, see R.D. Scott, The Thumb of Knowledge, New York 1930, 193-203. Sigurd and his thumb are also represented on carvings (dating back in some cases to the tenth century) over a wide area in Scandinavia, northern England, and the Isle of Man — see Scott, 204-10; H.R. Ellis in Antiquity 16 (1942), 216-36; and J.T. Lang in The Yorkshire Archaeological Journal 48 (1976), 83-9.

world was at its zenith, i.e., around the tenth century.[83]

Oral tradition gives more compact and rounded versions of the youth-biography than do the literary sources, which have a rather scattered effect as if the material has been edited and selected in order to convey information rather than for purposes of dramatic unity. The biography is of general interest, not least because of how it exhibits the special type of colouring which belongs to Fenian epic. The hero is born posthumously, after his father has been killed in battle by Goll son of Morna, who is Fionn's great rival in the cycle. Fionn is reared secretly in the forest, with a secluded dwelling in the hollow of a tree, for fear his father's enemies will kill him. Going to an assembly one day, he defeats all the other

83   The complicated problem of the relationship between the Fionn and Sigurd stories has occupied many writers — for lists of studies see Scott, *op. cit.*, 212-57; and Ó hÓgáin, *op. cit.*, (1982), 233-42, 438-9. The present writer regards the following as the most likely paradigm: Since knowledge was believed to be gained by eating certain kinds of flesh (note 74 above), and since the salmon of the Boyne was a celebrated source of knowledge (note 80 above), the idea grew up that Fionn had eaten that salmon or a morsel thereof. This invited another motif viz. the killing of a foe in the shape of a salmon (see T.F. O'Rahilly, *op. cit.*, 318-23). The result of this whole process was said to have gained knowledge through an adventure at the Boyne river which involved killing a seer and eating a salmon. Meanwhile, in Norse tradition, young Sigurd was reputed to have killed a dragon — which was an ally of his adult foe — and to have burned his finger by accident in its broth. Finding that this gave the finger a horny covering, he smeared himself with it so as to acquire invulnerability. The gaining of a magical gift from the dragon's broth attracted AT 673, and the resultant confusion gave rise to the account of how Sigurd gained knowledge of bird-language (as in AT 673) after he tasted the dragon-broth which burned his finger. The close Norse-Gaelic intercourse of medieval times enabled parallels to be drawn between this Sigurd tradition and that of Fionn (the youth of both heroes, their magical knowledge, and their victory over an adult foe). Accordingly, their images influenced each other. The plot of the Sigurd story was felt suitable for rationalising the strange lore which had the Boyne salmon as an alter-ego of Fionn's adult competitor, and in addition it provided a suitable context for the image of Fionn's celebrated thumb. In the opposite direction, Sigurd's finger was replaced by a thumb — on the Fionn pattern.

boys there at hurling and swimming and his true identity is
suspected. He flees along with his foster-mother through woods
and forests. When she tires he carries her on his shoulders,
and has travelled a great distance before he realises that she
has been torn asunder by the projecting tree-branches and
only the calves of her legs remain. Then follows the salmon
of the Boyne episode and that of how Fionn defeats the
burner of Tara and becomes leader of the Fianna, as his father
before him had been.[84] When faced with a logical obstacle,
of course, folk tradition is always ready to improvise. And so,
in the story of Diarmaid and Gráinne, it occurred to people
that the fleeing lovers could easily be discovered if Fionn
made sufficient use of his thumb of knowledge. So it was
necessary to find a way around this. The lovers are therefore
represented as sleeping on a bag of sand when inland and on a
bag of heather when near the sea, so that Fionn's clairvoyant
powers were confused.[85]

The consistency which oral narration demands is evidenced
also by the striking attribute of Diarmaid which I have already
referred to in passing. That is his love-spot (*ball seirce* or *ball
searc*), which caused women to be magically attracted to him.
This is in Gaelic folklore sources basically a peculiarity of
Diarmaid alone, although certain other characters have also
acquired it from him.[86] In the only full literary version of
the *Pursuit of Diarmaid and Gráinne* which has survived, the
plot begins with the betrothal banquet of Gráinne to Fionn
where she puts the Fianna warriors to sleep with a strong
potion and then compels Diarmaid to elope with her by invoking magical terms of coercion called *geasa*.[87] In place of
this, the oral versions have Gráinne accidentally seeing the
love-spot on Diarmaid, and the two thus become embroiled
in the adventure through no fault of their own.[88] The literary
version has borrowed the *geasa* motif from a more ancient
formulation of the same plot — the story of Deirdre in the

84 For discussion and some examples, see Murphy, *op. cit.*, l-liii.
85 Ní Shéaghdha, *op. cit.*, (1967), xxi; Bruford, *op. cit.*, 107-8.
86 For other characters, see Ó hÓgáin, *op. cit.*, (1985), 267-70;
    P. Ó Direáin, *Sgéalaidhe Leitir Mealláin*, Baile Átha Cliath 1926, 28.
87 Ní Shéaghdha, *op. cit.* (1967), 10.
88 References in Bruford, *op. cit.*, 108, 265.

Ulster cycle.[89] This leaves us with the sleep-potion having a
broadly similar function as the love-spot in the oral versions.
Interestingly, the function is fulfilled by a love-potion in the
third great Celtic formulation of the plot — the romance of
Tristan and Isolt.[90] Is there therefore some connection
between the love-spot and love-potions, a connection which
is not evidenced in the literary tradition?

It is as well to begin this quest in an empirical fashion by
describing the imagery of Diarmaid's love-spot. It was widely
referred to in the oral tradition of both Ireland and Scotland,
and it was situated on his face or his forehead.[91] We can regard
it as a way of concretising an idea which is to the fore in the
later literary sources — where he is described as being a darling
of women, a man with slow-moving eye, and a continuous
wooer.[92] Some texts use the epithet *dreachsholais* for him,
i.e., 'of lustrous countenance', which is intended to convey
how he appears in the eyes of women.[93] To demonstrate the
parallelism between this literary portrayal and the oral one
we can cite a literary story from the seventeenth century or
thereabouts which describes how he and some others were
being held captive by magic. They were being guarded by a
young lady and 'Diarmaid of the bright teeth' spoke amorously

89 V. Hull, *Longes Mac n-Uislenn*, New York 1949, 46.
90 For a discussion of this, see Gertrude Schoepperle, *Tristan and
    Isolt*, London 1913, 21-4, 401-10. Comparison with the Diarmaid
    and Gráinne romance on pp. 395-475.
91 See note 88 above, and also D. de hÍde, *An Sgeuluidhe Gaelach*,
    Baile Átha Cliath 1933, 125; IFC 1170:277.
92 Ó Siochfhradha, *op. cit.*, 6, 70, 234, 277 ('D. of the women');
    267, 274-6 (continuous wooing); 192 ('D. of the slow-moving
    eyes'). Also 'D. of the women' in O. Ó Aimhirgin, E. Mac Néill,
    Eachtra Lomnochtáin, Baile Átha Cliath, n.d., 29. For the same
    type of portrayal, see J.G. Campbell, *The Fians; or Stories,
    Poems and Traditions of Fionn and his Warrior Band* (= *Waifs
    and Strays of Celtic Tradition*, Vol. 4), London 1891, 62.
93 Ní Shéaghdha, *op. cit.* (1967), 8; P. Mac Piarais, *Bruidhean
    Chaorthainn*, Baile Átha Cliath, n.d., 24. He is said to be *déad-
    sholais*, 'of lustrous teeth', in Nessa Ní Shéaghadha and Máire Ní
    Mhuirgheasa, *Trí Bruidhne*, Baile Atha Cliath n.d., 13, 41. See
    also note 94 below.

to her and persuaded her to release them.[94] In oral versions of the same story, he secures her help by showing her the love-spot.[95] There can be no doubt but that this love-spot of Diarmaid goes back in the oral tradition for hundreds of years. It was already widespread in folk tradition from Scotland to Munster in the eighteenth century.[96] Moreover, in a fifteenth-century poem he is called 'a seducer of women with a great quality',[97] so it is reasonable to assume that the image was already current by then. There are examples of somewhat similar imagery in the medieval literature. In a text of the thirteenth or fourteenth century the wizard Mongán gives the appearance of beauty to an ugly woman as a prank: 'Mongán put a love-spell ("bliocht seirce") in the cheeks of the hag, and when the king of Leinster saw her he was immediately filled with amorousness and love for her.'[98] Even earlier texts use the word *oíbheall*, 'spark', with somewhat similar connotations, such as *aible serci*, 'love-sparks', on the face and *oible oitedh*, 'sparks of youth', also on the face.[99] But there is a certain definiteness about the image in the folk-lore sources on Diarmaid which these literary samples lack.

The earliest and most persistent portrayal of Diarmaid as a lover concerns Gráinne and their tragic elopement, so it is

---

94 The story, which is in ballad form, is published in Ó Siochfhradha, 137-45. *Déadgheal*, 'bright teeth', epithet on p. 142. The epithet also occurs *ibid.*, 112, 121, 193. Diarmaid is also described as *déadgheal* in a fourteenth-century text — Mac Neill, *op. cit.*, (1908), 45.

95 IFC 41:39-45, 79:6-10, 79:49-54; de hÍde, *op. cit.*, (1933), 156-8. These oral versions, in prose, are derived from the ballad, but include the love-spot.

96 Scottish versions of that time in J.F. Campbell, *Leabhar na Feinne*, London 1872, 154. For indirect proof of eighteenth-century versions in Munster, see Ó hÓgáin, *op. cit.* (1982), 229, 254-6.

97 *Revue Celtique* 33 (1912), 165, 168. A parallel to Diarmaid is instanced by the character Ciabhán in the *Acallamh* (Stokes, *op. cit.*, 107), who is exceedingly handsome and of whom all women are enamoured. The fact that this is not Diarmaid may indicate that he had not attained his fully-fledged image by then.

98 K. Meyer, *Voyage of Bran*, Vol. 2, London 1897, 1, 69.

99 K. Meyer, *Aislinge Meic Conglinne*, London 1892, 97; O. Bergin *et al.*, eds., *Anecdota from Irish Manuscripts*, 1, Halle 1907, 51.

clear that the original reason for the love-spot is to allow the
plot of the story to have Gráinne fall in love with him. In
this, as we have said, it is co-functional with a love-potion —
a motif which appears to have been in earlier forms of the
story. So, was a special manifestation on the face or forehead
regarded as part of love-magic in a similar context to drinks
and concoctions? There are some indications that it was, and
that such ideas were common in the ancient world. The Latin
writer Petronius refers to a concoction of spittle and dust
with which the forehead of a young man was marked in order
to awaken enthusiasm in his paramour,[100] while the Hindu
writer Kalayana Malla in the fifteenth century states that
whoever will place on his forehead a mark compounded of
certain herbs and other things 'will subdue the world of
women, and she who looks upon his brow cannot fail to feel
for him the most eager desire.'[101] The tenacity of these ideas
over a wide space of time and a wide area can be accounted
for by the perennial appeal of love-magic. We can be confident that the substances used for making these marks on
the forehead are of the same type, and probably identical
with, those employed in brewing love-potions.[102] So the
likelihood is that such a physical marking as a constituent part
of love-concoctions was known to Gaelic culture and was
attracted to the Diarmaid and Gráinne story by the image of a
magical drink. The rather more abstract imagery of Diarmaid's
attractive face which appeared lustrous to women would
then guarantee its entry into the story. Such a sequence of
development would also explain why Diarmaid had what was
in love-magic a deliberate charm but had no deliberate intent

100   *Satyricon*:131.
101   F.F. Arbuthnot and R.F. Burton, *Ananga Ranga*, New York
        1964, 69-70.
102   For references to such substances, see sources in notes 90, 100,
        101 above. For love-magic in Irish tradition, see T.P. Cross, *Motif-
        Index of Early Irish Literature*, Indiana 1952, Motifs D1355,
        D1900; Ó hÓgáin, *op. cit.* (1985), 267-72; S. Ó Catháin, *The
        Bedside Book of Irish Folklore*, Cork 1980, 87-91. A twelfth-
        century account has love-charms being secreted in nuts sent by a
        woman to Fionn — Best, Bergin, and O'Brien, *op. cit.*, Vol. 4,
        897-8, 945.

in applying it. The inherent unlikelihood of this situation may indeed be the very reason why his love-spot was rejected by the literary writers.

Once the love-spot was firmly established in oral tradition, of course, people would find it necessary to explain how it came to be on Diarmaid's brow. And so, throughout Irish-speaking Ireland was told a story which may be summarized as follows:

A group of the Fianna go astray in a fog while out hunting and arrive at a strange house. There they find an old man, a beautiful young woman, and a ram. Food is set on the table before them, but the ram butts the table and upsets it. Each of the Fianna try to tie the ram to the wall, but in vain. Then the old man does so without difficulty. The Fianna eat their fill, and then go to bed. During the night, Fionn tries to enter the young woman's bed, but he is rejected with the words: 'You had me once, you will never have me again!' Before they leave next morning, the old man explains that the ram is life, he himself is age, and the girl is youth. She then offers each of them whatever gift he desires. Diarmaid asks for the love-spot, Oisín for the grace of God, Oscar for a thong in his flail which will never fail, Conán for the ability to kill hundreds, and Fionn for the odour of clay to be removed from his body.[103]

The similarity between this story and the early thirteenth century Icelandic account of Tor's visit to Utgard has often been remarked upon, and scholars have generally agreed that the Icelandic story is based on an Irish original.[104] If so, some version of this allegory was current in Ireland in the tenth or eleventh centuries. At first glance, it seems unlikely that allegory would have been part of Fenian lore at that time. It may indeed be that some basic form of the story concerned characters other than the Fianna — we have several such

103 For lists and references, see Ó Duilearga, *op. cit.*, 427; Murphy, *op. cit.*, xxii; de hÍde, *op. cit.* (1933), 123-5; IFC Catalogue.

104 Text in G. Jónsson, *Edda Snorra Sturlusonar*, Akureyri 1954, 69-76. Discussion in Christiansen, *op. cit.* (1931), 30-2. A full study of the subject by Rosemary Power appears in *Béaloideas* 53 (1985), 217-94.

allegories, though unrelated to the one we are discussing, in medieval Irish literature.[105] Closer examination of the surviving Fenian literature, nevertheless, reveals that an origin for the allegory in the context of Fionn and his men is quite possible, even probable. The structure of the story, as well as certain constituent elements, can be identified in medieval texts concerning them. We have two versions of a narrative from the eleventh century relating how Fionn, Oisín, and Caoilte spent a night in a mysterious dwelling, where they met a giant, an old woman, and a headless man.[106] Again, in the twelfth century it is related in the *Acallamh* that a group of six (Fionn, Caoilte, Diarmaid, Oisín, Oscar, and Mac Lughach) sheltered from bad weather in a strange dwelling, in which a beautiful maiden brought them food and drink. The Fianna warriors learn the history of the inhabitants from their leader, join them in great battles against a rival otherworld band, and return to the ordinary world after the lapse of a year, a season, and a month.[107] These accounts are not allegories, but the mysterious atmosphere of them would suit such a narrative mode, and we may presume that an allegorical recension of the same type of plot was in existence at the time. The earliest real version of this Fenian allegory dates from about the fifteenth century. It occurs as one of a long string of stories in the text *Feis Tighe Chonáin*, and tells of how Fionn, Oisín, Caoilte, Mac Lughach, and Diarmaid were guests in the otherworld house of Cuanna.[108] The style is rather verbose and the plot disjointed, with the allegorical figures cluttered and their import not always clear; but from comparing the text with the Norse story of Utgard we can reach a few tentative conclusions. The most relevant of these here are that the beautiful maiden represented human intellect

---

105 References in Murphy, *op. cit.*, xlvi-xlvii. Some personalised characteristics are found in the *Acallamh* (Stokes, *op. cit.*, 183, 190). This tendency is presumably related to the type of allegory current in medieval Latin literature — for which see E.R. Curtius, *European Literature and the Latin Middle Ages*, London 1953, 117-27.

106 See sources in note 68 above.

107 Stokes, *op. cit.*, 136-47.

108 Joynt, *op. cit.*, 14-20.

in the original story, and that the idea of youth was not central to the interpretation.

When we set the house of Cuanna account against our folk versions, we can see what type of formulation the oral story-tellers judged to be necessary to the story. The more complex and unessential allegorical personalities had to be omitted, and the characterisation had to be centred on the Fianna — whose particularities were well-known and would accord with folk interest. This latter point explains why the gifts were added to the narrative. The motif of a magical object given to Fionn by a lady from an otherworld dwelling had been popular since the ninth century,[109] so there were precedents for the narrative technique. It will become clear, however, that in the present case the nature of the gifts springs from the developed images of the individual heroes at a late stage in the Fenian tradition. One particular gift may have had primacy, namely the gift conferred on Oisín, 'the grace of God', which refers to the well-known idea — described in the *Acallamh* — that he had survived into Christian times and had been baptised. [110] Oral tradition developed its own explanation as to how he had managed to bridge the time-gap. According to this, he sojourned for three hundred years in the otherworld — much as several other characters in early and medieval Irish tradition were reputed to have done.[111] It was especially easy for this motif to become attached to Oisín, for he was always allowed in Fenian lore to have a special connection with the other-world.[112] A poem written about the year 1750 describes how he had been brought away by a beautiful lady to the Land of

---

109   E.J. Gwynn, *The Metrical Dindshenchas*, Vol. 4, Dublin 1924, 36. A similar motif occurs in a thirteenth-century Fenian poem (Mac Neill, *op. cit.*, 42-5).

110   The ending of the *Acallamh*, missing in all surviving texts, doubt-lessly included Oisín being baptised, as Caoilte was (Stokes, *op. cit.*, 10) by Patrick. See also G. Murphy, *Duanaire Finn*, Part II, London 1933, 174.

111   For discussion, see Christiansen, *op. cit.* (1931), 10-3, 16-7. For references to Irish heroes brought away to the otherworld, see M. Dillon, *Early Irish Literature*, Chicago 1948, 101-31; and Murphy, *op. cit.* (1953), xxii-xxiii, 439-40.

112   See notes 134-6 below.

Youth. Admittedly this poem is extremely late, but we can be sure that the theme predated it by quite some time.[113] So it was claimed that, in effect, Oisín had become a Christian through the agency of a lady who represented — even personified — youth. It may be that this explanation was incorporated into the allegory at some time subsequent to the house of Cuanna version, thus transforming the leading lady's symbolism from intellect to youth and giving impetus to the notion of benefits or gifts bestowed by her. A date of around the sixteenth century would suit this line of argument, which possibly gets further support from the nature of the extra motif which is used, i.e. the rebuttal of Fionn's amorous designs. The frustration of such advances made by mortal men to beautiful ladies in otherworld dwellings was a very popular theme in Irish literature of that period.[114]

Since no definite original has been established, any theory as to the development of this strange allegorical story must be circumstantial. One editor of *Feis Tighe Chonáin* has remarked, very appropriately, that the house of Cuanna account 'forms a contrast to the rest of the work'.[115] That the redactor thought likewise is evident from the way in which he over-wrote the story, even forcing it into an uneasy union

113 B. O'Looney, *Laoidh Oisín ar Thír na n-Óg*, Dublin 1859. The author was Micheál Coimín. G. Murphy (*The Ossianic Lore and Romantic Tales of Medieval Ireland*, Dublin 1955, 27) believed that this story of Oisín was already in existence at the time the *Acallamh* was written but it is difficult to accept this at face-value. Even though the *Acallamh* has several instances of visits to otherworld raths, these seem to have no relationship to the story of Oisín in the Land of Youth. Coimín, however, did not invent the story, as it is a version of the international folktale AT 470*, 'The Hero Visits the Land of the Immortals'. The plot was found in late medieval literature on the Continent — see J. Stevens, *Medieval Romance*, London 1973, 113; J. Bédier, *Les Légendes Epiques*, Vol. 2, Paris 1926, 314-6. If based on some source like the latter, this story of Oisín can hardly be older than about the fourteenth century.

114 See reference in S. Watson, *Mac na Míchomhairle*, Dublin 1979, 65-7.

115 Joynt, *op. cit.*, 65.

with another and unrelated allegory known to him.[116] Furthermore, he does mention youth as a symbolic figure (though in
a minor role),[117] and we should not rule out the possibility
that he had, for some reason or other, reduced its importance
in the action. Of the gifts as a late addition we can be far
more confident, since they have in themselves no allegorical
purpose. So, just as Oisín got Christianity, Diarmaid must be
given his particular attribute — the love-spot. What Oscar got
was a marvellous thong for his flail. This also derives, ultimately, from the *Acallamh*, for it is there stated that St
Patrick arranged that the Fianna be released from hell into
heaven.[118] Oscar, the son of Oisín, has long been regarded as
the greatest warrior of all the Fianna. A well-known stanza
has Oisín say proudly to Patrick: 'If my son Oscar and God
were fighting hand-to-hand on yonder hill, if I saw Oscar
laid low, I would then believe that God was a strong man!'[119]
His devastating performance in battle was such that he was
known as 'Oscar of the strokes'.[120] He was ordinarily portrayed
as the fighter who saved the day for the Fianna when battles
seemed otherwise lost.[121] Already around the year 1400, a
ballad describes this 'battle-conquering Oscar' as playing a
prominent part in defending Fionn from the devils in hell.[122]
This situation was, of course, reminiscent of the indigenous
lore concerning the fierce encounters which Fionn and his
men experienced in the underworld. The escape from hell

---

116 We have a late redaction of this allegory in the fourteenth-century
Echtra Cormaic, W. Stokes and E. Windisch, eds., *Irische Texte*
3rd Ser., Vol. 1, Leipzig 1891, 183-229.

117 The beautiful girl who represents the intellect is portrayed as
being young, while a hag represents old age.

118 Stokes, *op. cit.*, 117.

119 Ó Siochfhradha, *op. cit.*, 85. It is part of the ballad 'Laoi an
Bhrait', and many versions of the stanza have been collected
from oral tradition — see IFC Catalogue.

120 J. O'Daly, *Laoithe Fiannuidheachta*, Vol. 1, Dublin 1859, 116;
Ó Siochfhradha, *op. cit.*, 6, 39, 198. Other references to his
strength in battle — Ó Cadhlaigh, *op. cit.*, 266-8; Mac Neill,
op. cit., 11, 18, 71; and Ó Siochfhradha, *op. cit.*, 4, 28, 45.

121 Mac Neill, *op. cit.*, 57, Cecile O'Rahilly, *Cath Finntrágha*, Dublin
1962, 14-6; Ó Siochfhradha, *op. cit.*, 30-1, 43-7, etc.

122 Murphy, *op. cit.* (1933), 170.

was the Fianna's greatest triumph, and gradually the power of Patrick's blessing in achieving it was replaced by the power of the Fianna's own arms.[123] So the story developed that, as the Fianna left hell, their retreat was covered by Oscar who stood at the gate driving the devils back. The weapon he used in this fight was a flail — hence the notion that he needed an unbreakable thong in it.[124] This oral tradition of Oscar certainly owes much to the influence of the international folktale AT 650A, 'Strong John', in which a marvellously strong man — who is a great thresher — masters the devils in hell.[125] Such influence of the international folktale would have been attracted by the common situation (hell), the common image (strong man), and the occurrence of the flail as a weapon of war in Fenian literature.[126]

'Fionn for knowledge, Goll for strength, Conán for victory', so goes an Irish dictum,[127] which refers to the ability to kill hundreds (*marú na gcéadta*) which the latter gained. Conán Maol son of Morna is the buffoon of the Fianna, but he is also the source of continual strife and destruction. In twelfth- and thirteenth-century sources he is referred to as 'headstrong Conán', and 'rugged Conán of horrid guise'. He is said to be 'mettlesome in company, contentious in family affairs, and critical of hosts and assemblies'.[128] A fifteenth-century ballad reference sets the stage for much of his later portrayal — according to it he is *fear millte na bhFiann*, 'the man who

---

123 Sources and discussions in Christiansen, *op. cit.* (1931), 17-9; Murphy, *op. cit.* (1933), 174; Murphy, *op. cit.* (1953), 56, 117.

124 Lists of versions in Murphy, *op. cit.* (1953), 116-7. Add *Irisleabhar na Gaedhilge* 2 (1884-6), 371; and IFC Catalogue.

125 This folktale was popular throughout Europe and beyond. Irish versions — excluding the Fenian derivative — listed in Ó Súilleabháin and Christiansen, *op. cit.*, under the Type. For general influence of the Type on Fenian lore, see Murphy, *op. cit.* (1953), xiii, xix (add IFC 84:357 to this).

126 Cecile O'Rahilly, *op. cit.* (1962), 31-2. This fifteenth-century text — in which Oscar defeats a fierce flail-wielding warrior — was well-known (Bruford, *op. cit.*, 118-20, 253). It probably helped AT 650A in introducing the flail image here.

127 *Béaloideas* 4 (1934), 83. Further references in Bruford, *ibid.*, 119, 121.

128 Mac Neill, *op. cit.*, 57, 60; Stokes, *op. cit.*, 61.

destroyed the Fenian band'.[129] This was a common phrase
with regard to him and merely refers to his malicious tongue
and capacity for mischief, but the word *milleadh* is commonly
used in folk speech in a more restricted sense to denote
'magical destruction'. An especially common usage is *súil
mhillte* which means the evil eye.[130] The transference of the
phrase to this more dramatic meaning would entail the idea
that he had a magically destructive eye. Probably in the background to this development lay some residues of the very
fertile ancient motif of Fionn's archetypal enemy with one
destructive eye.[131] A related myth seems definitely to have
influenced the imagery — that of the god Lugh overcoming
the tyrant Balor, whose destructive gaze wiped out whole
armies.[132] At any rate, realising the destructive effect which
Conán's gift would have — not only on the Fianna if he so
chose — but on the whole body of narrative, the storytellers
were anxious to limit it as much as possible. So the (rather
awkward) explanation provided was that Conán was indeed
given the gift, but that he himself remained unaware of it.
To exercise the power, he had only to gaze at a host through
his fingers, but Fionn — when he wished the power to be used
— used to direct all his men to adopt the same pose. So Conán
never discovered the invincibility which was his, and the
Fianna remained safe from the man who had enough malice
to destroy them.

Finally, we come to Fionn's strange request to be relieved
of the odour of clay which clung to him. This, it is explained,
was the result of an act of necrophilia which he once committed with a dead woman.[133] Naturally, the odour was a
source of great embarrassment to him on this account. A
study of this motif relative to Fionn involves a whole stratum
of lore concerning his dealings with women. First of all, we
have the very ancient tradition of his otherworld mistress Blái,

---

129 Murphy, *op. cit.* (1953), 258.
130 See DIL s.vv. *milliud, milltech, súil.*
131 For Fionn's archetypal enemy, see note 59 above.
132 For Balar and Lugh, see O'Rahilly, *op. cit.*, 58-61, 313-4.
133 Some versions referred to in note 103 above exclude the gift given
     to Fionn, due to the storytellers' sense of propriety.

the mother of Oisín, who was in the form of a doe.[134]. The
original idea seems to have been that she deliberately assumed
this form in order to divide him from his company in the heat
of the hunt, and then finding him alone seduced him by re-
assuming human form.[135] By the Middle Ages, however, the
story was being told in a different way — how Fionn's innocent wife was transformed into a deer by an evil druid.[136]
The imagery, because of its dramatic content, spread hori-

134 Philologists accept that his name 'Oisín' — attested from the
     earliest Fenian sources — originally meant 'little fawn'. The earliest
     reference we have to his deer-mother is in the twelfth-century
     Book of Leinster (Meyer, *op. cit.* [1910], xxvi), but it is clear
     (see notes 135-6) that this tradition is much more ancient.

135 The *Acallamh* has Oisín going into an otherworld dwelling to
     spend some time with his mother Blái (Stokes, *op. cit.*, 2). This
     Blái is represented as daughter of Derg, which is a frequent appel-
     lative for the god of the dead in early Irish tradition (T.F. O'Rahilly,
     op. cit., 117-29). Elsewhere, in an eighth-century text, a character
     called Derg is a foe of Fionn. This text already has an intrusive
     motif (the international one of Potiphar's wife) so the kernel —
     which is the conflict between Fionn and Derg — must be older
     still. Derg is in it represented as inhabiting the wilderness and
     going about 'on shanks of deer for his lightness'. The assumption
     must be that an otherworld deity — probably from the realm of
     the dead — appeared to Fionn as a deer in the forest, in pursu-
     ance of some definite objective. This seems also to be the rationale
     behind the idea that a goddess in deer form would seduce the
     hero. For references, see Murphy, *op. cit.* (1953), lvi, lxiii-lxiv,
     153-61; T.F. O'Rahilly, *op. cit.*, 125-8; Anne Ross, *Pagan Celtic
     Britain*, London 1974, 419-22; T.P. Cross in *Modern Philology*
     16 (1918-9), 156-62. See also Joynt, *op. cit.*, 34-40, 44.

136 A twelfth-century poem tells of how a beautiful young lady was
     transformed into a deer by the otherworld spirits, *na siabhra side*
     and was afterwards killed in that form by the High-King's fians —
     E. Gwynn, *Poems from the Dindshenchas*, Dublin 1900, 10-2.
     A contemporaneous passage in the *Acallamh* (Stokes, *op. cit.*,
     139) has a maiden being put into deer-shape by the otherworld
     community. These accounts — whether derived from the lore of
     Blái Derg or parallel with it — strongly suggest that the passive
     role of Oisín's deer-mother was current at that time. For a list
     of later oral versions — in which she is transformed by a druid —
     see Cross, *op. cit.* (1918-9), 159-60; *Béaloideas* 3 (1931-2), 146,
     and IFC Catalogue. For somewhat looser parallels, see Mac Neill,
     op. cit., 21, 31.

zontally in the Fenian lore. By the thirteenth century we are being told that Fionn's two great hounds had a human father and were born of a woman who had been transformed into a dog by an enemy.[137]

It is clear, then, that a sense of fantasy regarding the effect of magic on sexual matters was growing within the Fenian lore. Many examples of this are found in that collection of stories we have already referred to, *Feis Tighe Chonáin*, which was written about the fifteenth century by a scholar with a rather metaphysical turn of mind. He retells in great detail the birth-tale of Fionn's hounds,[138] and tells of a male member of the Fianna who became a woman every second year.[139] He also relates how the daughter of a dead warrior kissed her father's mouth and became pregnant thereby.[140] This curious type of speculation seems to go step by step with an increasing tendency to regard Fionn himself as an over-amorous hero. One early reference to him states that he had a woman in every district,[141] so there was a justification for the image in tradition. His father had a like reputation — the literature portrays Cumhall as a great abductor of women, while folk tradition held that few comely maidens were safe from him.[142] The attribution of many wives to Fionn results from the synchronising of various stories,[143] but this would underline the notion — which had no doubt grown up — that he simply took after his father in this regard. Thus the author of *Feis Tighe Chonáin* considers it appropriate to describe a

137 Mac Neill, *ibid.*, 40; Murphy, *op. cit.* (1933), 114-7; Murphy, *op. cit.* (1953), 103-5.
138 Joynt, *op. cit.*, 21-34.
139 *Ibid.*, 14. Sexual duality was a popular theme in medieval literature on the Continent — see Curtius, *op. cit.*, 113-7.
140 Joynt, *ibid.*, 7.
141 Meyer, *op. cit.* (1910), xix. This mode of living, free from ordinary social bonds, seems to be part of an original young man's perspective within the Fenian tradition.
142 *Béaloideas* 3 (1931-2), 188; Nagy, *op. cit.* (1985), 88. This portrayal of Cumhall seems to derive from his kidnapping of Muirn in the youth-biography of Fionn, and it seems to have been already established by the twelfth century (see Stokes, *op. cit.*, 35).
143 Mac Neill, *op. cit.*, 42-3, 85; Murphy, *op. cit.* (1933), 100, 104. See also note 144.

rather impolite haste on Fionn's part to sleep with women
he encounters in otherworld palaces.[144] This type of portrayal
lies behind the notion of his involvement in necrophilia. In
the twelfth century *Acallamh* it is stated that 'there was a
prohibition on Fionn to see a corpse, unless it had been killed
by weapons',[145] but this appears to mean simply that — since
he was a great warrior — death was appropriate to his character
only in the context of battle. As the notion of such a prohibition gained currency, however, it would lend itself to
other interpretations and invite some extraneous motif. It
found such a motif in necrophilia, a type of contact with the
dead which was most prohibited and which moreover fitted
in with the increasingly fantastic sexual imagery of Fenian
lore. This development seems to have taken place in or about
the fourteenth century. Perhaps it derives from the legend of
Charlemagne and his bewitched love of a dead woman;[146]
and certain other parallels with the Charlemagne lore suggest
that late medieval France could indeed be the source.[147] It
is clear that the motif had already become attached to Fionn
by the time *Feis Tighe Chonáin* was written, for in that text
he is pointedly asked: 'Why is there the stench of a corpse
from your offspring and the coldness of bronze in your
skin?'[148] Unfortunately Fionn's answer to the question is
not given, but elsewhere the author has him list among the
wonders of the Fianna 'a woman whom I myself have, and
she is dead every night and alive every day, and I hold no
woman I ever had in greater affection than her'.[149] This

144 Joynt, *op. cit.*, 42-3, 47.
145 Stokes, *op. cit.*, 150.
146 For this legend and its sources, see G. Paris, *Histoire Poétique de
     Charlemagne*, Paris 1865, 378-85; J.C. Payen, *Le Motif du Repentir
     dans la Littérature Française Médiévale*, Geneva 1967, 132-7;
     M. Moe, *Samlede Skrifter*, Oslo 1926, Vol. 2, 175-9, 319-21.
147 Like Fionn, and also due to attempts at reconciling varying nar-
     ratives, Charlemagne was invested with a series of consecutive
     wives — see Paris, *ibid.*, 385-99. See also note 150 below.
148 Joynt, *op. cit.*, 34, 60. The earliest surviving manuscripts read
     fuaire an umha, 'the coldness of bronze', and *fuaire anma*, 'the
     coldness of soul'. But these postdate the basic text by anything
     up to two hundred years, and the original reading might have
     been *fuaire ón uamha*, 'coldness from the grave', or such like.
149 Joynt, *op. cit.*, 14.

sounds suspiciously like an account of a fairy mistress whom Charlemagne had. This mistress was wont to become alive when the Emperor visited her, but to be dead when he departed.[150]

We may regret the way in which authors of old literary texts have edited folk themes, often giving a slightly strange colouring to them; but it is fair to say that folk tradition, in its turn, did not hesitate to alter and develop literary material to suit its own ends. A good example is provided by a passage in the house of Cuanna story, that strange allegorical narrative in *Feis Tighe Chonáin*. There the otherworld lady is 'human intellect, since she is the swiftest of all, since a person puts his intellect in the blink of an eye to knowledge which he would not find by experience in forty years'.[151] Manuscripts of this text were very plentiful in Ireland down to the nineteenth century,[152] and this remarkable passage had productive echoes in the oral stream. Thus we have Kerry lore telling us that Fionn would employ as messenger only 'a runner who was faster than the mind of a woman between two men' because such a messenger was faster than 'the closing of an eye'.[153] Traditionally, the great messenger and runner of the Fianna was Caoilte.[154] So I will end with a Galway anecdote which develops the imagery in a particularly artistic way:

> There was a king in Ireland long ago, and he wished to have the sand from each shore brought to him every morning — from north, south, east, and west. He would know

150 Paris, *op. cit.*, 384-5. The borrowing may have been prompted by the context of Fionn's prohibition referred to at note 145 above. There Fionn is talking to three strange men, who tell him they are dead every third night and do not wish to be seen in that state.

151 Joynt, *op. cit.*, 18. See note 155 below re speed of thought.

152 List of versions in Bruford, *op. cit.*, 261.

153 IFC 241:444, 242:74.

154 He was known as Caoilte *na gcos fada*, 'of the long legs'. For. folk accounts of him and his running ability, see IFC Catalogue, as well as de híde, *op. cit.* (1933), 190-6, and Murphy, *op. cit.* (1953), 85-9. He is portrayed as a great runner in the literature from at least the tenth century onwards — see Meyer, *op. cit.* (1910), xxiii; Stokes, *op. cit.*, 115; Mac Neill, *op. cit.*, 14, 57, 84; Murphy, *op. cit.* (1933), 2-14.

by examining the sand if any foe had landed in the country during the night. Three men applied for the job as his messenger. 'How long would it take you to collect the sands?' said the king to the first man. 'While the leaf is falling from a tree!' said the man. 'Oh, you would not be fast enough,' said the king. The second man said he would collect the sands as fast as a cat slipping between two houses. 'Not fast enough,' said the king. The third man was Caoilte. 'How long would it take you?' the king asked. 'As long as it takes a woman to change her mind!' said Caoilte. 'Did you set out yet?' asked the king. 'I returned just now!' said Caoilte.[155]

155 IFC 1010:85-6. The background to this narrative is the fifteenth-century text *Cath Fionntrágha*, ed. Cecile O'Rahilly, *op. cit.*, 1962, which describes an attempted invasion of Ireland by the king of the world. This king lands with his forces at Fionntrá, 'bright strand', and is defeated there by the Fianna. Several folklore versions of *Cath Fionntrágha*, which derive from manuscripts of the text, have been collected (see Bruford, *op. cit.*, 118-22, 253). Messengers play an important part in the text, and it is stated that 'there was not a landing port in Ireland without a watchman set there by Fionn' (Cecile O'Rahilly, *ibid.*, 5). Caoilte has been brought into the narrative, probably due to a medieval story of how he managed to fulfil the instructions of the High-King Cormac mac Airt by collecting a great variety of animals from all parts of Ireland in one day — references in Murphy, *op. cit.* (1953), 18-9. Elements of this story survived in folk tradition (Christiansen, *op. cit.* (1931), 46; and IFC 242:73). The motif of three applicants competing for a post is probably a recent borrowing from humorous anecdotes outside the Fenian context (AT 1950 is the pattern — cf. Ó Súilleabháin and Christiansen, *op. cit.*, Type 1950*). This format would have been attracted because of its imagery of extraordinary skills and its similarity to AT 513, 'The Extraordinary Companions', which has had a great influence on Fenian narrative (see Murphy, *op. cit.* (1953), xiv-xv, 177-88). The idea of a runner being 'swifter than thought' (Motif F681.1 in Thompson) is also found in *Culhwch ac Olwen*, a Welsh text which may be as early as the eleventh century (ed. J. Rhys and I.G. Evans, *The Red Book of Hergest*, 1, Oxford 1887, 111). A great runner in the same text is named 'Sgilti' (*ibid.*, 108), and he is probably derived from Caoilte. The speed of thought and the capricious nature of a woman's mind between two men are referred to in Fenian literature as early as the tenth century — see *Zeitschrift für celtische Philologie* 13 (1921), 270, 272.

MACPHERSON'S *OSSIAN*: BALLADS TO EPICS

DERICK S. THOMSON

(University of Glasgow)

Epics have come into being in a wide range of societies and eras, and in a variety of ways: some in heroic societies, some in post-heroic, and under the stimulus of local and national political ideals. There are various degrees of consciousness and sophistication involved, and at one end of the scale there can be very deliberate modelling on earlier known epic. In a context in which the history of the *Kalevala* is being commemorated, one of the more recent epics, and a very deliberately constructed one, it is not inappropriate to trace the genesis and growth of an eighteenth-century attempt to construct epics. In fact there is sufficient evidence to show that James Macpherson's Ossianic epics were both a stimulus and a warning to the group in Finland that eventually produced its epic spokesman in Elias Lönnrot. From the more domestic i.e. Irish/Scottish viewpoint there are of course many matters of interest in an analysis of how ballads turned into epics, with extraordinary suddenness and extraordinary repercussions, in the third quarter of the eighteenth century.

A quick reminder of the sequence of events, and the background to them, will allow us to concentrate later on a closer and more detailed analysis.

The Scottish Highlands had been regarded, by central government, first in Scotland and later in the U.K., as an uncontrolled and potentially dangerous sector. This attitude was an amalgam of political, cultural and religious attitudes, and the success of the Reformation in the mid-sixteenth century reinforced these. By the early seventeenth century a succession of initiatives was being undertaken to increase control over the Highland/Gaelic area, and in the course of that century a significant degree of cultural and political infiltration had taken place, so that the native leaders (the chiefs and their kin network) were moving perceptibly towards social and cultural norms that would eventually take them outside Gaelic society in any meaningful sense. The Jacobite campaigns of the eighteenth century, apart from their dynastic ambitions, can be seen as a reaction against these tendencies, and there can be little doubt that for at least a smallish number of Gaelic nationalists that was their prime significance.

The '15 and '45 Risings were succeeded by defensive and punitive measures, aimed at controlling the Highlanders from strategic strongpoints (forts and barracks) and improving communications (Wade's roads) to facilitate troop movements, while, particularly after the '45, culturally repressive measures were taken to undermine Gaelic pride and individuality. These measures meshed with the ongoing programme of reforming the religious beliefs and language loyalty of Highlanders through The Scottish Society for Propagating Christian Knowledge and other institutions.

It is against that background that we have to look at James Macpherson, who was born in 1736 in Badenoch, within sight of the Ruthven Barracks, built in 1718 to tame the Jacobite insurgents, and by an ironic coincidence the vicinity in which the Jacobite army disbanded after Culloden in 1746. Entering his teens about 1750 he could not fail to be conscious of the disaster that had overtaken his people, and we know that he had older relatives who had a high degree of Gaelic consciousness, and that he had friendly relations with them, a prime example being the Badenoch poet Lachlan Macpherson of Strathmashie.

James Macpherson was a student at Aberdeen's two Universities, King's College and Marischal College, in the 1750s, and seems to have studied briefly at the University of Edinburgh. He was employed as a tutor in Edinburgh by 1758, and in that year published a long poem, in English, entitled 'The Highlander'. By a succession of useful contacts and encounters he had met influential literary figures in 1758 and 1759, and with their involvement and encouragement he published his *Fragments of Ancient Poetry collected in the Highlands* early in 1760, and because of the excited response to these and the direct encouragement of friends and acquaintances, went on to assemble and publish two long poems, referred to as epics (*Fingal* and *Temora*) together with many shorter poems, all claimed to be translations from Gaelic, between late 1761 and 1763. The three publications of 1760 to 1763 were the basis of a large reputation which was sometimes controversial, especially in Scotland and the U.K., but which was firmly based in many parts of Europe. The nature of that reputation was strongly influenced by the emphasis that was placed on (a) authenticity and (b) creativity. To gain a balanced view of Macpherson's achievement we have to look carefully at these very different aspects.

We can begin by looking closely at the way in which Macpherson became involved in his collection and writing, considering in passing the network of sources that existed, and eventually moving to some analysis of how he constructed his larger works.

The evidence for Macpherson's early acquaintance with the ballad sources he was to use is in part circumstantial and in part direct. The matter is complicated because much evidence was assembled round about the year 1800, after Macpherson's death, and some forty years after the events recalled. Also, some of the witnesses were prejudiced in Macpherson's favour. But when we make allowances and adjustments, it is possible to reconstruct in some detail what the probable sequence of events, and development of attitudes, was.

It is admittedly difficult to pin down what Macpherson's early acquaintance with the ballads was, in his native Badenoch, and before he went to Edinburgh in particular. His own reference, in the Dissertation prefixed to *Fingal*, is fairly general: 'he admired the poems, in the original, very early, and gathered part of them from tradition for his own amusement'.[1] Thus we are mainly dependent on rather general statements about the ubiquitous practice of reciting Ossianic

1 *Fingal*, London 1762, xiv.

ballads. One such, made when the Highland Society of Scotland was collecting evidence for the *Report on the Authenticity of the Poems of Ossian*, (ed. H. Mackenzie, Edinburgh 1805), was by Ewan Macpherson, schoolmaster, a native of Badenoch and born c. 1727, and 'acquainted with the late Mr. James Macpherson' in his youth. Ewan Macpherson recollected that he —

> ... very often heard poems of Ossian, relative to the Fingalians repeated in his youth; and that, in general, the people of any taste with whom he was aquainted in his younger days, and had advanced in years, made it their entertainment, in the winter nights, to repeat the poems of Ossian, or hear them repeated to them; and as his profession made him reside in different parts of the Highlands, he found the same taste for Ossian's poems prevail among all classes of people ...[2]

This was the Ewan Macpherson who was apparently dragooned into accompanying James Macpherson to the Outer Isles in 1760 to write poems from oral recitation.[3] His general picture is confirmed by Archibald Fletcher, born c. 1735, who reported in 1801 that —

> ... in former times in the declarant's first remembrance, and he believes long before his time, it was the constant amusement or occupation of the Highlanders in the winter time to go by turns to each other's houses in every village to recite and hear recited or sung the Poems of Ossian and other songs and poems; which was particularly the practice of the McNicols in Arivean; but that for thirty years back [i.e. since c. 1770], this practice has been gradually wearing out in Glenorchay, and in every other part of the Highlands with which he is acquainted, so that it scarcely now exists at all any where.[4]

Of course this is an exaggeration, as can easily be shown from west coast and island evidence of continuing recitation

2 *Report*, App., 97.
3 *Ibid.*, 94 ff.
4 *Ibid.*, 271.

long after this time. Another Badenoch witness, though perhaps a less reliable one, is the Rev. Andrew Gallie, who wrote:

> I must confess, that I heard in early life among some of the most vulgar Senachies and singers, some parts of Ossian's poems interlarded with what was marvellous in the extreme; and I have heard them repeated by others, then and afterwards, without that disagreeable mixture.[5]

We shall return to Andrew Gallie later, as he gave evidence of what happened when Macpherson returned from his collecting tour, in 1760.

It may be useful to add at this point the testimony of Dr John Macpherson of Sleat, who reports in a letter of November 1763 that he had seen 'a Gaelic MS in the hands of an old bard, who travelled about through the Highlands and Isles about thirty years ago, out of which he read, in my hearing, and before thousands yet alive, the exploits of Cuchullin, Fingal, Oscar, Gaul, Dermid'. He goes on to say he was a MacMhuirich, 'a man of some letters', and had, 'to my certain knowledge, some manuscripts, in verse as well as prose, in his possession'.[6] This looks like a reference to Domhnall Mac Mhuirich, the last practising poet of the dynasty, and the reference to his reading from a Ms is of considerable interest. The general context of Dr John Macpherson's remarks would lead us to think that the Ms he refers to contained heroic ballads, rather than heroic tales, but the point can scarcely be taken as proven.

Accepting for the present that rather impressionistic view of Macpherson's acquaintance with Ossianic balladry at an early stage of his career, we can now seek to reconstruct his growing interest in such matters in his late teens and early twenties, and the connection between that interest and his writing ambitions.

We know that he wrote verse some years before the appearance of his Ossianic works, and the file of the *Scots Magazine* for the 1750s may credibly give us some idea of popular taste among the Scottish *literati* of the time. The

5 *Ibid.*, 41.
6 *Ibid.*, App., 10.

Augustan couplet, and the light wit that goes with it, are much
in evidence in the verse printed in the *Scots Magazine* in the
early 1750s. There are, however, clear signs of romanticism,
as in the poem 'Il Meditante' which was published in 1752.[7]
The author 'repairs'

> To the deep covert of some lonely wood,
> Where yews and cypress spread their mournful boughs,
> And the proud ruins of some stately palace
> Rear 'mid the trees their venerable heads
> There, while through rustling leaves and hollow vaults
> The wind howls mournful, and the list'ning ear
> Of tumbling waters hears the distant echo,
> With downcast looks and footsteps slow I'll tread,
> While the pale moon, in silent glory clad,
> Gilds with a trembling light the solemn scene.

It is not too fanciful, I think, to imagine Macpherson filing
away in his memory these lonely woods, mournful boughs,
rustling leaves, with the howling wind, tumbling waters and
the pale moon. Late in 1758 some verses by Macpherson,
signed 'J.McP.' and dated 'Ruthven, Oct. 31, 1758'[8] appeared
in the *Scots Magazine*, entitled 'On the death of Marshal
Keith'. The couplets are rather wooden and cliché-ridden:

> A pearly drop hangs in each warrior's eye,
> And through the army runs the gen'ral sigh.

There is evidence of Scottish national sentiment:

> Sad from his native home the chief withdrew;
> But kindled SCOTIA's glory as he slew;
> On far *Iberia* built his country's fame,
> And distant *Russia* heard the SCOTTISH name.

There is also, possibly, evidence of Highland sentiment,
and certainly a foretaste of the eerie, windy atmosphere of
his later work, though the regular metre detracts from the
impression of wildness and strangeness:

7   *Scots Magazine*, 14 (1752), 149.
8   *Ibid.*, 20 (1758), 550-1.

See! the proud halls they once possess'd decay'd,
The spiral tow'rs depend the lofty head;
Wild ivy creeps along the mould'ring walls,
And with each gust of wind a fragment falls;
Wild birds obscene, at noon of night, deplore,
Where mighty heroes kept the watch before.

But it is probable that the item in the *Scots Magazine* which made the deepest impression in the long run was an English version of a Gaelic ballad contributed in January 1756 by Jerome Stone, schoolmaster at Dunkeld. Macpherson had not quite turned twenty years of age. In his covering letter printed along with the translation, Stone says of the 'Irish' (i.e. Gaelic) ballads:[9]

> Several of these performances are to be met with, which for sublimity of sentiment, nervousness of expression, and high-spirited metaphors, are hardly to be equalled among the chief productions of the most cultivated nations. Others of them breathe such tenderness and simplicity, as must be greatly affecting to every mind that is in the least tinctured with the softer passions of pity and humanity.

And he goes on to say of the poems, and the criticism is much to the point, that in them 'energy is always more sought after than neatness, and the strictness of connection less adverted to, than the design of moving the passions, and affecting the heart'. The tone of the description and the criticism is one that would appeal more to a Romantic than to an Augustan.

The ballad contributed by Stone is that of Albin and the Daughter of Mey, or in Gaelic terms the ballad of Fraoch. This is a ballad version of an ancient story (not in fact belonging to the Ossianic cycle). The story is well told in Stone's version, and its narrative and dramatic strength must have struck the readers of *Scots Magazine* verse as quite unusual. The Northern literary motif of the fight with a dragon or monster was not so widely known to literary people then as it was to become later. Stone's translation was not a very

9 *Ibid.*, 19 (1756), 15-7.

close one, nor would this have been his intention. He retains the outline and sequence of the ballad plot, but frequently uses ideas and sentiments that have no counterpart in the ballad, but belong securely to the eighteenth century. There are unmistakable similarities in diction between Stone's and Macpherson's 'translation'. Stone left in Ms a collection of ten Gaelic ballads; many of these are versions of ballads used by Macpherson.[10]

Early in 1758 Macpherson published a long poem called 'The Highlander' which did not attract much attention at all, but which clearly foreshadows the ambitions and attitudes that were to mature further in *Fingal*. It foreshadows the plot of the later poems to some extent also, with its basic warring between Scottish Celts and Scandinavians, and in this respect also Macpherson was responding to the growing interest of his period in Northern antiquities.[11]

Late in 1758 Macpherson became tutor to Thomas Graham of Balgowan, near Dunkeld, and in 1759 he visited, with his pupil, the Manse of Logierait,[12] some eight miles from Dunkeld, where the minister was the father of Adam Fergusson, already well-known in Edinburgh literary circles. It is probable that Adam Fergusson was at home at the time. Much later, in the investigation into the authenticity of Macpherson's work, Fergusson wrote (20th March, 1798)[13] of how —

> about the year 1740, I heard John Fleming, a taylor, who in the manner of the country, worked with his journeyman at my father's house, repeat, in a kind of chiming measure, heroic strains relating to an arrival or landing of an host and a subsequent battle, with a single combat of two chiefs. This I took down in writing, and kept for some time.

10 For the Stone ballads, see *Transactions of the Gaelic Society of Inverness*, 14 (1887-8), 314 ff.
11 Evidenced, for example in P. Henri Mallet's books: *Introduction à l'Histoire de Dannemarck*, Copenhagen 1755, and *Monuments de la poesie des Celtes, et particulièrement des anciens Scandinaves*, Copenhagen 1756.
12 See *Celtic Magazine*, 5 (1880), 311.
13 *Report*, App., 62 ff.

Fergusson quotes two long lines or couplets of authentic Gaelic balladry in homespun orthography, and he goes on to say —

the principal use I made of them was to tell my friend and companion at College, Mr. John Home, that there were such relicks of ancient poetry in the Highlands, and which led him to the inquiries which produced Mr. Macpherson's communications.

Later in 1759, Macpherson met John Home in Moffat, apparently using an introduction from Adam Fergusson. We have corroboration from Home[14] of how Fergusson had awakened his interest in ancient Gaelic poetry but that it was Macpherson who at last had brought him into meaningful contact with it.

Within a mile of the Manse of Logierait there is the farm of Ballechin (Baile Eachainn), the home of James McLagan who was to collect close on 10,000 lines (including many variants) of heroic Gaelic verse. He had begun his active collection as early as 1755. McLagan was ordained by the Presbytery of Dunkeld in 1760, and in 1760-1 we find Macpherson corresponding with him, and acknowledging the receipt of specific ballads from him.[15] It seems probable that Adam Fergusson was Macpherson's contact in this instance also, and perhaps we are justified in seeing Fergusson, not himself at all expert, or deeply interested, in Gaelic matters, as a seminal influence in that remarkable resurgence of interest in the Gaelic verse tradition which we can see in the third quarter of the eighteenth century.[16] Several collectors have close connections with Perthshire, including MacDiarmid of Weem and Irvine of Little Dunkeld, and it is clear that such balladry had a continuous history there since the time of the Dean's collection in the early sixteenth century, and no doubt for long before that time.

14 *Ibid.*, App., 68-9 'Note from Mr. Home'.
15 *Ibid.*, App., 153.
16 Attention may be drawn to Fergusson's eloquent description of Gaelic's demotion in society, and Macpherson's courage in championing it. *Ibid.*, App., 65.

In the longer perspective, of course, the Dean's collection of heroic ballads is a relatively late item. According to Gerard Murphy's basic chronology many of the ballads had been composed in the twelfth and thirteenth centuries, and others in the fourteenth, fifteenth and sixteenth, while some of the themes and motifs in these ballads have a history which was already ancient by the twelfth century, and may go back to the very early Christian centuries if not beyond. What we are dealing with, and what Macpherson stumbled upon, is an ancient, widespread and long-lasting literary tradition which has its roots in myth and legend, was strongly cultivated by people who belonged to the professional literary orders, and ultimately came to be perpetuated as part of popular, and eventually non-literate, culture. Macpherson's general instinct as to the great age of this tradition, was sound, though he sometimes failed in a detailed understanding of it, and often made wilful distortions of it.

We may now return to September/October 1759, at Moffat, where Macpherson made the acquaintance of John Home. Home was the author of the play *Douglas*, which had attracted much attention, partly because Home was an ordained clergyman. The *Scots Magazine* in 1757 has many references to this play and reactions to it. When the two men met at Moffat, Home asked Macpherson for some information concerning the ancient poetry of his country, and Macpherson claimed to have in his possession several pieces of ancient poetry. When Home asked to see them Macpherson asked if he understood the Gaelic. 'Not one word', replied Home. 'How then can I show you them?' asked Macpherson. 'Very easily,' said Home, 'translate one of the poems which you think a good one, and I imagine that I shall be able to form some opinion of the genius and character of the Gaelic poetry'. According to Home, Macpherson was unwilling to try this, but was persuaded, and in a day or two brought 'the poem on the death of Oscar', and in a few days two or three more pieces, which greatly pleased Home. He showed them to Dr Blair and other friends in Edinburgh, and later in the year to friends in London, 'where they were equally admired'.[17] Some of

17 *Report*, App., 68-9.

the details of this account are corroborated in a letter written in 1802 by the Rev. Dr Alexander Carlyle.[18]

Yet it may seem to us that the matter came to a head all too easily. I am inclined to think that Macpherson had prepared himself for this important meeting, having been alerted by Adam Fergusson to Home's interest, and that he had his basic materials, including adaptations of the Gaelic ballads, to hand, however unwilling he appeared to be to show them.

The sequel to this crucial Moffat meeting may now be described briefly. Macpherson was introduced to Hugh Blair in Edinburgh, and with his and other people's encouragement published the *Fragments* early in 1760. The preface Blair later claimed to have written himself, but clearly it is a product of his discussions with Macpherson. The reception of this slim booklet was remarkable. The *Scots Magazine* for June 1760 gave over practically the whole review section to printing extracts, and the July issue also featured the book prominently. Already the work was being excitedly discussed in English literary circles, Thomas Gray being particularly impressed. Hugh Blair arranged a dinner in Edinburgh, to raise funds and encourage Macpherson to search for further Gaelic poetic treasures, including the epic at whose existence he had hinted in the preface to the *Fragments*.[19] Already on 23rd June, Blair had written to Lord Hailes, adumbrating such a scheme, and using the phrase 'and particularly for recovering our epic'.[20] Various prominent Edinburgh citizens fell in with Blair's scheme, and Adam Fergusson was among those at the dinner. As a result, Macpherson set out in August 1760, on a six-week trip, and went on a second expedition between late October 1760 and early January 1761.

There is much evidence of where he went and who he met on these trips, which took him to Perthshire, Argyllshire, Inverness-shire, and the islands of Skye, North and South Uist, Benbecula and Mull. He visited ministers, landlords, blacksmiths, and representatives of bardic lines such as the

18 *Ibid.*
19 *Fragments*, Preface, v, vii, viii.
20 Quoted by B. Saunders, *Life and Letters of James Macpherson*, London 1894, 90.

MacMhuirichs in South Uist, had his henchmen take down versions of ballads as they were recited, and collected manuscripts, often very persuasively, from people who were sometimes very unwilling to part with them. Perhaps it is as well he succeeded, for a good number of these manuscripts may not otherwise have survived. One such is the *Book of the Dean of Lismore*, which Macpherson probably got from the Rev. Thomas Fraser of Boleskine in Inverness-shire;[21] one of the *Books of Clanranald* was also in Macpherson's possession for a time, and other MacMhuirich Mss.

We have some vivid details of Macpherson's work on these relatively copious materials gathered in the Highlands. He does not seem to have claimed any great expertise in handling Gaelic, and the accounts of some of his collaborators make this clear also. On his return from the Outer Isles and Skye, Macpherson stayed for some time with Andrew Gallie and his wife, and in letters of 1799 and 1801[22] Gallie says that Macpherson 'was, for some years before he entered on that work, my intimate acquaintance and friend'. He reports that Macpherson produced several volumes 'in the Gaelic language and characters, being the poems of Ossian and other ancient bards', which he had got from the Chief of Clanranald. The next part of Gallie's letter is highly interesting, and revealing. He says:

> At that time I could read the Gaelic characters, though with difficulty, and did often amuse myself with reading here and there in those poems, while Mr. Macpherson was employed on his translation. At times we differed as to the meaning of certain words in the original.
>
> With much labour I have recovered some scattered parts of the translation made at my fire-side, I should rather say of the original translated there, and I communicate to you a few stanzas, taken from the manuscript.

There follow sixteen lines of Gaelic verse that are patently not traditional Ossianic balladry. A little later Gallie says

21 Information from Mr Ronald Black who is preparing a Catalogue of Gaelic Mss in the National Library of Scotland.
22 *Report*, 31 ff.

that these lines were 'taken out of the manuscript, by a friend who was at the time with Mr. Macpherson and me, a gentleman well known for an uncommon acquaintance with the Gaelic, and a happy facility in writing it in Roman characters'.[23] This friend is later identified as the poet Lachlan Macpherson of Strathmashie,[24] who died c.1797.

In this passage I believe we have very persuasive clues to what was going on. Lachlan Macpherson's involvement is clearly indicated, and in a careless phrase the aged Gallie refers to it as 'the translation made at my fire-side'. At the same time we have a picture of Gallie amusing himself by trying to read the manuscripts while Macpherson is employed on his translation. The passage of which Gallie claims to give the original in fact occurs in Book IV of *Fingal* (p. 55),[25] and it

---

23 *Ibid.*, 33.
24 *Ibid.*, 43.
25 The relevant passages are as follows:

A. Bha fer re fer, is cruaigh re cruaigh,
   Sgiatha fuaimneach, daoine air lar,
   Mur uird nan ceud air mac nan Eill,
   Dh'eirigh agus theirin gach lann.
   Ghluais Goll mar chrom osaig on aird,
   Gun ghlan e saoighin as
   Bha Sauran mar chaoir fasàich thall,
   Am fraoch fuaimar Gorm-mheall bras.
   Ach cia mur chuiram sios le fonn,
   Bàs trom na'n sleagh bha ann?
   Bu scrathoil stri bha san bhlàr,
   Bu lassach ard mo lann.
   Bu scrathoil Osgar mo mhac fein,
   Thar càch bu treubhach maith!
   Bha sòlas balbh am bhroilleach shuas,
   Bhi ghruaigh mar chaoir san chath.

(From Gallie's letter of 1799, in *Report*, 32).

is clear that Macpherson of Strathmashie had made a Gaelic version of this passage, probably in Gallie's house. The elaborate process of culling from the ballads, making an English epic, and translating it back into Gaelic, had already begun.

(footnote 25 continued)

> B. Man was opposed to man, and steel to steel,
> Shields sounding, men falling;
> Like hammers of hundreds on the son of the embers
> Swords rose and fell.
> Gaul went on like a blast descending from the height,
> As he destroyed heroes.
> Sauran was like a flame of the desert,
> That consumes the sounding heath of Gormal.
> But how shall I relate in song
> The heavy death of spears that was there?
> Terrible was the strife of battle.
> High flamed my sword.
> Terrible was Oscar my son,
> Whose deeds of valour exceeded all.
> Silent joy arose in my breast,
> As his countenance glowed in the battle.

(Literal translation, as given in *Report*, 32).

> C. Man met with man, and steel with steel.
> Shields sound, men fall. As a hundred hammers
> on the son of the furnace, so rose, so rung their swords.
>
> Gaul rushed on like a whirlwind in Ardven. The destruction of heroes is on his sword. Swaran was like the fire of the desart in the ecchoing heath of Gormal. How can I give to the song the death of many spears? My sword rose high, and flamed in the strife of blood. And, Oscar, terrible wert thou, my best, my greatest son! I rejoiced in my secret soul, when his sword flamed over the slain.

(*Fingal*, Bk. IV, 55).

The Gaelic translation that appeared eventually in the official text of 1807, was a somewhat different version, though the versification was similar.[26]

There seems little doubt that Gallie was a party to the deception planned by Macpherson. This appears again in the war-song enclosed with his letter dated 4th March 1801.[27] The metre of this piece is a lame strophic one, clearly fabricated as a Gaelic version of Macpherson's prose. The passage is again in *Fingal*, Book IV.[28]

26 Book IV, 11, 259 ff.
27 *Report*, 143.
28 The relevant passages are as follows:

A. A mhacain cheann
   Nan cursan strann
   Ard leumnach righ na'n sleagh
   Lamh threin 'sgach cás
   Croidhe ard gun scá
   Ceann airm nan rian geur goirt
   Gearr sios gu bas
   Gun bharc sheól bán
   Bhi snamh ma dhubh Innishtore
   Mar tharnanech bhaoil
   Do bhuill a laoich
   Do shuil mar chaoir ad cheann
   Mar charaic chruin
   Do chroidhe gun roinn
   Mar lassan oidhch do lann
   Cum suar (*sic*) do scia
   Is crobbhui nial
   Mar chih bho reul a bhaish
   A mhacain cheann
   Nan cursan strann
   Sgrios naimhde sios gu lar.

(From Gallie's letter of 1801, in *Report*, 143).

B. Son of the chief of generous steeds! high-bounding king of spears. Strong arm in every perilous toil. Hard heart that never yields. Chief of the pointed arms of death. Cut down the foe; let no white sail bound round dark Inistore. Be thine arm like thunder. Thine eyes like fire, thy heart of solid rock. Whirl round thy sword as a meteor at night, and lift thy shield like the flame of death. Son of the chief of generous steeds, cut down the foe; destroy.

(*Fingal*, Bk. IV, 56).

In a letter dated 16th January, 1761, to the Rev. James McLagan, Macpherson writes: 'I have been lucky enough to lay my hands on a pretty complete poem, and truly epic, concerning Fingal - - - - I have some thoughts of publishing the original, if it will not clog the work too much.'[29] This is no doubt mostly bluff, but he may have been thinking of the *Book of the Dean*, although, unlike Hugh Trevor-Roper, I do not believe Macpherson could have read it.[30]

We can observe a later stage in the production of the epic after Macpherson had got to work in Edinburgh. Hugh Blair, in a letter of 1797,[31] says of Macpherson:

> When he returned to Edinburgh in winter [i.e. 1760-1] laden with his poetical treasures, he took lodgings in a house immediately below where I then lived, at the head of Blackfriar's Wynd, and busied himself in translating from the Gaelic into English. I saw him very frequently: he gave me accounts from time to time how he proceeded, and used frequently at dinner to read or repeat to me parts of what he had that day translated.[32]

Blair and Macpherson had various shared literary experiences, including a knowledge of classical epic, the Authorized Version, Milton (and probably the work of Lauder, who had fabricated so-called originals for 'Paradise Lost'), and they probably also shared an acquaintance with ideas about the Sublime and the Beautiful being developed by William Hogarth and Edmund Burke in the 1750s. We can see that community of ideas if we compare the notes to *Fingal* with what Blair later published in his *Dissertation* (1763). Blair continually makes comparisons with Homer and Vergil, while Macpherson in his notes quotes from the *Aeneid*, Dryden's translations from the classics, and the *Iliad*.[33] Macpherson makes it quite clear that he is setting his 'translation' against the classical epics, and he is at pains to show in his notes that

29 *Report*, App., 155.
30 See article on 'The Ossian forgeries' in *The Spectator* for 16th March, 1985, 14-5.
31 *Report*, App., 56 ff.
32 *Ibid.*, 59.
33 *Fingal*, 22-3.

'Fingal' follows 'the rules of the epopoea' in the way it ends, happily, in contrast to the classical and Miltonic epics. Blair elsewhere chimes in with this view, in his *Dissertation*,[34] and we are left with a strong impression that there had been a close and purposeful collaboration between the Professor of Rhetoric and the young classicist who had produced, out of the mists of a romantic antiquity, epic works that were to be the wonder of Europe.

It is likely that both men played important parts in this achievement. Macpherson's was of course the greater by far, and we should not minimise his probable theoretical contribution, for he had himself been a student of Thomas Blackwell, at Aberdeen, and so was exposed to the ideas that had gone into Blackwell's *Enquiry into the Life and Writings of Homer* (s.l. 1735). Indeed Josef Bysveen, in a recent study suggested that Macpherson was putting Blackwell's theory into practice in *Fingal*.[35] But Blair's guidance was probably crucial at the earlier stage, in the presentation of the *Fragments*, and perhaps also in the presentation of *Fingal*, and especially in the working up of literary parallels. Blair's lack of knowledge of Gaelic may exonerate him to a significant degree from the disingenuousness, to put it gently, of Macpherson of Ruthven and Macpherson of Strathmashie.

That part of Macpherson's work that rested securely on genuine Gaelic ballads has been elucidated in a fairly definitive way, but it may promote clarity to recall the outlines of that elucidation. We can observe an interesting progression through his various Ossianic publications. In the *Fragments* there are several clear links with Gaelic ballads, though no close translations. Fragment 6, for example, later in *Fingal* to be identified with the 'Maid of Craca', is based on two Gaelic ballads, 'Cath Rìgh na Sorcha' and 'An Ionmhuinn'. Fragments 6, 7 and 8 refer to the theme of the 'Death of Oscar' ballad, which was to be used more fully in *Temora* (1763). Fragment 14 is partly based on the Garbh mac Stairn ballads. Fragment 15 has no Gaelic original, but was to be used again in *Fingal*.

---

34   E.g. 1797 ed. of *Poems of Ossian*, Edinburgh, Vol. 2, 214.
35   J. Bysveen, *Epic Tradition and Innovation in James Macpherson's Fingal*, Uppsala 1982, 54.

Fingal, appropriately enough considering the intensive collecting activity that preceded it, makes the most pervasive and detailed use of Gaelic ballads of any of Macpherson's books. The Garbh mac Stairn and the Manus ballads are used to provide the groundwork of the plot, and the main episodes are founded on three ballads: 'Fingal's visit to Norway', 'The Lay of the Maiden' and 'Ossian's Courtship'. He uses other ballads in a more restricted way, e.g., 'The Praise of Goll' as a stylistic model for Ullin's war-song, addressed to Gaul in Book IV, or 'Sliabh nam Ban Fionn' to provide names and other detail in a brief hunting scene in Book VI.

A number of shorter poems were published along with *Fingal* in 1761, and several of these have ballad originals, e.g., 'The Battle of Lora', unusually faithful to its Gaelic original 'Teanntachd Mhòr na Fèinne', of which Macpherson got one version from James McLagan, but used others also; or 'Carthon', in which he uses the Conlaoch ballads; or 'Carric-Thura', where the Spirit of Loda is probably based in part at least on the Muilgheartach; or 'Darthula', his version of the Deirdre story; or 'Calthon and Colmal', based more distantly on the 'Conn mac an Deirg' ballads.

From all this we can see that Macpherson had collected and studied a good range of Gaelic ballads, and had used variant versions of some, and probably many of these. He often misunderstood some of the linguistic detail, or guessed at the meaning of obscure words and phrases, as better Gaelic scholars than he would have to do at times. Certainly he manipulated plot detail to suit his own ideas, used or omitted detail, and transposed it, Scotticized or Anglicized nomenclature, and sometimes constructed names from Gaelic elements. It is in *Fingal* that he leans most heavily on his Gaelic sources, but after Book I of *Temora* he more or less floats free of them.[36] None of this would be regarded as particularly unusual or reprehensible in an acknowledged work of the imagination, but Macpherson had got boxed in to a situation in which he had assumed the character of translator, and this was what had given him his initial hear-

---

36 Interestingly, the Rev. John Smith put his finger on this difference between the two 'epics' in a letter of *1798, Report*, App., 76.

ing. It was therefore virtually impossible to abandon this stance, though there are occasional hints of his wish to do so. Adam Fergusson, in a letter of 1798, puts similar points neatly enough:

> When the poems of Fingal and Temora appeared, I was inclined to think some pains must have been bestowed, and even liberties taken, in piecing together what was found in separate or broken fragments . . .

and again:

> [Macpherson was] at times . . . not averse to be thought the author of what became so much celebrated and admired throughout Europe.[37]

The runaway success of the *Fragments* and the deep interest aroused by *Fingal* encouraged Macpherson to produce a second so-called epic, *Temora*, in 1763. Although it used the 'Death of Oscar' ballad fairly extensively in Book I, thereafter it makes scarcely any specific use of the Gaelic ballads. Whether for that reason or for another *Temora* suffers from a vagueness of plot and general dullness of execution. On publication it attracted little favourable comment, and Macpherson seems to have seen that this was the end of that particular road. In 1773 he wrote, with a flash of that honesty and directness that recur throughout his career:

> My first publication was merely accidental. Had I then met with less approbation, my after-pursuits would have been more profitable; at least I might have continued to be stupid, without being branded with dullness.[38]

In the apparatus to *Temora*, its introductory matter and footnotes, he took a quite different line from that taken in *Fingal*. He was sensitive, evidently, to the criticism of his classical parallels in *Fingal*. But in *Temora* he committed other excesses. Here his main concern was to construct a pseudo-history of the early Caledonians and Scots, and to press home his thesis that Scotland was the *maior Scotia*, and that the Irish Ossianic

37 *Ibid.*, App., 62 ff.
38 Quoted from 1797 ed., p. 156.

ballads were ultimately borrowed from Scotland. He had taken the trouble to read Keating and O'Flaherty on Irish history, and was apparently familiar with some of the matter later to appear in Dr John Macpherson's *Critical Dissertations on the origin etc. of the ancient Caledonians, their posterity the Picts, and the British and Irish Scots* (Dublin 1768). Also, as Matthew P. McDiarmid has persuasively argued, he used to good effect Father Thomas Innes's *A Critical Essay on the Origins of the Ancient Inhabitants of Scotland* (London 1729), which had 'demolish[ed] the pretensions of the earliest part of Boece's history', thus leaving some uncharted centuries to be mapped out.[39] He had presumably discussed Scandinavian antiquities with Blair.[40] He may well have been aware of the bias towards Scandinavian themes in the corpus of Scottish Gaelic ballads, and it is quite possible that his pro-Scottish thesis has some basis in his own beliefs, though he is quite unscrupulous at times in distorting the Irish evidence. But for all that we are probably justified in sensing a waning enthusiasm for Ossianic ploys, and perhaps the opening up of new vistas, as he began to find his way in London. He sums up this mood, cynically enough, in another sentence from his Dissertation to the 1773 edition of the Poems:

> To draw forth, from obscurity, the poems of my own country, has wasted all the time I had allotted for the muses . . .[41]

The mixed motives that came into play in the construction of the *Poems of Ossian* may make it more difficult to exonerate Macpherson, or to see his creative achievement in an uncluttered light. Had he not claimed authenticity so loudly we would not look for it; had he not busily falsified Scottish and Irish history his fabricated notes would not intrude on our appreciation of his fiction; had he been less of a nationalist his reception in England might have been kinder. The view from the Continent, and from farther afield, was less refracted.

39 See M.P. McDiarmid, '*Ossian* as Scottish Epic', in *Scottish Literary News*, Ossian Number, Vol. 3, No. 3 (1973).
40 Blair has an extended discussion of these in his *Dissertation*.
41 Quoted from 1797 ed., p. 162.

It could afford to ignore the more localised annoyances, and fasten on the novel and original features of the work, whether these came from the ballads or from Macpherson. I sometimes think there is a lesson for us in this. It is not enough to say that his folklore collecting wasn't up to modern standards, that his Gaelic and historical scholarship was suspect, that his personal and national propaganda was crude. If we fail to discern the source of that excitement that affected writers and artists and musicians across Euope, it is a failure of our historical imagination, or perhaps in part a victory for prejudice.

Thus it would be wrong-headed to talk at length about Macpherson's work without quoting some of it. Today I offer you only a *soupçon*, conscious of how tastes have changed:

(a) Morna, fairest among women, lovely daughter of Cormac-cairbar. Why in the circle of stones; in the cave of the rock alone? The stream murmurs hoarsely. The old tree's groan is in the wind. The lake is troubled before thee, and dark are the clouds of the sky. But thou art like a snow on the heath, and thy hair like the mist of Cromla . . . (*Fingal*, Bk. I, 8)

(b) The car, the car of battle comes, like the flame of death; the rapid car of Cuchullin, the noble son of Semo. It bends behind like a wave near a rock; like the golden mist of the heath. Its sides are embossed with stones, and sparkle like the sea round the boat of night. Of polished yew is its beam, and its seat of the smoothest bone. The sides are replenished with spears . . . (*Ibid.*, 11)

(c) My joy is in the unequal field; and my soul increases in danger [spoken by Cuchullin]. . . (*Ibid*, Book III, 40)

(d) Daughter of the hand of snow! I was not so mournful and blind; I was not so dark and forlorn when Everallin loved me [spoken by Ossian]. (*Ibid.*, Bk. IV, 49).

It is not difficult to see some of the individual features that attracted so much attention and enthusiasm. The wild scenery, the storms and mist, appealed to tastes which were in reaction from the sophisticated urban literature of the time. The women with flowing hair and flowing robes, wild gestures and uninhibited responses, fitted into the emerging landscape of early Romanticism, and we find these well represented in the etchings of Alexander Runciman in the 1770s. The elaborate introductions and notes would have some appeal for the well-established interest in antiquarian matters, linked as it was to classical studies.

Much of the imagery is Romantic in content, even if in form it is often traditional. One tires, of course, of the sameness of the imagery, as the earliest critics did, and after being carried away for a little by the sound and sequence of the words one begins to ask what lies behind them, to long for understanding of human motive, for anger and pity truly experienced: in short, for the insight which drives a creative writer towards memorable expression. Yet it would be wrong to deny to these works a quality of mesmerism, and it is still possible to fall briefly under their spell. Certainly many writers did, in Britain including Blake and Byron, in Germany Goethe and Herder, and in Ireland Yeats, to name only a handful of instances. We see this influence in Yeats' early poetry especially, as in 'Cuchulain's Fight with the Sea', and I suspect that Yeats' phrase 'a terrible beauty' came into his mind from a footnote of Macpherson's in *Temora*;[42] what Yeats did with this phrase is a different story.

We can point, in this way, to much influence, but it was not, one imagines, the kind of fame or influence that Macpherson dreamed of when he thought he saw the skeleton of that Gaelic epic emerging from the mists of the Highland past, and proceeded to put flesh on its bones.

42   1763 ed., p. 69.

CULTURE AND NATIONAL IDENTITY*

OLLI ALHO
(Finnish Film Archive, Helsinki)

I

At a seminar some time ago, a research project was being discussed. The project concerned the history of Namibia, a country where Finnish missionaries have been working for more than a hundred years. The problems of identity and nation building, and what a group of Finnish scholars might be able to do for the progress of such a country, were discussed. In the course of the debate, I asked the participants — among them Namibian scholars and students — if they could think of another country and of another historical situation where similar problems existed: a country which in spite of tribal and cultural differences among its people became a nation, a country where a small town with 5000 inhabitants, far from the established centre of political and cultural life was made into the new capital, a country which had to create a national language and a national history; a sense of cohesion and belonging together, a feeling of identity, a culture of its own; and its own national symbols: a flag and a national anthem.

*The writer wishes to acknowledge the help given by Ritva Poom in translating the text into English.

Most of those present believed I meant one or other of the African states which became independent during the 1960s — Kenya, Zambia, Tanzania, or Ghana. It was Finland I had in mind, of course, Finland in 1809, as it existed as a part of the great Russian Empire.

The annexation of Finland by Russia in that year and its becoming an autonomous grand duchy was a political manoeuvre that actually united the 'two Finlands', which had in many ways been living apart — the western and the eastern Finland. Both had their own intellectual, cultural and economical orientations; the former looked towards Stockholm, the latter towards St Petersburg. In both parts of the country the intellectuals had been showing interest in the ideas of the romantic movement emanating from Central Europe and spurred on by these, they were becoming increasingly interested in the common people, their traditions and way of life. In regard to commerce, however, as in language, and in other cultural and material aspects, they were closer to their own respective 'capitals' than to each other.

Before 1809 there would not have been many people either in the kingdom of Sweden or in western or eastern Finland, who would have wished to see the kingdom broken into two parts. As most historians now realise, this was caused by external factors, mainly the need of Russia to secure the geo-political position of the city of St Petersburg which had been founded in 1703. The annexation of Finland was an administrative measure which had little connection with the nationalistic or romantic ideas of the period. 'Finland was made, it was not born', as Professor Matti Klinge has it. The state of Finland came into existence, not as a result of a natural or inevitable development, but rather as an outcome of certain military and political necessities.

The country appeared alien and chaotic to contemporaries who visited the newly-born grand duchy. It was more like wilderness than a part of the order created by civilization. Of Finland in 1812, Madame de Staël wrote:

There is no centre here, no competition, nothing to say, nor much to do in this northern-Swedish and northern-

Russian countryside: and for eight months a year the living nature is in a deep sleep.[1]

Three years earlier, in similar vein, a Russian officer and author wrote to his fiancée in St Petersburg:

It is so cold here, that even the wings of time have frozen. It is terribly monotonous. The sadness lingers above the vast snowy plaines, and one may say without exaggeration that this wild, fruitless desert, where there are no books, no company, not even always wine, is so sad, that we cannot distinguish Wednesday from Sunday.[2]

For Sweden the loss of this wilderness was, nevertheless, a national catastrophy. It signified the end of Sweden as a major power and it was felt as a great national disaster. Sweden lost in 1809, one third of its territory and almost one fourth of its population. The famous Swedish general, von Döbeln, speaking to his Finnish troops in Umeå in 1809 stated:

Sweden has lost the Finnish people forever, its strongest support... the mother country has been broken and it has fallen into grief and agony at its incompensable sacrifices.[3]

In these times of national humiliation, Sweden tried in many ways to renew its national pride and regain its identity. At the political level there was a *coup d'état*: a new king from a new line was elected and a new constitution was drafted. At the national level, the country went back to its roots, through the study of folklore and ancient history. The virtues that characterized the early inhabitants of the country, simplicity, industriousness, love of freedom, formed the basis of a national revival and a new sense of national identity and national pride.

In Sweden these activities had an essentially local character; they gave birth to local, not national institutions —

1   Anne Louise Germaine de Staël, *Friherrinan Staëls Tioåriga Landsflykt. Af henne sjelft författad*, Stockholm 1822, 280. This and other English translations here are mine.
2   Quoted in M. Klinge, *Kaksi Suomea*, Keuruu 1982, 15.
3   Quoted in H. Pohjolan-Pirhonen, 'Kansakunta löytää itsensä', *Kanakunnan historia* 3, Helsinki 1973, 132.

historical societies and museums. Obviously Sweden's problem of national identity was a limited one; national or cultural independence was not all at stake. As a nation, Sweden was solid and its identity — even if badly hurt — merely needed to be reconstituted and fortified.

Things were altogether different in Finland, however. This was a sleeping country and, according to some observers, a wilderness; but it was also a country without a history of its own, without a written language (except Swedish), without literature, and without awareness of itself as a nation. In history, there was nothing to return to, in the present, very little to build upon — and in the future, great uncertainties.

Nevertheless, Finland was favoured by certain circumstances, specific to that period of time. Finland's situation was not unique in itself, but what may have been unique — as has been pointed out by Professor Lauri Honko — was that three things coincided in time: the national identity crisis, the growth of romantic ideas, and the birth of a national epic. 'This was a concidence of which Herder had perhaps dreamed, but never experienced', Honko writes.[4] This rare constellation, coupled with the political and administrative needs of Russia, formed the foundation for an exceptionally intensive period of development. The newly-created state was given a centre when Helsinki was made the capital in 1812. The new power demonstrated its status by having the heart of the new capital built in a most grandiose style. A new university was founded, rapidly and effectively developing into an important centre of learning.

The cultural life of the country came alive in 1831 with the founding of the Finnish Literature Society. The aim of the Society was to spread knowledge of the homeland, to develop the Finnish language and to create a Finnish literature. The constitution of the Society, not unnaturally, contained a clause to the effect that its minutes were to be written in Finnish. It is a significant reflection of the cultural situation in the country, however, that this rule had to be abandoned for practical reasons. Nobody knew Finnish well

4.　L. Honko, 'Upptäckten av folkdiktning och nationell identitet i Finland', *Tradisjon* 10 (1980), 45-6.

enough to do it and the minutes of the Society were written in Swedish for a further twenty five years. This fact — insignificant as it may appear — is illuminating. The *Kalevala*, one of the great products of world literature, appeared in a language, which, at the time, could hardly be used for serious intellectual purposes. This also explains the shock which the epic gave the intellectuals of the country after its publication in 1835.

It was precisely due to its influence on national identity that the *Kalevala* attained its primary significance when first published. The epic represented a turning point in Finnish cultural history. For those who stressed the position of Finnish as a language — along with Swedish — of both people and intelligentia, the *Kalevala* confirmed the potential of the Finnish language as a foundation for culture. To those who had been ashamed of the Finnish people's lack of history, the *Kalevala* constituted proof of greatness in antiquity and a high level of ancient culture.

The significance of the *Kalevala* lasted until almost the end of the century and it became the cornerstone of a developing national identity. The epic was taught to children in the schools. Some adults knew some lines or whole sections of it by heart. Artists were inspired by it. Jean Sibelius gave several of his works names derived from the *Kalevala* (The Kullervo Suite, The Swan of Tuonela). The artist Akseli Gallen-Kallela gave form to the most important characters of the epic in his paintings and depicted its best-known episodes (the defence of the Sampo, Lemminkäinen's mother weeping over her dead son, Joukahainen's revenge). The poet Eino Leino wrote one of his most famous collections of poetry in the *Kalevala* metre (*Helkavirsiä*, translated into English under the title 'Whitsongs'). Business concerns and insurance companies derived their names from the *Kalevala*. Later it became a source of names for restaurants and ice-breakers. The figures in the *Kalevala* became national prototypes. Even today personalities in literature and in real life are measured against these Finnish archetypes.

II

The nineteenth century was hardly over before the *Kalevala* was no longer considered to be a historical or a folkloristic document. However, its significance as a powerful national symbol continued until the end of Finland's period as an autonomous grand duchy. During the final years of Russian rule, when the pressures of russification threatened Finland's cultural identity, the role of the *Kalevala* was accentuated: it became the oppressed nation's proof of its right to exist. With the achievement of Finnish independence in 1917, the *Kalevala* began to lose its topicality and broader interest in it slowly began to wane. The epic had now become more an object of scholarly interest than of the love of the people. The majority of Finns today have little contact with the Finnish national epic after their obligatory familiarization with it at school. There are not many Finns who have read *Kalevala* in its entirety. Nevertheless, a copy of the *Kalevala* is found on the bookshelf in most Finnish homes — expensively bound and stylishly illustrated, in the more affluent ones.

During recent years, however, the *Kalevala* has somewhat surprisingly, become so topical that one is almost justified in speaking of the epic's renaissance. In 1974, the writer Paavo Haavikko (winner of the Neustadt Award in 1984) published a volume of poetry *Kaksikymmentä ja yksi*,[5] 'Twenty and One', in which he focussed on what may be the most enigmatic mythical theme of the epic, the tale of the Sampo, a wondrous object which mills wealth.

The Sampo, Haavikko explained in an interview, was a money-machine situated in Constantinople. The Byzantine coins minted by the Sampo spread throughout the entire world. According to Haavikko, the tale of the theft of the Sampo is based on a historical occurrence set in Viking times: the ancient Finns tried to steal the money-making machine and bring it north with them to mill wealth. Although the attempt failed, the memory of it lived on in the narrative poetry of the folk.

5   P. Haavikko, *Kaksikymmentä ja yksi*, Helsinki 1974.

The controversy over the nature of the Sampo created by Haavikko had not yet subsided before it was revealed that Kalle Holmberg, a well-known and controversial theatre director, was planning to feature the *Kalevala* as a television film, with Paavo Haavikko as text writer. This film, which Holmberg named *Rauta-aika*, 'The Iron Age' was completed in 1981 and awoke heated debate. Some scholars as well as ordinary members of the public felt that Holmberg had desecrated a relic, while others felt that Holmberg's powerful and personal film had, for the first time, given them a true feeling for this epic which had always seemed remote to them. In keeping with Haavikko's theory, the film depicts the Sampo as a money-minting machine. In the film, however, the machine has been constructed by the men from Kalevala themselves in order to make counterfeit Byzantine money.

The Iron Age went on to receive the prestigious Prix Italia award in 1983. That same year Professor Matti Klinge, one of the foremost Finnish historians, published a work in which he interpreted the Sampo as a cult statue located in the market-place of ancient Turku.[6] This statue evolved into a symbol of the trading rights of the particular market place, just as the Roland statues of the cities of the Magdeburg Archbishopric did. Klinge's theory was disputed by leading scholars of folk-lore and history.

Also in 1983, the debate about the Sampo was entered into by the Estonian ethnographer and author, Lennart Meri, in his work *Hopeanvalkea*,[7] 'Silverwhite'. Meri explained the Sampo as being the cosmic pillar of the world, the primary symbol of a cosmological order, centred around the North Star.

In 1984, the Finnish authority on the *Kalevala*, Professor Matti Kuusi, made a list of the Sampo interpretations which had appeared in print to date. There were about sixty of them. The magazine in which Kuusi's article was published[8] announced that it would draw up a 'complete listing' of Sampo interpretations to honour the *Kalevala*'s one hundred

---

6   M. Klinge, *Muinaisuutemme merivallat*, Keuruu 1983.
7   L. Meri, *Hopeanvalkea*, Jyväskylä 1983.
8   M. Kuusi, 'Päättymätön arvoituslaikki. Miten Sampoa on selitetty', *Kotiseutu* 2 (1984), 85-8.

and fiftieth anniversary. Readers were urged to add to Professor Kuusi's list — lest he may have overlooked any explanations — and also to send the editors any additional theories of their own about the enigmatic Sampo.

It is certainly natural that the Finns, when celebrating the anniversary of a national symbol like the *Kalevala*, see its very existence as a reminder of their own specific qualities and characteristics. It is equally natural, however, for us to realise that the *Kalevala* is not only there to distinguish the Finns from the rest of the nations of the world, but that it also joins the Finns with the rest of the world's peoples and cultures. This point of view — *Kalevala*'s global status, so to say — was already strongly to the fore in the development of folklore studies in Finland. Finnish folkloristics developed at an early stage into a science with two faces, combining the search for the national past and identity with the comparative approach in a search for global parallels to national themes. Thus the *Kalevala* and the old Finnish folk poems on which it is based contain two kinds of information: they inform the Finns about themselves, their ancient world-view, and, perhaps, history and, at the same time, they testify to the Finns' connection with other peoples and other cultures. Let me give a few examples of these latter relationships.

III

The myth of the creation of the world from an egg is known over a broad area extending from the Eastern Mediterranean to India, Japan, Polynesia and Peru. In the Balto-Finnic region, the theme of the diver is sometimes joined to the creation myth: the bird fetches a bit of land from the bottom of the cosmic sea and it is from this that the world is created.

In the same region where the myth of the cosmic egg appears, the concept of a mythical great tree (oak) is also known. It grows to the heavens and hides the sun and moon from sight. The second canto of the *Kalevala* relates how a tiny man rises from the sea and fells the oak. Once again, light can flow to the earth and fructify nature. The myth of the great oak is often explained as a depiction of the Milky

Way along which, according to the beliefs of the Finnic tribes, the souls of the dead travelled to the life beyond the grave. The song is sung in Estonia as a lullaby, in Ingria as a drinking song (to explain how a felled tree is used in making drinking utensils) and in Karelia as part of a healing drama — a good example of how one and the same myth may fulfill different functions.

The Sampo — an object which has attracted many explanations — has numerous parallels in mythology quite independent of how it is actually 'explained'. Scandinavian mythology offers the closest parallel in the description of the magical Grotti — a mill which ground whatever he wanted for the Danish king, Fróði.

An even more clearly Scandinavian impression is created by the tale of the theft of the Sampo: it is closely parallelled in the Old Norse *fornaldarsögur*. Thus, *Bósa saga* tells of Bósi, who steals the egg from the *gammr*, a huge bird. Bósi journeys to a distant land with a friend. They slay the elk which is guarding the egg, free a captive princess and return home. Soon Bósi and his friend go on a new journey — taking along a man named Smiðr ('smith'). In the distant land, the companions abduct a marriageable maiden against her will and hide her in their boat, inside a harp which performs miracles. The enemy attacks the boat. A furious battle ensues during which the enemy changes into a flying dragon and swallows Smiðr. The battle ends with the victory of Bósi and his companions. The similarities of this tale to the account of the theft of the Sampo are startling.

The tale of death and resurrection in the Lemminkäinen poems brings to mind an early parallel, that of the Egyptian Osiris myth, according to which Osiris is killed and cast into a river. His soul is later awakened by his sister, Isis. An obvious parallel is also found later on in Christian tradition. It is, however, more natural to compare Lemminkäinen to the Scandinavian god, Baldr who is killed by the arrow of the blind old god Höðr. Lemminkäinen also dies at the hands of a weak adversary, killed at the River of Tuonela by a small cowherd.

The tale of Väinämöinen's departure in the last song of the *Kalevala* is parallelled by the world-wide theme of the cultural hero who gives the people crucial knowledge and skill about community and cultural life and then departs from their midst after having promised to return when the people need his help again.

Scandinavian influence is also suggested by certain details in this poem: the place to which Väinämöinen sails is located between the earth and the sky. It is reminiscent of the 'Maelstrom', a whirlpool through which people and ships are sucked into the other world (in Olaus Magnus' map dated 1559, the Maelstrom is located in the Lofoten Islands). The episode in which the newborn child speaks, may be of the same origin as the French legend of St Goar, in which the child names his own father. In the *Kalevala*, the boy reproaches Väinämöinen, who decreed that the illegitimate child be cast into a swamp.

Widespread counterparts can also be found to numerous other themes of the *Kalevala*. Ilmarinen's despairing attempt to forge himself a wife of gold is reminiscent of Hephæstus' — or, in Indian mythology, Tvashtri's — similar efforts. Ilmarinen's creation, the golden maiden, is also widely known among Siberian peoples related to the Finns and in Lapland.

The tale of the capture of the sun and moon and their release is a northern version of the Prometheus myth. In a similar form this myth is known by many people of northern Eurasia. The tragic story of Kullervo has been compared to the legend of Amleth (Hamlet). Väinämöinen's kantele playing is reminiscent of the legend of Orpheus which was extremely popular in Europe during the Middle Ages as well as of the popular tale of 'The Singing Bone', well known in Europe, Africa and India. In this tale, a fisherman makes a wonderful musical instrument from the limbs of a drowned girl.

The charms and incantations (approximately 4,200 verses) which Lönnrot incorporated into the *Kalevala*, are also international in nature. Such magic charms were part and parcel of the life of the ancient Finns in every region and not even the advent of Christianity was able to effect any change over the centuries, other than the substitution of Christian saints for popular figures of pagan religion. The broad background of wedding songs in the *Kalevala* also belongs to folk tradition. The wedding laments, in particular, comprise the oldest and most interesting nucleus of material. Through these songs, the *Kalevala* provides insights into a folk tradition which reaches back further than the time of the creation of the songs themselves. Thus, though thoroughly national, *Kalevala* appears at the same time to be a deeply and thoroughly international and universal work, an epic of all peoples.

IV

The interplay between national and international — between Finnish and foreign — has always been a difficult thing for the Finns to cope with. This difficulty has produced in the cultural history of Finland many paradoxes and contradictions. I would like to touch upon one of them here.

What I have in mind is the fact that while Finland, as an autonomous part of Russia, went through a period that was intensively introvert, and deeply nationalistic, it had, at the very same time, a period of extreme internationalism, almost cosmopolitanism, especially in the arts and sciences. The second half of the nineteenth century and the beginning of the twentieth are generally considered a period when Finland, as a result of internal development, matured culturally to the extent that it could become a politically independent nation. It is seldom pointed out that this maturing was not only a national but also, to a considerable degree, an international process. To illustrate this, let us consider high points in the life of Elias Lönnrot — the maker of the *Kalevala* — and juxtapose them with some of the events of the nation's cultural history.

Lönnrot entered on his academic studies when he was eighteen years old, in 1820. In the same year the linguist, A.J. Sjögren, went to St Petersburg to launch a brilliant career in the Academy of Science there — a career that took him to many parts of the Empire, from Karelia to the Caucasus.

In 1841, Lönnrot made his tenth journey to collect folk poems for *Kalevala*'s second edition. In the same year the Academy in St Petersburg sent M.A. Castrén on a journey across Russia to West and East Siberia, beyond Baikal, all the way to the Chinese border. He became the founder of the study of Fenno-Ugrian languages.

In 1843, Lönnrot was editing the second edition of the

Kalevala (to be published in 1849) and planning his eleventh and last, journey into the field. The same year G.A. Wallin, a student of oriental languages, set off for Alexandria where he remained for six years. He became one of the leading experts of Arabic culture of his time and received — among other honours — the medal of the Royal Geographic Society in London in 1848 (one year after David Livingstone).

By the time Lönnrot had retired from his position as Professor of Finnish, A.E. Nordensköld, who had been forced by political circumstances to move to Sweden after having published his dissertation in the University of Helsinki in 1855, had gained fame for his journey through the Northeast Passage and for his research among the Siberian peoples in 1878-9.

Lönnrot died in 1884. The year before that, the Fenno-Ugrian Society had been founded in Helsinki. Over the following decades, a great number of scholars was sent by the Society to all parts of Russia and beyond. Many of them made expeditions lasting four or five years.

Certain political measures undertaken to counteract the cultural and political development of the country around the turn of the century — especially the so-called February Manifesto — evoked strong national sentiments among the Finns. At the same time the great era of Finnish scholarly expeditions began. C.G. Mannerheim, then a Russian officer, but who was later to become the supreme commander of the Finnish army, undertook an expedition through Russia and Mongolia to China yielding remarkable scientific results. The natural scientist, G.J. Ramstedt, studied northern Siberia in 1898-1912 and the geographer J.G. Granö, travelled in Mongolia and Central Asia during the years 1900-9.

The expeditions of Finnish scholars were not limited to various parts of the Russian Empire, or, to regions inhabited by Fenno-Ugric peoples. The orientalist, Arthur Hjelt, spent several years in the Near East from 1911 onwards; Edward Westermarck began his long field work in Morocco in 1897; Gunnar Landtman studied the Papuans in New Guinea in 1910-2; and Hilja Granquist spent the better part of the 1920s in Southern Palestine, investigating life in Arabic villages. Among these ethnographers was Sakari Pälsi, an individual who had taken part in Ramstedt's expedition to

Mongolia in 1909-10. In April 1917 he left home alone, with a camera for making moving pictures. His destination was the River Anadyr on the Kamchatka peninsula. He studied the lives of the Chuckchees, Lamutes and Koryaks, and photographed them. In 1919, when Pälsi returned to Helsinki the country had gained its independence.

Culture and civilization are not only conditioned by internal factors; for their harmonious development they are dependent upon contacts with other cultures, influence from outside and cultural and economic exchange. The national identity includes not only an image of ourselves in isolation, but also an image of ourselves in relation to others, an image of ourselves as one people among the peoples of the world. Finnish folklore scholars early discovered the relationship between the *Kalevala*, Finnish folk poetry and global tradition. Finnish scholars who travelled outside their own country widened and deepened this perspective.

All this was extremely significant, but a nation building its identity is not likely to appreciate such matters at the time. It is quite possible that the global character of Finnish mythology is a better-known fact abroad than in Finland – it is certainly true that, for instance, Westermarck, Karsten, Landtman, and Granquist are better-known abroad than in their home country. It is a telling fact that Westermarck's last work *Christianity and Morals*, published in England in 1939, did not appear in the Finnish language until 1984.

It seems a paradox that the intensively nationalistic period in Finland was at the same time intensively international. It is no paradox at all that the nation remembers those who worked for the national goals, but forgets those who worked within the wider context. But the value of the 'internationalists' for their country and culture becomes greater and more apparent when the formative period is over, and the nation has become part of the world community, and, accordingly, has established its right to be treated as an equal by others. Then knowledge of oneself, one's own nation, is not sufficient; instead, more and more knowledge about other peoples and cultures is required. With this comes a capacity to understand and co-operate with others, and to give and receive cultural stimuli.

Now, one hundred and fifty years after the *Kalevala*'s birth, it is possible to declare that Lönnrot and the great personalities of his time taught the Finns to understand themselves and to live with each other. But at the same time, other men and women, whether working in Swedish — or English, German, Russian and other international languages — gave substance and meaning to the other dimension of mature national existence, the capacity to live with others.

It may look strange at first sight — at least to an outsider's eye — that an old epic like the *Kalevala* has recently enjoyed such a renaissance in Finland, but a closer look at the phenomenon reveals its particular character, the differences from earlier approaches to the *Kalevala*. Characteristic of all these contemporary interpretations of the *Kalevala* is their concern with relating the epic, or its central themes, to an international context. The literary author takes the heroes of the *Kalevala* to distant Byzantium; the theatre director dresses the people of Pohjola in exotic costumes, brings Lemminkäinen's wife from Estonia and gives the heroes of the *Kalevala* a fascination for Byzantine money; the historian seeks the solution of the riddle of the Sampo by reference to central European mercantile customs and traditions.

This is no longer a 'looking for one's roots' or a 'searching for one's national identity'. This phenomenon must be seen against the background of a broadening consciousness within the nation sharing a common heritage with other peoples of the world. Previously it was expedient to regard the *Kalevala* as an epic distinguishing the Finns as a nation. Today, attention is focussed on the way in which *Kalevala* unites the Finns with the rest of the world.

The ways in which Finnish artists and scholars relate to international and global traditions and present-day trends are, of course, manifold. Nevertheless, I consider it to be somewhat of a miracle that they can still turn today to the old epic and — even without reference to its anniversary — find it an adequate source for inspiration. What has happened in Finland during the past ten years is a telling reminder of the cultural significance of the *Kalevala* — and of all epic poetry.

THE KALEVALA: MYTH OR HISTORY?

LAURI HONKO

(University of Turku)

Is the *Kalevala* primarily a historical or a mythical epic? This question has been worrying readers and scholars since the very start of the Kalevala process. For four decades the answer was sought in the *Kalevala* itself, until scholarly research into folklore began to be carried out in the latter half of the 1870s. One of its first tasks was to make scholars forget the *Kalevala* and concentrate on the original folk poetry recordings. The question thus became: Do the events and people in the folk poems used as the basic material for the *Kalevala* embrace features that link them up with historical facts obtained through other channels, or should they be regarded primarily as reflections of an ancient mythical world-view? In a way this meant a return from the time of Lönnrot to the time of Porthan. It was Porthan, after all, who outlined the rules for the publication and study of folklore which Lönnrot was forced to break in his desire to satisfy the order of society and to give the nation something more than a mere collection of unconnected folk poems.

The fledgeling science began to attract a limited band of followers, and the principles it applied in its methods gradually also began to be adapted to related sciences operating with elements of tradition. Scholarship placed the *Kalevala* under the protection of the banner of epic poetry. It became a useful reference in the debate on culture and national politics, and also in the headings to scholarly papers and articles. The *Kalevala* began to drift from folkloristics to literary research, leaving behind one, or at most two researchers to look into the source history of the epic and problems relating to Lönnrot's method. There were few people able to discuss their problems with them, and study of the *Kalevala* thus faced the threat of extinction in the hands of a small minority. The situation today is still very much the same — a regrettable state of affairs in view of the cultural-political significance of the *Kalevala* and the interest shown in it both in Finland and abroad. Elias Lönnrot himself seems to have wavered between the historical and the mythical interpretation in choosing the sub-title to the *Old Kalevala*. Undoubtedly *The Kalevala, or Old Karelian Songs from the Ancient Times of the Finnish People* points to history, but one of the alternative names considered by Lönnrot was *Finnish Mythology through Ancient Poems*. The question presents itself as to whether there was a true conflict here. Possibly the categories of history and mythology did not mean quite the same thing to Lönnrot and his contemporaries as they do to the scholars of the present century.

The earliest research interest was antiquarian: people became interested in folk tradition if it was believed that tradition could provide any insight into the way of life, occupations, history of settlement, rulers and pagan religion of ancient times. The cornerstone of Swedish and Finnish folklore collecting, the decree drawn up by Johannes Bureus and signed by Gustavus II Adolphus in May 1630 contains detailed instructions for the recording of relics of the past, including folklore. It contains the admonishment to inquire into 'all manner of chronicles and narratives, time-honoured legends and poems about dragons, gnomes and giants — likewise tales of celebrated persons, old monasteries, castles, the dwelling places of kings and towns, so that we may discover what used to be, the old poems about heroes and incantations, not forgetting their melodies'. This collecting programme was not, however, a sign of interest in tradition for its own sake: lurking in the background was the need to reinforce the national identity and to rank high among nations. The reasons given for the decree bear witness to a desire to prove 'that our ancestors were not barbarians', 'that we are the oldest of nations' and 'that our language is the oldest of all', and there is concern at the attempt by the Danes to appropriate this honour for themselves. The decree of Gustavus II Adolphus was a reaction to the summons concerning the collecting of Danish antiquities sent by King Christian IV of Denmark to the bishops of Denmark and Norway in 1622.

There was also a foreign example for the list of deities published by Mikael Agricola eight decades earlier, its aim being to root out remnants of paganism and popery. The needs and expectations channelling interest towards tradition have from the very beginning, and even in recent times, almost without exception, originated outside the communities upholding and maintaining the tradition. In speaking of interpretations of folklore it must be remembered that they are seldom the interpretations of the people actually producing and using this tradition. The discovery of tradition is usually followed by its transfer to some other sphere and its being put to some other use – archives, publication – as an instrument of cultural policy. The *Kalevala* too, is the result of such a transfer of tradition. The administrative or cultural elite setting the collecting of tradition in motion also bears the responsibility for the new use of the tradition in an environment quite unlike that in which it existed before its discovery.

The American professor William A. Wilson has examined the relationship between folklore and nationalism in Finland with the eyes of an outside observer. In the closing passage of his work he speaks of two ways of approaching folk tradition, one epitomised by Juslenius, the other by Porthan. A cautious scholar Porthan, used folklore as a mirror of Finnish culture, as a means of understanding man's way of thinking. The romantic, patriotic articles by Juslenius display a marked need, dictated by the plight of the nation, to find new faith in the future in the nation's heroic past. Then, however, the mirror of folklore ceases to reflect the people and tends to reflect the current political position of the holder of the mirror. Wilson claims that both approaches have lived on to the present day, and he says:

> To the extent that Finnish folklorists have been scholars first and patriots second, to the extent that they have used folklore to understand people but not to control them, to create a pride in the nation's heritage but not to shape its destiny – to that extent both folklore studies and the nation have profited. But when folklorists have stepped across the line of scholarly objectivity to devote themselves

and their research first and foremost to the service of the fatherland, when they have dreamed of a magnificent, powerful future or of a classless, communistic society, and have used folklore to mold the thinking of the people and to bring to pass these dreams — when they have done these things, both their research and their nation have suffered.[1]

The borders are strict in Wilson's black-and-white world; yet he is still worth listening to.

From an examination of the tidal fluctuation between the historical and the mythical interpretation of folklore in relation to the times of distress in the national identity, it appears that the historical interpretation is always resorted to when there is a marked need to reinforce the national identity. In the eighteenth century the high-flown theories of Juslenius were sorted out by the critical Porthan, who took a cautious attitude towards the historical evidence provided by folklore and instead began to speak with a sense of purpose of its cultural, artistic and literary value. Writings of his and of his colleagues and pupils display a strong interest in Finnish mythology and folk religion.

In the 1820s Elias Lönnrot, following the lead of such as Reinhold von Becker, began to apply the historical aspect to folklore as if in answer to the expectations aroused by the forerunners of the builders of national identity in autonomous Finland. He was also guided in this direction by his conception of the overall structure of the *Kalevala*, seeking help in the comments made by the rune singers and scientific information on the origins of the Finns. Lönnrot's guiding principle was his own view — half personal, half scientific — that the *Kalevala* poems described the life of ancient Finnish society. This vision of the ancient era was basically Christian and euhemeristic: the compiler of the epic believed that the religion of the ancient Finns bore monotheistic features, even though the fields and forests were still peopled by numerous spirits; very often the respect enjoyed by some historical figure led sub-

---

1   W.A. Wilson, *Folklore and Nationalism in Modern Finland*, Bloomington and London 1976, 206.

sequent generations to attribute divine features to him too, as
in the case of Väinämöinen and Ilmarinen. In seeking a time
and a setting for his vision, Lönnrot decided to place the
events related in the poems on the southern side of the White
Sea about a thousand years back in time, for according to
the scientific views at the time that was where the forefathers
of the Finns came from. In forming this quasi-historical view,
Lönnrot projected himself into the world of the *Kalevala*
more fully than we may imagine. As a scholar he wanted to
allow for all possible research results that might throw light
on the Finns' past; as a poet he wanted to tell about the past
in the words of folklore, as if calling on the rune singers, the
initial receivers of poetic communication as his witnesses.
The ancient era of the *Kalevala* unfolded before him as a
period in history of which the *Kalevala* was proof. Seen from
this angle it is, perhaps, possible to understand the astonishing
fact that from time to time Lönnrot spoke of the *Kalevala* as
a source for scientific research, illuminating the life of ancient
society. We see from this that he underestimated his own
contribution and overrated the historical or ethnographic
source value of the *Kalevala*. This was, however, no intentional
oversight, for Lönnrot was always completely frank about,
for example, his methods in compiling the *Kalevala*.

Although not everyone accepted Lönnrot's ancient historical
interpretation of the *Kalevala* – Snellman, among others.
doubted it and Jacob Grimm suggested that it be replaced by
a mythical interpretation – it became the dominant one and
was the one adopted for teaching in schools. Julius Krohn
was the first to turn the study of folklore on to a new track
though he took great care not to offer offence to the *Kalevala*
and its creator. It is indicative that the studies of both Julius
Krohn and his son Kaarle Krohn were at this stage based on
the theory of evolution and the nature-mythical interpretation.
The Finnish historical-geographical research method was
undergoing intensive development and an extensive international comparative study, mainly of folktales, was begun
in this spirit; within a short time this created a wide range of
foreign contacts for Finnish folkloristics. Narrow, factional
views broadened out into cosmopolitan perspectives. Comparative research proved its worth: a foreign background was

discovered for a growing number of poetic motifs and tradition elements once thought to be indigenous. Folk tradition became the tradition of many peoples: 'Borrowings, borrowings and more borrowings . . .' was soon the cry heard from scholars everywhere.

The promising developments towards an overall view of Finnish folklore, balanced by findings from abroad, were interrupted by the First World War. Even before this the Finnish identity had been in dire straits, and this also began to disturb the peace of researchers. In 1910 a number of articles appeared in the press criticising the Krohn school: it was accused of lowering the value of the *Kalevala* and of stressing the occurrence of late mediaeval Christian loans at the expense of the ancient, free, warlike era of heroes. National identity was again in need of fuel. Four years later Kaarle Krohn announced that his concept of Finnish poetry had undergone radical change: contrary to what he had believed so far, the poems contained historical remnants of pagan society and the heroes it revered. Shedding most of his former theories, Krohn adopted a new historical paradigm, later forming an alliance with the most notable authority on Finland's early history, Jalmari Jaakkola. Between the two World Wars, these men created the scholarly atmosphere in which the subsequent generation of folklorists, above all Martti Haavio, grew up and which internalised the idea of heroic poetry composed during the Viking Era in Finland. Folklore also became a weapon of Finnish expansionist propaganda. At least one observer — William A. Wilson — appears to be convinced that the choice of subjects for research in the first few decades of independence and the results obtained were regulated by political expediency. The research front was not, however, entirely united, for the nature-mythical interpretation, for example, found a strong advocate in E.N. Setälä.

In view of all that had happened, research after the Second World War might be expected to have been in a state of bankruptcy, but in fact the inevitable change meant a welcome release from a research tradition that was becoming something of a burden. Fresh breezes swept through both methods and subjects. This is evidenced, for example, by Martti Haavio's work *Väinämöinen* (1950, in English 1952). The question posed in the heading to the first chapter dealing with previous research on Väinämöinen, 'God or man?', received such a comprehensive reply, indicating an intimate familiarity with tradition, that the reader is made aware of the impossibility of the unadorned either/or. The poems recognise at least two Väinämöinens, the shaman and the cultural hero, whose characters include stratified motifs from archaic belief systems and international myths and legends. It is no longer possible to discern from the poems any real historical core, such as some shaman or sage of centuries past, but it is possible to see in them a fairly complete picture of the mythical world-view of a specific cultural era.

The work by Matti Klinge *Muinaisuutemme merivallat* (The Naval Powers of Finnish Antiquity, 1983), published on the eve of the *Kalevala* jubilee, has revived the old controversy. If only for the reason that Klinge lacks a logical, overall method for the analysis of traditional elements it is, in general, easy to agree with the critical comments made by Väinö Kaukojen and Heikki Kirkinen. Kirkinen speaks emphatically of the mythical interpretation raised by post-war folklore research, which he considers as having replaced the historical interpretation. This being so, Klinge's work is more or less an anachronism stimulated, as he says, by the fight between Western and Eastern Finland for the ownership of the old epic and thus for the Finnish soul and identity. Kirkinen takes up arms in the same cause but uses more measured devices in attempting to strengthen the image of Karelia as an independent cultural region of influence, extending far into Savo and Ostrobothnia. Certain old features of this area which are also encountered in Western Finland, have, according to him, a Proto-Finnic rather than a mediaeval origin. In any case, it is interesting that debate over the potential of the historical and the mythical interpretation has once again become part of the moulding of identity, even though not an identity crisis as such.

Our survey of the history of learning would appear to suggest that we are at present living in an era of the mythical interpretation of the *Kalevala* and ancient epic. To begin with, this means the collapse of the idea cherished by Lönnrot of the *Kalevala* at least as an indicative source of ancient Finnish history. It can no longer be considered much more than an idle amateurish entertainment to try to link Väinämöinen, Ilmarinen, Lemminkäinen or Joukahainen with any historical figure, or even with any precise place or time, or even to suggest that they together belonged to any particular era. The stratification of these characters and partly also the regional differences in their development make scientifically watertight historical reconstruction in this respect impossible. The proportion of poetry indubitably based on historical fact, such as Elina's Death, Duke Charles and possibly Bishop Henry, is infinitely small in the entire Finnish epic repertoire; our indigenous poetry has not taken kindly to historical themes — a fact worth noting in debating its mythical nature. The question of the historical verity of the figures and events described in the *Kalevala* is abortive — a fact that many of Lönnrot's contemporaries, such as Snellman, seemed to realise immediately on making acquaintance with the work.

The question of the ethnographical reliability of the *Kalevala* is somewhat more complex. The question is: Do the customs and practices, the tools and materials, the vehicles and weapons described in the epic reflect the true folk culture of some particular region or period? It is not possible here to study any examples in detail. In general, however, it is true to say that the objects and customs mentioned in the *Kalevala* really did exist in living folk culture, or have a basis there. In other words all the practices described are not fictive, poetic. Undue enthusiasm for the ethnographic source value of the *Kalevala* is, however, curbed by two basic caveats. The first concerns Lönnrot's method: in combining poems by different singers and from different regions, he did not adhere to any known cultural model in a logical manner, instead heeding his intuition and the vision flashing before his mind's eye of ancient Finnish society. Having gone through this process, the material of the songs no longer had any geographical domicile and no clear fixed point in time. Lönnrot thus destroyed the authenticity of his original recordings in chopping them up into lines and segments to suit his own ends. He tried to replace it by a new authenticity ultimately relying on his own view of the *Kalevala* way of life. The result is

a patchwork quilt whose colourful patches may momen-
tarily correspond to a feature of some existing folk culture
but only as fragments. Thus, whatever reflection of true folk
culture the original recordings contained could no longer
come across in the *Kalevala*.

But did even the original folk poems reflect folk culture with photographic precision? The answer to that differs
slightly according to genre – incantations, wedding poems,
bear poems, lyrics, epic proper, and so on – but in all instances there are more reservations than one may imagine.
Ritual poetry, for example, did, after all, reflect authentic
contexts and the lyrical poetry described the basic emotional
constellations and problems that recurred again and again
in everyday life. In spite of this 'closeness to life' the poems
from the oral tradition were neither the rite poems nor the
epic poems proper; they are not photographic copies of
reality. They were not intended to be so, and it was not in
their nature. There is always a gulf between the reality depicted
in the poems and the singer's reality, the discerning of which
calls for familiarity with the real environment of the singer
and also genre analytic source criticism. To take an example,
bears were in reality killed with a firearm, in songs always
with an arrow or a spear. It was probably observations just
such as these that emboldened Lönnrot to construct a fictive
way of life for the ancient Finns. The customs and practices
communicated by the poems often seemed rather poorly
suited to the present day, but they might be better suited
to some earlier era. This may have been true, but not necessarily so. And there was no guarantee that the communications
from ancient times preserved by memory came from comparable sources, in other words that they reflected a specific
level or stage of culture.

There is still a third level at which we may speak of historical
verity, and that is the level of social structures and the world-
view based on them. We are not speaking here of photographic
precision but of the values and attitudes expressed in the
poems. It may be assumed that they were filtered in the
singer's consciousness in a way that must of necessity have
influenced his concept of reality. Even when they did not
correspond to concrete everyday experience, and precisely

then, they helped the singer to understand, to analyse and to express reality. At this point we nevertheless begin to move away from history and ethnography to the domain of world-view and myths. In the case of the *Kalevala* the question of the relationship between the poems and social reality becomes: What was Lönnrot's attitude to the social structure he encountered in the poems and how did he mould it? In other words the filter is once again Lönnrot.

In order to come to grips with the discrepancy between the historical and the mythical interpretation we must turn to the conception of time. Historical time is linear, continuous and irreversible, whereas mythical time is cyclic, recurring, and born of the merging of two time dimensions, the great primaeval time and the present moment.

To borrow the definition used in comparative religion, a 'myth' (Greek *mȳthos*, 'true word, speech') is 'a story about gods', a narrative based on a religious world concept of fundamental happenings that took place in primaeval time (at the creation of the world, the decisive moment in time), and of the exemplary deeds of the gods (saints, cultural heroes, founders of clans, etc.). It was thanks to these that the world, nature, culture and our social group with all its many phenomena came into being and was ordered in a way that still influences the present day. The myth is thus the charter for world order, referred to in arguing forms of behaviour, social institutions, moral laws and systems of norms, along with the efficacy of a religious rite and the sacredness of a cult. The actual living environment of the myth is the rite, the religious ceremony. The ritual performance of the myth is the defence of world order: the world is prevented from plunging into chaos by imitating sacred example events. The events reported in the myth are sacred and real to the believer and the community around him, in other words the myth is part of a socially acceptable, internalised world-view. From the point of view of the myth, history is profane time, which the myth in fact destroys and replaces with sacred time; the myth may thus be characterised as 'sacred history'. According to Mircea Eliade, archaic man, who is still present in us all, tries to withstand the pressure created by the onslaught of historical events by transferring to mythical time, and by believing as true and as happening, only that which has an example and model in the events of primaeval time. We may add to Eliade's idea by saying that man draws from these primaeval models and ideas, projected into the present day by means of, for example, a rite, both knowledge and strategy for his action. Archaic man's behaviour is thus a prototype through and through, recalling the models of primaeval time and linking them up with events in everyday life. In this way the events of profane everyday life are 'translated' into the language of the myth and transferred to mythical time, which takes the place of profane time.

Myths are more persistent than their ritual contexts, and the thought mechanism itself may be preserved for a long time outside religious behaviour proper. In this respect the concept of the myth provides the reader with the keys both to the *Kalevala* and to folk poetry on mythical subjects. Many narratives and points in them become more readily understood if we do not try to force them down to the level of historical time and everyday experience but try to hear in them the message aimed at man operating in mythical time.

The way to do this starts with the acceptance of folk poems as such. For example, there is no need to submit genuine, original folk poems to textual analysis, to compare them with variants, to seek remote parallels. It must be accepted that they were in their own performing context fully meaningful and were part of a living world-view. If there is sufficient information about the context, the message of the poem may reach us even across cultural and linguistic borders. What is important is to listen to other poems from the same region or community, for this may place the reader on the track of the systematic features of the world-view concerned.

Well, what about the *Kalevala*? Can it be approached by the same method? Undoubtedly it can. The myths in the *Kalevala* are, of course, Lönnrot's variants, but we can see through them into the basic structure of the myths — and that is sufficient. The messages of the archaic myths reach us through both the *Kalevala* and folk poems. A wealth of variants is part of the life of the myth: on receiving a myth we create our own variant of it. A certain structural basic meaning, which we may not always be capable of verbalising, is nevertheless retained from one culture to another, and on it we build our current meaning of the myth. Since listening to myths is based on interaction, involving ourselves and the performer or source of the myth, there is neither reason nor need for not considering Lönnrot as one of the transmitters of myth. In this sense, Lönnrot's version is just as authentic as Ontrei Malinen's. We are dealing with one basic form of human communication, the means being myths and the mythical concept of time.

It is not possible here to go deeper into the myths of the *Kalevala*, but they are relatively easy to discern in the work. The origin of the world is the basic myth, which Finnish poetry tries to link up with the origin of numerous other natural and cultural phenomena. Typical tales of creation in the *Kalevala* are the planting of the forests, the sowing of the first barley, the origin of beer, the origin of fire, the origin of iron and the origin of music. Alongside the god of creation appears the cultural hero Väinämöinen, or rather the pair of heroes Väinämöinen and Ilmarinen. Their participation in the primaeval events is also reflected in their later deeds, in the cantos telling of the Sampo and the journeys to woo the maiden of Pohjola, in which there are sufficient references to mythical themes in between and behind the 'adventurous' elements of the plot. Lönnrot also drew extensively on incantations for mythologems. Although their place in the *Kalevala* is by no means always in keeping with oral folklore, they nevertheless become part of the mythological world-view transmitted by the *Kalevala*. Special colour is added to this world-view by the great ritual dramas, such as the wedding and the bear feast, likewise the prayers which appear in the most varied of contexts and which though they cannot necessarily be classified as myths, nevertheless contain references to myths and in principle operate at the same level, i.e. within the mythical conception of time.

I have here outlined two ways of approaching the *Kalevala* and folk poetry. One of them is the folkloristic approach centred around the transmitter of the poem or myth. Viewed in this light the *Kalevala* must immediately be branded as unauthentic if used as a reference work on folk culture, since such a work must be ethnographically correct. But the same criticism may in principle be levelled at original folk poems too, since they are not ethnographically correct either. Neither the *Kalevala* nor folk poetry conveys a picture of the real world as such. Even so folk poetry is part of the ethnographical real world and can, mainly by the means of genre analysis and tradition-ecology, be integrated into that world. The *Kalevala*, on the other hand, does not belong to the world of the rune-singers; it is a product of literary culture, a brilliant synthesis by an epic poet also incorporating elements from outside Finnish-Karelian folk poetry and inspired by the long epic tradition and the tastes of the chosen target group — educated Finnish circles.

My second approach is based on the communication of tradition in culture, not excluding our own culture. We can take part in the folklore process, which nowadays relies more on books and the electronic media than on oral tradition. In actual fact we cannot avoid myths. And among them is the *Kalevala*, and why not also the myths contained in the original folk poems? We react to them in the manner of archaic man: we step out of the present moment, from linear, historical time into the midst of primaeval events and sacred history, whose models and structural meanings spell out the present-day message of contemporary events. In this set-up we not only receive myths, we also reproduce them and create them. The question of the message contained in the *Kalevala* and folk poetry is thus bound to the present day and age, to our ability to receive it, to our problems, fears and hopes. But it is important to note that this process of giving meaning is constantly structured by the old myths, many of which also found their way into the *Kalevala*.

SELECT BIBLIOGRAPHY

M. Eliade, *Der Mythos der ewigen Wiederkehr*, Düsseldorf 1953.

M. Haavio, *Väinämöinen*, Porvoo 1950.

L. Honko, 'Kansallisten juurien löytäminen', *Suomen kulttuurihistoria 2*, Porvoo 1980.

V. Kaukonen, *Lönnrot ja Kalevala*, Pieksämäki 1979.

— 'Mielikuvituksellista varhaishistoriaa 1-2', *Suomenmaa* 2-3.12.1983.

H. Kirkinen, 'Kalevalainen epiikka, historiaa vai myyttiä?', *Kotiseutu* 1 (1984).

— 'Intiasta Atlantille — kalevalaisen epiikan juuret', *Kotiseutu* 2 (1984).

— 'Suomi kohoaa idän ja lännen väliin', *Historiallinen Aikakauskirja 3* (1984).

M. Klinge, *Muinaisuutemme merivallat*, Keuruu 1983.

'Myytti', *Otavan Suuri Ensyklopedia 12*, Keuruu 1979.

Anna-Mari Sarajas, *Suomen kansanrunouden tuntemus 1500-1700-lukujen kirjallisuudessa*, Helsinki 1956.

— 'Snellman ja Kalevala. Lönnrotin aika', toim. P. Laaksonen, *Kalevalaseuran vuosikirja 64*, Pieksämäki 1984.

W.A. Wilson, *Folklore and Nationalism in Modern Finland*, Bloomington & London 1976.

THE *KALEVALA*, THE SOUTH SLAVIC EPICS AND HOMER

ALBERT B. LORD

(Harvard University)

The differences among the three epic traditions represented in this essay are great. The *Kalevala* is the last of a series of compilations made by Elias Lönnrot of shorter songs collected by himself and others from epic singers in various parts of Finland. The oral traditional epics of the South Slavs are independent, individual songs, both short and long, ranging from several hundred lines to three, five, and even upwards of ten thousand lines. In respect to length some of them are close to the Homeric poems. The Homeric poems, i.e. the *Iliad* and the *Odyssey* of Homer, are also independent, individual songs, but their lengths are over ten thousand lines.

The *Kalevala* emerged in the period when the *Liedertheorie* was in fashion as a means of understanding the composition of both the *Nibelungenlied* and the Homeric poems, when the prevalent opinion was that these great poems were stitched together from shorter songs. That theory is no longer widely held. The Classicist Milman Parry believed that the Homeric poems were composed in the same manner as the longer songs in the South Slavic tradition, and that each was the unified work of a single traditional singer.

In this paper I wish to speak first about the various kinds of relationships among the three epic traditions of the title. Second, I shall speak about the techniques of composition and transmission in the three traditions, Finnish, South Slavic, and Ancient Greek. Third and last, I shall comment on shared epic subjects and narrative patterns among the three areas.

I

The idea of concatenating Karelo-Finnish traditional songs into an epic-like whole was first advanced by Kaarle Akseli Gottlund in 1817:

> ... if one should desire to collect the old traditional songs [*National-sångerna*] and from these make a systematic whole, there might come from them an epic, a drama, or whatever, so that from this a new Homer, Ossian, or *Nibelungenlied* might come into being.[1]

In the Preface to the *Old Kalevala* Lönnrot wrote:

> Already while reading the songs previously collected, particularly those collected by Ganander, I at least wondered whether one might not possibly find songs about Väinämöinen, Ilmarinen, and Lemminkäinen and other memorable forebears of ours until from these had been got longer accounts, too, just as we see that the Greeks [in the Homeric poems] and the Icelanders [in the *Poetic* or *Elder Edda*] and others got songs of their forebears.[2]

What Lönnrot created was in at least one respect closer to the Old Icelandic Eddic poems than to the Homeric because the individual shorter poems from which the *Kalevala* was made are visible in the final work. Lönnrot succeeded however, in producing a 'national epic' for the Finns, which had never existed before. He did not realize, of course, that the *Iliad* and the *Odyssey* were not really 'national epics' for the Ancient Greeks, any more than the *Elder Edda* was a 'national epic' for the Icelanders.

Although all, or almost all, of its ingredients were oral traditional songs, the *Kalevala* itself is not one. Domenico

---

1   Quoted from *The Kalevala, or Poems of the Kaleva District*, compiled by E. Lönnrot. Prose Translation with Foreword and Appendices by F. Peabody Magoun, Jr, Cambridge, Mass. 1963, Appendix I. *Materials for the Study of the Kalevala*, B, *The Kalevala*, 350.

2   Also quoted from Magoun's translation of the *Kalevala* cited in the previous note, Appendix I, D, *Lönnrot's Prefaces to the Kalevala*, II, *Preface [1835] to the Old Kalevala*, 366.

Comparetti pointed this out in 1898 in his extraordinary book, *The Traditional Poetry of the Finns*:[3]

> That a whole popular, traditional poetry, living and bringing forth for centuries, should come to furnish the material for one single poem is a strange and abnormal phenomenon. Confronted with such a fact we have the right of doubting whether the poem can be defined as a popular production, collective and not individual; as is without doubt the poetry from which the poem was composed.[4]

The *Kalevala* was created by a collector, and it is unique. There are no variants other than the two which Lönnrot himself composed in the process of reaching the final version, created in the same way in which he composed it. They are not the natural variants formed in the normal processes of a living tradition. Lönnrot's material was traditional, but he altered it, and he devised the sequences of songs of different genres, which were usually sung singly and on different occasions. He believed himself to be a traditional singer, since he was thoroughly conversant with the traditional style.[5]

Yet Lönnrot was not really a traditional singer, in the strictest sense of the words, because he was not brought up in a traditional community and did not inherit the specific traditional songs of a specific group. He was an outsider, but, I hasten to add, he was a very special kind of outsider. He could, and did, create poems, and a poem, in an oral traditional style. Formulaic analysis would surely show a very high percentage of formulas and formulaic expressions. In spite of the fact that everything in the *Kalevala* is traditional, the poem itself, as a whole, is an individual construct by a non-traditional person, a song that did not come into being, as Comparetti noted, under the normal circumstances of the tradition.

3   D. Comparetti, *The Traditional Poetry of the Finns*, translated by Isabella M. Anderson, with introduction by A. Lang, London 1898. The original has the title *Il Kalevala; o, la poesia tradizionale dei Finni; studio storico-critico sulle origini dele grandi epopee nazionali*, Roma 1891.

4   *Ibid.*, 328.

5   See Appendices A and B.

Lönnrot was a man of some education, acquainted with books. He merged variants of songs from different regions, using his knowledge of many parts of the country, a knowledge no traditional singer of the 'old days' or even of his own, would have had.

It is necessary to emphasize that it was not only Lönnrot's knowledge of the world of books that made him an outsider, but he also had access to manuscript collections containing variants of songs from various regions, as just outlined, and he chose elements from those variants. Both the availability of those variants and his manner of using them distinguished him from the traditional singer. Theoretically, a traditional singer could have travelled all over Finland and acquired acquaintance with the songs and variants of many regions, picking up what he heard as he journeyed and keeping what he found to his liking. His sources in that case would have been live songs heard in living circumstances; they would not have been set down in manuscripts from which he might cull his favorites at leisure. He would have assimilated them under the normal associative processes of the tradition of which he was a part. Moreover, with his education, there is a possibility, even a probability, that Lönnrot's criteria for choice of elements would not be those dictated by the traditional, subconscious association of ideas and phrases, but by those inculcated by written literature.

It is remarkable that a number of other long epics are also, in reality, compilations of short narrative songs. Alexandra David-Neel collected Tibetan songs about Gesar of Ling and constructed an epic from them.[6] Daniel Biebuyck did the same for the Mwindo Epic of Zaire, the former Belgian Congo.[7] The Kara-Kirghiz epics of Manas and of Er Töshtük were formed from individual shorter songs.[8] In all these cases,

---

6 Alexandra David-Neel and the Lama Yongden, *The Superhuman Life of Gesar of Ling*, New York 1934.

7 *The Mwindo Epic from the Banyanga {Congo Republic}* edited and translated by D. Biebuyck and K.C. Mateene, Berkeley 1969, and *Hero and Chief, Epic Literature from the Banyanga Zaire Republic*, Berkeley 1978.

8 Examples of the 'short' songs — some have over 2,000 lines — about these two heroes can be found in German translation in W. Radloff,

the real epic songs were the shorter ones which were put together in sequence. In this respect, the *Kalevala* is quite different from either the South Slavic or the Homeric oral traditional epics, which correspond, in spite of differences of length, to the single narrative songs of the Finnish tradition rather than to the *Kalevala*. On this subject Comparetti is also enlightening:

> The *Kalevala* is a poem inferred and put together by Lönnrot from the whole of the popular, traditional poetry of the Finns... Hence the poem is unique; a fact which does not repeat itself in the poetry of any other people. .. The Homeric poetry, the Nibelungen, the Chanson de Roland are not unique. They have their places in a period of production of numerous large poems, or in one in which national poetry has already elaborated and matured much material for such poems. .. The epic songs of other peoples who never reached the point of having large poems, as, for instance, the Russians, Servians, Kelts, Siberian Tatars, ancient Scandinavians and others, do not converge towards one poem, but if ever they reached or should reach the maturity of large compositions they would give many poems of different subjects.[9]

It is necessary to add that the Serbian tradition to which Comparetti refers actually did produce songs of several thousands of lines, comparable, for example, to the length of those in the Old French tradition. Most of these Serbo-Croatian epics of such length belong to the Moslem singers in South Serbia, Bosnia, and Hercegovina, and until recently were not so well known as the shorter Christian songs. Curiously enough, the first publications of the Moslem songs were by Kosta Hörmann in 1888-9, and Luka Marjanović in

Proben der Volksliteratur der nordlichen türkischen Stamme, Part V, St Petersburg 1885. A composite epic of Manas can be seen in Russian translation in *Manas, Kirgizskij epos velikij pohod*, Moskva 1946, and one of Er Töshtük, in French translation with introduction and notes by P. Boratav and L. Bazin, can be found in *Adventures merveilleuses sous terre et ailleurs de Er-Töshtük, le géant des steppes*, Paris 1965.

9 Comparetti, *ibid.*, 327-8.

1898-9, at the very time when Comparetti was writing. The longest song published by Hörmann, however, had only 1878 lines and the longest published by Marjanović had 1862 lines.[10] The longest songs in the Milman Parry Collection at Harvard have 12,311 and 13,326 lines. These lengths are exceptional, but songs of two to four or five thousand lines are not unusual.

There are a number of instances in South Slavic literature in which a previously non-existent long literary epic has been created by concatenating and expanding short oral traditional published songs. For example, in the nineteenth century Vuk St Karadžić published in his classic collection of oral traditional epic songs in Serbo-Croatian nine or ten short songs, more balladic in nature than epic, connected with the battle of Kosovo in 1389 in which a Christian coalition under Prince Lazar was defeated by Turkish forces under Sultan Murat. Not a single one of those songs, however, related the central event of the battle, namely, the killing of the sultan by the Serb Miloš Obilić.[11] Karadžić's famous nineteenth century Kosovo texts were not, as a matter of fact, the first recorded songs about the battle. Among our oldest manuscript collections from the eighteenth century there is a Kosovo song which puts together material found later only in short songs or fragments. This bugarštica[12] is thought by some scholars to be written literary text rather than an oral traditional epic. However, it, too, is not of epic length, having only 252 lines. There are also Kosovo texts in the unpublished collections made by Vuk Vrčević in the middle of the nineteenth century, some of which seem to be of the same kind, although they, too, are not very long.[13]

---

10 K. Hörmann, *Narodne pjesme muslimana u Bosni i Hercegovini*, Sarajevo 1888-9; L. Marjanović, *Hrvatske narodne pjesme*, Odio prvi, Junačke {muhamedovske}, 3 and 4, Zagreb 1898-9.
11 See Vuk St Karadžić, *Srpske narodne pjesme*, II, Beograd 1958, Nos. 44-52.
12 See V. Bogišić, *Narodne pjesme iz starijih, najviše primorskih napisa*, Biograd 1878, 3-10.
13 Matica hrvatska, Ms. Collection No. 62, Knjiga I, No. 21, Knjiga II, No. 14, Knjiga III, Nos. 1-3. One of the reasons given by the Serbian Academy of Sciences for not publishing these texts is that they are

It is noteworthy, however, that *long, written* epics of the battle of Kosovo in 1389 were composed during the nineteenth century, and later, using the shorter songs from published or unpublished collections from traditional singers, including the Vuk Karadžić collection of oral tradition epic songs, although Karadžić himself made no such longer songs from his materials. In 1927 one of these, by Sr[eten] J. Stojković,[14] appeared in a sixth edition. Unlike Lönnrot, Stojković did himself not collect any songs. He simply assembled and arranged songs already collected, composing some transitional passages himself — as did Lönnrot. Like Lönnrot, he produced an epic, which he called 'national', but which was his own creation, not an oral traditional epic.

It is clear from these efforts to produce long epic songs, that one of the most important factors in the minds of those who created them was length; an epic poem was thought to be long by definition. Had Lönnrot not had such epics as the Homeric poems in his mind, he would not have striven for a long song.[15] Like others before and after him, he thought of an epic as a long narrative poem recounting in a high style the deeds of heroes of the past. This concept of epic was derived from a consideration of the Homeric poems and of Vergil's *Aeneid*.

The length of the Homeric poems, however, may well be

Vrčević's own compositions and not traditional songs dictated by a traditional singer. Cf. Radmila Pešić, *Vuk Vrčević*, Beograd 1967. Yet Vrčević's texts have affinities with an Albanian version collected by Elezović earlier in the present century. See G. Elezović, 'Jedna arnautska varianta o boju na Kosovu', *Arhiv za arbanašku starinu, jezik i etnologiju*, 1 (1923), 54-67. See also Parry Text No. 650, a Serbo-Croatian version collected by Milman Parry in 1934 from a Yugoslav Albanian in Novi Pazar. For more on these Kosovo texts and others see A.B. Lord, 'The Battle of Kosovo in Albanian and Serbocroatian Oral Epic Songs', in *Studies on Kosova*, New York 1984.

14 *Lazarica, ili boj na Kosovu, narodna epopeja u 25 pesama, iz narodnih pesama i njihovih odlomaka sastavio Sr. J. Stojković*, 'Lazarica, or the battle of Kosovo, national epic in 25 songs, from traditional songs and their fragments, put together by Sr. J. Stojković.'

15 See Appendix A.

due to the role of writing in their creation at the moment, or during the hours and days when Homer dictated them to a scribe. It is very likely, in my opinion, that Homer never sang the songs of the return of Odysseus from Troy or of the wrath of Achilleus at the great length in which they appear in our *Iliad* and *Odyssey*. Like the *Kalevala* they were special poems in their composition. But the manner of composition of the Homeric poems was far different from that of the *Kalevala*. Homer was a *bona fide* traditional singer who had sung many songs many times in a tradition of singers like himself and songs like his. He expanded two of the songs in his normal repertory, when he dictated them. He did not stitch songs together to make his 'monumental' songs, but he composed them in the manner of a living tradition such as those of the Slavs, which on occasion 'mix' songs in order to create other, often carefully unified, songs. This is a different process, and one that has not yet been adequately described, from that of Lönnrot in compiling the *Kalevala*. The Homeric poems, on the contrary, were composed, I believe, in dictation in the same way in which Avdo Medjedović's 'The Wedding of Smailagić Meho' was composed in dictation.

In composing the *Kalevala* Lönnrot gained length in various ways. One of the most striking was the inclusion of ritual songs, i.e., for example, incantations and wedding cycle songs. This type of expansion is absent in the South Slavic and in the Homeric songs. It is true that in describing the mourning of Achilleus for Patroklos, Homer tells how his mother Thetis and the Nereids came out of the sea to comfort him, and Thetis led in singing a threnody for Patroklos, the words of which Homer realistically gives us, in the manner of fulness of narration and description typical of Homeric epic. Homer includes other ritual laments in the *Iliad*.[16] They are not, however, generic laments such as the generic wedding

16   E.g., in addition to the laments of Achilleus and of his mother Thetis and the Nereids for Patroklos in *Iliad* 18, 22ff., see especially Achilleus' lament for Patroklos in 23, 13ff. and the laments of Andromache and Hekabe for Hektor in 24, 723ff. For more on the ritual lament in Ancient and Modern Greek literature, oral and written, see Margaret Alexiou, *The Ritual Lament in Greek Tradition*, Cambridge 1974.

ritual songs in the *Kalevala*, which are independent songs.

Although there are scenes in some of the South Slavic heroic songs which could serve as background for the singing of ritual or lyric songs, the songs themselves that might accompany such rituals are not actually inserted into the epic, as Lönnrot did in composing the *Kalevala*. For example, some epic songs begin with a group of youths and maidens going to harvest grain in a field near the border with the enemy's country.[17] There are many traditional harvest songs, and it would have been quite appropriate to insert them into the epics, but they were not incorporated, either entire or partially, into the epic songs. Similarly, in South Slavic epic song there are many heroic tales of bride capture, which end with an elaborate wedding, but one does not find any wedding ritual songs included.[18]

In the *Kalevala* Lönnrot on occasion inserted separate stories, such as the tragic one of Kullervo, thereby interrupting the flow of another narrative. Even though the events of Kullervo's life are intertwined with that of Ilmarinen, since he eventually murders Ilmarinen's wife, the prophecy of a heroic life for the child Kullervo is inconsistent with the boy's actual future, and the unusual results from the tasks which he performs so badly also are indicative of a glorious life when they occur in other traditional contexts. The joinings are not felicitous. In the *Odyssey* Homer tells, through the Phaeacian bard, the story of Ares and Aphrodite. Like the laments of which I spoke earlier, that tale is the result of Homer's desire to tell the story fully. It is not an interruption but a lingering over the details of a scene. On the other hand Homer does interrupt the forward movement of the Telemachy to recount the story of Odysseus, whose

---

17 See 'The Ragged Border Warrior Wins the Horses', *Serbocroatian Heroic Songs*, collected by M. Parry, edited and translated by A.B. Lord, Vol. 1, Cambridge and Belgrade 1954, No. 17.

18 An excellent example of a song telling of the attaining of a bride by the hero, combined with an initiatory journey and a tale of succession, is A. Medjedović's, 'The Wedding of Smailagić Meho', in *Serbo-Croatian Heroic Songs*, collected by M. Parry, translated with introduction, notes, and commentary by A.B. Lord, Vol. 3, Cambridge 1974.

adventures in turn are held up at one point for him to recapitulate everything that had happened to him up to the time of the telling. But these strands of narrative are related and the juxtaposition of the several portions is the product of a particular technique of narration. The Kullervo poems, on the other hand, are not intimately related to the other narratives in the *Kalevala*. The many deceptive stories in the *Odyssey* are important, integral elements in the main narrative of Odysseus' return. Such stories are found in abundance in South Slavic return songs as well. But they are a different matter from an inserted ritual, lyric, or narrative songs such as those which are so common in the *Kalevala*.

The short Finnish songs, even the narrative ones, are more comparable to the South Slavic 'women's songs' than to the South Slavic epics. This is especially true of the Finnish lyric and ritual songs, such as the charms and songs used in the ceremonial acts and speeches attendant upon weddings. For example, South Slavic women's songs have a rich cycle of ritual songs associated with weddings, including the lament of the bride on leaving her home, instructions for the bride from her mother, and so forth. These separately are like the corresponding Finnish songs. They exist independently, but they are not included in epic texts. Here is an example from the South Slavic wedding cycle:[19]

---

19 M.S. Milojević, *Pesme i običaji ukupnog naroda srpskog*, II, K. Svatovske, Beograd 1870, No. 171, from Miss Stana Stojanović of Prizren.

Sunce mi je na zahodu,	'The sun is setting,
Hoće da zadje,	It will set,
Hoće da zadje,	It will set.
I devojka na pohodu,	The maiden is leaving,
Hoće da podje,	She will leave,
Hoće da podje,	She will leave.
Žali oca na pohodu,	She is sorry for her father as she leaves,
Oće da podje,	She will leave,
Oće da podje.	She will leave.
Žali majku na pohodu,	She is sorry for her mother as she leaves,
Oće da podje,	She will leave,
Oće da podje.	She will leave.
Žali seju na pohodu,	She is sorry for her sister as she leaves,
Oće da podje,	She will leave,
Oće da podje.	She will leave.
Žali brata na pohodu,	She is sorry for her brother as she leaves,
Neće da podje,	She won't leave,
Neće da podje.	She won't leave.
Za svekrvu upituje,	She asks about her mother-in-law,
Hoće da podje,	She will leave,
Hoće da podje.	She will leave.'

Variants of this song add a number of other members of the family, whom the bride is sorry to have to leave. Here is another example:[20]

---

20 *Op. cit.* No. 173, from Mr Nikola Andrejević, priest, in Sretačka-sirinačka, a *župa* on Mount Sar, and he wrote it down from his brother's wife.

Odvoji se devojka od tatka,	'The maiden is separated from her father,
Odvoji se devojka od majke,	The maiden is separated from her mother,
Odvoji se devojka od braće,	The maiden is separated from her brothers,
Odvoji se devojka od sestri,	The maiden is separated from her sisters,
Odvoji se devojka od roda,	The maiden is separated from her family,
Svoga roda i rodbine svoje.	Her family and her kin.
Ona kreče tekne u tudjine.	She leaves for someone else's home.
Tudjeg tatka tatkom zove,	She calls father someone else's father,
On je ćerkom ne nazivlje.	He does not call her daughter.
Tudju majku majkom zove,	She calls mother someone else's mother,
Ona je ćerkom ne nazivlje.	She does not call her daughter.
Tudjeg brata bracom zove,	She calls brother someone else's brother,
On je sejom ne nazivlje.	He does not call her sister.
Tudju ćerku sejom zove,	She calls sister someone else's daughter,
Ona je sejom ne nazivlje.	She does not call her sister.
Tudjeg roda rodom zove,	She calls family someone else's family,
Tudjeg roda i rodbina,	Someone else's family and kin,
Ona je rodom n nazivlje.	They do not call her family.'

The ritual songs in the *Kalevala* are long, having been expanded by Lönnrot, so I have chosen an example from the *Proto-Kalevala*:[21]

The poor girl sighed deeply,   sighed deeply, gasped;
sorrow weighed on her heart,   tears came to her eyes,
she uttered a word, spoke thus: 'Now I am really setting
    out from here,

---

21   Magoun's translation of lines 539ff. of Poem 8.

from this lovely home, from the house acquired by my
father,
from my mother's dancing ground. I thank you, father,
for my former life, for the lunches of days gone by,
for the best snacks. I thank you, mother,
for rocking me when young, for always washing my head,
for suckling me earlier, for your sweet milk.
I thank the whole family, all the companions I grew up
with . . .'

Lönnrot also added to the length of his new poem by
expansion of episodes and songs from within, a method used
by both Homer and the South Slavic singers. This element is
so clear in all three traditions that it seems superfluous to
illustrate it.

In sum, both the *Kalevala* and the South Slavic epic songs,
different as they are from one another, have something to
teach us about the Homeric poems. Of the two, the Slavic
tradition is closer in t y p e to the Homeric poems than is the
Finnish *Kalevala*. In both the Slavic and the Homeric traditions we find independent, integral songs of some length. If
there were separate songs telling the story of Telemachus, or
of the wanderings of Odysseus, apart from the Homeric
Odyssey — and I believe there were — they were integrated
into the long Homeric poem rather than concatenated in
Kalevala style.

II

The second part of my paper deals with the method of composition of the shorter songs of the *Kalevala*. Fortunately,
the shorter songs have published variants, and we have also
the forms of them that occur in Lönnrot's own three versions
of the *Kalevala*, namely, the *Proto-Kalevala*, the *Old Kalevala*,
and the [New] *Kalevala*.[22]

22 All three were translated into English by F. Peabody Magoun, Jr
as follows: *The Old Kalevala and Certain Antecedents*, compiled
by Elias Lönnrot. Prose Translations with Foreword and Appendices by F. Peabody Magoun, Jr, Cambridge, Mass. 1969. *The
Kalevala, or Poems of the Kaleva District*, compiled by E. Lönnrot. Prose Translation with Foreword and Appendices by F. Peabody Magoun, Jr, Cambridge, Mass. 1963.

The songs from which the *Kalevala* was made were shorter than the South Slavic epic songs or the Homeric. They never attained great length, by which I mean several thousands of lines. This has been true of some parts of the South Slavic terrain, for example in Bulgarian and in general in the Christian songs among the Serbs. In comparing the three traditions, one must keep in mind that one is not properly comparing the whole *Kalevala* with the *Iliad* or *Odyssey*, but the Finnish songs which were used in the *Kalevala* with the Homeric poems and with individual songs among the South Slavs. Although we do not have variants from ancient Greece of the Homeric songs, we have variants from South Slavic and from Finnish. The variants tell us how the traditions worked.

In his Preface to the *New Kalevala*[23] Lönnrot gave his version of the way in which songs were transmitted:

> As for the authenticity of the songs, the matter runs about as follows: At a feast or some other social gathering someone hears a new song and tries to remember it. Then on aother occasion when this person himself is now singing it before a new audience, he remembers quite exactly the material proper rather than its narrative word for word in every detail. Those passages which he does not remember in just the original words he tells in his own, in places perhaps better even than they were before. And if some rather insignificant incident among them is left out, another can take its place out of the singer's own head. In the same way, then, second and third persons who hear it proceed to sing it and the song is changed, changed rather in individual words and details than in the material itself.

This is a description by someone who knew the tradition very well and it is a very perspicacious one. I believe that by the 'someone' he speaks of who hears a new song he means a singer, i.e. someone within the singing tradition itself. Otherwise he would not be able to compose 'new' lines and passages. Lönnrot continues in a remarkable way:

---

23 Quoted from Magoun's translation of *The Kalevala* cited above, Appendix I, D, III, *Preface [1849] to the [New] Kalevala*, 376.

Parallel to this kind of versified story there runs, however, another which keeps closer to the old words and their linking together, namely, a child's learning from its parents from generation to generation. But at the same time that this prevents the other migratory sister-song from deviating too far, it must itself at times follow the other lest it be left far behind.

Lönnrot recognized two kinds of transmittal, one closer to the 'original' (my quotation marks) and one more removed. The first recipient, it would seem, tried to *memorize*, that is to get by rote every word through mimicking, as a child learning from his parents; the other, already, I assume, a competent singer, *remembered*, rather than consciously memorized, the 'material', including, presumably, some of the words, naturally enough, but in reality he retold the story in his own way. It is extremely important to realize the distinction between *memorizing*, with its conscious attempt to reproduce every word of an 'original', which must be fixed for that process to be meaningful, and *remembering*, the basic, normal process of recall, which is more potent, I believe, than it is generally credited with being. It is through learning the art of verse-making and through remembering given, discrete, units of composition, rather than through word-for-word memorization that the South Slavic songs were both composed and transmitted. I believe that it was in this way that the epic songs in ancient Greek tradition were transmitted from one generation to another.

One of the methods of composition of the *Kalevala* songs which aids in transmission, is the repetition of a memorable pattern. An excellent example of what I have in mind is found in songs 15, 16, and 17 in *Finnish Folk Poetry. Epic.*[24] The songs do not tell exactly the same story, but each has at its beginning a scene in which a girl, bleaching clothes, spies a boat approaching, and asks the boatman where he is going and why. Two or more lying answers are given and finally the truth is told.

24 M. Kuusi, K. Bosley and M. Branch, eds. and trans., *Finnish Folk Poetry. Epic. An Anthology in Finnish and English*, Helsinki 1977.

No. 15, 'The Sampo IV', begins with a stanza devoted to the departure of Väinämöinen for Pohjola to woo the maid. The second stanza is on the left below. The opening stanza of No. 16, 'The Courtship I', is on the right below:

The girl Anni, matchless maid	Annikki the island maid
	smith Ilmorini's sister
was washing her little things	went off to do her washing
	on the shore of the blue sea
at the end of the long quay	at the end of Laisa Quay
when she saw a shoal of fish.	

Finally, for comparison, on the right below we have the opening stanza of No. 17, 'The Courtship II', still keeping the second stanza of No. 15 on the left below.

The girl Anni, matchless maid	The girl of night, maid of dusk
was washing her little things	was rinsing clothes she had washed
bleaching what she'd rinsed	what she had bleached was bleaching
at the end of the long quay	at the end of the long quay
	a bright-carved bat in her hand
when she saw a shoal of fish.	

The singers of these three songs are not the same.[25] Without another text from the same singers one cannot tell whether they held them in a fixed form in their own mind. But one can say that even the lines which are similar in meaning could come from a fixed 'original' text. The line 'at the end of the long quay' is a fixed traditional line, a whole-line formula. In No. 16 it seems to be adapted through substitution of the name of the quay for the epithet to its immediate context, but there the English translation leads us astray. In Finnish the lines are different:

---

25 Nos. 15 and 16 are from A.A. Borenius' collection of 1872 and were written down in Archangel Karelia. No. 17 is from the collection of D.E.D. Europaeus of 1845, written down in North Karelia.

No. 15   pitäm portahan nenässä.
No. 16   Laisan laiturin nenällä.
No. 17   pitkän portahan nenässä.

Let us pursue the textual comparison of the three songs.
No. 15 continues on the left and No. 16 on the right:

> She spied a black speck on the
>   sea
> something bluish on the waves
> herself put this into words:
> 'If you are my father's boat
> turn homeward, turn to your
>   house
> away from other havens!
> Or else if my brother's craft
> away from other havens!
> Or yet Väinämöini's boat
> bring yourself here for a talk!

> If you are a shoal of fish
> then away with you, swim
>   off!
> If you are a flock of birds   If a darling flock of ducks
> Then begone with you, fly   spread out into flight!
>   off!
> If you are a water-rock   Or again a water-stone
> then roll off in the water!   draw the water over you!'
> If you're old Väinämöine
> bring yourself here for a talk
>   come here for a word!'

> The old Väinämöine came   It was Väinämöine's boat
> took himself there for a talk took itself there for a talk.
>   went there for a word.

The above passage does not have an equivalent in No. 17,
which continues simply with:

> A red boat went by:
> one side of the boat was red.

There follows immediately the conversation in which the

questions and answers concern the destination of the boat and/or its occupant, which we shall consider shortly.

Typical of versions of the same theme by different singers, our texts of the girl's words exhibit variant readings where the subjects are the same. One of the items concerns a flock of birds, another, a water-rock. Here, in Finnish, are the four lines involved; the first two tell of the birds, the last two of the water-rock. No. 15 on the left, No. 16 on the right:

Jos lienet lintuine *karja*	Olit armas alli*karja*
niin sie *lendoho leviete*!	sinä *lentohon levie*
Jos lienet *vezikivoine*	Elikkä *vesikivoni*
niin sie *vezin* vierekkänä!	*vesi* peälläsi vetähys!'

I have italicized the words which are alike in both versions, except for morphological differences. The singers were certainly not going back to the same memorized 'original', the similarities come from the traditional subject matter. Memorization is not needed; only remembering 'flocks', 'fly off', 'water-stone', 'water'. The alliteration of *lendoho leviete* and *vezikivoine, vezin vierekkänä* helps in the remembering as well.

The same is true of the final words of the girl's speech in No. 15 and their corresponding lines in No.16. Here they are in Finnish:

Jos lienet vanha *Väinämöine*	Eli pursi *Väinämöisen*
pakinoilla painustoate	sie *painu pakinoilla!*
sanomilla soahustoate!	

These lines are, of course, repeated in the description of the action after the girl's words:

Tuli vanha Väinämöine	Se oli pursi Väinämöisen
pakinoilla painustihi	se om painu pakinoilla.
sanomilla soahustihi.	

In short, the elements which remain textually alike in all versions of a theme, i.e. a repeated p a s s a g e, are the essential ideas as expressed in the traditional word combinations, parts of lines, lines, or groups of lines, especially couplets, that singers have used for generations. These are adapted to the context of the particular song being sung. The similarities are thus the natural ones stemming from the narration of the subject of the passage in traditional garb; they are not the result of memorization of a fixed text, a process which could not have produced the patterns of repetition outlined above.

What we have seen in these examples from the *Kalevala* songs in Finnish is demonstrably true as well of both South Slavic and Homeric oral traditional narrative song. A single illustration from each will have to suffice for this paper, but they can easily be multiplied. First, an example from a South Slavic 'return song' at the moment when the hero, who has been long in prison in an enemy city, asks a recently captured prisoner for news of home.[26] Here are two versions of the same passage from the same singer, the one on the left collected Nov. 24, 1934 and the one on the right Nov. 20, 1934:

Sedi lj' moja kula na ćenaru?	Sedi lj' moja na ćenaru kula?
Je lj' se moja kula podurvala,	Da se nije kula oburvala,
Alj' se moja kula harap učinela?	Alj' je kula joste na nogama?
Je lj' mi živa ostarela majka?	Je lj' mi živa u odjaku majka,
Je lj' mi živa svijet mijenila?	Alj' je majka svijet mijenila?
A sedi lj' mi sestra neudata,	A sedi lj' joj Huso kah-vedjija?
Sestra Fata u odjaku mome?	Cini lj' staroj hizmet do odjaka?
Čeka lj' brata Djulić bajraktara?	A sedi lj' mi sestra neudata,
A sedi lj' mi dorat u podrumu?	Sestra Fata Djulić bajrak-tara?
Držu lj' konja dobro u podrumu?	A sedi lj' mi vijernica ljuba?
Dalj' mi Huso sedi kahved-jija?	Da se nije ljuba isprosila?
Čini lj' staroj hismet u odajk?	
'Is my old mother alive?	'Is my mother alive by the hearth?

26 *Serbocroatian Heroic Songs*, collected by M. Parry, edited by A. Bates Lord, Vol. 2, Beograd and Cambridge 1953, No. 4, lines 50-63 and No. 5, lines 33-43, 65-70.

Is she alive, or has she
changed worlds?
Is my sister unmarried,
My sister Fata by the hearth?

Does she await her brother
Djulić the standard-bearer?
Is my chestnut horse in the
stable?
Do they care well for the
horse in the stable?
Is Huso the steward there?'

Has my mother changed
worlds?
Is Huso the steward there?
Does he serve the old
woman by the hearth?
Is my sister unmarried,

Fata, sister of Djulić the
standard-bearer?
Is my true-love there?

My true-love has not been
bethrothed?'

After the answer to the above has been given, the hero continues:

Sedi lj' moja vijernica ljuba?

Da se ljuba nije isprosila?

A sedi lj' mi dorat u
podrumu,
Sedi lj' dorat u toplom
podrumu?
Hranu lj'dora konja mojega,
A goru lj' mu četiri svijeće;
Sve mu goru danjem i po
noći,
Ka' što ga je Djulić naucijo?

'Is my house standing on the
border?
Has my house fallen in,
Or has it been destroyed?
Does he serve the old woman
in her chamber?
Is my true-love there?

My true-love has not been
betrothed?'

'Is my house standing on
the border?
My house has not fallen in?
Is the house still standing?
Is my chestnut horse in the
stable?
Is the chestnut horse in the
warm stable?
Are they feeding my chest-
nut horse?
Are the four candles burn-
ing for him?
Burning day and night,
As Djulić taught him to
expect?'

There are at least two things which we can learn from a study of those two passages. First, I believe that it is clear that the singer had not memorized a fixed original. I can assure you, indeed, that there never was a fixed original. Yet the text may seem to be amazingly close, so close that in the minds of some the closeness can be explained only by the existence of a fixed original that has been memorized. That leads to the second fact, which we can learn from studying these passages and others like them. They consist of easily remembered, more or less stable, units of two or three lines. Those lines may have one or more lines added to them in elaboration, as the third line in both passages, or the couplet in the passage on the left asking about Djulić's sister. In the question about the chestnut horse in the passage on the right the elaboration is greater and includes a group of three lines at the very end, which themselves form a unit of composition used elsewhere. I should like to suggest that these units of composition are the ones that are more overtly in the mind of the singer than are the individual formulas that make them up, important though they be. It is these units, too, from which 'themes' are constructed, as the above passages illustrate, for they are 'themes'.

Let me turn, finally, to an example from the Homeric poems. In recounting the speeches in the assemblies of men or of gods in the *Iliad* Homer has several ways of noting the reactions of the assembly to a speech that has just been made. In three cases he reports that the men shouted, and in several instances the words of the speaker were met with silence. After he has indicated the reaction, Homer has a line leading to another speech. Two of the three shouting passages begin with the same couplet, and vary only in the third line, which introduces the next speaker. Here is the couplet:[27]

῍Ως ἔφαθ', οἱ δ' ἄρα πάντες ἐπίαχον υἷες 'Αχαιῶν,
μῦθον ἀγασσάμενοι Διομήδεος ἱπποδάμοιο.

'So he spoke, and all sons of the Achaians shouted acclaim for the word of Diomedes, breaker of horses:'

27 *Iliad* 7, 403-4; 9, 50-1. This and other English translations from the Greek quoted here below are from R. Lattimore, trans., *The Iliad of Homer*, Chicago 1951.

The third shouting passage differs from the above couplet in its first and second lines:[28]

"Ὣς ἔφατ', Ἀργεῖοι δὲ μέγ' ἴαχον, ἀμφὶ δὲ νῆες
σμερδαλέον κονάβησαν ἀϋσάντων ὑπ' Ἀχαιῶν,

'So he spoke, and the Argives shouted aloud, and about them the ships echoed terribly to the roaring Achaians.'

The third and fourth lines of the preceding passage are:[29]

μῦθον ἐπαινήσαντες Ὀδυσσῆος θείοιο.
τοῖσι δὲ καὶ μετέειπε Γερήνιος ἱππότα Νέστωρ·

'as they cried out applause to the word of godlike Odysseus. Now among them spoke the Gerenian horseman, Nestor:'

Note that these two lines are variants of the second and third lines of the other two passages:[30]

404, 51   μῦθον ἀγασσάμανοι Διομήδεος ἱπποδάμοιο.

405   καὶ τότ' ἄρ' Ἰδαῖον προσέφη κρείων
         Ἀγαμέμνων.

52   τοῖσι δ'ἀνιστάμενος μετεφώνεεν ἱππότα
         Νέστωρ·

'acclaim for the word of Diomedes, breaker of horses.
and now powerful Agamemnon spoke to Idaios:
and now Nestor the horseman stood forth among them and
    spoke to them:'

When the reaction to a speech is silence, the passages (there are five of them) bridging that speech to the next begin with the line:[31]

"Ὣς ἔφαθ', οἱ δ'ἄρα πάντες ἀκὴν ἐγένοντο σιωπῇ,

'So he spoke, and all of them stayed stricken to silence.'

Four of the passages end with a line introducing another speech by the same speaker. In three of them the speaker is Diomedes, and the line is the same:[32]

---

28 *Iliad* 2, 333-4.
29 *Iliad* 2, 335-6.
30 *Iliad* 7, 404-5, and 9, 51-2.
31 *Iliad* 8, 28; 7, 398; 9, 29; 9, 693 and 10, 218.
32 *Iliad* 7, 399; 9, 31; 9, 696, 10, 219.

ὀψὲ δὲ δὴ μετέειπε βοὴν ἀγαθὸς Διομήδης·

'but now at long last Diomedes of the great war cry addressed
them:'

In the fourth the speaker is Athene, and the line is varied
to accommodate her name:[33]

ὀψὲ δὲ δὴ μετέειπε θεὰ γλαυκῶπις Ἀθήνη·

'But now at long last the goddess grey-eyed Athene answered
him:'

In the fifth case, although the next speaker is Diomedes,
he is not resuming after the preceding speech, and the line is
slightly different. It is like *Iliad* II, 336 in the shouting passages, except for the change of speakers:[34]

τοῖσι δὲ καὶ μετέειπε βοὴν ἀγαθὸς Διομήδης·

'but now Diomedes of the great war cry spoke forth among
them:'

In two cases there are only two lines in the passage, and
they have been discussed. In the remaining three cases there
are one or two lines of varying content between the beginning
and the ending lines. It is to be noted, however, that the
intervening lines have relatives in the other passages, both
those with shouting and those with silence. Here are the
three cases in question in their entirety:[35]

Ὣς ἔφαθ', οἱ δ' ἄρα πάντες ἀκὴν ἐγένοντο σιωπῇ
μῦθον ἀγασσάμενοι μάλα γὰρ κρατερῶς ἀγόρευσεν.
ὀψὲ δὲ δὴ μετέειπε θεὰ γλαυκῶπις Ἀθήνη·

'So he spoke, and all of them stayed stricken to silence,
stunned at his word, for indeed he had spoken to them
very strongly.

But now at long last the goddess grey-eyed Athene answered
him:'

Ὣς ἔφαθ', οἱ δ' ἄρα πάντες ἀκὴν ἐγένοντο σιωπῇ
δὴν δ' ἄνεῳ ἦσαν τετιηότες υἷες Ἀχαιῶν.
ὀψὲ δὲ δὴ μετέειπε βοὴν ἀγαθὸς Διομήδης·

'So he spoke, and all of them stayed stricken to silence.

33 *Iliad* 8, 30.
34 *Iliad* 10, 219.
35 *Iliad* 8, 28-30; 9, 29-31; and 9, 693-6.

For some time the sons of the Achaians said nothing, in
    sorrow;
but at long last Diomedes of the great war cry addressed
    them:'

῝Ως \ἔφαθ', οἱ δ' ἄρα πάντες ἀκὴν ἐγένοντο σιωπῇ
μῦθον ἀγασσάμενοὶ μάλα γὰρ κρατερῶς ἀγόρευσεν.
δὴν δ' ἄνεῳ ἦσαν τετιηότες υἷες 'Αχαιῶν.
ὀψὲ δὲ δὴ μετέειπε βοὴν ἀγαθὸς Διομήδης·

'So he spoke, and all of them stayed stricken to silence
in amazement at his words. He had spoken to them very
    strongly.
For a long time the sons of the Achaians said nothing, in
    sorrow,
but at long last Diomedes of the great war cry spoke to them:'

The study of these passages indicates clearly that Homer,
like the Finnish and South Slavic traditional poets in the
passages from them analyzed above, had in his mind a more
or less stable unit of composition, with some lines very stable
but others flexible enough to fit the contexts in which his
narrative expressed itself.

As I pointed out earlier, the *Kalevala* is unique, although the
songs that went into its making were not. They were, indeed,
like the South Slavic and the Homeric epics in that they had
many variants, many other poems, or songs, around them.
They were not isolated as is the *Kalevala* itself, a lone monu-
ment, without variants.

Yet, having said all that, the *Kalevala* songs are very likely
far closer to tradition than those of many edited and published oral traditional epic texts. The editing process itself,
except when it limits itself to correcting such things as spelling or grammatical mistakes, argues the existence of two
poetics at odds with one another. When one of the finest of
the Croatian collectors of oral tradition epics at the end of
the last century edited his carefully written down texts for
publication he changed them. He standardized the normal
variations of metrics, and in many cases he eliminated the
regular repetitions which are so much a part of the oral
traditional style but which grated against Marjanović's literary

sensibilities, in spite of his great acquaintance with the oral traditional epic style. We can see from his edited manuscripts, copies of which are in the Parry Collection at Harvard, exactly what he disapproved of. Sometimes he omitted whole passages or wrote new ones to be inserted into the text. The editor and the singer had different ideas of what constituted acceptable poetics. I have not seen any better proof of the existence of two poetics, one for oral traditional poetry and the other for written literary poetry.

III

There are two main patterns of story in the *Kalevala*. One is that of gaining a bride, the other is the stealing of the Sampo. Clearly the two patterns have much in common. The Trojan legend is concerned with the regaining of a bride, although that is only part of the background of the Homeric poems, not their main focus of action, which is on Achilleus in the *Iliad* and on Odysseus in the *Odyssey*. The *Odyssey* is a 'return song', to which is joined a story of an initiatory hero setting out on a journey to find his father, and a series of incidents in a tale of wanderings. While there is an abundance of 'return' stories in the South Slavic tradition, as well as many tales of initiatory heroes setting out to find their missing father or uncle, there are no 'wanderings', insofar as I can recall, in South Slavic epic.

Comparetti[36] has analyzed and described the composition of the *Kalevala* in detail. In what follows I shall examine some of the patterns of narrative in that poem to see whether they agree with the traditional patterns in the Homeric poems and in the South Slavic epics with which I am acquainted. I shall first consider the 'wedding' sequences. In spite of the differences in the traditions involved, one might expect that some patterning, different though it might be from the Homeric or South Slavic songs, would emerge in repeated traditional sequences in the *Kalevala*. I will thus be treating Lönnrot's epic poems for the sake of the experiment, as if it were itself an oral traditional epic.

Väinämöinen is twice offered a bride. In the first case,

36 *Ibid.*, Chapter III.

that of Joukahainen's sister, the pattern is as follows: 1) a bride is offered to the hero by someone else (Joukahainen) under duress; 2) the bride refuses to marry the hero (because he is too old); 3) the bride kills herself (by drowning); 4) Väinämöinen returns without a bride.

In the second case too, when the eagle carries Väinämöinen to North Farm, the pattern is in part repeated: 1) a bride is offered to the hero by someone else (the mistress of North Farm) for a price (forging the Sampo); 2) the offered bride refuses to marry the hero (by setting three impossible tasks, two of which Väinämöinen accomplishes, although he fails in the third, building and launching a boat. The third element in the pattern (the bride kills herself) is missing in this instance; 4) Väinämöinen returns with a bride, although he still has the task set by the mistress of North Farm, yet to be fulfilled, namely, to forge a Sampo. The patterns of gaining a bride in the traditions of ancient Greece and of the South Slavs do not fit Väinämöinen's marital adventures, at least not up to this point, although the element of setting tests or a series of tasks for the bridegroom is familiar enough.

We find the pattern again in the exploits of Ilmarinen: 1) a bride is offered to him by the mistress of North Farm (for forging the Sampo — in Väinämöinen's place); 2) the bride demurred; 3) again the third element is missing, since the maid of North Farm does not kill herself; but 4) Ilmarinen goes home empty-handed.

There is indeed a repeated pattern here, which we might call that of 'the jilted bridegroom', an unheroic sequence, the hero being frustrated. Either the girls are unwilling, or the hero cannot meet the requirements set by the girl! While I do not know this pattern in South Slavic epic, it is reminiscent, as is the setting of impossible tasks, of English ballads such as 'The Elfin Knight', in which the suitor is an otherworldly figure who seeks to lure the girl into the world of magic and death. By setting him impossible tasks, she is able to save herself. There may be some ambiguity in the pattern in the *Kalevala* caused by this suggestion, because both Väinämöinen and Ilmarinen are certainly associated with the world of shamanism.

The impasse between Väinämöinen and Ilmarinen is solved

by one more occurrence of 'the jilted bridegroom' pattern for Väinämöinen, and a true wedding sequence for Ilmarinen, who finally wins the maid of North Farm, after performing dangerous tasks set by the mistress of North Farm. The element of testing the bridegroom occurred before, of course, with Väinämöinen, who failed the test! 'The successful bridegroom' pattern, if we may call it that for the moment, is: 1) someone offers the hero a bride; 2) a series of tests is imposed on the hero, which he succeeds in performing — sometimes with outside help; 3) the hero wins the bride.

Lönnrot accomplishes the transition to the adventures of Lemminkäinen in the direct way in which the South Slavic singers make the same kind of transition, that is, by saying simply: 'It is time to speak of Ahti, to go on about the rascal.' In his version of the Song of Bagdad, Salih Uglijanin, having told of the gathering of the Bosnian armies, changes the subject with: 'Now let me tell you about Fatima.'[37]

Interestingly enough, Lemminkäinen is also a 'successful bridegroom', but in his case no tests are imposed on him. That element is replaced by a straightforward 'abduction of the bride':

Now on a certain day   on a certain evening,
the maidens were sporting,   the fair ones dancing
secretly on the land side of the island,   on a lovely heath,
Kylliki supreme over the others,   most famous flower of
    the Island.
The ruddy-cheeked rascal came along,   reckless Lemmin-
    käinen drove
his own stallion,   his choice colt
to the middle of the playing field,   of the fair one's dance.
He snatched Kylliki into the sleigh,   dragged the maiden
    into his sled,
put her on his fur rug,   tied her to the slatted bottom of
    his sleigh.
He struck the horse with the whip,   cracked the lash,
then started sliding along.

37 *Srpskohrvatske junacke pjesme* collected by M. Parry and edited by A.B. Lord, Vol. 2, Belgrade and Cambridge, Mass. 1953, No. 1, line 659.

In South Slavic epic it is not uncommon to find the hero —
or sometimes the villain — riding up to a group of maidens
dancing the kolo, with the heroine at the head of the dance,
and taking her onto his horse, tying her three times to him
with his long sash, and galloping home. If this pattern were
being followed in the *Kalevala*, one would expect pursuit to
complete the pattern, or at least a later rescue.

Lemminkäinen's journey to North Farm for a bride follows the pattern of the 'unsuccessful' — but not 'jilted' —
bridegroom, but there are some differences in the pattern
from what we have seen so far. 1) The hero s e e k s   a
b r i d e (he is not offered one by someone else); 2) he is asked
to accomplish three tasks, two of which he does successfully;
3) in doing the third task (shooting the swan of Tuonela) he is
killed (by Soppy Hat), but brought back to life — and to home
— by his mother. This wedding trip of Lemminkäinen is like
that of Väinämöinen, in which he is unsuccessful in accom-
plishing the third of the tasks set him (the building and
launching of a boat), but the tests for Lemminkäinen were
not imposed by the maid of North Farm, but by her mother.
Setting tests of the bridegroom, as has already been remarked,
is common, and has its place in ritual as well, but it is not
common for the hero to be unsuccessful in overcoming all
obstacles. Ritually this would not be proper.

These, then, are the 'wedding songs' in the *Kalevala*. They
fit indifferently into traditional patterns elsewhere, agreeing
in great part, but disagreeing in some important ways. The
main difference is in the element of frustration of the bridegroom, which gives to some of the hero-bridegrooms in the
Kalevala a note of pathos, which is missing in the South Slavic
epics.

There are no 'wanderings' in South Slavic epic, but some of
the single incidents in the wanderings of Odysseus, such as
encounters with man-eating monsters, can be paralleled there.
The adventures of Lemminkäinen in the *Kalevala* come close
to forming a series of 'wanderings', when the hero sets out to
hide on the island where his father had once hidden. In the
Proto-Kalevala and in the *Old Kalevala* he returns home
directly from the island, but in the *New Kalevala* he is ship-
wrecked and swims to another island, where the lady of the

island provides him with a boat, with which he reaches home. There is something Odyssean about both the sequence, 1) island of women, 2) acquiring a boat (by building), 3) shipwreck, and 4) arriving at an island where a woman provides a boat to take the hero home.

Then reckless Lemminkäinen   proceeds on the blue sea.
He proceeded one day, proceeded a second.   In the third day, indeed,
a wind got to blowing,   the horizon to rumbling,
a great northwest wind,   a strong northeast wind blew.
It caught one plank, caught a second,   it capsized the whole boat.
Then reckless Lemminkäinen   fell straight into the water,
began to row with his fingers,   to paddle with his feet.
a wind got to blowing,   the horizon to rumbling,
a great northwest wind,   a strong northeast wind blew.
It caught one plank, caught a second,   it capsized the whole boat.
Then reckless Lemminkäinen   fell straight into the water,
began to row with his fingers,   to paddle with his feet.
After he had swum a night and a day,   after he had paddled along quite a distance,
he saw a little cloud,   a cloud patch in the northwest.
That, indeed, changed into land,   became a headland.
He went onto the headland into a house,   found the mistress baking,
the daughters shaping loaves. . . .
The gracious mistress   went out to the storehouse,
sliced some butter in the storehouse,   a sliver of pork;
she puts it to roast   for the hungry man to eat,
brings beer in a stoup   for the man who has been swimming to drink.
Then she gave him a new vessel,   a really well-equipped boat,
for the man to go to other lands,   to proceed home.

One thinks, of course, of Circe and Calypso, and even of the Phaeacians. In fact, since the final incident is not in the earlier versions of the *Kalevala*, I wonder if Lönnrot, in inserting it in the *New Kalevala*, was influenced by Homer's *Odyssey*.

In addition to the narrative patterns mentioned above, there are journeys to the world of the dead in both the *Kalevala* and the *Odyssey*, different though they be. Väinämöinen seeks special, magical knowledge, the words of a charm, in several places, among which is Tuonela, the Land of the Dead. There he is almost ensnared, but he is unsuccesful in his quest for charms. Not until he encounters Antero Vipunen and penetrates to his interior, is he able to obtain the words he needs. The correspondence between this episode and Odysseus' consultation with Teiresias has been noted by Martti Haavio.[38]

There are actually two episodes in the *Odyssey* in which someone seeks, and obtains, information. They are multi-forms of one another. In the first Menelaos inquired of the Old Man of the Sea how he could leave Egypt and continue on his journey home. The scene is not in the Land of the Dead, to be sure, but it is in the magic land of Egypt. In the second episode, just referred to, Odysseus questioned Teiresias, who was really in the Land of the Dead, about many things, and he learned much even without asking, including his own fated death. As a matter of fact, Väinämöinen's journey to Tuonela has little in common with Odysseus' journey to the Land of the Dead; it is more nearly akin to the episodes in which Odysseus is almost killed, or detained forever in the other world, from which, however, he manages to escape.

The world of the dead, as such, like the 'wanderings', is missing in the South Slavic tradition, but there are journeys into 'other worlds' in the Balkan Slavic epics. In the other world heroes seek, and usually gain, brides, horses, and artifacts; and from the other world they rescue people who are being held there against their will. Such a world is usually the world of the enemy — appropriately enough, because it is truly a land of death. One must pass barriers and guardians, which are sometimes monstrous, before one can enter it, and at the barriers, or in the foreign land itself the hero has some-times to hide his identity, through disguise. He is asked to identify himself, and his answers are often deceptive at first, and tests are made prior to his recognition by a friend in the

38   *Väinämöinen, Eternal Sage*, FF Communications 144, Helsinki 1952, 134.

enemy land. Such questions are reminiscent of those put to Väinämöinen at the approaches to Tuonela.

The fundamental difference between the Finnish tradition and those of the Slavic Balkans and of Ancient Greece is the prevalence and force of shamanism in the *Kalevala* and in the songs and their variants which went into its making. Heroism by magic spells rather than by swords and spears gives the *Kalevala* a very special atmosphere, and it is exciting to enter into that strange world.

It is useful and necessary to be aware of the similarities among traditions, to understand that traditions are not watertight compartments. But it is also important to comprehend the peculiar features of each tradition and to have as firm and sympathetic a grasp as possible of the details and meanings of the traditions in which one works. The haunting tragic beauty of the *Kalevala* cannot be easily matched anywhere else. Lönnrot expressed in it, however, the same sense of human personal loss that one finds in the *Iliad*. The *Kalevala* also shares with it the ultimate sense of reconciliation with the reality that is symbolized by the fact that only portions of the Sampo can ever be possessed by any one people, ironical though it be that they were clever enough to create it.

APPENDIX A

From *The Traditional Poetry of the Finns*, by D. Comparetti, translated by Isabella M. Anderton, New York 1898, 157.

'The order in which the singers chant their runes should certainly not be entirely overlooked. At the same time I have not thought well to attach too much importance to it, as it is a matter in which they differ much from each other. This very difference in the ordering of the runes confirmed me in the idea I have already conceived: that all runes of this kind could be combined among themselves. For I had observed that the disposition adopted by one singer was not the same as that adopted by another; so that, after a great copying of runes recited by various singers, I found very few that had not been sung, by one or another, in various connections. I could not consider one singer's ordering of the runes as more original than that of another; but explained each case by the natural desire of man to bring order into his knowledge, a desire which produces differences according to the different conception of the individual singers. As a consequence, since none of the singers could compare with me in the mass of runes I had collected, I thought that I had the same right which I was convinced most of the singers assumed: the right, that is, of ordering the runes according as they best fitted into each other.'*

*Helsingfors Litteraturblad, 1849, 16. We may here remind the reader of other words of Lönnrot given in chapter I, 9.

APPENDIX B

From *The Traditional Poetry of the Finns*, by D. Comparetti, translated by Isabella M. Anderton, New York 1898, 9, note 1.

'We may refer here to what Lönnrot wrote in this connection after the new edition of the *Kalevala* in *Helsingf. Litteraturblad*, 1849, n. 1, p. 20: No discussion as to the mode of origin of the Homeric poems could ever have arisen had those who have written on this subject had the experience which I have acquired through the Finnish poems, of the influence of tradition on poetry. They would all have agreed that some poet first briefly sang contemporary events, and that tradition then expanded the songs and produced variants of them. He who afterwards collected these variants did much the same as I have done in ordering and weaving together those of the songs of the *Kalevala*; only I beg that no one takes these words amiss, as though I wished to place my abilities or the subject I have treated on a par with that other collector and his work. The various dialectic forms which occur so often in the Homeric poems render impossible the belief that the latter were the work of one man or were handed down by tradition without many variants. He who orders and puts together these pieces of a cycle of songs must sometimes insert a connecting line, and I doubt not that such lines can be found, if we look for them, in the Homeric poems. I also have had to introduce some of them into the runes of the *Kalevala*; but it seemed to me, and to others also, that it would have been mere pedantry to draw attention to them, especially as they have nothing to do with the poem itself, and consist generally in such phrases as "He expressed himself in words and spoke thus" (*Sanon virkkoi, noin nimesi*), or, "Then he spoke and said" (*Siita tuon sanokisi virkki*), etc.'

ELEMENTS OF EASTERN ORIGIN IN THE *KALEVALA*.
A PRELIMINARY REPORT

FELIX J. OINAS
(Indiana University)

I

The materials used in compiling the *Kalevala* do not only consist of genuine Finnish and Balto-Finnic songs, but are also derived from borrowings from either the West or the East. The attitude of scholars toward these sources varies. Kaarle Krohn and Antti Aarne were inclined to see a preponderance of Western elements in the *Kalevala*. Martti Haavio found the origin of the songs he investigated primarily in the East. Matti Kuusi, on the other hand, has established the genuineness of several songs in the *Kalevala*, which other scholars considered to be foreign origin. Since the *Kalevala* was compiled from songs collected primarly in eastern Finland, Karelia and Ingria, it is, in general, natural to expect the Eastern traditions to dominate.

In the following, I will briefly discuss a number of typical Eastern elements — songs and individual motifs — in the *New Kalevala* (1949), identified by various scholars. About half of them consist of my personal contributions. The elements whose Eastern origin has, in my opinion, not been fully proven (like 'The Song of the Release of the Sun', 'The Golden Maiden'[1] and others) will be bypassed. The final part of the paper will summarize the findings.

---

1 It is not impossible that the Finnish-Estonian song of the golden maid has some connection with the folklore of the Arctic areas, since e.g. the Lapps and Ob-Ugrians have cult objects and places called 'golden wife'. The background of the song requires further study. See M. Kuusi, *Kalevalaista kertomarunoutta*, Helsinki 1980, 224-5; M. Kuusi, K. Bosley and M. Branch, eds. and trans., *Finnish Folk Poetry. Epic*, Helsinki 1977, 532.

II

1. *The Creation Song* (1:201-244).

The scaup duck makes a nest and lays its eggs on the knee of the mother of water. As eggs roll into the sea and break into pieces, the bits give rise to the earth, the heavens, the sun, the moon, the stars and clouds.

'The World Creation Song' served as the basis for this episode in the *Kalevala*. According to Kuusi, it takes the following original form among the Balto-Finns: The world bird (an eagle?) is flying above the sea, looking for a nesting place and, having found it (a tussock?), lays one or three eggs; a gust of wind causes the eggs to roll into the sea, break, and out of them arise (the earth and the sky and) the sun to shine, the moon to glow, and the stars in the sky.

In the Estonian and Ingrian redaction of the song, the bird is specified as a swallow. The East Karelian redaction is different through the presence of the active creator — Väinämöinen. Kuusi suggests that the poet who recreated the epic of Väinämöinen in Karelia linked the creation song with Väinämöinen's maritime creation work: the eagle was changed into the scaup duck or goose, and the tussock was replaced by Väinämöinen's knee, which he thrust out of the sea. In the *Kalevala*, Lönnrot introduced several changes. The role of the active creator was shifted from Väinämöinen to the water mother (transformed from a godly being — the virgin of the air), and the act of creation was placed at the beginning of the world.

The myth of the creation of the world from an egg is widely known in an area extending from the eastern Mediterranean to India, Japan, Polynesia and Peru. It is probably of ancient Aryan origin.[2]

---

2   M. Haavio, *Väinämöinen*, Folklore Fellows Communications (= FFC) 144, Helsinki 1952, 45-63; G. Stipa, 'Der Weltursprungsmythos des Kalevala' in *Fabula* 5 (1962), 1-14; M. Kuusi, *Suomen kirjallisuus* 1, Helsinki 1963, 68; H. Fromm, *Kalevala: Kommentar*, München 1967, 20-1, Kuusi, Bosley, Branch, *op. cit.*, 522-3; Kuusi, *op. cit.*, 220.

2. *The Sower (Sampsa Pellervoinen)* (2:13-32; 16:13-100).
Sampsa Pellervoinen, the Spirit of Growth, appears in the
Kalevala as Väinämöinen's helper at the creation: he sows the
lands with crops and trees. He also procures timber for
Väinämöinen's boat.

The figure of the Spirit of Growth comes from the folk-
song 'The Sower', in which he is usually called Sämpsä. In
Ingria Sämpsä is the sower of grain, and in the northern
regions the sower of various trees. An Ingrian version tells us
that grain and grass do not grow, because Sämpsä is asleep.
The winter boy is sent to wake him up, but Sämpsä refuses,
because of the damage done by the winter winds. However,
he heeds the call of the summer boy. In a North Karelian
version, Sämpsä fled to the North after he lay with his sister
or stepmother. The summer boy ('wolf') went, and on his
second trip, proved successful. Upon his arrival, Sämpsä
sowed fields and forests.

Finnish scholars, from Kaarle Krohn to Kirkinen, have
suggested several foreign models for the song. I contend that
it has grown out of a Hittite-Greek myth. The Hittite story
describes the god Telipinus, who disappears and takes all life
with him; grain no longer grows and trees shrivel. The Storm-
god first sends the eagle, then goes himself to look for him,
but to no avail. Finally, the bee discovers Telipinus lying
asleep in a meadow and awakens him with its sting. The god
returns, is appeased with a ritual, and re-establishes the good
life.

This story, as shown by Burkert, is related to a Greek myth
about Black Demeter. Angered by Poseidon's rape, she hides
in a cave, is sought for, found, and brought back. The earth's
fruit returns.

The Near-Eastern myth and the Ingrian-Karelian 'The Sower'
have an identical basic pattern and show additional similarities
in some details (an unnatural sexual incident that caused
Demeter's and Sämpsä's departure, the role played by the
wind, etc.). It can be assumed that the Anatolian myth was
passed on to the Greeks, and through intermediaries migrated
to the north — to Ingrians and Karelians. A Mordvin (originally
Russian) and a Belorussian song represent a link in this migration. The Mordvin song tells of the gods' feast to which the

fertility goddess or (in some variants) St Nicholas have not come. Messengers are sent to the field to invite them, but only rarely do they comply. In one variant Christmas and Easter are sent for St Nicholas, who is said to be angry. In the Belorussian song St Nicholas is walking along the boundary strip and refuses the invitation. As Kirkinen has shown,[3] some details of Sämpsä's garment have obviously been taken over from his namesake St Sam(p)son.

3. *The Great Oak* (2:43-224).

When Väinämöinen goes to look at the land seeded by Sämpsä, he sees that the oak tree has not grown. Later four girls prepare the soil and the oak grows so tall that it extends to the heavens, obscuring the light of the moon and sun. A little man emerges from the sea and, on the third attempt, fells the tree. Now the sun and moon begin to shine again.

The Karelian-Finnish folksong 'The Great Oak', the basis for this episode, has correspondences in Estonian and Mordvin. Shown to belong to the most ancient stratum of the Finnic aetiological and ritual songs (probably created in the Common Balto-Finnic period), it derives from an ancient Oriental myth of the world tree, which is widely known from the Mediterranean to the Pacific (including the Bible [*Ezekiel* 31:3-18], Indo-China and Japan) and in South America. It is also connected to northern Eurasian ideas about the world tree. One explanation of the myth contends that it reflects ancient ideas about the Milky Way.

In the course of time this song has developed in various areas in different ways — from a gay swinging song in Estonia

3　H. Kirkinen, 'Oliko Sampsa historiallinen henkillö?' in *Kalevalaseuran Vuosikirja* 47 (1967), 103-32; W. Burkert, *Structure and History in Greek Mythology*, Berkeley and Los Angeles 1979, 123-6; A. Turunen, *Kalavalan sanat ja niiden taustat*, Lappeenranta 1979, 295-6; Kuusi, *op. cit.*, 229-30; F.J. Oinas, *Studies in Finnic Folklore: Homage to the Kalevala*, Helsinki 1985, 108-14.

to a lusty drinking song in Ingria and to the prologue for healing incantations in Karelia.[4]

4. *The Creation of the Sea-Bed* (3:215-244).

During the singing match between Väinämöinen and Joukahainen, Joukahainen brags of remembering how he created the floor of the sea, but Väinämöinen rejects this as a lie.

Väinämöinen's reference to Joukahainen's bragging as a 'lie' in the *Kalevala* is a mild understatement. In the Ingrian-Karelian folk song used for this episode, Väinämöinen emphasizes that it is he who plowed the sea, hoed out its hollows, dug deep spots for the fish, heaped up blocks of stone, etc. Remnants of the plowing of the sea motif appear also in Estonia.

The motif of the creation of the sea-bed is obviously of Eastern origin. Correspondences are found in the Eastern earth-diver myth, in myths of the earth-carrying and -shaping animals, and — most importantly — in the Old Indian myth of Brahma, who, in the shape of the boar, breaks up the bottom of the primeval sea.[5]

5. *'He Took His Straw Stallion'* (6:5-14).

Following the suggestion of his dead mother, Väinämöinen vowed to set out to woo the beautiful maiden of the North. 'He took his straw stallion, his peastalk horse', and rode easily on the surface of the sea. However, he could not get far.

---

4 M. Haavio, *Kirjokansi*, Porvoo-Helsinki 1952, 233-8; Kuusi, *op. cit.* (1963), 73-9; M. Haavio, *Suomalainen mytologia*, Porvoo-Helsinki 1967, 345-57; Anna-Leena Kuusi, 'Finnish Mythology' in *Ancient Cultures of Uralic Peoples* (ed. P. Hajdú), Budapest 1976, 260-1; Kuusi, Bosley, Branch, *op. cit.*, 546-7.

5 Haavio, *op. cit.* (1952), 64-82; M. Kuusi, 'Suomalaisen luomisrunon jäänteitä' in *Kalevalaseuran Vuosikirja* 39 (1959), 43-72; Kuusi, *op. cit.* (1963), 72, 219-21; Fromm, *op. cit.*, 36-43; Kuusi, Bosley, Branch, *op. cit.*, 525; Turunen, *op. cit.*, 75-6; Kuusi, *op. cit.* (1980), 222; M. Kuusi, 'Ein estnisches Mythenrelikt' in *Folklorica: Festscrift for Felix J. Oinas* (ed. E.V. Žygas and P. Voorheis), Bloomington 1982, 155-64.

Joukahainen, who bore a grudge against him, shot the horse from under him, and Väinämöinen found himself drifting on the waves.

The description of Väinämöinen's horse in the *Kalevala* is identical with that in Karelian-Finnish folk songs. The 'straw stallion, peastalk horse' has been explained by scholars as being light as straw, or the color of straw, or fed with peastalk, made of straw or peastalk, etc. None of these explanations turned out to be acceptable. Setälä considered Väinämöinen's mount a phantasy horse, and Haavio thought it originally to have been a boat; Fromm rightly found these ideas 'not quite satisfactory'.

In my opinion, the explanation of the 'straw stallion' is to be sought in shamanism. A Hungarian *táltos*, 'shaman' is said to have gone 'to a wedding on a reed horse, that is, he put a reed between his legs and galloped away and was there before the men on horseback'. Close parallels to Väinämöinen's ride are also found among the Altaic and other Siberian peoples. Holding his staff, called 'my horse', like a hobby horse on his left side, the Tuvan shaman feigns the act of riding. The Buryat shaman hits two sticks, carved like horses, together while shamanizing. The Mongolian shamans use the same kind of horse-shaped sticks with attached stirrups. The Uzbek dervish is believed to be able to fly on a stick decorated with human features, which he puts between his legs. More commonly in Asia, the drum functions as the shaman's mount. It is variously called the shaman's 'horse', 'white horse', or 'reindeer bull', depending upon the kind of animal used for riding in the area. The drum is equipped with reins, and the drumstick is the whip. The shaman's 'flight' or 'riding' are, according to Eliade, 'figurative expressions for ecstasy, that is, for mystical journeys undertaken by superhuman means and in regions inaccessible to mankind'.

The expression 'blue deer' occurs occasionally in parallel verses of the Finnish folk song for the 'straw stallion'. The deer is a well-suited parallel image.[6]

6   E.N. Setälä, *Sammon arvoitus*, Helsinki 1932, 517-8; Fromm, *op. cit.*, 55; Louise Bäckman and Å. Hultkrantz, *Studies in Lapp Shamanism*, Stockholm 1978, 16; W. Heissig, *Geser-Studien*,

6. *Väinämöinen's Knee Wound* (8:145-196).

Väinämöinen was building a boat on a mountain. As the devil turned the ax handle, the ax cut into his knee. The blood ran like a river and flooded the field of berry-stalks and tussocks. The flow of blood was finally stopped by charms.

The Finnish-Karelian folk song about Väinämöinen's knee wound has been used as the historiola of an incantation to stop bleeding. It is the Arctic version of the biblical flood myth (*Genesis* 1:7-8). Haavio, following Erkki Itkonen's suggestion, connected the myth of Väinämöinen's knee wound with that of the Lapp flood hero Naainas (< Nooa), who hit his leg while making a boat and, after death, occupied a place in the realm of those who had died a blood-death. The Northern Lights are believed to have arisen from his blood.

Some motifs of the Finnish-Karelian myth coincide with the Vogul flood myth, e.g., the tightening of the boat with birch bark and fat and equipping it with a cover from fish skin. The tightening is found also in the Altai myth. Haavio suggests that these similar motifs came from an unknown Russian redaction.[7]

7. *The Demon's Elk* (13:27-270, 14:1-270).

When Lemminkäinen asks Louhi for her daughter, he is assigned to catch the Demon's elk on skis as his first wooing task. Boasting arrogantly, Lemminkäinen sets out in pursuit. He almost catches the elk, but the animal manages to free itself. Only after entreating the mistress of the forest with huntsmen's charms does he capture it and take it to the North.

Göttingen 1983, 319; Oinas, *op. cit.*, 154-69. For additional information on the staff and drum as the shaman's magic mounts, see M. Hoppál, *Shamanism in Eurasia*, Göttingen 1984, 76, 348 *et passim*.

7 E. Itkonen, 'Kolttien satu revontulten synnystä', in *Virittäjä* 63 (1959), 96-100; M. Haavio, 'Naainas' in *Kalevalaseuran Vuosikirja* 43 (1963), 53-96; E. Itkonen, 'Älteste Elemente der lappischen Volksüberlieferung' in *Suomalais-ugrilaisen Seuran Aikakauskirja* 74 (1976), 47; Kuusi, *op. cit.* (1980), 221.

For the Demon's elk in the *Kalevala*, Lönnrot made use of the corresponding Karelian folk song, but changed its ending. Whereas in the folk song the elk escapes, in the *Kalevala* — because of the plan of the epic — it had to be caught. The charms were added by Lönnrot.

Jouko Hautala showed that the folk song was created around 1000-1300, west and northwest of Lake Ladoga, from where it migrated to the Ingrians in the south and the Karelians in the north.

According to Hautala, the song is based on the North Eurasian redaction of the world-wide Orion myth. The myth appears, e.g., among the Lapps, Samoyeds, Yenisei Ostyaks, Buryats, Teleuts, Mongols, etc. Typical of the North-Eurasian redaction is the length of time it takes to make the skis and their extraordinary speed. The Vogul myth is especially close to the Karelian version.[8]

8. *Lemminkäinen's Death and Resurrection* (14:373-460; 15).

As the third wooing task, Lemminkäinen must shoot the swan in the river of Death's Domain. The cattle herder, who is on the lookout for Lemminkäinen, kills him with a cowbane-poisoned tube and throws him into Death's river. His body is cut to pieces. At Lemminkäinen's home his mother notices blood oozing from his brush and suspects the worst. She hastens to the North, assembles all the pieces of his body, and restores him to life.

The song of Lemminkäinen's death and resurrection in the *Kalevala* has been taken from the second part of Lemminkäinen's song (except for the charms). In some versions Lemminkäinen, changed into a fish, goes 'clattering down the rapids, whizzing downstream'.

The second part of Lemminkäinen's song, like the first, was considered to be of foreign origin. Castrén, the Krohns and others pointed to the similarities between Lemminkäinen and Baldr and Christ. Haavio concluded that the song of

---

8 J. Hautala, *Hiiden hirven hiihdäntä*, Helsinki 1947; Haavio, *op. cit.* (1952), 240-3; Kuusi, Bosley, Branch, *op. cit.*, 548-9; Turunen, *op. cit.*, 49; Kuusi, *op. cit.* (1980), 232.

Lemminkäinen's death was based on the ancient Egyptian myth of Osiris, who is killed by his jealous brother, cut into pieces and scattered far and wide. His wife-sister reassembles his body and revives him. The Osiris myth, according to Haavio, could have reached Karelia through Byzantium and Russia, carried by the *skomorokhi*, the wandering singers. Kemppinen's position is close to Haavio's. He considers both the myth of Lemminkäinen and that of Baldr as going back — partly by different routes — to the Eastern myths of the death and resurrection of Osiris and some other mythical beings.[9]

9. *Antero Vipunen's Song* (17).

Väinämöinen visits Antero Vipunen, a deceased great shaman, to learn necessary words to finish building the boat. Trees and bushes have grown out of Vipunen's body. Väinämöinen tries to open Vipunen's mouth with a cowl-staff, but instead slips inside. In Vipunen's stomach, he sets up a smithy and torments him in order to extort the words. The spells Vipunen utters are not effective against the intruder. Finally, Vipunen reveals the words and Väinämöinen leaves.

In Karelian-Finnish folklore, there are two versions of Antero Vipunen's song. The first, found primarily in Border Karelia and Olonets, describes the trip Väinämöinen (originally obviously Lemminkäinen, Vipunen's son) makes to Vipunen's grave to learn the words. Väinämöinen's efforts to wake him are in vain: Vipunen's flesh has decayed and his soul is far away, in a whale. This song has a close parallel in Lapp and was obviously created under Lapp influence. It is also known in Estonia.

The second version, used by Lönnrot in the *Kalevala* (with some motifs from the first version added), was sung primarily in East Karelia. It tells of Väinämöinen's adventure in Vipunen's stomach. According to Finnish folklorists, the singer may not have properly understood the metaphor of the shaman's

9 I. Kemppinen, *Johdatus muinaissuomalaiseen mytologiaan*, Helsinki 1957, 143-79; Fromm, *op. cit.*, 300; Kuusi, *op. cit.* (1963), 321-3; Haavio, *op. cit.* (1967), 249-64; Kuusi, Bosley, Branch, *op. cit.*, 538-40; Turunen, *op. cit.*, 173-5.

mouth and belly as the source of spells, and let Väinämöinen slip into the monster's mouth to obtain them there.

The second version is, in my view, a different song as to its origin. Whereas the Vipunen of the first version is a father figure, whose son approaches him for advice, in the second version he is a man-eating monster.

About a century ago, Afanas'ev connected the detail of the torment in Vipunen's stomach with the Russian tale of 'The Prophetic Dream', which tells of a young boy, who was carrying wood and was swallowed by a whale. In the whale's stomach he built a bonfire and caused the creature to fling itself to all sides in pain. When the whale died, the boy cut a hole in its side and crawled out.

In Karelia and Olonets, this Russian tale has given rise to the tale of the Old Hag of Hiisi or a pike-swallowing smith Ilmarinen (Ilmoillinen). The Russian tale (or its derivative in Karelia and Olonets) with its Jonah motif also affected Antero Vipunen's song. The Karelians knew the first version of Vipunen's song at the time when they heard the tale of the whale or huge pike. Vipunen was identified with these aquatic beings, since the shaman was believed to assume their shape for his missions or to have his soul imbedded in them. The singer recreated the song accordingly.

The Russian tale is obviously of Turco-Tatar origin. The Altai Kizhi tale 'Täktäbäi Märgän' about the prophetic dream has basically the same plot as the Russian. The theme of the hero's getting into the stomach of a cannibalistic monster also appears in the folklore of the Mongols.[10]

10. *The Great Ox* (20:17-118).

An enormous ox grew in Karelia. It was taken to be slaughtered for the wedding of the maiden of the North. Virokannas and other gods came to kill it, but when the ox shook its head, the gods jumped up into trees. Finally a black man who rose from the sea killed the ox easily.

10 Haavio, *op. cit.* (1952), 261-8; Kuusi, *op. cit.* (1963), 255-9; Kuusi, Bosley, Branch, *op. cit.*, 535-6; Turunen, *op. cit.*, 22-3; Oinas, *op. cit.*, 131-45.

The folk song of the great ox appears in Finland, Karelia and Ingria. Two versions of it have been united in the *Kalevala*. The first, concentrated in Savo, tells of a black man who comes from the sea and kills the enormous ox. Originally it was sung at the Kekri festival. The song also spread to Estonia, where it was sung during the harvesting bee.

The second version is found farther to the east, mainly in the north of East Karelia. Here a group of gods come to slay the ox; but when the ox shakes its head and moves its ears, the frightened gods run to hide in trees.

As demonstrated by Haavio, 'The Great Ox' is connected with the Orient. The first version derives from the Iranian Mithras myth, which tells of the capture and slaughter of the sacrificial bull. The second version, in my view, is linked with the Near-Eastern (Old Iranian and Mesopotamian) beliefs of the earth-carrying bull, beliefs which have spread far and wide with Islam — to the Caucasus, Western Asia, East and Southeast Europe, Egypt, Oceania, etc. Since the earth was believed to rest on one or both horns of the bull, the shaking of its head or its movement caused earthquakes.

In Babylonia the role of the earthquake bull has obviously been transferred to Labbu, a lion-like gigantic serpent that causes people to lament and cry. When Labbu raises its tail, all the gods of heaven prostrate themselves before the moon-god Sin and grasp his robe. When Labbu is finally killed by one of the gods, the event is accompanied by natural phenomena resembling volcanic activities and earthquakes.

It can be assumed that the Oriental myth of the earth-carrying and earthquake bull was disseminated to the northeast to Russia. After reaching East Karelia, it blended with the first version of 'The Great Ox' song and gave rise to the second version. Since earthquakes were not known in these regions, the earthquake motif was dropped. Thus the gods' fright followed immediately after the ox's shaking its head, a sequence that rendered the song unintelligible and even illogical.[11]

---

11 M. Haavio, *Karjalan jumalat*, Porvoo-Helsinki 1959, 39-78; Kuusi, *op. cit.* (1963), 161-3, 336-7; Oinas, *op. cit.*, 142-3.

11. *Lemminkäinen's Trip to the North* (26; 27:1-396).

Lemminkäinen, who is plowing the field, learns about festivities in the North. He decides to go there uninvited. His mother warns him not to go, because three deaths lurk along the way and a magic fence bars the entrance. Lemminkäinen nevertheless leaves and overcomes all the obstacles. In the North he is received in an unfriendly manner. The master sings up a pond on the floor and some animals, but Lemminkäinen disposes of them one by one. Finally they have a duel in the yard, during which the master is killed.

The first part of the Lemminkäinen's song was used for this poem in the *Kalevala*. As Haavio has shown, this portion is based on the Russian *bylina*, 'Vavilo and Skomorokhi', which shares all the basic motifs: Vavilo's plowing the field; his departure with a group of *skomorokhi*, 'singers-entertainers' to King Sobaka, 'Dog'; the warnings about death and dangers; the duel in charms with the king; Vavilo's victory. Haavio claims that the Vavilo *bylina* is based on an Egyptian story of the first century A.D.

One detail in Lemminkäinen's and Vavilo's song, in my opinion, definitely demonstrates a genetic relationship, viz. the fact that Lemminkäinen's song contains the remnants of the death/danger series as well as the duel series of the Vavilo *bylina* as the last motifs. It can be concluded that the Egyptian story passed through Greece to Byzantium. The *skomorokhi* spread it to northwest Russia, where it was taken over by the Karelians.[12]

12. *The Snake-Fence* (26:225-236; 583-594).

Lemminkäinen's mother warns her son not to go to the North, because of the three deaths lurking on the way. Over there he would come to an iron fence, reaching from earth to heaven, wattled with reptiles, interlaced with snakes and bound together with lizards, whose heads are outward, tails inward. When Lemminkäinen comes to the fence, he sends the reptiles away.

---

12 Kuusi, *op. cit.* (1963), 253-7; Haavio, *op. cit.* (1967), 232-49; Kuusi, Bosley, Branch, *op. cit.*, 538-40; Kuusi, *op. cit.* (1980), 227-8; Oinas, *op. cit.*, 115-30.

The snake-fence occurs in Finnish-Karelian folk songs and incantations. Turunen connects this fence with notions about the Otherworld, whereas Kuusi associates it with the witch-doctor's belt, equipped with numerous paraphernalia. I am inclined to see in the magic fence the shaman's protection of his area against hostile intruders. Snakes and lizards are generally known to be the helping spirits of the shaman.

Similar ideas are found in northern Siberia. Anna-Leena Siikala, following Anisimov, states that 'To prevent spirits [of disease and death] sent by the shaman of an alien clan from attacking, the shaman erected a *marylya*-fence, i.e., he ordered his assistant spirits to keep guard round the clan's land'. The same idea also appears among the Lapps. A Lapp shaman's assisting spirit is hurt by a hostile shaman's assisting spirit in the guise of sharp poles standing up from the bottom of the sea.[13]

13. *'Is That Dense Smoke or a Dark Cloud?'* (31:53-64).

A feud flares up between two brothers, Untamo and Kalervo. One day Kalervo's daughter-in-law looks out of the window and wonders: ' "Is that dense smoke or is it a dark cloud at the end of those fields?" It was not a misty mist nor indeed a dark smoke; those were Untamo's men getting ready to come to battle.'

The description of the coming of Untamo's men involves the stylistic figure of the negative analogy — affirmation by denial. It found its way into the *Kalevala* from an Ingrian folk song of Kullervo. In variants of this song, the approaching gang is compared to atmospheric phenomena — dark clouds, heavy rain, dense smoke, misty mist, etc. This construction also occurs in other songs in Ingria and Olonets.

The negative analogy is, as I have shown, derived from Russian *byliny* and historical songs. Menacing atmospheric phenomena — clouds, heavy rain, spreading fog — in them symbolize an attacking army or the arrival of a hero, e.g.,

---

13 Kuusi, *op. cit.* (1963), 36, Anna-Leena Siikala, *The Rite Technique of the Siberian Shaman, FFC* 220, Helsinki 1978, 245; Bäckman and Hultkrantz, *op. cit.*, 54; Turunen, *op. cit.*, 16.

'Fellows, it was not a storm-cloud that came up, it is not fog spreading over the field, it is . . .'[14]

14. *'You Killed Your Former Wedded Wife'* (38:95-102).

When Ilmarinen goes to the North to woo the younger sister of his former wife, he receives only abusive words from her mother and others. The girl herself retorts: 'You killed your former wedded wife, . . . you would kill me too'.

These lines come from a North Karelian wooing song, and have entered from the song, 'The Maiden of Kaloiniemi'. The latter song describes Hannus' wooing the daughter of a dignitary. When the girl suggests that he should first kill his wife, Hannus does so. However, the girl still refuses him, because, having killed his wife, he may kill her too.

I have shown that the Finnish-Ingrian song was created on the model of the Russian song, 'Fedor and Marfa'. A Mordvin folk song about a man who murders his wife and children at the instigation of his girl friend comes from another version of the same Russian song.[15]

15. *'What Has Run across here?'* (38:111-124, 180-286).

After he has been refused the young daughter of the North, Ilmarinen flings her into the sleigh and rushes away. The girl sees the footprints of a hare, a fox and a wolf on the snow and, in each instance, comments that she would rather run in those tracks than ride in this suitor's sleigh. While Ilmarinen, wearied by the journey, sleeps soundly, the girl lies with another man. Ilmarinen gets angry and sings her into a seagull.

The dialogue between the girl and Ilmarinen comes from 'Iivana Kojonen's Son', recorded by Lönnrot in Uhtua, White Sea region. In the song, the girl has been taken forcibly from her home. Following the dialogue, the girl and her abductor start 'measuring their swords'. The girl's sword turns out to be longer; the man cuts her head off and sends parts of her body to her mother.

---

14 Oinas, *op. cit.*, 83-90.
15 Fromm, *op. cit.*, 245-6; Oinas, *op. cit.*, 17-31.

A century ago, Julius Krohn proved that 'Iivana Kojonen's Son' was based on the Russian *bylina*, 'Ivan Godinovič', in which the abductor's party chances upon the footprints of three animals, and Ivan's companions proceed to follow them. When the girl's real groom arrives, a fight breaks out between him and Ivan. In the fight the girl helps her groom, for which she is savagely killed by Ivan.[16]

16. *'One Wing Brushed the Clouds'* (43:165-166; 19:209-210).

In the pursuit of the thieves of the Sampo, Louhi changes herself into an eagle, takes a hundred men under her wings, and flies swiftly along: 'One wing brushed the clouds, the other grazed the water'. This image of the enormous wingspan is also used in the song of the fight between the eagle and the pike.

The formula of the eagle's wings appears in the corresponding Finnish-Karelian folk songs. It is also found in the song of 'The Goose Lost', where it describes the ordinary goose. From Ingria the motif of the goose with fantastic wings has spread to the Setus in Estonia.

The earth-sky formula occurs widely in Altaic folklore as a characteristic of monstrous gigantic beings. Such are, e.g., the Altai Kizhi monster, Ker Jutpa, whose one lip is snapping the sky, the other, the earth; an Osmanli Turk Negro with a lip on the earth and the other in the sky; and a Kumandin monster, who plows the earth up with its lower jaw and the sky with its upper jaw. Further examples are encountered in Mongolian, such as the giant sister with enormous tusks in thirteenth century Mongolian literature, the black-spotted tiger with huge lips, and the wild bull with horns touching both the sky and golden earth in the Peking block-print of 1716. The monsters represent one basic type — the monstrous 'devourer' (*avaleur*), primarily the incarnation of the shaman. The formula describes the paired parts of the face and head; one of them touches (or snaps, plows, stirs, etc.) the sky,

16 J. Krohn, *Suomalaisen kirjallisuuden historia*, Helsinki 1883, 480-2; Fromm, *op. cit.*, 245-6; F.J. Oinas, *Studies in Finnic-Slavic Folklore Relations*, FFC 205, Helsinki 1969, 8-9.

while the other touches (or snaps, plows, tears up, etc.) the earth. The formula underscores the overpowering size of these beings. Since there is no exact counterpart of the Finnish-Karelian bird with enormous wingspan in Altaic folklore, we may have in the earth-sky formula an instance of parallel development.

It should be noted that the growth as high as (or approximating) the sky also appears in the Finnic and Asian fantasies about the great oak and great ox.[17]

17. *The Bear Song* (46).

Väinämöinen hunts the bear sent by Louhi. He kills it, but blames its death on the beast itself. After having skinned the bear and boiled its meat, he prepares a traditional ceremonial banquet. During this so-called wedding party, Väinämöinen sings of the bear's birth in heaven and its lowering to the surface of the earth in a cradle suspended from golden chains. Finally Väinämöinen takes the bear's teeth (i.e., its skull) to a tree in the forest.

The dramatized bear rituals were customary all over the polar areas. The Finnish-Karelian bear rites have grown out of the paleo-Arctic shamanistic tradition. Correspondences to these rites are found among the Lapps, Samoyeds, Ob-Ugrian and other North Siberian hunting nations and North American Indians. The myth of the bear's birth and youth has its closest equivalent among the Ob-Ugrians. The Ostyaks tell at the bear funeral that Numi-Torem, the supreme god, lowered the cradle with the young bear in it to the earth by gold and silver chains.

In Finland the song of the birth of the bear frequently was preserved as part of an incantation, sung while sending the cattle out in the spring for the first time to graze in the forest. Occasionally it was sung while going bear hunting, and only exceptionally at bear funerals.

The bones of the bear were preserved to ensure resurrection and, thus, the survival of the species. The skull was taken in

17   Y.H. Toivonen, 'Vaakalintu' in *Virittäjä* 35 (1931), 433; U. Harva, *Sammon ryöstö*, Porvoo-Helsinki 1943, 125-6; Heissig, *op. cit.*, 322-3; F.J. Oinas, *Studies in Finnic Folklore*, Finnish Literature Society/Indiana University Uralic and Altaic Series, Vol. 147, Mäntää 1985, 146-53.

procession to the forest and fastened to the sacred tree among the skulls of beasts killed previously. This procedure was to show the bear the way back to its forefathers in heaven.[18]

18. *The Origin of Fire* (47:67-364; 48:1-192).

Ukko of the air strikes fire. The fire drops to earth, causes much harm, and finally lands in Lake Alue, where a white-fish swallows the spark, a lake trout swallows the whitefish, and a pike swallows the trout. Since the pike cannot be caught with a bast net, a flax-cord net is made, with which the fire is captured.

This episode is based on the Finnish-Karelian folk song of the origin of fire, amplified by additions and repetitions to comprise two poems in the *Kalevala*. In the folk song it is usually Ilmarinen and Väinämöinen, sometimes Ukko or the bird of the air, etc., who strike fire with three eagle's feathers. Older variants of the song reveal features that have parallels throughout the Arctic regions as far as the North American coastal areas. The striking of the spark with three eagle feathers by the bird of the air can be compared with the Arctic myth about the gigantic bird (a metaphor of thunder), which scratches trees with its stone claws. The motif of carrying the spark in the belly of fish is likewise a feature belonging to the Arctic myth tradition. In the Finnish-Karelian folk song as well as in the Northwest American Indian tale it is usually a red salmon, in whose bowels fire is found. With the capture of the fire-swallowing fish, fire — originally possessed by animals — becomes human property.[19]

19. *'I am Forging a Neck Ring'* (49:345-362).

After Louhi has hidden the sun and moon inside a hill, Ilmarinen forges tools to tear the hill open. Louhi assumes the shape of a bird and flies to see what he is doing. Ilmarinen says that he is forging a neck ring with which to fasten Louhi

18 Kuusi, *op. cit.* (1963), 41-4; Haavio, *op. cit.* (1967), 26-31; Anna-Leena Kuusi, *op. cit.* (1976), 252-3.
19 Kuusi, *op. cit.* (1963), 55-60; U. Harva, *Finno-Ugric, Siberian* in *The Mythology of All Races*, ed. C.J.A. MacCulloch, New York 1964, 235-8; Anna-Leena Kuusi, *op. cit.* (1976), 261; Kuusi, Bosley, Branch, *op. cit.*, 524-5.

to the mountain. Louhi gets frightened and releases the luminaries.

The song about the forging of the neck ring in the *Kalevala* is based on the Finnish-Karelian folk song about chaining the smith of Hiisi or the devil. The smith-devil is forging fetters to chain the Creator. When the smith asks God about the thickness of the Creator's neck, God responds that it is as thick as his (the smith's) own. The smith puts the ring on his neck, and God locks it.

The legend of the chaining of the devil is international. It appears widely in Europe — in Estonia, Lithuania, Belorussia, Ukraine, Germany, Italy, etc., and further in the Caucasus and Near East. Haavio argued that in Karelia and Finland the legend is of Russian origin. The Russian prose legend was converted into a poem in the eastern song area, whereas in Northeast Finland it was retained in prose.

The fact that the legend is known in Belorussia and the Ukraine, but not in Russia, would strengthen our view about the significant role that Belorussia and the Ukraine have had in the migration of southeastern and southern traditions to the Balto-Finns.

The Estonian version, which is in prose and appears primarily in the southeastern corner of Estonia and sporadically in Central Estonia, has obviously come directly from Belorussia.[20]

20. *Marjatta's Search for Her Son* (50:347-424).

After Marjatta's son slips away from her knee, she searches for him. She asks the star and the moon, but they do not tell. Then she asks the sun, and the sun discloses his whereabouts.

The song of Marjatta's son is identical with the Ingrian-Karelian folk song, 'The Search for the Lost Child', which describes St Mary's search for the Child Jesus. Jesus, like Marjatta's son, disappears, and she inquires of the road, the moon and the sun. The latter tells where he is. The song has grown out of the motif in *Luke* 2:41-52, in which the twelve

---

20 K. Krohn, 'Der gefangene Unhold' in *Finnisch-ugrische Forschungen* 7 (1908), 120-84; M. Haavio, 'Hiiden sepän kahlinta' in *Kalevalaseuran Vuosikirja* 18 (1938), 20-52.

year old Jesus disappears from the temple. It is known widely in Europe.

As I have shown, the closest variants to this song appear in the Ukrainian *koljadas*, glorifying songs sung at Christmas. The song with its sun-moon-star symbolism may reflect the Iranian-Slavic sun cult.[21]

III

In the songs and motifs of Eastern origin in the *Kalevala* several strata can be distinguished.

1. The Arctic tradition in the *Kalevala* is represented by hunting myths ('The Bear Song' — 17, 'The Demon's Elk' — 7), cosmological myths ('Väinämöinen's Knee Wound' — 6), and shamanism ('The Snake Fence' — 12). These myths occur in Northern Eurasia among the Lapps, Samoyeds, Ob-Ugrians, and other North Siberian peoples, partly (17, 18) also in the coastal areas of the North American continent. Several of them (7, 6, 17) have their closest correspondences among the Ob-Ugrians.

2. Numerous ancient songs in the *Kalevala* go back to the myths of Oriental high cultures. Here belong the songs based on cosmogonic myths ('The Creation Song' — 1, 'The Creation of the Sea-bed' — 4), on the cult and culture myths ('The Great Oak' — 3, 'The Great Ox' — 10, 'The Sower' — 2), on shamanism ('Lemminkäinen's Trip to the North' — 1, 'Lemminkäinen's Death and Resurrection' — 8), and on religious myths ('I am Forging a Neck Ring' — 19). The corresponding myths are found in the Eastern Mediterranean and in Southern Asia as far as Japan, some (1, 3), even in South America. Lemminkäinen's songs are of Egyptian origin.

3. A couple of shamanistic songs or individual motifs have their correspondences in the folklore of Turko-Tatar and

---

21 M. Haavio, *Suomalaisen muinaisrunouden maailma*, Provoo-Helsinki 1935, 67-77; Kuusi, *op. cit.* (1963), 292-300; Oinas, *op. cit.* (1969), 86-92; Kuusi, *op. cit.* (1980), 233-4.

other Altaic peoples in Central Asia. Such is the earth-sky formula of the gigantic bird ('One Wing Brushed the Clouds' — 16) and Väinämöinen's riding on the sea ('He Took His Straw Stallion' — 5). The second version of the song of the visit to a deceased shaman ('Antero Vipunen's Song' — 9) is obviously a hybrid; it is basically Lapp, but recreated under the influence of a Russian tale of Altaic origin.

4. From the Slavs (primarily Russians) come some cruel songs or recurrent motifs, connected with kidnapping and murder ('What Has Run Across here?' — 15, 'You killed Your Former Wedded Wife' — 14), and with a bloody family feud ('Is That Dense Smoke or a Dark Cloud?' — 13); the latter has become a formula and has been introduced into various songs. The tender biblical song ('Marjatta's Search for Her Son' — 20), though primarily Slavic, may have its roots further southeast.

The oldest songs of Eastern origin in the *Kalevala* belong to the first two groups. The songs of Group 1 are based on the myths of the Arctic, circumpolar tradition, and those of Group 2 on the Oriental tradition. In his classfication of the ancient strata of Finnish-Karelian folk songs, Matti Kuusi has shown that these two groups differ in one respect:
    Whereas the paleo-Arctic components of the Finnish-Lapp folk tradition are almost completely unknown to the Estonians, the Oriental myths occur in the most cases in Estonian-Finnish common tradition.[22]
This difference can be interpreted as testifying to the fact that most of the songs of Arctic origin were created after the Finns had arrived in Finland, but the majority of the myths of Oriental provenance must have come to the Balto-Finnic area before the forefathers of the Finns and Estonians separated. As the Oriental myths were in prose, they had to be clothed in verse form by the Balto-Finns. This was done either before the splitting of the group, or afterwards, by the Estonians and Finns individually. To the songs created before the splitting up of the group (i.e., to the common Estonian-Finnish stratum

22 Kuusi, *op. cit.* (1982), 162.

belong 'The Creation Song', 'The Creation of the Sea-bed', and 'The Great Oak', as the syntactic-stylistic analysis testifies.

The songs and motifs of Group 3 were created on the basis of the Central Asiatic tales and songs, which reached the Karelians and Finns around the end of the Middle Ages. Those in Group 4 arose somewhat later.

In the migration of the Oriental myths to Karelia and Finland, Byzantium and the Slavs (among others, the Ukrainians and Belorussians) played an essential role. The Arctic myths and songs arrived there through the Lapps and other Finno-Ugric peoples, partly through the Russians. The songs and motifs of Turco-Tatar origin reached the Finnish area through the mediation of the Russians.

It should be pointed out that some of the elements listed as of Eastern origin, may actually represent parallel developments, caused by the similarity of the ideas of peoples on a comparable cultural level.

THE ROOTS OF FINNO-UGRIAN FOLK EPIC

HEINRICH WAGNER
(Dublin Institute for Advanced Studies)

I

When I came to Ireland for the first time in October 1945 I had the good fortune to establish a close scholarly relationship with Ernst Lewy who at that time was one of the few specialists in Finno-Ugrian languages in Central and Western Europe. Lewy, a former Professor of General Linguistics in Berlin University, had escaped with his family from Germany during the thirties and was living in Dublin. Later he became a Professor at the Royal Irish Academy and spent the rest of his life in Dublin. In the course of my Irish studies I found time, again and again, to visit and work under Lewy who introduced me systematically to the field of little known Finno-Ugrian languages, in particular Čeremiss and Mordvin, languages of Fennic origin spoken on both sides of the river Volga.

Lewy possessed a first-hand knowledge of these languages because, during World War I, he had made, in Germany, vast collections of linguistic and folkloristic material from native speakers in prisoner-of-war camps which were inhabited by members of many non-Russian-speaking nationalities. As a matter of fact, also in a prisoner-of-war camp, he studied an Eastern Caucasian language too. Another special subject of Lewy's was Basque which, like other scholars, he believed to be connected with Caucasian. Not only myself but also some young Irish scholars, in particular Conn Ó Cléirigh, the present Professor of Linguistics at University College Dublin, and Patrick L. Henry, the Professor of Old English at University College Galway, profited greatly from Lewy's teaching of all these languages. He also entertained visitors from abroad who studied his work.

In 1934 Wolfgang Steinitz, one of Lewy's pupils in Berlin

347

published a pioneer work concerning the most characteristic
stylistic features of the Kalevala and of Finno-Karelian folk
poetry in general, namely parallelism. His monograph was
published in the *Folklore Fellows Communications* series of
which Séamus Ó Duilearga, founder member of the Irish Folklore Commission and its long-serving Honorary Director, was,
at a later stage, an editor. On account of his Jewish background and his idealistic Communist convictions, Steinitz, like
Lewy, had to leave Germany and went to Russia where he
became an authority on Ostyak, the most remote of all Finno-
Ugrian languages, spoken east of the Ural mountains on the
river Ob. After the war he became Lewy's successor in the
old Humboldt University of East Berlin. Steinitz's work on
Ostyak is now continued by a school of scholars in the University of Munich.

A third member of Lewy's Finno-Ugrian school in Berlin
was the Indo-Europeanist Hermann Jacobsohn. Because of
his Jewish origin he was dismissed from Berlin University and
he committed suicide in 1933. Jacobsohn's book entitled
Arier und Finno-Ugrier, which, according to its author, could
not have been written without Lewy's help, is a classic and
has been reprinted recently. In it he discusses the prehistoric
links which must have existed between Finno-Ugrian in
Central and Southern Russia and an archaic form of Indo-
Iranian from which Old Persian and Sanscrit are derived. A
considerable amount of Finno-Ugrian words are loan-words
from Indo-Iranian or perhaps from a primitive form of Indo-
European itself. The key-language in these studies is, as Lewy
and others before him saw clearly, Mordvin, which was the
most southerly of all Finno-Ugrian languages and is still spoken
in a wide area on both sides of the Volga river south of
Kazan. I met Steinitz once in Helsinki and discussed with him
all these problems. His death occurred shortly before Lewy's.
Much of what I have to say here derives directly from what I
have learnt from Lewy and Steinitz as well as from Jacobsohn's book. The main ideas, however, are my own.

Needless to say, Finnish scholars might well describe me as
a dilettante in the field of Finno-Ugrian studies. It is a fact,
however, that comparative studies on such a wide scale can
only be carried out by people who know a little of everything

or, alternatively, by teams of specialists who, however, can seldom be housed under one roof. Visits to Lapland and Northern Finland have provided me with some limited practical knowledge of the Finno-Ugrian languages of Scandinavia, and Dr Öpik, a physicist at Queen's University, Belfast and an Estonian by birth, gave me an adequate introduction to his native language which is closely related to Finnish.

All these biographical details indicate that I have profited from various personal upheavals which affected scholars in the thirties and forties of this century and which have brought together people who otherwise would never have met. I may add that the main reason for my being a Professor of Celtic in Ireland over the last 27 years is Julius Pokorny's departure from Berlin and his escape to Switzerland in 1943. Pokorny, also of Jewish background, had been Professor of Celtic in Berlin and belonged to the same school of scholars as Lewy, Jacobsohn and Steinitz. It was on Pokorny's recommendation that I went to Ireland in October 1945 and he also introduced me to Lewy, who at that time had published his great work on *Der Bau der europäischen Sprachen* for the Royal Irish Academy (*Proceedings of the Royal Irish Academy*, Section C, Vol. 48, No. 2 [1942]).

II

By way of introduction to the main subject, I now wish briefly to analyse the first lines of Lönnrot's *Kalevala* which with the help of Anton Schiefner's German translation of 1852, an original copy of which I inherited from Lewy's library, I have been able to analyse even though with some difficulty. I must emphasise, however, that my knowledge of Finnish and in particular of the language of Finnish folk poetry is minimal. My English translation is as literal as possible.

1	*M*ieleni *m*inun tekevi,	'My mood urges me,
1a	*A*ivoni *a*jattelevi	My brain drives me,
2	*L*ähteäni *l*aulamahan,	That I go to sing,
2a	*S*aa'ani *s*anelemahan,	That I proceed to recite,
3	*S*ukuvirttä *s*uoltamahan,	To tell the song of the tribe,
3a	*L*ajivirttä *l*aulamahan;	To sing the song of the kin;

4	Sanat suussani sulavat,	Words melt in my mouth,
4a	Puhe'et putoelevat,	Sounds slip out,
5	Kielelleni kerkiävät,	They escape from my tongue,
5a	Hampahilleni hajoovat.	They open up my teeth.'

It is not my intention here to discuss the metre of these lines. The recently published *Finnish Folk Poetry. Epic* tells us that 'Kalevala poetry is cast in unrhymed, non-strophic trochaic tetrameters'[1] (cf. *lähteäni laulamahan*). Instead of rhyme, alliteration is used though not quite regularly. The most striking feature of this poetry, however, is parallelism. As our specimen shows, in each pair of verses the second line echoes the first line in different synonymous or analogous words. There are exceptions; unparalleled verses do occasionally occur. These often contain a personal name, cf. Runo III, 51: *sanoi nuori Joukahainen*, 'said the young J.'. As I mentioned earlier, parallelism in Finnish folk poetry was studied by Steinitz in his doctoral thesis. His work, however, is not based on the Kalevala itself but on the poetry collected from the folk poet, Arhippa Perttunen, who lived in the first half of the nineteenth century. Perttunen's repertoire of almost 6000 verses exceeded the amount of material collected from any other folk-singer known in his time. The following is a specimen of Perttunen's parallelistic poetry:

Rekehensä reutosihen,	'Into his sledge he threw himself,
Korjahan korentelihen[2]	Into the sledge he climbed'

In a short appreciation of the Finnish folk epic in 1910, on the occasion of the 75th anniversary of the publication of Lönnrot's *Kalevala*, a Norwegian authority on Finno-Ugrian languages, J. Qvigstad, said that the *Kalevala* reminded him of Hebrew poetry through its parallelism and of Old Norse poetry through its alliteration.[3] But as early as 1697, Er.

1 K. Bosley, M. Kuusi, M. Branch, *Finnish Folk Poetry. Epic*, Helsinki 1977, 62.
2 W. Steinitz, *Der Parallelismus in der finnisch-karelischen Volksdichtung*, FF Communications 115, Helsinki 1934, 30.
3 *Finnisch-Ugrische Forschungen*, 10 (1910), 26.

Cajanus, in a thesis entitled *Linguarum ebraeae et finnicae convenientia* (Åbo 1697)[4], referred to parallelism as being a characteristic feature both of Finnish and Hebrew poetry. Finnish parallelism, however, has its closest counterpart in Mordvin folk epic. The systematic collection of Mordvin folk poetry is largely due to the efforts of the Finnish scholar Heikki Paasonen who began his work at the end of the last century. He not only collected an enormous amount of material himself, but also engaged the assistance of some native Mordvins in collecting material for his archive in Helsinki. These collections were published after Paasonen's death under the title *Mordwinische Volksdichtung*.[5] Thanks to Paasonen and his successors, in particular Paavo Ravila, a former Chancellor of the University of Helsinki, we now possess in print many thousands of lines of Mordvin folk poetry. As Lewy and others before and after him have seen, Mordvin is, for various reasons, a language of the greatest historical importance.

First of all, Mordvin is of Finno-Ugrian stock, like Čeremiss (called Mari by the natives who were known as Merja in mediaeval times) and the Permian languages, Ziryene and Votyak. The same applies of course to Finnish and Estonian, as well as to some other minority languages in the Baltic area. These languages are known as West-Fennic. Lappish, though divergent from West-Fennic, in particular in phonological matters, is also a Finno-Ugrian language. It is probable that the Lapps spoke an entirely different language before Finnish was imposed on them by the advancing West-Finns.[6] We know that most of Eastern Scandinavia as far south as Lakes Onega and Ladoga was originally occupied by Lapps who gradually retreated northwards when the West-Finns began to penetrate modern Finland and Karelia. The origin of the West-Finns and of the primitive Finno-Ugrians in general must be sought in an area of central Western Russia near the river Volga, an

---

4 Cf. Steinitz, *op. cit.*, 14, 3.
5 Henceforth *MV*; Vols. 1 (1938), 5 (1977), 6 (1977) = *Mémoires de la Société Finno-Ougrienne* 77, 161 and 162. Two further volumes which have not been available to me have since been published.
6 Cf. H. Wagner, 'Nordeuropäische Lautgeographie', *Zeitschrift für celtische Philologie* 29 (1964), 230ff.

area bordering on and partly covering that now occupied by the modern Volga-Finns and Permians. This means of course that Mordvin is spoken on old Finno-Ugrian territory while the historical position of the West-Finns is due to migrations of Finno-Ugrian speaking people from central Western Russia to the Baltic.

Mordvin, Čeremiss, Ziryene, Votyak, West-Fennic and Lappish as spoken in mediaeval and modern times are quite different languages, though the differences between them, especially in grammar, may not be as great as those between Indo-European languages such as primitive Celtic and Germanic. In its grammar, with its suffixed definite article and its objective pronominal affixes of the verb, Mordvin also shows certain structural affinities with Balkan and Caucasian languages. This was at least Lewy's view. From a very early period Finno-Ugrian of Central and Southern Russia is certain to have been in contact with Indo-Iranian. These contacts persisted from prehistoric to mediaeval times; Iranian-speaking tribes, descendants of the ancient Scythians, can be traced in Southern Russia and Hungary in historical times. Some of them moved into the Caucasus where Ossetic, an Iranian language, is still spoken north of Georgia. Linguistic contacts between Finno-Ugrian and Indo-Iranian consist mainly of Indo-Iranian loan words in the Finno-Ugrian languages. In this respect, Mordvin, since it used to be the most southerly of all Finno-Ugrian languages, is undoubtedly itself deserving of special study, particularly from the point of view of Indo-European studies.

Another special aspect of Mordvin is that its phonological system, as shown by Steinitz and others before him,[7] is similar to that of Russian. In my own opinion, it is most likely that Russian owes its phonological development to a southern Finno-Ugrian substratum which became active when Slavonic extended itself from the Pripjet area in South-Western Russia to northern territories previously occupied by Finno-Ugrian speaking populations. Mordvin is, therefore, also of paramount interest to Slavonic scholars. I may add that there are

7 Cf. *Geschichte des finnisch-ugrischen Vokalismus*, Stockholm 1944.

some grammatical features which link Mordvin not only with Russian but also with Ossetic. Čeremiss, on the other hand, shows closer affinities with Čuvash, a language of Turkish origin, still spoken west of Kazan between the territories of the Mordvins to the south west and those of the Čeremiss to the north. The territories of these non-Slavic-speaking populations are now known as the Mari (i.e. Čeremiss), Čuvash and Mordvin Autonomous Soviet Republics, respectively.

Undoubtedly the study of Finno-Ugrian languages and folk literatures is a very complicated subject. Before you can enter into it, you have to know Finnish, Hungarian, Russian and German, as the standard works on this subject are written in these languages. To understand the history of Čeremiss and Mordvin, one also has to involve oneself in Slavonic, Baltic, Turkish and Indo-Iranian studies. Only a few scholars, among them the Finns Paasonen and Ravila, the Hungarian Munkácsi, the Russians Šachmatov and Serebrennikov and, in Western Europe, Ernst Lewy complied with all these demands.

With regard to parallelism in Finnish and Mordvin folk poetry one has to go even further afield. First of all I shall present here a specimen of Mordvin folk poetry. It is taken from *MV* 6 (cf. note 5), the contents of which were collected by a Mordvin scholar of the name Ignatij Zorin, who collaborated with Paasonen. It is the beginning of a song which was sung by village girls on the occasion of the Easter festival. The girls dress the most beautiful of their number in festive clothing and send her out of the village towards the east where she hides herself. The other girls proceed — singing — to the entrance gate of the village in order to receive Easter in the person of the dressed-up girl. They bring with them some beer and sing the following lines (*MV* 6, 2):

Ťejťeŕ-kakat, ťejťeŕ-ejť!	'Girls, Girls!
Bojar-avat, azrafkat!	Bojar-women, Ladies!
Ḿeźeń koŕas ḿiń sịńek,	What purpose-for we came,
Ḿeźe ťezẹj purnịḿiź?	What here gathered-us?
Śeń koŕas ḿiń ńej sịńek,	This purpose-for we now came,
Śe ńej ḿińek purnịḿiź.	This now us gathered-us.
Purnaýińek ťejťeŕ-ejť,	We gathered, girls,

Míń ińe-čiń učomo,   We great-day to expect,
Mazį čińeń śŕečamo.   Beautiful day to receive.
Ko jondo sį ińe-čiś?   Which direction-from comes great
                             day?

Ko jondo sį mazį čiś?   Which direction-from comes beau-
                             tiful-day?

Či-ĺiśima son jondo,   Sun-rise it direction-from,
Ńiške-pazoń ikeĺde.   Sky-god's front-from.
Mazįńestę naŕažaś,   Beautifully it adorned itself,
parińeste son purnaź.   Best it is made up.'

Among the words included in this text are the following which may serve to illustrate the historical complexity of Mordvin vocabulary: *tejteŕ*, 'daughter, girl', borrowed from Baltic, cf. Lith. *duktė*, 'daughter', also in Finn. *tytär*, 'daughter'; *ava*, 'mother', compared by Paasonen with Čuvash *aBa* id.; *azrafka*, 'Lady', from *azoro*, 'Lord' + *ava*, 'woman', *azoro* from Indo-Iranian *asura-*, Sanscrit *asura-*, Old Persian *Ahura*; *mazi*, 'beautiful' = Iranian *maz-*, 'great', *ińe*, 'great = Sanscrit *inas* id.[?]. *naŕažaś*, 'adorned itself', borrowed from Russ. cf. *naražjatı-sja*, 'dress oneself beautifully'. There may also have been early connections between the primitive Baltic people, the ancestors of the Lithuanians and Latvians, and the Finno-Ugrians of central Russia; Mordvin *tejteŕ*, dialectically *texteŕ*, is almost certainly a borrowing from Baltic (cf. Lithuanian *duktė*, gen. *dukteŕs*), cf. *Suomen Kielen Etymologinen Sanakirja* 6, 1463.

Taking Finno-Karelian folk poetry in general and comparing it with the vast bulk of Mordvin folk poetry, there seems to me to be no doubt that there is a direct historical connection between the two folk literatures, namely with regard to the feature of parallelism. Paasonen thought that the metres exhibited by Mordvin poetry were of eastern Slavonic origin. In Mordvin we can distinguish various syllabic types. Roman Jakobson, however, a pupil of the famous Trubetzkoy, the father of modern linguistics, has maintained more recently that Paasonen's view is unlikely to be correct.[8] According to

8 Cf. R. Jakobson, *Selected Writings* 5, The Hague: Mouton 1979, 160 ff.'

Jakobson, the Mordvins may have preserved a type of poetry which was current before the expansion of Slavonic civilisation and language to Central and Northern European Russia.

In his book of 1934, Steinitz referred briefly to the fact that parallelistic poetry is characteristic also of the folk epic of the Ostyaks and, to a lesser extent, that of the Voguls. As I have said before, Ostyak and Vogul are representatives of the Ugrian branch of Finno-Ugrian from which Hungarian is also derived. The Ostyaks and Voguls, generally described as Ob-Ugrians, now live east of the Ural mountains on both sides of the river Ob. Ostyak folk poetry became known on account of the activities of the Hungarian scholar Anton Reguly, who studied among the Ostyaks in the forties of the last century, though his collections were not published before the end of that same century, long after Reguly's death at the age of 39. As the language of Ostyak folk poetry is beyond my comprehension, I can only judge from the German translations given by Josef Pápay in the edition of Reguly's and his own Ostyak material published in 1905, a rare book in Western Europe, which I have also inherited from Lewy's library. Since then a metrical and stylistic analysis of Ostyak and Vogul folk poetry has been presented by Robert Austerlitz.[9] From this study it becomes clear that we might be entitled to speak of parallelism as being the most characteristic feature of Finno-Ugrian folk poetry. The Ob-Ugrians separated themselves from the Finno-Ugrian stock in prehistoric or early historical times and at an unknown date moved to areas east of the Ural mountains. The fact that the Ob-Ugrian and the Volga-Fennic tongues, though related, are very different, is perhaps in itself proof of the antiquity of parallelism as the most characteristic feature in the poetry of both these linguistic groups. The apparent absence of a similar type of folk tradition in the literature of the Čeremiss may be due to the strong Turkish over-layer in the traditions of this nation. But I am speaking here rather from instinct than knowledge.

9   R. Austerlitz, *Ob-Ugric Metrics*, FF Communications 174, Helsinki 1958.

III

Pursuing completely different problems, I have also been involved since my student days in Semitic and Hamitic linguistics. From time to time various scholars have asked themselves why Insular Celtic shares important phonological and grammatical features with the Hamito-Semitic languages of Northern Africa and adjacent Asia. Among the languages concerned are Berber, Egyptian, Hebrew, Arabic and Aramaic. In 1899, Morris-Jones, one of the greatest of all Welsh scholars, published a paper in which, on strong linguistic grounds, he promoted a theory according to which the pre-Celtic people of the British Isles spoke Hamito-Semitic dialects, which, as a substratum, contributed to the making of Insular Celtic. Pokorny and myself as well as a few other scholars have further developed this research which, however, has remained controversial up to the present day, particularly when taking into account the views of those scholars who know nothing about Hamito-Semitic.

The study of Hamito-Semitic languages compelled me to have a close look at the language of Ugarit. Ugarit, modern Ras Shamra, was an ancient city on the Syrian coast about a hundred miles north of Tripoli. One of its later archaeological layers yielded archives containing texts written in a cuneiform alphabet. The texts contain the religious literature of a Semitic-speaking people whose language proved to be fairly close to the language of the Old Testament. As Ugaritic was written in a period between 1400 and 1200 B.C., it precedes chronologically the oldest stratum of Hebrew poetry which dates from about 1000 B.C. The period between 1400 and 1200 B.C. is known as the Tell Amarna Age and was a period of great political and cultural activity among the various powers of Mesopotamia, Syria, Egypt and Eastern Asia Minor. According to the specialists Ugaritic literature is of importance, not only for the study of the Old Testament but also of Homeric Greek literature, because Ugarit was centrally situated between the various cultures of the Eastern Mediterranean world. Practically all Ugaritic texts are mythological in content and clearly poetical, i.e. non-prosaic. Like Finnish, Mordvin and Homeric poetry, Ugaritic poetry is non-strophic. In each line there is a restricted, but not clearly defined number of syllables. To detect any sort of metre is difficult because the Ugaritic alphabet, like the Hebrew and Egyptian alphabets, is purely consonantic. It has been maintained, perhaps correctly, that Ugaritic poetry, from a modern point of view, is non-metrical. It exhibits, however, the same kind of parallelism which is found in Finnish, Mordvin and Old Hebrew poetry. It could be said, therefore, that parallelism is the one and only metrical feature of Ugaritic poetry. Gordon's *Ugaritic Manual* contains a detailed chapter on this feature from which I quote the following specimens:

(a) wrgm lktr wḫss   'and speak to Ktr-w-Ḥss,
    tny lHyn dhrš ydm   declare to Hyn of craft of hands'

(Ktr-w-Ḥss and Hyn are names of one and the same god).

(b) klb arḫ lᶜglh   'like the heart of the cow towards her calf,

    klb tat limrh   like the heart of the ewe towards her lamb,

    km lb ᶜnt atr bᶜl   so is the heart of Anat after Baʿlʼ[10]

Steinitz in his description of Finnish parallelism, distinguishes between synonymous parallelism and analogous parallelism. The same distinction is borne out in these specimens from the Ugaritic corpus. In the first of these the two lines are strictly synonymous, the poet using two names of one and the same god. He also makes use of two synonymous verbs meaning 'to speak'. A systematic comparison of the parallelism of the Finno-Ugrian folk epic with that of Ugaritic mythological poetry, could yield astonishing results. One has also to consider the fact that important sections of the West-Finnish and Mordvin epics, not to mention the epic of the Ob-Ugrians, contain mythological material. It is probable that Ugaritic literature reflects the pre-monotheistic religion

10 C.H. Gordon, *Ugaritic Manual*, Vol. 1, Roma 1955, 109.

of the Canaanites and precedes that which is laid down in the
Old Testament.

Ugaritic parallelism, however, does not mark the end of
our road. Gordon, in his *Ugaritic Manual* (*op. cit.*, 108) says:

> ... it should be stated that unit lengths, types of parall-
> elism, strophic structures etc., can be duplicated in the
> literatures of Mesopotamia, Asia Minor, Phoenicia, Egypt ...

It becomes clear that parallelism in Hebrew poetry is
inherited from a type of mythological literature which was
current in Syria and Palestine in the second millennium B.C.[11]

In search of a solution to different linguistic problems[12] and
in attempting to trace the roots of Celtic mythology,[13] I
embarked, some twenty years ago, on the study of Sumerian,
the oldest attested language of the world, spoken in the third
millennium B.C., in what is now modern Iraq. Like Ugaritic
poetry, a great deal of literature transmitted in this language
contains mythological material reflecting the religion or
religions of the ancient Mesopotamian populations. It does
not require much reading of Sumerian mythological texts to
recognize that parallelism is the most outstanding feature
of Sumerian poetry. As in the case of Ugaritic poetry the
specialists seem to think that, apart from parallelism, there
are no other metrical features inherent in Sumerian poetry.
Parallelism, therefore, is the only criterion which enables us
to distinguish between prose and poetic language. Like Ugaritic
and Finno-Ugrian poetry, Sumerian poetry is non-strophic
and was probably accompanied by some sort of musical instruments. I present the following specimens from a Sumerian

---

11 I have been informed on this subject by Professor Cathcart, Depart-
    ment of Semitic Languages, University College Dublin, but I shall
    leave the problems connected with Hebrew poetry aside, as I am
    not qualified to speak about them. For further information on this
    subject, cf. W.G.E. Watson, *Classical Hebrew Poetry*, Sheffield
    1984.

12 H. Wagner, 'The Typological Background of the Ergative Con-
    struction', *Proceedings of the Royal Irish Academy*, Vol. 78, C,
    No. 3 (1978), 37 ff. and H. Wagner, *Das Hethitische vom Stand-
    punkte der typologischen Sprachgeographie*, Pisa 1985.

13 H. Wagner, 'Origins of Pagan Irish Religion', *Zeitschrift für cel-
    tische Philologie* 38 (1981), 1ff.

myth composed around 2000 B.C. Specimens (a) and (b) illustrate synonymous, specimen (c) analogous parallelism:

(a) a-a-zu duga-ni mah-àm   'father-thy (of) word-his great-is

Enki-ke daha-ni mah-àm   Enki's remark-his great-is'

(i.e. 'what your father has said is great, what Enki [the god of water and creator of all civilisation] has remarked is great').[14]

(b) a šu-zu nu-tag   'water hand-your not-touched
a meri-zu nu-tag   water fingers-your-not-touched'[15]

(c) lugal-e gu hé-emma-b-gaz-e,   'the king cattle may slaughter,
udu hé-emma-b-šár-e,   sheep he may slaughter,
kaš bur-a hé-em-dé-e   beer he may pour into a vessel'[16]

As I have already said, parallelism is the one and only feature which distinguishes prose from poetry in the old Mesopotamian literary tradition and the same can be said of the ancient North Western Semitic literature preserved in Ugarit. The striking similarity between Finno-Ugrian parallelism, documented in the Finnish, Mordvin and Ob-Ugrian folk epics, and parallelism in Sumerian and Ugaritic religious poetry of the third and second millenium B.C. can hardly be purely coincidental and of no historical significance at all. Since prehistoric times, the Balkans and Southern Russia have been constantly influenced by the civilisations of Asia Minor, Mesopotamia and Syria. Sumerian tablets of the so-called Djemdet Nasr period, about 2800-2700 B.C., have been found in the Romanian province of Siebenbürgen (cf. *Ériu* 26 (1975), 12, n. 26). They imply that Sumerian culture must have affected South Eastern Europe at a very early date. There

14 Gertrud Farber-Flügge, *Der Mythos 'Inanna und Enki'*, Rome 1973, 2, iii, ll. 50-51.
15 *Ibid.*, 2, iii, l. 37.
16 *Ibid.*, 2, iv. ll. 45-6.

can be hardly any objection to the view that Finno-Ugrian-speaking people populated territories adjacent to Southern Russia and the North Eastern Balkans as early as the beginning of the second millennium B.C. I strongly suspect, therefore, that parallelism of the type found in the Mordvin, Ob-Ugrian and Finnish folk epics is ultimately borrowed from ancient Mesopotamian poetry as transmitted in Sumerian and Akkadian texts of the third and second millennium B.C.

The kind of parallelism which dominates the structure of Finnish folk poetry is reflected in somewhat different form in ancient Germanic poetry, in particular in Old Saxon and Anglo-Saxon literature. The Old Saxon *Heliand*, a ninth century paraphrase of the New Testament, narrated in Old Germanic style and poetical language, and the Anglo-Saxon heroic epic, *Beowulf*, are characterized by a stylistic feature which Germanists call variation, half-lines of one verse being echoed by different words in the next line. Thus:

(a) *Beow. 258f.*

| Him sē *y*ldesta *o*nds-warode, | 'Them the eldest answered, |
| *W*erodes *w*īsa, *w*ord-hord onleac | people's leader, word-treasure he opened up'.[17] |

(b) *Beow. 102ff.*

Waes sē grimma *g*ǣst *G*rendel hāten,	'Was this grim ghost Grendel called,
*M*ǣre *m*earcstapa, sē the *m*ōras heold,	the famous borderland walker, he who moors held,
*F*en ond *f*aesten.	moorland and stronghold'.[18]

(c) *Heliand 115f.*

| Hêt that *fr*ôd gumo *f*orht ni wâri, | 'Said that (the) wise man frightened should not be, |
| Hêt that he *i*m ni *a*nd-rêdi | Said that he himself not should fear'.[19] |

---

17 F. Holthausen, ed., *Beowulf*, 7th ed., Heidelberg 1938, 258f.
18 *Ibid.*, 102ff.
19 O. Behaghel, ed., *Heliand*, 4th ed., Halle 1933, 115f.

(d) *Heliand 1381*

So sprac he thô *sp*âh-	'So spoke he then wisely and
lîco endi sagda *sp*el	told God's word,
godes,	
*L*êrde the *l*andes uuard	taught the land's protector his
*l*iudi sîne	people'.[20]

Semantic repetition of lines or half-lines — as Finnish parallelism as well as Germanic variation may be described — is not the only link between the two literatures. There is of course also the feature of alliteration which is of paramount importance in both poetries. Alliteration, on the other hand, is not characteristic of Mordvin nor of Ob-Ugrian poetry and the same applies to Ugaritic and Hebrew poetry (although examples of it can be found in any of these literatures).

Alliteration in Finnish folk poetry may be a borrowing from ancient Germanic tradition. In Germanic as well as in Finnish tradition, it seems to be connected with the fact that both languages exhibit initial word stress. The West Finnish languages and Lappish are the only Fennic languages which possess this stress-system. The others lack, therefore, the linguistic pre-condition for the development of alliteration as a more or less strict metrical device. There must have existed close contacts between the Baltic Finns and Early Germanic tribes, because early Finnish has borrowed a number of words from primitive Germanic (such as Finnish *kuningas*, 'king'). These borrowings must have taken place in the course of the first centuries A.D. at the latest. The fact that the Finnish word *ja(h)*, 'and' is identical with its Gothic counterpart suggests strongly that Eastern Germanic language and civilisation had considerable influence on the early Finnish language and institutions.

Since, however, alliteration is also the most striking feature of the oldest Insular Celtic poetry I may be allowed to discuss briefly Early Irish poetry. First of all it must be mentioned that Old Irish also possessed initial word-stress and the same feature may have applied to primitive Brythonic. I shall confine myself to archaic Old Irish poetry as discovered and

20 *Ibid.*, 1381.

described long ago by Kuno Meyer. Archaic Old Irish poetry consists of a small number of fragments embedded in the genealogies of the Leinster people. Some years ago I re-edited what can be described as one of the oldest if not the oldest poem written in the Irish language. Its subject is the destruction of *Dind Ríg*, lit. meaning 'The Height of the Kings', a pre-historic citadel situated in Co. Carlow. Similar *Togail-*, i.e. destruction-poems, are preserved in archaic Welsh. From the subject point of view one is reminded again of Near Eastern poetry, in which destruction of holy citadels is a familiar theme. The oldest example is the poem 'Lamentation over the Destruction of Ur', a long parallelistic composition in Late Sumerian published by S.N. Kramer in *Assyriological Studies*, No. 12, Chicago 1940. This Old Irish poem is transmitted in a number of manuscripts and its original form, therefore, is somewhat uncertain. I would read it now as follows:

1. Dind *R*íg *r*úad — *r*opo *t*úaim *t*enbath,
2. *T*richa **r*íg — *r*o- *b*rón *b*ebsat.
3. *B*ruisius *b*reosius — *b*ár-nia *l*ond Labraid,
4. *L*áith *E*lgae — *a*ue Luirc *L*oegairi.
5. Lugaid *l*oeg — *l*ond *s*anb Sétne,
6. Sochla *C*oel *C*obthach — *c*ond *M*áil Muiredach.
7. *M*andrais *a*rma — *a*thair *a*thar Ollomon,
8. Oirt *M*oen — *m*accu *á*in *A*ugaini.

'Dind Ríg red — the hill-face has become a kindled-fire!
Thirty kings have died in sorrow.
He crushed them, he broke them down, the fierce boar-champion Labraid,
The warrior of Elgae (i.e. Ireland), the grandson of Loegaire.
Lugaid a bull-calf, fierce (and) eager for spoils Sétne!
Famous Cobthach Coel, a chieftain Muiredach Máil!
He trod down the weapons, the father of the father of Ollom.
Moen killed the sons of glorious Augaine.'[21]

The metre of this poem is accentual. Each line consists of two half-lines containing two main stresses. This is also the

---

21. H. Wagner, 'The Archaic *Dind Ríg* Poem and Related Problems', *Ériu* 28 (1977), 1.

metre of Germanic verse as found, for example, in the famous
Old Saxon song of Hildebrand. Alliteration is prominent in
our Irish poem but, without going into details, different from
that found in Germanic poetry. We notice synonymous or
analogous parallelism between the first two half-lines and
between lines 3 and 4, 5 and 6, 7 and 8. Only the second line
stands out on its own. A detail of special interest concerns
the last pair of verses. The conqueror of Dind Ríg is Labraid
Loingsech. Labraid is called *loingsech*, 'the exile' because he
was believed to have attacked from Britain. The tradition
that the Leinstermen came from Britain is strong in semi-
historical Irish literature. But Labraid was also known as
Moen, 'the Dumb', while *Labraid* itself means etymologically
'the Speaker'. This name has undoubtedly a mythological
background. O'Rahilly compared *Labraid*, 'the Speaker' with
Aius Locutius, a divinity who in 390 B.C., according to
Roman tradition, had announced to the Romans the imminent
invasion of Gallic tribes. *Gudea* meaning 'the Speaker' was
the name of a famous Sumerian king who reigned at the end
of the third millennium B.C. In the last two verses of our
poem, apparently in order to produce a parallelistic couplet,
Labraid is mentioned in the first line as 'the father of the father
of Ollom' and in the second one by his epithet *Moen*, 'the
Dumb'. There are other examples in archaic Irish poetry which
exhibit a similar procedure: Another figure in semi-mytho-
logical Leinster tradition is *Fiachu Raiphtine* (or *Sraiphtine*),
raiphtine[22] meaning 'lightning'. Another poetic fragment
contains the following line:

daith-ruire *R*aiphtine — *r*opo *F*iachu *f*orderg
'a swift chieftain (was) Raiphtine, Fiachu was all red'.[23]

With this one may compare what Gordon[24] has to say
about mythological names in Ugaritic poetry:

'Some gods have names of the type 'A- and B-' [cf. K̲tr-
w-Ḫss in the specimen quoted above], which apparently
arose by identifying and combining names in the pantheon

22 Cf. *Ériu* 13 (1942), 184ff.
23 Cf. *Ériu* 28 (1977), 7.
24 *Op. cit.*, 51. Cf. also *Ériu* 26 (1975), 8.

or in some cases by combining a god's name with one of his epithets ... The names can be split for use in poetic parallelism'. Example: hlk ktr ky^cn wy^cn tdrq ḥss, 'the gait of K̲tr he sees, yea he sees the tread of Ḥss'.

The god in question is normally known as K̲tr-w-Ḥss (cf. specimen above (p. 357). It is not difficult to find similar examples in Mordvin songs:

Śeśke ńesį ńiśke-pazoś	'Immediately sees-it Niškepas-
sįnst oznumast	the their offering-their
Maŕasįńže veŕe-pazoś sįnst	hears-them Verepas-the their
valost	words-their.'[25]

Niške-pas and Vere-pas are different names of one and the same sky-god, the second part of these compounds (*pas*, dialectically *pavas*) being a borrowing from primitive Iranian *baga-*, 'god'.

In this context I may briefly refer to another stylistic feature which provides a link between archaic Irish and Finnish poetry. In his description of Finnish verse, Steinitz,[26] refers to the type of lines which he calls *Kettenverse* ('chain-verses'):

*Pilvess' p*ität *pisar*at,	'In the cloud long drops,
*pisar*issa *l*aajat *lammi*t,	in the drops great seas,
*Lammi*ss' on *veno* punaset,	in the seas are red boats,
*Vene*hessä nuoret miehet	in the boat young men'.

This kind of poem is also found in the corpus of archaic Irish and Welsh verse:

(a)   In an archaic Irish legal poem:[27]

5 sabaid *cuirm* thige	'Sticks (quarrels) in an ale-house,
6 *cuir* mescae;	Contracts made in drunkenness;
11 mórmaín *mrug*rechta:	The great substance of land-law:

25 *MV*, 5, 38, 4.
26 *Op. cit.*, (1934), 100.
27 D. Binchy, 'An archaic legal poem', *Celtica* 9 (1971), 156ff.

12 *mrogad* coicrích	Marking out (fresh) boundaries.
15 rann eter *com*orbu,	Partition among co-heirs,
16 *com*aithig do garmaim,	Summoning of neighbours.
24 cuirther *gellaib*,	(Neighbour-law) that is contracted by pledges
25 *gell*tar smachtaib miach,	(And) secured by fines (consisting) of sticks
27 lóg *ndíre*,	The value of penalties,
28 *díre* n-aurbai,	The penalty for breaching (a boundary fence)
67 dringid co fedo *forball*,	It extends to the undergrowth of the wood
68 *forball* ratho	The undergrowth of the fern.'

(b) *LL* 1634ff.[28]

Ailiu iath nHerend hermach muir . *mothach*	'I greet the land of Ireland, Rolling (is) the sea rich in product,
mothach sliab, *srathach*	Rich in product (is) the mountain-land full of glens,
srathach caill . *cithach*	Full of glens (is) the woodland endowed with showers,
cithach aub . *essach*	Endowed with showers (is) the river full of waterfalls,
essach loch lindmar	Full of waterfalls (is) the lake-land abounding in water.'

---

28 *The Book of Leinster* (= *LL*), 6 Vols., Dublin 1954-83. Cf. also A. Knoch, 'Ein irischer Sonderfall von Epizeuxis', *Zeitschrift für celtische Philologie* 22 (1941), 54-7.

(c)   *CT* iv, 4ff.[29]

     a chein tired imi yn *ryfed*,
     a *ryfed* mawr ac eur ac *awr*;
     ac *awr* a chet a *chyfriu*et
     a *chyfriuyant* a rodi *chwant*
     chwant oe rodi yr vy llochi etc., etc.

IV

We have dealt with those poetic traditions of Northern and Eastern Europe which are free of any influence from Classical Greek and Roman tradition or from the waves which swept through European poetry in mediaeval and modern times. In early Mesopotamia we have traced a type of poetry which is solely characterised by parallelistic verse. From Mesopotamia parallelism spread to neighbouring Syria and Palestine where it is prominent in the mythological literature of Ugarit and in the poetic sections of the Old Testament. Furthermore, I assume that the same feature spread in prehistoric times from Mesopotamia to the Finno-Ugrians of Central and Southern European Russia. I am convinced that a detailed comparison of parallelism in Sumerian and Ugaritic poetry with that of Mordvin, Ostyak and Finnish poetry will render it difficult to believe that their similarity is based upon pure coincidence and, therefore, historically irrelevant. It could be that the Baltic Finns brought the parallelistic folk epic from their original Finno-Ugrian home between the river Volga and the Ural mountains. Finnish poetry, however, has also links with ancient Germanic poetry. Alliteration, which is not a regular feature in Mordvin or ancient Near Eastern poetry, must be considered as the most striking feature linking the poetry of the Baltic Finns with that of the ancient Germanic peoples. Furthermore, alliteration as well as the accentual metre links

29   For the interpretation of these lines, which presents a number of difficulties, cf. Sir Ifor Williams, ed., *The Poems of Taliesin* (= *CT*). English translation from the Welsh by J.E. Caerwyn Williams, Dublin 1968. Cf. also H. Wagner, 'Wortstellung im Keltischen und Indogermanischen' in *Indogermanisch und Keltisch*, ed. K.H. Schmidt, Wiesbaden 1977, 219f.

Germanic poetry with Celtic poetry as preserved in the fragments of archaic Irish verse and also in the rhetorics of the sagas and the fragments of *fénechas*, the remains of preliterary Old Irish law. How far parallelism was developed in Celtic verse is difficult to say considering the fragmentary character of archaic Irish poetry. It is probable, however, that variation of the Germanic type is related to Finnish parallelism. With regard to the subject-matter of Mordvin, Ob-Ugrian, Finnish, Germanic and Celtic poetry, it contains very old mythological themes, a fact which provides another link with Sumerian and Old Semitic poetry, which consist almost entirely of mythological material. The antiquity of parallelism as a poetic device is underlined by the fact that in Sumerian literature it is probably the only device which distinguishes poetry from prose. The same may be true for Ugaritic literature. This would mean that other metrical features recognizable in Mordvin and Finnish poetry are due to later developments. Some years ago I pointed out that alliteration of the Insular Celtic type which Meyer has called *Kettenalliteration*, 'chain-alliteration', is also found in late Egyptian poetry of the Demotic period.[30] Chronologically this would bring use close to the Early Christian period, when there were close connections between the monastic institutions of Egypt and Ireland. It has also been seen by various scholars, for example, Rudolf Much in his authoritative edition of Tacitus' *Germania*, that Egyptian religion must have exercised a considerable influence on the pantheon of Germanic tribes. Egyptian influences reached the Celtic and Germanic world via Southern France.

Alliteration is also a specific feature of the fragments of archaic Latin poetry. By archaic Latin poetry we mean the kind of poetry which was current among the Italic tribes before the adoption of Greek metres in the third century B.C. The Italic dialects of the fourth century B.C. were characterised by initial word stress, a feature which provides a significant link between the Italic, Celtic and Germanic branches of Indo-European, in whatever way this fact is to be

30 Cf. Wagner, *op. cit.* (1977), 231.

explained historically. The situation in Old Italic poetry does not, of course, exclude the possibility that alliteration as a metrical device was introduced from Egypt. The cult of the Egyptian goddess Isis was prominent in the Rome of the early emperors as well as in North Western Germany and in Denmark.

To illustrate alliteration in Italic poetry, I shall discuss briefly a fragment of an Oscan dialect which is contained in a funerary inscription from Cumae near Naples (c.100 B.C.). This kind of inscription was hidden in graves or death-chambers and was addressed to the powers of the netherworld in order to bring destruction upon an enemy. In Rome it was called a *malum carmen*, 'a bad spell' and as such was condemned in the famous 'Law of the Twelve Tables', a proof that it was popular among the ordinary people of rural Italy:

stenim . kalauiiúm . tri / *a*ginss . *u*rinss . *ú*lleis . / *f*akinss .
(Stenium Calavium Tre(bi ? filium), *a*ctiones, *o*rationes *i*llius, *f*acinora,)
*f*angvam / *b*iass . *b*iítam . *a*ftiím . / *a*namúm . *a*itatum / *a*mirikum
(linguam, vires, vitam, spiritum ?, animam, aetatem, quaestum)
tifei (– –?).
(tibi)[31]

Only the name and the last word of this inscription stand outside the alliteration system, which recalls that of archaic Irish verse. An interesting detail which this inscription has in common with Celtic and Germanic alliteration concerns the way in which a vowel alliterates with any other vowel (cf. *a*ginss . *u*rinss . *ú*lleis). As in Germanic, and perhaps also in primitive Celtic, words beginning with a vowel were preceded by some kind of a glottal stop.

V

Finally, two further points ought to be made. Roman Jakobson, in a wide-ranging article on poetic parallelism remarks that 'the only living oral tradition in the Indo-

31 E. Vetter, *Handbuch der italischen Dialekte* 1, Heidelberg 1953, 29.

European world which uses grammatical parallelism as its basic mode of concatenating successive verses is the Russian folk poetry both songs and recitatives.'[32] To me it seems most likely that parallelism in Russian folk poetry is due to the Finno-Ugrian substratum in the Russian language and tradition. In the same article Jakobson refers to the literary tradition of the Chinese which as he states 'has never abandoned parallelism as the cardinal poetic artifice'.[33] He also refers to a paper entitled 'On the poetry of the Chinese' read by J.F. Davis in 1829 at a meeting of the Royal Asiatic Society in which parallelism is declared to be the most interesting feature in the construction of Chinese verse, 'as it presents a striking correspondence with what has been remarked of Hebrew poetry'.[34]

The Chinese case seems to destroy my argument for an historical connection between early Mesopotamian and Finno-Ugrian poetry. It rather supports R. Jakobson's view according to which 'those poetic patterns where certain similarities between successive verbal sequences are compulsory or enjoy a high preference appear to be widespread in the languages of the world'.[35] Finnish, Mordvin, Ugaritic and Sumerian parallelism however, are so much alike that it is impossible for me n o t to suspect an historical link between them. If it is true, and I have no means of checking it, that Chinese parallelism represents a striking correspondence with that of Hebrew and, therefore, also Ugaritic and Sumerian parallelism, one could also raise the question as to whether Chinese and Early Mesopotamian poetry are historically connected in some way or other. I am inclined to subscribe to a view expressed by various scholars that Sumerian is related to an archaic form of Western Indo-Chinese. According to V. Christian, the Sumerians invaded Southern Mesopotamia early in the third millennium B.C. from India.[36]

---

32 R. Jakobson, 'Grammatical Parallelism and its Russian Facet', *Language* 42: 2 (1966), 405.
33 *Ibid.*, 401.
34 *Ibid.*, 401.
35 *Ibid.*, 399.
36 V. Christian, 'Die Herkunft der Sumerer', *Oesterr. Ak., phil.-hist. Kl., Sitz.b.*, Vol. 236: 1. Abh. Vienna 1961.

SELECT BIBLIOGRAPHY

B. Collinder, *Comparative Grammar of the Uralic Languages*, Stockholm 1960.

H. Jacobsohn, *Arier und Ugrofinnen*, Göttingen 1922 (repr. Göttingen 1980).

A.J. Joki, *Uralier und Indogermanen* = *Mémoires de la Société Finno-Ougrienne* 151, Helsinki 1973.

E. Lewy, *Kleine Schriften*, Berlin 1961.

E. Lönnrot, *Kalevala*, Porvoo 1963.

H. Paasonen, *Mordwinische Chrestomathie mit Glossar und grammatikalischen Abriss*, Helsingfors 1909.

J. Pápay, *Sammlung Ostjakischer Volksdichtungen*, Budapest & Leipzig 1905.

A. Schiefner, trans. *Kalevala, das National-Epos der Finnen*, Helsingfors 1905.

W. Steinitz, *Ostjakische Volksdichtung und Erzählungen*, Tartu 1939.

PROSE AND VERSE IN ICELANDIC LEGENDARY FICTION

DAVÍÐ ERLINGSSON
(University of Iceland)

I

By means of a survey of the main kinds of poetry which have been used as vehicles of storytelling in Iceland and the main types of prose narratives, I hope to elucidate the interaction of prose and verse in storytelling in a particular society. At the same time such a survey might provide a basis for the discussion of the most pertinent questions about the varying narrative modes that operate both simultaneously and at different times in that society. These questions deal with how and why the living world of storytelling develops historically, both as a whole and in its component parts. Obviously, verse and prose are the two chief means of transmitting a story, and each of these can be divided into several sub-categories or modes.

I believe that it is still commonly thought that in terms of chronology, verse antedates prose as a vehicle of story. According to most scholars, including Heusler and the Chadwicks, heroic poems originally came into being in early Germanic society at a time close to the persons and events they reflect. Indeed, Heusler and others believed that poetry was the only medium for that society's heroic tales.

The evidence mustered in this field is unfortunately bound to remain incomplete; hence the view that in pre-literate Germanic society heroic tales in prose did not exist, can be only an article of faith. To my mind it is wise to be cautious and more sensible to think of other possibilities than verse in this context. It is my belief that man has always had an intrinsic and essential need for news, vital or otherwise, and that in this need lie the seeds of story in everyday language. In this sense, therefore, prose must be more original and more basic than poetry. Consequently, I tend to be in agreement with Hans Kuhn that in early Germanic culture there must have been *Heldensage vor und ausserhalb der Dichtung*, 'heroic prose tales before and aside from the poems'. Similarly, I also believe that, say, an Irish ballad on the tragic fate of a freedom-fighter is probably always a creation secondary to prose reports which, however, might not yet have reached a fixed form. At the very moment when the hero's fate stood out in popular or individual consciousness as something of wider and deeper significance than the events themselves, when the story had acquired mythical or paradigmatic value, then it was time for it to be moulded in the more elaborate elevated form of a poem to be performed on solemn occasions.

An attempt to survey the eco-system of Icelandic story-telling might assist in providing sensible answers to such questions as: how and why is it that an essentially heroic *fornaldarsaga*, like the saga of Hrólfr kraki, King of Denmark, and his heroes, came to be turned into various sets of *rímur* and how and why is it that such stories were enjoyed through the centuries as entertainment and became known to a larger public in metrical form rather than in the form of prose narrative? The task of surveying Icelandic literature is not easy, but one, nevertheless, that must be attempted. To be sure, everyone who has tried to give a scholarly account of some part of Icelandic tradition has also adopted a particular attitude as to the nature of that tradition as a whole, but this has often been done implicitly rather than explicitly, so that the authors of such surveys cannot be said to have consciously proceeded with some unified concept in mind. Essential to me in this context, seems to be the notion of an eco-system — a developing but basically independent life-body of tradition, with the constituent parts often in some way or another conflicting or interacting with each other, at the same time as they constitute a dynamic whole. Such an ecological point of view might offer a more promising approach than the general attitude to cultural tradition as an endlessly complex maze of ideas, stories, motifs, etc., thrown together in the melting-pot of human society by the accidents of history and processed by accidents of human nature.

Every society's tradition is, of course, unique by reason of different and varying circumstances historical and otherwise, but the ecology, the biological facts of life, are bound to be common to all. Epic traditions are one important part of the life of the mind, and one of the purposes of studying them must be to come as close as possible to knowing their biological world; the scholar is like the forester who cannot explain the characteristics of an individual tree without knowing the forest.

II

Prior to our survey of the Icelandic epic tradition, a few points must be briefly considered. A description of the kind I propose would be difficult or even impossible to attempt in many parts of the world, but there are some basic conditions that make such an attempt more plausible and promising with regard to Iceland.

Iceland stands apart geographically and has no border problems. It has a short history of only some eleven hundred years, a history that in its entirety is relatively well-known. The country was settled only once and there has been no invasion or real re-settlement. To be sure, there have been foreign domination and foreign influences on both the texture of Icelandic society and culture, but there has never been any radical breakdown in the cultural milieu, such as would have ensued from a change of language.

That the history of the Icelandic people is well-known is due partly to its shortness and partly to the interest taken in its beginnings by historians only two or three centuries after it commenced. Little more than a century after the settlement of Iceland, Christianity was adopted by the predominantly pagan nation, and with it came writing. This art was soon turned to use in the vernacular and from the twelfth century onwards an amazing quantity and variety of literature has been preserved: prose works on the history of Iceland and other countries; law; the chronicle of the Settlement; genealogies; the family sagas; and sagas of ancient prehistoric times, to name a few of the prose genres with roots in the pre-Christian period, but there is also a wealth of saints' legends, homilies, etc., as well as literature relating to the more or less contemporary history of the twelfth to fourteenth centuries. The antiquarian interest that bore its richest fruits in the thirteenth century has also left us the invaluable corpus of Eddic poetry and Snorri Sturluson's work on mythology and poetics. All of the above is well-known, but needs to be borne in mind when one considers the relationship between the poetic and prose traditions.

We think of folk epic poetry primarily as an oral cultural phenomenon. In Iceland with its relatively rich written sources, we find ourselves faced with the usual dilemma, of assessing oral phenomena of the past on the basis of written texts alone, texts which may or may not be faithful to oral versions once current. In addition to this customary limitation to our knowledge, however, we are also in Iceland dealing with a culture in which the distinction between oral and literary form would appear to be less clear than elsewhere.

A more or less watertight division between a layer of society being the predominant carriers of native oral culture and a learned and aristocratic class, writing and thinking in Latin, may be applicable in parts of continental Europe, but it is not of any great relevance in Iceland where the group that created written works did so mostly in the vernacular. Unlike their European colleagues these writers did not stand apart from society at large. In all likelihood, literacy was more widespread or had a more permeating effect on life in Iceland than elsewhere, in the Middle Ages. It may not be possible to prove this, but it is clearly borne out by the strong ties between literature and tradition, or, in other words, the tradition-boundness of Icelandic literature. This can be partly explained by certain features of the social fabric. As might be expected, the roles and functions of the epic in Iceland have been studied mainly by literary historians. These have always acknowledged the extraordinary indebtedness of Icelandic medieval literature to oral folk culture. Though the literature itself is our main source of information about the traditions and popular entertainment of early times, it does not always and of necessity facilitate the study of them. In this context, we need only recall the well-known dispute among scholars as to whether the sagas of Icelanders, the *Íslendingasögur*, should be regarded as more or less faithful recordings of oral legends (or even oral sagas), or as fiction making arbitrary use of oral legends. Traditions, sometimes of an epic nature and often including verse, have played a decisive role in the formation of the sagas and in their subject matter. The writers were steeped in this lore and at the same time they often were well acquainted with foreign literature and literary theory. They made use of all their resources in an independent fashion, committed neither to an exact recording of traditions nor to rigorously observing learned literary precepts.

Prior to writing, native oral traditions, in prose or verse or both, had developed according to their own laws, subject to the accidents of transmission. Their entry into literature was a major, critical step. The changes introduced by the writer at this stage might be of at least three kinds: 1. development and formation along the same lines as in oral tradition; 2. development according to certain precepts, perhaps learned ones; and, 3. transformation in order to adapt the legend to the larger unit of the saga, or conflation of different versions of the legend. Changes of all three kinds might occur together, thus reminding us how difficult it is to distinguish between oral and literary elements in written works. A saga writer steeped in the lore of a largely oral culture, including epic traditions in prose and verse, uses and, indeed, cultivates oral forms of art in writing.

At the outset it has been necessary to emphasise the integration of the oral and the literary in the society that formed saga literature. It is a truism that the saga is the form taken by the epic in Iceland. This statement appears to reflect the notion that the epic, or epic poetry, was something intrinsic in society, at least in Germanic society, and this again implies that epic is something needed by man in that society, and perhaps by social beings in general.

One might say that the prose saga is the form of narration which in Iceland took on the function fulfilled by epic heroic verse in the pre-literate society from which it descended.

III

The society that created the written saga has also left us a heritage of poetry, and a considerable part of this had been composed prior to the settlement. From the beginning, there were two kinds of poetry, quite distinct in nature, Eddic and scaldic: Eddic was associated with the ancient lore of heroes and gods and the wisdom needed to live in this world, in other words, didactic matter. It was popular poetry, and the poets were always anonymous. Scaldic poetry was the vehicle of panegyric and imaginative description, the highly self-conscious art of individual poets, often court poets, dealing mostly with contemporary matters.

The original and basic metrical form of Eddic poetry, the *fornyrðislag*, was inherited from earlier Germanic alliterative verse. In Icelandic it continued to be the main vehicle of epic narration, but developed from a stichic to a stanzaic form. Each stanza usually consists of eight lines each carrying two metrical stresses and alliterating in pairs. The number of unstressed syllables was not strictly fixed, but two unstressed syllables gradually became optimal, so that the line would consist of four syllables. Almost invariably the metrical stress admirably coincides with the natural language stress. Of the four metrical stresses in a pair of lines, two or three of them carry alliteration. The rhythmical pattern varies from line to line, and this variety is felt to be essential to counterbalance monotony.

Of other measures the *ljóðaháttr* is the most important. It is seldom found outside Iceland. With its six lines it became the main medium of didactic matter and wisdom, and also of dialogue.

As distinct from Eddic poetry, scaldic poetry was presumably a new form of poetic art exercised in the much stricter and more complicated *dróttkvætt* metre, with eight lines each containing three stresses to a stanza, alliteration connecting each pair of lines, internal rhyme in each line, and a very elaborate poetic language of *heiti* and kennings based largely on mythology. The core of this poetic art is imagery — an intellectual play with pictorial ideas which is sometimes quite far-fetched. Though this kind of poetry would hardly strike one as a likely medium for epic, it is, nevertheless, intimately tied up with epic traditions.

While all Eddic poetry is anonymous, scaldic verse is ascribed to individual poets. Most of the Eddic poems are handed down in a single collection which doubtless owes its existence to antiquarian interests, and this collection survives in a single manuscript of the thirteenth century. Scaldic poetry is preserved mostly in bits and pieces entered and quoted in sagas and in Snorri Sturluson's work on poetry and mythology, the Prose Edda (which is also an invaluable source for Eddic poetry). Scaldic poetry has not been collected in the same way as Eddic; it has not enjoyed the same kind of antiquarian interest. Nevertheless, the corpus of scaldic poetry, amounting as it does to some six thousand stanzas, is impressive. Considering that we know the scalds mainly as court poets and taking into account the fact that their poetry is preserved in the sagas of kings and other rulers, it is not surprising that the two predominant topics seem to be battle and praise. It may be, however, that the source situation gives a slightly distorted picture of the full spectrum of the scaldic art.

Eddic poetry is not epic in the sense in which this word has been used by romantic scholars of the past. They are not long, heroic poems with a wide, slow and heavy stream of narrative. The Eddic poems are all shorter by far and more tightly structured than, for instance, the Homeric epics or Beowulf. To a lesser degree, the same holds true of Icelandic heroic poems in comparison to the heroic poetry of other Germanic peoples. The closest we get to a continental heroic poem in the Edda is *Atlakviða*.

Some of the Eddic poems bear a close resemblance to the popular ballad. In many cases they present a single event or situation instead of telling a complete story from beginning to end. A surprisingly large number of them consist, exclusively or almost exclusively, of dialogue or monologue with only a minimal narrative framework. In this sense the Eddic poems are predominantly dramatic. In other cases we have a mixture of dialogue or monologue with narrative verse. This is sometimes termed the epic-dramatic form.

It is really only *Atlakviða* and *Atlamál* (the two poems about Atli), *Hamðismál*, *Hlöðskviða* and *Völundarkviða* that relate a lengthy chain of events. In these poems the epic narrative may be said to hold its own and contain the dramatic element. These poems are also presumably the oldest in the corpus, doubtless descended from continental folk epics transmitted orally to Iceland.

The poems in the single manuscript, the *Codex Regius*, have obviously been arranged according to a plan. There is a primary division between the poems about gods (and other supernatural beings) and those about heroes. The arrangement of the poems within each of these groups is also evidently the work of an intelligent mind, whose method, nevertheless, is not always easily understood. In the portion devoted to the gods, which comes first, the compiler moves from the cosmological and general poems to those about individual gods and other supernatural beings, and the poems on the gods begin with Oðinn, move on to Þórr, and then to others in a hierarchicial sequence.

In the heroic section of the *Codex Regius* there has been an attempt to superimpose a chronological order of events on the poems, and to present the most prominent heroes and heroines as related to each other by blood. The only poems about heroes of Nordic (Danish) origin — the two poems about Helgi Hundingsbani and the poem about Helgi Hjörvarðsson — with which the heroic section begins, are connected to the following series of poems on Sigurd, by making Sigurd the Völsung a half-brother of Helgi Hundingsbani. The result of this is that the collection of poems on South-Germanic heroes and the Goths and Huns, that is, the majority of the heroic poems, are in a sequence determined by family connections. The sequence of poems may be likened to a Family Saga covering several generations, and, indeed, Finnur Jónsson called this principle of structure the saga-principle.

At the point of transition from the Danish Helgi poems to the matter of Sigurd the Dragon-Slayer has been inserted *Grípisspá*, a very late poem which with its *spá*-prediction serves as a starting point and, at the same time, as a cohesive factor for the series of poems about the later career of Sigurd until his death, and even for the events after his death. It has been suggested that *Grípisspá* might have been composed by the compiler of the *Codex Regius* for that very purpose.

Even if the shape of the heroic collection can be explained by the saga-principle, which suggests the hand of a single editor, there are indications that more than one editor had been at work. My impression is that a cyclic tendency may have come into play earlier, perhaps in the oral stage, maybe even a tendency similar to that assumed in the history of the Homeric poems. I cannot enter into this here, however, nor do I wish to attempt to demonstrate the existence of a more or less fixed cycle of heroic poems before the extant collection was formed.

The oldest stratum of Eddic poems, the epic-dramatic ones with *Atlakviða* as the prime example, is generally accepted to be as near as one can get to the Nordic manifestation of Germanic heroic epic. The oldest Eddic poems also provide the closest approximation of the classical notion of epic in Icelandic tradition. Still, compared to what exists of comparable texts on the Continent and in England, it would appear that the Icelandic epic-dramatic poems have already moved a bit in the direction they were later to take, that is, to a diminution of their narrative element (which became less elaborate and detailed and thereby more effective) and towards an increased role for their dramatic element, the dialogue (which became more prominent, dramatically poignant, and polished than in the Continental and English counterparts). In the event that this thesis is correct, the development is a continuous one.

In the transmutation from these oldest poems to the youngest stratum from the twelfth and thirteen centuries, several tendencies may be observed. In metrical form there is a move towards normalisation and regularity, in diction, towards increased use of scaldic figures of speech and ideas. From beginning to end, we can discern the increasing influence of scaldic taste. Of greater interest in our context, however, is what I would like to describe as a development in the direction of saga.

Several important Eddic poems have been preserved outside the main collection, in Snorri's *Edda* and in some sagas, mostly the mythical-heroic sagas, the *fornaldarsögur*. These are distinct from the late medieval romances that succeeded them. In the *fornaldarsaga* proper, which often contains legends about ancestral heroes prior to the time of the settlement of Iceland, Eddic verse is integrated in such a manner as to deserve being designated a constituent element.

Similarly, it is true to say that scaldic verse was a constituent part of the *Íslendingasögur* and the *Kings' Sagas*. This was felt to be so, and is borne out by the observations that saga-writers, short of verses in support of the authenticity of their stories, or for other purposes, sometimes themselves resorted to composing the verses.

We know less than we would wish about the performance of poetry. Court poetry was recited by the poets before their lord. The sagas tell us as much, but they are silent about the manner in which the verses were spoken, chanted or intoned. As to Eddic poetry, we do not know whether or in what manner it may have been accompanied by an instrument such as the harp. Norna-Gestr — whose story, which contains important fragments of Eddic poetry, and which is often referred to as an important source on poetic entertainment — did play the harp, but seemingly not to accompany his recitals of Eddic verse. This story is likely to have been written about the year 1300, but the story matter is older. It may then also have contained something about poetic entertainment, but we have no way of knowing that. The writer may have been in touch with a living tradition in Eddic entertainment in the thirteenth century and used that experience in the *þáttr*. Norna-Gestr, a Nordic Meleager, in his extraordinary old age, visited the court of King Ólafr Tryggvason of Norway. At the end of his stay, when he had been baptised, his life-candle was made to burn out, and he died happily. Before that he had entertained the court with his memories of ancient kings and heroes, told them some old stories, and recited old poetry. He tells of the events of antiquity in his own words and recites only verses in direct speech. What Gestr told is in fact *fornaldarsaga* material, and his performance as it is described in the *þáttr* is likely to be a reflection of the way old lore was used in entertainment in the twelfth or thirteenth centuries. It also fits in with what we would assume about performances of *fornaldarsögur* and *Íslendingasögur*: a form of story entertainment, where verse, often drama in dialogue, functions within the frame of prose narrative.

In the Edda collection there are many prose passages. It is obvious that some of these are editorial, inserted in order to explain and connect the poems. These, however, do not contain anything that is not also expressed in the poems in one way or another. In other instances, the prose is necessary to provide a background which could not be deduced from the poems themselves; a story leads up to the scene of the poem. In some cases such passages are quite extensive, encompassing more narrative matter than is strictly necessary in order to provide the poetry with its essential context.

The use of prose is not confined to such introductions to individual poems. There are narrative pieces joining verse passages or at the conclusion of some poems. Good examples of this procedure are the poems about Helgi Hjörvarðsson and the older of the two Helgi Hundingsbani poems, as well as the two poems about Sigurd's youth, *Reginsmál* and *Fáfnismál*. For the most part the action is advanced in the prose interludes while the dramatic dialogue is in verse. Among the poems about gods we find the same system operating, for example, in the Óðinn-poem called *Grímnismál*, which is prefaced by a lengthy and intricate prose story which tells of two young princes who are lost and fostered by a mysterious couple who turn out to be Óðinn and Frigg. Each of these gods have their own favourite, and they try to outwit each other in furthering the interests of their respective protégés. With Óðinn's help Geirröðr becomes king, but his brother suffers a miserable fate, outside human society. Later Óðinn visits Geirröðr to prove Frigg wrong in her accusations about Geirröðr's stinginess — a vice ill-becoming a king. Then Óðinn is captured and put between two fires. The poem itself consists of Óðinn's monologue in this predicament. Geirröðr's son, the only person who shows him the kindness of offering him a drink, is given a lesson in mythology. As is the rule on similar occasions, Óðinn travels in disguise, only in the end revealing his true identity. Geirröðr then rises to meet him, but falls on his own sword and dies. The conclusion of the story, like the involved tale at the beginning is told in prose, only the lesson in mythology directed by Óðinn to the young prince is in verse.

In addition to this kind of poem and the poems about the young Sigurd dating from the end of the creative period of Eddic poetry in Iceland, there are also poems consisting entirely of dialogue which encompasses everything needed for an understanding of the action. *Alvíssmál*, the poem about Alvíss and the god Þór offers an example of this.[1]

We witness a general development in Eddic poetry away from the form of *Atlakviða*, where epic narrative and drama were balanced, where the elevated narrative still carried the action effectively from event to event, and dramatic direct speech was used to convey the psychologically important points and scenes. This general development takes us either towards a form where all is built into the dialogue and no narration is needed — as in *Alvíssmál* — or towards a form with narration in prose, and drama and didactic matter in dialogue verse.

This development consisted in the cultivation of the two elements, narrative and drama, each gradually refined, leading to separation of the two. In the poems accompanied by narration in prose we see the results of a development toward saga. This development must be thought of in direct connection with the mode of transmission in entertainment. It agrees broadly with what can be seen in *Norna-Gests Þáttr*. Even in the absence of such a source, we would be bound, on the internal evidence of the *fornaldarsaga* and Eddic poetry, to think in terms of performances where prose must have alternated with verse.

The resultant epic form, where prose and verse interact in this manner, has been called prosimetrum by some scholars. In relation to heroic tales, in particular, it is no doubt an important question, whether this form is to be regarded as a development of tales entirely in verse, or whether stories entirely in prose as well as stories composed partly in prose and partly in verse were in existence in addition to the known tales told entirely in verse. All this may be regarded as of minor importance in the context of the Icelandic tradition. Whatever way we look at it, this form, whether we call it prosimetrum or something else, is fundamental to the development of saga literature. Verse was felt as essential

1 Admittedly, there are also some poems which, like Þrymskviða, really are verse narratives, whose metrical stringency and scaldic tendencies point to a late origin. I am not sure how these should be placed but, on the whole, I find the evidence for a gradual transformation of Eddic poetry convincing.

and necessary in the saga. There is scarcely an *Íslendingasaga* without *dróttkvaett* verses, and hardly a *fornaldarsaga* deserving of the name without some Eddic verse. The straightforward, objective prose is obviously well suited to advancing the action but dialogue, direct speech, often in verse, was the main vehicle for finer characterisations and psychological interpretation. To quote an excellent article of Lars Lönnroth's which has been of great use to me:

> The verses provide exactly the kind of thing that could not be provided by the cool, objective prose of the sagas, i.e., didacticism, passions, rhetoric.[2]

IV

Some time after the division of roles between prose and verse in narrative had reached its completion in saga-literature, a new kind of narrative verse, the *rímur*, stepped onto the stage. By the time it appears in writing, this genre was close to having developed its trappings and resources fully. It is, therefore, difficult to account for the processes involved in its creation. If we had a fuller knowledge of how the genre originated, we might have a deeper insight into how it came to play the role it was to occupy in the world of storytelling and in Icelandic social life. Whatever opinions we might otherwise hold about them, the *rímur* are, undeniably, the most important kind of verse in Iceland for the five or six hundred years of their existence. The *rímur* are, without equal, the popular narrative verse genre most used and enjoyed by the ordinary people and a genre that was probably in some respects a more important cultural factor than prose storytelling.

The word *ríma* in the singular is used to refer to the series of stanzas intended to be recited at a sitting or without a break, usually corresponding to a section or chapter of the story. The plural form, *rímur*, refers to the sequence or cycle of *ríma*s which together tell the whole story. It became

---

2   L. Lönnroth, 'Hjalmar's Death-Song and the Delivery of Eddic Poetry', *Speculum* 46:1 (1971), 7.

intrinsic to the genre to divide a story into *rímas* and to vary
the stanzaic form from one *ríma* to the next. Single *rímas*
may have been more common when the genre first emerged;
at all times these were versifications of simple, short stories,
not of romances with long and involved action. The division
of the story into *rímur* ordinarily gives due regard to natural
segmentation like chapter division in prose. Occasionally,
other considerations prevail. A poet may end his *ríma* with
'let us now leave him there', even though it might be the
critical moment of a battle; thus the plot is left suspended
and the audience in suspense until the next occasion for
rímur-chanting. For different reasons, the length of the
individual *rímas* may vary considerably but commonly contain from between 30 or 40 up to between 70 or 80 stanzas;
only rarely do they contain one hundred or more. The total
number of *rímas* in a cycle may be as few as two or three or
amount to a dozen or even more. Generally *rímur* from later
times tend to be longer than the earlier ones.

The basic unit, the stanza follows a number of patterns.
In the course of time varied and elaborated stanza forms
emerged. The poets took pride in their ability to compose in
intricate measures. In the medieval period, however, the metres
for the most part remain simple, and the number of stanza
forms is limited. The original *rímur* measure is *ferskeytt*, a
quatrain, a regular four-line structure with four stresses in
lines 1 and 3, three stresses in lines 2 and 4, and end-rhyme
and cross-rhyme, *abab*. Another basic feature is alliteration
connecting lines 1 and 2 and lines 3 and 4 of the stanza.

Apart from the *mansöngur*, 'love-song' (which shows
clear traces of its descent from the works of troubadours and
Minnesinger), with which each *ríma* almost always beings, the
genre is wholly devoted to transmitting stories. The source of
the story is usually a written prose work. Wherever this is preserved, it can be demonstrated that the versifier followed his
source more or less slavishly. Consequently, we may assume
that the *rímur* poets often had the prose-text at hand while
composing. In some instances, however, the wording of the
prose and the verse shows such discrepancies that we may
reasonably assume that the versifier composed from memory,
whether he had once heard the story or himself read it in a

manuscript (or even read it in a printed book). The *rímur* frequently allude to books and although phrases like 'as the book says' may be line-fillers, they doubtless reflect objective truth. Original compositon in *rímur* is exceedingly rare. From the medieval period only one instance is known with certainty, and this *ríma* is exceptional in other ways too. There are also some other instances in which the story matter is preserved exclusively in the form of *rímur* but there we have good reason to suspect that they are based on a lost prose saga. In the manuscript tradition of *rímur* one may often see the signs of oral transmission, that is, the *rímur* have been written down from memory. The order of the verses may be mixed up, or parts of the original replaced by more commonplace passages in order to fill in gaps of memory. A reciter of *rímur* who had performed the same cycle a number of times would rely less and less on the written word and, perhaps resort totally to his memory. Those who listened to him would also pick up passages and, perhaps, later on commit them to writing from memory. In such ways there was a constant interplay between oral and literary transmission of the *rímur*.

From the early period, there is no direct evidence for oral composition of *rímur* comparable to, say, the famous story of how Egill Skallagrímsson composed *Höfuðlausn*, 'head-ransom', in the field of scaldic poetry. This story, however, fictitious it may be, demonstrates the author's notion of how a poet might compose and memorize a difficult poem. This kind of composition was probably frequent in the instance of *rímur* too. Poets are likely to have versified sections of stories perhaps one *ríma* at a time, before committing or having them committed to writing.

A woman living in the north of Iceland tells us, in her memoirs, of her youth on a farm shortly after the middle of the nineteenth century. She and her sister were reading a novel that was serialized in a newspaper, and, in the winter while they were attending to the sheep in the shed at that farm, they used to versify this story one chapter at a time in *rímur* form. One of them would extemporize stanza after stanza and the other would help out by occasionally contributing words and verse lines. They kept in memory each section of verses and committed it to paper before they had forgotten it. They clearly enjoyed doing all this. A look at the *rímur* they composed shows that they mastered most of the tricks of the trade, then between five and six hundred years old. Similar methods of oral composition are likely to have been employed quite frequently. The women I refer to were not generally recognised as *rímur* poets and it may have been exceptional for two poets to co-operate in this fashion. In the case of the more or less professional *rímur* poets of the sixteenth to eighteenth centuries, such methods would have been out of the question. The transformation of a long story into a *rímur* cycle might have taken place bit by bit or *ríma* by *ríma*, beginning with deliberative composition and followed recital from memory before the material was committed to writing.

Both the extreme length and the general knowledge of writing make it unlikely that memorization of a whole cycle ever took place. Though many sections and even whole individual *ríma*s with popular appeal were retained in memory, by and large the role of the book is central in the *rímur* tradition. When *rímur* finally made their way into print, it was, therefore, no wonder that they should be so much in demand, frequently published and used in traditional entertainment from the eighteenth century on and even up to our own time.

Whatever factors may have been at play, when the *rímur* were first created and whatever the proportions between them may have been it is certain that the characteristic features of the poetic language were inherited from scaldic poetry. The *heiti*, poetic synonyms, and *kenningar* (kennings) are at the heart of their style and diction. This clearly demonstrates the firm grip scaldic poetry held on the public mind, as well as giving us an insight into the minds of the poets at the time. Apart from these stylistic figures, the narrative language and technique of *rímur* is essentially rather simple and straightforward and remained so for the most part in the early period. A story is told from beginning to end and though the verse form in itself constitutes a relatively rigid frame, it is not a particularly difficult task to fit a narrative into it. *Heiti* and kennings are obviously used to facilitate the provision of the correct number of syllables and proper rhythm and rhymes.

However important, this function should not be thought of as the basic *raison d'être* for these poetic figures. Their basic function certainly was to elevate language to a level higher than that of prose narrative.

In the *rímur* we must not expect to find the high degree of artistry met with in the best of scaldic poetry, where the possibilities of the kennings are fully and imaginatively exploited in a way that brings to mind the intricacies of *l'art pour l'art*. *Rímur* use *heiti* and kennings quite mechanically. The metaphorical quality is lost, or nearly so, and the amount and frequency of wrongly constructed kennings and kenning-types increases as the genre develops; all the same, a certain creativity always prevails, and what amounts to serious degeneration when seen from a historical perspective does not diminish the role of the elevating differentiation from plain narrative.

Both *heiti* and kennings fulfill the same function as oral formulas in epic style, in as far as they serve to fit concepts into the metre, but there is also an important difference. Far from repeating identical phrases, the *rímur* poet has to vary his *heiti* and especially his kennings. Ideally, exactly the same kenning should occur only once in a cycle. This is a total inversion of the rule of economy applying to formulas or oral epic style.

Such a demand for variety would seem to indicate a literary taste rather than a popular one. All the same, there is most definitely a popular and oral aspect to the *rímur* style. In order to appreciate a *rímur* performance, the audience has to be at least passively familiar with the main features of the system of kennings and to comprehend at least the more common elements of the considerable vocabulary of the *heiti*. The fact that the use of kennings increased in later *rímur*, and the fact that the genre not only survived, but enjoyed growing popularity, proves beyond doubt that the kenning-*heiti* apparatus was a factor to be counted on in the public mind. It was already in existence when the genre came into being, and it lived on until the present century. People must have become acquainted through listening to entertainments at home from early childhood with the *rímur* rhythms drumming on their ears. Those who were themselves poets some-

times studied the rules of the art as explained by Snorri in
the *Edda*, but above all they learned from each other. We
may assume that the basis of the kennings had to be explained
to younger members of the audience. Their participation,
initially passive, might later have become active, however,
because essentially the kennings may be considered as a kind
of intellectual toy offering opportunities for play and fun,
but also mental exercise.

In our day, those who have not been brought up in the
living tradition not only find it impossible to follow a recital
of *rímur* but they will not even be able to read and fully
understand simple *ríma* stanzas containing some kennings.
This would hold true even though the concept of kennings
had been explained to them and examples given. The intellectual apparatus is not to hand since they lack the mouth-to-
ear training which every generation of Icelanders from about
1400 to 1900 received. Although the written or printed word
was never distant, that intellectual apparatus was in every
essential a popular oral phenomenon. In the *rímur*, then, the
scaldic stylistic features serve to elevate the diction and to
facilitate transmuting narrative matter into metrical form.
Though the flow of events may be quite fast, and frequently
is so, especially in the earlier period, it is often slowed down
by the weight of detail, most of which is taken over from the
original prose sources. When a versifier follows his original
closely and does not trim it by careful omission of non-
essential detail, the inevitable consequence is a long text in
which the action cannot proceed quickly and the presence of
the poetic language may even result in *rímur* versions that are
longer than the prose texts.

In many respects the narrative technique of the *rímur* was
taken over from prose sagas. For example, a *rímur* version
of an *Íslendingasaga* might include formal passages introducing the characters of the story, though some of these will not
enter the stage of action until much later. Information that
provides the setting for the action and gives scope to the
story is normally included. When such details are missing, one
often has reason to suspect that the *rímur*-writer is writing
from memory rather than having the written text in front of
him at the time of composition.

The composer addresses his audience personally in the *mansöngur* at the beginning of each *ríma*. Apart from this, his presence is not prominent, but he is never as anonymous as the storyteller in the classical sagas. He often steps forward in the first person at the beginning and end of the narration in each *ríma* to remind his audience where the action left off last time and to wind up the action at the end of a *ríma*. Occasionally the author speaks in the first person in the body of a *ríma* but usually only in stereotyped phrases.

Many of the medieval *rímur* can be seen to be under the influence of the romances of chivalry, the *riddarasögur*, in which persons tend to be depicted in terms of absolute good and absolute evil. The narrator of the courtly romance at times steps forward — passing judgement on the characters and events, and such judgements are sometimes directly carried over into the *rímur* versions. In the versification of native sagas this is rare, but the black-and-white view has had a strong influence on native fiction. In *rímur* style this is apparent from the fact that words and phrases denoting binary oppositions are used in reference to the characters in the compositions whether the subject matter is based on native or foreign sources.

Usually the *rímur* narrative moves forward by steps, stanza by stanza, but even in the events where versifiers have sensibly omitted much detail, there still remain certain descriptive passages that are not subject to such thrift. These are above all descriptions of battles and fights, of feasts frequently held at weddings of the heroes, and of splendid fleets of ships sailing the sea. Such descriptions were also favourite subjects with the scalds of earlier times.

On the whole, creative alterations of the stories are disappointingly rare in the *rímur*. The changes that are made are such as to make for less originality, and more formalisation of certain episodes and adaptations in accordance with prevailing taste. Nevertheless, there are examples of entertaining descriptive passages giving evidence of considerable powers of fantasy and skilled narrative craftsmanship in their authors. In the *rímur* from the medieval period, the subject matter may be almost any kind of story with the exception of religious legends. There is a marked predeliction in favour of fictitious and fantastic material, however. *Fornaldarsögur*, *riddarasögur* and late medieval Icelandic romances descended from these account for about two-thirds of the preserved corpus of medieval *rímur*. The remaining one-third is divided between Kings' Sagas, Sagas of Icelanders, popular legends, *Märchen* and *exempla*. There are two *rímur* cycles on mythical poems from the *Edda*.

In later centuries the subject matter of the *rímur* became more varied, yet they were still primarily concerned with the transmission of legendary fiction. In that large field it seems that almost every story worth its salt was versified sooner or later. Indeed, some stories have been turned into *rímur* more than once. *Rímur* have also frequently been rendered back into prose, and such prose versions have sometimes formed the basis of new *rímur*. In this manner, verse and prose went hand in hand in popular entertainment; the tales oscillated between these two forms in ways that cannot always be easily delineated by the philologist.

Hrómundur Gripsson, an ancient Nordic hero who seems to have been well-known in Scandinavia, makes his first literary appearance in Iceland in the earliest extant description of popular story entertainment – þ*orgils saga ok Haflida* in the *Sturlunga saga*. This saga tells of a wedding feast at Reykjahólar in the west of Iceland in 1119. This oft-cited passage refers to two stories with which the guests were entertained. One of these stories was told by a certain Hrólfr of Skálmarnes. He had composed the story himself and there were many verses in it. He told of the 'viking Hröngviðr, Ólafr liðsmannakonungr, the breaking up of the burial-mound of þráinn, and of Hrómundr Gripsson'. This story was told to King Sverrir who said that he found such *lygisögur*, i.e., 'lying stories' or 'fictitious stories', the most entertaining. 'All the same, there are people who claim to be descended from Hrómundr Gripsson', the saga tells us. These indications of content are enough to classify the story as a *fornaldarsaga*. No such saga exists, but there is an early *rímur* cycle about Hrómundr called *Griplur*, in which the other three persons mentioned in *Sturlunga* also figure. *Griplur* doubtless drew its matter from a lost *fornaldarsaga*, and that saga was probably quite different from the story Hrólfr told at the wedding. Late in the seventeenth century a prose saga was written on the basis of *Gríplur* and this found its way into Rafn's classic collection of *fornaldarsögur* (1830). In 1859 a poet retold the story in *rímur*, perhaps using as his source the prose tale printed by Rafn which had as its basis the early *rímur*, though I cannot prove this. In Scandinavia there is a heroic ballad about Hrómundr a figure who, according to some, is commemorated in place-names and associated legends in Sweden.

The long symbiosis and persistent interaction between *rímur* verse and story prose clearly indicates that both were considered necessary and that plain prose narrative could not fulfill popular need or demand, in other words, that there was a socially intrinsic demand for epic narration in the elevated language of poetry.

The power of the *rímur* mode of narration was recognized around 1600, when the main protagonist of Lutheran doctrine in the country — for the good of the cause, in the hope of making people forget their gory heroes and turning their minds instead to pious matters — instigated adaptation on a considerable scale of stories from the Bible into *rímur*. These *rímur* were printed and distributed, but never attained popularity. Apart from *rímur*, there were other types of narrative poetry, but none of them could compete with *rímur* in popularity. The late Middle Ages saw the creation of a variety of end-rhymed metres in which religious legends, miracles, and *exempla* were transmitted. Some of those poems have had a long life in tradition. *Dróttkvætt* was also used in religious poetry long after its role in court poetry had come to an end.

The popular ballads were brought to Iceland from Scandinavia, and some of them have survived tenaciously in oral tradition until recent times. It is an uncertain and very much debated matter when ballads were first introduced into Iceland, but I tend to side with those who believe that they might have been known there in the fourteenth century. Though there are a *few* native ballads, the great majority bear clear signs of foreign originals. There are fewer ballads in Iceland than elsewhere in Scandinavia. In particular, it is noticeable that the so-called heroic ballad, or *kæmpevise*, so prominent in Faroese and Norwegian tradition, is totally absent in Iceland. The explanation is likely to be that the same subject matter was treated in Iceland in *fornaldarsögur* and in *rímur*. An Icelandic audience must have preferred the *rímur* with their more intricate style of language. According to several scholars, the *ferskeytt* metre of the *rímur* grew out of the ballad quatrain and some other *rímur* metres have also been connected with ballad metres. But it is difficult to assume a direct connection since both style and narrative method in the ballad are quite different from those of the *rímur* and, especially, if we also bear in mind that it cannot be ascertained that ballads were known in Iceland at the time when the *rímur* genre was formed.

To complete the picture, the so-called *sagnakvæði* must also be mentioned. This is a group of poems in Eddic metre *fornyrðislag*, narrating legends and fairytales. Some of them are beautiful poems, serene in tone. It is conceivable that narrative composition in Eddic metre never died out completely, but these poems, which probably originated in the sixteenth century, flourished only for a short while, and may, perhaps, rather represent a renaissance attempt to revive Eddic verse. The genre was creative only for a short while, but some of the poems lived on for a long while in oral tradition.

Scanning the whole panorama of Icelandic narrative verse, one will of necessity focus on the only point in history when there was a profound change: the time of the formation of the *rímur* in the fourteenth century. I have tried to describe the nature of this poetry and by way of conclusion I would like to say that the study of *rímur* may be a healthy exercise for people who tend to think in antithetical terms such as written *versus* oral or literary *versus* folk or learned *versus* popular. Our survey will have demonstrated that such oppositions are lacking in validity in Iceland. Instead of being 'either-or', *rímur* tend to be 'both-and'.

V

If we assume that tradition in its widest sense, forms an eco-system, and that narrative constitutes an important part of that system — a sub-system in which, it seems to us, prose and verse are not mutually exclusive, and each claimed its own right to exist — one can summarize the interaction of verse-and-prose in the mixed oral-and-literary Icelandic narrative tradition in the following manner:

Dominant at the beginning were Eddic, narrative verse and scaldic, non-narrative verse; prose narration must have existed alongside the verse. The two elements of Eddic verse, the epic narrative and the dramatic, developed apart, and prose narrative gradually replaced Eddic narrative. In connection with this development, the narrative method and style of the sagas evolved. When this development had reached its climax, epic verse was no longer being composed and the mixed 'prose-interspersed-with-verse', or verse with accompanying prose, had become the dominant narrative form. *Dróttkvætt* verse lives on, but there is no epic poetry.

At this point a new epic genre, the *rímur* entered and filled the vacuum. On the basis of my argument, there is no event or change as momentous as this one.

SELECT BIBLIOGRAPHY

B.K. Þórólfsson, *Rímur fyrir 1600*, Safn Fræðafjelagsins um Ísland og Íslendinga, Vol. 9, Copenhagen 1934.

W.A. Craigie ed., *Specimens of Icelandic Rímur from the Fourteenth to the Nineteenth Century* I-II, London etc. 1952.

R.J. Glendinning and H. Bessason, eds., *Edda, A Collection of Essays*, Winnipeg 1983.

W.P. Ker, *Epic and Romance*, 2nd ed., London 1908.

H. Kuhn, 'Heldensage vor und ausserhalb der Dichtung', in *Festschrift F. Genzmer*, Heidelberg 1952, and repr. in the author's *Kleine Schriften* II, Berlin 1971.

L. Lönnroth, 'Hjálmar's Death-Song and the Delivery of Eddic Poetry', in *Speculum* 46:1 (1971).

V. Ólason, 'Nýmæli í íslenskum bókmenntum á miðöld', in *Skírnir*, Vol. 150 (1976).

H. Pálsson, *Sagnaskemmtun Íslendinga*, Reykjavík 1962.

E. Ól. Sveinsson, *Íslenzkar bókmenntir í fornöld* I, Reykjavík 1962.

E. Ól. Sveinsson, 'Lestrarkunnátta Íslendinga í fornöld', in his *Við uppspretturnar*, Reykjavík 1956, and in *Skírnir* 118 (1944).

THE HEROIC BALLAD IN FAROESE TRADITION

MORTAN NOLSØE
(Academia Færoensis)

The heroic ballad in Faroese tradition can only be understood against the background of the country's history. It will therefore be necessary to give some account of this.

It is generally accepted that the islands were first settled by Christian hermits coming from Ireland at the beginning of the eighth century, but only a century later they were driven away by raiding Vikings. These new colonizers were of Norwegian stock, mostly from Western Norway, but some of them came via the Hebrides and other parts of the British Isles. They were christianized about the year 1000 through the efforts of the Norwegian king and later, in 1035, the islands were made a Norwegian province. In medieval times the connection between the islands and Norway was mainly with Bergen, especially in the period 1134-1319, when that town was the residence of the Norwegian kings, and when it became a Hanseatic trade centre with wide foreign contacts. In medieval times there were also quite close contacts between the Faroese and the Norse-speaking inhabitants of the other islands in the North Atlantic, especially with the Icelanders who visited the Faroes on their voyages between Iceland and Norway. These contacts are likely to have grown stronger when Iceland came under the Norwegian crown after 1262. We have reason to believe that close contacts of a similar nature existed between the Faroese and the Shetlanders during this period, up to 1469 when the Shetland Islands came under the Scottish crown. Together with Norway, the Faroes passed to Denmark in 1380, but the contact with Bergen seems to have continued, more or less, until the end of the seventeenth century. In 1709 the islands were separated administratively from Norway and came under the diocese

of Zealand. At the same time a Danish royal trade monopoly
was established in the islands, a measure which barred contact
with the outside world. When the royal trade monopoly was
finally abolished in 1856, the Faroese community soon
emerged from its primitive economy, revolving around sheep-
farming, to its present economy, almost exclusively based on
fishing. The cost of this rapid economic progress was radical
social change.

The traditional peasant life in the small villages gave way
to a more modern type of life in the new fishing centres with
their fast growing population of people moving in from the
villages. However, the anxiety for the future of the Faroese
language and traditional culture soon led to a national movement which among other things created a greater interest in
the old ballad dance and especially in the heroic ballads in
the Faroese language.

Although everyday speech in the islands is an archaic dialect
of distinct West Scandinavian origin, the official written
language for centuries after the Reformation was Danish.
However, the wish among scholars to record in writing the
extensive oral poetry existing in the native tongue gradually
led to the creation of a modern written language. The first
step in this direction seems to be connected with the recording of some supposedly old ballads which were sent in 1639
to Denmark in a manuscript now lost. A further attempt to
create an orthography took place in the 1770s, when the
Faroese scholar, Jens Christian Svabo, started to collect
Faroese ballads and lexical items. The phonetic spelling he
used was discarded, however, when another Faroese scholar,
Vencel Hammershaimb, in 1846 introduced the orthography
still current. Our present orthography may with reason be
termed a true product of the Romantic era. There can be
little doubt that the choice of a 'medieval' linguistic model,
close to Icelandic, was to a considerable extent promoted by
the archaic language of the Faroese ballads with which Hammershaimb, himself an ardent ballad collector, was thoroughly
familiar.

The heroic ballad repertory sung to the Faroese dance of
today is bilingual; the ballads are represented not only by
Faroese, but also by Danish texts. A significant result of this,

indeed age-old, situation is that different words have developed in popular usage for a heroic ballad belonging to each language tradition. The normal designation for a heroic ballad composed in the Faroese language is *kvæði* (the word is used in this meaning already by Jens Christian Svabo [1746-1824] in his *Dictionarium Færoense*) while a heroic ballad composed in the Danish language is called *kempuvísa*. The latter word primarily refers to such ballads as came to the islands with the printed Danish ballad books of Anders Sørensen Vedel and Peder Syv which were first published respectively in 1591 and in 1695 and soon became very popular in the Faroes. The Danish topographical author and clergyman Lucas Jacobsøn Debes who lived in the islands in the period 1651-1675, gives in his description of the Faroes, which was published in Danish in 1673 and in English in 1676, the following information concerning the linguistically mixed heroic ballad repertory among the Faroese of his time:

> ... almost all of them know most part of the Old Gyant Ballads: not only those that are Printed in the Danish Book of Ballads, but also many more of the Champions of Norway, that may be are forgotten elsewhere, here in fresh Memory, being usually sung in their Dances.[1]

There can hardly be any doubt that the author when speaking of 'Old Gyant Ballads' other than those printed, refers to heroic ballads current in oral tradition in the Faroese language. This piece of information is of great interest to the question of oral composition versus memorization in Faroese heroic ballad tradition. Here we must bear in mind that in connection with the performance of the Danish heroic ballads, there exists in the Faroese ballad community of today an unbroken tradition based on fixed texts, reaching back almost four centuries. This age-old habit of memorizing Danish texts may also have influenced the performance of the heroic ballads in the Faroese language at an early date, especially when copies of such ballad texts had been made available to performers of heroic ballads through the work of collectors. We should

---

1   L.J. Debes, *Færoæ, & Færoa Reserata*, London 1676, 337-8.

hardly imagine that the two traditions existed in separate compartments; the contact between them is evidenced by a certain Danish influence on the Faroese heroic ballad language.

As far as we know interest in the collecting of Faroese ballads was first awakened by the Danish scholar Ole Worm when upon his initiative a royal decree was sent out in 1622 to the bishops in Denmark and Norway to collect what was described as all kinds of antiquities. The now lost manuscript of ballads he received from the Faroes in 1639 was sent in by the Faroese clergyman Hans Rasmussøn, who was the predecessor in office in Tórshavn of Lucas Debes. Although the manuscript is no longer extant, information given about it by Peder Syv, and a knowledge obtained from more recent recordings enables us to identify five of these poems. We find traces of the following three heroic ballads in the manuscript, namely 'Hermundur illi' (*TSB* E 85), 'Samsons kvæði' (*TSB* E 136) and 'Torsteins kvæði' (*TSB* E 110).[2] The first of these is also known in Norwegian tradition, while the other two have only been recorded in Faroese tradition. Although the geographical distribution of the said heroic ballads naturally is accidental, it corresponds astonishingly well with the picture given in *TSB* of the general geographical distribution of heroic ballads in Faroese and in Scandinavian tradition. Moreover, we also find in the three ballads a representative difference between the heroic ballad in Faroese and in Norwegian tradition in the composition of the narrative, because not only the so-called short type is present in the ballads 'Hermundur illi' and 'Samsons kvæði', but we find also the long type, composed in narrative sections, or fits, in 'Torsteins kvæði', which is divided into three or four fits (Far. *tættir*), totalling in its longest known version 265 quatrains. The narrative subject matter of all three ballads is taken from unknown sources, although in 'Samsons kvæði' we find a twisted version of the events connected with the hero whose exploits are recorded in *Judges* 13-6 in the Old Testament. It is curious that the Biblical story about Samson and Delilah

---

2 *TSB* = *The Types of the Scandinavian Medieval Ballad*, eds., B.R. Jonsson, S. Solheim and Eva Danielson, Stockholm & Oslo 1978.

has been turned into a so-called 'troll' ballad. The three
ballads so far mentioned are exceptional, however, in that no
Old Icelandic sources exist for them. However, for the two
remaining poems mentioned in the manuscript, i.e. 'Koralds
kvæði' and 'Berrings vísa', we are able to point to romantic
sagas as specific sources, namely *Konráds saga keisarasonar*
and *Bærings saga*. Both sagas are known in Icelandic manuscripts from the fourteenth century. 'Koralds kvæði' is composed in the stanzaic form of Icelandic *rímur*, and this poem,
no doubt, had its origin in Iceland, although it is no longer
preserved there.

Apropos Faroese ballads mentioned in seventeenth-century
sources, reference should be made to 'Sigmundar kvæði', (*TSB*
E 30) which is mentioned by Lucas Debes in 1673 as an old
Faroese ballad and which is undoubtedly derived from the
Icelandic Saga of the Faroe Islanders. The quatrain is the
dominant stanzaic form of the Faroese and Scandinavian
heroic ballad, but 'Sigmundar kvæði' is in couplets.

Nearly a hundred and fifty years passed from the time of
the collecting work of Hans Rasmussøn before someone else
undertook the collection of Faroese ballads from oral tradition.
The pioneer was, in this case, Jens Christian Svabo, who in
the 1770s and especially from 1781 to 1782 brought together
a large collection of what he called in Danish *Gamle Kjæm-
pesange*, i.e. old heroic ballads. About some of the subjects
dealt with in these ballads, Svabo says:

> These *kvæði* generally are full of fighting, bloodshed and
> heroic feats of kings, earls, supernatural or human giants
> (...) and in them are mentioned countries like Norway,
> Denmark, Sweden, Iceland, Faroes, The Empire of Gardar,
> The Empire of Mikle-garth, Britain, Saxonia etc.[3]

With Svabo also began the main work of collecting ballads,
which lasted approximately a hundred years. In this period,
which coincided with the Romantic Movement and the collection of folk poetry in Europe, one collector after another
in the Faroes made collections, some large some small, which

3 J. Chr. Svabo, *Indberetninger fra en Reise i Færøe 1781 og 1782*,
ed. N. Djurhuus, Köbenhavn 1959, 121. My translation.

together represent all the heroic ballad types in the great ballad corpus, *Føroya kvæði* (*Corpus Carminum Færoensium*) brought together by the famous Danish ballad scholar Svend Grundtvig.

Among the collectors we find both clergy and laymen. Among the former there were especially two who had an important influence. One was J.H. Schrøter (1771-1851) who carried out the larger part of his collecting in Suðuroy while he was pastor there from 1804-26. The other was V.U. Hammershaimb (1819-1909), who travelled through all the islands on his collecting expeditions, mainly during the years 1847-8. Most of the collectors, however, were laymen who wrote down ballads primarily in their respective home districts. Their ballad manuscripts have, therefore, often taken the name of the place where the collection was made. The largest of these collections is the *Sandoyarbók* (named after Sandoy), which Johannes Clemensen assembled in 1821-31.

The collection of Faroese ballads in the Faroes did not end here, however. It has continued over the past hundred years. The result of this collecting work has mainly been that further variants of the already-known types have been saved — but a number of new types have also been found. Among the collectors from this period, two names are especially worthy of mention. One is the well-known Faroese linguist and folklorist, Jacob Jakobsen (1864-1918), who undertook his collecting at the turn of this century. The other is the Faroese nationalist and ballad singer Jóannes Patursson (1866-1946), whose ballad books appeared in six volumes between 1922 and 1945. These booklets were intended primarily for the use of dancers in the Faroes.

While the collecting of Faroese heroic ballads has a history of some 350 years, publication did not begin until after 1800. There are three principal works which are of great importance for contemporary Faroese culture as well as for international scholarship. The first of these principal works (also the first printed book in the Faroese language) was H.C. Lyngbye's *Færöiske Qvæder on Sigurd Fofnersbane og hans Æt* (i.e. Faroese heroic ballads of Sigurd the Dragon Slayer and his kin), which appeared in 1822. The next two were both collections of Hammershaimb, *Færöiske Kvæder* I-II, 1851-5.

Both these authors based their work on their own collecting, although the former, who was Danish, received valuable assistance from Faroese collectors, for example, Pastor J.H. Schrøter. Co-operation worked both ways, however, for the Faroese, Vencel Hammershaimb, at an early period met the Dane, Svend Grundtvig, who was then preparing his great scholarly Danish ballad corpus, *Danmarks gamle Folkeviser*. Grundtvig therefore, urged Hammershaimb to undertake further collection of ballads in the Faroes. For Grundtvig himself, this ballad collaboration with Hammershaimb later resulted in the fortunate arrangement that he joined with his brother-in-law, Jørgen Bloch, to arrange all the Faroese ballads from oral tradition in the great ballad manuscript *Føroya kvæði* (*Corpus Carminum Færoensium*). Their work, carried out between 1872 and 1905, appeared in print in six volumes, issued between 1941 and 1972 and edited by the Faroese scholars Chr. Matras and N. Djurhuus. Furthermore, it should be mentioned that important ballad manuscripts of individual collectors, like Svabo, Schrøter and Johannes Clemensen, have also been published since 1939.

Of the 236 types printed in *Føroya kvæði*, about 200 belong to the following ballad genres into which it is customary for scholars to subdivide the types of the Scandinavian medieval ballad in oral tradition: ballads of the supernatural, legendary ballads, historical ballads, ballads of chivalry, heroic ballads and jocular ballads. Of these, approximately 200 ballad types, more than half belong under the heading of the heroic ballad.

By heroic ballads we understand, first and foremost, orally transmitted poems in ballad form which tell of champions of the past and of their wonderful deeds, most often, in faraway places. These ballads are closely connected with late Icelandic sagas, the so-called *fornaldarsögur*, with their descriptions of romantic and fantastic adventures. The hero in the heroic ballads is the foremost warrior of warriors in contest or in battle, particularly in single combat. This warrior is full of desire to carry out feats and eager to meet his opponent whether he be human or a supernatural, e.g. giant, dragon or dwarf. It is also the practice among ballad scholars to divide heroic ballads into two groups according to the type of adversary, i.e. ballads of champions (*TSB* E 1-112) and ballads of champions and supernatural beings (*TSB* E 113-67).

The heroic ballad hero's reasons for joining contest or battle can be varied and various: to try his valour, to help or to avenge a kinsman, to subjugate or to defend possessions (land or treasure), to win or to defend a lady, or to force heathens to become Christians. Compared to the ballads of champions, the ballads of champions and supernatural beings are more like folktales, although the hero in such ballads is generally more powerful and self reliant than in tales of magic.

Among the main themes of ballads of champions and supernatural beings are the following: a hero travels to the supernatural world and rescues a captive maiden (often a princess); a giant (*risi*) comes to the land of humans to carry off a maiden, but a champion kills him and saves her; a giant plays dice with a champion for his head and loses, but ransoms his head with treasure; a stepmother of supernatural race married in the world of humans sends a stepchild to the supernatural world to remain there; a maiden carried off by a giant rescues herself and returns to the world of humans. Most of the themes of Faroese heroic ballads are also met with in the heroic ballads of the other Scandinavian countries and especially those of Norway. All in all, however, the Faroese have more heroic ballad themes (or motifs) than any other Scandinavian country and this together with other characteristic features gives the Faroes a central position in Scandinavian heroic ballad poetry.

An important difference between heroic ballads in the Faroes and those of other Scandinavian countries is that the former are longer and contain a greater number of episodes. This allows one and the same ballad to relate several events concerned either with the same central character or with more than one central character, usually kinsfolk or friends of the original hero. Such long Faroese ballads can, as previously mentioned, run to many hundreds of stanzas and are usually constructed in several sections, called *táttur*, pl. *tættir*, each of which can be, more or less, considered a free-standing part of the narrative and can therefore be sung in isolation. A long heroic ballad constructed in sections (or fits) would thus seldom be sung in its entirety in one evening. In the instances when this happened, however, it was considered a feat of endurance, which only a few exceptional singers (Far. *skipari*, pl. *skiparar*) would have been able to accomplish. Jóannes Patursson relates an interesting example of this from Skúvoy in the nineteenth century, recounting that 'Sniálvs kvæði' (with 9 sections and more than 600 stanzas) is seldom sung in its entirety. It was, therefore, a memorable occasion (N. Winther the sheriff of Sandoy said to Jóannes Patursson) when Jógga sung all the sections of 'Sniálvs kvæði', one after another, on his attending the gift-giving day of the wedding of Jóhan á Rípuni on Skúvoy. Then the lamp had been lit long before he finished the final section.[4]

The question of the origin of the *tættir* composition in Faroese ballads is disputed. Such a composition is found in one single Icelandic heroic ballad (i.e. *TSB* E 4, 'Þorgeirs rímur') and, furthermore, this technique is well-known from Icelandic *rímur* poetry. However, it is not certain that the technique is derived from Iceland, since it is also found in British ballads, for example in 'A Gest of Robyn Hode' (Child 117), dating from the late Middle Ages and consisting of 456 quatrains divided into 8 fits. As to the shorter Faroese heroic ballad without sectional division, the view is commonly held that it is modelled on the Norwegian heroic ballad of the late Middle Ages, and it has also been suggested that the long Faroese heroic ballad, composed in sections, came by the same general route and particularly via Bergen.

In the Faroese heroic ballads there are two champions who have received fuller treatment than others. Foremost of these is unquestionably Sigurd (Far. *Sjúrður*), the slayer of Fafnir, who is not only mentioned in the widely-known 'Sjúrðar kvæði' with its fits, *Regin smiður*, *Brynhildar táttur*, *Høgna táttur* and *Aldrias táttur*, but also in many shorter Faroese heroic ballads.

I

In 1853, when few Faroese ballads were being printed other than those concerning Sigurd, this caused the well-known Norwegian ballad collector and editor, M.B. Landstad to give the following rather unbalanced description of the Faroese ballads:

4   J. Patursson, *Kvæðabók* 5, Tórshavn 1945, 5.

They move no doubt in a narrower circle than ours and treat principally with the saga of Sigurd the slayer of Fafnir who has become for them a permanent legendary character who must be present in almost all of their poems, whether he belongs there or not.[5]

The other champion is Charlemagne, about whom many heroic ballads, particularly those concerning his battles with the pagans, have been composed both in late medieval and more recent times. The ballads of these two champions have held a central place in research on the Faroese heroic ballad. As soon as H.C. Lyngbye's book, *Færöiske Qvæder om Sigurd Fofnersbane og hans Æt*, appeared in 1822, the question arose as to the relationship between the Faroese heroic ballad about Sigurd, old Icelandic sources — Eddic poems and legendary sagas — and Old German poetry, especially the *Nibelungenlied*. Most earlier scholars in this field of research held the opinion that the Faroese heroic ballads about Sigurd were derived from Old Icelandic or Norse heroic lays and, therefore, very old, while the majority of later scholars tend to regard them as based on written sagas, like *Völsunga saga* and *Þiðreks saga*, in which case the ballads must have been composed after c.1300. It must also be borne in mind that the oldest version of 'Sjúrðar kvæði' was written down as late as 1817, although the 62 year-old informant could tell Lyngbye that he had learned this long heroic ballad of nearly 600 quatrains as a 10 year-old boy from his 92 year-old grandmother. A puzzling problem is also that Svabo makes no mention whatsoever of 'Sjúrðar kvæði, but, on the other hand, we must remember that the custom of keeping secret for generations certain heroic ballads is not unknown within the Faroese ballad community.

Concerning the research on Faroese heroic ballads about Charlemagne, the question of source connections was clearer in that there were fewer possibilities to choose between. Here, the discussion centred on whether ballads were composed on the basis of the romantic work *Karlamagnús saga*,

---

5 M.B. Landstad, *Norske Folkeviser*, Kristiania 1853, XVIII. Translated from the Norwegian.

which was translated into the Old Norse language at the end of the thirteenth century from Old French heroic epics, e.g., *Chanson de Roland*, or on the basis of later treatments of the same subject matter, i.e. in the form of long printed chronicles. If the latter alternative holds true, it would prove that heroic ballad composition continued longer in the Faroes than in the other Scandinavian countries, that is to say, after the end of the Middle Ages and into modern times. When Thomas Tarnovius in 1669 states about the Faroese: 'Moreover, they practice composing long rhymes and songs about one thing or another in a way one would think quite impossible', it may, therefore, be easily imaginable that he is referring to the living heroic ballad composition of his day.[6]

In the late Middle Ages, our heroic ballads show connections not only with Norway, with which the Faroes has many ballads in common, but also with Iceland. Here, it is rather the narrative material which is often found in written Icelandic sagas — not only in the legendary or romantic sagas, but also in the sagas of the kings and the sagas of the Icelanders. This indicates that in the Faroes in the Middle Ages there were Icelandic saga manuscripts which formed the basis for the composition of the ballads. This custom of composing heroic ballads based on Icelandic sagas was revitalized in the Faroes in the nineteenth century and continued into this century, although printed saga editions then formed the sources.

In our oldest sources for the Faroese ballad dance, i.e. those from the seventeenth century, it is stated that heroic ballads were sung especially at weddings and at Christmas. This is still the usual practice although there is also dancing on other occasions, The period Christmas to Lent remains the main season for dancing. The custom in some southern villages, notes Hammershaimb in 1846, has been that the dancers should not sing any ballad more than once during the dancing season, which gives an idea of the extent of the ballad repertory in such places. The reason for this custom appears to have been, first, to make the singing as varied as

6   T. Tarnovius, *Feröers Beskrifvelser*, ed. H. Hamre, Köbenhavn 1950, 76 = *Færoensia* 2. My translation.

possible; secondly, to prevent anybody other than the dance leader (*skipari*) from learning a ballad which was not 'free'; thirdly, to see to it that as few ballads as possible should become hackneyed. For practising and passing on the tradition, singing at home without dance was of great importance. This took place in connection with indoor work during the dark evenings of autumn and winter.

During the years in which the collection of Faroese ballads mainly took place, the population was between five thousand and ten thousand. In such a society, where the population was both sparse and scattered, the vast repertory of Faroese ballads has been kept alive by relatively few tradition bearers, each of whom has as a rule stored more than one ballad in his memory. Thanks to a source from 1821, referring to the champion ballad singer Jógvan Danielsen, we obtain a glimpse of the number and different kinds of ballads a good tradition bearer was capable of retaining.

First, he had to sing the first section of 'Sjúrðar kvæði' for me . . . Then he sung the ballad of 'Grímur kongur á Bretlandi' which lasted more than one hour. And then he listed for me the names of 20 ballads which he knew from beginning to end. When I did not understand a particular word and asked him for an explanation, he gave it to me and to illustrate his interpretation, would cite another stanza where the meaning was quite clear. *Jógvan*, said my hostess, is a strange man; he speaks a language which we scarcely understand.[7]

From the list which Forchhammer made of the titles of the ballads on Sandoy, which certainly also includes the repertory of Jógvan, we can see that they are 23 in number, nearly all falling into the category of heroic ballads. Since all ballads in the list have been written down from other informants on Sandoy, it is possible to make an approximate estimate of the number of stanzas Jógvan knew by heart — they would have amounted to at least 2,500. It therefore

7 J.G. Forchhammer, *Rejse til Færöerne. Dagbog 8, April til 21. August 1821*, ed. Ad. Clément, Köbenhavn 1927, 47-8. The English translation is by S. Sweeney.

remains a mystery why the collector of *Sandoyarbók*, Johannes Clemensen, only took down one single heroic ballad from Jógvan, but perhaps Jógvan did not want to expose the full spectrum of his repertory to a local collector; there are later parallels from Skálavík for such behaviour.

In an article about the Faroese ballads, printed in *Nordisk Kultur* in 1931, the Norwegian scholar Knut Liestøl expresses the opinion that the dancing function generally has had a detrimental influence on the texts of the ballads. Since the Faroese like to dance they have a predilection for long ballads. An easy way to expand a ballad text is to make frequent use of so-called parallel-stanzas and to insert many stereotype stanzas when depicting certain themes, such as voyages. This, according to Liestøl, has the effect that many Faroese ballad texts seem rather lengthy and watered down to a reader. As the general and the stereotype has expanded, the ballads have lost poetically and what is individual and essential to a given subject has been suppressed. When Jan de Vries in an article about stereotype and individual characteristics of Scandinavian poetry, printed in 1923, went so far as to consider the Faroese ballad composer as a *vísasmiður* — a song-smith — rather than a real artist, the editor of the periodical in question very sensibly asked the Faroese Jóannes Patursson, himself an excellent ballad dance leader (*skipari*), for his comments.[8] Rather than have his article take the shape of a formal refutation of Jan de Vries, Patursson fortunately chose to give as his contribution a presentation of three outstanding Faroese ballad singers, whose ballad dance performance he had personally experienced.[9]

Here we shall only refer to two of them, starting with 'Jøkil Buason', a singer who did not want his identity disclosed, although his name and birthplace on Suðuroy are known to us. The event took place in Vesturvík, which is another name for the village of Fámjin, and the occasion is the ballad dance, the so-called 'Grindadansur', after the

8 J. de Vries, 'Stereotype og individuelle sermerke ved den skandinaviske folkediktning' in *Norsk Aarbok* 1923, 23-46.

9 J. Patursson, 'Tríggjar föroyskar kvæðakempur' in *Norsk Aarbok* 1924, 28-37. The English translation is by Sheila Arnskov.

slaughter of pilot whales. Jóannes Patursson observed this thirty years earlier and left us the following vivid description:

It was almost dark when we reached the village. The flock of whales had been slaughtered. The Grindadansur was in full swing on the green pasture. We approached. It was then I saw Jøkil the first time; he was leading 'Einars rímu Tambarskelvar'.[10]

Twelve of the men from his own village were nearest him and sang along with him, a hundred or so people singing the refrain. The others who had been at the killing of the whales sat in small groups on the grass around the dance and watched and listened, nobody went into the dance ring. 'We had better not join in', I said to my companion, 'let's sit down too.' 'Yes, indeed', he answered, 'to join in the dance now is sacrilege.'

The sky was clear and the wind still. Dark blue mountains encircled the village fields. Ridges, clefts and peaks stood out against the last light which was fading in the west. Cliffs were reflected in the mirror surface of the bay. Side by side three hundred whales at rest on the white sand.

In the midst of the scenic beauty, on this green turf, this ancient people in their age-old dress, with age-old steps, danced this age-old Faroese dance. And in an ancient language and ancient melody the singer told the story of ancient heroes of Norway.

History was lived out in the dance and we who sat watching lived it too.

We have been in Norway and visited King Olav and Einar Tambarskelv; we have been to Iceland to fetch Ílint, the strong one, to kill the evil giant who troubled the people and king of Norway. We have once again been in Norway and listened to the dragons howling on the Dovrefjell and seen the giant clambering over hill and dale to Trondheim, and we saw Ílint kill him.

Now we are once more in the Faroe Islands, in the atmosphere of a Faroese village on a gentle mild summer

10   *TSB* E 120, *Einars tættir*.

night. Jökil and all the others who took us on this journey into history are now tired and have sat down on the grass. Those who sung the *kvæði* and we who watched and listened have experienced a moment of sanctity. This moment and many others like it explain how these few Faroese, living under foreign domination, cut off generation after generation, have been able to maintain their spirit, as it was the day they landed on these skerries.

The other ballad singer, i.e. the farmer Tróndur á Trøð from Skálavík, mentioned by Jóannes Patursson, describes his background and life thus:

I was born on the 17th of November, 1846. From my earliest years I loved our *kvæði*. My first memory is of father spinning in the winter evenings and singing in his strong beautiful voice. He was one of the great *kvæði* singers, well known in his time. At first I didn't understand much, but soon I began to catch what he was singing about. I wept when Roland brought together on a scarlet shield his dead companions, but when the heathen, Dosmar, dared to seize the horn from his hand, and Roland struggled to open his dying eyes and whacked Dosmar on the head with the horn so that the brain burst and stuck to the horn, then I thought that that was a great feat and I must admit that I felt it served him right.

Then I started to go to the dance. I was scarcely more than 8 years old. First I went with my father and mother, later with my sisters and then on my own. At that time old men went to the dance, old lads with white beards; then there was real dancing. It wasn't without grounds that I was afraid of these huge old fellows; they tramped on the floor; at times their arms were up over their heads, and then they jumped nearly to the ceiling; their eyes blazed; it was as if sparks shot from them, and I didn't dare to go near them. But when the *kvæði* was over – it could last for hours – then they sat down to get their breath, and I saw that they were gentle. Then they would discuss the *kvæði* that had been performed, censured what they considered worthy of censure, and praised what was good. They liked great heavy blows; then neither shield nor helmet was of avail and everyone was split in two and cast into the sea. They sat and boasted until they were rested, then they went again and had a look at the dance. If a *kvæði* that they liked was in progress they went into the dance again.

About his repertory of *kvæði* and their origin Tróndur informs us:

I didn't know very many *kvæði*, but enough for me not to have to sing the same *kvæði* in the course of a year. My father knew far more, but none of them was written down; however, I learned a number from him. Jóannes í Króki (i.e. Johannes Clemensen, the collector of the ballad manuscript *Sandoyarbók*) had *kvæði* that were written down, and anyone who wanted them could get them from him. I collected *kvæði* from different places; I can hardly remember all those I have known. Now my sons know all of them, but I myself will end by forgetting them all.

Jóannes Patursson's own contribution to the portrayal of Tróndur as a ballad singer refers to his own experience of him in Skálavík, five years previous to his article. He was dance leader (*skipari*) on a so-called Last Night Dance, i.e. on the last Sunday before Lent. His account runs like this:

I was in Skálavík. Several of us went and asked Tróndur to sing 'Ilingstáttarnir' — there are between 600 and 700 stanzas — which have been preserved by Tróndur's forefathers and they are not found anywhere else.[11] Tróndur has often been asked for them, but he has refused. It took a long time to persuade him, but at last he came along. When we got to the place where the dance was being held, the dancing stopped at the end of the *kvæði* that was in progress. Everyone knew that Tróndur had come, he had come to sing, and he was held in such an esteem that it was self evident that he should take charge of the dance. 'It is best to take a short *kvæði* first to loosen up my voice', said Tróndur, and he started on 'Seyðaríman', which he sang right through.[12] There are 60-70 stanzas in it. It seemed

11   *TSB* E 127, *Ílints tættir*.
12   *TSB* E 149, *Seyða ríma*.

to me characteristic that these 60-70 stanzas should be to 'loosen his voice' and to get the dance going before he started on the main *kvæði*. When he had finished the last stanza he went out of the dance and rested for a little while. During this time the dance waited for him. He came into the dance again and started 'Ílingstáttarnir', which he and his sons sang alone, while the rest of the dancers joined in the refrain. Tróndur himself says that when at the age of 8 he went to the dance and the old men sang 'then there was real dancing'. I say, 'The evening that Tróndur led 'Ílingstáttarnir', then there was *real* dancing in Skálavík!'

More than 50 years had to pass after this event before Jógvan, the son of Tróndur and the last possessor of the heroic ballad in question, decided to let me tape-record it in its entirety, i.e. 507 quatrains divided between three *tættir*. His main reason for permitting me to record it was, as he stated himself, that there was no longer any suitable successor to it within the family.[13]

13 The recording was made in Skálavík on 14th and 15th June, 1970 in the home of Jógvan's youngest brother, Leifur Tróndarson (1901-80); present also was another brother, Jørundur. Jógvan Trondesen (1889-1983) sung the ballad in a so-called 'sitting performance' (Far. *í sitandi kvøðing*), being assisted in singing the refrain by Leifur. During the performance Jógvan had at his disposal his father's handwritten ballad book (from 1865); the fluency of his performance, however, seemed to indicate that he knew most of the ballad by heart. Afterwards, Jógvan told me that he had never sung the ballad in its entirety in a dancing performance. He had, however, sung the first two fits of it, numbering about 430 stanzas and, together, forming a narrative whole, at a dance in the village of Dalur. On the other hand, his brother Leifur informed me that he himself had only sung the third fit of the ballad in dancing performances in Skálavík and in Tórshavn. With regard to Jóannes Patursson's earlier description of his father — Tróndur á Tröð (17.11.1846 — 7.3.1933) — and his singing of the ballad in a 'Last Night' dance performance in Skálavík, Jógvan

(who was one of the participants) wanted to make it clear that his father had not sung all of the ballad on that particular occasion. As well as that, I was told by Jógvan and his brothers that, according to family tradition, their grandfather, Pætur, had once sung the whole ballad in a dance performance in the village of Hvalvík on Streymoy after a whale hunt. He was said to have sung the ballad very rapidly. In Jógvan's opinion this was probably done in order to prevent others present from learning the ballad.

THE CAULDRON OF REGENERATION: CONTINUITY AND FUNCTION IN THE WELSH FOLK EPIC TRADITION*

ROBIN GWYNDAF
(Welsh Folk Museum, Cardiff)

I

There has been in Wales a very long and rich bardic and folk narrative tradition.

In 1188 Giraldus Cambriensis (Gerald the Welshman) — who, as his name indicates, was of Welsh descent, but who also had Norman blood in him — made a journey through Wales, and in his two classic books, *Itinerarium Kambriae* (The Journey through Wales) and *Descriptio Kambriae* (Description of Wales), although he freely discusses some dishonourable features of the Welsh people, he also writes of many praiseworthy aspects.[1]

> No one of this nation ever begs, for the houses of all are common to all; and they place liberality and hospitality above all other virtues . . . those who arrive in the morning are entertained till evening with the conversation of young women and the music of the harp.

It is difficult to know of anyone who has captured the atmosphere of entertainment in early Wales better than Morys Clynnog at the beginning of Gruffydd Robert's Welsh Grammar, *Dosparth Byrr ar y rhann gyntaf i ramadeg cymraeg*. Both Morys Clynnog and Gruffydd Robert were Catholic exiles, and publication of this Grammar was begun in Milan in 1567.

*I am most grateful to my colleagues Dr William Linnard, Miss Verona Pritchard, Mr Niclas Walker and Dr Anne E. Williams for their kind assistance in preparing this paper for publication, and to Mr Tony Bianchi for his valuable guidance with the selection relating to Anglo-Welsh novelists and poets.

1 For English translations, see L. Thorpe, *The Journey Through Wales* and *The Description of Wales*, Harmondsworth 1978. See also B.F. Roberts, *Gerald of Wales*, Cardiff 1982.

In its prologue we find the two men one warm afternoon in a pleasant orchard and, being far away from their native country, they converse about the days gone by. I cannot hope to convey in English the excellence of Morys Clynnog's Welsh prose, but here, at least, is the meaning of his words:

Although the place where we are now is very beautiful, although it is pleasant to see the green leaves offering shelter from the sun, and although it is wonderful to feel this northern breeze blowing beneath the vines to give us joy in this unreasonable heat, which is heavy on everyone who was born and bred in a country as cold as the land of Wales is, yet I have a longing ['*y mae arnaf hiraeth*'] for many things which were to be had in Wales to pass the time away pleasantly and happily while sheltering from the sun on long summer days. Because there, however warm the weather, there would be comfort and joy to every sort of man. If one wished entertainment, one would have a musician with his harp to play sweet tunes and a melodious singer to sing harp verses according to his desire, whether praise of virtue or satire of evil. If you wish to hear of the custom of the country during our grandfathers' time you would find grey old men who could relate to you by word of mouth every remarkable and famous deed which happened throughout the land of Wales a long time ago.

'A long time ago . . .' The earliest written Welsh poetry takes us to the second half of the sixth century and to districts which today form part of Southern Scotland and Northern England. Until about the middle of the seventh century the Brythonic (or British) people occupied the country south of the modern Glasgow and Edinburgh as far down as Wales and even Cornwall, Devon and Somerset.[2]

2 See T. Parry, *A History of Welsh Literature*, translated from the Welsh by H. Idris Bell, Oxford 1955, and G. Williams, *An Introduction to Welsh Literature*, Cardiff 1978. For a standard history of medieval Wales, see J.E. Lloyd, *A History of Wales from the Earliest Times to the Edwardian Conquest*, 1-2, London 1911. For English translations of early Welsh poetry referred to in this paper, see A. Conran and J.E. Caerwyn Williams, *The Penguin Book of Welsh Verse*, Harmondsworth 1967; J.P. Clancy, *The Earliest Welsh Poetry*, London 1970; K.H. Jackson, *A Celtic Miscellany: Translations from the Celtic Literatures*, Harmondsworth 1971; G. Jones,

According to Nennius, Cunedda Wledig and his eight sons came down to Wales in the fourth century from Manaw Gododdin — the land around Stirling between the rivers Forth and Tyne, and he can truly be regarded as one of the founding fathers of the Welsh nation. The Brythoneg (or British) tongue gradually developed into Welsh between this time and the sixth century, and the poet Taliesin (referred to as *Taliesin Pen Bardd*, 'Taliesin Chief Poet,' made a masterful use of the new language in his poems of praise to Urien, king of Rheged (the present counties of Wigtown and Kircudbright), and his son Owain. The poems have been preserved in a thirteenth century manuscript, known as *Llyfr Taliesin*, 'The Book of Taliesin'.[3]

By the sixth century the English had settled in kingdoms along the eastern coast and were a continuous thorn in the side of the Brythons. The conquerors from the Continent, and Deodric, king of Bernicia in particular, attacked Rheged, but Urien, says Taliesin, was 'the land's anchor'. His generosity in court and his courage in battle will long be remembered. 'When you attack the Angles have no answer . . . You are the bridge from the past to the future, the best of your breed, the head of your race.' When his son Owain slew Fflamddwyn ('Flame-bearer', a nickname given to the English King by the Brythons) it was, according to the poet, 'no more to do than sleeping'.

Pan laddawd Owain Fflamddwyn
Nid oedd fwy nogyd cysgaid.

And this statement is followed by a most vivid description of the fallen warriors of the English army:

The Oxford Book of Welsh Verse in English, Oxford 1977; G. Williams, *An Introduction to Welsh Poetry from the Beginnings to the Sixteenth Century*, London 1953; G. Williams, *The Burning Tree: Poems from the First Thousand Years of Welsh Verse*, London 1956; and G. Williams, *Welsh Poems: Sixth Century to 1600*, London 1973. I have used the above anthologies (and others not yet mentioned) in translating the poetry quoted in this paper.

3 See J. Gwenogfryn Evans, *Facsimile and Text of the Book of Taliesin*, Llanbedrog 1910. For an edited text of the Taliesin poems, see I. Williams, *Canu Taliesin*, Cardiff 1960. For a translation into English, see J.E. Caerwyn Williams, *The Poems of Taliesin*, Dublin 1968.

Cysgid Lloegr llydan nifer
  A lleufer yn eu llygaid.[4]

'Sleeps now the wide host of England with the light in their eyes.'

A contemporary of Taliesin was a poet called Aneirin, according to tradition the author of the classic and comparatively long poem 'Y Gododdin' — the name also of the tribe who lived in the land between the rivers Forth and Tyne, Manaw Gododdin, with Caer Eiddyn as its chief city (on the site of the modern Edinburgh). Mynyddawg Mwynfawr, 'Mynyddawg the Wealthy', was its King, and for a whole year he trained and entertained a choice band of three hundred youths of noble blood to recapture Catraeth (Catterick) from the English of Deira.[5]

It was a tragic but glorious failure, a daring expedition doomed to destruction. All but one of the warriors were killed, and in this splendid poem the poet expresses his deep sense of loss for the young men who fell one after another, but also his praise for their unyielding courage in the face of death.

Gwŷr a aeth Gatraeth oedd ffraeth eu llu;
Glasfedd eu hancwyn, a gwenwyn fu.
Trichant trwy beiriant yn catau —
A gwedi elwch tawelwch fu.
Cyd elwynt i lannau i benydu
Dadl diau angau i eu treiddu.

'Men went to Catraeth, ready for battle; fresh mead was their feast, bitter was the after-taste. Three hundred by command giving battle — and after exultation there was silence. Though they went to churches to do penance, the certain doom of death encountered them.'

---

4 *Marwnad Owain ab Urien*, 'Elegy to Owain, the son of Urien'.
5 See I. Williams, *Canu Aneirin*, Cardiff 1938, and K.H. Jackson, *The Gododdin: The Oldest Scottish Poem*, Edinburgh 1969. The poem has been translated metrically in J.P. Clancy, *The Earliest Welsh Poetry*. See also Rachel Bromwich, ed., *The Beginnings of Welsh Poetry, Studies by I. Williams*, Cardiff 1972.

The main qualities of this early poetry are clarity, restraint, vividness and sincerity, and, to quote Dr Gwynfor Evans:

> This is one of the great wonders of our history — that the Welsh language was the medium of such beauty and civility in such an uncivilized age; that a radiance streamed through it when the lights of Christian Europe had been extinguished... when the darkness over England was so profound that only a few fragments are known about its condition and its history ... this is when a superb and shimmering stream of Welsh literature began upon its course down fourteen hundred years.[6]

One by one the Brythonic kingdoms of the Old North fell to the enemy, but through the poems of Taliesin and Aneirin the memory of the heroic valour of their defenders was kept alive for generations to come.[7]

In no other country in Europe is the poet given a higher place of honour today than in Wales (the National Eisteddfod and the hundreds of local *eisteddfodau*, for example, attest to this).[8] As Emyr Humphreys in his book *The Taliesin Tradition: A Quest for the Welsh Identity*[9] has admirably demonstrated, the Welsh poetic tradition can be traced unbroken through the centuries. To use a phrase of Saunders Lewis, we cannot 'pluck a flower of song' in our own days without 'stirring a great northern star in the sixth century'.[10]

6 *The Land of my Fathers: 2000 Years of Welsh History*, translated from the Welsh *Aros Mae*, by Elin and R. Garlick, Swansea 1974, 55.

7 See A.O.H. Jarman, *The Cynfeirdd: Early Welsh Poets and Poetry*, Cardiff 1981, and A.O.H. Jarman, 'The Heroic View of Life in Early Welsh Verse' in R. O'Driscoll, ed., *The Celtic Consciousness*, Toronto 1981, 161-8.

8 See the annual bilingual *Illustrated Programme: Proclamation Ceremony of the Royal National Eisteddfod of Wales*. For a concise history of the National Eisteddfod, see H. Teifi Edwards, *Yr Eisteddfod*, Llandysul 1976.

9 London 1983.

10 Quoted in E. Humphreys, *op. cit.*, 2. Saunders Lewis refers to Ioan Siencyn, a minor eighteenth-century poet from Pembrokeshire.

II

The earliest written reference to Welsh folk narratives appears in Nennius' *Historia Brittonum* (c.800).[11] To him, as to most early historians, the boundary between history and legend was very unreal and, fortunately, he relates traditions not only about past heroes, such as Arthur, Gwrtheyrn (Vortigern), Taliesin, and Garmon, but also about wells, lakes, stones and other physical features. Even so, we are reminded that what he relates, however valuable, is but a small reflection of a much larger collection of now lost tales and traditions.

No mention of the early folk narrative tradition can be made without reference to the eleven classic tales known as 'The Mabinogion', described by Professors Gwyn and Thomas Jones as being among 'the finest flowerings of the Celtic genius and, taken together, a masterpiece of our medieval European literature'.[12] The tales have been preserved in two Welsh collections: *Llyfr Gwyn Rhydderch* (The White Book of Rhydderch), written about 1300-25, and *Llyfr Coch Hergest* (The Red Book of Hergest), belonging to the period 1375-1425, but many of the narratives must have been known in their present form well before the time of the earliest of these manuscripts.

Although Wales since the Middle Ages has not seen professional storytellers with a large repertoire of long, heroic tales, romantic tales or *Märchen*, yet, throughout the centuries the role of the active and passive folk narrative tradition-bearers has been an important one. It is they who have kept the old and the new tales alive by retelling them to others

---

11   For an English translation, see J. Morris, *British History; and the Welsh Annals*, London 1980.
12   *The Mabinogion*, Everyman edition, London 1948, IX. See also W.J. Gruffydd, *Folklore and Myth in the Mabinogion*, Cardiff 1958; K.H. Jackson, *The International Popular Tale and Early Welsh Tradition*, Cardiff 1961; A. and B. Rees, *Celtic Heritage*, London 1961; and P. Mac Cana, *The Mabinogi*, Cardiff 1977.

and have thus ensured that the magic of folklore still delights and sustains the spirit of man.[13]

In the fourth Branch of the Mabinogi (composed probably during the second half of the eleventh century) you may recall the scene where Gwydion and his company enter Pryderi's court in Dyfed in the guise of bards:

'Lord', said Gwydion, 'it is a custom with us that the first night after one comes to a great man, the chief bard shall have the say. I will tell a tale gladly.' [*Yntau, Wydion, gorau cyfarwydd yn y byd oedd*.] And he, Gwydion, was the best storyteller in the world.[14]

Here we are reminded that the poet and the storyteller in medieval Wales, as elsewhere, often combined the same role.

We are reminded also of the following words in the *Trioedd Cerdd*, 'The poetic or song triads':[15] *Tripheth a beir y gerddawr vot yn amyl: kyvarwyddyt ystoryeau, a barddoniaeth a hengerdd*: 'Three things that give amplitude to a poet: knowledge of histories, the poetic art and old verse.' *Ystoryeau* in this context, to quote Rachel Bromwich, means 'the national inheritance of ancient traditions'.[16] The word is a late borrowing from the Latin *historia*; and the repertoire of a number of cultured tradition-bearers in Wales today — men who often combine the roles of local historian, storyteller

---

13 For works relating to Welsh folk narratives, see I. Williams, *Hen Chwedlau*, Cardiff 1949; A.O.H. Jarman, *Chwedlau Cymraeg Canol*, Cardiff 1957; J. Rhŷs, *Celtic Folklore*: Welsh and Manx, 1-2, Oxford 1901; T. Gwynn Jones, *Welsh Folklore and Folk Customs*, London 1930 (reissued 1979 with a new introduction and bibliography by A. ap Gwynn, Woodbridge and Totowa, N.J.); T. Jones, 'Y Stori Werin yng Nghymru' in *Transactions of the Honourable Society of Cymmrodorion* (1970), 16-32; and R. Gwyndaf, 'The Welsh Folk Narrative Tradition' in Venetia J. Newall, ed., *Folklore Studies in the Twentieth Century, Proceedings of the Centenary Conference of the Folklore Society*, Woodbridge and Totowa 1980, 218-25.

14 *Loc. cit.*, 56-7.

15 As recorded in *Llyfr Coch Hergest* (The Red Book of Hergest) version of the *dwned*, 'grammar', attributed to Einion Offeiriad.

16 *Trioedd Ynys Prydein. The Welsh Triads*, Cardiff 1961, LXXI.

and poet — is a remarkable reminder of the eleventh century triad.[17]

Medieval storytellers and poets in many countries were expected to be well versed in history, traditions and genealogy of their people; for example, the Teutonic *scop*, the Hindu *suta*, the Irish *fili*, the *bardos* of the Continental Celts and the Welsh *pencerdd*. In certain countries the same is true also of post-medieval storytellers and poets. It is true, for example, of the Irish *seanchaí* and, to a lesser extent, of the Welsh storyteller.[18] In Wales the link between the present and the past was a very real one. Folk memory made people conscious of a long and vivid history. Giraldus Cambrensis wrote:

> Even the common people retain their genealogy, and can not only readily recount the names of their grandfathers and great-grandfathers but even refer back to the sixth or seventh generation or beyond them . . .

And the Welsh term *hyd y nawfed ach*, 'to the ninth generation', is still in common use today.

Thus, in this paper, I shall not draw a strict dividing line between verse and prose, poetry and narrative. Although we usually link the great epics of the world with verse, in outlining the Welsh epic tradition, form, as such, is not the crucial factor. The most important consideration, in my opinion, is content and function. It so happens that occasionally in the Welsh material both verse and prose forms are intermingled. Characters in the Mabinogion tales at times speak in *englynion* — short, concise stanzas. And, as Sir Ifor Williams has ably demonstrated, the ninth-century Llywarch Hen and Heledd cycle of poems are probably relics of long-lost *cyfarwyddyd* — tales and traditions in which the story would be told in prose and the conversation between the characters in verse.

17 See R. Gwyndaf, 'The Folk Narrative Repertoire of a Passive Tradition-Bearer in a Welsh Rural Community', Part I in *Folk Narrative Research, Studia Fennica* 20 (1976), 283-93, Part II in *Fabula* 22 (1981), 28-54.

18 See K.J. Holzknecht, *Literary Patronage in the Middle Ages*, Philadelphia 1923, 21-2; J.H. Delargy, *The Gaelic Story-Teller*, London 1946 and J.E. Caerwyn Williams, *Y Storiwr Gwyddeleg a'i Chwedlau*, Cardiff 1972, 15.

Furthermore, there are certain passages in the early Welsh tales which, when we listen to them, fall on our ears as sweet music. It is poetry in prose form. Mention should be made also of the fact that both prose and verse form reflect similar stylistic formulae and characteristics of the epic, such as the use of stereotyped phrases, stock epithets, hyperbole, parallelism, contrast and repetition.

III

In this paper I confine my remarks mainly to historical characters, men who trod the land of Wales and the Old North hundreds of years ago. But they are men who are born anew and belong to all ages. They are celebrated men of valour and good deeds who are not allowed to die, as if they had been gently carried into the great cauldron of rebirth which, you may recall, Matholwch, King of Ireland, had received as a gift from Branwen's brother, Bendigeidfran, 'Brân the Blessed', and was eventually used by the Irish to revive their own dead in that tragic encounter between the two nations, as told in the second branch of the Mabinogi.

High Kings and warriors of the sixth and seventh century had by the eighth and ninth centuries become characters in legends. Llywarch Hen, 'Llywarch the Old', was a chieftain in the Old North, and in a cycle of ninth-century stanzas by an unknown poet, probably from Powys, in mid-Wales, he mourns the death of his cousin Urien Rheged.[19] His body lies still on the battle-ground: *Ac ar y vronn wenn vran du* — 'And on his white breast a black raven'. Llywarch carried Urien's head away from the battlefield, probably in order to prevent its mutilation by the enemy, and addresses it in a series of moving stanzas. And in another series he laments the loss of Urien's home — the hearth of Rheged, now in ruins:

---

19 For an edited text of the Llywarch Hen and Heledd cycle of poems, see I. Williams, *Canu Llywarch Hen*, Cardiff 1935. See also I. Williams, *Lectures in Early Welsh Poetry*, Dublin 1944, and P. Ford, *The Poetry of Llywarch Hen, Introduction, Text and Translation*, California 1974.

Yr aelwyt hon, neus clad hwch.
Mwy gordyfnassei elwch
Gwyr, ac am gyrn kyuedwch.

'This hearth, the sow digs there. More customary of the old
the exultation of heroes, and around the drinking-horn
carousal.'

Llywarch when he lived in Powys had, according to the
poet, twenty four noble sons who valiantly defended the
Marches against the English. All were killed. Llywarch in his
old age became a herdsman in poor circumstances. He addresses
his wooden staff:

Baglan brenn, neut kynteuin.
Neut rud rych; neut crych egin.
Etlit ym edrych y'th yluin.

'Wooden staff, it is early summer, brown the furrow, curly
the young corn, the sight of your cook makes me groan.'

Wyf hen, wyf unic, wyf annelwic oer,
    Gwedy gwely keinmic,
Wyf truan, wyf tri dyblic.

'I am old, and alone, and shapeless with cold, my bed was
once splendid. I'm doubled in three, and wretched.'

Y deilen honn, neus kenniret gwynt,
    Gwae hi o'e thynghet!
Hi hen; eleni ganet.

'This leaf, the wind drives it; alas for its destiny. It is old;
this year was it born.'

Urien is also mentioned in a Welsh version of the 'Washer
at the Ford' legend, recorded in a mid-sixteenth century
manuscript — an onomastic legend connected with Llanferres,
Clwyd, which endeavours to explain the birth of his son,
Owain, and his daughter, Morfudd.[20]
Owain, praised by Taliesin in the sixth century for his
valour in battle, by the thirteenth century plays chess with
King Arthur in the Mabinogion tale 'The Dream of Rhonabwy',

20 Peniarth Ms. 147. See Gwenan Jones, 'A Washer at the Ford', in
    Aberystwyth Studies, 4 (1922), 105-9.

and he is also the hero of 'The Lady of the Fountain' (one of three Welsh Romances in the Mabinogion with a strong Norman-French influence). Indeed, a few people in Wales even today still call chess-pieces *Brain Owain ab Urien*, 'the ravens of Owain, son of Urien'.

Cynddylan, the son of Cyndrwyn, with his court at Peng-wern, near Shrewsbury, was killed by the English, probably some time in the seventh century, and generations later stories also grew about him and his family, but, doubtless, there was a kernel of truth in them. In a series of well-known *englynion* (one of the finest examples of poetry in Welsh literature, again belonging to the ninth century), Cynddylan's sister, Heledd, mourns his death and that of her other brothers. She wanders, almost insanely, from grave to grave, from hill to hill, and ends her days as a cowherd, stricken with grief. Their beautiful home is now destroyed:

Stauell Gyndylan ys tywyll heno,
    Heb dan, heb wely.
Wylaf wers; tawaf wedy.

Stauell Gyndylan ys tywyll heno,
    Heb dan, heb gannwyll.
Namyn Duw, pwy a'm dyry pwyll?

'The hall of Cynddylan is dark tonight, without fire, without bed. I shall weep awhile, then I will be silent.'

'The hall of Cynddylan is dark tonight, without candle. But for God, who will give me sanity?'

IV

The poet in medieval times, as we well know, was often endowed also with the gift of prophecy, and just as the great Virgil eventually became a magician and prophet, two sixth-century Welsh poets had by the ninth century become legendary characters with superhuman and prophetic powers.

One was Myrddin (Merlin) whose legends became so widespread in the Celtic countries and on the Continent. In the Welsh version, founded upon the primitive theme of the Wild Man in the Woods, Myrddin after his defeat at the Battle of Arfderydd (the modern Arthuret, near Carlisle) in 573, lost his reason and fled to Coed Celyddon, the Caledonian Forest in the then Welsh-speaking Scottish Lowlands. While wandering in misery for half a century with only a wild pigling as his 'rude bedfellow' he became a prophet. From the ninth century onwards his prophecies were contained in poems claimed to have been written by Myrddin himself, many of which are included in *Llyfr Du Caerfyrddin* (The Black Book of Carmarthen), written about 1200.[21] Most of the more recent traditions about Myrddin are centred around Caerfyrddin (Carmarthen), 'the fort of Myrddin'. Many stones in the district are connected with his prophecies, and his famous oak tree in the town was for many years carefully guarded by the municipal authorities. And well should they take such care! Had not the great Merlin himself prophesied:

When Myrddin's tree shall tumble down,
Then shall fall Carmarthen town.

A few years ago the old tree's remaining stub was eventually taken down to make way for road improvements, but the good people of Carmarthen took the precaution of keeping it safe in the County Museum!

According to one tradition the great magician is still alive in a cave in Bryn Myrddin, 'Merlin's Hill', kept in bonds of enchantment for ever by his once beloved Vivien, and at certain times of the year people used to hear his groans bewailing his folly in allowing a woman to learn his secret spell.[22]

The other sixth-century poet, of course, was Taliesin who, in the process of time, became a figure of the greatest importance in Celtic myth and romance. This is attested to, for example, in the wide-ranging and often complicated collection of prophetic, legendary and religious poems attributed to him in the manuscript known as *Llyfr Taliesin*, 'Taliesin's Book',

---

21 See A.O.H. Jarman, *Llyfr Du Caerfyrddin*, Cardiff 1982; A.O.H. Jarman, *The Legend of Merlin*, Cardiff 1960; and A.O.H. Jarman, *Ymddiddan Myrddin a Thaliesin*, Cardiff 1951.
22 J. Ceredig Davies, *Folk-Lore of West and Mid-Wales*, Aberystwyth 1911, 265-71.

written c.1275; these poems, in fact, were composed much later than the age of Taliesin himself, mainly in the ninth and tenth centuries. By then a widespread and most amusing legend had grown up around him which must have formed an essential part of the repertoire of medieval storytellers. It explains vividly the circumstances of his birth and the source of his magical powers.[23]

A powerful witch called Ceridwen had the most ugly son in the world, Morfran, also named Afagddu, 'Darkness'. In order that he would be accepted in society she conjured up a plan which would enable him to know all about the past, the present and the future. And this was how she set about it — she boiled for a whole year and a day in her cauldron of inspiration all the known virtuous herbs that would at the end of that period produce a magic essence — three shining drops — which were to be swallowed by the ugly son at the appropriate time. A blind man was employed to keep the fire burning and a young boy called Gwion Bach to assist him. But this Gwion Bach was a clever lad and when the witch accidentally fell asleep just before the end of the year he changed places with the ugly son at the crucial moment and swallowed the three sacred drops. Gwion Bach, now the wisest man on earth, fled in fear of Ceridwen's wrath. During the chase both of them transformed themselves into various animals. Finally Gwion became a grain of wheat, but he was swallowed by Ceridwen when she turned herself into a hen and in nine months she gave birth to a beautiful son. She sewed the baby up in a skin bag and threw him into the sea in a tiny coracle. The bag was picked up by Elphin at Cored Wyddno, 'Gwyddno's weir', on the edge of the Mochno bog, near where the village of Borth is today. Marvelling at his lovely forehead (*tal*), Elphin called the baby Taliesin, 'beautiful brow'. Elphin was the son of Gwyddno Garanhir, king of Maes Gwyddno or Cantref Gwaelod, 'the lowland hundred', where Taliesin was brought up. When it was drowned by the sea, Taliesin, we are told, escaped.

23 See I. Williams, *Chwedl Taliesin*, Cardiff 1957, and Juliette Wood, *A Study of the Legend of Taliesin*, unpublished M.Litt. thesis, University of Oxford, 1979.

That is the legend of the shape-shifting Taliesin. His name has been commemorated since 1820 in a tiny village near the Mochno bog, called Tre Taliesin, where his grave is said to be.[24] But wherever Taliesin was actually buried, his spirit lived on as a constant source of inspiration.[25] The great eighteenth-century genius and eccentric Edward Williams (Iolo Morganwg), founder of the Bards of the Island of Britain (1792), to name but one admirer, had the greatest respect for druidic lore and Taliesinic mysteries.[26] It is little wonder that he named his first-born son Taliesin, and in a letter to his friend William Owen (Pughe), (who, apparently, christened his own first-born son Aneurin, in commemoration of the sixth-century poet) he wrote the following words:

> I hope my Taliesin will live to be the Editor and Translator of the works of his ancient namesake ... There will be a dawning of a New Age in Welsh Learning and it will be known to posterity as 'The Age of Taliesin'.[27]

Iolo Morganwg's motto: *Y Gwir yn Erbyn y Byd*, 'the truth against the world' was also adopted by the famous Welsh-American architect Frank Lloyd Wright, whose Unitarian grandfather and inheritor of druidic lore emigrated to the New World in 1841 and settled in Wisconsin. When building his own homes Frank Lloyd Wright named all three of the houses in memory of the sixth-century poet and all he stood for:

> I began to build Taliesin to get my back against the wall and fight for what I had to fight ... All my people had Welsh names for their places ... So I too chose a Welsh name for mine and it was Taliesin. Taliesin, a druid ... He

24 See R.J. T[homas], *Bedd Taliesin*, Tre'rddôl 1968, and Juliette Wood, 'Bedd Taliesin' in *Ceredigion: Journal of the Ceredigion Antiquary Society* (1979), 414-8.
25 E.g. 'Taliesyn Jewellery' is the name of a company of craftsmen who design items in gold and silver at Pontsenni (Sennybridge), Powys.
26 See G.J. Williams, *Iolo Morganwg*, Cardiff 1956, and P. Morgan, *Iolo Morganwg*, Cardiff 1975.
27 Quoted in E. Humphreys, *The Taliesin Tradition*, 110.

sang the glories of fine art ... so I chose Taliesin for a
name — it means 'Shining Brow'.[28]

V

'They are passionately devoted to their freedom and to the
defence of their country.' Thus wrote Giraldus Cambrensis
about the Welsh people towards the end of the twelfth century in his *Itinerarium Kambriae*. Until 1485 when the Welshman Henry Tudor became King of England, Wales was a nation
living under constant fear of attack, mainly from its mightier
conqueror and neighbour — England. The only exceptions
were brief periods of uneasy independence notably during
the two centuries prior to the death of Llywelyn ap Gruffydd,
known as 'The Last Prince of Wales'.

In the Lansdowne Collection of manuscripts in the British
Library, a Government official writing a secret report, sometime around 1600, on the state of religion in North Wales,
has given us a vivid description of how the Welsh people in
Gwynedd were constantly reminded of their long struggle with
their alien neighbours, and reminded also of the deeds and
valour of their own national heroes:

> Upon the Sondaies and hollidaies the multitude of all
> sortes of men woomen and childerne of everie parishe doe
> use to meete in sondrie places either one some hill or one
> the side of some mountaine where theire harpers and
> crowthers singe them songs of the doeings of theire aun-
> cestors, namelie, of theire warrs againste the kings of this
> realme and the English nacion, and then doe they ripp upp
> theire petigres at lenght howe eche of them is discended
> from those theire ould princs. Here alsoe doe they spende
> theire time in hearinge some part of the lives of Thalaassyn,
> Marlin Be[u]no, Kybbye, Jermon [Garmon], and suche
> other the intended prophets and saincts of the cuntrie.[29]

Reminding the Welsh people of their past — its glory and
tragedy — made them conscious also of the ever-present pos-

28 *Ibid.*, 160-1. See F. Lloyd Wright, *An Autobiography*, London
    1945.
29 Lansdowne Ms. 111, fol. 10.

sibility of a better future. In upholding this banner of hope the Welsh poets played a central role. After the days of Taliesin and Aneirin hundreds of poems have been composed in honour of kings, princes and other noble leaders of society. These poems are mostly in strict traditional *cynghanedd* metre a highly developed art of an intricate system of alliteration and repeated rhyme.[30] Much emphasis was placed on craft, and although the poems were preserved eventually by being written down in manuscripts, they were intended primarily for oral presentation — to be recited, chanted or sung and to have a direct appeal to the listeners.

It is true at times it was difficult even for the poets themselves to see any glimmer of hope. With the loss of a great prince, brave in battle and generous in court, who now would man the breach? At no time in our history was this more deeply felt than in that dark and gloomy winter of 1282, when Wales lost her independence with the death of Llywelyn ap Gruffydd, affectionately known ever since by the Welsh people as *Llywelyn ein Llyw Olaf*, 'Llywelyn our last Prince'. On the 12th December that year after he and a small band of his men had unsuccessfully defended Irfon Bridge, at Cilmeri, near Builth Wells, against the might of Edward I's army, he was returning almost alone to rejoin his own soldiers on the land above the river when an English knight, Stephen de Franckton, probably ignorant of the Prince's identity, pierced his body with a spear. Later Edward arranged for Llywelyn's severed head to be crowned with ivy and carried on a pole through the streets of London to the sound of horns and trumpets and great merriment. Legend tells us that the land in Cilmeri where Llywelyn died was once full of broom, but since that fateful day it has never grown again.

As the great historian J.E. Lloyd remarked: 'It was for a far distant generation to see that the last Prince had not lived in vain, but by his life work had helped to build solidly the enduring fabric of Welsh nationality.'[31] To his own people,

---

30 For a concise description of *cynghanedd*, see H. Idris Bell, 'Cynghanedd and the Welsh Metrical System' in *History of Welsh Literature*, 121-6.

31 *The History of Wales*, 2, p. 764.

however, there was little consolation, now that 'the candle of kings' and 'the lion of Gwynedd' was with them no more. It was no less than a national catastrophe, and the anguish and grief is clearly felt in Gruffydd ab yr Ynad Coch's renowned elegy — a poem described by Gwyn Williams as:

> One of the most splendid utterances in Western European literature . . . [moving] . . . to a tremendous climax in which the Poet's whole world comes to an end, and in which, as in the tragedies of Shakespeare, nature and the order of the universe seem to be imperilled by the disaster.[32]

Poni welwch-chwi hynt y gwynt a'r glaw?
Poni welwch-chwi'r deri'n ymdaraw?
Poni welwch-chwi'r môr yn merwinaw'r tir?
Poni welwch-chwi'r gwir yn ymgyweiriaw?
Poni welwch-chwi'r haul yn hwylaw'r awyr?
Poni welwch-chwi'r sŷr wedi r'syrthiaw?
Poni chredwch-chwi i Dduw, ddyniadon ynfyd?
   Poni welwch-chwi'r byd wedi r'bydiaw . . .
  Pen Llywelyn deg, dygn o fraw — i'r byd
    Bod pawl haearn trwyddaw.
   Pen f'arglwydd, poen dygngwydd a'm daw;
    Pen f'enaid heb fanag arnaw.
Pen a fu berchen ar barch naw — canwlad,
    A naw canwledd iddaw.
   Pen tëyrn.

'Do you not see the rush of wind and rain? Do you not see the oak-trees crashing together? Do you not see the ocean scourging the shore? Do you not see the truth is portending? Do you not see the sun hurtling through the sky? Do you not see that the stars have fallen? Have you no belief in God, foolish men? Do you not see that the world is ending? . . . Head of fair Llywelyn, sharp the world's fear, an iron spike through it; head of my lord, harsh pain is mine; head of my spirit left speechless; head that had honour in nine hundred lands; nine hundred feasts for him; head of a king.'[33]

---

32 G. Williams, *An Introduction to Welsh Poetry from the Beginnings to the Sixteenth Century*, London 1953, 92-3.

33 For an English translation of this poem, see the anthologies mentioned in note 2.

The deep sense of loss in the Welsh eulogies, as in this poem, is indeed truly sincere. And yet, in essence, Welsh poetry is celebration poetry. The eulogies, and even most of the elegies, celebrate the continuation of all that is good and lasting in life. The poets were the social conscience of their people, and through their poems, and the eulogies in particular, they were carrying on a centuries-old Celtic tradition of 'holding a mirror up to society, and especially to the leader, and — through this picture of what it and he should be — inflaming their love of that image'[34] — uniting and inspiring and sustaining the highest standards.

In times of distress the Welsh poets from the ninth to the fifteenth centuries would endeavour to raise the spirit and patriotic zeal of their countrymen by forecasting a great revival and the coming of the long-awaited *Mab Darogan*, 'the prophesied son', who would lead his people once again to victory. The great deliverer was one of the remarkable heroes of the past: Cynan, Cadwaladr or Owain. People came to believe that such super-warriors were not dead but asleep in some cave, awaiting for the day to be recalled to battle. The anonymous authors of many early vaticination poems attributed their work to some poet in the distant past, in particular the sixth century Taliesin and Myrddin (Merlin).

A special place of honour was given to the mighty King Arthur, who by the seventh and eighth centuries had become to be considered a supreme warrior, the *dux bellorum* (the commander in battle), as Nennius describes him in his *Historia Brittonum* (c.800). He was the champion defender of the Britons against the attacks of the Angles and Saxons from the Continent, especially in East and South East Britain. Later, more and more fabulous feats were attributed to him, and these, undoubtedly, formed an essential part of the repertoire

34 D. Myrddin Lloyd, quoted in G. Evans, *Land of My Fathers*, Swansea 1974, 74.

of Welsh storytellers in the Middle Ages, and have done so ever since.[35]

Twelve of his battles are listed by Nennius (a list probably based on a lost Welsh poem).[36] In all these he was victorious, and in the last one of all (according to the Nennius text) — the Battle of Badon (c.500) — 'there fell in one day nine hundred and sixty men from one charge by Arthur, and no one laid them low except he himself.'

Arthur was the ultimate standard by which all other kings and warriors were judged. An early popular triad mentions the 'Three Generous Men of Britain: Nudd the Generous, Mordaf the Generous, Rhydderch the Generous.' *Ac Arthur ehun oedd haelach no'r tri*, 'And Arthur himself was more generous than the three.'[37]

In *Y Gododdin* the poet Aneirin describes a valiant young warrior called Gwawrddur attacking the enemy with such ferocity that he left a carnage behind for the crows to feast on: *Gochonai brain du ar fur caer*, 'He glutted black crows on the wall of the stronghold.' He then adds the following brief remark: . . . *cyn ni bai ef Arthur*, 'although he was not Arthur.' There was no need to elaborate. The audience were well aware of the traditions about Arthur's feats in battle. We are reminded of this, for example, when a ninth-century poet who praised the courage and sacrifice of the seventh-century Cynddylan ap Cyndrwyn and his brothers, refers to them as: *Canawon Arthur fras*, 'the whelps of the mighty Arthur'.

The Battle of Camlan in which, according to the *Annales*

---

35. See R.S. Loomis, *Wales and the Arthurian Legend*, Cardiff 1956, L. Alcock, *Arthur's Britain: History and Archaeology, AD 367-634*, London 1971 and B. Lewis Jones, *Arthur y Cymry. The Welsh Arthur*, Cardiff 1975. For a comparison between Arthur (and other early heroes, such as Merlin) and contemporary heroes in literature and film, see G. Thomas, *Arwyr Geiriau, Arwyr Lluniau*, Rhyl 1985.

36 Cf. the two references to Arthur in *Annales Cambriae* (Harley Ms. 3859). See E. Phillimore, 'The "Annales Cambriae" and the Old Welsh Genealogies from Harleian MS 3859' in *Y Cymmrodor*, Vol. 9 (1888), 141-83.

37 Bromwich, *op. cit.* (1901), 5.

Cambriae (Harleian Ms 3859, c.1100), Arthur and Medrawd fell, also became an important point of reference to the Welsh poets. In Gruffydd ab yr Ynad Coch's elegy to Llywelyn, the Last Prince, already mentioned, for example, we read the following words: *Llawer llef druan fal ban fu Camlan*, 'Many a wretched cry as at Camlan.'

The Welsh native tales and the three Romances in the Mabinogion clearly reflect how Arthur during the Middle Ages had developed from a skilled and notable warrior into a most wonderful superhuman mythic figure, half god, half man. In *Culhwch and Olwen* (c.1100), the earliest and most important Welsh Arthurian tale, he is the sovereign King of the whole Island of Britain, with his great court at Celliwig in Cornwall. With the valued assistance of his host of noble knights (Cai and Bedwyr were two of them) he successfully hunts the wild boar called Twrch Trwyth and fulfils other tasks which seemed quite beyond the powers of ordinary men; all this, so that the young Culhwch could marry Olwen, the beautiful daughter of Ysbaddaden Bencawr — the 'Chief Giant'.

A reference to a lost tale mentioned in an obscure poem in the *Book of Taliesin* seems to suggest that Arthur was challenging even the powers of the Otherworld.[38] In his ship called Prydwen he mounts an attack on some fairy fort — – Caer Siddi — far away beyond the sea. Arthur and his men fought bravely. Only seven returned.

As with the other world-famous heroes, we are not told where the grave of Arthur is. And this is understandable. In the minds of ordinary people such a wonderful figure as the great King Arthur was not allowed to die, and a brief three line stanza in the *Black Book of Carmarthen* conveys well this mystery of his death:

Bedd i March, bedd i Gwythur;
Bedd i Gwgawn Gleddyfrudd;
Anoeth byd bedd i Arthur.

A grave for March, a grave for Gwythur; a grave for Gwgawn of the Red-sword; the world's wonder a grave for Arthur.'

38 *Preiddiau Annwfn*, 'The Spoils of Annwfn'. See R.S. Loomis, 'The Spoils of Annwn: an early Welsh poem' in *Wales and the Arthurian Legend*, 131-78.

In c.1136 Geoffrey of Monmouth published his epoch-making *Historia Regum Britanniae* (The History of the Kings of Britain),[39] a book which Koht called 'the most famous work of nationalistic historiography in the Middle Ages'.[40] Geoffrey in this colourful history portrayed Arthur within a historical framework — a heroic king and defender of the Britons in the first half of the sixth century. Yet, in essence, his vivid portrayal is the creation of his own imagination. He brings in Merlin, the great magician, to give him parents of royal blood. Arthur is not only king of Britain, he also conquers Ireland, Iceland and Norway with ease. He kills the great Frollo, King of Gaul (France) by giving him such a mighty blow with his sword, Caledfwlch, that his head is cut in two. With an army of 183,000 men he eventually succeeds even in overcoming the Emperor of Rome himself:

> His enemies fled before him as sheep run from a fierce lion . . . Their armour gave them no protection against the thrusts of Caledfwlch, when wielded in the hand of this mighty King.

He is preparing to march triumphantly to the city when he receives news that his nephew Medrawd, whom he had left in charge of Britain, has made himself king. He is also living adulterously with Arthur's beautiful wife, Gwenhwyfar. In the fierce battle that follows between the two — the Battle of Camlan — Medrawd is killed and Arthur is fatally wounded. He is gently taken away in a ship by three young women dressed in white to the Isle of Afallon (*Insula Avallonis*) to be healed of his wounds.

In Welsh folklore many placenames, stones and caves still preserve Arthur's memory: *Bwrdd Arthur*, 'Arthur's Table'; *Cadair Arthur*, 'Arthur's Chair'; *Coetan Arthur*, 'Arthur's Quoit'. And all these are of gigantic size — stones and hill-tops worthy only of an undying hero who himself had become a giant of superhuman powers. A game known as *'Torri*

---

39 For an English translation, see L. Thorpe, *The History of the Kings of Britain*, Harmondsworth 1966. See also A.O.H. Jarman, *Sieffre o Fynwy. Geoffrey of Monmouth*, Cardiff 1966.
40 Quoted in G. Evans, *op. cit.*, 202.

Cleddyf Arthur', 'Breaking Arthur's Sword', was once played
by the children of Glamorgan. A Welsh riddle reads: '*Beth yw
diod ceffyl y Brenin Arthur?*', 'What does King Arthur's
horse drink?'. And here I may be allowed to add a personal
note. I was brought up in the rural area of Uwchaled, in
Clwyd, North Wales, an area steeped in folklore and onomastic
traditions. Fifteen miles to the north from my home you
may still see on the square in Rhuthun town today a stone
called *Maen Huail*, 'Huail's Stone', upon which, legend tells
us, Arthur beheaded Huail because he had dared to dance
with one of his favourite young women. About fifteen miles
to the south of my home is Aran Benllyn, a mountain in
Merionethshire where King Arthur is said to be asleep. And
in the parish of Llangwm, little more than one mile from my
home, a small river is called today Afon Medrad, and on its
banks many centuries ago, we are told, was *Llys Medrawd*,
'The Court of Medrawd', one of the most famous of King
Arthur's noble knights.

Geoffrey's *Historia* had a tremendous influence on the
literary world. So too did his portrayal of Arthur. It inspired
poets and storytellers. To the people of Wales in their constant struggle for the independence of their country Geoffrey's pseudo-history was of particular importance. It had
given them what they wanted to hear. He presented as historical truth the myth that the whole of the Island of Britain
had once belonged to the Cambro-Britons and that the mighty
Arthur had been its sovereign king. The land had been taken
from them by the English, and that with the help of a Welshman — Gwrtheyrn (Vortigern) — who had betrayed his own
people. As Emyr Humphries remarked:

> The notion of this lost paradise and treachery by which
> it had been stolen from them took firm root in the Cymric
> imagination and provided a new source of intense fuel for
> the engines of praise poetry.[41]

And also, we may add, vaticination poetry. Past heroes
proclaimed as the 'prophesied sons' or the 'men of destiny',
who were to deliver their countrymen from bondage, were

---

41 *Op. cit.*, 9.

national heroes in the true sense. Like the brave and defiant Caradog in the first half of the first century, who was marched in chains to Rome, they had unselfishly fought not for themselves, but for the good of their country.

Cadwallon, who ruled Gwynedd, was a Christian and one of the ablest military leaders since Maelgwn Gwynedd.[42] Cadwaladr (Cadwallon's son) died young of the yellow plague in 664. Yet he, like his father, must have made a lasting impression on his day and age. He became known as Cadwaladr Fendigaid ('Cadwaladr the Blessed'), and in 'Armes Prydain' (c.900) and other early prophetic poems, it is prophesied that he would again return to lead the Welsh to victory.

Of all the names mentioned in the vaticination poetry, Owain is by far the most common. Usually we are not told to which particular Owain in Welsh history the poets refer. But one thing is certain: there were a number of worthy leaders bearing that name, Owain ab Urien (6th century); Owain Gwynedd (c.1100-70); Owain Cyfeiliog (c.1130-97); Owain Lawgoch (d.1378); and Owain Glyndŵr (c.1354-?1416).

Owain Lawgoch (lit. 'Owain the Red Hand'), or Owain ap Thomas ap Rhodri, also known as Yevain de Galles, was eagerly expected to return from France to reclaim his right to the ancient throne of the princes of Wales when he was murdered by an officer of the English Government who had received £200 as payment for his callous task.

But of all the great heroes of the past called Owain, the most famous *Mab Darogan* was Owain Glyndŵr. He won the loyalty of the people of Wales in his own day, and captured their imagination in later centuries. Trevelyan, the English historian, described him as a 'wonderful man, an attractive and unique figure in a period of debased and selfish politics'.[43]

And J.E. Lloyd, author of a standard biography of Glyndŵr, commented:

---

42 For an account of the sixth-century Maelgwn Gwynedd, see Juliette Wood, 'Maelgwn Gwynedd: A Forgotten Welsh Hero' in *Trivium* 19, 103-17.
43 Quoted in G. Evans, *op. cit.*, 257.

Throughout Wales his name is the symbol for the vigorous
resistance of the Welsh spirit to tyranny and alien rule and
the assertion of a national character which finds its fitting
expression in the Welsh language . . . For the Welshmen of
all subsequent ages, Glyndŵr has been a national hero, the
first, indeed, in the country's history to command the
willing support alike of the north and south, east and west.
. . . He may with propriety be called the father of modern
Welsh nationalism.[44]

Nobody knows when or where Owain Glyndŵr died. It is
said that many of his men remained outlaws in the mountains
and forests of Wales. They were called *Gwerin Owain*, 'Owain's
men', and in Welsh oral tradition one of them is linked with
a beautiful and popular folk song:

Mi a glywais fod yr hedydd
Wedi marw ar y mynydd,
Pe gwyddwn i mai gwir y geirie
Awn â gyrr o wŷr ac arfe,
I gyrchu corff yr hedydd adre.

'I was told that the lark has died on the mountain. If I knew
those words were true I would go with a band of armed men
to bring the body home.'

As with Arthur and Owain Lawgoch, there are caves in
Wales where, it is said, Owain Glyndŵr is asleep, awaiting the
day to be called to lead his men again.[45] A popular legend
relates how he was one morning wandering alone on the
Berwyn Mountain in North Wales when he met the Abbot of
Valle Crucis, Llangollen. 'You have risen early,' remarked
Owain. 'No,' replied the Abbot, 'it is you who has risen early,
a hundred years too early.'[46]

---

44 *Owen Glendower. Owen Glyn Dŵr*, Oxford 1931, 1,146.
45 See e.g., J. Rhŷs, *Celtic Folklore*, 2, Ch. 8, 'Cave Legends', 456-97.
46 The legend is recorded in the mid-sixteenth century Chronicle of Elis
    Gruffydd, 'The Soldier of Calais' (1490-1552). See J. Gwenogfryn
    Evans, *Report on Manuscripts Commission*, London 1898-1910, 1,
    p. 221.

During the fifteenth century, following the death of Owain Glyndŵr, there was yet again a profound desire for a Deliverer, a desire vigorously expressed, if at times obscurely, in the numerous prophetic poems of such poets as Tudur Penllyn, Lewis Glyn Cothi and Dafydd Llwyd Mathafarn. But now there was a distinct difference. The poets henceforth addressed their poems to specific persons and to a specific cause. To avoid actually naming the 'man of destiny' he was alluded to by the names of such animals as a bull, boar, bear, wolf, leopard, snake, and eagle. But the poets had no misgivings at all about naming the specific cause. With the turmoil of the Wars of the Roses and the continuous fighting between the Yorkists and the Lancastrians, the poets called on the *Mab Darogan* to seize not only the throne of Wales, but also the throne of England, thus fulfilling Merlin's words and centuries-old prophecy that a Welshman one day would wear the Crown of England. They rekindled the fire under the crucible of myth which had been so successfully concocted by Geoffrey — the false notion that the Welsh could rightly lay claim to the whole of Britain.

When Henry Tudor, from Penmynydd, Anglesey, in North Wales, won the Battle of Bosworth Field, 1485, and was eventually proclaimed King Henry VII of England, then the Welsh people (or at least the majority of them) did indeed believe that the old prophecy had been well and truly fulfilled. At long last they had arrived in the promised land. As the poet Spenser had expressed in his famous poem 'The Faerie Queen', they too saw the Tudor dynasty as a 'restoration of the Kingdom of the Britons'.

Henry as king wisely emphasized his Welsh descent. He made use of Welsh flags: the Red Dragon and the Banner of Cadwaladr. He kept Welsh poets and harpists at his court. He called his eldest son Arthur and proclaimed him Prince of Wales. He celebrated St David's Day on March 1st. And he conferred high offices and honours on many of his fellow countrymen. The Welsh were happy with symbols, and it paved the way for the majority of them to accept without opposition the Act of Union of 1536 (and 1542) which stated quite clearly that Wales was to be 'for ever henceforth incorporated, united and annexed to and with' the realm of England.

In 1483, two years before the Battle of Bosworth Field, the poet Robin Ddu had written:

Y mae hiraeth am Harri;
Y mae gobaithoi'n Hiaith ni.

'There is a longing for Henry; there is hope for our Language.'

He would not have said this about his son's attitude to the language. It was the policy of the Act of Union 'utterly to extirp all and singular the sinister Usages and customs differing from his realm of England'. And this included the language: 'a speech nothing like, nor consonant to, the natural mother tongue used within his realm'.

The Tudor dynasty ensured that there was peace and stability in Wales for many years. Yet it was due to other factors, such as the translating of the Bible into Welsh, that the Tudor policy of extinguishing the language did not succeed. Although Wales since 1485 was no longer challenged with the force of arms, it became a country once more under threat and in peril of losing its sense of national consciousness. It now became endangered by more subtle alien influences, such as the introduction of English as the official language. And yet, from the sixteenth to the nineteenth century, the language and culture of Wales flourished.[47]

During the nineteenth century, however, we see a deliberate Government policy to introduce English in the schools of Wales. In 1846 three monoglot Englishmen were sent to prepare a report on the state of Education in the Principality. The conclusion of the Commission was devastating. It stated clearly that:

The Welsh language is a vast drawback to Wales and a

---

47 See D. Williams, *A History of Modern Wales*, London 1950, and Davies, Griffiths, Jones and Morgan, eds., *Welsh Society and Nationhood. Historical Essays Presented to Glanmor Williams*, Cardiff 1984.

manifold barrier to the moral progress and commercial prosperity of the people.[48]

Eight years later such an influential person as Matthew Arnold (who had written much about Celtic Magic and similar topics) expressed his opinion that:

> Sooner or later ... the difference of language between Wales and England will be effaced ... an event which is socially and politically desirable.[49]

In order to force children to learn the English language, one system practised in Wales during the nineteenth century was the 'Welsh Not'.[50] This was a small piece of wood with the letters 'W.N.' carved on it. Any child caught speaking Welsh in the classroom — even in monoglot Welsh-speaking areas (as most areas were in the nineteenth century) had to wear this piece of wood until some other child had been caught. The unfortunate child who wore it at the end of the day would be caned.

The result of the Government's education policy eventually was to link the Welsh language with ignorance and inequality. To 'get on in the world', even in Wales, English was the important language. Welsh men and women were made to feel second-class citizens in their own country.

From the second half of the nineteenth century onwards, however, there was a resurgence of Welsh patriotism, reflected, for example, in the work of the movement known as *Cymru Fydd* (lit. 'the Wales of the future'), founded in 1886. Arthur, Llywelyn ap Gruffydd, Owain Glyndŵr, and other Welsh princes became the subject of numerous cantatas, librettos, and especially poems and songs, composed by such popular lyric poets as John Jones (Talhaiarn, 1810-70); John Ceiriog Hughes (Ceiriog, 1832-87); and Richard Davies (Mynyddog, 1833-77).[51]

48 *Report of the Commissioners of Inquiry into the State of Education in Wales*, Part II, London 1848, 309.

49 Quoted in G. Evans, *op. cit.*, 370.

50 Two such examples are exhibited in the Gallery of Material Culture at the Welsh Folk Museum, St Fagan's, Cardiff.

51 For a catalogue of songs, solos, cantatas and librettos, see H. Williams, *Canu'r Bobol*, Denbigh 1978.

These compositions were an expression of patriotism. The authors, like so many of their fellow countrymen, suffered from what Dr Gwynfor Evans called 'a sort of national schizophrenia. They did not know properly who they were ... were they Welsh, or were they British? Of the two, was it Wales, or was it Britain that claimed their first loyalty?'[52] During the twentieth century, however, there has also been in Wales an increasing new sense of national consciousness, and especially after the formation of *Plaid Cymru* (The Welsh Nationalist Party) in 1925, and *Cymdeithas yr Iaith Gymraeg* (The Welsh Language Society) in 1962.[53] Yet, once again, whilst sincere homage is paid to new heroes of our own day and age (such as the three men who sabotaged the Government's Bombing School at Penyberth in the Llŷn Peninsula in 1936: Saunders Lewis, Lewis Valentine and D.J. Williams), the insight and noble leadership of the early Welsh Princes, notably Llywelyn ap Gruffydd and Owain Glyndŵr, is a constant source of inspiration to a small nation in its age-long struggle for survival. The names of Arthur, Taliesin and Myrddin, and the heroic characters of the Mabinogion, such as Branwen, Bendigeidfran, Rhiannon and Blodeuwedd, are also as well known and referred to today as ever: the tragic and human figure of Branwen who was given as wife to Matholwch, King of Ireland, and then cruelly mistreated; the great Bendigeidfran, 'Brân the Blessed', her brother, who led his men to Ireland to avenge the wrong done to his sister (he was so mighty that he allowed the soldiers to walk over his body where the sea was narrow, and his words uttered then are still a common saying in Wales today: '*A fo ben, bid bont*', 'Whoever is chief, let him be a bridge'; the mysterious Rhiannon — the folk memory, probably, of an old horse goddess — and the beautiful, but frail, Blodeuwedd (lit. 'flower-faced'), created through magic from the flowers of the field.

An ever-increasing number of parents during the last twenty

---

52 *Op. cit.*, 417.
53 See K.O. Morgan, *The Rebirth of a Nation: Wales 1880-1980*, Oxford 1981; D. Hywel Davies, *The Welsh Nationalist Party, 1925-1945: A Call to Nationhood*, Cardiff 1983; and N. Thomas, *The Welsh Extremist*, London 1971, and Tal-y-bont 1978.

or thirty years have christened their children with traditional Welsh names. Tales of the Mabinogion inspire artists and craftsmen. Taliesin was the name given to the Welsh Academy's literary journal, first issued in 1961. Furthermore, scores of novels and poems have been published in this century based upon or inspired by heroic characters and events in Welsh history and legend.[54]

Novels written in English and relating to the Mabinogion, for example, have been published by such authors as: Lloyd Alexander (*Prydain* cycle, 1964-8); Padraic Colum (*The Island of the Mighty*, 1924); Alan Garner (*The Owl Service*, 1967); John James (*Not for all the Gold in Ireland*, 1971); and Robert Nye (*Taliesin*, 1967). Merlin is the subject of novels by Susan Cooper (*The Dark is Rising*, 1965-7), and T.H. White (*The Sword in the Stone*, 1938). King Arthur is the subject of novels by Rosemary Sutcliff (*The Light Beyond the Forest*, 1979), and Mary Stewart (*The Last Enchantment*, 1979). John Cowper Powys is the author of the novel *Owen Glendower* (1950), and Edith Pargetter is the author of a series of novels based on the life of the Welsh princes — Llywelyn ap Gruffydd in particular. To commemorate the 700th anniversary of the death of Llywelyn in 1282 three Welsh language novels were also published, the authors being Marion Eames, Rhiannon Davies Jones and Gweneth Lilly.[55]

Welsh poets writing in English since the Second World War — the Anglo-Welsh poets as they are called (for example, David Jones, Vernon Watkins, R.S. Thomas, and Harri Webb) — have been particularly inspired by Welsh historical and mythical characters. Identifying themselves with Welsh history and

---

54 One contemporary Welsh novelist, Gweneth Lilly, has given an excellent account of how Welsh history and legend have inspired her work in her article 'The Deep Streams: Welsh History and Folklore as the Inspiration of the Novelist' in F. Keyse, ed., *Loughborough '83: Proceedings of the 16th. Loughborough International Seminar on Children's Literature*, Aberystwyth 1984, 82-90.

55 For an anthology of Welsh poems composed to Llywelyn ap Gruffydd, see A. Llwyd, ed., *Llywelyn y Beirdd*, Caenarfon 1984.

legend seems to play an important role in their search for a new and sometimes lost Welsh identity.[56]

In what is probably the most important and well-known Arthurian poem in the Welsh language, 'Ymadawiad Arthur', 'The passing of Arthur', composed by the great poet T. Gwynn Jones in 1902, Arthur before being borne away in a ship to the Island of Afallon (Avalon), bids farewell to Bedwyr, his faithful knight, in these words:

> Mi weithion i hinon ha
> Afallon af i wella,
> Ond i'm bro dof eto'n ôl.
> . . . yn fy nghledd
> Gafaelaf, dygaf eilwaith
> Glod yn ôl i'n gwlad a'n iaith.[57]

'I go now to the halcyon summer of Afallon to be healed, but I shall return to my land . . . my sword I shall grip, I shall bring back honour to our country and language.'

Bedwyr pleads with Arthur that he too may be allowed to accompany him to Afallon (we all at times want to escape to such an island). No, replies Arthur, you must return to carry on fighting. And the poem ends with a brief but significant couplet:

56 The following is a small but representative selection of poems by such authors: Anthony Conran, 'Four Welsh Personae, 1. Llywarch Hen Meditates the Moon'; Jon Dressel, 'Llywelyn Speaks from Hell'; Christine Furnival, 'Rhiannon'; Raymond Garlick, 'Dyfed'; Cyril Hodges, 'Myrddin in the woods of Celyddon', 'The Mead Song of Taliesin', and 'Blodeuwedd'; David Jones, 'The Sleeping Lord'; Sally Roberts Jones, 'Gwyn ap Nudd's Palace, Glastonbury Tor', 'The Lost World', and 'New World'; T. Harri Jones, 'Rhiannon', and 'Anoeth Bid Bedd i Arthur'; Roland Mathias, 'Madoc' (a major poem on the subject of Madog who reputedly sailed from Gwynedd in 1170 and landed on the Gulf Coast of North America, thus giving birth to the myth that the Mandans, of what is now North Dakota, were Welsh Indians and descendants of Madog and his company); Brian Morris, 'State'; R.S. Thomas, 'Taliesin'; Vernon Watkins: a series of five poems to Taliesin; Harri Webb, 'A Crown for Branwen', 'Cilmeri', 'Abbey Cwmhir', and 'The Stone Face'.

57 *Caniadau*, Wrecsam 1934.

Bedwyr yn drist a distaw
At y drin aeth eto draw.
'Bedwyr with grief quietly returns to the battleground.'

VI

This is what is happening in many areas in Wales today: men and women, and young people in particular, fighting once again for their country — its culture and language. But no longer with the force of arms, but through hard work and personal sacrifice. The poetry which is an expression of this 'rebirth of a nation' is characterised by sincerity and a direct appeal to the readers and listeners. I will refer briefly to poems by two acclaimed young poets: Gerallt Lloyd Owen and Dafydd Iwan.

In his poem 'Cilmeri', where Llywelyn, the Last Prince of Wales, was killed, Gerallt Lloyd Owen writes:

Fan hyn yw ein cof ni.
Fan hyn sy'n anadl inni.
Fan hyn gynnau fu'n geni.[58]

'This place is our memory. This place is our soul. Here some time ago we were born.'

The famous folk-singer Dafydd Iwan is the author of numerous nationalistic songs which have become very popular with Welsh-speaking young people.[59] One such song is 'Cerddwn Ymlaen', with its refrain: 'We will march forward with confidence in our hearts.' The poem 'Owain Glyndŵr' is another of his popular songs. Here follows an English translation of the second verse:

I hear the voices of the soldiers,
I hear the sound of their feet
Marching from Snowdonia on their mission.
Put aside all despair
And the many doubts,
Owain is again ready for the day.
From his hideout in Snowdonia

58 *Cerddi'r Cywilydd*, Bridgend 1972.
59 One hundred of his songs were published in *Canto Ganeuon*, Tal-y-bont 1982.

He will come with his faithful band
To lead us at dawn to a free Wales.
Like the tide after the ebb,
Like the rainbow after the rain,
Like the dawn after the night,
In the name of God! I know that he will come.[60]

These twentieth-century popular poems and songs recited, or sung to the accompaniment of the harp or guitar, will in the future probably, become part of the Welsh folk epic tradition. There are many other nationalistic, but lesser known, poems and songs being composed today, however, that may never become part of the epic tradition. It is doubtful, for example, if the following poem has ever been published, although the sincere and optimistic message of its young author is similar to that which has been expressed by Welsh poets for many centuries. It is a poem about King Arthur, composed by a pupil of the Rhydfelen Welsh Secondary School in Glamorgan, c.1967, and was the winning entry for the Chair competition at the school's annual Eisteddfod. The poem ends with this verse:

A welaist y gloch fawr swynol
    Wrth ochr yr ogof fawr?
A glywaist ti sŵn y chwyrnu
    Gan filwyr y Brenin mawr?
Ni welais i Arthur erioed yn fy myw,
Ond credaf o'm calon fod Arthur yn fyw.

'Did you see the large enchanted bell on the side of the big cave? Did you hear the noise of the great King's soldiers snoring? I never in my life saw Arthur, but I believe with all my heart that Arthur is alive.'[61]

'I believe . . . I know that Arthur is alive . . .' In this paper I have confined my remarks mainly to poetry relating to historical heroic characters who have not been allowed to die a

60 *Ibid.*, 91-3.
61 For a discussion of caves connected with Arthur, see J. Rhŷs, *op. cit.*, 2, 456-97, and T. Jones, 'A Sixteenth Century Version of the Arthurian Cave Legend' in *Studies in Language and Literature in Honour of Margaret Schlauch*, Warszawa 1966, 175-85.

natural death. But what has been said about historical characters could also be said about pseudo-historical and even
mythical figures. Why? Because they belong, not only to their
own age, but to all ages. Because we ordinary men and women
of the twentieth century somehow can, and want to, identify
ourselves with them — with their fears and hopes and deepest
aspirations. As our forefathers longed for a Deliverer, so we
in Wales today hope that there will always be men and women
ready to lead their country and safeguard its inheritance.

Any folk epic tradition which is a living tradition is relevant to all ages. It inspired people yesterday; it will inspire
people yet again today and tomorrow. The great scholar and
playwright Saunders Lewis (1893-1985) wrote a play called
Buchedd Garmon, 'The Life of St Garmon'[62] in which Emrys
pleads with the fifth-century saint to come and lead his men
against the pagan invaders. But the plea of Emrys so many
centuries ago has also a meaningful message to us today, and
the famous words of Saunders Lewis, therefore, (here translated into English) have become well-known throughout
Wales:

Garmon, Garmon,
A vineyard placed in my care is Wales, my country,
To deliver unto my children
And my children's children
Intact, an eternal heritage:
And behold, the swine rush on her to rend her.
Now will I call on my friends,
Scholars and simple folk,
'Take your place by my side in the breach
That the age-old splendour be kept for ages to come.'

In his grief of having lost all his twenty four noble sons in
battle, the old Llywarch, according to a ninth-century poet,
remembers a place known as Abercuawg.

---

62 Aberystwyth 1937. The passage quoted is from a translation by
D. Myrddin Lloyd, in D.M. and E.M. Lloyd, *A Book of Wales*,
London and Glasgow 1953, 268.

> Yn Abercuawc yt ganant gogeu
>> Ar gangheu blodeuawc.
> Gwae glaf a'e clyw yn vodawc.

'In Abercuawg the cuckoos sing on blossoming branches. Woe to the sick man who hears them and cannot stir.'

We do not know today where Abercuawg is (it was probably somewhere in Powys, mid-Wales), but, as the poet R.S. Thomas in an illuminating lecture[63] has emphasised, it no longer really matters where Abercuawg is. It has now become a symbol of beauty and peace and all that is good and lasting in life — Abercuawg, where the 'cuckoos sing on blossoming branches . . .' It belongs to all ages. We may never find it, but in our search for it we may get a glimpse of it and experience something of its everlasting joy. The Abercuawg of the ninth-century poet, therefore, has a meaningful message to us in the twentieth century — a message vividly expressed by R.S. Thomas also in one of his poems, entitled 'Abercuawg':

> I am a seeker
> in time for that which is
> beyond time, that is everywhere
> and nowhere; no more before
> than after, yet always
> about to be . . .[64]

John Roderick Rees, the poet who won the Crown at the 1985 Rhyl National Eisteddfod of Wales, composed a poem describing his elderly mother when her mind had gone.[65] One line of this poem reads: *Ystafell yr ymennydd sy dywyll heno*, 'The hall of the mind is dark tonight'. When we read these words we become conscious of a thousand years of Welsh history, because the line is a direct echo of similar and often quoted words composed by a ninth-century poet

---

63 *Abercuawg*, The National Eisteddfod of Wales annual literary lecture, Cardigan 1976.
64 *Frequences*, London 1978. For an appreciation of this and other poems by R.S. Thomas, see W. Moelwyn Merchant, *R.S. Thomas*, Cardiff 1979.
65 *Cyfansoddiadau a Beirniadaethau*, the compositions and adjudications of the Rhyl and District National Eisteddfod, 35-42.

about Cynddylan, prince of Powys, in the seventh century, killed in battle defending his country: *Stafell Cynddylan ys tywyll heno*, 'The hall of Cynddylan is dark tonight'.

Similarly when we today hear or read the well-known words of the sixth-century Aneirin: *Gwyr a aeth Catraeth . . .* , 'Men went to Catraeth . . .', we are reminded not only of the death of 300 noble young warriors of the Old North, but we also become conscious of the sacrifice and grief of men throughout the centuries. Thus, in their elegies to their own fellow-men in their own age the poets (to quote Martti Haavio's words relating to Balto-Finnic lament poetry) have expressed 'the sorrow of all people'.[66]

Nowhere in Welsh verse or prose is this sorrow expressed in more memorable manner than in the story of Branwen in the Second Branch of the Mabinogi. Only seven men, we are told, returned alive from the war in Ireland. They travel to Aber Alaw in Anglesey with Branwen, carrying the head of her beloved brother Bendigeidfran:

> And they came to land at Aber Alaw in Talebolion. And then they sat down and rested them. Then she looked on Ireland and the Island of the Mighty, what she might see of them. 'Alas, Son of God,' said she, 'woe is me that ever I was born: two good islands have been laid waste because of me!' And she heaved a great sigh, and with that broke her heart. And a four-sided grave was made for her, and she was buried there on the bank of the Alaw.[67]

The tale, however, does not end there. And here we have another common theme in epic tradition, namely the super-natural passage of time, as expressed, for example, in the Second Epistle of St Peter in the New Testament (ch.3, v.8): 'One day is with the Lord as a thousand years and a thousand years is as one day.' The seven men (with Bendigeidfran's head) journey to Harlech, in North Wales:

---

66 *Suomalaisen muinaisrunouden maailma*, Porvoo 1935. See also L. Honko, 'Balto-Finnic Lament Poetry', *Studia Fennica* 17 (1974), 9-61.
67 *The Mabinogion*, 38.

And then they went on to Harlech, and they sat them down and began to regale them with meat and drink; and even as they began to eat and drink there came three birds [the Birds of Rhiannon] and began to sing them a certain song, and of all the songs they had ever heard each one was unlovely compared with that. And far must they look to see them out over the deep, yet was it as clear to them as if they were close by them; and at that feasting they were seven years.[68]

Here we are reminded that man has, and always will, endeavour to reach that point of the 'still centre'; to experience, even for a short while, those everlasting moments when time seems to stand still, and when we, too, like the poet Gwenallt (1899-1968), desire to hear the Birds of Rhiannon:

Come again this evening, Birds of Rhiannon,
Sing us a song from o'er the blue wave . . .
All is not well in Wales or Erin . . .
Raise the dead with your soul-stirring music,
Give hope to the living in their transient day,
Weave a tune from our glorious story . . .[69]

But in the epic tradition we are reminded also that we are, after all, only mortal men and women — human beings who are the creatures of time and space. The seven men in Branwen's tale then journey to Gwales in Dyfed, carrying with them the 'wondrous head' of Bendigeidfran:

And there they passed the fourscore years so that they were not aware of having ever spent a time more joyous and delightful than that. It was not more irksome than when they came there, nor could any tell by his fellow that it was so long a time. Nor was it more irksome having the head with them then than when Bendigeidfran had been with them alive.[70]

68 *Ibid.*, 39.
69 *Ysgubau'r Awen*, Llandysul 1938, 17. The quotation is from a translation by D. Myrddin Lloyd, *A Book of Wales*, 254-5.
70 *The Mabinogion*, 39.

But there was a condition. There was one door facing Corn-wall and Aber Henfelen that was on no account to be opened. There are certain things in life which are prohibited to us. As the poets constantly reminded the audience in their eulogies of kings and princes, there are standards to be kept by all leaders of men — a certain code of honour to be respected — just as, in folklore, there was treasure under various stones that was not to be disturbed, and one tree in the Garden of Eden whose fruit was forbidden to man. The price of dis-obedience is destruction. When Heilyn, son of Gwyn, opens the door the seven men were reminded of all their grief and tribulations:

> . . . they were conscious of every loss they had ever sus-tained, and of every kinsman and friend they had missed, and of every ill that they had come upon them, as if it were even then it had befallen them.[71]

Yet, there is one other theme which must be mentioned. There is more to man than mere flesh and blood. He has a mind of his own and he will at times 'reach for the stars'. In the midst of death even, he can and will occasionally be able to rise as a Phoenix from the ashes to be born anew. Then he shall proclaim with Dylan Thomas: 'And Death shall have no dominion.' And here we have a theme that, as we have already seen, is central to the Welsh folk epic tradition. In times of despair the poet-prophet raised the spirit of his people with his messianic message: all was not lost, the 'Prophesied Son' was coming.

In the First Branch of the Mabinogi, Pwyll, Prince of Dyfed, wishes to sit on the magic throne or mound at Arberth, although he knows that one of two things would happen to him: he would either be grievously wounded or he would experience a wonderful revelation. Pwyll ventures, and it is then that he sees the beautiful Rhiannon on her white mys-terious horse. Pwyll represents man in all ages. Though faced with the possibility of harm and even death, his greatest desire is to experience the wonder and joy of life: to revisit

---

71 *Op. cit.*, 39-40.

Abercuawg, to see as he has never seen before, and to hear, even for a short while, the cuckoos singing on 'blossoming branches' or the wonderful song of the Birds of Rhiannon.

VII

In one of his poems to Taliesin, Vernon Watkins describes the seer-poet wandering inside a dark cave:

> Taliesin took refuge under the unfledged rock.
> He could not see in the cave, but groped with his hand,
> And the rock he touched was the socket of all men's eyes.
> And he touched the spring of vision . . .

> He still held rock. Then three drops fell on his fingers,
> And Future and Past converged in a lightning flash . . .[72]

'Future and Past . . .' — inspiration, creativity, relevance, vision — these, in my opinion, are the important words in defining the nature of the Welsh folk epic tradition, its continuity and function.

I have already mentioned that the Latin word *historia* gave us the Welsh word *ystoreau*, that is 'an inheritance of old traditions'. Now we are reminded that *historia* also gave us the Welsh word *ystyr* (meaning). We are reminded, too, that the early Welsh word for storyteller was *y cyfarwydd*, 'the familiar one'. His task was *cyfarwyddo*, 'to direct'. It is believed that the Welsh word *gweled*, 'to see', and the Irish word *fili* (gen. *filed*) both derive from the same Indo-European stem. The *cyfarwydd*, like the Irish *fili*, was a poet — a visionary, an interpreter — the one who helped his people to 'see' — to visualize the invisible; to give meaning to the meaningless. That is one reason why the Welsh folk epic tradition, like that of many other countries, is so rich and valuable. And that is one reason also why we are proud in 1985 to celebrate the one hundred and fiftieth anniversary of the first

---

72 *Unity of the Stream. A New Selection of Poems*, Llandysul 1978, 32-3. See also Dora Polk, *Vernon Watkins and the Spring of Vision*, Swansea 1977.

publication of the great Finnish epic, the *Kalevala*, and the fiftieth anniversary of the founding of the Irish Folklore Commission, because, in the words of the old Irish proverb:

Is buaine port ná glór na n-éan,
Is buaine focal ná toice an tsaoil.

'A tune is more lasting than the song of birds, and a word (or tale) is more lasting than the wealth of the world.'

EPIC ELEMENTS IN EARLY WELSH AND SCOTTISH HAGIOGRAPHY

JOHN MacQUEEN

(University of Edinburgh)

Milton asserted that *Paradise Lost* possessed greater epic qualities than the poems of Homer and Virgil. The argument of his poem was, he claimed,

> Not less but more Heroic than the wrath
> Of stern *Achilles* on his Foe pursu'd
> Thrice Fugitive about *Troy* Wall; or rage
> Of *Turnus* for *Lavinia* disespous'd,
> Or *Neptune's* ire or *Juno's*, that so long
> Perplex'd the *Greek* and *Cytherea's* Son.

> (9. 14-19)

He described himself as a poet

> Not sedulous by Nature to indite
> Wars, hitherto the only Argument
> Heroic deem'd, chief maistry to dissect
> With long and tedious havoc fabl'd Knights
> In Battles feign'd; the better fortitude
> Of Patience and Heroic Martyrdom
> Unsung.

> (9. 27-33)

The second quotation refers, of course, not to the poems of Homer or Virgil, but to the many later epic romances dealing with Arthur, Charlemagne and their followers. Milton writes as if no one had previously attempted the task which he is now undertaking, a point true at least in terms of his own level of accomplishment. At a rather humbler level, many others, however, had attempted the same task, not least, as I hope to show, the authors, often anonymous, of the early

Lives of the Celtic saints. Those who wrote in mainland Britain resembled Milton in that they sometimes had in mind tales about Arthur and others associated with him, tales which from the point of view of the early church might be regarded as secular, no matter what their ultimate origins in fact were. These formed the heroic ideal, which the church partly opposed, partly attempted to modify and even transform.

The two processes are often combined in a curious way, most readily illustrated by those *Lives* in which the saint is set against a recognised secular hero, as the Welsh Cadog, for instance, is more than once set against Arthur. Such occasions generally involve the discomfiture or discredit of the secular hero. Thus, in chapter 22 of the *Life* of Cadog by Lifris[1] (c.1100), the saint for seven years gives sanctuary to Ligessaug Llaw Hir, who has killed three of Arthur's followers. When Arthur eventually discovers his enemy's place of refuge, he comes with a very great force of soldiers, to the northern and eastern boundary of Cadog's territory, the River Usk, but is afraid to issue a direct military challenge by making a crossing. He chooses instead to appeal to law — in itself a somewhat unheroic procedure. The judgement of the mainly ecclesiastical court, summoned on the spot, is that Arthur should receive one hundred cows in compensation for the loss of his men. This is a little too straightforward for the king who insists that he will accept only cattle 'distinguished in their fore part with a red colour and in their hind part with white'. Where this combination of colours occurs in other Welsh tales, it usually indicates that the animal in question is of other-worldly origin (from Annwfn), and otherworld cattle, for the normal person, are difficult to obtain. The king is in fact challenging the saint to a display of supernatural power, and Cadog obliges, transforming the colour of a herd of ordinary cattle, not with help from Annwfn, but by the force of prayer. As the contending parties have situated themselves on opposite sides of the river-boundary, the proper place for the transfer is the middle of the ford (which also, incidentally, is a place of great supernatural significance), where they are

---

1   A.W. Wade-Evans, *Vitae Sanctorum Britanniae et Genealogiae* (here-after, 'Wade-Evans, *Vitae*'), Cardiff 1944, 24-141.

accepted by Arthur and his two chief followers, Cai and Bedwyr. The legal transactions are thus concluded. No sooner has Arthur's side accepted the cattle, however, than the beasts are transformed, like fairy gold, into bundles of fern. Arthur is compelled to recognise his own presumption, and come to a more reasonable agreement with Cadog. As soon as this is ratified, the original owners find the transformed cattle back in their stalls, restored to their proper colour. The origins of several local placenames are traced to this sequence of events.

Arthur's humiliation here is to be contrasted with his triumph over the saints of Ireland related in *Culhwch and Olwen*, an almost contemporary Welsh tale which belongs entirely to the secular tradition. I quote the version of Patrick K. Ford:[2]

> And then Arthur assembled all the warriors there were in the three Islands of Britain and their three adjacent islands, and in France, Brittany, Normandy and the Summer Land; he assembled choice foot-soldiers and renowned horses, and all those multitudes went to Ireland.
>
> There was mighty fear and terror in Ireland at his coming, and after Arthur disembarked, the saints of Ireland came to seek protection from him. He gave protection to them, and they in turn gave their blessing to him. The men of Ireland approached Arthur with a tribute of food.

By comparison with the story in Lifris, there is a striking reversal of roles between saint and king.

A number of additional points may be noticed. Because the saint comprehensively vanquishes the hero, who is compelled to beg forgiveness, and accept terms which are less profitable to himself than those originally offered, much of the *mana*, the numinous quality originally associated with the secular figure is transferred to the ecclesiastical. The process is almost like that associated with early church sites; Gregory the Great, it will be recollected, advises Mellitus, later Bishop of London, to destroy only the idols in the temples of the English, once they had been converted, but to preserve the

---

2 *The Mabinogion and Other Medieval Welsh Tales* (hereafter 'Ford'), Berkeley 1977, 153.

buildings and turn them into churches. 'In this way, we hope
that the people, seeing that their temples are not destroyed,
may abandon their error and, flocking more readily to their
accustomed resorts, may come to know and adore the true
God.'[3] The *mana* of the temples was retained, but transferred
to the victorious Christian church. Something of the same
kind happens to the victorious Christian saint, to whom is
transferred the *mana*, often itself of pre-Christian religious
origin, appertaining to the secular figure.

The methods used by the saint, secondly, do not differ
essentially from those of the magician-ruler of much popular
tradition in Wales as elsewhere. In this instance, Cadog is
protecting his territory from the encroachments of a rival
power. He despises it, as is shown by the biblical quotation
used in illustration: 'Fear not those who kill the body, but
cannot kill the soul, but rather fear him who is able to cast
soul and body into hell'; but recognises that it may possess
powers not dissimilar to his own. Arthur himself is not usually
depicted as illusionist or shape-shifter, but in *Culhwch and
Olwen* several of his retinue possess at least the second of these
powers, and in the secular 'Math son of Mathonwy', the fourth
branch of the *Mabinogi*,[4] both Math himself and his nephew
Gwydion are capable of changing their own appearance, and
that of others, or of producing what in effect are hallucina-
tions. There is nothing specifically Christian about these
powers; rather, hagiographic traditions have adapted themselves to cultural patterns more familiar from the sometimes
pre-Christian secular tales — the prose-epics — characteristic
of the insular Celts. The process is one of acculturation.

The third point is that the story is put into what might be
called the landscape of the saint by way of placenames. It
forms a kind of charter-myth, consecrating, as it were, certain
places — Tredunnock, Rhyd Gwrthebau, Llandewi Penn bei,
Merthyr Tegfedd and Llanddyfrwyr — by associating them
with Cadog and the fellow-saints, who on this occasion were
his subordinates. Other episodes are linked to the names of
the greater centres of the saint's power; most notably Llan-

3 *Historia Ecclesiastica*, I.30.
4 Ford, 89-109.

carfan, his principal church, where again there is a strong charter-element in the story, as well as many elements of the secular tale. The saint discovers the site by the help of an otherworld beast – in this case a white boar, which shows him where the various buildings are to be placed – and it receives its name, Llancarfan or Nantcarfan, by a popular etymology from the two stags (*carw*, 'stag') which in a time of emergency were yoked to a wagon by his Irish disciples, Finian and Macmoil.[5]

One of the main functions of a saint's legend is thus to authenticate the major and minor cult-centres associated with him, or with his disciples. Often the legend itself is a kind of epic guide-book to these places. One might readily compare it with the tales which form the basis of the Greek hero-cults, typical objects of which 'are the traditional ἥρωες of Homer and other writers of saga'.[6] Of necessity, the legend, like that of a Greek hero, contains some account of the birth, and often the childhood, of the saint, his mature exploits, his death and burial, and often of his posthumous exploits, usually performed at the tomb. This last is another link with the Greek cults, defined as 'the worship, as being superhuman, of noteworthy dead men and women, real or imaginary, normally at their actual or supposed tombs'.[7] This worship might involve receiving oracles or having the sick cured. The first of these is exemplified by the oracular cave of Trophonius at Lebadea in Boeotia, the other by the cures, the result usually of incubation, performed in the temples of Asclepius in Epidaurus and elsewhere. The most elaborate narratives associated with Greek cult-heroes (apart, that is, from those celebrated by Homer), are probably those of Heracles, Oedipus, Theseus and Perseus. Heracles, it should be noticed, especially in private worship, 'was commonly appealed to as a warder-off of evils and victor over them'.[8] His role in parti-

5 Wade-Evans, *Vitae*, 44, 52-5.
6 *Oxford Classical Dictionary*, 2nd ed., Oxford, s.v. 'Hero-Cult'. For more detail, see especially L.R. Farnell, *The Cults of the Greek States*, 1-5, Oxford 1896-1909, *Greek Hero Cults and Ideas of Immortality*, Oxford 1921.
7 *Loc. cit.*
8 *Oxford Classical Dictionary*, s.v. 'Heracles'.

cular may therefore be compared with that of the fourteen
Christian 'auxiliary saints' (who include George and Chris-
topher), particularly venerated for the efficacy of their prayers
on behalf of human necessities.

In Celtic lands generally, the vehicle for this kind of ecclesiastical epic narrative is prose, usually Latin, which may be
assumed to be substantially based on earlier vernacular
traditional narrative, probably in the same medium. This, as
has been mentioned, is the form usually found in insular
Celtic heroic narrative, whether Welsh or Irish. *Lives* composed
in Latin heroic verse are not however uncommon (in Britain,
usually where cult-centres fell under Anglo-Saxon influence),
especially in the eighth and ninth centuries.[9] So too such
Anglo-Saxon poems as *Andreas*[10] give the full panoply of the
Germanic vernacular epic to the *Life* of a saint. The text of
Lifris, finally, contains a number of passages in verse, the
function of which seems not dissimilar to that of the verse
passages which are found in Irish prose epic.

Lifris did not confine Cadog to Wales. Chapter 26 contains
the story of a journey to Scotland made by the saint in order
to visit the shrine of St Andrew. On his homeward journey,
he received angelic instructions to remain for seven years at a
place on this (i.e. the Welsh) side of Mount Bannog, 'which is
said to be situated in the middle of Scotland'. The place in
question is somewhere to the south of the Campsie Fells and
Kilsyth Hills to the north and east of Glasgow, and has sometimes been identified with Cambuslang on the Clyde, the
parish church of which in medieval times was dedicated to
Cadog.

During the construction of a monastery there, the saint
uncovered a gigantic human collar bone, 'through which,
wonderful to relate, a champion on horseback could (or
might) ride without check. Which being found, saint Cadog,

9   A good example is the anonymous *Miracula Nynie Episcopi*, written
    at Whithorn in the last quarter of the eighth century. Text and
    translation by W.W. MacQueen, *Transactions and Journal of Pro-
    ceedings of the Dumfriesshire and Galloway Natural History and
    Antiquarian Society* (hereafter '*Dumfries Transactions*'), 37 (1961),
    21-57.

10 Ed. G.P. Krapp, Boston 1906.

wondering, said, "I will not approach meat or drink, but prayer in place of food and tears in place of drink will be mine, until this prodigious thing, what it may be, is revealed to us by God".' As a result of his efforts, the former owner of the collar bone, the giant Caw of Prydyn (Pictavia), was resurrected from Hell, where he had been suffering torments for the sins committed during his former incarnation. His story was that he had been a king of the Picts, killed in the course of a plundering raid which he had made south of Mount Bannog into the territory of the Strathclyde king. During his time in Hell, he had come to see the error of his former ways, and the repentant giant gained ultimate salvation by acting as *fossor*, 'digger', for Cadog during the remainder of his second incarnation.

Caw is known in the Welsh secular tradition, as hero and as ancestral figure. The list of Arthur's warriors in *Culhwch and Olwen*[11] includes one of his daughters and nineteen of his sons. A twentieth son is killed during the hunting of Twrch Trwyth. Caw himself has an organic role to play in one section at least of the action; the tusk of Ysgythyrwyn Chief Boar and the blood of the Black Witch, daughter of the White Witch are both necessary (one as razor, the other as a kind of pre-shave lotion) for the shaving of Ysbaddaden Chief Giant, whose daughter can be married only after this ceremony; Caw obtains both, and finally himself shaves Ysbaddaden to the bone, cutting off his ears in the process. After such humiliation, Ysbaddaden wishes only for death, and thus leaves the way open for Culhwch to marry Olwen, the gian't daughter, and so live happily ever after.

It is to subordinate this secular hero to the saint that he is given the humble final role of *fossor*, and to this extent the tale parallels the other examples already quoted. But the method by which Caw is introduced, resuscitation from the dead, also has a place in the secular heroic tradition, best seen in two Irish stories. *The Spectral Chariot of Cú Chulainn*,[12] where St. Patrick summons the great hero of the Ulster Cycle

---

11   Ford, 126-31.
12   Translated in T.P. Cross and C.H. Slover, *Ancient Irish Tales*, repr. Allan Figgis, Dublin 1969, 347-54.

from the dead to testify of his doings and his ultimate fate to the as yet unregenerate King Laegaire, is partly adapted to ecclesiastical requirements, but *The Recovery of the Táin*,[13] in which the ghost of Fergus mac Roig is summoned by a poet to retell the ancient epic, the precise memory of which had faded from the world, belongs wholly to the secular tradition. It seems not unlikely that the story underlying this ecclesiastical version laid much more stress on Caw's exploits as a king beyond Mount Bannog, and his defeat and death at the hands of the Strathclyde Britons than is to be found in the present, and only surviving, version. The difference is to be explained by the transfer from one cultural milieu to another.

In some saints' *Lives*, the influence of secular epic tales extends to the actual literary form. The *Life* becomes, in effect, a heroic biography which follows, so far as is possible, the international pattern for hero-figures, discussed by a sequence of scholars from J.G. von Hahn (1876) to Tomás Ó Cathasaigh (1977).[14] Ó Cathasaigh's summary of what is involved deserves quotation, in itself, and also for the illustration which it provides of the mythological and religious elements present in the adaptation of a pre-Christian form for use in a Christian community:

> By means of the heroic biography the human person (real or imaginary) is transmuted into something *quite other*, that is, into a sacred personage. Thus we may speak of the heroic biography as it operates in each cultural tradition as a 'trans-historical model' for the prestige legends of the group. The hero is a mortal personage whose life is characterized by certain definable features which mark him off as sacred.   (p. 5)

Pre-eminently, a saint is a sacred person, and it is thus entirely appropriate that his life-story should fit the heroic mould. This involves miraculous circumstances during conception, birth and fosterage in secret; the death or disappearance of the father; a series of boyhood deeds performed in the face

13 Translated in T. Kinsella, *The Táin*, London 1970, 1-2.
14 See especially T. Ó Cathasaigh, *The Heroic Biography of Cormac mac Airt* (hereafter '*Cormac mac Airt*'), Dublin 1977, 2-4.

of general hostility on the part of the hero's foster-fellows, a series which normally at some point entails the gift to the hero from some old and wise person of a hero-name; the departure of the hero from his fosterparent, and the subsequent establishment by him of a kingdom or sphere of political influence; exile from his kingdom and subsequent triumphant return, which may, where appropriate, be combined with a meeting with the lost father; a notable death, often heralded by prophecy, and residual posthumous influence focussing on the hero's grave.

Elements of this can be seen in the *Life* of Cadog, but they are better exemplified elsewhere. For the remainder of this paper, I intend to focus on the *Life* of the Glasgow saint, Kentigern[15] (Mungo, Mochoe; ob. 612, according to *Annales Cambriae*[16]), and in particular on the earlier form of the *Life*, generally known as the *Fragmentary Vita*. This was composed during the episcopate of Herbert, bishop of Glasgow from 1147 to 1164, by a foreign ecclesiastic, perhaps a Tironensian monk of Kelso, the house of which Herbert was abbot until he succeeded to the bishopric. The anonymous author made use of 'a little book of his (Kentigern's) virtues' or perhaps better 'of his miracles', and of 'the oral communication of the faithful'. In the unique manuscript, British Library Cotton Titus A. xix, the text is preceded by the so-called Lailocen fragments,[17] which may well derive from the same original. An Office of the saint, preserved in the manuscript Sprouston Breviary, now in the National Library of Scotland, seems to have been made from a text of the *Fragmentary Vita* more complete than that which we now possess. The later *Life* by Jocelin of Furness was put together during the Glasgow episcopate of another Jocelin (1175-1199), specifically, perhaps, in connection with the dedication in 1197 of the new cathedral, the building of which was begun in 1181. This *Life* was based partly, in all probability, on the Frag-

15 Most of the material is gathered in A.P. Forbes, ed., *Lives of S. Ninian and S. Kentigern* (hereafter 'Forbes'), Edinburgh 1874.

16 A.W. Wade-Evans, *Nennius's 'History of the Britons'*, London 1938, 89.

17 H.L.D. Ward, 'Lailoken (or Merlin Silvester)', *Romania* 22 (1893), 504-26.

mentary *Vita*, or its source,[18] partly on a *codiculum alium
stilo Scottico dictatum*, composed, that is to say, either in
Gaelic, or in the style which Jocelin felt to be characteristic
of Irish *Lives* of saints. Jocelin's biography is complete, but
he revises and bowdlerizes his basic material in what he
probably saw as the interests of twelfth century orthodoxy
and decorum.

All in all, there is thus considerable material for a reconstruction of the epic or heroic biography of the patron saint
of Glasgow.

The Fragmentary *Vita* itself narrates the story of the conception and birth of Kentigern and the circumstances under
which he acquired the special name 'Mungo' from the lips of
St Servanus, by whom he was accepted into fosterage.
Jocelin adds details,[19] presumably derived from the Scottic
Life, to explain his other names, 'Kentigern' and 'Mochoe'.
The *Fragmentary Vita* also indicates that the part now completely lost gave some account of the meeting between the
adult Kentigern and Ewen son of Erwegende, the father
whom he had never previously seen.[20] The Office combines
with Jocelin to provide details of the saint's boyhood spent
in Servanus' monastery at Culross in Fife, of the hostility of
his fellows, triumphantly overcome, and of his eventual
departure for Glasgow. The Lailoken fragments give some
account of the saint's relations with a wild man of the woods,
in some ways a figure parallel to himself, but one which
Marie-Louise Sjoestedt[21] would have described as living outside rather than within the tribe, whose prophecy that Kentigern and others would die in the course of the current year
receives strong preliminary confirmation from the three-fold
death which he accurately foretells for himself. An abbrevi-

---

18   J. MacQueen, 'Yvain, Ewen and Owein ap Urien', *Dumfries Trans-
      actions*, 33 (1956), 107-31; K. Jackson, 'The Sources for the
      Life of St. Kentigern', *Studies in the Early British Church*, ed.
      N.K. Chadwick, Cambridge 1958, 273-357; J. MacQueen, 'Reply
      to Professor Jackson', *Dumfries Transactions*, 36 (1959), 175-83.
19   Cap. IV: Forbes, 41, 169.
20   Cap. III: Forbes, 128, 247.
21   *Gods and Heroes of the Celts*, trs. Myles Dillon, London 1949,
      81-91.

ated, not to say emasculated, version of this appears in Jocelin's final chapter XLV. For other incidents, in particular, the exile of the saint to Wales and his eventual triumphant return, we depend on the sole authority of Jocelin. Each of the accounts, it may be added, abounds in references to placenames, many of which are 'explained' by the narrative. During the twelfth and succeeding centuries, as probably also in earlier times, these places had a particular significance in the cult of St Kentigern. The legend is the charter-myth of the cult-centres or places of cult-pilgrimage so named.

There is, finally, a good deal of evidence for the existence of a secular tradition, which also made use of the material preserved in the ecclesiastic legend of Kentigern. Much of this survives primarily in Old French — the *Yvain*[22] of Chretien de Troyes — of which in Middle Welsh we have a cognate, the prose *Countess of the Fountain*.[23] The substance of these romances is probably derived from the activities of travelling bards and storytellers, whose first language was Welsh, Cornish or Breton, but who came into contact with French courtly circles, the influence of which eventually extended back as far as Wales. The *Fragmentary Vita* contains a reference[24] to *gestae histrionum*, 'stories told by minstrels', which itself indicates the existence of such a secular tradition. Many of the names which occur in the biography are also to be found in the earliest Welsh poetry and in early historical and genealogical compilations. A line of transmission may be traced with some considerable probability from Welsh-speaking Strathclyde through Wales itself and Cornwall to Brittany. The transition to French most probably occurred at one of the last three stages, though direct transmission even from Strathclyde is not wholly unthinkable.

22 Ed. M. Roques, Paris 1967.
23 This is not included by Ford in his translation. See G. and T. Jones, *The Mabinogion* (hereafter 'Jones and Jones'), London 1949, 155-82.
24 Cap. I: Forbes, 125, 245. Forbes's reading *historiarum* for *histrionum* is erroneous.

As I have pointed out elsewhere,[25] the story of the conception, birth and fosterage of Kentigern is paralleled by that of
the Greek hero Perseus, the ultimate source of which may
have been a lost Greek epic, and which, as Hartland long ago
demonstrated,[26] is only the most familiar of a series of
related stories of the birth of a hero to be found in many parts
of the world. (The Perseus epic, incidentally, is itself, as Lord
Raglan, for one, recognised,[27] a specimen of heroic biography).
Leudonus, the king of Lothian, Kentigern's grandfather,
corresponds to Acrisius, king of Argos and grandfather of
Perseus; Thaney, Kentigern's mother, corresponds to Danae,
and like Danae, she finds that the punishment for her pregnancy is exposure to the mercy of the sea. Danae and Perseus
are rescued by the fisherman Dictys, from whom they
receive sanctuary in the little island of Seriphos; the corresponding figure in the legend of Kentigern is Bishop Servanus
at Culross in Fife. Childbirth in both cases is the result of a
conception which takes place, more or less miraculously, in
spite of all the precautions adopted by the girl's father; the
birth in effect is virgin, though in both cases a father is named
— Zeus for Perseus, Ewen son of Erwegende for Kentigern.
There are, of course, differences of detail; in the most familiar
version Zeus, for instance, approaches Danae in a shower of
gold, whereas the beardless youth Ewen deceives Thaney when
he comes to her disguised as a girl; but those differences for
the most part reflect, not essential differences in the story,
but differing social and cultural assumptions in the two
societies concerned.

The most notable difference between the two versions is
the presence in the *Fragmentary Vita* of the mysterious
swineherd whom Leudonus appoints, in effect, as Thaney's
foster-father, to humiliate her, and yet, at the same time to
be guardian of her virginity.[28] No more satisfactory explanation of his presence is ever given in the text, and he is said,

---

25 'Yvain, Ewen and Owein ap Urien'; see also 'Myth and the Legends
   of Lowland Scottish Saints', *Scottish Studies* 24 (1980), 14.
26 *The Legend of Perseus*, 1-3, London 1894-6.
27 *The Hero. A Study in Tradition, Myth and Drama*, London 1936,
   177.
28 Cap. I: Forbes, 125ff., 245ff.

like Thaney herself, to be a Christian, a disciple of Servanus. Thaney's eventual pregnancy leads Leudonus, very naturally, to assume that the swineherd is the father of her as yet unborn child, and pursue him with the intention of putting him to death, but instead he is himself killed, struck by a javelin which the swineherd hurls. Leudonus' place of death is commemorated by a standing stone 'about a mile to the south of Mount Dumpelder' or Traprain Law in the modern East Lothian.[29]

The swineherd has here taken on the role which in the Greek version is reserved for Perseus himself, who fulfils his prophesied destiny by accidentally killing Acrisius with a discus which the wind blows aside during the games celebrated at Larissa, where the old king had taken refuge. It was a prophecy of just this event which led to Acrisius' original cruel treatment of Danae, and indeed this motif seems an essential part of the basic story (AT 934C*, 'Man will Die if he ever Sees his Daughter's Son'). The northern version has been influenced presumably, by the feeling that it is unfitting for a bishop, actual or potential, to be the murderer of his own grandfather, even under circumstances of extreme provocation.

This of itself, however, scarcely explains the introduction of the swineherd. In the *Vita*, his proportions are merely human. Not so in the more secular variants of the tale. The corresponding figure in Chretien's *Yvain*, and its cognate, the Welsh *Countess of the Fountain*, is much more formidable. Here is the Welsh description:[30]

And when I came there, what wild animals I saw there were thrice as remarkable to me as the man had said; and the black man was sitting on top of the mound. Big the man told me he was: bigger by far was he than that. And the iron club in which the man had said was the full load of two men, I was sure, Cei, that there was therein the full load of four warriors. It was in the black man's hand. And I greeted the black man, but he spoke nothing to me save incivility. And I asked him what power he had over the animals. 'I will show thee, little man,' said he. And he took

29 Cap. VII: Forbes, 130-1, 249.
30 Jones and Jones, 159.

the club in his hand, and with it struck a stag a mighty blow
till it gave out a mighty belling, and in answer to its belling wild animals came till they were as numerous as the
stars in the firmament, so that there was scant room for
me to stand in the clearing with them and all those serpents
and lions and vipers and all kinds of animals. And he looked
on them and bade them go graze. And then they bowed
down their heads and did him obeisance, even as humble
subjects would do to their lord.

Clearly we have here an otherworld figure, a Monstrous
Herdsman, whose flock is made up of wild rather than
domesticated animals. In immediate context, his apparent
role is simply to watch the frontier which separates the realm
of everyday things from the region of supernatural adventure.
Since the crossing of the frontier entails for any traveller
mortal combat by means of which he may obtain the hand of
the Countess of the Fountain, his role becomes comparable
to that of another herdsman, the equally monstrous shepherd
Custennin, who in *Culhwch and Olwen,*[31] together with his
wife (also a monster), the maternal aunt of Culhwch, acts as
the guardian of the giant's daughter, Olwen. In the *Fragmentary Vita*, the figure has been, as it were, euhemerized as a
consequence of the transition from secular to ecclesiastical
narrative: he is not distinguished in colour, shape, size, or
the nature of his flock. Even so, it is enough, perhaps, that he
is a herdsman. The Irish tradition is familiar with such figures,
for example, Olc Aiche in the cycle of stories which forms
the heroic biography of the high king, Cormac mac Airt. Of
this figure Ó Cathasaigh observes,[32] 'In his role as a Herdsman, Olc Aiche is doubtless to be classed among the avatars
of the "divine" Herdsman of which Irish myth provides many
examples - - - Olc's role must now be clear: he is the guardian
of the domain and of the maiden'. He combines, that is to
say, the role of the herdsman in *Yvain* and the *Countess of
the Fountain* with that of Custennin in *Culhwch and Olwen*.
It should perhaps be added that Ó Cathasaigh regards what he
calls the 'domain' as in fact a form of the otherworld.

31 Ford, 133-4.
32 *Cormac mac Airt*, 31.

When, after earlier repulses, the disguised Ewen approaches Thaney, she is engaged in the lowly task of tending the herdsman's swine, 'sitting alone without any companion, beside the stream of a little fountain which flowed by the edge of a certain wood, whither she was wont to come frequently to drink and to wash her hands'.[33] Ewen entices her into the wood on the pretext of helping 'her' (himself, that is to say, in disguise) lift a bundle of kindling-sticks. In the wood, he assaults her once only, with results so swift that he assumes she must already have been seduced by the swineherd, and in his disappointment and disillusion immediately abandons her. The motivation is different, but the sequence of events is very similar to that in the summary made by Ó Cathasaigh[34] of two Irish tales about Cormac, one (which he refers to as SEC) dealing with Art, Cormac's father, and the maiden Achtan daughter of the Olc Aiche already mentioned, the second (ETB) with Cormac himself and Ethne, foster-daughter of the hospitaller Buchet. Cormac is the child of the first encounter, Cairbre, son and successor to Cormac, of the second:

1. The hero has journeyed/is absent from Tara, and
2. He encounters a maiden.
3. The maiden is engaged in menial tasks, for her father (SEC), or her foster-father (ETB).
4. The girl's (foster-) father is a herdsman.
5. The hero desires the girl, but he is at first refused.
6. In SEC, the Herdsman grants the girl to the hero; in ETB, the hero takes her by force.
7. The hero sleeps only once with the girl, impregnates her and in due course
8. She gives birth to the future king.

Even in quite fine detail, the parallel is striking.

Ó Cathasaigh makes a valuable distinction between the martial and the kingly hero,[35] Achilles and Cú Chulainn being

33 Cap. II: Forbes, 127, 246.
34 *Cormac mac Airt*, 29.
35 *Cormac mac Airt*, 9-11.

examples of the first, Cormac and Arthur of the second. A
hero who is a bishop as well as a saint finds a more appropriate place in the second class, with his diocese taking the place
of a kingdom. So at least it would seem to be with Kentigern,
and there are a number of interesting consequences.

The secular kingly hero is usually heir-apparent to his
father's or grandfather's kingdom, but cannot immediately
take his due place in society because of some natural or supernatural obstacle. For Cormac, it is the death of his father at
the hands of the usurper Lugaid mac Con; for Perseus, the
hostility roused in his grandfather by the prophecy that he
will die at the hands of his daughter's son. As a consequence,
the future king is necessarily reared in secret, usually at some
distance from the seat of his future royal power. His childhood, in other words, is spent in exile. The childhood of a
future bishop is unaffected by such problems of the succession;
thus Kentigern is fostered by Servanus in obscurity, not primarily because he is heir to the throne of Lothian, but because
he must be trained in the monastic ideals of the church. His
childhood is a preparation rather than an exile, and when he
leaves Servanus, it is to go, not across the Forth back to
Lothian, but westwards to the seat of his future authority in
Glasgow.

Although the eventual outcome is as yet hidden from him,
he is prepared for episcopal power by the three stages of his
journey. He crosses a magical river boundary, and so severs
relations with Servanus. When he reaches Kernach (Carnock
in Stirlingshire), he is greeted by the aged Fergus (Fregus) in
words which echo those of Simeon to the young Christ in the
Temple, the *nunc dimittis*. On the death of Fergus, Kentigern
entrusts his body to a cart drawn by two bulls which had not
previously been yoked; these bring it to a neglected cemetery
at Cathures, 'which is now called Glasgow', a cemetery which
Kentigern's great predecessor, Ninian, had long ago con-
secrated, but which since then had remained unused. Fergus
is the first to be buried there, and Kentigern establishes his
community on the same site. The reputation which he acquires
for sanctity soon leads the king of Strathclyde and his clergy
to have him made bishop.

The symbolic heart of this narrative is that the future

bishop finds his kingdom, not in a palace or royal hall, but in a cemetery. From this he rules austerely, wearing no fine clothes, fasting rather than feasting, and subjecting his body to a harsh discipline. Like a peasant, he works the fields, although on occasion, like Cadog's disciples, Finian and Macmoil, already mentioned, he is prepared to exercise supernatural power to keep his people from starvation. His diocese includes at least part of his ancestral principality of Lothian; Jocelin is careful[36] to point out that it 'extended according to the limits of the Cambrian kingdom, which kingdom reached from sea to sea, like the rampart once built by the Emperor Severus' — Grim's Dyke, that is to say, or the Antonine Wall, the eastern end of which touches the Firth of Forth at Bridgeness in West Lothian. Kentigern is later said to have lived for eight years at Lothwerverd (Borthwick) in Midlothian, where he erected a cross of simple sea-sand.

By his actions, Kentigern also separates himself from what one must assume to be the more local and provincial kind of Christianity represented by Servanus, and links himself to the more exalted Roman tradition of Ninian.

As has been noted, the fosterage of Kentigern by Servanus is thus in no real sense the exile, demanded by heroic biography, and leading to a return to the ancestral kingdom, in episcopal terms, the corresponding feature is reserved for a later period, and is eventually brought about by the kindred of the wicked Morken,[37] who on his accession to the throne of Strathclyde, set himself up in opposition to the saint and bishop, and so brought about, not merely his own destruction, but also the taint of hereditary gout in his family and successors. In face of the hostility which followed Morken's death, Kentigern departed for Wales, where he continued his good works, founding, among much else, the community of Llanelwy or St. Asaph.

The kingly character of Kentigern's episcopate is demonstrated by the crop failure, famine and disease which followed his departure, and only came to an end when a new king, Rhydderch (*Rederech*), sent messengers to beg him to return,

36 Cap. XI: Forbes, 55, 182-3.
37 Caps. XXI, XXII, XXIII: Forbes, 69-73, 195-9.

and on his return conceded to him power over himself and his posterity. In return, not only were the crops and the health of the people restored, but the queen, Languoreth, who had long been barren, at last conceived and bore a son. Kentigern possesses what in the Irish tradition was called *fír flathemon*, 'the prince's truth', through which, as Professor Binchy has remarked,[38] 'come prosperity and fertility for man, beast and crops; the seasons are temperate, the corn crows strong and heavy, mast and fruit are abundant on the trees, cattle give milk in plenty, rivers and estuaries teem with fish; plagues, famine and natural calamities are warded off; internal peace and victory over external enemies are guaranteed'.

J. de Vries summarised[39] the essential shape of heroic biography in a ten point system. Six of these are certainly present in the story of Kentigern, others may have, as it were, a subliminal presence. Ó Cathasaigh finds seven in the Cormac material which he studies, and concludes[40] that 'the incidence of seven items out of ten already argues a high degree of correspondence between Cormac's life and the international pattern, and suggests that he should be treated as a hero'. Much the same is true of Kentigern, and if we equate the epic with the heroic, it would seem to follow that the totality of the material discussed constitutes an epic narrative, and that it is at least possible for the biography of a saint to have something like full epic qualities.

38 *Celtic and Anglo-Saxon Kingship*, Oxford 1970, quoted in *Cormac mac Airt*, 64.
39 *Heroic Song and Heroic Legend*, London 1963, 211ff.
40 *Cormac mac Airt*, 24.

THE FUNCTIONING OF LONG FORMULAE IN IRISH
HEROIC FOLKTALES

KEVIN O'NOLAN

(University College Dublin)

In the archives of the Department of Irish Folklore at University College Dublin, in the manuscript material transcribed from oral recordings made on the Ediphone, there is a heroic folktale called 'Ócha, Mac Rí in Éirinn, agus Manannán', 'Ocha, a King's Son in Ireland, and Manannán'. It was recorded by Liam Costello from the great Connemara storyteller, Éamon Búrc on the 20th of March, 1936. Costello's manuscript carries a note at the end of the tale to the effect that on the day following the recording the storyteller requested Costello not to 'set the story working' for the present, as he had not given it to him in full: he had not remembered it properly, he said, and he would have to record it again some other time.

The story, nevertheless, was transcribed. Anyone who reads the tale can at once understand the storyteller's dissatisfaction with his own performance, for the tale consists almost entirely of formulae or long 'runs' of traditional narrative. It is a curiosity and would remain so except for the fact that Búrc, the storyteller, retold the tale to Costello on the 5th and 6th of August of the same year and we have Costello's transcription of that retelling. In the second case the tale runs to thirty manuscript pages (as against twelve in the first version), and the tale runs its course in a satisfactory way. It may therefore be useful to examine this traditional feature itself and whether its operation in these two versions of a tale gives any insight into the way the storyteller's memory and creativity work.

The type of formula we are dealing with is often called a 'run' or, to use Búrc's own term for it, *culaith ghaisce*, 'battle-dress'. Let us take a fairly plain example from a tale, 'Céadach', collected by Seán Ó hEochaidh in Teelin, Co. Donegal, in the 1920s.

471

Thóg siad a gcuid seolta go bucóideach go bacóideach go barr na gcrann díreach, le croidhe córacha, sa chruth 's nach rabh dadaidh le móchtáil aca acht caoineadh rónta, plé péisti móra, scairteach na n-easconn, feadalach na bhfaoileann; agus ní thearn siad stad mara nó mór-chomhnaidhe gur sheol siad isteach suas ar an taoibh thoir de Éirinn.[1]

'They raised their sails, bulging and billowing, to the top of the straight masts, with a fair wind, so that they could hear nothing but the wailing of seals, the converse of great beasts, the calling of eels, the crying of gulls; and they made no sea-stop nor long stay until they sailed up into a harbour on the east coast of Ireland'.

This is an example of a sea travel formula. When the particular storyteller who uses it has recourse to it, he always repeats it exactly, unless he chooses to curtail it.

For purposes of comparison let us recall a voyage description in the *Odyssey* (Bk. 2, 420 ff):

And now out of the West, Athene of the flashing eyes called up for them a steady following wind and set it singing over the wine-dark sea. Telemachus shouted to the crew to lay hands on the tackle and they leaped to his orders. They hauled up the fir mast, stept it in its hollow box, made it fast with stays, and hoisted the white sail with plaited oxhide ropes. Struck full by the wind, the sail swelled out, and a dark wave hissed loudly round her stem as the vessel gathered way and sped through the choppy seas, forging ahead on her course.[2]

The description here is mostly a formula. It recurs in great part, for example in the *Iliad* (Bk. 1, 481 ff.) where Apollo sends the following wind and where all the description of hoisting the white sail and the dark wave hissing and the vessel forging ahead, and so forth, recurs exactly. Homer pre-

---

1 *Béaloideas* 7 (1937), 198, 199-200.
2 Homer, *The Odyssey*, translated by E.V. Rieu, 48-9. Penguin Classics, Harmondsworth and New York 1945-.

fers realism, the Irish storyteller loves the fantastic. Homer is less fond of the long fixed formula, he may use a large part at a time and what is otherwise a fixity tends to be tailored to the particular context. The folktale, on the other hand, does not allow the context to violate the formula and thus the formula is detachable from the context.

The late Professor James H. Delargy, in his notable lecture, *The Gaelic Story-Teller*, published in the *Proceedings of the British Academy* (1945), had some things to say about this narrative feature:

> Most story-tellers have difficulty in appreciating our interest in the shorter types of narrative, as in their opinion the only tales worthy of any sensible person's attention are the long folk-tales, especially the Finn-tales (*Fiannaíocht*) and the hero tales (*sgéalta gaisce*). And both the narrator and his audience held in low esteem the tale which did not include the traditional and often semi-obscure 'runs' without which they held no hero-tale was complete. This characteristic feature of Gaelic story-telling is almost exclusively confined to hero-tales or to *märchen* which have been fitted into the traditional pattern of oral heroic narrative, e.g. Irish 'ecotypes' of Aarne-Thompson 301, 'The Kingdom Underground'. The main function of the most elaborate of these embellishments is to impress the listener, and the more corrupt and unintelligible they are the greater the effect; but they serve also as resting-places for the story-teller in the recital of the long, intricate tales, from which he can view swiftly the ground he has to cover. They are recited at greater speed than the narrative proper.[3]

These observations are too well supported by the experience and notebooks of collectors to be easily disputed. The fact that such passages do impress the audience, are often unintelligible and are recited at high speed are all interdependent factors. But these results cannot have been the intention of the long tradition which devised these elaborate and fixed formulas. This can be seen from the innumerable examples of such passages in medieval manuscript tales where the language

3 *Op. cit.*, 34-5.

is both clear and stylish and full of recurrences, and where, on the other hand, the ideas of the passage are severely limited to produce a vivid and economic tableau. Economy is both the taskmaster and the paymaster of the teller of long stories.

We must remember that the oral folk tradition in the long tale has been in steady decline for at least one hundred and fifty years. In some cases the borrowing of some of these passages from a higher tradition led directly to corruptions which once received were impossible to alter and hence lack of comprehension led to admiration for the *crua-Ghaeilg*, 'the hard Irish' of the storyteller. On the other hand, when we come across an exceptional practitioner like Búrc, even in this late and final stage of the tradition, the runs are found to be stylish and clear.

The natural and original function of the run may be seen in miniature in a type of brief formula very common in the Irish tradition, namely, the coupling of two, usually alliterating synonyms. Such synonyms are quite common also in Homer who uses such formulae as 'fate and death', 'his mind and his spirit', 'he died and met fate', 'weeping and wailing', and so forth. However the device runs riot in the Irish tradition. For example, in the manuscript tale, *Bodach an Chóta Lachtna*,[4] the hero, who arrives by ship, is said to vault from deck to land using his two spear-shafts as levers — much in the way skiers propel themselves. This very habit of heroes is itself part of the economy of ideas of heroic narrative. In this case the story says they saw him rise *d'urlannaibh a shleagh agus do chrannaibh a chraoiseach*, 'by the poles of his lances and the shafts of his spears'. Here the composer piles on the agony by using two synonymous expressions each with two matching synonyms. Incidentally, this method of landing is familiar to Búrc's hero in the tale we are considering. He does not use spears but such is the thrust of his feet as he rises from the deck that the ship sinks behind him. The fact is, dozens of these pairs of synonyms can be met with in any Finn tale, expressions such as *cuan agus caladphort*, 'harbour and haven', *cath agus comhrac*, 'battle and combat', etc. etc.

4 S.H. O'Grady, ed., *Silva Gadelica*, London 1892, 289.

The folk tradition is the heir to this formula just as it inherits the more elaborate 'run' formula.

Pairs of synonyms function in exactly the same way as the noun-epithet formula studied in depth by Parry.[5] The true Homeric epithet adds nothing to the intrinsic quality of the noun: we may think of *hollow* ships, or *hollow* caves, or *many-holed* sponges. These epithets are chosen by the tradition, just like the synonym, to underline, not to add to the picture. That is why they come so readily to the lips of the storyteller; to use a vivid expression of Professor Lord's: 'they emerge like trained reflexes'.[6]

In practice the widespread use of these formulae has two important effects: they slow the pace of the narrative and ease the demands on the hearer's attention.

In the case of the long traditional 'runs' the same is true but to a more emphatic degree. A travel formula, for example, could easily be passed over; all the storyteller conveys is that the hero went to the East. The essence of the tale would not suffer but length would suffer. And the audience, unlike the reader who quickly skims through the familiar, is nothing loath to view yet again the vivid scene which the storyteller projects on the screen of their minds, to listen again to the well-known and well-loved expressions. For the teller and his audience to travel is better than to arrive.

At this stage let me quote in translation some of the 'runs' which occur in the versions of the tale by Éamon Búrc with which we are concerned. His travel formula is as follows:

> He went down to the sea and threw his gold ring out on the sea with all his force, and made (of it) a great capacious ship. He himself with a second leap went in amid ships. He raised up its great billowing bulging sails from the bottom to the top of the masts; the rough sand going down, the fine sand coming up. He did not leave a mooring rope without hauling nor an oar without shattering; the small fish, the large fish of the eastern sea and the western sea coming on the end and blade of his oar; the small eels and the large

5 M. Parry, *L'Épithète traditionelle dans Homère*, Paris 1928.
6 A.B. Lord, *The Singer of Tales*, Harvard 1964, 58.

eels of the eastern sea and the western sea weaving together for him on deck, rendering a service of sport and
music to Mac Rí in Éirinn as he went to the eastern world.
And when he went to the eastern world he struck three
waves upon the ship, a wave of the wind going through
her, of the sun splitting her; till he had tied her up for a
year and a day even supposing she would be there for
only a moment, until he had made her into a green stone
on the shore and seaweed growing on her.

As we see the storyteller here has a short introductory
formula describing the magical production of the ship and a
conclusion describing how it was magically transformed on
arrival.

This tendency to string formula upon formula is particularly noticeable in the case of the main business of the
hero, namely, combat. A common preliminary formula met
with many times in these versions is this:

He struck the challenge pole. He did not leave a foal in
a mare, a lamb in a sheep, a child in a woman that he did
not turn nine times in its mother's belly and from there
back again; he did not leave the old castle unbroken, the
new castle unbent; the old tree unbroken and the new tree
unbent; and it said on the flat of his sword that there was
not a hero under ground or above ground able to beat him.

This remarkable effect of the striking of the challenge pole
may at times be omitted. In that case the bare facts are related
that he struck the challenge pole and the herald came out and
asked what he wanted. If the lord or giant of the castle has
forces he asks for combat with the forces and there is a formula to describe their coming: 'He saw the darkening of the
hills and the mottling of the glens as they came from east and
west.' The combat is described and very often ends with an
old formula borrowed from a higher oral tradition: 'He made
three heaps of them, a heap of their heads, a heap of their
bodies, and a heap of their arms and dress.'

Finally he asks for combat with the king or giant:

'You won't have long to wait', says the herald. 'The
giant is dressing himself from the top of his head to the

soles of his feet in armour plate. Devil a blow', says he, 'he will deal you, that he will not drive from the skin to the flesh, and from the flesh to the bone, and from the bone to the marrow'.

The actual combat has various formulations and the difficulty of the combat and its length varies according to its importance. The end, however, is always the same:

> He struck him at the juncture of his spine and his neck. He took the head off him. The head was whistling as it went up and humming as it went down, in hope of coming on the same body again. But he made no mistake: he sent (the head) a ridge and seven acres away.
>
> 'Well you did', says the head, says he. 'If I came upon the same body again, half the Fianna would not take me down.'
>
> 'Well it was not to let you up, weakling', says he, 'that I took you down.'

The audience knows, as the hero knows, that the enemy has magic and the danger is not over when the head is merely cut off. Incidentally, in Búrc's formula, the hero kicks the head away *iomaire agus seacht n-acra*, 'a ridge and seven acres'. This does not seem right for a measure of distance, but a similar medieval formula reads *naoi n-iomairi agus naoi n-eitreacha*,[7] 'nine ridges and nine furrows'. This perhaps exemplifies how mistakes can become fixed in oral transmission.

A better example, perhaps, of faulty transmission is another formula met with in both these versions:

> They spent the night as they spend the three thirds, a third at storytelling, a third at *Fiannaíocht*, and a third at slumber and steady sleep until the morrow.

In this formula not only is the word for slumber corrupt and in itself unintelligble, but the other two activities of the night, storytelling and *Fiannaíocht* are one and the same thing. Now in medieval Finn tales the night is better divided by formula into three parts: the first part is spent at drinking,

---

7   See O'Grady, *op. cit.*, 264; *naoi nimaireda ocus naoi neitreda.*

the second at singing and regaling of spirits, and the third at sleep.[8]

A frequent way of motivating action in Búrc's tales, including these versions, is to lay the hero under a binding obligation. This is done often by inducing him to play a game of cards and if he loses he is bound to pay a forfeit which can be any task. A dying enemy can also lay on him an obligation without further ado. This brings me to my last example of traditional formula. When the particular task is enjoined on the hero, it is done in a simple form of words such as 'I put you under binding obligation.' The hero accepts the situation as a matter of course and goes home. Here is where the formula comes in. When he goes in, he invariably leans against the gable-end of the house and lets a sigh out of him. The gable-end splits in two. His father, no mean diagnostician in these matters, immediately says: 'You are a King's son who is under binding obligation.' The son tells what has happened and what a distant quest lies ahead. The father then utters this formula in the shorter version – it is omitted in the longer version: 'Do not bother to go there', says the father, says he. 'I will give you a new house, a new cup, a new table, a new dish, a new bed', says he, (every day) for as long as you live, and there is no need for you to go there.'

This may seem at first glance to be a strange proposal, a *non sequitur*. But the hero and his father understand, and of course the audience and the storyteller, even though he does not say so, that the binding force is so exigent that the hero may not sleep twice in the same bed or drink from the same cup or sit at the same table, stay twice in the one house, and so forth, but must press on to fulfill the task he has been set. The father is proposing an unheroic way out of the obligation and the hero invariably rejects the proposal.

The folktale hero's ordinary activities such as getting up, dressing, preparing for rest, eating and so on are covered by

8 *Ibid.*, 268.

traditional formulae which extend the length of the tale but do not advance the essential action. Even the more heroic activities such as long travel, the undergoing of trials, the prominent feature of dialogue and verbal exchanges, arming and even combat, the chief activity, cannot of themselves constitute a tale. These are the features and occasions which the storyteller inherits from the tradition by way of formulae. They are ingredients indifferently of one tale or another. They add length to tales and give them their heroic tone. Judiciously used they improve and escalate the action. But they cannot provide that essence which make one tale different from another.

Finally let us examine the two versions of 'Ócha and Manannán' in so far as space permits. First I shall summarize the shorter version, that which is made up almost entirely of the formulae above described and others. It is difficult to give a clear picture and in the interests of brevity and clarity I omit features like the formal opening of the tale and the formal ending which is common to both versions. Sentences like 'he fights the giant' can be taken to cover a narrative involving several formulae.

An old man approaches Ócha, the hero, puts him under obligation, gives him a sword and sends him to the eastern world to bring back a certain black hound. Ócha sets out and arrives. He fights and slays an opposing host. Next day he fights their master, giant number one. He proceeds again on his travels and encounters giant number two. On being asked what he wanted, the hero says the black hound which the great Hag of Bun an Chroic had, that or combat. He gets combat and kills the giant who with his dying breath obliges him to go to the Hag and tell her he has killed himself and the other giant. The hero does so, reaches the Hag's abode and demands combat against the hosts of her realm. He kills the host and next day demands combat with the Hag herself. They fight and when the Hag is overcome she asks for quarter, promising gifts such as half her kingdom. The hero says all he wants from her is the black hound. This is provided, he kills the Hag and returns home. He meets Manannán, gives him the hound and thus fulfils his obligation.

It will be seen that the tale has no real motivation — we do not know why the hound is being sought. In quite simple tales the object sought may often be of such value as to justify the quest or the object may have a magic potency which is urgently needed. Furthermore there is incoherence in the matter of the two giants. They were not mentioned in the task originally set, which was to get the black hound from the Hag of Bun an Chroic. This would not matter provided some advance notice of these encounters were given. It is the rule in oral narrative that action to come is in some way programmed in advance, otherwise the audience are lost. If an action lies ahead which has not been scheduled, a helper may warn the hero, thus letting the audience know what lies ahead. Or an extra obligation may, in course of transit, be laid on the hero. For example, as mentioned in the summary, the second giant at the point of death laid an obligation on the hero to go to the Hag. This is strictly unnecessary since he is reiterating an existing obligation, but at least it lets us know where finally the hero is going and ties these two points of the story together.

There are also certain lapses — in one case the storyteller starts afresh on a formula saying he has forgotten part of the tale; and in the case of the giants he wrongly names the second giant by the name of the first. These are superficial lapses but they confirm the storyteller's own impression that his recollection was at fault.

The second version starts differently. Ócha is sent for a year abroad to learn athletic feats and valour. When he returns he receives much welcome and gifts. Last to offer a gift is an unknown young woman who gives him a sword and spear and departs. He follows and questions her, but she is under obligation to give no information. When out hunting later he rests and falls asleep. When he wakes an old man is beside him who claims to know past, present and future. He asks who the girl is. He tells him that he himself is Manannán; that his brother married an Irish princess and brought her to the eastern world. They had a daughter. Meanwhile giants attacked that country and deprived his brother, the younger Manannán, of his kingdom. The girl had come with her father's sword and spear to the only person who might get back the kingdom, a king's son in Ireland.

Ócha sets forth and meets the two giants as in the first version. He next encounters a hag who as she dies lays him under obligation to go and inform an even more formidable hag of what he has done. He kills this second hag and turns round to find an old man beside him who turns out to be the deposed king, the younger brother of Manannán. He welcomes Ócha and tells him that his own oppressor is the Blue giant, a very formidable enemy. Manannán's daughter, the girl who had come to Ócha with the gift of her father's sword and spear, is not at home because she was kidnapped a year before by a giant from the western world. Ócha takes on the Blue giant and, spurred on by the younger Manannán, kills him. He then makes his ship and travels to the Western world. He kills the guards who protect the castle. The girl is overjoyed to see him. She tells him the giant is shortly to return. He often assumes the shape of a whiteheaded dog but combat is hopeless since he can die only by choking on an egg which is inside a duck which is in the stomach of a ram which is locked up in the castle. The hero gets the egg and in the course of a combat with the giant, he watches his chance, and when the giant assumes his dog form he throws the egg down his throat. This novel use of a well-known motif leads to the freeing of the princess and her marrying the hero, as well as to the restoration of his kingdom to her father.

This long though very bald summary of the second version may seem to describe a different story, but in reality the course of each version is very similar. But the new element, the initial appearance of the girl who gives the hero the sword and spear, is the real key which gives coherence to the tale. The old man Manannán explains the matter and Ócha feels compelled to go to her father's rescue. In the first version the omission of the girl is a fatal flaw. Manannán indeed, in the first version sets the hero on his travels but his mission even if accomplished leads nowhere.

The middle course of both tales is the same, namely the combat with the giants and hags. In neither version is this part quite at home: these combats are not programmed in advance. Their purpose seems to be to lengthen the tale. However, the second version has not two but four of these in-transit combats, there is escalation of the hero's difficulties and a sense of progression. The discovery of Manannán's brother, just after the last of these combats, brings the story line into accord with the early projection, namely, the rescue of the girl's father from his wretched state and his restoration to the throne. The full circle is now about to close when a snag arises — the hero indeed has already been apprised of it: the girl is missing — kidnapped a year before. There follows a further narrative culminating in the rescue of the girl, marriage and return. This may seem at first sight an afterthought, but if we look at the bald plot of the tale, the girl with her gift of sword and spear, Manannán who explains why she came with these gifts, the in-transit combats with giants and hags, Manannán's brother, the injured king who explains his own situation and his daughter's kidnap, and finally the rescue of the daughter, we see a plan of almost perfect symmetry with reverse order in the second half. Further, there is the subtlety that the real compelling force is love for the girl, not any binding spell: for when the son comes home from hunting, he leans against the gable and sighs and splits the gable. His father makes the usual diagnosis, but in fact there has been no obligation laid on the hero in this version. Nevertheless, he answers that he must go to rescue the girl's father from the giants. The magnet that draws him is love, as is made clear in the tale.

From a comparison of these versions we may conclude perhaps that the activities of the hero which are enshrined in fixed formulae are not in themselves enough to sustain a tale, a conclusion which indeed might have been assumed from the very nature of formulae and their transferability from tale to tale. But this conclusion entails another conclusion: that however much these elaborate 'runs' may have helped the storyteller to remember a tale, he must also have had some additional aid to hold in mind or recall a synopsis of a tale.

It is true that combat is the main business of the hero and therefore a large part of the on-going or essential narrative. But the reduction of combat to a formula is at variance with the practice of more aristocratic traditions. For example, combat which is a main part of the Iliad never becomes a formula, though there is a pattern to it which is very like the pattern of the Búrc formula. This pattern is a verbal exchange, the actual combat, a further verbal exchange between the dying man and the victor, the victor having the last word. But although the pattern contains formulae, everything is variable according to the occasion and the characters, except perhaps that the victor has the last word. One might think that the victim who dies with his last words would deprive the victor of his privilege but Homer has a formula to ensure otherwise. When Hector meets Patroclos there is no initial exchange of words because he wounds him in the back. When Patroclos dies with his last word Homer says 'Shining Hector addressed him, dead though he was' (*Iliad* 16.858). Equally when Achilles kills Hector the same formula is used: 'Godlike Achilles addressed him, dead though he was' (*Iliad* 22.364).

Though using the same pattern and much formular language, Homer makes one fight distinct from another and thus combats are absorbed into the running narrative. The same is true to some extent of medieval Irish tales. Alan Bruford, for example, in his study of the Medieval Romances remarks that 'it is often hard to decide when the run ends and the normal process of narration . . . begins again.'[9] This is so because the monolith run is avoided and also the spread of traditional formulae throughout the narrative is more profuse than in the folktale.

In the folktale the verbal exchange is always the same, the fight follows the same course, the death blow is always a beheading stroke, and though the severed head has a final remark or two, the hero has the last word.

It is difficult then, to lay much structural weight on the combat formula, because it is a formula and is frequent. Búrc indeed, by his repertoire of combat formulae and by varying the length from one or two days to eight or by making it go hard for the hero, does distinguish one combat from another and brings in an element of escalation. But he does this by inserting a further traditional element. For example,

9 *Gaelic Folk-tales and Medieval Romances*, Dublin 1967, 36-7.

when the fight is so evenly balanced that neither can beat the other, a bystander exhorts the hero by reminding him that no loved one is near to lament or bury him if he should go down, and this tips the balance. If there is no bystander, this gloomy thought occurs automatically to the hero.

I suppose we should be thankful that the same thought never strikes his opponent otherwise we would have even longer fights. But in storytelling, though it may not seem so, the dice is always loaded in the hero's favour.

FORMULA IN YUGOSLAV AND COMPARATIVE FOLK EPIC: STRUCTURE AND FUNCTION

JOHN MILES FOLEY

(University of Missouri/Columbia)

I

Perhaps only seldom does a scholar interested in elucidating an intellectual problem or set of problems propose to do so by making matters more complex. The more customary academic route, perhaps especially in the field of folk epic, has led away from divergences, idiosyncrasies, and contrasts towards syntheses, universals, and similarities. But what I hope to demonstrate in a modest way in this paper is precisely the importance of adding complexity to the study of folk epic. In a general way, I would argue that comparisons become meaningful, permanent aids to interpretation only when they are fashioned against the background of realistic distinctions. More particularly, it seems apparent that the modern critical trend away from such forbidding, out-of-date pursuits as philology has stamped much recent research with a lack of regard for linguistic and textual essentials. I say 'essentials' simply because I believe that, even in an area where the idea of 'text' must be much modified if it is to have true meaning, we should begin our investigations of the formula and other elements characteristic of folk epic with a consideration of the uniqueness of the language and tradition of the individual work. Although each language and tradition will naturally share a number of features with other languages and traditions, perhaps even under the Indo-European blanket or more closely within language families, no two works will be composed out of exactly the same cloth.

Thus in the opening section of this study I shall focus on the necessity of viewing folk epic first in its most immediate context before moving on to the broader strokes of comparison. In doing so I shall advocate three principles of analysis which are intended to establish the uniqueness of the individual

485

folk epic and then to calibrate the comparison that follows. The first of these principles, tradition-dependence, refers to the language-based set of idiosyncrasies that characterize a formula in any given work; my core assumption is that since the language and meter of any one tradition differ to some degree from those of any other, then it is imperative to establish the difference among the structures they support, such as the formula. The second principle, genre-dependence, has to do with a work's singular generic form and function; here we should address not only the crude distinctions such as that between epic and lyric but also the finer divisions among, for example, subgenres marked by varying story patterns or modes of performance. The final principle, that of text-dependence, concerns the nature of the document with which we are presented. That is, do we have a recorded or even videotaped text, a manuscript (if so, what were the circumstances of the commission to writing), or something else?

With these added complications introduced and briefly exemplified in relation to Serbo-Croatian and other folk epics, I shall turn in the second part of the paper from structure to function. From philological differentiation the discussion will proceed to a consideration of the impact of the formula on a traditional audience. Put most directly, the question to be grappled with in this latter section is: 'What and how does the formula mean?' It has been clear for some time that recurrent phraseology characterizes many folk epics, but there has been little agreement about the core significance of their 'essential ideas', as Milman Parry and Albert Lord have called them.[1] We know that such phrases are not boringly repetitive, as they would be for the modern, post-traditional sensibility, but beyond that point opinions vary. I shall propose that formulas (and other traditional structures)

---

1 See the basic works: *The Making of Homeric Verse: The Collected Papers of Milman Parry*, ed. Adam Parry, Oxford 1971, hereafter cited as *MHV*, and A. Lord, *The Singer of Tales*, Cambridge MA 1960 *et seq*. For a brief history of oral theory and a digest of the more than 1900 books and articles associated with this approach, see my *Oral-Formulaic Theory and Research: An Introduction and Annotated Bibliography*, New York 1985, hereafter cited as *OFTR*.

generate meaning by indirection, that is, by reference to the extratextual world of the tradition. But this is more than a generic reference. What the formula does is to bring up into the individual performance the significance of a character, location, or whatever from all other performances within the audience's experience, so that 'swift-footed Achilles' is not simply a hero who is generally fleet of foot but an entire heroic presence conjured, as it were, by his noun-epithet formula. This process of the formula serving as the key to the traditional wordhoard I call *metonymy*, and understand as the nominal part standing, *pars pro toto*, for the unexpressed and inexpressible whole.

First, then, to the philological perspective and the structure of the formula. As one reads over the scholarship on formulaic phraseology in various folk epic traditions, it quickly becomes only too apparent that a single, canonical definition of the traditional phrase is not a realistic goal.[2] Milman Parry's concept of 'a group of words which is regularly employed under the same metrical conditions to express a given essential idea' (*MHV*, 272) is useful as far as it goes, since it does point the way toward the aspects of surface phraseology, recurrence, metrical texture, and an underlying core idea. But since these 'metrical conditions' may vary widely from one tradition to the next, the comparatist is soon faced with a corresponding variance in wording, pattern of recurrence, and even of morphology. The Homeric hexameter encourages certain kinds of phrase-making and -retention, and on the whole provides a rhythmic frame that promotes the generation of relatively long and stable formulaic elements. The Serbo-Croatian epic decasyllable or *deseterac* shares many metrical characteristics with Homer's line, but is of course not an exact match: one discovers that certain kinds of malleability are more typical of Yugoslav than of ancient Greek diction. The Old English alliterative line is the least 'conservative' of these three meters,

2 For an idea of the variation possible among different traditions, see, e.g. J.J. Duggan's concept of the Old French formula (*The Song of Roland: Formulaic Style and Poetic Craft*, Berkeley 1973), as contrasted with Patricia Arant's notion of the phraseological unit in Russian ('Formulaic Style and the Russian Bylina', *Indiana Slavic Studies* 4 (1967), 7-51).

allowing and even promoting many different sorts of meta-
theses, additions, and substitutions unknown in the other
two folk epic poetries.

Even these few examples illustrate the problems inherent
in a unitary, global definition of the formula. If we choose to
ignore tradition-dependence and continue to seek a linguistic
universal where none can logically exist, we are doomed to an
endless search for a chimera. Nor will the distinction between
'formula' and 'formulaic system'[3] save the investigator from
this plight; since different traditions make different metrical
demands upon their traditional phraseologies, verbatim repeats
will be more common in some epic poetries than in others.
What is more, what can be classified as a formulaic system
under the metrical rules of one tradition might not qualify
for the same designation in another poetry. Quite clearly, we
must begin by asking for a definition of the formula in a single
tradition. Only after establishing the morphology of the
diction on its own terms can we proceed to informed comparison between and among formulas from different traditions.

As an example of how this kind of preliminary work might
proceed, let us examine a few features of the three meters
mentioned above and their symbiotic relationships to folk
epic phraseology. The decasyllable or *deseterac*, the metrical
foundation for much of the Yugoslav folk epic tradition,
reveals its Indo-European heritage in its regular syllable count,
succession of quantities, caesura placement, and 'right justification'.[4] This last quality amounts to an increasing con-

3 Parry's definition of a 'formulaic system' was 'a group of phrases
   which have the same metrical value and which are enough alike in
   thought and words to leave no doubt that the poet who used them
   knew them not only as single formulas, but also as formulas of a
   certain type' (*MHV* 275). On later notions of the system, see
   further Foley, *OFTR*.
4 Other studies of the Indo-European origins of the *deseterac* start
   with R. Jakobson, 'Studies in Comparative Slavic Metrics', *Oxford
   Slavonic Papers* 3 (1952), 21-66, and continue with J. Vigorita,
   'The Antiquity of Serbo-Croatian Verse', *Južnoslavenski Filolog*
   32 (1976), 205-11, and J.M. Foley, 'Tradition-dependent and
   -independent Features in Oral Literature: A Comparative View of
   the Formula', in *Oral Traditional Literature: A Festschrift for
   Albert Bates Lord*, Columbus OH 1980, rpt. 1983, 262-81. See

servatism as one moves from beginning to end at the levels of both the colon and the line; Roman Jakobson located one aspect of 'right justification' when he reported an Indo-European echo in the 'quantitative close' of the last four syllables of the decasyllable. Another reflex of the same tendency is the longer second colon of six syllables following the shorter one of four, and we notice within each colon greater regularity of stress placement toward the end of the unit. These are a few of the ways in which the *deseterac* deserves its charactization as an archaic meter.

The Homeric hexameter shares many of the same tendencies, but not to the same extent or in the same way. It shows conservatism in syllable-count (more precisely, in mora-count), to be sure, but the line is about half again as long and thus open to many more permutations even on this simplest of levels. The succession of quantities is also regular, but idiosyncratically so; on the synchronic level, we may say that the sites for substitution are different. The ancient Greek epic line has recurrent caesuras as well, but there are three rather than one of them, and they demarcate a variety of cola rather than two. And although we find evidence of 'right justification' in the Homeric hexameter, it once again takes a form that compares to, but does not exactly correspond with, the increasing conservatism of the Serbo-Croatian line. To summarize telegraphically, while both meters reveal their Indo-European lineage, they also reveal individuality in their idiosyncratic evolution from the hypothetical Ur-meter.

The alliterative verse of *Beowulf* is quite another matter, however. It demonstrates no regular syllabicity, succession of quantities, caesura, or right justification, the loss of which features may well be traced to the shift of stress in Proto-Germanic that turned the meter into a stress-based rather than a syllabic medium.[5] An Old English verse line may be from eight to sixteen syllables in length, with wide variation

further this last entry for a selective bibliography on related research in other traditions.

5   This amounted to a shift in prosodeme from syllable to stress; see further Winfred P. Lehmann, *The Development of Germanic Verse Form*, rpt. New York 1971, especially 26-63.

in verse-types; the mid-line break cannot be termed a caesura since it does not demarcate consistent units; there is little or no trace of right justification; and, perhaps most importantly, the verse-form actually encourages the lack of what Parry called 'thrift' as well as frequent necessary enjambement. One could hardly imagine a metrical frame more different in its essentials from the Yugoslav and ancient Greek lines.

As for the phraseologies in symbiosis with these varying meters,[6] we must expect them to differ correspondingly — and they do. Whereas four- and six-syllable formulaic phrases are the building blocks of the Serbo-Croatian folk epic, Homer's verse is made up of a more complex selection of colonic types.[7] Of course, the accounts are levelled a bit by the Yugoslav diction's relatively more numerous adaptive mechanisms; though the cola are simpler, the morphology shows greater variety. The Old English traditional phraseology closely resembles neither of its counterparts: formulaic phrases consist most often of lines or parts of lines with recurrent core elements within otherwise quite variable contexts. One begins to understand why there has been so much discussion about the formula in Anglo-Saxon, for in comparison to the Yugoslav *guslar* and to Homer, the *Beowulf*-poet seems at first sight very un-formulaic indeed.[8]

Thus the principle of tradition-dependence, which really demands nothing more or less than taking account of the contribution of the given language and meter to a formulaic

6 I use the phrase 'in symbiosis with' to indicate that I believe the most accurate way to speak of the interrelationship between prosody and phraseology in these works is to give the dominant, determining role to neither one, especially from a diachronic point of view (see further G. Nagy, *Comparative Studies in Greek and Indic Meter*, Cambridge MA 1974). As discussed below, it seems to be a set of traditional rules — dependent upon language and meter but much more specialized than simple metrical constraints — that shapes formulaic phraseology.

7 See, e.g., B. Peabody, *The Winged Word: A Study in the Technique of Ancient Greek Oral Composition as Seen Principally through Hesiod's* Works and Days, Albany 1975, 68ff.

8 Thus, for example, the conclusions of L. Benson in his 'The Literary Character of Anglo-Saxon Formulaic Poetry', *Publications of the Modern Language Association* 81 (1966), 334-41.

phraseology, helps to determine what we can reasonably expect in the way of traditional structure and thus assists us in assessing what we find. As a principle it is most crucial at the levels of meter and diction, where differences are directly reflected, but we may also mention its importance at the level of typical scene or, as Albert Lord and others have called it, 'theme'.[9] For while narrative structures as groups of ideas are naturally not directly influenced by linguistic realities, their expressive content – formulaic phraseology – most certainly is. At one remove, then, in their actual verbal identity, typical scenes will also show idiosyncratic structure.

In addition to tradition-dependence, the investigator committed to precise and productive comparisons must observe the complementary principle of genre-dependence. The focus of this congress on folk epic eliminates gross errors such as adducing non-narrative genres as comparands for narrative forms, or mixing various narrative forms in the same inquiry. But there are further differentiations which can and must be made. One of these is the general matter of 'subgenre'; the folk epic is arguably a rather broad designation, and many kinds of works may qualify for admission to the category. For example, the Serbo-Croatian epic, as collected most thoroughly by Parry and Lord, boasts a number of story-types, among them wedding songs and return songs. While comparison of these subgenres will no doubt yield some interesting and valuable results, the inherent differences between them will preclude certain kinds of comparative analysis.

Other concerns also enter the picture in the Yugoslav situation. For one thing, material drawn from collections other than that of Parry and Lord is often a mélange of texts, some quite short and undeveloped, and thus hardly deserving the name 'epic'. Then, too, there is the discrepancy between Moslem and Christian epic. Parry especially sought the Moslem material because it was characteristically longer and more developed and thus served as a better comparand

---

9 Lord defines 'themes' as 'the groups of ideas regularly used in telling a tale in the formulaic style of traditional song' (*op. cit.*, 68). For further studies of the theme, see *OFTR*.

for the magisterial works of Homer and his tradition; Avdo Medjedović, for example, was a member of this part of the tradition. The Christian songs, on the other hand, were much less extensive. There is evidence – in the collection made by Vuk Stefan Karadžić, for instance – that poets could rework these shorter Christian songs from memory, so that their works approached the kind of consciously designed texts we have come to expect of so-called 'literary' works. It should be emphasized here that Parry's and Lord's sense of what was the most finely wrought comparison, that between Homer and the Moslem epic poet, was unerring; in effect, by matching the two, they were observing the principle of genre-dependence.

But if Parry and Lord succeeded in fashioning a comparison of similar genres, it must be admitted that scholars interested in *Beowulf* as a folk epic have not done nearly so well. Apart from indefensible juxtapositions with riddles or with ornate lyrics such as the elegies, even comparisons with the verse hagiographies cannot stand up. As traditional as the diction of the Old English narrative of St Andrew may seem, for example, we must remember that it has a source, however remote, in the Greek *Praxeis Mattheou kai Andreas*, and that the two genres represented by *Beowulf* and this saint's life could hardly be more disparate. If, realizing this discrepancy, we point to phraseological similarities as an indication of how, even in spite of their vastly different origins and generic identities, these two works testify to continuity in the Anglo-Saxon *Kunstsprache*, then we have made a reasonable statement that may be of use to later interpretation. But we cannot begin by ignoring the discrepancy in genre and proceeding blindly to textual analysis.[10]

Another discrepancy that has plagued students of folk epic is that addressed by our third principle, text-dependence. Is it *prima facie* reasonable to directly compare formulaic phraseology in, for instance, a manuscript of uncertain

10 Compare A. Lord's remarks on the Christian poetry in the Old English canon in his 'Perspectives on Recent Work on Oral Literature', in *Oral Literature: Seven Essays*, ed. J.J. Duggan, Edinburgh 1975, 19-24.

provenance and a transcribed record of an oral performance? Once again, Albert Lord has shown us that even sung and dictated versions of the same song by a single singer vary in characteristic ways.[11] My own work with the Parry Collection material seconds his findings, most clearly in the case of the singer who easily adapts to the dictation method, namely that the dictated song is usually longer and fuller, more ornate than the sung version.[12]

When an unambiguously oral performance and a manuscript are juxtaposed, the uncertainties begin to multiply. Instead of accepting such strange bedfellows as equivalent documents, we should be asking (even if we cannot provide complete answers) questions like the following: What were the conditions under which the text was set down in writing? How was that original text transmitted to the present time? What editing procedures were involved, either at the initial recording or at any point in the history of transmission? If, for example, there is any evidence of significant editing, then any study of formulaic morphology should take that into account. Moreover, if the comparison treats both edited and unedited texts, the results of comparative analysis must be qualified accordingly.

Although Parry and Lord were scrupulous about the collection of their texts, all investigators who have worked in Yugoslavia were not so careful. Matija Murko reports from about 1910 onward that there were numerous *guslari* who could read and write to a degree and who learned the greatest part of their repertoires from printed songbooks;[13] certainly their performances were quite different from those of their

---

11 'Homer's Originality: Oral Dictated Texts', *Transactions of the American Philological Association* 84 (1953), 124-34.

12 'The Traditional Structure of Ibro Bašić's "Alagić Alija and Velagić Selim" ', *Slavic and East European Journal* 22 (1978), 1-14.

13 Examples of such singers abound throughout Murko's major work, *Tragom srpsko-hrvatske narodne epike: Putovanja u godinama 1930-32*, 2 Vols., Djela Jugoslavenske Akademije Znanosti i Umjetnosti, knjige 41-42, Zagreb 1951; see, e.g., the section on singers in Serbia (Vol. 1, 71-93). My translation of this and other of Murko's works into English will be issued by Charles Schlacks Publishers in later 1987 or early 1988.

preliterate colleagues, who learned by listening. The case of
the Homeric poems presents a baffling array of factors that
bear on the principle of text-dependence, from the various
theories about the fixation of the *Iliad* and *Odyssey* in their
present forms through the lacuna-riddled story of their
transmission and on to modern editing procedures. Especially
intriguing in this regard is Stephanie West's demonstration
that the Ptolemaic or so-called 'wild' papyri of Homer share
what she terms 'concordance interpolation',[14] an insight that
amounts to evidence that some vestige of Homeric oral
tradition existed long after the supposed canonization of the
texts at the Panathenaic Festival in the sixth century B.C.
And why not? The work of Parry and Lord has taught us that
the simple recording of a version need not necessarily leave
any imprint at all on an oral tradition. In this particular case,
we are left to ask (or to hypothesize about) what effect such
a continuing tradition — however transmuted — might have
had on the text that has reached us.

Once these three principles — tradition-dependence, genre-
dependence, and text-dependence — are applied to the study
of folk epic, first to the individual tradition and then to comparative analysis, we can begin an informed discussion of the
meaning of the various structures so defined. With a clear
grasp, in other words, of exactly what a formula is in Serbo-
Croatian, ancient Greek, or Old English epic, it is then possible
to ask what and how that formula means. The path toward
interpretation, toward an understanding of function, leads
necessarily through a philological investigation of morphology.

II

And what do we find when we turn from philology to
criticism and interpretation? At present there seem to be two
schools of thought on the meaning of formulaic phraseology,
and they amount in effect to old answers to the Homeric
Question. One side holds that, after the research initiated by
Parry, we must speak only, that is, exclusively of 'utility', of

14　*The Ptolemaic Papyri of Homer*, Papyrological Coloniensia 3, Köln
　　and Upladen 1967, especially 12-3.

the usefulness of a given phrase to the composing poet or singer. Under such conditions aesthetic manipulation of formulaic elements is impossible, since the value of a phrase is purely as a metrical entity that makes possible the telling of tales in oral performance. This group would interpret the 'essential idea' of 'swift-footed Achilles' as 'Achilles', or of 'wily Odysseus' as 'Odysseus'. Art as we know it in post-traditional works, which emphasizes the artist's creative manipulation of the audience's expectations, is for them simply not part of folk epic.

The other school, chiefly Homerists reacting against an over-stringent version of Parry's ideas, would save Homer and his fellows from perdition's flames by showing that certain instances of formulaic phrases bear special, situation-specific meanings.[15] In short, they would make folk epic into a literary creation, complete with ready opportunities for conventional literary criticism.

Perhaps too obviously, neither of these positions is very satisfactory: we cannot force folk epic into a mindless, machine-like exercise, nor can we seek to redeem it by calling it literary. Even if we subscribe to another version of the first position, to wit, that the formulas mean only g e n e r i c a l l y and not particularly, the folk epic must suffer indignities in interpretation. For the generic meaning thesis is a wolf in sheep's clothing: 'swift-footed Achilles' is not simply a formal and somewhat clumsy approximation for 'Achilles', useful because it fills up a certain section of the line. What the idea of generic meaning fails to recognize is that we are dealing not with a single poem, but with a tradition, an entire mythos. The generic-particular dichotomy may convey something of the applicability of the diction, in that it describes elements of phraseology that are appropriate to manifold situations, but it misses the most fundamental issue of all — precisely what this item of diction conveys and how it accomplishes the transmission.

As indicated above, what I propose as an answer to this as

---

15 A recent contribution to this line of argument is P. Vivante, *The Epithets in Homer: A Study in Poetic Values*, New Haven 1982.

yet unsatisfactorily solved problem is an approach through
the richness of the folk epic tradition. I suggest that a formula
conjures its meaning metonymically, *pars pro toto*, by indirect
reference to the tradition. Some phrases will naturally carry a
heavier association than others, so that the truest concept of
the diction would be a spectrum of phraseology ranging from
'nonce' formulas created by a single singer for a certain purpose
all the way to formulas repeated verbatim in texts from
widely varying times and geographical areas. Many formulaic
phrases will at least tend toward the latter, tradition-wide
pole in the spectrum, and so we need to confront their
metonymic character.

Let us turn to Serbo-Croatian folk epic for a few examples
of this latter kind of metonymic formula, specifically to songs
collected by Parry and Lord in the region of Stolac in 1933-35
and 1950-51. (I stress that these examples are all drawn from
the Moslem epic, the natural comparand for folk epics such
as Homer's, and further that they are all taken from texts
belonging to the subgenre of Return, the same tale-type as
instanced in the *Odyssey*.)

I begin with two examples of noun-epithet formulas for
heroes, the category of phrases on which Parry concentrated
in many of his writings on Homer.

| lički Mustajbeže | 'Mustajbeg of the Lika |
| Tale od Orašća | Tale of Orišac' |

The first of these designates the great hero Mustajbeg, who
appears throughout South Slavic epic, customarily at the
head of a band of troops. He is a curiously ambiguous character,
one who leads the Turks and yet may turn treasonous at any
moment. In one song from the Stolac region, for example, he
refuses to open the gates of his city for a fellow Turk who is
being pursued by the enemy Christians; the result is that his
comrade, the central figure in the story, is captured and
imprisoned. In another song he plays the role of a South
Slavic Antinoos, heading up the band of suitors who seek to
force a departed hero's wife to remarry. Only when the
supposedly deceased hero doffs his disguise and appears
before the suitors does Mustajbeg cut his losses and flee. But
we should not overemphasize his occasional (and, except by

traditional association, unpredictable) disloyalty to his constituency, for he can and does perform quite heroically in battle.

Were a literary poet to wish to create such ambivalence in a character, he might use a battery of adjectives such as 'scheming', 'two-faced', or 'wily'. But even this ploy could not instill in a literary character, who is almost always the prisoner of a single canonical text, the kind of resonance Mustajbeg has in the Yugoslav folk epic tradition at large. The audience actively expects some sort of double-dealing from him, because they have heard other stories in which his actions are questionable. The key concept here is that the audience is able to bring extratextual experience to bear on the present text or performance, and they can do so to an extent unknown to the reader of written literature. Mustajbeg lives not as an original creation in this or that specific situation, not even as a generic character imported from one situation to another, but as a fully formed, multidimensional actor in a drama larger and more involved than the present single scene. The tremendous advantage of characterization in such a medium as folk epic is that the character need not be, and is not, simply the hero who walks through the present narrative sequence, but rather the hero who lives in the larger tradition. To this single, present situation he brings a lifetime of achievement, reputation — perhaps even ignominy; in short, he brings the heroic personality developed in all of the stories in which he appears, the personality given him by the tradition.

And the cue that summons the heroic personality to take his place in this particular scene of the larger drama is the noun-epithet formula. By focusing on one particular aspect of a hero's identity, and often an apparently nominal one at that, the tradition summons the whole of the character by metonymy, with the designated part standing for the whole. Thus 'Mustajbeg of the Lika', a seemingly innocent enough way to refer to this hero, becomes charged with extratextual meaning, as do its variants. And in this case the epithet *lički* is not without supportive connotations, for the Lika is not only a geographical area (the 'borderland') at the edge of Turkish territory but also a mythically liminal land of uncertain dimension and contents. It is, in other words, just as

ambiguous a territory as Mustajbeg is a hero. All forces
converge to characterize this Turkish leader as a powerful,
mysterious, liminal, and finally not altogether trustworthy
individual.

Another example of a noun-epithet formula rife with
associations is 'Tale of Orašac'. Here I am speaking of the
'trickster' figure in South Slavic folk epic, the character
without whom, we are often told, there can be no battle or
wedding. But while no father of the bridegroom would consider omitting Tale from the invitations list, this honoured
guest is not quite the picture of decorum. His usual mount is
a mouse-grey swayback horse, his customary outfit amounts
to rags, and his standard-bearer is in the habit of riding backwards carrying his banner upside down. All this and more
constitute the traditional personality conventionally referred
to with one of a few epithets, among them 'Tale of Orašac',
and it is such elements that conjure that identity in whatever
tale makes use of the rhetorical shorthand. And again the
designation 'of Orašac' turns out to be more than nominal.
Orašac is Tale's home, the place from which messengers are
sent to fetch him, upon arrival in that woebegone locale,
they not occasionally find him literally in midstream sharpen-
ing his sword, with his troops either on the riverbank or
getting wet with him. The various versions of this scene and
others are visually arresting in their stark incongruity, and
are only one aspect of the personality which is brought up
into the narrative at hand through the traditional magic of
metonymy.

But what of other formulas which do not name a person
and a quality in this classical way? Are they also metonymic,
or is that quality reserved for only one type of formula?
Consider, for example, the following three phrases:

sužanj nevoljniče	'unwilling captive
knjiga sǎrovita	decorated letter
grada bijeloga	white town' (gen. case)

The first of these names an unspecified prisoner held against
his will. So much for the denotation; the connotation, however, carries much more weight. Although we do not know
from this phrase specifically who the prisoner is, we do

associate the formula with the incarcerated hero of the Return Song, who, like his Indo-European compatriot Odysseus, will bargain for and obtain his release, return home, and confront a situation in which his wife or betrothed is held hostage in their own home. This is the metonymic import of the simple and apparently general phrase 'unwilling captive'. Likewise, the 'decorated letter' has many associations in the folk epic tradition: it is what an estimable father sends out in great numbers to invite his guests to the wedding; it is what the commander of a substantial force sends to summon his allies to join him in battle; it can also be a treacherous missive that subverts the well-laid plans of one leader and contributes to an unlikely turn of events. To gloss *knjiga šarovita* simply as 'letter' is to miss these overtones. Our third example in this group, *grada bijeloga*, is less focused yet, but it also has metonymic range. A 'town' is not spoken of as 'white' simply to eke out the six syllables of the second colon in the deca-syllable; this designation echoes against other instances of the phrase in the experience of the reader or listener, indicating a place of some importance where some important event will take place. Almost on the level of myth (as with the toponym of the Lika), this last phrase creates a setting rife with expec-tation so that, while its traditional connotations are not as distinct as those associated with other formulas, it still pro-vides extratextual cues from the folk epic tradition at large.

I have purposely chosen a range of formulaic phrases for these few examples in order to illustrate how metonymy can function at a very specific and focused level — as with the noun-epithet formulas that designate individuals — and at a more general and 'mythic' level which is nonetheless evocative of traditional ideas and concepts.

III

To close this presentation and to bring together the strands of thought developed in the two sections, I now offer a final word about formulaic structure and function. These closing remarks are based on my research on the structure of the three meters and phraseologies that have provided the examples given above, that is, on the Homeric hexameter, Serbo-Croatian *deseterac*, and Old English alliterative line as well as the phraseologies associated with each.[16]

To put it most economically, I have found that one can fully explain formulaic structure and morphology only by recourse to what I call t r a d i t i o n a l r u l e s. In each folk epic tradition these rules take shape in symbiosis with the idiosyncratic features of the individual language and meter, and they provide guidelines, as it were, for the formation of the diction both synchronically and diachronically. That is, these rules can be demonstrated to be at the basis of all cola and lines in the given work, whether those lines and parts of lines are as well established as the most hackneyed of noun-epithet formulas or whether they seem, on the evidence of available material, to have no formulaic relatives whatever. Perhaps that deserves repeating: the traditional rules, which of course vary significantly from one tradition to the next, underlie both regular, verbatim formulas and apparently 'nonce' expressions, as well as all diction in between these poles. To my way of thinking, these rules are what make the phrases traditional, whether the actual elements of diction can be proven to recur in the available corpus or not.

And just as the variety of traditional phraseology is in my opinion best construed as a spectrum with verbatim formulas at one end and 'nonce' diction (but still diction governed by rules) at the other, so the metonymic function of that phraseology also reveals a whole range of possibilities. To the extent that a phrase formed according to traditional rules attracts to itself over time and through usage a distinct, detachable meaning — so that it summons by itself a network of associations, it becomes a recognizable formula, an element in and of itself. Such a phrase is neither situation-specific nor generic, for on the one hand it is free of the constraints of any one situation and on the other it is a highly charged nexus of traditional meaning which mediates a network of complex

16 These and other areas are treated in my book in progress, *Studies in Traditional Oral Epic: The Odyssey, Beowulf, and the Serbo-Croatian Return Song.*

significations.[17] Noun-epithet formulas naming specific heroes or gods, like the ones described above, fall into this category.

But many phrases do not attain such status, and are essentially made anew each time according to traditional rules. These are what many scholars have called 'formulaic systems', and this description has served well for studying the interrelationships among similar elements. The concept has the authority of what Dan Ben-Amos[18] would call an 'analytic' category, that is, a quite viable construct introduced from the outside to lend some order to a set of linguistic or cultural data. While I would not for a moment advocate doing away with such a productive concept, I would recommend complementing this 'analytic' category with what I take to be an internal, 'ethnic' one: the set of traditional rules that underlies the formation and morphology not just of formulas or systems or 'nonce' diction but of all of these kinds of phrases. Ultimately, resemblances among elements in a folk epic phraseology must be due to the pervasive influence of these rules and not to separately existing systems.

Thus it is that phrases which do not reach the status of 'Mustajbeg of the Lika' or 'Gerenian Nestor' may yet show many similarities over time and from place to place. They will not bear the detached, context-free meaning of their more stable and more celebrated counterparts, but they will still carry with them some metonymic associations, however general and undefined those associations may be. We have seen above, in the examples of 'unwilling captive', 'white town', and 'decorated letter', phrases which remain stable and yet whose connotations tend toward the mythic, nonspecific level of narrative pattern. Phrases which lack this verbal consistency — that is, elements that from a synchronic point of view seem to form a 'system' rather than separate formulas — cannot of course command the same specificity of extratextual reference. Another way to say the same thing is to observe that such 'systemic' phrases also lack specificity in their essential ideas, in their potential for referentiality.

17 Compare M. Nagler, *Spontaneity and Tradition: A Study in the Oral Art of Homer*, Berkeley 1974, especially 1-63.
18 'Analytic Categories and Ethnic Genres', *Genre* 2 (1969), 275-301.

As a general rule, then, those phrases most worthy of being designated as formulas will be those which have established themselves as elements that c o n t r i b u t e to rather than a r e d e p e n d e n t on their textual surroundings. Only when phraseology has escaped, at least for the moment, the curse of continual reincarnation and has become a unit unto itself can it attract multiple associations and then bring them into the narrative through metonymic reference. As I mentioned above, the qualifications necessary for advancement to this status will vary in each folk epic tradition, simply because it is the nature of languages and meters — and therefore of the traditional rules which they foster — to be different one from the next. And there will always be exceptions, as there should be in any program of poetics. In the traditions discussed in this presentation, for instance, one perhaps thinks first of the formulas for speech introduction, which remain relatively stable and which are nonetheless usually quite empty of any special connotation. While I have no time to treat such exceptions in this format, I might observe in passing that, from the perspective of 'speech act' theory, even such apparently empty phrases may well have a certifying, normative meaning that goes well beyond mere denotation.

IV

In summary, then, I have proposed two new directions for the study and interpretation of folk epic, directions that I hope prove complementary and move toward an integrated perspective on the special properties of such works. The first section has been devoted to emphasizing the importance of viewing the structure of each tradition and each work on its own terms, with philological scrutiny, before trying to grapple with questions that ultimately depend on a firm grasp of structure. In this connection, I introduced the ideas of tradition-dependence, genre-dependence, and text-dependence in order to illustrate various dimensions of a given work's identity *sui generis*. After we have established an epic's individuality, comparisons to other works and traditions will have meaning and permanence. The second section of the paper has attempted to open up the matter of the referentiality of structures like the formula by concentrating on the associative process I have called m e t o n y m y. By gathering to itself extratextual connotation, a traditional structure may bring into a given narrative whole worlds of significance — the textual transaction being accomplished via the metonymic 'switch', as it were. The salient part stands traditionally for the unexpressed and inexpressible whole. Both parts of the paper thus attempt to move toward a poetics that is both exacting in its philological analysis and sensitive to the traditional art of folk epic.

FORMULAIC ANACHRONISMS AND THEIR EPIC FUNCTION
'MARKO KRALJEVIĆ AND HIS BROTHER ANDRIJAŠ'

SVETOZAR KOLJEVIĆ
(University of Sarajevo)

Even the commonest formulaic expressions suggest that Serbo-Croat epic conventions reveal a thoroughly dislocated sense of historical realities in language. So, for instance, 'the white palaces' (*bijeli dvori*) of the early feudal *burgarštice* migrate with this poetic tradition to a later peasant setting and often begin to denote just ordinary village houses in decasyllabic epics.[1] *Grozne suze*, initially denoting 'tears as big as grapes', (from *groždj*, 'grapes'), suggests to the later listener merely 'terrible tears', although in many places it would be difficult to tell that they were terrible at all.[2] T. Maretić thinks that even by *rujno vino* — which could suggest only red wine or rosé today — the singer meant what we call 'white' wine, which, incidentally, is also a misnomer. Maretić supports his argument by suggesting that *ruj*, the *sumac*, *'Gelbholz'* in German, bears a yellow flower, and adds that *rujnice* are yellow mushrooms. However, if the *sumac* indeed bears a yellow flower, it is also true that most people become aware of it in the autumn when the shrub is brilliant red; and one would have to be colour blind not to see that

---

1 See, for instance, '*Šta osveta čini*', 'What Vengeance Does', V.S. Karadžić, *Srpske narodne pjesme*, III, ed. V. Nedić, Belgrade 1976, No. 68, ll. 45, 66. Unless otherwise specified, this will be the edition referred to in all the subsequent footnotes. *Bugarštice* were sung in the so-called 'long lines' (fourteen to sixteen syllables); they mostly flourished along the coast and had a far more feudal imprint than the later decasyllabic epics which flourished in patriarchal peasant settings, particularly in Herzegovina, Montenegro, mountain parts of Serbia and along the Turco-Austrian and Turco-Venetian frontiers.

2 See T. Maretić, *Naša narodna epika*, Belgrade 1966, 73-4.

rujnice are always pink or orange. And who can tell what colours were dancing before the eyes of the singer of Russian *bylyny* when he began to talk about a wine that was 'green'?[3] He must have had quite a lot of it, whatever it was.

However, the varied colours of wine do not dance only in front of the eyes of epic singers; 'white wine', widely used in many European languages, seems to suggest that this liquid is as innocent as milk, and as regards *crno vino*, which is a standard Serbo-Croat term for red wine, it can, of course, vary in colour, but it is never actually black. So similar things happen — for analogous and usually forgotten reasons — in the history of non-poetic, so-called 'ordinary' language. Why do we say in Serbo-Croat that someone is 'as drunk as a mother' (*pijan kao majka*) or that he stares at something 'like a young bull at a coloured gate' (*kao tele u šarena vrata*)? Few modern speakers will remember that plum-brandy was used as an anaesthetic at child-birth, and it was only recently that we were told by a French scholar that back in Roman times, in the gladiatorial arenas in southern Yugoslavia (e.g. at Stobi), skilful gladiators used to shut multicoloured doors in front of the bewildered and curious animals.[4] A language, in short, has a better memory than do the people who use it; and it often remembers metaphorically what it has 'physically' forgotten. Even in the urban Yugoslav setting there are still many 'capricious' women, or, for that matter, men, long after goats (in Italian '*capra*') were banned in the countryside.

However, such metaphorical and material deposits of elements of lost worlds and bygone times in the language of oral epics are not simply a matter of particular expressions and formulaic features; they also create a special anachronistic world which has never existed, a realm of astonishingly interlaced imagery and narrative. In the Serbo-Croat epic tradition it is a realm where the cults of pre-Christian, pagan Slav times live on, interwoven with various customs and social norms of the medieval feudal world in the Balkans, set into the village, patriarchal civilization of Turkish times, chiefly along the

3 *Ibid.*, 74.
4 See S. Radojčić, *Uzori i dela starih srpskih umetnika*, Belgrade 1975, 101-2.

Turco-Austrian and Turco-Venetian frontiers, where clan identity and family ties were sacrosanct, because they were the basic means of physical, social and spiritual survival. And it was this communal linguistic and imaginative epic convention that united such different areas as Montenegro, Herzegovia, Dalmatia, Bosnia, Lika, Slavonia and the wild mountain regions of Serbia — where life went on for several centuries either under Turkish rule or in the shadow of its constant threat over the border. Of course, the forms of life in each of these regions, their political and cultural set-up, were often quite different; and they also changed considerably in the period preserved by epic memory — a period which extended from the use of clubs and arrows in the times of dragons and *vilas*, to the days of rifles and canon, battle tactics and calculations.

This world has sometimes the illusory credibility of science fiction films based on fairy-tale patterns — of something that has never really existed but is structured on archetypal patterns. And just as it is very difficult to draw the line between imaginary and documentary details in such films, between the metaphorical and the real, so the Serbo-Croat epics present us with an assembly of things which were never, strictly speaking, united at any moment in history, but which exercise a rich, distorting imaginative pull over one another in their new co-existence and create a narrative space which becomes an artistic norm unto itself. This can be seen in the anachronistic interplay of formulas, truncated realism and heterogeneous social cults and norms in the first recorded full-length poem, the *bugarštica* 'Marko Kraljević and His Brother Andrijaš'.

When Petar Hektorović, a Hvar literary nobleman, recorded this poem from one of his fishermen some time around 1555, he was nearly seventy years old. But as a grand and cultivated man of letters, he still kept up the tradition of fishermen's eclogues, the Renaissance pastoral poetic form in which fishermen took the place of shepherds. However, his *Fishing and Fishermen's Conversations* (*Ribanye i ribarscho prigovaranye*, Venice 1568) was very different from the highly literary Italian eclogues abounding in fantastic elements, probably because the old gentleman was trying to live this literary form while writing his work. Looking for a few days outing, he took two of the best fishermen he could find and went with them for an actual boating expedition. During the expedition, apart from the excitement of fishing, the two fishermen, 'young and gaudy' Nikola Zet, and elderly Paskoje Debelja, 'a good and upright man',[5] entertained their master by telling stories, singing songs, solving riddles and discussing all sorts of questions — sometimes perhaps with a theological penchant of obvious provenance and certainly unexpected among Dalmatian fishermen. There is, of course, no doubt that the fishermen's conversations as described in this work are thoroughly imbued with their master's culture. It is highly unlikely, for instance, that the two illiterate gentlemen accosted each other in rhymed alexandrines when the young dandy begged his elderly, upright friend to sing a fine poem 'in the Serbian manner':

> To while away time let us each tell
> a fine *bugarščina*, not to feel the toil,
> in Serbian manner, my dear comrade,
> as we have always done among our friends.[6]

But in spite of this ventriloquism, which helps Hektorović to make his fishermen poetically presentable, there is more truth than we might suspect in his statement to his learned friend Nikša Pelegrinović, in which he claims that he has described his outing accurately and noted down the songs from his simple-minded fishermen 'without adding the single smallest word'.[7] It is significant, for instance, that in the quoted lines where he r e p o r t s on what the fisherman said, he uses the contemporary, local Dalmatian form of his own, and presumably the fishermen's dialect of the word *meu*, 'among', but when he q u o t e s what Nikola Zet sang in his *bugarštica* 'Duke Radosav of Severin and Vlatko of Vidin', we twice find the older form *meju*, which cannot be traced

5 P. Hektorović, *Ribanye i ribarscho prigovaranye*, Venice 1568, f. 12[r] (photographic edn., Zagreb 1953).

6 *Ibid.*

7 P. Hektorović, 'Poštovanom gospodinu Nikši Pelegrinoviću', *Hanibal Lucić — Petar Hektorović*, ed. M. Franičević, Zagreb 1968, 224.

anywhere else in Hektorović's works.[8] This indicates that the language of this epic poem and, as we shall see, some of its epic conventions and norms, were 'introduced into the Dalmatian čakavian area, or into the čakavian region of central Dalmatia, or into Hvar itself, quite some time, at least half a century, before the author of *Fishing* wrote his work'.[9]

This reflects the astonishing fidelity of Hektorović's recording as to linguistic detail, but hardly suggests the width of implication embodied in the discrepancies between the language of the recorded epics, Hektorović's written language and the spoken language of his fishermen. This becomes more evident when Paskoje Debelja, the 'upright' singer, 'cries out' the first line of his poem about 'Marko Kraljević and His Brother Andrijaš':

Two poor men were good friends for a long time.[10]

The ikavian form *vrime*, 'time', like by far the largest number of ikavian word forms in the recorded poem, clearly reflects the Dalmatian linguistic norm,[11] i.e., the song is an integral part of the Hvar fisherman's living oral culture, however conscious he may be of 'the Serbian manner', of the origin of the convention which he is using. But this origin is also reflected in the dual verb enclitic *sta*, 'were' — the old linguistic form which is otherwise unknown to Hektorović and must have been unknown to his singers, because it never appears in the written records after the fifteenth century, save in the manuscripts of folk poetry, which obviously retain it because poetic convention remembers what 'ordinary' language forgets.[12] But if the language of this poem often

8   See A. Mladenović, *Jezik Petra Hektorovića*, Novi Sad 1968, 164.
9   *Ibid.*
10 This poem is quoted in the translation of A. Pennington and P. Levi, *Marko the Prince*, London 1984.
11 Depending on the development of the old Slavonic *jat* ('ѣ') three types of pronunciation are differentiated in Serbo-Croat: 'ekavian' (*e*), 'ijekavian' (*ije*) and 'ikavian' (*i*). Disregarding the complexities of the Serbo-Croat dialect map, in this context 'ikavian' features point to the local Dalmatian dialect, whereas 'ekavian' elements suggest the more distant Serbian origin.
12 See A. Mladenović, *op. cit.*, 173.

reaches back into the distant past and outwards into contemporary life, it also points forward to future octo- and decasyllabic verse. Three variants of the opening formula ('three friends were long friendly'; 'two brothers grew up in love'; 'three brothers grew up in love') are found in the *Erlangen manuscript*,[13] written down in the early eighteenth century in beautiful Habsburg calligraphy in Slavonia. In a decasyllabic metrical adaptation, the same formula emerges again in the early nineteenth century, on the lips of Karadžić's anonymous singers from Bosnia and Montenegro, and again in the opening lines of two outstanding poems about fratricide: 'two brothers dearly loved each other', 'two brothers lived wonderfully together'.[14] How far epic language travels, and what it picks up on its historical journey, is clearly revealed in the Muslim elements in the heroes' names in these poems (Milan-bey and Dragutin-bey, Mujo and Alija). The first two suggest the time when Christian feudal lords became the Sultan's vassals, and the second pair reflects islamization.

Of course, many other formulaic features of 'Marko Kraljević and His Brother Andrijaš' will also make a long journey, particularly such linguistic structures as questions and answers, imaginary counsels and noble lies, truthtelling (*kazovanje istine*) and cunning evasions, the 'drawing' (*potrzanje*) of a sword, usually 'a bright sword' (*svitle sablje*), 'the good horses' (*dobri konji*) and 'the black mountain' (*crna gora*).[15] They all traverse numerous other *bugarštice* and decasyllabic poems, remembering and forgetting their original contexts, mingling their forms and effects. This intermingling of linguistic features which never co-existed historically, leads at an imaginative level to more significant encounters of discrete times and places, of diverse social norms and mythical insights into the nature of human life. One such encounter takes place in the opening lines of this poem: the picture of the two poor brothers, living in harmony together and always sharing their

---

13 G. Gesemann, ed., *Erlangenski rukopis*, Sremski Karlovci 1925, No. 52, l. 1, No. 121, l. 1, No. 149, l. 1.
14 V.S. Karadžić, *Srpske narodne pjesme*, II, No. 10, l. 1, No. 11, l. 1.
15 See S. Koljević, *The Epic in the Making*, Oxford 1980, 50-1 (particularly footnotes 101-10).

booty justly, reflects an outlaws' idyll, but the idyll which achieved an epic status only during the rule of the Turks, when outlawry became the 'choice' of people with no other choices. But this idyll, historically rooted in the fifteenth and the sixteenth centuries of Balkan history, is soon revealed as an illusion in a remarkable poetic ploy, a nascent Slavonic antithesis:

My friends I tell you, they were not two poor men,
But one of them was Sir Marko King's son,
Sir Marko King's son and his brother Andrijaš,
The young knights.

Is the idyll, then, set in historical outlawry? Or is its setting high and feudal: by the end of the poem the two heroes will have been referred to as 'knights' several times, and Marko will have been called four times 'prince'?

But throughout the poem the relationship between the two knights is also conceived in the spirit of outlaw norms and customs. So for instance when Andrijaš begs Marko not to give their mother 'a crooked share', but to give her both her share and his, since he will never be able to share with her again, he reflects the outlaw obligation in peasant and patriarchal, not feudal communities, to divide the booty with the other members of the family. This is why the Slavonic antithesis, suggesting that they are knights and not outlaws cannot be taken as a full, straightforward denial; it is, as usual, a stylistic ploy to create a kind of musical counterpoint in which the outlaw or the feudal melodies sound more audibly by turns, before they take us outside historical realities into the realm of pure epic imagination. In this sense it is analogous to the ultimate effect of the famous poem 'God Leaves No Debt Unpaid' where the natural harmony of two pines growing beside a fir-tree seems to be contradicted when we are told that the pines and the fir-tree are, in fact, two brothers and a sister. The contradiction, however, is a means of metaphorical identification: at the end of the poem, after the innocent sister is killed, this metaphorical, cosmic harmony is again established in the natural imagery of 'basil' growing on her grave.[16]

16 'Bog nikom dužan ne ostaje', *Srpske narodne pjesme*, II, No. 5.

In the same way 'Marko Kraljević and His Brother Andrijaš'
is imbued with Serbian medieval chivalry as with the world of
outlawry and its patriarchal values, and this is not so much a
contradiction as the source of its epic life and imaginative
power. The abbreviated Slavonic antithesis — suggesting, first,
that the two heroes are outlaws and then apparently denying
this proposition, by telling us that they are in fact two feudal
lords — embodies a duality which will govern the poem. For
as soon as we are told that Marko and Andrijaš fall out over
'three good horses', we have to assume that they are quarrel-
ling about outlaw booty. But around this outlaw conflict
play the shades of feudal times gone by: times when a good
horse (*dobri konj*) was, like a sword, a spear or a shield, not
only a battle requisite, but a symbol of power and right. This
is why a family could never inherit one, but was obliged to
pass it over to the sovereign. To be precise, as the forty eighth
article of Dušan's *Code of Laws* explicitly states: 'When a
nobleman dies, his good horse and weapons are to be given
to the emperor.'[17] The 'good horse', of course, had to be a
very good one — in order to carry a medieval warrior in full
armour, but it is only in medieval legal context of this phrase
that we can understand the epic struggles and jealousies over
a horse, not only in this poem but also in 'The Death of Duke
Prijezda',[18] and the many other epics in which a horse, sometimes combined with a sword, or even a wife, figures as a
symbol of honour and status. One should not forget, however, that inside this epic romance of historical greatness and
status, the good horses have, for Marko and Andrijaš, also a
straightforward, outlaw value, and they are certainly more
genuinely vital to the epic excitement of the poem than any
mere power symbol could be. This is not only shown in the
way the knights do not fall out over the first two 'good horses',
but only over the third, and also in the way they quarrel,
swearing at each other with genuine outlaw passion and
vocabulary, falling out as only true brothers, in a patriarchal
setting, can do.

17 N. Radojčić, ed., *Zakonik Cara Stefana Dušana 1349. i 1354*,
    Belgrade 1960, 102.
18 'Smrt vojvode Prijezde', *Srpske narodne pjesme*, II, No. 84.

This interpretation of the worlds of outlawry and chivalry is not peculiar, of course, to the poem 'Marko Kraljević and His Brother Andrijaš'. It was immensely widespread both in epic poetry and in historical reality, particularly in the coastal region extending from Boka Kotorska to Senj. In fact there were so many Slav fighters, ex- or honorary outlaws, in the Venetian service, that both the Dubrovnik and the Venetian soldiers were often officially called 'outlaws' (*hajduci*), and their paid captains *harambašas*. One of the greatest epic heroes of this type, Old Vujadin, must have been a historical outlaw in the Venetian service fighting with the Turkish border guards around Livno at the end of the seventeenth century when Livno, after the Turkish defeats in the Morean War, was reduced from a major administrative centre to a frontier outpost; the way in which he is dressed is a kind of combination of Oriental costume and the clothes of European feudal lords, together with the silver feather in his helmet, which was an actual Venetian decoration given to the outlaws and their captains in recognition of their service in regular Venetian military units,[19] certainly reflects – in an epic fashion which can be corroborated by contemporary paintings[20] – the historical realities of this region.

However, at the very centre of this epic world that combines distant historical realities, there beats a strong pulse of patriarchal emotion, a sense of the sanctity of family ties which turns this chivalric-outlaw drama into a tragic story of fratricide, in which other family relations also loom large. It is significant, for instance, that at the moment of dying at his brother's hand Andrijaš begs Marko to tell their mother a noble lie and explain that his 'hero sword' is blood-stained because he had to plunge it into the heart of 'a quiet deer', which would not get out of his path. The deer provides a story within the story: as the deer's 'soul parts from him on the road', Marko begins to understand what he has done; he

19 See 'Beleške i objašnjenja', V.S. Karadžić, *Srpske narodne pjesme*, III, ed. N. Banašević, Belgrade 1958, 668.
20 This comes out clearly on the portrait of Stojan Janković, a famous seventeenth-century captain of border-raiders (Historical Museum of Croatia, Department of Serbs in Croatia, Zagreb).

mourns for the deer 'like his brother' and recognises that he would not kill it if he could find himself again in the same situation. Of course, the imaginative power of these lines springs from their dramatic location: it is the dying Andrijaš who puts these words into the mouth of the fratricide, in order to spare their mother's feelings, and to give free play to the uprush of filial love and fraternal remorse. This drama of patriarchal love, not the less deep and instinctive for being drenched in blood and wrapped in a noble lie, is also visible in Andrijaš's plea that Marko tell their mother he has fallen in love with 'a fine-dressed girl' and given up battles and wars ever since. Thus Andrijaš, as he dies, takes on his shoulders heavy sins. He is telling lies, he is betraying his sacred heroic obligation in a community where 'warring' was the basic mark of a man, and also the chief form of support for his family; but these mortal sins are so imagined in the poem that they become the ultimate expression of filial love, an imaginary consolation for the mother, because a mother can be relied on to forgive her son even a vice that makes him happy. At the same time this is also an illusory comfort for Marko and a great, if illegitimate happiness for the dying Andrijaš.

The linguistic features of this drama also throw significant light on the diverse social and historical worlds which meet in this poem. So, for instance, diminutives like *drumak* (instead of *drum* — 'road') certainly point to an aristocratic milieu; for peasants and fishermen augmentatives were much more characteristic[21] — and, indeed, *drumčetina*, 'great highway' would much more accurately convey the experience of travel in the poor man's world. Of course, this hint at an aristocratic background could well be the reflection of Hektorović's usage, but this could not be possibly claimed for the ekavian form *gizdava devojka*, 'a fine-dressed girl' which, admittedly, we find elsewhere in Hektorović and which is a highly characteristic formula in the *bugarštice*. Such an ekavianism in a formula is analogous to the *bele ruke*, 'white hands' and *verne sluge*, 'faithful servants' which we find in Hektorović only in the poem which he wrote down from his other,

---

21 See A. Mladenović, *op. cit.*, 175-6.

younger fisherman on the same occasion.[22] It is not very probable, surely, that Hektorović should have hit on two ekavian singers in the ikavian Hvar; it is more natural to suppose that these ekavianisms betray the fact that 'the origin of these poems' — we would prefer to say of the formulaic language in which they are sung — 'must be sought in an ekavian-štokavian dialect'.[23] And the mixing of the two different active participle verb forms (the older ending in -l, the later in -o: *pošal*, 'went' and *obljubio*, 'loved a girl') points to the end of the fourteenth and the beginning of the fifteenth century, to a time 'when the old feature l was not yet completely replaced by the innovation -o.'[24] And this was approximately the time when Kraljević Marko lived and died (1395).

This does not mean, of course, that the poem laments some kind of historical occurrence: Kraljević Marko did not kill his brother Andrijaš; indeed, in later epic 'memory' he will come to avenge his death in a decasyllabic Dalmatian poem, and kill all nine of the Turks who got Andrijaš drunk and cut his head off by a trick![25] However, it would not be quite accurate to say that Kraljević Marko merely lent his heroic name to a fratricide in a poem which must have existed in innumerable variants, in a region where the story of Cain and Abel could not have been unknown and must have been alluring to many a patriarchal imagination. Marko was important to the singer both because he could give the necessary feudal status to the story and, perhaps, because he is the only one of the Serbian medieval lords who is notoriously irascible in epic memory: he chops off the right arm of Novak the Blacksmith when the latter tells him that he has forged a better sword for a better hero;[26] he can even catch a *vila* in the clouds and

22 *Ibid.*, 155-7, 185.
23 *Ibid.*
24. *Ibid.*
25. See 'Marko Kraljević osveti brata Andrijaša koga mu Turci pogiboše' ('Marko Kraljević Avenges the Death of His Brother Andrijaš Killed by the Turks'), V. Bogišić, *Narodne pjesme*, Belgrade 1878, No. 89.
26 'Marko Kraljević i Musa Kesedžija' ('Marko Kraljević and Musa Kesedžija'), *Srpske narodne pjesme*, II, No. 38, ll. 140-63.

punish her for her misconduct to his blood-brother;[27] and
when he dies, the heguman of Chilandarion thinks that he
is asleep and goes round a long way because he knows what
Marko can be like when he has just woken up.[28] This is why
Marko is an ideal character for this poem, not just more
suitable than, say, Tsar Lazar or Saint Sava. However, if this
arrangement is not acceptable to the epic tradition as a whole,
the tradition will rebel and, in a later poem, Marko will come
to slay the Turks who killed his brother.

Moreover, the conversion of Prince Marko into an outlaw
of the village patriarchal world is not just an accidental
anachronism; it is an essential constituent of Marko's epic life
in the Serbo-Croat heroic tradition: he has to be put into
situations and settings in which he never lived in order to give
his invaluable historical dimension to the contemporary world
of the singer's mind and that of his audience. The fact that,
strictly speaking, he was a Turkish vassal is neither here nor
there; the illusions and the realities of the here-and-now always
loom large in the poem, whatever it pretends to be 'about';
this Hvar *bugarštica* could hardly live if the distant feudal
world, which gives it an epic aura, had not been subordinated
to the contemporary patriarchal drama of an outlaw quarrel
over the division of booty, a drama in which outlawry and
family ties constitute the very pith and marrow of existence.
And this is why the climax of the poem comes at a moment
when the singer is most deeply personal and most thoroughly
anachronistic, when Andrijaš takes his last farewell, and all the
cruelties of life and history come together in the timeless
focus of devotion and love:

> When pirates drop on you in the black forest,
> Do not fear them, my brother, my dear,
> Cry out to Andrijaš, to your brother,
> Though you will call in vain to me, brother,
> When they hear you call my name,

27 'Marko Kraljević i vila' ('Marko Kraljević and the *Vila*'), *Srpske
narodne pjesme*, II, No. 38, ll. 75-109.
28 'Smrt Marka Kraljevića' ('The Death of Marko Kraljević'), *Srpske
narodne pjesme*, II, No. 74, ll. 135-9.

The cursed pirates,
Heroes will scatter from before your face,
As they have always scattered, my brother,
Whenever they have heard you call my name.

What are pirates — not outlaws — doing in Marko's homeland, an area which lies hundreds of miles from the Adriatic
coast? They surely did not come from Hvar to Prilep; it is
far more likely that they are the offspring of historical reality
in Hvar, who have come to inhabit the epic world of Prilep.
For in the course of the sixteenth century, piracy did indeed
become a general plague in the Adriatic. Apart from the
traditional, local Italian pirates, many newcomers put in an
appearance: Sicilian pirates and, in particular, African Berbers
who became much more lively 'in the first decade of the
century, after the Turco-Venetian truce of 1503 when, after
many years of war, famine and plague, shipping and maritime
trade revived.'[29] Hvar at this time was the richest Venetian
settlement in the Adriatic, and the winter quarters of the
Venetian fleet, so that it is not surprising that it was plagued
by all who could reach it, including the notorious *uskoks*,
'border-raiders' of Senj, who for the length of the sixteenth
century were a source of fear and trembling to the Turks, as
well as to the Venetian fleet itself, which undertook, unsuccessfully, large-scale naval operations against them.[30] Finally,
this piratical *melée* was further enriched by a not insignificant
number of Turkish pirates who appeared in Albania at the
end of the fifteenth century; in addition, at this time 'piracy
and the interception of shipping was undertaken not only by
professional robbers at sea, but also by ships in the war fleets
of some states, pre-eminently by the Turks and the Vene-
tians.'[31] Thus the Turks' plundering of Hvar in 1539 was as
much a military attack as a quick pirate raid, which inspired

29 B. Hrabak, 'Dubrovnik i rodski pirati', *Istoriski glasnik*, 2, Belgrade
    1956, 1.
30 See G. Stanojević, 'Venecija protiv uskoka', *Senjski uskoci*, Belgrade
    1973, 95-141.
31 B. Hrabak, 'Gusarstvo i presretanje pri plovidbi u Jadranskom i
    Jonskom moru u drugoj polovini XV veka', *Vesnik vojnog muzeja*,
    4, Belgrade 1957, 97.

some of Hektorović's most authentic lines, since he himself
spent eighteen days on that occasion 'sailing in a vessel across
the vast seas'.[32] He himself tells us that 'the great number of
us all' were forced to flee,[33] but it is most unlikely that his
fishermen's flight was also so well-planned and sufficiently
subsidized as to carry them to Italian landscapes where they
could reminisce on their native soil and compose pastoral
poetry in peace. This is perhaps why Andrijaš thinks of
'cursed pirates' when he tries to imagine the greatest misfortune that could befall his brother Marko at the climax of
the poem, and it is at this moment that the ultimate patriarchal ideal of brotherly love triumphs, both literally and
metaphorically, over death: Andrijaš tells Marko that if
attacked by pirates, he would only have to call his brother's
name and the call will drive the pirates away. Again, the
dramatic arrangement of this scene — Andrijaš promises to
help his brother, who has killed him, beyond death — shows
an artistic instinct of the highest order.

The ikavian linguistic standard of the poem, together with
an occasional ekavian formulaic element and the phonetic
and morphological forms which existed when Kraljević Marko
was alive but disappeared before the poem was written down,
show that it was composed in a language readily understood
by the audience, although nobody ever actually spoke it quite
in that form; just as the mingled elements of feudal, outlaw,
patriarchal and piratical life also create an exciting and easily
recognisable imaginative realm which is genuinely close to its
audience, although it never actually existed. For the power of
epic poetry depends as much on the forms of life which language remembers as on the dramatic sense of the historical
moment in which the poem is sung. If its language is chained
to an ossified sense of the past, as in very many of the *bugarštice*, then it cannot detach itself from the outworn soil of a
lost world. If its language is overloaded with a sense of the
contemporary so that it cannot move away from it, as happens
in many of the decasyllabic poems of the Slavonian frontier,

---

32   See M. Kombol, *Poviest hrvatske književnosti*, Zagreb 1945, 122.
33   *Ibid.*

then it cannot break through the limitations of chronicle, and the poem lives only 'as long as the intensity of its audience's interest in a particular historical event'.[34] It is only when the poem brings together diverse and freely anachronistic and 'anatopical' historical realities inside the force-field created by a contemporary emotion that the story begins to take wing and that we become ready 'to transfer from our inward nature a human interest and a semblance of truth sufficient to procure for these shadows of imagination that willing suspension of disbelief for the moment, which constitutes poetic faith'.[35] It is this, in fact, that marks out the best of the Serbo-Croat ballads about patriarchal family life and very many of other decasyllabic epics recorded by Vuk Karadžić around the time of the first and the second Serbian uprisings at the beginning of the nineteenth century. But even here we can notice the same difference between some of the poems which are weak because exclusively focussed on the present ('The Battle of Deligrad' with its long enumeration of the names and the toponyms)[36] and, say, such poems as 'The Beginning of the Revolt against the Dahijas' in which a sharp sense of the contemporary history evokes almost the whole epic landscape from Murad and Kosovo to the miraculous 'heavenly apparitions'.[37]

Anachronisms and 'anatopisms' in oral epics should not exclusively interest us as evidence of the singer's inadequate grasp of facts, but also by their poetic function, as a response to the basic challenge of the epic imagination. Paskoje Debelja, that 'good and upright man', rose to this challenge: the outlaw customs and attitudes give flesh and blood to the great patriarchal and chivalric drama, and the ideal of brotherly love triumphs over reality at the very moment the pirates are appearing where they never were before. The poetic voice is so much stronger than the errors on which it draws that each of them becomes an invaluable

---

34 M. Maticki, *Srpskohrvatska graničarska epika*, Belgrade 1974, 167.
35 K. Raine, ed., *Coleridge — Poems and Prose*, Harmondsworth 1957, 192 ('Biographia Literaria', ch. XIV).
36 'Boj na Deligradu', *Srpske narodne pjesme*, IV, No. 31.
37 'Početak bune protiv dahija', *Srpske narodne pjesme*, IV, No. 25.

thread in a rich tapestry. In much the same way, the best of the later poems about the battle of Kosovo span the widely distant shores of biblical stories, feudal toasts and defiant outlaw manners ('The Building of Ravanica', 'Pieces from Various Kosovo Poems', etc.).[38]

This is not to say, however, that every mistake, every example of 'anatopism' or anachronism, is a great source of epic inspiration. There is a limit to what a singer, or even his audience, can swallow. There are also mistakes which bring absurd comic elements into the foreground of the heroic landscape. So, for instance, when a Dalmatian singer exults over the Turkish disaster at the siege of Vienna and cries out that under the Viennese walls all the seas were red with Turkish blood,[39] this is not only testimony to his ignorance but also an emblem of malicious, 'patriotic' feeling, not wholly uncharacteristic of Serbo-Croat epic poetry at its worst. Such examples are undoubtedly many, and not far to seek, but the point, surely, is that the mixture of diverse, anachronistic or 'anatopical' elements, can be a runway for the epic imagination. After all such and similar discrepancies are also often found in some of the best-known lines in the *Iliad*, when, for instance, the warrior's world of cruel fighting is represented in the peaceful pastoral imagery of country life. And surely it is the pagan pyres and rites inside a largely Christian feeling for the transitoriness of this earthly life, that inspired some of the most moving lines in *Beowulf*. It could hardly be otherwise in a poetic convention where the language comes down to us through the ages and weaves its ultimate artistic design out of everything it has picked up in the course of that journey.

---

38 'Zidanje Ravanice', 'Komadi od različnijeh Kosovskijeh pjesama', *Srpske narodne pjesme*, II, No. 35 (another variant No. 36), No. 50.
39 See 'Od Beča kralj razbi Turke pod Bečom' ('The Viennese King Defeated the Turks at Vienna'), V. Bogišić, *Narodne pjesme*, No. 114, ll. 28-30.

FOLK EPIC IN THE WILDERNESS: ARABIA AND THE NORDIC WORLD

H.T. NORRIS
(University of London)

Introductory

Runo 1 of the *Kalevala* tells of the meeting of two men from two regions:

> Shall I start to sing
> shall I begin to recite
> with a good man as partner
> two who grew up together?
> Come, let us put hand in hand
> and finger in finger-gap
> each grip in the other's grip.
> One word from you, one from me
> splendid speech from both:[1]

Rare indeed, one might think, could be the meeting, whether in the flesh, or in the mind, of the fair, fur-clad, helmeted man of the North, and the swarthy, robed and turbaned man of Arabia. That both did meet, however, cannot be denied. The archaeological evidence of coinage from the Islamic East deep within Scandinavia, the accounts of Arab travellers who visited Scandinavia and Russia from Moorish Spain and the Eastern Caliphate, and the sea and land encoun-

---

1 M. Kuusi, K. Bosley and M. Branch, eds. and trans., *Finnish Folk Poetry. Epic*, Helsinki 1977, 81.

ters between the Arabs and the Vikings (al-Majūs)[2] at the Pillars of Hercules; one and all testify to a constant contact between the Arabs and the peoples of the North.[3]

To most Arabs, and to most Muslims, the furthest North was a region of diabolical darkness. Sharaf al-Zamān, Ṭāhir of Merv (who died shortly after 1120), physician at the courts of the Seljuk sultan, Malikshāh (1972-92) and his successors furnishes a dramatic description of the Arctic lands of the Finnish *Ves* (Veps), and other peoples who were either Karelians or Lapps:[4]

At a distance of twenty days from them [the Bulghār], towards the Pole, is a land called ISŪ, and beyond this a people called YŪRA; these are a savage people, living in forests and not mixing with other men, for they fear that they may be harmed by them. The people of Bulghār journey to them, taking wares, such as clothes, salt and other things, in contrivances (*lit.* 'utensils') drawn by dogs over the heaped snows, which (never) clear away. It is impossible for a man to go over these snows, unless he binds on to his feet the thigh-bones of oxen, and takes in his hands a pair of javelins which he thrusts backwards into the snow, so that his feet slide forwards over the sur-

2 According to Professor D.M. Dunlop ('The British Isles according to the Medieval Arabic authors', *Islamic Quarterly* 4, April 1957, 13-4, 13, note 2): 'It is well known that the term *al-Majūs* is standard for the Vikings in western Arabic sources (The confusion with 'Magians', strictly the priestly caste among the Zoroastrians, but in general for Zoroastrians, arises from the fact that the pagan Vikings also burned their dead). Al-Masʿūdī conjectured that they were the same as the Rūs, i.e. the Vikings, mainly Swedish, who followed the 'Eastern route' (G.M. Trevelyan) and were well known to the Arabs!'

3 For example, see T.D. Kendrick, *A History of the Vikings*, London 1930, 200-2, *Rūs* by V. Minorsky, in the *Encyclopædia of Islam*, and in his *A History of Sharvān and Darband in the 10th-11th centuries*, Cambridge 1958, and, at an earlier date, V.L.P. Thomsen, *The Relations between Ancient Russia and Scandinavia and the Origin of the Russian state*, Oxford and London 1877.

4 V. Minorsky, *Sharaf al-Zamān Ṭahir Marvasi, on China, the Turks and India*, Arabic text (c.A.D. 1120), *James G. Furlong Fund Series*, The Royal Asiatic Society, Vol. 22 (1942), 4-5, 112-5.

face of the ice; with a favourable wind (?) he will travel a great distance by the day. The people of Yūra trade by means of signs and dumb show, for they are wild and afraid of (other) men. From them are imported excellent sable and other fine furs; they hunt these animals, feeding on their flesh and wearing their skins.

Beyond these are a COAST-DWELLING PEOPLE who travel far over the sea, without any (definite) purpose and intention; they merely do this in order to boast of reaching (such and such a remote) locality. They are a most ignorant and stupid tribe, and their ignorance is shown by the following. They sail in ships, and whenever two (of their) boats meet, the sailors lash the two together and then they draw their swords and fight. This is their form of greeting. They come from the same town, perhaps from the same quarter, and there is no kind of enmity or rivalry between them; it is merely that this is their custom. When one of the parties is victorious, they (then) steer the two ships off together. In this sea is the fish whose tooth is used in hafting knives, swords and suchlike. Beyond them is a BLACK LAND which cannot be crossed. As for the sea-route, the voyager sailing towards the Pole reaches a part where there is no night in the summer and no day in the winter; the sun rotates visibly over the land for six months, circling the horizon like the revolution of a mill-stone; the whole year thus consists of one day and one night.

The Arab, and here I specifically mean the urban and the bedouin Arab of the Peninsula, the Arabian nomad who made his home in the deserts of Asia and Africa which were conquered by the Arabs in the seventh century or later, was no stranger to a pitiless and harsh environment. He was constantly threatened by it and spent much of his short life trying to survive in it, protecting his precious herds of camels, sheep and goats, travelling great distances for pasture, sustaining his family, fighting for his tribe, carrying bars of salt or raiding richly laden caravans. The icy North and the sun-baked emptiness of Arabia have moulded the mentality of those who dwell there. It is this paradox, this human reaction and response to the severity of the terrain and the climate, which above all explains similarities which we find in the folk epics of the North and of Arabia.[5]

There have been historians and linguists, and more than one of them an Arabist, who have explored the history and the literature of the Norsemen and the Arabs in order to discern elements in their life which disposed them to compose epic poetry and tales of adventure. These fill their oral literature and have marked some of the greatest literary masterpieces committed to writing in the languages of the North on the one hand, and, on the other, the Arabic language, the language of the Koran. Arabic tales which spread the faith of Muḥammad, also influenced the literature of other peoples in Africa and in Asia who were converted to that faith. Nevill Barbour, a distinguished Arabist, explained this in a lecture which he delivered to the Fifth Congress of Arabic and Islamic Studies held in Brussels in 1970, his subject being 'Arabs and Norsemen':

> Both Arabs and Scandinavians had inhabited peninsulas which lay just beyond the borders of the Roman Empire, the Arabs on the southeast, the Scandinavians on the northwest. The Arabian peninsula was almost a continent, very hot and very dry. Its people solved their problems of desert transport largely by the use of their own speciality, the camel, which also supplied them with milk. Arab agriculture was limited by the lack of water; the movements of the nomads were determined mainly by the need to find vegetation for their animals to eat. They received payments for protection from travellers passing through their tribal area. They also raided other tribes and, when conditions permitted, the settled lands. They possessed a language of remarkable complication and a sophisticated system of verse, subject to strict conditions of metre and content — descriptions of desert scenery and animals, reminiscences of camping grounds, accounts of inter-tribal wars, and love of poetry. In the hilly south, they possessed sizeable cities and irrigated agriculture; and carried on transit trade between the Orient and the West. The Scandinavians, on

5   See W. Thesiger, *Arabian Sands*, London 1959, xvii.

the other hand, lived primarily by agriculture, fishing and raiding, but also, like the Arabs, by trade, transporting goods by sea and river and when necessary drawing their boats overland till they reached the next waterway. By these means the Swedes travelled across Russia to Constantinople and Central Asia. Evidence of this extensive trade with the Caliphate are the Arab coins, amounting to over 80,000, of the eighth and ninth centuries, which were buried in moments of trouble, particularly in the Swedish island of Gotland, and only recovered in modern times. The Scandinavian Sagas, in their present form, date from centuries after the events which they purport to describe, but they contain much verse and many traditions from earlier times. Less sophisticated than Arab poetry, they are more varied in theme, saying much about agriculture, as well as about the internecine warfare of family groups which corresponded, after making the necessary adjustments, to the tribal warfare of the Arabs.[6]

6 N. Barbour, 'Arabs and Norsemen, The Expansion and Settlement of the Arabs between 632 and 1100 and of the Scandinavians between 789 and 1250', paper delivered to the Fifth Congress of Arabic and Islamic Studies held at Brussels, August 31-September 7, 1970.

Gotland was particularly important as a centre for trade. Arthur Spencer writes in his *Gotland*, Newton Abbot 1974, 51, 52:- 'With their safety and commercial rights thus guaranteed, the Gotlanders concentrated on building up the lucrative trade assured to them by their favourable position in the Baltic, remaining rather apart from the main political developments in North-Western Europe in the next few centuries. Their main trade was with Byzantium and the prosperous Arab realms of Western Asia, whose silver mines financed the trade of the known world. The runic inscription on an eleventh-century whetstone succinctly records the situation. "Ulvar Ormika [the names of two Vikings] Greece [the Byzantine Empire] Jerusalem Iceland Arabia" it says, commemorating the travels of its owners and dramatically symbolising the range of Gotland's interests at the time.

The Vikings developed their northern routes to replace the Mediterranean ones blocked by the mutual hostility of Christian West and Muslim East. Religious differences ironically gave them another advantage. As Foote and Wilson put it: 'Human beings were probably the commonest commodity the Vikings dealt in, both as traders and raiders.' The Arabs had an insatiable demand for slaves

Pre-Islamic Arabic folk epic

Professor R.A. Nicholson in his classic *Literary History of the Arabs*[7] likewise wrote:

It has often been remarked that the Arabs have no great epos like the Iliad or the Persian *Sháhnáma*, but only prose

but Christians were prohibited from selling them (at least to heathen customers). No such scruples hampered the Norsemen, who dragged off impartially both distant Christians and Scandinavian neighbours to sell for profit. They also sold furs and weapons to the Eastern lands, receiving in payment silver coins (*dirhams*), of which over 60,000 (about a quarter of the total found in northern Europe) have come to light on Gotland, the centre of this trade. Thus in a less monopolistic form Gotland in the ninth and tenth centuries achieved a pre-eminence in East-West trade comparable to that of Venice a couple of hundred years later. The Gotlanders' familiarity with Christianity before their conversion was attributed as a matter of course in the Saga to their contact with many pilgrims visiting the island — 'For at that time the way to Jerusalem and Greece was through Gotland.'

Dr Vilhelm Thomsen in his three lectures, *The Relations between Ancient Russia and Scandinavia and the Origin of the Russian State*, Oxford and London 1877, 82, 83, makes the following observation in regard to that period of the greater part of Arab coins in Scandinavia: 'The testimony of the historical records as to the connection between the Scandinavians and the eastern lands is supported, in the clearest manner, by archaeological discoveries. We see from numerous coins which have been found in Russia and the North, that just at the time of the great Viking expeditions an extremely lively trade existed between Scandinavia, the East and the Byzantine empire. This intercourse was carried on through the interior of Russia. Thus in Sweden great quantities of Arabian coins (nearly 20,000) have been found, which date from between 698 and 1002, but the far greater part are from between 880 and 955, the very time when, according to all evidence, the Scandinavian element was playing so important a part in the history of Russia. It seems that from the tenth century, especially, the island of Gothland was the central point of trade between Scandinavia and the East; for the largest discoveries of coins have been made here (about 13,000). With these Arabian coins were intermixed other foreign coins which must also have been brought there by traders from the East; among them were many Byzantine coins which bear dates of the tenth and eleventh centuries.'

7   R.A. Nicholson, *A Literary History of the Arabs*, Cambridge 1969, 325.

narratives which, though sometimes epical in tone, are better described as historical romances.

Nicholson's observation is basically sound, yet perhaps it is flawed in two respects. It ignores the undatable corpus of oral literature in verse or rhymed prose, which, the Arab *littérateurs* derided and then disowned. Secondly, it seems to discount the probability, if not certainty, that the zeal of the men of Islam to erase any trace they could of their past from the age of barbarism, the *Jāhiliyyah*, was so successful, that what has survived is insufficient to enable us to arrive at any fair assessment of the scope and nature of the bardic tradition of the poets (the *shu'arā'*) in pre-Islamic Arabia.

W. Robertson Smith, a predecessor of Nicholson, in his Burnett Lectures of 1888-89, on the religion of the Semites, drew attention to the paltry evidence which distorts our vision:

> That the Semites never had a mythological epic poetry comparable to that of the Greeks is admitted; but the character of the Semitic genius, which is deficient in plastic power and in the faculty of sustained and orderly effort; is enough to account for the fact. We cannot draw inferences for religion from the absence of an elaborate mythology; the question is whether there are not traces, in however crude a form, of the mythological point of view. And this question must be answered in the affirmative.[8]

The deeper the folk epic of the Arabs is studied whether in the scrappy early texts, or in the sung cycles of the tales of the Banū Hilāl describing their march into Africa and their wars and heroic exploits — cycles still performed by the bards of Upper Egypt to this day — the more the corpus of a genuine tradition of Arabian folk epic is made apparent.[9]

What were the earliest Arabian tales? They were certainly oral and some were in verse. Even the Koran itself was by

---

8 W.R. Smith, *Lectures on the Religion of the Semites*, London 1894, Lecture 11, p. 49.

9 For a recent comprehensive and authoritative presentation of the Tunisian material, see *Histoire des Beni Hilal*, by M. Galley and A. Ayoub, Paris 1983.

repute, first written down on skins and bones. One theme of almost certain ancient origin in Arabic oral literature is that one which we know from the tale of 'Saint George and the Dragon'. It is still told amongst the Mahrah of Southern Arabia and it is about Bū Zayd of the Banū Hilāl and his comrades.

The daughter of a ruler is tied up as food for a *jinnī* serpent which, if deprived of sustenance, will lay waste the land. Bū Zayd and two companions release her. Then each one takes a part of the night to watch for the monster. During the first third of the night one comrade distracts the serpent by propping its jaws open with a branch. During the subsequent third another comrade entertains it by singing. Then in the last third of the night Bū Zayd slays it by cutting off its head, which he places on the top of a castle wall. The ruler offers his daughter without a dowry to anyone who can prove, by a leap to seize the head on the wall, that he is the saviour of the princess and the kingdom. Only Bū Zayd, initially disguised, is able to seize the head.

The number three is an obsession of this tale and in many other tales[10] there are three companions, three parts to the night and in the competition to leap upwards to seize the serpent's head, it is Bū Zayd, at the third attempt, who is the triumphant suitor.

Countless stories are told, or are influenced by, the figure of Luqmān, a slave, then a vagabond or a sage, then king of the prehistoric people of ancient 'Ād, and lastly a prophetic macrobite, whose life span of a millenium equalled that of seven companion vultures. Like the one-eyed Arabian Cyclops, Shiqq, the character of Luqmān seems to reflect the influence of ancient Greek mythology. René Basset has observed:

There existed perhaps in pre-Islamic antiquity an

---

10 On this tale, see B. Thomas, *Arabia Felix*, London 1932, where a cycle of Bū Zayd stories is introduced in his travelogue, pages 246-51, and also S. Thompson, *Motif-index of Folk-Literature*, Bloomington and London 1966, H335.3.1. *Suitor's task to kill dragon to whom the princess is to be sacrificed.*

adventurer noted for his cunning and his adroitness who was at an early date identified with the mythical king of 'Ād, to whom the legend of the vultures was attached. The Qur'ān, which has made use of the best-known names of previous epochs, employed the name of Luqmān to apply to a man, or to describe saws, adages of general wisdom, and anecdotes, attributed to Aesop by the Greeks. This confusion of the two imaginary beings grew and grew, and it was complete at the time when the fables of Aesop were translated from Syriac into Arabic.[11]

Luqmān may have been chosen by the Prophet, Muḥammad, in *Sūrah* 31, in the Koran, to illustrate the wisdom of Aesop or to warn the idolators. However, in the *Kitāb al Tījān*, 'the Book of Crowns', attributed to the Yemenite storyteller, Wahb ibn Munabbih (died 732), Luqmān retains his pre-Islamic, giant, troll-like, personality. He is a troglodyte, jealous of his wife, law-giver, king, constructor of the Mārib dam in the Yemen. His cave is a store house of weapons and it is amongst these weapons that a Yemenite named Hamaysa[C], who covets Luqmān's wife, is hauled unknowingly by the latter into his inaccessible cave. Luqmān then leaves to journey afar. The inevitable outcome of the story is disclosed, stage by stage, by the storyteller, employing the motif of a triple elevation and debasement and an association between weaponry and male prowess to add drama and colour to his story:

When Luqmān left, Hamaysa' spoke to Sawdā', Luqmān's wife, and said: 'I am Hamaysa' b. al-Samaydā''. She released him, and he satisfied his desire with her. She gave him food and drink, then she put him back among the weapons. She acted with him thus, until he slept with her on Luqmān's bed. Then he spat and ejected phlegm on the ceiling of the cave, and there it stuck.

After that Luqmān returned. He was weary and threw himself down on his bed. He cast his eye on the roof of the cave and saw the phlegm. He said to his wife: 'Who

11 On three (or thirty) being the number of a band of heroes in the Old Testament, see Samuel II, Chapter 23, vv 8-39 and Chronicles I, Chapter 11, vv 10-25, and R. Basset, *Loqmân Berbère*, Paris 1890, lxix.

spat so?' She replied, 'I did.' 'Spit then!' So she spat but could not reach [the roof of the cave]. 'But I was sitting up.' 'Sit up, then!' She did so, she did, but all to no avail. 'I was standing up.' 'Stand up, then!' She did so, but with no greater success. 'The weapons, then, are the source of my misfortune.' Luqmān hurried to them, uncovered them and brought out Hamaysaʿ.

He summoned Ḥimyar and asked them, 'What is your opinion?' 'O Luqmān,' they said, 'Banish the Banū Karkar b. ʿĀd from the land of Ḥimyar, since they are a treacherous and crafty people. Let them not sow cunning amongst us, nor burden us with hatreds, not bequeath malice unto us.' Luqmān said to ʿĀd, 'Depart from my protection!' Next he climbed the mountain, tied Sawdāʿ, his wife, to Hamaysaʿ among the weapons which had hidden him. Then he cast them down from the top of the mountain and stoned them. All those with him followed his example. Luqmān was the first who stoned according to the penalty for adultery, and he killed them both.[12]

Kings of Ḥimyar

Another story of the ancient kings of the Yemen recounts the adventures of Asʿad Kāmil, one of the greatest Yemenite heroes, and his encounters with his foes. As a youth he had met three witches who had predicted his rise to fame. Nicholson has vividly translated the scene in the Arabic poem:[13]

O the fear that fell on his heart when he
Saw beside him the witches three!
The eldest came with many a brew —
In some was blood, blood-dark their hue.
'Give me the cup!' he shouted bold;
'Hold, hold!' cried she, but he would not hold.

12 See my 'Fables and legends in pre-Islamic and early Islamic times', in *The Cambridge History of Arabic Literature*, Vol. 1, *Arabic Literature to the end of the Umayyad period*, Cambridge 1983, 379-81. See also S. Thompson, *op. cit.*, J1142.3. *Adultery detected by spit marks.*
13 Nicholson, *op. cit.*, 19-21. See also S. Thompson, *ibid.*, G201. *Three Witch Sisters.*

She gave him the cup, nor he did shrink
Tho' he reeled as he drained the magic drink.

Then the second yelled at him. Her he faced
Like a lion with anger in his breast.
'These be our steeds, come mount,' she cried,
'For asses are worst of steeds to ride.'
"Tis sooth,' he answered, and slipped his flank
O'er a hyena lean and lank,
But the brute so fiercely flung him away,
With deep, deep wounds on the earth he lay.
Then came the youngest and tended him
In tears; but he averted his face
And sought a rougher resting-place:
Such paramour he deemed too base.
And him thought, in anguish lying there,
That needles underneath him were.

Now when they had marked his mien so bold,
Victory in all things they foretold.
'The wars, O As'ad, waged by thee
Shall heal mankind of misery.

Hassān, the son of this As'ad Kāmil, was the Yemenite
monarch who captured Zarqā', the black-eyed maiden, who
could see a distance of three days' journey. The story also
introduces a camouflaged army which reminds one of the
march of Birnham wood to Dunsinane in Shakespeare's
Macbeth. The tribe of Ṭasm were almost exterminated in a
feast by Jadīs, their rivals. The latter tribe were incensed at
the way a noble woman had been the victim of a kind of jus
primae noctis which the dominant Ṭasm enforced upon them.
Riyāḥ ibn Murrah, a Ṭasmite, escaped. He sought refuge with
King Ḥassān of the Ḥimyarites who promised him his aid.
Riyāḥ warned the king that Zarqā', his sister, who was married
to a man of Jadīs, had such remarkable vision that she could
see a rider at a distance of three days' journey. He told the
king to order each Ḥimyarite soldier to uproot a tree and to
bear a branch of it before him as he advanced towards Jaww,
the capital of Jadīs. His advice was heeded.

Zarqā' al-Yamāmah watched the horizon. She told Jadīs

that she had observed bushes marching towards the city.
There were humans behind them. Her report was received with
disbelief. When the king of Ḥimyar and his men were at a
night's distance from Jaww the order to attack was given. All
the citizens were slain. Zarqā' was brought before the king
who found that her eyes were impregnated with antimony.
This had dyed the arteries and had given her exceptional
vision. Zarqā' died, crucified, or suspended from a gibbet,
above the gate of Jaww.[14]

In the Koran are introduced several ancient Yemenite
stories which are told for spiritual edification. Shaddād, king
of 'Ad was the builder of a fabulous city of columns, though
he was destroyed for his pride. The invisible city was lost in
the desert and remained to be discovered by the lucky few.
In time the tale was confused with that of another city, the
City of Brass or Adamant Castle. Bilqīs, the Queen of Sheba
and the spouse of Sulaymān, the master of *jinn* and talismans,
fills the verses of *Sūrah* 27, (the Ant). The Two-Horned,
Dhū'l-Qarnayn in the verses of *Sūrah* 18, (the Cave), marches
to the water of life in the west and to the wall of Gog and
Magog in the north-east. Several Yemenite kings bore this
noble title. It should be noted that the Koran pre-dates a
translation or paraphrase of Pseudo-Callisthenes into Arabic
by 'Umārah ibn Zayd. The 'green one' al-Khiḍr, *wazīr*, seer
and drinker of the water of life is the faithful counsellor of
this two-horned king.[15]

The Ṣa'ālīk

A famous figure in the pre-Islamic age, about whom many
stories were told, was the raiding vagabond Ṣu'lūk, who,
with his tongue and his sword and his guile, faced his foes
unto death, and even beyond death if the code of blood
revenge for himself, his family and his tribe demanded it. An
early Yemenite tale tells how such vagabonds — Ṣa'ālīk —

14 Nicholson, *ibid.*, 25. The influence of this tale on Western Saharan
    folk epics is explained in my *Saharan Myth and Saga*, Oxford
    1972, 125-59. See also S. Thompson, *ibid.*, K1872.1. *Army appears
    like forest*, and F642ff.

15 See my 'Qiṣaṣ elements in the Qur'ān' in *The Cambridge History of
    Arabic Literature*, *op. cit.*, 246-59.

stumbled on the treasure of Shaddād ibn ʿĀd, guarded by talismans and monsters.

Certain famous poets were Ṣaʿālīk. Two of them were especially famous, Taʾabbaṭa Sharran and Shanfarā. The former carried a sword, or a demon (ghūl), or both, beneath his armpit, when he was an infant. He gained notoriety by escaping from a cave, surrounded by his foes, down a gluey slide of spilt honey which he had gathered. Shanfarā slew one hundred men of Salāmān by the skill of his sword, by a blow from his severed hand, and by a fragment of his skull lying bleached in the sand. This bone poisoned the foot of his hundredth victim.

T.M. Johnstone made a special study of these poets and found several parallels between their exploits as tribal heroes and those of other heroes in Celtic and Nordic literature. Both these Arab vagabonds were famous runners and had abnormal powers of hearing and sight. Both could be killed without incurring blood-debt or bringing retaliation on the head of the killer. Shanfarā was captured and brought up by the Banū Salāmān. As he grew older he swore that he would take revenge for a humiliating insult amongst them. He returned to the tribe of Banū Fahm, the tribe of his birth. When he had killed ninety-nine of the Banū Salāmān, he was surrounded at a well. He was shot in the eye and his hand was severed. He then recited his famous verse:

> Bury me not! Me you are forbidden to bury,
> But thou O hyena, soon wilt thou feast and make merry,
> When foes bear away mine head, wherein is the best of me,
> And leave on the battle-field for thee all the rest of me.
> Here nevermore I hope to live glad-a stranger
> Accurst, whose wild deeds have brought his people in danger.[16]

Then he was hanged. His skull rolled from his skeleton hanging on the gibbet. When one of the Banū Salāmān kicked it with his foot, a splinter entered his foot and he died of the wound. Now Shanfarā had claimed his hundredth victim.

16 Nicholson, op. cit., 79-82.

Parallels can be found to this story. Johnstone examined a number of them: they include the story of the Scottish chief, Maelbrigte Tusk. The *Orkneyinga Saga*, tells how Sigurd was slain by the skull of this formidable earl. Another story of similar type is the revenge of Cú Chulainn through his severed head as told in the *Book of Leinster* and elsewhere. This hero's marvellous feats in battle, his body revolving beneath the skin and a light streaming from his head, are like those in a number of 'Antar's tales. This Ulsterman's death, together with the terror which the sight of his body inspired in his pursuers, recalls the most famous Arab hero of all 'Antar and his heroic death.[17]

'Antar and Imru'ul-Qays

In the West, the name of 'Antar, the Arabian Black Knight of the high Middle Ages, is better known than 'Antarah ibn Shaddād, the historical pre-Islamic poet, whose battle ode ranks as one of the great seven 'hung' poems (*al-Mu'allaqāt*), which, according to legend, were written in golden letters and suspended on the walls of the Ka'ba, the holy sanctuary, in the heart of Mecca. The most famous of the master poets of that age was Imru'ul-Qays al-Kindī, a wandering king who was out to avenge the death of his father, and who was also a passionate lover.[18]

Imru'ul-Qays, who was nominally a Christian yet who only too obviously epitomises the spirit of pagan Arabia in its decadence, is by almost all Arabs regarded as the poetic embodiment of the bardic age of their literature. His fame spread as ancient Arabic culture was carried into Africa and

17 Professor T.M. Johnstone, 'Heads you lose', in *Oriental Studies presented to Benedikt S.J. Isserlin*, edited by R.Y. Ebied and M.J.L. Young, Leeds University Oriental Society, Near Eastern Researches 11, Leiden 1980, 131-5. There is an extended comparison between the exploits of 'Antar and those of Cú Chulainn in *The Cattle Raid of Couly* in E.L. Ranelagh's book, *The Past We Share*, London 1979, 152-4. Ranelagh draws attention to the common obsession with livestock and cattle raiding, the protection of the weak by the strong, the physical abnormalities of both 'Antar and Cú Chulainn, the training of the heroes, when lads, by women, and the promise of a maiden's hand if the hero will fight relatives.

18 A.J. Arberry, *The Seven Odes*, London 1957, 33-5, 62 and 63.

Asia through conquests of Islam. Yet what a paradox! The sentiments in the verses of Imru'ul-Qays were forthrightly condemned by the Prophet Muḥammad himself.

Imru'ul-Qays is revered by the modern Arab as an incomparable poet. However, he has been metamorphosed in the past amongst the Islamised Tuareg of Niger. Whether this be due to popular folk epic (in the Sīrat 'Antarah both pre-Islamic characters are rivals for the prize at the Meccan Eisteddfod), or by the diffusion of Arabic tales deep into Africa, Ghantarata and Amerolqis reveal pagan Arabia absorbed into Tuareg mythology. Amerolqis is a cultural hero, and is by far the more interesting of the two. He is a nocturnal gallant and a Don Juan deeply loved by all women, even if none of them could bear him offspring, so deadly was his potency. He invented the Tifinagh script to express the Tuareg Berber language with the aid of a sharp piece of straw. Some maintained that he invented their Tamajeq language as well. He sought to humiliate the Tuareg's enemies, the Arabs, by use of secret codes. The violin, the flute, popular song itself, are based on the example of Amerolqis. None knows whether he was a son of Paradise or Hell. When he sang, even female animals came to listen to him.[19]

The Nordic World in Arabic Literature: Trade and Commerce

The contact between the Muslim East and the Nordic World, whether in the remotest North itself, at the Straits of Gibraltar, in the region of the Caspian and Black Seas, or along the waterways of Russia, made its mark in the writings of the Arabs and the Persians. Despite the strangeness of the northern lands and their peoples, they are little to be seen in Arabian or Oriental stories of wonders and enchantments; rather they appear in the writings of travellers, geographers and historians. The Arab storytellers preferred spice-filled islands in southerly oceans. To the north, the divinely commanded wall built to thwart Gog and Magog was a little too close for comfort. Even so, Yaḥyā ibn Ḥakam al-Bakrī al-

19 M.A. Zakara and Jeannine Drouin, *Traditions Touarègues Nigér-iennes, Amerolqis héros, civilisateur pré-islamique et Aligurran archétype social*, Paris 1979, 21-48.

Ghazzāl, accompanied by Yaḥyā ibn Ḥabīb, both emissaries
sent by the Umayyad ruler of Spain, 'Abd al-Rahmān II, in
the ninth century, in order to arrange terms of peace with
the anonymous King of the Norsemen, describe an island in
the North (probably to be identified as either Jutland or
Ireland) 'in which are flowing waters and gardens', and where
the Norsemen's Queen wore shining buttons in her dress.[20]
Earlier than this, al-Mas'ūdī said that he had seen in the books
of al-Kindī (died c.870), and his pupil, al-Sarakhsī, that the
utmost extremity of the land of the north was a great lake
under the North Pole, and that close by was sited a city
called Tūliyah (Thule, [the Shetlands?]). The Spanish geographer al-'Udhrī, writing about 1058, describes whaling
in the vicinity of Ireland. The following passage is to be
found in a work of al-Qazwīnī who died in 1283:

> Al-'Udhrī said: 'The Norsemen have no capital (qā-
> idah) save this island in all the world. Its circumference is
> a thousand miles. Its people have the customs and dress
> of the Norsemen. They wear rich mantles, one of which is
> worth 100 dīnārs. Their nobles wear mantles ornamented
> with pearls.' He related that on their coasts they hunt the
> young of the whale (ablīnah), which is an exceeding great
> fish. They hunt its calves, regarding them as a delicacy.
> They have mentioned that these calves are born in the
> month of September, and are hunted in the four months
> October to January. After this their flesh is hard and no
> longer good for eating. As to the manner of hunting them,
> al-'Udhrī mentioned that the hunters assemble in ships,
> having with them a great iron blade with sharp spikes. In
> the blade is a great strong ring, and in the ring a strong
> cable. When they find a calf, they clap their hands and
> shout. The calf is delighted by the clapping and approaches
> the ships, wanting to be friendly with them. A sailor speci-
> ally appointed for the task rubs the calf's forehead briskly,
> and the calf finds pleasure therein. Then he places the
> blade in the middle of its head and, taking a powerful
> iron mallet, he strikes with it upon the blade with all his

20 Dorothee Metlitzki, *The Matter of Araby in Medieval England*,
Yale 1977, 120-6. See note 21 below.

force three times. It does not feel the first blow, but at the second and third it struggles violently. Sometimes it hits part of the ships with its tail, and destroys them. It does not cease struggling till weariness overtakes it. Then the crews of the ships take turns to drag it, till it is brought to the shore. Sometimes the mother of the whale-calf sees the struggle and follows them. They prepare much powdered garlic, which they scatter on the water. When the whale smells the garlic, she lets (the calf) go, and turns backwards in her tracks. Then they cut up the meat of the calf and salt it. Its meat is white like snow, and its skin black as ink.[21]

It was relatively rare that Arab voyagers took this north-westerly sea route. More common was the Russian overland route, where Arabic and Islamic and indeed Oriental ideas and stories, in general, reached the furthest North. J.H. Kramers observed:

It appears from the written Arabic sources that the country of the Volga Bulgars, on the middle course of that river, was the final goal of their trade expeditions and their embassies, the faith of Islam, too, penetrated as far as those regions at an early date. The route generally followed by trade went from Transoxania to the Delta region of Khwārizm (Khiva) at the mouth of the Oxus; the way up the Volga from its mouth was less usual. The fact, however, that the coins are found over so wide an area is a symptom of cultural influence, and proves that the Muhammadans purchased in the Bulgarian markets a good many wares from the peoples living in the north-west. Amongst these the Scandinavian Russians were the most important. We know from geographical works, principally from al-Maqdisī, what were the wares that the Islamic merchants acquired in this way: 'sables, miniver, ermines, the fur of foxes, beavers, spotted hares, and goats: also wax, arrows, birch bark, high fur caps, fish glue, fish teeth, castoreum, amber, prepared horse hides, honey, hazel nuts, falcons,

---

21   D.M. Dunlop, *op. cit.*, page 14 and 19-20. The whole article is in one way or another relevant to the discussion.

swords, armour, maple wood, slaves, small and big cattle'.[22]

With trade went tales. Professor H.A.R. Gibb wrote that the furthest North did not escape the irresistible fascination of the Oriental fables:

Arabic travel-literature and cosmography have also left their traces in western literature, as was only to be expected when to travel implied for Europe mainly going on pilgrimage to the Holy Land. It was almost inevitable with oral transmission that the fabulous and marvellous elements should have spread farthest. They supplied embroideries for Marco Polo and 'Sir John Mandeville' amongst others, but their range was not limited to the Latin countries of the West. They penetrated even to Ireland and Scandinavia — possibly by way of the Caspian-Baltic trade-route — and reappear in such monastic tales as the *Legend of St Brendan*.[23]

The Arab, himself, was equally fascinated and amazed with what he saw. Ibn Faḍlān describes many of the customs of the Viking Rūs[24] during his mission from Baghdad to Bulghār in 922. He describes their wooden houses on the Volga, and the sale of girls to merchants in front of wooden idols. He is dazzled by the rich silver, copper and gold brooches and rings of the wives of the Rūs merchants.

Perhaps Ibn Faḍlān's most graphic description is that of the cremation of a chief in a boat together with a number of his servants and slave girls. The whole ritual, even myths about it, are set before us in the Arabic account. Beside the burning fire of the boat, Ibn Faḍlān remarks:

A man of the Rūs was standing beside me, and I heard him talking to the interpreter, who was near him. I asked him what he had said to him, and he answered: 'He said: 'You Arabs are stupid'. I asked: 'Why so?'. He answered: 'Why, because you take the people you most love and honour and throw them into the ground, and the earth and

---

22 J.H. Kramers, 'Geography and Commerce', *The Legacy of Islam*, Oxford 1931, 100-1.

23 *Ibid.*, 193.

24 J. Simpson, *The Viking World*, London 1980, 100-1 and 181-5.

creeping creatures and growing things destroy them. We, on the other hand, burn them in an instant, so that they go to Paradise in that very hour'. Then he gave a roar of laughter, and when I asked him about this, he replied: 'For the love of him, his Lord has sent this wind to carry him away at the right time!' And, in fact, not much time passed before the ship and the timber and the slave-girl and her master had all turned into ashes and so into dust.[25]

Other Arab accounts of Swedish traders in Russia describe witch-doctors (*aṭibbā'*) who demanded sacrifices of women, men and cattle. They tell of the burial of musical instruments. Extremely detailed is the report of a Muslim from Córdoba, Ibrāhīm al-Ṭurṭūshī, who in the 950s visited Hedeby in Schleswig. He describes the feast in honour of Sirius, the cosmetics of the women and the hideous singing of its people.[26]

The Baltic in the writings of Arab geographers

The most comprehensive coverage of the northern lands is to be found in the geographical work, *Nuzhat al-Mushtāq*, the so-called *Book of Roger*, (the Norman Roger II, King of

25 See above. For a later description of Bulghār region see H.A.R. Gibb, *Ibn Battuta, Travels in Asia and Africa*, New York 1939, 150-1. See also A. Zeiki Validi Togan, *Ibn Faḍlān's Reisebericht*, *Abh. für die Kunde des Morgenlandes* 24, 3, Leipzig 1939.

26 *A Description of Europe, and the Voyages of Ohthere and Wulfstan*, ed. and translated, J. Bosworth, London 1855, 5; G. Jacob, *Arabische Berichte von Gesandten an germanische Fürstenhöfe aus dem 9. und 10. Jahrhundert*, Berlin and Leipzig 1927, 3, and G. Jacob, *Der Nordische-baltische Handel der Araber im Mittelalter*, Leipzig 1887. On recent discoveries at Hedeby, see J. Simpson, *op. cit.*, note 24. O. Klindt-Jensen in his *The Vikings in England*, Copenhagen 1948, 23-4, remarks: 'Money circulated, and the people of Hedeby even began to mint silver coins thus imitating Dorstadt in Friesland. Commoner than these, however, were the coins of the rest of Western Europe and of Arabia. The latter came in a steady glittering stream by the trade routes of the Swedes along the Russian rivers. A few Arabs, dark types of perhaps the most cultured people of the time, walked down the streets of Hedeby among the tall, fair Northmen. We have some notes written by one of them. He did not feel so comfortable up here as at home. The singing reminded him of the howling of dogs, and the exposure of small children who could not be reared was alien to him'.

Sicily), completed by the *Sharīf* Muḥammad al-Idrīsī, in January 1154. His description of the islands of Britain and Ireland and the Orkneys, then under the rule of Norway (*nrbāgha*), in the second section, his third, fourth and fifth sections of the seventh clime; each have much to tell us of the towns, peoples and beliefs of the northern lands, Finland amongst them.

The informants of al-Idrīsī, be they Swedes or Germans, portray the shore of the Baltic as a broad, highly disfigured coastline, with a series of ports along the coasts of Wendland, Poland, Lithuania, Latvia and Estonia, matched by a further series bordering on Finnmark and the Sea of Bothnia, ports such as Kalmar and Sigtuna which are described as attractive towns. Particularly striking is the fact that two regions of the Baltic are mentioned in much greater detail than the rest, namely the 'Island of Denmark', which in fact is confined to the peninsula of Jutland and to Schleswig, in the far west, and in the extreme east the territories of Finland, Estonia and Baltic Russia. Trade, it would seem, was funnelled for security across southern Jutland and Schleswig through the Viking town of Hedeby with its massive fortifications.

The toponyms mentioned by al-Idrīsī in the area of Schleswig and Jutland are often difficult or impossible to identify. They seem to lie to the east and the west of the Haervejen which ran north from the area of the Elbe through the centre of Jutland. From al-Sīlah, Slien or Sly, Sliesthorp, Schleswig itself, or possibly Sylt on the opposite coast, the road went north through Ṭardhīrah, either Tyraborg west of Hedeby on the Danevirke ramparts or the region of Ribe, to another port or haven, well-sheltered from the wind. The fort of Khūw yet further to the north might be Hobro, beside Fyrkat, with its giant Viking ramparts, dating from the beginning of the eleventh century. At Wandalsgādah, Vendelsgade, the route arrived at the tip of Jutland in the region of Vendssysel, possibly Lindholm Høje and Aalborg. Here was the point of departure for Jazīrat Narfāghah, the peninsula of Norway. Turning southwards the route passed through Hursh Hunt, a beautiful town, probably Horsens, a place of abbeys and fortresses founded in the twelfth century, when the *Book of Roger* was written. The route then passed out of Jutland again, via Landwīnah, to the town of Sīsabūlī, which must have been situated in the vicinity of Seebüll in the Schleswig region, today in Germany.

The occasional detail about the eastern Baltic, a centre of trade with the East via the waterways of Russia is prominent. The study by O. Tallgren-Tuulio and A.M. Tallgren,[27] shows how much Finland, especially Ṭabast, the district of Häme, Swedish Tavastland, in south-western Finland, appears in these accounts, likewise the opposite coast of Estonia and its hinterland, the fortress of Qalawrī, possibly Kalvaria in Lithuania, Barnū, namely Pernu, Falmūs, Palamuse and its troglodyte dwellers, the Chuds, in their fiery caves in winter, who return to their fortress in the rainy days of summer. The account speaks of Jintiyār on high ground well within Estonia, possibly at Sventoji, or even Novgorod itself, where Russian wizards or ṣhamans could be found. The scattering of tiny details here illustrates the importance of the eastern Baltic for traders, some of them having links with the Muslim World, everywhere shown by the presence of Arabic coinage.

Lying in the Baltic are many islands. Al-Idrīsī mentions two in particular: 'The islands of the Viking Amazons' (*Amazaniyūs al-Majūs*). The western island is only inhabited by men, the eastern only by women.

Every year, the men cross the passage betwixt them in skiffs which they possess. It is in the spring. Each man

27 Idrīsī, *La Finlande et les autres pays baltiques orientaux*, (*Géographie*, 7: 4) by O.J. Tallgren-Tuulio and A.M. Tallgren, Societas Orientalis Fennica, *Studia Orientalia*, 3, Helsingforsiae 1930. This exhaustive study of the eastern Baltic also discusses Denmark and Sweden *passim*. See also P.A. Jaubert, *La Géographie d'Edrisi*, translation of *Kitāb Nuzhat al-Mushtāq*, Amsterdam 1836-40, 427-33.

Since I wrote this paper, my friend, Haakon Stang of the University of Oslo, has drawn my attention to the exhaustive monograph of H. Birkeland, *Nordens Historie i Middlealderen etter Arabiske Kilder*, Skrifter Utgift av Det Norske Videnskaps-Akademi i Oslo, H. Histo-Filos Klasse, 1954, No 2, Oslo I Kommisjon Hos Jacob Dybwad, 1954, 177 pages and two plates. Birkeland has alternatives to offer in regard to Scandinavian toponyms in Arabic texts of the medieval period. I have, however, not discussed these and have not altered my original text.

hunts for a wife and makes love to her and remains several days with her, up to a month, and then the men journey back to their island and they remain there until the next year, and to that time. Then once more they make for the island of their women and act with them in the manner of the preceding year, in that the man makes love to his wife and stays a month with her. Then he returns to the island where he lives. All of them behave in this way. It is a well known custom amongst them and a prevailing way of life amongst them.[28]

It is to be noted that a predecessor of al-Idrīsī, the Andalusian traveller, Ibrāhīm ibn Yaʻqūb al-Ṭurṭūshī, (c.968), does not mention two islands:

To the west of the Rūs (Vikings) is the town of women. They have lands and male slaves. They become pregnant from their slaves. If a woman gives birth to a male she kills him. They ride horses and engage in battle and they are both heroic and courageous. Ibrāhīm ibn Yaʻqūb al-Isrāʼīlī said that the report about this city is true and that he had been told of it by Otto the Great (king of the Germans, al-Rūm[29]).[30]

---

28   For the Arabic text, see A. Bombaci *et al*, *Opus geographicum* . . . Naples-Rome 1970, in progress, 955-6. Jaubert's translation, page 433, *op. cit.*, reads *Amazaniyūs* as *Imrāyinas*. According to Tallgren, *op. cit.*, 140:- 'The information supplied is manifestly fabulous and one can hardly give these islands a location. Let us mention, however, that facing Tallin there lies a low island called *Naissaare* (Island of the Woman or Island of Women), Nargen in Swedish (in 1250 Narigeth, Nargethen), which for a long while was Swedish. If the name *Naissaare* is ancient, it could have given birth to the localisation of the tradition of an Island of the Amazons.' An Arab coin has been found on *Naissaare*, *op. cit.*, 140. Lemminkäinen's adventures with the Maidens of Saari, in the *Kalevala*, takes place on an unspecified 'island' — Saari. For al-Bakrī's references, see A. A. el-Hajji, *The Geography of Al-Andalus and Europe*, Beirut 1968, 169-70.

29   Literally 'Byzantines', although here applied to Otto the Great and his subjects, see P. Hitti, *History of the Arabs*, London 1946, 201.

30   El-Hajji, *ibid.*, 170, and his article, 'Ibrāhīm ibn Yaʻqūb aṭ-Ṭur-

Westberg sited this town in Lithuania. A.M. Tallgren suggested that the island was off the coast of Estonia, namely the low island of Naissaare, facing Tallinn. On the other hand this legendary town, or island, could have been imagined further to the west. Bornholm and Gotland cannot be excluded.

The Arab geographer, al Bakrī, who quotes al-Ṭurṭūshī, wrote that there lived to the west of the city, or realms of women, a Slavonic, Scandinavian, or Baltic people called the 'nation of the Waltābah/Udbābah'. Al-Hajji, the editor of the text, suggests that this name should be Wulīnānā. This reading is suspect. Three possible explanations for the people suggest themselves. They could be the Volynians. The Volynian Chronicle says that they were ruled by dukes, several of whom were 'elders'. The Lithuanians had regional strongholds, fortified hillocks, where settlements were established. This is not a strong case. Several scholars maintain that Waltābah is the correct reading and that the people are the Veletians, settled between the Odra and the Elbe.

Professor T. Lewicki writes:

> The Slavs living westwards of the Odra river, the so called WALITAB or WELETABE (Veletians or Liutici). Their former prince called Māğik (MAŽăKZ) had presumably been the ruler of all the Slavs in the earlier days. Together with them are mentioned the people NāMğIN or NĕMğIN whom we recognise as the Germans.[31]

It is possible that Wīlinānā is derived from the Latin name of Tallinn, namely Vironia, *terra Virorum, terra Revalorum*. But this would site it to the east, not to the west of Naissaare. A third suggestion is that the life of the town relates to the legendary settlement of Wollin/Jomsborg (Vineta) in Wendland. According to the *Jómsvikinga saga*, the Jomsvikings lived a monastic type existence, though they harried far in

tūshī Andalusian traveller', *Islamic Culture* 40 (1966), 39-46. For full details on Ibrāhīm ibn Yaʿqūb and his European travels, see M. Canard, *Miscellanea Orientalia*, Variorum Reprints, London 1973, 503-8.

31 *al-Masʿūdī Millenary Commemoration Volume*, ed. S. Maqbul Ahmad and A. Rahman, India 1960, 12.

the Baltic. They built a huge harbour for three hundred and sixty longships, and the harbour entrance had a stone arch, iron doors and a great tower in which catapults were installed.[32]

That this is largely legend is well-known. Some of this story may have been inherited from the Slavic Wends, whose religion and mythology of tree cults, oracles, amulets and symbols was derived from contacts with Iranians and Turkomans. Al-Bakrī, citing Ṭurṭūshī, remarks that there was a town sited in thickets or marshes in the land of Miesco (Mashaquh), Duke of Poland, who allegedly reigned over the Slavs from 964 to 992. The city was out to sea in the Surrounding Ocean. It had twelve gates and a harbour. The men of this town used 'strict laws in administration' (shuṭūran ḥarlan). Al-Hajji suggests 'just rules' or 'equitable rules', qawā'id 'ādilah), a statement which agrees closely with the alleged laws imposed on the warrior community of Jomsborg by the mythical hero, Pálna-Tóki.[33] Muslims might describe such a community as a semi-monastic Ribāṭ — though their war was hardly holy jihād. No one must have a woman in the city and no one must be away longer than three days. Every summer they went harrying in various lands and won fame. According to al-Ṭurṭūshī, 'they fight Miesco and their furor of fighting is intense. They have no king and owe allegiance to none. Only their "elders" are their governors'.[34]

Is there anything Islamic in this tale? It is not impossible. Otto the Great, who told al-Ṭurṭūshī about the Island of Women legend, had, in 953, sent as his envoy, John, a Lotharingian monk to Córdoba for three years to learn Arabic and

32 N.F. Blake, The Saga of the Jómsvikings, London etc. 1962, viii, xi, 18. See also S. Rapoport, The Slavonic and East European Review, London 1929, Vol. 8, No. 23, 331-41. One of the most thorough investigations into the Oriental and Classical origins of the City of Women story is by Professor T. Lewicki, 'Pónocna kraina Amazonek w opisach średniowiecznych geografów arabskich', in Odbicle ze Sprawozdań Polskiej Akademii Umiej, Tom 49 (1948) nr 7, str 352, 352-5. For a detailed study of the Dulebian League (supposedly destroyed by the Avars in the seventh century) see H. Paszkiewicz, The Origin of Russia, London 1954, 362-4.

33 N.F. Blake, op. cit., viii.

34 El-Hajji, The Geography of Al-Andalus and Europe, op. cit., 174-5.

to bring back Oriental learning. Reminiscent of this same dedicated equality, warrior males and a fortress established in thickets appear much later in the Arab geographers' description of the *Ribāṭ* of the Saharan Almoravids in the eleventh century. There may be common classical elements in these stories. Arab storytellers sited the exploits of the two-horned Dhū'l-Qarnayn in the desert regions of the Western Sahara, and also, in the furthest North, where the fount of life might also be discovered. Al-Tha'labī, a tenth-century author of *Tales of the Prophets*, like the Yemenite storytellers before him, mentioned a heroic march to the Wall of Gog and Magog near the fount of life and to regions of darkness where the Angel of the Last Trump blows his horn near the North Pole. Throughout this Islamic literature the Sea of Darkness extends from the region of the Canaries to the Baltic and beyond.[35]

Arabic folk epic: fantasy, formula and function in the Northern sagas and the *Kalevala*

Reading W.F. Kirby's translation of the *Kalevala* in the Everyman's Library, one is made aware of similarities with, if not borrowings from, Oriental folklore. Parallels with Islamic, especially Arabic popular literature of the high Middle Ages, may be seen in the Island of Women, the forging of a magic sword, heroic flights in the imagination, if not in the body, amidst the stars, copper men appearing from the ocean, and an obsession with talismans, especially one supreme talisman a dazzling *baht* stone or store house of treasure, guarded by serpent monsters, the power house of prosperity and the key to mastery of mankind. This stone talisman or treasure is usually inaccessible or hidden, frequently in a mountain or a fortress of copper. Several of Kirby's notes to the *Kalevala* mention the *One Thousand and One Nights*. Elsewhere in his writings, in his *The Hero of Esthonia*,[36] he devotes a chapter to 'Oriental Tales', the 'Maidens who bathed in the Moon-

---

35 See the article '*Yādjūdj wa-Mādjūdj*', by A.J. Wensinck, in the *Shorter Encyclopædia of Islam*, Leiden and London 1961, 637.

36 W.F. Kirby, *The Hero of Esthonia and Other Studies in the Romantic Literature of That Country*, Vol. 2, London 1895, 233-60. The story of The Northern Frog bears a superficial resemblance to pas-

light', and 'The Northern Frog', or monster, which could be overcome with the aid of Solomon's Seal and the understanding of its inscription. This needed to be interpreted by an Eastern sorcerer. The ring enabled the hero to fly through the air.

However, if one reads *Finnish Folk Poetry. Epic*, such 'Orientalism' is usually un-noticeable. One suspects that an Oriental colouring is, occasionally, Kirby's own contribution wherever he senses a possible relevance. That the Northern *sagas* have Oriental borrowings is well-known.[37] Margaret Schlauch in her *Romance in Iceland* draws attention to this influence on Icelandic literature:

> Some of the incidents in the *lygisögur* recall to a modern reader the *Arabian Nights* and other typical Eastern Romances. Nichulás Leikari, in the saga named from him, disguises himself as a jewel merchant in order to win the haughty Princess Dorma of Constantinople, who has refused all wooers. The episode of the ring desired by two brothers, Helgi and Hróarr, in the *Hrólfs saga Kraka* (Chapter X), is almost identical with one of the *Arabian Nights*. In the *Gibbons saga ok Gregu*, the hero makes use of a flying cloth or carpet to transport himself from one place to another; there is a flying mantle also in the *Jóns saga Leikara*, in the *Sigrgarðs saga Frœkna*, and the *Egils saga Einhenda*. We have already spoken of the use of a favorite motive, namely, the love between a prince and princess who have never met, but only beheld each other in dreams — a motive frequently used in the East. It is to be found in *Inclusa* (of *The Seven Sages of Rome*), and also in the *Vergiliús saga*. These features of our sagas are, however, too widely used and too banal to be definitely traced.

She concludes even if one disagrees with the implication that sensuality was the hallmark of the East:

> sages in the tale of Ḥasan al-Baṣrī in the *Nights* and episodes in the *Sīrat Sayf ibn Dhī Yazan*, even so it suggests that kind of borrowing to be found in Icelandic and other sagas, rather than the importation or borrowing of an essentially Oriental tale.

37 B. Lewis, *The Arabs in History*, London 1950, 88.

But despite the large number of disputable cases, it is evident that much Oriental material did reach Iceland in the latter Middle Ages. It formed the most exotic, the most incongruous, and the most un-Icelandic elements in the multicolored patchwork of the *lygisögur*. No one can conceive of a more violent contrast than the restraint and nobility of tone of any truly Icelandic saga — even of a 'romantic' one like the *Völsunga saga* — and the *Dinus saga Dramblátá*, with its struggle for erotic domination by means of vulgar tricks, talismans to produce lust, and the abject humiliation of man by woman or woman by man.[38]

Something similar is discernible in the poems of the *Kalevala*. Most obvious is The Island of Women, an East Viking tale, which is the *milieu* of the Kaukamoinen folk epic. In Arabic tradition Amazon 'knights' grace the Romance of 'Umar al-Nu'mān in the *Arabian Nights* or this island is located in the China Sea, in the Indian Ocean or the western regions, and appears in Ḥasan of Basra's tale, and in the Sīrah of Sayf ibn Dhī Yazan. Akin to it is the story of an island which rises in the sea. János Honti has remarked in his *Studies in Oral Epic Tradition*:

> The traditions of the Hellenistic novels of adventure continued by a flourishing Arabic literature: Arabic expansion conquering practically half of the world, and Arabic trading calling at practically every port of the known world, have such an enormous increase that the emergence of travel-literature was almost an inevitable consequence. We can refer at least to one of these novels of adventure which has been well known in the whole of Europe, these are the travels of Sindbad, the Sailor. We can find in them at least one episode which embraces an interesting idea of Hellenistic-Arabic mythical geography: it is a country which is famous for not having either this or that. Sindbad arrives in a country where neither the saddle nor the stirrup are known — and the people naturally reward Sindbad very richly when he teaches them the use of these objects.[39]

38 M. Schlauch, *Romance in Iceland*, London 1934, 92, 94.

Copper men and metal men who rise from the sea resemble
the warrior-*jinn* imprisoned in cucurbites in a lake or sea by
Solomon near the meeting place of the two seas — in the
Koran itself (*Sūrah* 18) and the Tale of the City of Brass. The
magical sword is exemplified in the cutting power of *Ḍāmī*,
the sword of 'Antar, which could sever a man in twain, even
the most fearful foe, whose revolving head might endeavour
to continue the battle. A magic whip is found in the *Kalevala*
and also in the *Sīrah* of Sayf ibn Dhī Yazan. The *sampo* as
a magic mill would find little response in an ancient Arabian,
who regarded the mill wheel as the symbol of war and its
terrors. Yet, viewed as an example of a source of all prosperity, it resembles those varied talismanic objects around
which every segment in the articulated structure, which the
Arabic *Sīrah* represents, is built, for example, the Book of
the Nile in the *Sīrat Sayf*. Fabulous treasure in a monster-
guarded cave is found in Yemenite tales, the treasure of
Shaddād in Jabal Shimām, the pulpit of the Prophet, Hūd, the
treasure of Quadā'ah, objects of plunder for a trio of Ṣa'ālīk,
heroes, poets, outcasts of society, who consistently band
together to search for treasure hoards beyond imagination.[40]

Conclusion

Some of the parallels between the epic storytelling of the
Arabs and the peoples of the North, and some of the few
instances where specific borrowings may be identified, have
been discussed. Yet in most respects, it is the artistry of the
bard himself, his mode of recitation, singing, acting and the
spell which he casts upon his hearers, that seems to unite
two worlds — the Arab and the Nordic — in their love of
adventure, tragedy and love and struggle against an unfriendly
destiny.

39 J. Honti, *Studies in Oral Epic Tradition*, Budapest 1975, 45-6
    and the comment on the vertical cosmology of the Central Asian
    peoples, 113.
40 Such talismanic protected treasures and sources of prosperity fill
    the pages of the *Kitāb al-Tījān*, attributed to Wahb ibn Munabbih,
    of the Ḥasan al-Baṣrī Tale in the *Nights*, of the Tale of the City of
    Brass and Iram Dhāt al-'Imād, also in the *Nights*, and of Hamdānī's
    Iklīl, see N.A. Faris, *The Antiquities of South Arabia*, Princeton
    1938.

The Egyptian bard, the *shā'ir*, the reciter of the 'epic' of the Banū Hilāl, the only really oral 'Arab epic' which survives, is no mere poet or storyteller. His art has nothing to do with the *Nights* or even the exploits of 'Antar and Sayf which are recited from books. Often the *shā'ir* is illiterate. His repertoire is confined exclusively to the heroes and heroines of the post eleventh-century *Sīrat Banī Hilāl*; Abū Zayd, Dhiyāb, Jāziyah a self-sacrificing lover and mother, and the noble enemy, the *Sulṭān* Khalīfah of the Zenātah Berbers; it is part history, part legend and folk memory of the Bedouin. In Upper Egypt, the *shā'ir* is an important person and he is very often a gypsy. To be proficient in his art he must be able to sing for ninety-nine nights in succession from sundown to dawn. His audience, often elderly, is discerning and is conversant with the plot: how Dhiyāb slew Khalīfah, how he became a tyrant, tormented Jāziyah, killed his relation Abū Zayd, and how he was finally done to death by the young Hilālīs and Zenātah who combined to overthrow him. To the accompaniment of the rebec (*rabābah*), on occasions the tambourine and drum, the poet begins with a prelude, then praises the Prophet in hymns, then extols the virtues of the heroes, then unravels the story. The stanza forms are a *mawwāl* (AAAA or AABA etc), or single rhymed *qaṣīdah* which includes parts in prose, free verse or quatrains. Much use is made of similes, antithesis, periphrasis and paronomasia. It is the social occasion which decides the performance.

One Egyptian scholar, Ṭāhā Ḥusayn, recalls his boyhood days when he leaned on the fence of his hut and listened spell-bound, as the audience clamoured for a repetition of the poet's tale. He writes:

> The *shā'ir* would hold his peace until they had finished with their clamour, be the time short or long, then he would start up afresh his sweet melodious recitation which hardly ever seemed to change.

Rabābah or *kantele*, it is the poet's artistry which unites time in North and South, East and West. Splendid speech is indeed the only universal tongue.

SELECT BIBLIOGRAPHY

A. Abboudy, *La Geste Hilalienne*, trans. T. Guiga, Cairo 1978.

Bridget Connelly, 'The Structure of Four Banī Hilāl Tales', *The Journal of Arabic Literature*, 4 (1973), 18-47.

Mia Gerhardt, The authoritative work on the 1001 Nights — *The Art of Storytelling*, Leiden 1963.

E.W. Lane, *The Manners and Customs of the Modern Egyptians*, Chapters 21, 22 and 23, London 1963, first ed. London 1836.

A. Miquel, *Un conte des mille et une nuits: 'Ajīb et Gharīb*, Paris 1977.

H.T. Norris, 'The Adventures of Antar', *Approaches to Arabic Literature*, No. 3, Warminster 1980.

R. Paret, *Sirat Saif b. Ḏī Yazan, ein arabischer Volkroman*, Hanover 1924.

E.I. Ranelagh, *The Past We Share*, London 1979.

Diana Richmond, *'Antar and 'Abla, a bedouin romance*, London 1978.

Discography: Only one disc can be recommended: *Egitto Epica 1*, text by Professor G. Canova, in Italian, English and Arabic transcription, with musicological notes by H.H. Touma. *I Suoni*, Musica di Tradizione Orale, *Cetra/SU 5005*, 1982. This disc is indispensable for a study of the *Hilāliyya* and the dying art of its reciters.

THE USE OF THE SUPERNATURAL IN THE TURKISH EPICS OF *DEDE KORKUT* AND *KÖROGHLU*

AHMET EDIP UYSAL

(Orta Doğu Teknik Üniversitesi, Ankara)

I

The Turkic peoples comprising such Turkic-speaking groups as the Uzbeks, Kirghiz, Kazakh, Türkmen, Tartar, Azeri and the Anatolian or Western Turks, as well as many smaller communities or sub-groups scattered over a very wide area stretching from the Balkans to the borders of China on the one hand, and from the Himalayas to Siberia on the other, are known to have had a rich and long tradition of minstrelsy, fed and fostered by a common linguistic and cultural heritage, a tradition which still preserves much of its original vitality. Although studied extensively by such well-known scholars both from the east and west as Barthold, Radlov, Zhirmunsky, Chadwick, Köprülü and others, the vastness of the area and the bewildering richness of the oral material so far gathered, require a good deal more research. It is regrettable that even now at the end of the twentieth century, most of these territories are inaccessible to Western scholars and that it is impossible to conduct unhampered fieldwork in them.

We must, however, be grateful to a small number of energetic collectors who were able to surmount all difficulties and brought to light an extraordinary wealth of oral materials, sufficient to give us a fairly good idea of the nature of the oral epics of the Turkic peoples.

It is generally believed that the epics of the Turkic peoples first made their appearance between the seventh century B.C. and the first century A.D. and that they mostly dealt with tribal conflicts over land and pasture. Warriors drawing attention by their outstanding exploits in the service of their community formed the models or prototypes for the heroes of many Turkic epics which show structural similarities. First of all, each epic is the life story of a hero who often has a legendary birth and, as he grows, he performs a series of remarkable exploits. He is given a name on the basis of these achievements, which also mark the end of his childhood period and the beginning of his adult life. This is followed by the search for a wife and marriage. Subsequently, the hero encounters problems of a more serious nature, related to his family or tribe. He rescues a kidnapped father, brother or sister, and fighting against the enemies of his people, succeeds in restoring peace and order in his community and eventually creates a large empire in which he unites all Turkic peoples. The epic celebrates the hero's achievements and comes to an end with his death. A second epic story follows describing how the hero's son succeeded in restoring his father's shattered empire, executing many acts of heroism in the pursuit of his task. As in the epics of many other nations, the fights of the heroes of the Turkic epics sometimes take place in the sea and below the surface of the earth. In these fights, the hero's sole asset is his superhuman power and the supernatural qualities of his horse. The hero may be a legendary figure involved in actual historical events. He is often said to be accompanied by 40,365 or 1999 companions.

In the Turkic languages the word *destan*, originally a loan-word from Persian, is used for an epic tale. Singers of epic tales are sometimes called *kam*, *bakshi*, *ozan* or *ashik*, individuals who are often believed to have been endowed with powers of clairvoyance and prophecy. Their function in the community, therefore, did not consist of merely reciting an epic. They also sought remedies for the serious problems of their community. Although this function is no longer valid, singers of epic tales of great length are still revered and they enjoy prestige throughout the Turkic-speaking world, where the epic singer is considered to be a divinely inspired man. When Radlov, a nineteenth-century investigator of Central Asian epics, asked an epic singer how and from whom he had learned his art, he received the following reply:

The art of singing epic tales was put into my heart by Allah. I never search for words and lines when reciting an epic, they just pour out from my inside on their own.[1]

There is a belief still prevailing throughout the Turkic-speaking parts of the world that the ability to create spontaneous poetry, lyric or epic, is granted to the artist by some divine agents in the form of a sweet drink (*bade*) in a dream state.[2] In Turkey such minstrels are distinguished from those who did not have this experience by the epithet *badeli ashik*, 'minstrel who has had the cup'. Such minstrels recite and create spontaneous poetry as if in a state of trance.

It is believed by the epic singers of the Turkic world that the spirits of the heroes attend a session of epic recital, and if the performance is a good one they are extremely gratified, if bad they become very angry.

Although this belief in divine inspiration is very common among Turkic epic singers, it must be pointed out here that the Turkic epic singer cultivates his art by arduous training and exercise through apprenticeship to a master (*usta*). This traditional master – apprentice system is still followed in Turkey.

Zhirmunsky writes as follows about the training of Uzbek singers of epic tales:

Central Asian tale-singers were professionally trained in their art. The most detailed information exists on the training and schools of Uzbek tale-singers. In early times many outstanding Uzbek *bakshy* were also teachers of poets (*ustoz*). The most prominent singer-teachers had several pupils at a time. Training lasted for two or three years and was free of charge; the teacher provided his pupils with food and clothing, the pupils helped the teacher about the house.

The young singers listened to the tales of their teacher and accompanied him on his trips to villages. At first, under

---

1 V.V. Radlov, *Proben der Volksliteratur der türkischen Stamme Südsibiriens*, V. Tiel, Der Dialekt der Kara-Kirgisen, St Petersburg 1885, xvi. (Quoted after D. Yıldırım.)
2 S. Kazmaz, 'The Theme of Initiation through Dream in Turkish Folk Literature', *ERDEM, Atatürk Kültür Merkezi*, Vol. 1, No. 1, January 1985.

the teacher's guidance, the pupils memorized the traditional passages of dastans and epic clichés, and at the same time learned how to recount the rest of the poem through their own improvisation. The end of the training was marked by a public examination: the pupil had to recite a whole dastan before a selected audience of tale-singers, after which he received the title of *bakshy* with the right to perform independently.[3]

Manas, the well-known Kirghiz epic, is the most remarkable Turkic epic as far as length, content and form are concerned. Dursun Yıldırım, a Turkish scholar who worked extensively on this work, writes as follows about its importance:

> The Manas epic cycle is comparable only to the *Iliad* and *Odyssey* of the Greeks, the *Kalevala* of the Finns, the *Mahabarata* of the Indians, the *Shahnama* of the Persians and *Jangar* of the Kalmuks as regards both length, content and poetic quality. It is longer, beyond any scale, than any of the above-mentioned epics.[4]

The same scholar informs us that the *Manas* epic is six times longer than the *Shahnama* and forty eight times longer than the *Iliad*. The Manas epic recounts the exploits of a Kirghiz hero in uniting the scattered Kirghiz tribes into a powerful state.

After this brief introduction to the Turkic epic, I now turn to the supernatural elements in the *Book of Dede Korkut* and *Köroghlu*.

II

The *Book of Dede Korkut*, consisting of twelve epic tales, recounting the heroic exploits of the Oghuz Turks, ancestors of the Turkish peoples of Turkey, survived in two sixteenth-century manuscripts, one of which came to light in the Dresden National Library in the early nineteenth century and the other in the Vatican Library in the twentieth century. The

---

3 V.M. Zhirmunsky and N. Chadwick, *Oral Epics of Central Asia*, Cambridge 1969, 330.
4 D. Yıldırım, 'Manas Destanı ve Köketay Hannıng Ertegüsü', unpublished dissertation, Ankara 1979, 16-7.

epic must have circulated in oral tradition for many centuries before it was written down and finally published in Turkey first in the old Arabic script in 1916 and later in the new Turkish alphabet i.e. in Latin characters in 1938. Numerous more recent editions, including a facsimile edition, have been made since then. It was translated into Russian in Baku in 1950, Italian in the Vatican in 1952, German in Zürich in 1958, and English in Texas, USA, in 1972.

The manuscript contains three pages in the form of an introduction listing a number of proverbs with no direct relation to the tales which are titled as follows: 1. 'The Story of Bugach Khan, Son of Dirse Khan' 2. 'The Sack of the House of Salur Kazan' 3. 'The Story of Bamsı Beyrek, Son of Kam Büre' 4. 'The Story of the Capture of Uruz Bey, Son of Kazan Bey' 5. 'The Story of Delü Dumrul, Son of Duha Khoja' 6. 'The Story of Kan Turalı, son of Kanlı Khoja' 7. 'The Story of Yigenek, Son of Kazılık Khoja' 8. 'The Story of Basat, Killer of the One-eyed Giant' 9. 'The Story of Emrem, Son of Begil' 10. 'The Story of Seghrek, Son of Ushun Khoja' 11. 'The Story of Salur Kazan's Captivity and his rescue by his son Uruz' 12. 'The Story of the Revolt of the Outer Oghuz against the Inner Oghuz and of the Death of Beyrek'.

The Vatican Ms[5] of the *Book of Dede Korkut* containing the introductory part and only six of the tales is believed to be a more carefully written text than the Dresden Ms.

Tales Nos. 2, 4, 7, 9, 10 and 11, all tales with political themes recounting the conflicts between the Oghuz and their neighbours are closely related to each other. Tale No. 12, describing an internal conflict within the Oghuz community, can also be classified as a political tale. Tales 3 and 6 can be called love stories in which the heroes risk their lives in daring exploits. Tale 1 is the story of a father led by some conspirators to kill his son. Tales 5 and 8, being of a mythological character, belong to a separate category altogether.

In the absence of any concrete evidence to help us in dating the compilation or creation of the *Book of Dede Korkut*, it is merely a matter of conjecture to say that the

---

5 E. Rossi, 'Un nuovo manoscritto del Kitab-i Dede Qorqut', *Estratto dalla Rivista degli Orientali*, 25 (1950), 34-43.

tales must have circulated in oral tradition for many centuries previous to the Oghuz people's acceptance of Islam in the tenth century. The two manuscripts, which are now almost universally accepted to have been written in the second half of the sixteenth century, are full of Islamic references. It is highly probable that, like *Beowulf*, for example, these tales were originally pagan but later went through a phase of Islamic transformation.

Contrary to the claims of some scholars, Islam is not merely a thin veneer in the *Book of Dede Korkut*, rather is its presence felt strongly throughout. Dede Korkut, after whom the tales are named, combines the functions of a shaman, advisor, name-giver, tribal wise man and preacher. He is often invited to officiate on ceremonial occasions. After the audience has heard of the heroic achievements of the Oghuz heroes, Dede Korkut exhorts the members of the audience to learn from their example, saying:

> Where now are the noble heroes who thought the world
> was theirs?
> Where are those men who once claimed the whole world?
> Now death has carried them off, and the earth concealed
> them.
> To whom the mortal world remains? The world where men
> come and go,
> The world which is rounded off with death.[6]

Most serious scholars are now unanimous in their evaluation of the religious sentiments expressed in the *Book of Dede Korkut*. They accept them as sincere, deep and pure.

Time and space allow me to present only a very brief treatment of some of the supernatural elements in this epic. The references to Gabriel, Adam, Satan, Noah, Abraham, Nimrod, Moses, Jennet and Jehennem in the tales hardly need any explanation. However, some of the more obscure supernatural references may require clarification.

In *Bogach Khan, Son of Dirse Khan*, the first tale in the epic, Dirse Khan is a childless lord in the Oghuz community

6 F. Sümer, A.E. Uysal and W.S. Walker eds., *The Book of Dede Korkut: A Turkish Epic*, Austin, Texas 1972, 114.

and he is stigmatized on that account. Many believed he was cursed and that Allah had condemned him to sterility. At the suggestion of his wife, Dirse Khan fed the poor, dressed the naked and gave a huge banquet and implored Allah to give him a son. Finally his wife bore him a male child. According to Oghuz tradition a male child was not given a name until he had performed some remarkable act. This child fought the king's bull and sent it crashing down with a blow directly to its forehead. He then severed the bull's head with his knife. This feat took place under the eyes of many lords. Therefore, Dede Korkut was called upon and the child was ceremoniously given the name *Bugach*, 'bull killer'. Bugach grew into a fine young man and succeeded to his father's throne. As a ruler he ignored his forty companions, who being thus offended planned a conspiracy against him. They told his old father Dirse Khan that his son Bugach had become a tyrant and that he was planning to destroy the Oghuz state. Upon this, Dirse Khan decided to kill his son during a hunting expedition, which he had specially arranged. Bugach was shot and seriously wounded by an arrow shot by his father. As he was left there bleeding, wild birds were trying to descend upon him to eat his flesh, but they were chased away by his dog. Soon, Hızır, riding upon his gray horse appeared, stroked his wound gently three times saying that an ointment made of his mother's milk and mountain flowers would heal it. He then disappeared.

Hızır,[7] the Islamic counterpart of St George, is the most popular saint in Islamic countries. Among the many roles he plays is that of rescuing people from disaster at the last minute when all hope has been abandoned.

When word reaches the hero's mother she comes upon the scene and addresses her son as follows:

7 For Hızır, see W.S. Walker and A.E. Uysal, 'An Ancient God in Modern Turkey: Some aspects of the cult of Hızır', *Journal of American Folklore*, Vol. 86, No. 341 (July-September, 1973), 286-9, *Tales alive in Turkey*, Cambridge (Mass.) 1966, 42-3, 210; P.N. Boratav, 'Türk Folklorunda Hızır', *Islam Ansiklopedisi*, 5, 463-71; I. Friedlaender, 'Khıdr', *Encyclopaedia of Religion and Ethics*, 7, 693-5; F.W. Hasluck, *Christianity and Islam under the Sultans*, 2 (ed. M.M. Hasluck), Oxford 1929, 315-36.

Your slit black eyes now taken by sleep — let them open.
Your strong healthy bones have been broken,
Your soul all but flown from your frame.
If your body retains any life, let me know.
Let my poor luckless head be a sacrifice to you.
Kazılık Mountain, your waters still flow;
Let them, I pray, cease their flowing.
Kazılık Mountain, your deer still run fast;
Let them cease running and turn into stone.
How can I know, my son, if it was lion
Or tiger? How can I know, my son?
How did this accident happen to you?
If your life is still in your body, my son, let me know.
Let my poor luckless head be a sacrifice to you.
Speak a few words to me now.[8]

In *The Sack of the House of Salur Kazan*, the second tale of the epic, there are lines which seem to bear testimony to certain important Turkish cults such as the tree, water and wolf cults. Here is the passage in which these references occur:

My beautiful home — oh, how did the enemy find you?
My big white tent is gone, and only the ground beneath it remains.
Now there is only the place my old mother used to sit.
Now only the target remains at which Uruz my son used to shoot.
Now quite empty is the square where the Oghuz once pranced their mounts.
Now only the hearth remains where once the black kitchen stood.

When Kazan saw his camp in this condition, his black eyes filled with bloody tears. His veins boiled, and his breath came in gasps. He spurred the flanks of his chestnut-brown horse and set off after the enemy. When he reached a stream, he said to himself: 'This water must have seen the face of Allah. Let me talk with it.' Let us hear what Kazan said to this stream:

8   *Book of Dede Korkut*, 18.

Oh, water that gushes from under the rocks!
Oh, water that tosses the ships made of wood!
Oh, water once sought by Hasan and Huseyin!
Oh, water, a treasure for gardens and vineyards!
Oh, water so cherished by Ayshe and Fatma;
Oh, water, the drink of all beautiful horses;
Oh, water drunk deeply by thirsty red camels;
Oh, water near which lie the flocks of white sheep.
Do you know what disaster has come to my camp? Oh, speak!

But how could the water inform him?

After he had crossed the stream, he met a wolf. He said to himself: 'This wolf has a blessed face. He may know. Let me speak to him.' Let us see what he said to the wolf:

When the night grows dark, then comes your day.
When it rains and snows, then you stand erect.
When big black stallions see you, they neigh.
When big red camels see you, they cry.
When you see some white sheep, you drive them along with your tail.
You destroy with your back the strong walls of the fold.
You carry away fat sheep two years old;
You swallow with greed their bloody tails.
You fight with the fierce barking dogs;
You make run through the night the shepherds who kindle their fires.
If you know what disaster has come to my camp, oh, speak!
May my luckless head be a sacrifice to you.[9]

The hero's invocation of water in the earlier part of the above quotation may be taken as traces of an ancient Turkish shamanistic water cult.[10] The ancient Turks held water to be a sacred element and worshipped rivers. For them drowning was believed to be an honourable form of death.

In their pre-Islamic, animistic period, the ancient Turks

9 *Ibid.*, 27-9.
10 See in this connection: A. Inan, 'Türklerde su kültü ile ilgili gelen-ekler', *Fuat Köprülü Armağanı*, Istanbul 1953, 249; *Samanizm*, 49. *Samanizm*, 49.

considered trees as sacred and some Turkish tribes traced their origin to trees. According to a Turkish myth, mankind grew out of a beech tree (father) and a hazelnut tree (mother). One night when a column of sacred light fell upon these trees, the hazelnut tree became pregnant. Nine months later a door opened in the trunk of this tree and from it jumped five babies.

The wolf was the official symbol of the Göktürk Empire founded by the Tu-kiu Dynasty. On the Göktürk standard there was a small emblem showing a wolf's head. In a fourteenth-century Oghuz legend written in Uigur script the Oghuz ruler is said to have been led by a gray wolf in his conquests.[11] Michael the Syrian Patriarch mentions that the Oghuz Turks under the Seljuk Dynasty in the eleventh century carried before them in their conquests of the Near East an animal resembling a dog, undoubtedly a wolf. Originally the official emblem of the Republic of Turkey carried a wolf's head along with the star and crescent, although this head later disappeared. In European literature, Atatürk himself was sometimes referred to as 'The Gray Wolf'. All Turkish tribes once called the wolf *boru* or *börü*, but, from the eleventh century onwards, the Oghuz used the word *kurt* instead. *Kurt* is also the name of the common earthworm, and the deliberate ambiguity here is probably brought about by a kind of word magic. Although admired as a Turkish totem, the wolf is also feared as a destroyer of flocks. By avoiding its real name and using instead the name of a harmless creature, the Turks must have hoped to keep him away.

As in most medieval and ancient legends, dreams have an important place in the *Book of Dede Korkut*. As told in Tale 7, *The Story of Yigenek, Son of Kazılık Khoja*, one day, Kazılık Khoja, a vizier of Baynındır Khan, the Oghuz ruler, was taken prisoner by the infidel commander of a castle on the Black Sea coast. This infidel was sixty yards tall and carried a huge club weighing sixty batmans. A rescue party headed by Yigenek, his son, and including some of the greatest Oghuz heroes was sent by the Oghuz ruler. During the night before

11 See the notes of wolf in the *Book of Dede Korkut*, 186.

the rescue operation Yigenek had a dream which he told his companions in the morning. This is the dream Yigenek told his friends in the tale:

O, beys, while asleep last night, this poor and unfortunate head of mine had a dream. When I opened my eyes, I saw the world crowded with heroes riding on gray-dappled horses. I took the white-helmeted heroes with me, and then I received advice from the white-bearded Dede Korkut. I crossed the long ranges of black mountains and reached a sea lying below me. There I built myself a boat and made a sail for it out of my shirt. I sailed through the sea lying under me. On the other side of the black mountains I saw a man whose head and forehead were shining. I rose and went toward him, holding my spear in my hand. I went and stood before him. When I was about to pierce him, I looked at him out of the corner of my eye and realized that he was my maternal uncle Emen. I greeted him and asked him who he was among the Oghuz. Lifting his eyes, he looked at me and asked, 'Yigenek, my son, where are you going?' I replied, 'I am going to Düzmürd Castle, where I have heard my father is imprisoned.' My uncle spoke to me as follows:

I once had seven warriors faster than the wind.
My warriors were like wolves out of the seven mountains.
My bowstring then was pulled by seven men
To shoot my beechen arrows with gold fins.
Winds blew, rains fell, and fog descended —
I tried to take that castle seven times, and then returned.
You cannot show more courage than I;
My Yigenek, turn back!

Yigenek in his dream spoke as follows to his uncle:

When you arose from where you sat,
You did not lead forth brown-eyed princely men with you;
You did not gallop out with well-known beys.
You must have taken mercenary troops for five akchas
    apiece,
And that is why you failed to take the fort.
He continued,

Stewed meat is good to eat, slice after slice.
A powerful horse is good in time of need.
Good luck is good while it lasts.
The mind is good if it does not forget;
And valour, too, is good if there is no retreating from the
    foe.[12]

This was a telepathic dream, because it turned out that
Yigenek's uncle Emen was not very far away. He soon joined
the party and the Oghuz warriors finally reached the Düzmürd
Castle.

Sleep and dream are among the important motifs in the
book. The Oghuz heroes have a reputation for sleeping long.
It is said that they often slept for seven days. *Küçük ölüm*,
'little death' was a synonym for sleep. Bamsı Beyrek in
Tale 3 and Salur Kazan in Tale 11 were captured while they
were asleep. In Tale 3, Segrek falls asleep at a most critical
moment and was awakened by his horse. In Tale 6, the narrator
states that in days gone by, most of the misfortunes of Oghuz
beys were the result of untimely sleep.[13] The heroes' falling
into long sleep is a frequently encountered motif in the tales
of other countries, too. Oghuz heroes are often warned about
important events through dreams. Salur Kazan's dream in
Tale 2 is a dream of this kind. It is a nightmare which comes
true:

> As it happened, Salur Kazan, the hope of the strong Oghuz
> people . . . had a dream that night. Waking up with a start,
> he said: 'My brother Kara Göne, do you know what I saw
> in my dream? It was a terrible dream. I saw my falcon
> dying in my hand. I saw a lightning bolt strike down my
> tent with the golden top. I saw a black cloud descending
> upon my camp. I saw mad wolves attacking my house. I
> felt the black camel biting my neck. I saw my black hair
> rise like spears and cover my eyes. I saw my ten fingers
> dipped in blood to my wrists. I wonder why I had such a
> dream? Ever since I had this dream I have been unable to
> think clearly. My brother khan come and interpret my
> dream for me.'

12 *Book of Dede Korkut*, 117-8.
13 *Ibid.*, 108.

Kara Göne said: 'What you say about a black cloud has to do with power. Snow and rain from such a cloud would mean troops. Hair represents sorrow, and blood means trouble. I cannot interpret the rest. May Allah interpret it.'[14]

What actually happened was that while he was hunting his own house was sacked by the troops of an infidel ruler.

No discussion of the supernatural would be complete without reference to the theme of bargaining with the Angel of Death, Azrail, in Tale 5, 'The Story of Delü Dumrul', Son of Duha Khoja', and to the fight with the One-eyed Giant (Tepegöz) in Tale 8, 'The Story of Basat, Killer of the One-eyed Giant'.

Tale 5, 'The Story of Delü Dumru', is obviously a variant of the story of Admetus and Alcestis. In the Greek myth Hercules wrestles with Thanatos, the Angel of Death and, winning, saves the life of his friend's wife. In the Turkish tale, Delü Dumrul, 'Dumrul the Mad', decides to put an end to Azrail's terrorizing people and taking their lives, so he declares openly that he would fight with him. One day Azrail comes quite unnoticed and asks Delü Dumrul to deliver his life to him. Delü Dumrul tries to reason with him and asks if there is a way out. Azrail suggests that there is only one way out, namely to find somebody else who is willing to give his life as a substitute. He goes to his parents, but they refuse to sacrifice their lives for their son. He finally appeals to his wife who agrees to give her life to save her husband. This is reported to Azrail but he is not pleased with the arrangement. He takes the lives of the parents and grants 140 years to Delü Dumrul and his wife. I suppose Azrail showed this generosity, not for the sake of Delü Dumrul, whose behaviour towards his parents can never be considered a noble gesture in any culture, but for his deep sympathy for his wife, who gave a perfect example of love and loyalty to a man even though he did not deserve it. As portrayed in this tale Delü Dumrul does not display exemplary behaviour fitting an Oghuz hero. He may be forgiven, perhaps,

14 *Ibid.*, 27.

on one point. His motive is a noble one, as he wants to save mankind from the curse of death once and for all; but the means he employs is far from being noble and honest.

The second supernatural element in these tales is a theme also found in Greek mythology i.e. the fight with the One-eyed Giant (Cyclops). Similarities between the Turkish Tepegöz (the One-eyed Giant) and Homer's Polyphemus in Book IX of the *Odyssey* are obvious. The direction of the borrowing is controversial. It cannot be argued, of course, that all tales of one-eyed giants derive from the Polyphemus story and that other models did not exist for the giant called Tepegöz. There are examples of similar monsters in ancient oriental legends some of which may well precede Homer and Hesiod. See for example S. Thompson and J. Balys, *Motif and Type Index of the Oral Tales of India*, Bloomington 1958, Motifs F512.1.1 and F31.1.1. Even more closely related to the Turkish tradition is Dua (Dev) the One-eyed Mongol character whose exploits are narrated in the opening lines of the Secret History of the Mongols.[15]

III

The *Köroghlu* is a more popular epic tale than the *Book of Dede Korkut*, which is now considered a subject fit for scholarly study rather than for public recitation on the occasion of such social events as village weddings and minstrel gatherings. Although some traces of the Dede Korkut tales are still found in many living Turkish folktales, they are no longer a part of the repertory of Turkish minstrels, whereas The *Köroghlu* is still narrated to the accompaniment of the *saz*, the six-stringed national musical instrument. The tradition of narrating long epic tales and tales of romantic adventure is still alive, particularly in such eastern provinces as Kars and Erzurum. A village wedding without a minstrel reciting traditional tales would be unthinkable in those provinces.

Among the Turkish folk heroes, Köroghlu, the chivalrous outlaw, occupies a very prominent place; few Turkish folk

15 A. Waley trans., *The Secret History of the Mongols*, London 1963, 217.

heroes stir sentiments as deeply as he does. Like Robin Hood, Köroghlu for many Turks stands as a symbol of freedom and defiance of arbitrary authority. Köroghlu is by no means a simple bandit. He is an embodiment of some of the highest Turkish ideals: physical strength, courage, charity, courtesy, manliness and honour. Like Robin Hood and Rob Roy, he is the protector of the oppressed and the enemy of the tyrant. Like them he robs from the rich in order to give to the poor. What makes him a very unusual hero is that he is a *saz*-playing minstrel who frequently resorts to verse in his dealings with both friends and enemies. Köroghlu is a compound name formed from *kör*, 'blind man' and *oghlu*, 'son of', i.e. literally, he is 'the son of the blind man'.

Originally called Rushen Ali, he was renamed after his father, a groom, who was blinded for failing to carry out the orders of his master, the Bey of Bolu. He had been ordered to find a high-bred colt for him, while, instead, he brought home a mangy colt. This was taken as a serious insult and in punishment he was blinded, by having red-hot skewers driven through his eyeballs, and dismissed with the worthless colt he had brought with him. The blinded groom and his son Rushen Ali depart with the colt. The groom had reason to believe that the colt he had chosen was going to grow into an extremely good horse. Let us continue with the rest of the story from the mouth of Sergeant Hasan, the town crier (Tellal Mehmet Chavush), a man of seventy five, from the town of Nallıhan, not far from the Köroghlu Mountain, in the province of Bolu. He narrated to me the very beginning of the epic 'How Köroghlu became an outlaw', right in the middle of a field. Here is his account:

> When Köroghlu's father reached home, he said to his son, 'Build four walls here.' After Köroghlu had built the four walls, his father said, 'Now cover these four walls with a roof so that not even a single ray of sunshine can penetrate it.'
>
> The horse was put in this dark stable, and there it was groomed for six months. After that time had passed, Köroghlu's father ordered that a field be plowed twelve times and watered after each plowing. After this was done,

he ordered Köroghlu to mount the horse and ride through the plowed field. When Köroghlu had done this and returned, his father felt the horse's hoofs with his hands, but he was not satisfied with what he felt there.

'There must be a leak in some corner of the stable', he said to Köroghlu. 'This horse must be kept in complete darkness in the stable for another six months.' Köroghlu found the place in the roof where a small amount of light leaked and fixed it. Then he cared for the horse for another six months.

At the end of that time, his father ordered that the field be again plowed and watered twelve times. Köroghlu then mounted the horse and rode around the field several times, jumped over a high wall, and returned to his father, who again felt the horse's hoofs with his hands. This time he was satisfied, for he found some dry earth on the hoofs and knew that the horse had been able to reach down through the mud to the firm earth.

'As long as you have this horse', he told Köroghlu, 'nobody can defeat you. Now I want you to go and take my revenge against Bolu Bey.'[16]

What made Kirat, the Gray Horse, a remarkable animal was that it was sired by a sea stallion (*deniz kulunu*). He understood his master's speech and actually talked with him. He warned him of approaching danger. He could fly like a bird. He was immortal. In fact, Köroghlu himself was immortal, too, because he purposely drank the *abu hayat*, 'water of life', given him by Hızır, the Turkish counterpart of St George, as already mentioned in connection with the epic of Dede Korkut. This elixir, called *abu hayat*, was to be administered to his father's eyes, but Köroghlu could not resist the temptation of drinking it himself, as in this way he would acquire superhuman power which he needed to exact revenge for his father from the Bey of Bolu. While drinking this elixir he spilled part of it on his horse making him immortal, too.

Taking the Gray Horse and 365 warriors with him, Köroghlu built a castle at Chamlıbel in the Köroghlu Mountains for

16 Uysal and Walker, *op. cit.* (1966), 193-4.

himself and his companions. From this base he carried out raids on the territories of the Governor of Bolu, his father's former master, and the man who had blinded him. He robbed caravans, went on hunting expeditions and engaged in amorous pursuits. He possessed many of the attributes of a medieval knight. He was a hero of the days of man to man combat with sword and shield. He is said to have stated that the days of heroism and bravery were over with the invention of the 'iron pipe', as he called the rifle. He disappeared mysteriously. It is said that he joined the Forty Saints and still lives in their company since he has gained immortality, having drunk the Water of Life, and that his horse Kırat is also with him.

IV

In conclusion, I would like to express the view that, like other types of folklore, the epic tale is also waging a struggle for survival against the motion picture and television. Perhaps something can be done to save the epic if the cooperation of some television producers can be engaged. Surely, there must be at least a few sufficiently imaginative, easily convertible, sensitive people in the profession somewhere, people who can appreciate the power, beauty and mystery of this ancient means of entertainment and education. The supernatural element in the epic has great appeal to all kinds of audiences, be they naïve or sophisticated. In a way, these elements of the epic provide the same kind of excitement and create the same spell as science fiction does. Great actions expressed in forceful language will always produce vibrations deep in the heart of man.

EPIC TRANSMISSION AND ADAPTATION: A FOLK RĀMĀYAṆA IN SOUTH INDIA

STUART H. BLACKBURN

(University of California, Berkeley)

Introductory

Folk epics are not without a certain ambiguity, an ambivalence of a marked category. Of all the major narrative genres, epic is that least associated with folk tradition; rather, it has been considered a literary form, so much so that even folklorists have argued that the folk epic only develops from contact with writing.[1] That position may be overstated, but the role of literary tradition and written models in the emergence of a folk epic can also be easily underestimated. This uneasy status of the folk epic is revealed in the curious fact that the major theoretical advance in its study was made in an effort to settle an issue in Homeric scholarship. In truth, we know very little about what distinguishes folk and classical epics, or what might unite them.

Nowhere is the ambiguity of the folk epic more patently clear than in the *Kalevala*. Its unclear boundaries between oral and written compositions, folk and classical forms, were controversial when Elias Lönnrot first created the epic and they continue to stir folkloristic debate even today.[2] For most scholars who (like myself) study the folk epic in other parts of the world, the *Kalevala* thus represented the extreme case of fabrication; but a more accuate view, I believe, is that

---

1 See Ruth Finnegan, *Oral Poetry: Its Nature, Significance, and Social Context*, Cambridge 1977, 22-4, 160-8; Ruth Finnegan, *Oral Literature in Africa*, Oxford 1970, 108-10; D. Tedlock, *The Spoken Word and the Work of Interpretation*, Philadelphia 1983, 250; J. Opland, *Xhosa Oral Poetry*, Cambridge 1983, 143-6, 232.

2 See A. Dundes, 'Nationalistic Inferiority Complexes and the Fabrication of Fakelore: A Reconsideration of Ossian, the *Kinder- und Hausmärchen*, the *Kalevala*, and Paul Bunyan', in *Journal of Folklore Research* Vol. 22, 1 (1985), 5-18.

its ambiguity, far from being idiosyncratic, is actually sympto-
matic of the folk epic. A combination of oral and written
compositions, and the associated political, ideological questions
— For whom does the epic speak? Who controls its dissemina-
tion? — are characteristic of other folk epics, though often
less visible.[3] A consideration of them leads not to the unusual
but to the typical.

These issues have particular salience in a complex culture
like India that has produced (and continues to produce)
epics in all shapes and sizes, and has transmitted them by every
possible combination of oral and written media. Until very
recently, epic in India meant the two great Sanskrit epics, the
Rāmāyaṇa and the *Mahābhārata*, but now we know that
these are only a small fraction of the total epic tradition in
India. Good textual and contextual data is available on a
dozen folk epics, less complete reports on another dozen,
and more are being reported.[4] None of these folk epics in
regional languages has the pan-Indian reach of the Sanskrit
epics (through their translations in regional languages), but
some cover thousands of square miles and require hundreds
of hours to perform; as historical chronicle, or story entertainment, or religious cult, all play an extraordinary cultural
role in their regions and localities.

The relations between these folk epics and the Sanskrit
epics are varied. Some have no significant link with the pan-

---

3 The ideological dimensions of Indian oral epics are discussed in
   V. Narayana Rao, 'Epics and Ideologies: Six Telugu Folk Epics',
   in *Another Harmony: New Essays on the Folklore of India*, eds.
   S.H. Blackburn and A.K. Ramanujan, Berkeley 1986, 131-65.
4 For overviews of the Sanskrit epics, see B. van Nooten, 'The
   Two Sanskrit Epics' in *Heroic Epic and Saga: An Introduction to
   the World's Great Folk Epics*, ed. F. Oinas, Bloomington 1978,
   49-75; J.D. Smith, 'Old Indian: The Two Sanskrit Epics' in *Tradi-
   tions of Heroic and Epic Poetry*, ed. A.T. Hatto, London 1980,
   48-78. On Indian oral epics, see the essays in *The Oral Epic in
   India*, eds. S.H. Blackburn, P.J. Claus, Joyce B. Flueckiger, Susan
   S. Wadley (forthcoming); Brenda Beck, *The Three Twins: The
   Telling of a Folk Epic in South India*, Bloomington 1982; G.H.
   Roghair, *The Epic of Palnāḍu, A Study and Translation of the
   Palnāṭi Vīrula Katha*, Oxford 1982.

Indian epics, but many do. Of the latter folk epics, some are sequels to the Sanskrit epics, whose heroes and heroines are reincarnated to carry on the business left unfinished in the earlier telling. Even if they are sequels, however, the folk epic stories are often entirely unrelated to the Sanskrit epics; the folk hero may be identified as Rāma who battles someone identified as Rāvaṇa (as in the *Rāmāyaṇa*), but the resemblance extends no further. Another group of folk epics, however, is more substantially linked to the Sanskrit ones; they do not continue the action (as the sequels do), they repeat it (like a re-run). For some as yet unknown reason these folk epics (in Southeast Asia as well as in India) are very often in dramatic form, dance-drama or shadow puppetry.

These drama forms are consciously understood by performers and audiences as reproductions of the Sanskrit epics. Herein lies the ambiguity: are these folk epics or classical epics? If they are folk 'variants' of the Sanskrit epics, what relation does this signify between folk and classical epic? Performers, audiences, patrons, and settings are certainly folk, but how do these local traditions retain their link to the Sanskrit epics? These problems are recognizably those associated with the *Kalevala*, but with a fundamental difference: the process of epic formation has been reversed. In the Indian examples, we are concerned not with how a 'folk' epic was transformed into a literary epic, but with how a literary epic has been transmitted and adapted to a folk setting.

In the specific case discussed in this essay, the processes of transmission and adaptation are unusually transparent. Briefly stated, a medieval, classical Rāmāyaṇa has been transferred almost verbatim to a village-based tradition of shadow puppetry. This remarkably close textual correspondence between the classical source text and the modern folk text draws a sharp line between them and throws into bold relief other forms of divergence. Whereas most models of epic formation discussed in the literature — compilation, expansion, fragmentation — turn on the alteration of textual material, the example at hand illustrates a process of epic development that has taken other, non-textual forms.[5]

Classical Text and Folk Tradition

Sometime between 885 and 1185 A.D. in the Tanjore area of Tamil-speaking South India (see map, p. 590), a court poet named Kampaṉ composed a Rāmāyaṇa of approximately 40,000 lines in Tamil.[6] Kampaṉ's epic, although heavily indebted to the Vālmīki Rāmāyaṇa, is neither a translation nor an imitation of that earlier Sanskrit work. As leading Brahmin scholars first declared when they heard Kampaṉ sing it, and as Indian and Western scholars have reiterated, it is the finest narrative poem in the two thousand years of Tamil literature.

Yet, the history of Kampaṉ's Rāma story – its composition, transmission, and performance – is virtually unknown. We may infer from the existence of several versions of the text in palm-leaf manuscripts, before these were conflated into authoritative editions beginning in the 1930s, that the classical epic had circulated through different channels in various parts of South India.[7] It also appears that Kampaṉ's epic influenced the composition of classical Rāmāyaṇas in other Dravidian languages (particularly Kannada and Malayalam).[8] Very possibly its popularity is linked to the curious

---

5 These models of epic formation are discussed in J. de Vries, *Heroic Song and Heroic Legend*, trans. by B.J. Timmer, London 1963, 250-66; Wm. F. Hansen, 'The Homeric Epics and Oral Poetry' in *Heroic Epic and Saga: An Introduction to the World's Great Folk Epics*, ed. Felix Oinas, Bloomington 1978, 14-5; Merle Simmons, 'The Spanish Epic' in Oinas, *op. cit.*, 228-32; J.W. Johnson, 'On the Heroic Age and other Primitive Theses', *Folklorica: Festschrift for Felix J. Oinas*, eds. Egle Victoria Zygas and P. Voorheis, Bloomington 1982, 121-38.

6 On Kampaṉ, see K. Zvelebil, *The Smile of Murugan*, Leiden 1973, 207-17.

7 The first complete commentary on Kampaṉ was by Vai. Mu. Kōpālakirusnamāccāriyār (1928); references in this essay are to the Kampaṉ edition with commentary by Ti. K. Cupparāya Ceṭṭiyār (1937).

8 Malayalam Rāmāyanas influenced by Kampan include *Rāmacaritram* and *Rāma Katta Pāṭṭu*; see K.M. George, *Rāmacaritram and the Study of Early Malayalam*, Kottayam 1966; P.K. Narayana Pillai, *Rāma Katta Pāṭṭu*, Kottayam 1970.

proliferation of Rāma temples in the Tanjore area that dates from Kampan's time;[9] no doubt the epic was recited as liturgy in some of those temples and commented upon in a form of stylized, public discourse (in which one or two verses are sung and then elucidated for several hours), a practice that continues even today. The only hard evidence, however, is a fourteenth-century A.D. inscription from a temple in the Kannada country that mentions the recitation of the epic.[10]

In the face of this near-total ignorance, it is of extraordinary importance that the Kampan text is still preserved in a folk tradition in central Kerala.[11] Throughout Palghat District and contiguous parts of Trichur and Malappuram districts, it is performed as part of a leather shadow puppet play held in local temples of the goddess Bhagavati. The text, accompanied by a voluminous commentary, is recited by a small group of men as a ritual presented for the goddess; the puppet play performances are held overnight (10 p.m. to 5 a.m.) and continue from a minimum of eight nights to a maximum of twenty-one nights.

The history of this folk tradition is as obscure as that of Kampan's epic. Tamil scholars have managed to dig up stray references to a leather puppet play (tol-pāva-kūttu) in old Tamil poetry, but any connection to the present folk tradition in Kerala is conjectural.[12] Whether the art of puppetry (practised in five neighbouring states) was found in Kerala before the arrival of Kampan's text or was developed in order to present it, and how and when the text and folk art reached

---

9 See R. Champalaksmi, *Vaisnava Iconography in the Tamil Country*, New Delhi 1981, 273-6.

10 T.P. Meenaksisundaram, *Tamiḻum Pirapanpātum*, Madras 1973, 28-9.

11 My field research on the Kerala shadow puppet tradition was conducted for three months in 1984 and five months in 1985, and was supported by a Senior Fulbright Fellowship of the Council for the International Exchange of Scholars.

12 See M. Arunachalam, 'Vindication of T.K.C.'s Reconstruction of the Valin Episode', in *Proceedings of the Fifth International Conference-Seminar of Tamil Studies, Madurai*, ed. by M. Arunachalam, Madras 1981, 86-105; S. Ramaswamy, 'Tamiḻaka Tolpāvaniḻal Kūttu', Ph. D. Dissertation, Madurai University 1978, 21-3.

Kerala, are all unanswered questions. Other research on
South India shadow puppet traditions has indicated that this
folk art is connected to the movement of Marathi armies to
South India in the seventeenth and eighteenth centuries
since most contemporary performers of the art are Marathi
speakers.[13] But the Kerala tradition seems to have followed
a different line of development since its performers speak
a mixture of Tamil and Malayalam (and sing in them).

Unfortunately the limited literature on the Kerala folk
tradition has done little to clarify this obscurity. By focusing almost exclusively on the puppets themselves (production,
iconography, and theatrical role, and so forth) the text has
been ignored.[14] But the text is our surest link to the historic
past. From a comparison between the text performed by the
puppeteers in Kerala and the printed editions of Kampaṉ, we
can say that folk text follows the classical text very closely.

Not all of Kampaṉ's 10,000 verses are sung in performance. Instead, the puppeteers commonly sing either 1,400
verses (if the story is begun from the Araṇya Kāṇḍa) or 825
verses (if begun from the Yuddha Kāṇḍa); in rare instances
when the full story is performed, a little more than 2,000
verses are sung. In any form of performance, approximately
90% of the verses are borrowed directly from Kampaṉ (the
remainder are discussed later in this paper). Of these, more
than half correspond letter-by-letter with the Kampaṉ verse,
the only difference being a systematic change from indirect
to direct speech. In other verses, the puppeteers might sing a
new word or phrase, or occasionally an entire line.

The verses sung in the folk tradition correspond to the
classical text not only in wording, but in sequence as well. To
illustrate both, we may compare the shadow puppeteers'

13 See J. GoldbergBelle, *Tōlubommalāṭa: The Andhra Shadow Puppet
    Theatre*, Ph. D. Dissertation, University of Wisconsin, Madison
    1984, 185ff.
14 See K.B. Iyer, 'The Shadow Play in Malabar' in *Bulletin of the
    Rama Varma Research Institute*, Vol. 11, 1 (1936[1971]), 3-12;
    M.D. Raghavan, *Folkplays and Dances of Kerala*, Trichur 1947;
    F. Seltmann, 'Schattenspiel in Kerala', in *Bijdragen tot Taal-Land,
    en Volkenkunde* 128 (1972), 458-90; C. Ravindran, 'Kirusṇaṉ
    Kuṭṭi Pulavar', *Yātra* 37 (1982), 8-20.

version of one episode with the standard Kampaṉ version of the same episode. Choosing the *nakar niṉku paṭalam* episode as an example (see chart below), we find that the puppeteers sing only 39 of the 327 verses in Kampaṉ's text.[15] And these 39 verses have not been selected at random. Skipping the first two verses in Kampaṉ (which set the scene), the folk performers sing the following four in sequence, skip the next verse, sing the following verse, skip seven in a row, sing the following two (in reverse order), etc.

The general pattern is that the folk tradition tends to omit verses that are descriptive (of persons, places, or mental states) and to select those with speech or action. The latter verses normally occur in small clusters (of two, three, or four verses) which the folk text preserves, skipping the many verses between the clusters. This pattern is followed by all five performing troupes which I observed. In addition, these troupes show very little variation in either the wording or sequencing of the verses they sing. There is, however, some variation in which verses a given troupe will sing on a given night; that is, they do not all sing exactly the same 39 verses when they present the *nakar niṉku patalam*. But when they do sing the same verse, they do so with the same words and in the same sequence.

This degree of accuracy in textual transmission and standardization of performance suggests written records. Indeed, from the particular pattern by which the folk text has followed the classical epic, one is led to conclude that some person(s) actually sat down with a manuscript of the Kampaṉ epic and deliberately adapted it to the shadow puppet play. Today some troupes do possess palm-leaf manuscripts of the performed verses, and some own printed editions of Kampaṉ. But more important and common are handwritten (pen on paper) notebooks which are recopied and passed on to young learners. The learners then read and memorize the verses, practice them orally, and then recall them by reference to the first two syllables of the initial line of each verse. Many

---

15 This particular episode usually covers most of one night's performance.

young singers also write out these syllables on a cardboard
sheet for easy reference during the long and exhausting performances that continue night after night. Accuracy of transmission is also ensured by the presence of a senior puppeteer
in each troupe who sometimes proves more infallible than
any written record.[16] Accurate transmission is also demanded
by the ritual function of the shadow puppet performance,
and this brings us to context.

Adaptation to Folk Context

Textual reproduction is only one aspect of transmission;
the other is what takes place when the reproduced text is
performed within a new context. Here transmission involves
adaptation. But this adaptation does not necessary alter the
text itself (although that is possible); rather, by simply framing and embedding the preserved text, the new context produces even more fundamental shifts in meaning. Adaptation
in the Kerala shadow puppet play occurs in five primary
forms, each a layer of the folk tradition, as illustrated below:

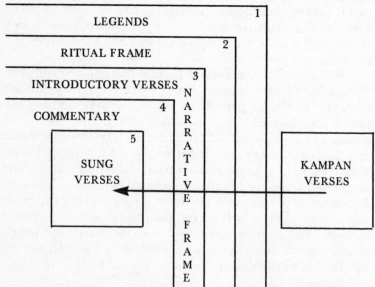

---

16 Even if (as often happens) this senior puppeteer is half-asleep, a
    mistaken or garbled line sung by the others will bring him quickly
    to his feet to correct the error.

Folk and Classical Versions (*Nakar Niṅku Paṭalam*)

Folk	Kampaṉ	Comment
1	3	folk skips first 2 verses in Kampaṉ
2	4	minor changes in first two lines
3	5	meaning altered by shift in single word
4	6	verbatim
5	8	minor alteration
6	15	substitution of single word
7	18	verbatim
8	26	verbatim
9	25	verbatim
10	—	new verse
11	—	new verse
12	32	verbatim
13	33	two words changed
14	44	verbatim
15	45	verbatim
16	48	verbatim
17	49	verbatim (spelling of single word differs)
18	57	verbatim
19	58	verbatim
20	59	verbatim
21	117	verbatim; note folk skips 58 verses
22	121	verbatim
23	122	verbatim
24	127	verbatim
25	128	verbatim
26	133	verbatim
27	134	verbatim
28	138	new first line
29	150	verbatim
30	151	two words changed
31	165	verbatim
32	166	new last line
33	221	verbatim; note folk skips 55 verses
34	222	verbatim
35	224	verbatim
36	225	verbatim
37	226	verbatim
38	231	verbatim
39	232	verbatim

233 to 237 omitted in folk tradition

As I will attempt to demonstrate, each layer acts as an interpretative frame for the transmitted classical epic text and for
the other levels contained within it. Cumulatively, then, the
folk tradition as a whole provides an interpretive framework
for the classical epic that it has absorbed.

The first layer, the extreme outer frame of the folk tradition,
consists of cultural perceptions and expectations of it: of
Kampaṉ, his text, the puppeteers, their gurus (*pulavar*), etc.
The most fundamental of these perceptions are those about
Kampaṉ and his text which, in setting forth perspectives on
the origins of the tradition, influence all other perspectives.
These perceptions are most developed in a series of folk
legends that are current today in oral tradition in Kerala.
Time permits us to consider only a few of them and those
only briefly.[17]

The dominant theme in these Kampaṉ legends is the classical poet as a 'man of the common people'. In part this
portrayal stems from the fact that Kampaṉ composed in
Tamil and not in Sanskrit (known only through special
training and restricted to Brahmins), and also because his
own language is relatively accessible. But folk tradition has
told its own tales about Kampaṉ. Perhaps the best known
describes Kampaṉ's defense of his composition by appeal to
colloquial speech (see Appendix). When a fellow poet questioned the usage of a particular word, Kampaṉ led his rival
and a party of kings and patrons to a village where, with
some magical assistance from a goddess, he showed them a
hut and inside a woman, who used the disputed word. In
another legend, a woodcutter (and would-be-poet) entered
the assembly of court poets and began to recite. When the
other poets scoffed at his incoherent mutterings (and in
Tamil they are complete nonsense), Kampaṉ stepped forward
and explained how each phrase could be construed as metrical
verse, thereby displaying his own prosodic skill. Elsewhere
the poet is a gallant lover of many women, a cook, and a

---

17 Some of these legends are discussed in Cu. Turaicuvāmi Piḷḷai,
   Tamiḻar Nāvaḻar Caritai, Madras 1949 and Me. Vī. Veṇukōpāla
   Piḷḷai, *Vinota Mañcāri*, Madras 1953.

brother of a barber (near-Untouchable caste). In yet another story, Kampan plays the role of folk healer using his verses as a charm to revive a child killed by a snake-bite.

All this stands in contrast to the portrait of Kampan developed in classical sources and scholarship. In this literature he is a 'saint' (*ālvār*, lit. 'deep-one'), a devotee of Visnu and his *avatāra* Rāma; his poem is certified not by the common speech of village women, but by rigorous examination from Brahmin scholars in wealthy temples.[18] In developing their image of Kampan, the folk legends represent the essential role of the adaptive process: they do not actually change the original identity of Kampan as a classical poet (for this would rob the folk tradition of prestige), but only enlarge upon it, presenting him as more than a poet, as a person and a personality.

Another group of legends enlarges on the image of Kampan in the opposite direction, by presenting the poet as a form of the god Śiva. Once, when the goddess Laksmi was guardian of the treasury of the gods, she became haughty and was cursed to be reborn as a guard in the palace of Rāvana (demon king and enemy of Rāma) where she spent many years. When Rāma's army approached, she tried to prevent the entrance of a monkey general who slapped her with his powerful tail and brought her spiritual liberation (*moksa*) in Śiva's heaven. But there she complained to Śiva: 'I spent so many years in Rāvana's palace and now will miss the chance to see that demon killed by Rāma.' Śiva replied that he would grant her a vision of Rāvana's death, and not just once but repeatedly: she would be reborn again, this time as goddess Bhagavati and he as Kampan, whose epic of Rāma would be enacted for her every year in her temples.

A second and equally popular variant of this legend provides another reason for the goddess' absence at the original death of Rāvana: she herself was away killing another demon (Mahisāsura). She then appeals to Śiva who grants her the boon as in the first variant. In both variants, Śiva is then born to a childless woman who has practiced bodily austerities in a

---

18 The 'orthodox' biography of Kampan can be found in several sources, see for example, *Kalai Kalañciyam* 3 (1966) and A.K. Naidu, *kaviccakkaravartti Kampar Varalāru*, Madras 1963.

temple. But, because her husband is away at the birth, she abandons the child to avoid scandal; the child is found in the temple courtyard at the base of a pole (*kampu*) from which he is given the name 'Kampaṇ'. Kampaṇ composes his Rāmāyana, which is performed as a shadow puppet play for the goddess Bhagavati so that she can finally witness and rejoice in the death of Rāvāna.

This second group of legends thus adapts the image of the classical poet and his composition more directly into the local context. They explain that Kampaṇ was born, his epic composed and then transformed into the shadow puppet play to fulfil a boon given to the goddess (Laksmi/Bhagavati) by Śiva in order that she be pleased by sight of Rāvāna's death. And this is precisely how Kampaṇ's story of Rāma is performed in Kerala today — as a form of worship to Bhagavati who watches the spectacle from inside her temple.

This performance context and its ritual frame is the second level of adaptation. Here the classical text is presented in a particular fashion: the transformations are not narrative, but performative. At present, the shadow puppet play is enacted in at least one hundred Bhagavati temples in central Kerala as part of the temple's annual festival. At each site a special building (*kūttu maṭam*) has been constructed for the performance; it is set apart from the main temple complex, but linked to it by a series of rituals conducted on each of the several nights of performance. About 10 p.m. each night, after a number of other rituals, a flame is brought from the temple's central oil-lamp to the puppet stage by a procession of officials, patrons, and singers. At the puppet stage, it is used to light the many smaller lamps inside the building whose flames cast the puppets' shadows on a white cloth that hangs from the roof and separates the puppeteers inside the building from the audience on the outside. After the goddess (in the form of her medium) blesses the performance, the small crowd of on-lookers disperses and the play proper begins. From that point (around 10.30 p.m.) until five o'clock sharp the following morning, as the puppeteers manipulate the leather puppets, sing the Kampaṇ verses and comment on them, the only audience is Bhagavati herself who sits at a small distance inside her temple.[19]

As mentioned earlier, the shadow puppet play may begin at two or three different points in the Rāma story, depending on how many nights it is to continue in a particular temple (which in turn depends on the extent of local patronage). However, the play always concludes the series of nights on the same event (as requested by the goddess): the death of Rāvaṇa and the coronation of Rāma. Here, again, the classical text has not been altered for this is the conclusion of Kampaṉ's epic, too. But these events are not just story; they are the ritual culmination of several weeks of a temple festival. In thus transforming a classical epic into a ritual instrument, the folk tradition produces more far-reaching changes than it would by narrative alterations. The linear end-point of a narrative has become the centre point of a complex; when the story ends, it does not simply break off into everyday reality but resonates within.

This ritual function of the shadow puppet play affects also the actual frame for the narrative, the third level of adaptation. This narrative frame consists of two parts, placed at either end of the performance; each is intended to win the favour of the goddess and is approximately one hour in length. The first part of the frame is a long series of verses sung at the very beginning of a night's performance; the second part, the closure of each performance, is a repetition of a single verse for each and every person who contributed a few rupees to the performance. The present analysis considers only the first part of this narrative frame.

These introductory verses begin with two praise-poems to Gaṇapati (elephant-faced god and remover of obstacles), followed by several others to various gods and goddesses (including the particular Bhagavati in the temple), a verse thanking sponsors of the night's performance (who contribute hundreds of rupees), and finally a prose segment that

19 This curious fact — that through the long night performances there is no human audience (save at a few temple sites where the festival has become a fair that keeps a crowd all night) — indicates an extreme example of performance as ritual act.

recapitulates the previous action as background to the episodes sung that night. Following directly on the prose summary is the narrative itself which begins when the puppeteers sing the first verse and then comment upon it in a pattern that will continue without interruption until the next morning.

Within this introductory string of verses are several examples of performative adaptation; two seem significant. The first concerns the identity of the singers: although the puppeteers who actually sing the verses are non-Brahmins, the puppets on the screen who are presented as singing them are Brahmins. In the center of the screen is fixed a puppet of Gaṇapati who is flanked by two Brahmin puppets singing the introductory verses as part of a ritual conducted to him. In this way, the larger ritual frame of the temple festival (level two) is recreated on a smaller scale within the performance of the Rāma story. Even more importantly, this framing voice gives the puppet performance a status it would not otherwise enjoy. While performances are a central ritual in temple festivals, the tradition has a relatively low status; its singers and patrons are from middle-level castes and the puppet stage itself is carefully set outside the temple compound. By contrast, other performing arts are enacted within the temple by Brahmins and other high castes.

In other words, the folk tradition must compensate for its low status by reintroducing the Brahminical sanction which Kampaṉ's text originally had but loses in the hands and mouths of the puppeteers. The legitimizing Brahmins, however, have become 'puppets' who confer status only within the stage, that portion of the total tradition over which the puppeteers have most control. Again, adaptation is interpretive rather than substantive; more consequential than altering the text is controlling the identity of those who present it.

The other adaptation in the introductory verses that frame the performance concerns not who speaks, but what is said. Many of the prefatory verses invoking deities are drawn not from Kampaṉ but from oral tradition; by naming various local gods and goddesses, they fix the performance firmly in the local context. But a more subtle effect is achieved by a verse which is borrowed from the classical epic. In translation it reads:

There is wealth, wisdom and fame
with Lakṣmi's lotus smile,
and even a path to salvation.
For those who tell of Rāma's strong shoulders
when he destroyed the demons' great armies
and wore the *vākai* victory flower.

This verse is an example of a convention common to most traditional literature in India and known in Tamil as 'benefit [gained from] the text' (*nūl payaṉ*). It is used in both Kampaṉ and the shadow puppet performance with the same intention, in the same introductory position, and with precisely the same wording. Even the oral commentary given by the puppeteers agrees with the classical commentary in its essential points. Yet this accurate transmission of the classical text does not preclude its adaptation in extra-textual forms. The verse is borrowed verbatim from Kampaṉ, but it is given special attention: because it is sung in the introduction to every performance, it is sung more frequently than any other verse borrowed from Kampaṉ; it is the first verse learned by a student; it is often placed at the head of palm-leaf and hand-written manuscripts used by the puppeteers; some written folk texts use it as a heading for each division in the narrative. Moreover, during performance, it is delivered in an unusual style when all the performers join together and sing in a high pitch, followed by a long, dramatic pause before they move on to the next verse in the introductory string.

In short, this verse has become an epigram for the folk Rāmāyaṇa. It tells the essence of the story — that Rāma kills Rāvaṇa (and wore the *vākai* flower) — and carries the promise that those who tell (and listen) to it will achieve life's goals. The verse does this in the classical text as well, but the folk tradition develops it performatively, by repetition, by vocal style, and by emphasis. Through these means, the verse has come to function as a condensed commentary upon the text from which it was taken; in its small way, it illustrates the more general relation of folk tradition to classical epic, the relation of commentary to text.

An amusing hermeneutical twist in this relation occurs in the shadow puppet play when Rāma is exiled to the forest.

Sadly he turns to his wife, Sītā, and tells her that he must
leave her for fourteen years; but she refuses to be left behind
and argues that she must accompany him. Rāma says no, the
hardships of the forest will be too great. The argument is
finally broken when Sītā says, 'But of course I will go with
you — is there any Rāmāyaṇa in which Sītā does not accompany Rāma to the forest?'[20] Here the text upon which the
folk tradition comments is the total tradition of Rāma stories,
including itself; the Kerala tradition calls attention to itself
as a variant of the Rāmāyaṇa, with the ironic intention of
maintaining narrative uniformity.

Such self-reflexivity is possible through the use of the oral
commentary, the fourth level of adaptation in the folk tradition. The commentary, which follows each verse, takes two
forms: a line-by-line gloss in formal prose which leads (sometimes) into a more informal and extended discussion incorporating parables, folk tales, cosmology, architecture, medicine,
and so on. This complicated and lengthy commentary, which
accounts for the many nights of performance, is entirely oral
and independent of the written transmission of the classical
text which it interprets. Its commentarial function is the
essence of that relation between folk tradition and classical
text discussed in other forms of adaptation: it maintains the
text but interprets it for the local context (see the Appendix
for an example of this commentarial role).

On each of the four levels considered thus far, we have
seen that the folk Rāmāyaṇa tradition in Kerala adapts Kampaṉ's epic without altering the text. On the fifth level of the
embedded text, however, adaptation is necessarily textual.
As pointed out earlier, verses borrowed from Kampaṉ are
changed to suit the puppet play by a systematic shift from
indirect to direct speech and by minor substitutions of words
and phrases. A more substantial textual alteration is represented by the 5%-10% of the sung verses which are not from
Kampaṉ and have been added to his text by the folk tradition.

Although the number of these added verses (perhaps 150-
200) is small, the incidents that they narrate are not insig-

20 This humorous twist is found also in folk Rāmāyaṇas in Kannada
     (A.K. Ramanujan, personal communication).

nificant. Perhaps the most important of those incidents is the killing of Sambukumāran (son of Śūrpaṇakhā who is Rāvaṇa's sister) by Lakṣmaṇa (Rāma's brother). This event is unknown in Kampaṉ (in any version) or in Vālmīki in which Śūrpaṇakhā has no son to be killed. In the Kerala folk epic, when Rāma, Lakṣmaṇa, and Sitā, arrive in the forest, Sambukumāran is already deep in meditation in a tree, the same tree that Lakṣmaṇa soon chops down. Accidentally, then, Sambukumāran is killed in a verse that ends with Lakṣmaṇa's fear: 'What evil consequences will arise from this act I do not know.' And, indeed, the remainder of the epic story can be seen as those consequences: Śūrpaṇakhā finds her dead son, vows revenge, and later entices her brother Rāvaṇa to steal Sitā, an act that forces Rāma to war against the demon king.

The killing of Sambukumāran is described by the puppeteers in eight verses, none of which appears in Kampaṉ. But it would be wrong, therefore, to conclude that this incident is the innovation of the Kerala folk tradition for it is found also in other folk and literary Rāmāyaṇas in India and Southeast Asia.[21] The actual wording of the verses (which is virtually indistinguishable from Kampaṉ) might well be the work of a folk poet, even a learned puppeteer, from Kerala, but is more likely borrowed (like the rest of the text) from a literary source. Even in this textual realm, the principle of adaptation is the same as in the other areas discussed above: adaptation is primarily additive and interpretive. The folk tradition does not replace episodes in the classical text with episodes of its own; instead it adds to the received text by incorporating new verses that provide a commentary. The Sambukumāran episode, for example, supplies another level of motivation (Śūrpaṇakhā's revenge) to the already complicated plot.

In conclusion, the ambiguity of the folk epic is present in

---

21   The killing of Śūrpaṇakhā's son is found in several folk Rāmāyaṇas in Tamil, Telugu, and Kannada, and in the more literary *Ananda Rāmāyaṇa* (Sanskrit), *Paumacariyam* (Prakrit), *Rāmakien* (Thai), and *Hikayat Seri Rama* (Malay). On this episode in the Kerala tradition, see also Pe. Nā. Appucāmi, 'Curpaṇakaiyiṉ Makaṉ' in *Arupatantu Nirai Vila Malai*, ed. M. Raghava Aiyangar, Madras 1942, 161-5.

the Kerala shadow puppet tradition, but in a form that reverses that found in the *Kalevala*. Rather than a folk or oral epic written down and transformed into a literary epic, the Kerala text is a classical epic transmitted, adapted, and now orally performed in a context very different from the courtly milieu in which it was composed. This process of adaptation has been achieved through various forms of adaptation, identified on five levels.[22] Only on the last of these levels does adaptation involve alteration of narrative material. And on all levels, adaptation is interpretative; it frames and orients the text but does not substitute for it. This maintenance of relative textual stability over a thousand years of oral performance may challenge standard presuppositions of variation in oral and folk tradition, but it also suggests that the creativity of the folk epic may lie in other, extra-textual spheres.

APPENDIX

The following translation of a commentary to one verse from a shadow puppet performance (March 1985, Puttūr) presents one version of a legend about Kampaṉ, the classical poet whose epic the folk tradition has preserved. The excerpt picks up the story when Rāma and his monkey army have reached the shore of the ocean that separates them from Lanka where Rāvaṇa holds Sitā, Rāma's wife, captive. Unable to cross the water, Rāma forces Varuṇa (god of oceans) to appear; Varuṇa tells Rāma to build a bridge by throwing stones and boulders into his water.

The performer begins by singing a verse in which a monkey

---

22 Although the notion of adaptation runs counter to presuppositions (in both Western and Indian scholarship) of unified composition and unitary authorship in classical epics, these texts also have a history. However deeply Kampaṉ's text, for example, is felt to be the creation of the court poet, it is as much an adaptation (of pre-existing Rāma stories in Tamil) as are the folk Rāmāyaṇas (like the Kerala tradition) which adapt it. These Rama stories in Tamil are discussed in M. Rākava Aiyaṅkār, 'Irāmāyaṇamum Tamil Valakkuṅkalam' in *Ārāycci Tokuti*, Madras 1964, 16-51; A Pandurangan, 'Ramayana Versions in Tamil' in *Tamil Culture* 21 (1982), 58-67.

throws a large mountain into the sea which sends drops of
water into the heavens; he then speaks in a formal, stylized
prose:

(*Kampan's verse*: A monkey throws a mountain into the sea
which sends drops of water all the way to heaven where the
gods think it is ambrosia and begin to dance.)

(*Puppeteer's Commentary*: This is a verse that carries many
meanings. It's said that it was the very first verse that Kampan
wrote and that he wrote it to make a point. It also contains the
story of how that point was demonstrated to the court poets.
So much history lies behind this single verse, but we can begin
with what we all know — that the earth was ruled by the
Chola, Pandyan, and Chera kings. The Chola kings ruled over
the region of Tanjore, and each king kept sixty four learned
men, thirty two poets and thirty two scholars. At that time
in Tanjore there also lived a great man named Cataiyappan
who had the reputation of helping everyone who brought
their troubles to him; he offered them support and so was
given the title *vallal* or 'Great Benefactor'.

This generous Cataiyappan was also a close friend of the
Chola Raja and would often visit his court. One day he spoke
to his friend, 'Oh Raja, you have sixty four poets and scholars
in your court, but we have no Rama story in the southern
language, in Tamil. It's only in the northern language, in the
Sanskrit written by Valmiki with many, many meanings
condensed in each line. If it were in Tamil, all of us could
follow it and enjoy the benefit that comes from understanding that great story. Therefore, summon your best poets —
Ottakuttan and Kampan — and order them to compose a
Ramayana in the southern language.' The Raja called the
poets, made the request, and they agreed.

From that day, Ottakuttan began to write; he finished the
Bala Kanda, Ayodhya Kanda, Aranya Kanda, Sundara Kanda,
and came to the beginning of the Yuddha Kanda when Sri
Rama,[6] Laksmana, and the monkey army travelled for twelve
days and reached the edge of the salt ocean. When Ottakuttan
told the Raja he had completed this much, Kampan was
embarrassed: 'I've not yet written a single verse. But if I

admit it, the name of Kampaṇ, which is praised everywhere
as a great poet, will become inferior to Ottakūttaṇ. Certainly there are books which admonish us not to lie; but
there are other books which say we can lie. How do we know
when to lie and when not to? Well, if we do lie, the most
important thing is that it should not cause any trouble or
evil. If you lie in order to accomplish a good deed, then it's
not wrong; in fact, it ceases to be lie and becomes the truth.
The *sastra* rule books say you can tell not just one lie, but
two, three, a hundred, even hundreds of lies, and all at the
same time. There is that verse:

Getting a woman married, or a spy spying,
Creating good, or teaching the three essences,
And saving an innocent man from death —
At these times, a hundred lies may be told.

This is what philosophy teaches us. In order to get a woman
married and give her a good life, you have to tell a hundred
lies. Those lies become the truth; if you don't tell lies, how
can you arrange a marriage? Or to create a good thing, to
avoid evil, you may tell a hundred lies. Likewise, if a cruel
person goes to kill an innocent man, we may tell lies to save
him. At times like these, lies act like truths.'
    Now Kampaṇ thought about this and said to himself, 'The
lie I'm going to tell won't have any evil consequences.' So he
looked at the Raja and said: 'I have written up to the point
when Rāma comes to the ocean, is unable to cross, does
meditation, fires arrows at Varuṇa (sea-god), waits for Varuṇa
to appear, then strings the Brahma-*astra* and Varuṇa places a
garland on Rāma, worships him and asks forgiveness, and then
tells Rāma that to cross to Lanka he may build a bridge by
throwing rocks into his ocean. Then . . .'

Kumutaṇ threw a mountain into the sea,
    whose roaring, frothy water
Reached to the heavens where the gods danced
    hoping the ambrosia would rise again.

When Kampaṇ told the Raja he had written that verse, he lied
and Ottakūttaṇ knew it. He had seen him wandering about

and knew he hadn't written a single verse. He also saw that
some of the wording was ungrammatical and so, hoping to
expose Kampaṉ's lie, Oṭṭakūttaṉ challenged him: 'Kampaṉ,
your verse may sound fine, but look at the line about the
gods dancing when the water (*tumi*) reached the heavens. I
ask you: Is the use of *tumu* grammatical? Does it have any
basis in common speech?'

Kampaṉ had to stop and think because at that time the
word *tumi* was not used: 'Oh, even if it were grammatical,
that's not enough; it must be used by common people.' Then
Oṭṭakūttaṉ continued, 'No one speaks the word *tumi*; if it
were common speech, lots of people would use it, wouldn't
they? You must prove to me that they do.' Kampaṉ simply
answered, 'All right; I'll prove it tomorrow.'

Without taking any food, he went straight to the temple
of Ampikai and called to her: 'Goddess, with your blessings
I am a poet sitting in the Raja's court; he ordered us to compose a Tamil Rāmāyaṇa and I told a lie about a verse with
the word *tumi* in it. Now the other poets have challenged me
to prove it's used in common speech. Of course if you don't
want to help, it's no loss to me.' With this plea, he fell into a
half-sleep; then Ampikai appeared and spoke: 'Kampaṉ, why
worry like this? Tomorrow morning, before the night has
gone, bring them all to the shepherds' lane and I will prove
to their ears that the word is used.' Suddenly she vanished
and Kampaṉ felt relieved.

Early next morning, he finished his duties and went quickly
to the Raja who greeted him: 'Well, Kampaṉ, can you show
us the word *tumi* today?' 'I can,' he replied, 'but we must go
now before the light. Come along, all of you.' The Raja,
Oṭṭakūttaṉ, Caṭaiyappaṉ, the ministers, and other poets had
stayed awake and were ready. Off they went to the shepherds'
lane where they saw two lines of houses. They looked on
both sides, but nowhere was there an open door or a burning
lamp. Going ahead, they looked carefully and then, at the
very end, saw a single house with a light. Inside was a woman
surrounded by four children: 'Get back, the *tumi* will fall on
you; watch out for the *tumi*.'

The Raja, poets, and ministers were amazed. Why, among
all these houses with no one awake and no light, does this

single house have a lamp? Who is that woman? And who are the children? They ran forward to find out, but when they reached the spot, there was no house, no children, no woman, no lamp – only a deserted place! They stopped for a minute and then cried out: 'This is the work of Ampikai; it can be nothing else. And Kampaṉ has her powers so we can't debate with him about poetry. What goddess or god can we summon to prove our point?' And so they all returned to the palace.

Then Kampaṉ began to write; with the help of the best Tamil scholars and Sanskrit pandits, he composed 700 verses between sunrise and sunset every day. In the evening he would go to Ampikai's temple and worship her, placing his manuscript near the shrine. After his rituals, he would look again at it and all the errors would have been corrected. This is how Kampaṉ wrote his Rāmāyaṇa in 12,116 verses and six chapters.

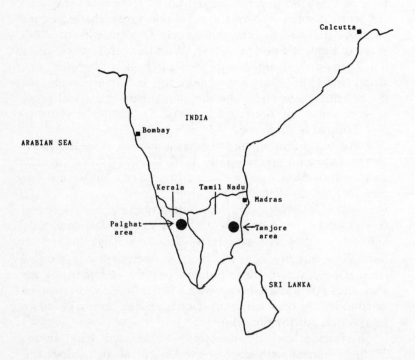

FORMULAIC LANGUAGE IN THE EPICS OF INDIA

JOHN D. SMITH
(University of Cambridge)

Sad to say, this century has seen the virtual extinction of the oral epic in many parts of the world where it once flourished. Traditional epics seem not to be compatible with Communism, and Communism has spread throughout those areas of East Europe and Central and North Asia which until comparatively recently were noted for their rich epic traditions. It is thus a relief, as well as a pleasure, to discover that South Asia too boasts a wealth of such traditions, few of which appear to be in any immediate danger. For the present, then, it is still possible to study oral epic in the field, though no doubt the day will come when such study will be confined to the archive and the library.

To say that India 'boasts' many oral epics is not in fact strictly true, for India has kept extremely quiet about them. It is only in the last two decades that scholars have even become aware of the existence of many of these traditions, and serious studies only began to appear in the late 1970s. This is thus a subject still very much in its infancy; but it is certainly one that has got off to a good start in life. At a conference devoted exclusively to Indian oral epics held in 1982 in Madison, Wisconsin, no fewer than twenty specialist papers were read by scholars of North American, Indian and European origin; and a forthcoming volume of essays by a number of those scholars should prove to be of interest to students of epic as well as to Indologists.

A major feature of the conference — one fully reflected in the book — was an emphasis on the comparative approach. In a country as vast and diverse as India there can be no *a priori* reason to assume that there will be significant similarities between epic traditions from different regions, operating in

591

different languages (even different language families). Of the traditions currently known to us, some are found in the Indo-European speaking North — Rajasthan on the Pakistani border, and the more central Hindi area; others belong to the Dravidian-speaking South of the subcontinent, with epics composed in Tamil, Telugu, Kannada, Malayalam and Tulu. Thus the discovery that there are in fact many close and profound resemblances between these widespread and linguistically various traditions is an important one. Since my title refers to 'the epics of India' as forming, by implication, a coherent group, I shall start by giving a brief indication of some of that group's most salient common characteristics.[1]

To start with, it is noticeable that most Indian epics are performed by members of relatively low castes — sometimes, indeed, by untouchables. Brahmins have little or nothing to do with them, and this is all the more striking since in a great many cases the epic performance represents a liturgical invocation of a hero who is also a deity. (In some cases — for instance the Hindi epic *Lorikī* — the heroes are not themselves incarnate deities; but even here the gods play important, if more marginal, roles in the narrative.) The epic deities are not recognised by Indian brahmanical orthodoxy: their cults are limited both geographically and socially. For example, Pābūjī, the subject of epic performances by untouchable Nāyaks, is worshipped throughout most of Rajasthan, but the bulk of his devotees are drawn from a single caste (Rebārīs); the epic of *Palnāḍu*, similarly performed mainly by untouchable Mālas, appeals to a broader social spectrum but has no currency outside a rather small area of Andhra Pradesh.

There are no hard-and-fast boundaries between entertainment and ritual in India, a fact strikingly illustrated by the folk epics. The stories are stories of heroes and heroines, and it would be foolish to pretend that entertainment forms no part of their function; if there were any doubt about this it would only be necessary to point to the quite frequent occurrence in them of straightforwardly comic passages. This

---

1 The following paragraphs summarise arguments put forward in 'Scapegoats of the Gods', my contribution to the forthcoming book on the oral epic in India.

is not seen as being in any way at odds with the fact that most of them are performed as ritual propitiations of those same heroes and heroines *qua* deities. Indeed, it is plain that the stories reinforce the ritual, for it is in the stories that each cult expresses its world-view. Once again, comparison of different epic traditions reveals remarkable similarities of outlook. The narratives are essentially pessimistic: they present man as being in thrall to a hostile fate, a fate which is imposed on him by the ill will of the gods. As the hero's story progresses he will find himself forced into impossible situations which endanger his honour or his life. Women and kinsfolk are represented as the greatest sources of danger, and the conflicts they spark off escalate into massive wars of annihilation. Worst of all, though, is man's own internal conflict: confronted with the gods' hostility, should he struggle against it or accept his fate with dignity? To this question no answers are given; some heroes take one course, some the other, while some waver between the two. The one thing that is made clear, however, is that ultimately one's attitude towards fate will make no difference, for the will of the gods always prevails.

The Sanskrit epic *Mahābhārata* is conventionally dated c. 400 B.C. − 400 A.D.; it is a written text in a classical language; and it is recognised as a major holy text of brahmanical Hinduism. It is thus far removed in time, in nature and in social status from the oral epics of present-day India − or so it would seem. Yet despite these apparently profound differences, the *Mahābhārata*, too, shares many of the characteristics already mentioned as typifying the Indial oral epic. Its language is not in fact very 'classical' at all: epic Sanskrit is notorious for its willingness to sacrifice correct grammar in favour of more-or-less correct metre, or sometimes for no evident reason at all. 'Our' *Mahābhārata* may be a written text, but there is no doubt that it had an oral origin. It may now be a brahmanical work, but that is the result of the centuries of brahmanical interpolation indicated in that 800-year period allowed for its formation (the work contains references to its own textual inflation); its inception belongs with the Sūtas, a 'mixed' − i.e. low − caste of charioteers and bards. Most telling of all, its mythology is non-Vedic and

points clearly to an ideology closely similar to that propounded
in the modern epics: hostile fate, hostile kinsmen, dangerous
women, and heroes torn between acceptance and rejection of
the gods' will.

It is thus plain that the present-day oral epics known to us
have a great deal in common with each other, despite the
major geographical and linguistic differences between them;
and it is also plain that the Sanskrit *Mahābhārata*, despite its
even greater apparent remoteness, shares in many of the
resemblances. A more formal comparison of these works is
clearly a legitimate undertaking. In particular, what light can
the standard theories of formulaic composition shed on them,
and what light can they shed on the theories?

S.M. Pandey's description of the use of formulaic language
in the Hindi epic *Lorikī* appears only in the Hindi edition
of his work on the subject, and has therefore not attracted
the attention it merits. Without ever actually mentioning Parry
or Lord by name, Pandey makes it clear that he is familiar
with their theories and has found them of value in coming to
an understanding of the performance techniques employed
by the singers he has studied.

> If a single performer's version is recorded and transcribed
> on several occasions, it will contain considerable differences.
> The singer of a folk epic always has to face his audience,
> and when he sings there is little time [to think], so these
> formulae are helpful to him. He casts his own compositions
> in a formulaic style ... which he employs repeatedly with
> little modification. Folk epic audiences do not consider
> these kinds of repetitions a fault, but regard them as a
> characteristic.[2]

Pandey's emphasis in his examples is in fact less on individual formulae than on 'runs' extending over several lines,
but it is clear that he has *The Singer of Tales* much in mind
and finds the model proposed there to be applicable to the
Hindi epic. A point of some interest is that he describes the
same formulae being used in passages of differing metre,

---

2 Śyāmmanohar Pāṇḍey, *Lok Mahākāvya Lorikī*, Allahabad 1979, 26.

something we shall encounter in the Sanskrit *Mahābhārata*; however, his approach to the analysis of metre is clearly a standard 'literary' approach (with the result that his description is not notably precise). It seems on the face of it rather more likely that what Pandey treats as different metres are in fact different musical forms requiring different verbal adjustments and fillers.

Pandey's second book, which deals with another version of the same epic known under the name *Canainī*, treats the question of oral formulaic composition in greater detail (and, this time, with due acknowledgement of the work of Parry and Lord). Not unreasonably in the land of the Vedas, he places greater stress on the fact that no two epic performances are textually identical than on the formulaic nature of the language used. A series of comparisons is made, of which the first is typical: the same part of the narrative (the beginning) is recorded from the same singer on two successive days, and —

> we can see the similarity in the events but the sequence of the words and lines is very different ... a few lines are similar in the two texts, although in the sequence of the words they are not identical.[3]

Pandey's conclusions read, naturally enough, like a summary of Lord's work:

> From what we have discussed above, it is clear that the singers do not produce a memorized fixed text ... [the epic singer] remembers the sequence of his events, his models of formulas, themes, meters and the styles of singing and with their help he produces a new text in each new performance.[4]

Students of other Indian oral epic traditions have not, however, been able to see so immediate a parallel between their material and the South Slavic epics. Nineteen eighty two was something of a boom year for Indian epic studies, for it saw not

3 Shyam Manohar Pandey, *The Hindi Oral Epic Canainī*, Allahabad 1982, 45-6.
4 *Ibid.*, 82.

only the Madison conference and Pandey's second book but
also the publication of two works on South Indian epics by
American scholars. Both of these are well aware of the work
of Parry and Lord, but both are compelled by the nature of
their material to be cautious in discussing the use of formulaic
language. To start with, a significant part of these epics is
performed in prose (a medium also used, though less prominently, in *Lorikī*). As is well-known, Parry's very definition
of the formula, a definition reproduced unchanged by Lord,
assumes metricality: it allows formulae to be used only 'under
the same metrical conditions'. Gene Roghair, discussing the
Telugu epic of *Palnāḍu*, finds himself constrained by this
criterion:

> ... even a brief look at the style adopted by the Vīra
> Vidyantuḍu reveals narrative elements which are repeti-
> tive and which might be called formulaic in any except the
> most restricted sense used by Lord. Furthermore, these
> formulas appear to play an important role in allowing the
> Vidyantuḍu rapidly and effectively to sing a long story
> which is basically prose.[5]

On the other hand, Roghair also allows that 'much of the
[prose] material is not formulaic',[6] and the only specific
examples he gives of prose formulae consist simply of 'stock
form[s] of address' of the sort that can be heard in any
western court or committee room. So while we may accept
that 'the contents of the verse lines ... are repeated formulas
that are regularly used in the same places for the same purpose',[7] there would seem to be little reason to assume that
the prose narrative is also strongly formulaic.

Brenda Beck's study of the Tamil epic *Aṇṇaṇmār*, also
published in 1982, gives slightly firmer information on this
subject. Like *Palnāḍu*, *Aṇṇaṇmār* is performed largely in prose:
70% prose in a normal performance, 82% in a dictated version
by the same performer.[8] In the passages of song, writes
Beck:

5   G.H. Roghair, *The Epic of Palnāḍu*, Oxford 1982, 60.
6   *Ibid.*
7   *Ibid.*
8   Brenda E.F. Beck, *The Three Twins*, Bloomington 1982, 60.

Just as Parry and Lord predicted [*sic*], Rāmacāmi used essentially the same song lines in both versions. Yet he continually shifted whole and even part phrases around, using a different sequence of those pieces on the two occasions.[9]

The prose passages, by contrast, are characterised by 'the freest use of words'.[10] Again, Beck provides a percentage figure:

> ... if one searches for formulas in the prose portions of the performed version, only 2% or 3% of the material can be so classfied. Many prose formulas are quite short, and they are generally addressed to personages of higher or lower status than that of the speaker. That is, prose formulas are used most in formal interaction settings.[11]

All of this sounds very similar to Roghair's description of the epic of *Palnāḍu*: a narrative delivered in prose interspersed with song; the songs highly formulaic, the prose passages much less so, except for the frequent use of 'stock form[s] of address'.

If the Hindi epic *Lorikī* follows Professor Lord's 'predictions' and the two southern epics *Palnāḍu* and *Annanmār* mingle formulaic verse with less formulaic prose, the Rajasthani epic of *Pābūjī* provides a third pattern. Here we find the same alternation of sung and spoken passages that occurs in the other traditions I have mentioned; but the spoken passages in *Pābūjī* are not prose. Rather they are the same verse couplets as are sung, but delivered more-or-less 'straight'; whereas in the sections of song they are subjected to an extraordinary process of 'inflation' with meaningless fillers and repetitions, in a singing-style which I have encountered in Indian folk song and in western rock music, but never before in the performance of an epic.[12] What is more, some ten different tunes are used by the performers, and each of these requires a different form of 'inflation'; so that one and the same couplet

9   *Ibid.*, 69.
10 *Ibid.*
11 *Ibid.*, 64.
12 See further my article 'Words, Music and Memory', in P. Ryan, ed., *Memory and Poetic Structure*, London 1981, 50-65.

may appear in up to ten utterly different guises, in all of which it is submerged under a veritable verbal flood (filler-words always greatly outnumber 'nuclear' words). Under these circumstances it is clearly easier to restrict any attempt at formula-analysis to the spoken sections of epic performances, where textual embellishment, though it still occurs in almost every line of every couplet, is on a more manageable scale.

The picture that emerges from the study of many different performances of the epic of *Pābūjī* is of 'an e x t r e m e [textual] stylisation, that is to say an extreme reliance on themes and formulae'.[13] Whenever similar events occur, they are described in the same formulaic words; and similar events occur all the time. Allowing for substitution of proper names as appropriate, every battle in *Pābūjī* is the same battle, every journey the same journey, every meeting the same meeting. The western scholar undertaking fieldwork on oral epic thus begins to find himself in the eerie position of being able to predict what a performer is going to say next. As an example, here is a fairly literal translation of one account of a journey — one of probably about one hundred journeys described in the course of the complete narrative.[14] The situation is this: Pābūjī needs to choose one of his companions to send on a dangerous mission, so he asks his closest companion Cãdo to travel to the home of the lady Deval, in order to ask Deval to come and make the choice.

1. (Pābūjī said,) 'O Cãdo my courtier, make great haste; quickly summon the lady Deval to my palace.'

2. Cãdo tied his low-hanging Rāthor turban; on his feet he fastened his velvet shoes.

3. Cãdo the courtier set off walking like geese or peacocks; he trod hesitantly like a frightened wild peacock.

4. The stars were shining at frosty[15] midnight; in the middle of the night Cãdo went and called out to Deval.

5. Deval was sleeping in her palace tall as a stooping cloud; when she heard Cãdo's call she woke up.

---

13 See my unpublished article 'The Words and Music of Pābūjī's Epic'.
14 That of Parbū Bhopo, my chief informant for Pābūjī, recorded in 1976 in Jodhpur.
15 Literally 'dripping (with dew)': the point is that it is very cold.

6. Deval woke up; she threw off sleep and rose at once.

7. Deval filled a tray with gems and excellent pearls; she went out to do Cãdo honour with pearls.

8. (Cãdo said,) 'Listen, Deval, the rising Sun with its spotless rays has already done me honour; now come and do honour to Pābūjī's mare Kesar Kālamī.'

9. (Deval said,) 'O courtier Cãdo, stay a little while; enter Deval's palace to clean your teeth.'[16]

10. (Cãdo said,) 'O lady Deval, you are a Cāran by caste; a Rajpūt cannot clean his teeth in the house of a Cāran.'

11. (Deval said,) 'O courtier Cãdo, tell me what is on your mind; on what business have you come to my palace?'

12. (Cãdo said,) 'O lady Deval, the rising Sun with its spotless rays will deal with matters of moment; I have come to your palace on a small domestic matter.

13. O Deval, make great haste; Pābūjī summons you to his palace.'

14. The lady Deval took the trident of Karnī Mātā[17] in her hand; over her shoulders she spread her costly cloak.

15. The lady Deval set out as the stars were shining at frosty midnight; at daybreak she arrived and reverenced Pābūjī.

16. Pābūjī's warriors and headmen were seated in a throng; in the crowded assembly Deval reverenced Pābūjī.

17. The lady Deval stood in Lord Pābūjī's court; she stood and spoke to Pābūjī.

18. (Deval said,) 'O protector Pābūjī, tell me what is on your mind; on what business have you summoned me to your palace?'

19. (Pābūjī said,) 'O lady Deval, the creator Sun with its rays will deal with matters of moment; I have summoned you to my palace on a small domestic matter.'

Etc.

In these nineteen couplets there is not a line that does not occur — and occur repeatedly — elsewhere in the narrative; indeed several lines recur more than once within this one

16 I.e. 'accept hospitality from me'.
17 A Rajasthani goddess: Deval too is in fact a goddess, hence her right to a trident.

passage. Whenever anyone goes anywhere, meets anyone, tells anyone anything, this is how they do it. The fact that Deval lives in another part of the same village as Pābūjī and his companions does not, it seems, justify any curtailment of the full theme 'X goes on a journey': if she had lived on the other side of India the only difference would have been an extra couplet saying 'three nights Cãdo spent on the road; on the fourth day he cast off his stirrups in such-and-such a place'. (In fact the performer does accidentally say just this in the preceding sung version of this passage.)

This 'predictability' extends beyond mere diction. It should cause no surprise that the overall narrative is invariable, since it is not 'just a story' but an account of the deeds of an incarnate deity. But in the middle realm between diction and narrative content, the realm of episodes and their constituent themes, there is the same fixity. A transcription of a performance by a particular performer will serve as an approximate transcription of a n y performance by that performer; it will be perhaps 75% correct for other performers from the same 'family'; it will still be somewhere around 35% correct for unrelated, unknown performers from other districts. The epic of *Pābūjī* has achieved a level of textual stability that contrasts strikingly with the South Slavic epics described in *The Singer of Tales*.

Study of Indian oral epics thus leads to the conclusion that, whilst they may have much in common in terms of performance context and the messages they contain for their audiences, they differ markedly in matters of diction. The Hindi *Lorikī* appears to follow the Parry/Lord 'norm'; the two South Indian epics discussed intersperse formulaic verse with largely non-formulaic prose; whilst the Rajasthani epic of *Pābūjī* is highly formulaic but also highly unLordian in that it is always performed the same. How are we to account for this diversity?

The most obvious explanation to present itself is a geographical one. *Lorikī* is performed in central North India, *Aṇṇanmār* and *Palnādu* in eastern South India, *Pābūjī* in western North India. The distances between these areas are enormous, their languages very different, even their cultures by no means the same. What more natural than that their epic performers should use formulaic diction differently? Surely what is surprising is not the differences between the various oral epic traditions in India, but the similarities?

This argument looks very strong, and I am certainly not able to demolish it. There may well be regional differences of approach to epic performance — indeed, put as broadly as that, there are bound to be differences. But I still suspect that the geographical argument does not fully explain the nature of the differences we can perceive, and I find support for this idea in a very interesting article by Paul Kiparsky. Kiparsky examined the Finnish epics collected in the nineteenth century by Lönnrot, and used by him as the basis for the *Kalevala*. He writes:

> In order to check to what extent the songs are products of composition-in-performance I compared repeated performances of a song by the same singer, and the versions of father and son wherever several generations in bardic families are on record. I did this for the epic songs of the White Sea district, which included some of the greatest singers, among them those who contributed the bulk of the *Kalevala*. The results were interesting. The repertoire of the Finnish singers, unlike those of Yugoslavia, must be regarded, at least for the epic poetry, as consisting of fairly stable compositions. Performances recorded even many decades apart are, as a rule, far more alike than the corresponding Yugoslav cases presented by Lord. Changes in the content and organization of the story are rare. Usually, differences within lines are a matter of small changes of wording, most of them changes of word order or substitutions of synonyms.[18]

And he concludes:

> It is evident that the differences in stability between the Finnish and the Yugoslav oral epic poetry spring from their different roles in their respective cultures. Where the Yugoslav poetry functions largely as storytelling and enter-

18 P. Kiparsky, 'Oral Poetry: Some Linguistic and Typological Considerations', in B.A. Stolz and R.S. Shannon III, eds., *Oral Literature and the Formula*, Ann Arbor 1976, 95.

tainment, the Finnish poetry has strong elements of *myth* and ritual.[19]

Kiparsky's proposal is helpful in trying to explain the very diverse Indian situation. *Lorikī* is a largely romantic epic; Lorik is not a deity, and there is no cult. Performance thus 'functions largely as storytelling and entertainment'. *Pābūjī*, by contrast, 'has strong elements of myth and ritual': the story is a story about gods and men, and performance is a religious rite. It is surely in this contrast, rather than in mere geography, that we should see the reason for the differences between the two. The South Indian epics on the other hand, though also concerned with myth and ritually performed, are composed for the most part in prose. They therefore c a n n o t be formulaic in the strictest sense of the term, and they prove to be not very formulaic even if Parry's original definition is stripped of its metrical criterion. Having derived much benefit from Kiparsky's article I feel somewhat mean-spirited in pointing out that the South Indian evidence thus does nothing to support his other main proposal, which is precisely that the metrical criterion should be abandoned.

What of the *Mahābhārata*, which I was so careful to include in my discussion early in this paper, and which I have ignored ever since? Clearly any attempt to analyse the use of formulaic language in that text has a somewhat different purpose, and probably involves a somewhat different *modus operandi*, from the kind of study I have dealt with so far. Eight hundred years is a long time for a text to undergo active interpolation, and the result is a text-critic's nightmare. 'What cannot be found here cannot be found anywhere', proclaims the *Mahābhārata* proudly of itself,[20] not without justice. On top of the ancient epic story have been piled:

Expanded accounts of parts of that story (e.g. the war);

'New' episodes, sometimes very long ones (e.g. the entire *Book of Virāṭa*);

Relatively early didactic material (e.g. the *Bhagavadgītā*);

19 *Ibid.*, 98.
20 1. 56.34.

Stories totally unconnected with the central narrative (e.g. almost the whole of the *Book of the Forest*);

Later didactic material (e.g. the Books entitled *Śānti* and *Anuśāsana* — the latter consists of some 6000 stanzas on right behaviour delivered by the hero Bhīṣma on his death-bed, and the two Books together constitute about one quarter of the entire received text);

Numerous other secondary passages of various sorts (e.g. the lists of contents and summaries of the Books with which the work opens).

It has been a besetting sin of Indologists to act as if only what is old can be interesting, and I do not want to give the impression that I hold that view. Nonetheless, to understand any given section of the *Mahābhārata* aright we need to be able to place it at its correct point in the overall development of the text. This can be difficult, for though the general lines of development are well-known and not controversial, 'placing and dating' of particular passages requires the application of distinguishing criteria. Textual study of the *Mahābhārata* has been likened to work at an archaeological dig,[21] an analogy which seems to me extremely apt: the text-critic's task is not, in this case, to separate the 'authentic' from the 'spurious', but rather to identify the stratum, and to whatever extent possible the provenance, of any textual fragment that he encounters. (It may be said that the Poona critical edition's failure to recognise this fact is greatly to be regretted.)

In very general terms, the criteria which have been employed in studying the archaeology of the *Mahābhārata* have been three in number: content, language and metre. All three raise problems. As far as content goes, absolute dating is impossible and even relative dating very risky for ancient India, so clear synchronisms and anachronisms are few in number. Instead there has been — and still exists — a tendency to appeal to theories of literary development which are presumed *a priori*, often producing arguments of the self-fulfilling or circular

---

21 Mary Carroll Smith, *The Core of India's Great Epic*, unpublished Ph.D. dissertation, Harvard 1972, 63.

variety. Linguistic questions may be less prone to vagaries of personal judgement — but here there is a circularity in the evidence itself: later authors took the language of earlier authors as a model, so the occurrence of, for instance, an 'incorrect' grammatical form does not necessarily prove anything. Metre is probably the best and safest single criterion, but it too carries its inbuilt problems: correct metrical analysis requires a text that is reliable down to its smallest, subtlest details — which in our case we have not got. Yet again there is a circularity: establishment of a text permits analysis of the metres used in the text, which assists in the establishment of the text.

Used singly and absolutely, these criteria are thus less helpful than one could wish. But it is a different story when they are used jointly or proportionally. A few brief examples are in order, since they will help to establish a general principle. I have already mentioned that the *Book of Virāṭa* (Book 4) is a later addition to the text. This is a narrative section, describing the adventures of the Pāṇḍava heroes after they complete their twelve years of forest exile and undertake the stipulated thirteenth year dwelling incognito in a populated place (the city of Virāṭa). Hopkins's comments on the c o n t e n t of this book, and that of other passages referring to the terms of the Pāṇḍavas' banishment, are worth quoting (his heated language is in response to Dahlmann's claim that the *Mahābhārata* did not develop, but was composed complete in much its present form sometime round 500 B.C.):

> Let us take the fourth book. The heroes are dressed up as eunuchs, cooks, and servitors, and play pranks in Virāṭa's palace. Between the grimness of the gambling-scene and the fierceness of the battle, this episode stands like an interlude of pantomime inserted to cover a thirteenth year of exile, which in other parts of the book is not recognized. Is it of no importance that such harem-stories as are here given are found nowhere else in the epic; that only here, in laudation unparalleled elsewhere, Arjuna alone routs the whole Kuru army? But the text itself hints that the fourth book as at present composed is a late addition. There are two passages . . . where the thirteenth year is ignored alto-

gether, as if it were an afterthought . . . and a verse alluding
to the exile after it is all over distinctly states that the Pāṇḍavas passed all thirteen years as hermits in the wood . . .[22]

Taken by themselves, these strictures have a dangerous
sound to them. Perhaps Hopkins's conception of what is
appropriate in an epic does not coincide with what the ancient
Sūta bards felt; perhaps they w a n t e d an 'interlude of
pantomime' at this point in the story; perhaps it is not the *Book
of Virāṭa* but the passages which seem unaware of the events it
describes that are ill-thought-out later additions. But when
we link the criterion of content to a second one, that of metre,
doubt is resolved. Mary Carroll Smith's computer-based
analysis of *Mahābhārata* stanzas in *triṣṭubh* metre demonstrates that throughout the *Book of Virāṭa* there does not
occur a single 'old-style' *triṣṭubh* of the type in which the core
narrative is composed.[23] Two different approaches thus coincide in suggesting that the fourth book is not part of the
earliest stratum.

In other cases it is necessary to calculate the proportionate
frequency with which certain features appear in the text.
Hopkins's *magnum opus, The Great Epic of India*, contains
many instances of linguistic and, especially, metrical 'patterns
of irregularity'. To quote him again:

> In the careless writing of the pseudo-epic, Sanskrit
> grammar is flung to the winds. I do not mean that irregular
> forms are not found outside of it. . . . The cases in the older
> epic are, however, not frequent . . . , but in the late epic
> they flourish like reeds . . . and it is just here that new
> irregularities are found.[24]

Chapter Four of Hopkins's work, entitled 'Epic Versification', is a monster of 171 pages, and embodies a wealth and
detail of analysis unlikely ever to be surpassed; again, he is
able to detect subtle differences in the frequency with which

---

22 E. Washburn Hopkins, 'The Bhārata and the Great Bhārata', *American Journal of Philology* 19 (1898), 1-24, esp. 4.
23 Mary Carroll Smith, *op. cit.*, 77-8.
24 E. Washburn Hopkins, *The Great Epic of India*, New York 1901,
265.

certain unusual metrical forms occur in different parts of the
Mahābhārata. I permit myself a final quotation, not because
it adds to our understanding of the *Mahābhārata* but because
it adds to our understanding of the greatest of *Mahābhārata*
scholars, here apparently approaching the end of his tether:

> No doubt this parisaṃkhyā [enumeration] philosophy is
> tiresome reading, but as it is even more tiresome to obtain
> the facts than to glance at them, I shall beg the reader to
> have patience while I give the results of a few more reckon-
> ings, since I believe they are not without a certain value.[25]

I think many scholars must recognise how he felt.

Since *Mahābhārata* textual scholarship is thus dependent
on the evaluation of various types of evidence in combination,
and since some of that evidence is statistical in nature, it is
reasonable to ask whether a further contribution to the subject could be made through the study of formulaic language
in the text. Grintser has already demonstrated that narrative
sections of the *Mahābhārata*, especially those describing battle-
scenes, are rich in formulae, didactic passages less so;[26] the
question is whether such distinctions can be refined to the
point where they might provide information that could be
reliably used in textual criticism. The rest of this paper is
devoted to a brief consideration of this question; but it should
be emphasised that this can represent no more than a pebble
sent skimming over the surface of a great ocean. R e a l study
of this topic would be a truly gigantic undertaking. I understand that Professor Daniel H.H. Ingalls, the distinguished
retired Professor of Sanskrit at Harvard, is working on a com-
puter-assisted project in this field, but have not been able to
secure any further information on the nature of his undertaking. What I present here are summaries of the results of a
mere few weeks of investigation, and are intended as no more
than possible indications for future lines of research.

---

25 *Ibid.*, 228.
26 P.A. Grintser, *Drevneindijskij epos: genezis i tipologija*, Moskva,
    1974, esp. ch. 3. See also J.W. de Jong, 'Recent Russian publications
    on the Indian Epic', *Adyar Library Bulletin* 39 (1975), 1-42.

The diversity evidenced by the present-day oral epics of India dashes any hopes we might have entertained of finding some characteristically 'Indian' use of formulaic language that might throw light on the *Mahābhārata* also. It is plain that all we can do is to examine sample passages which on other grounds can safely be assigned to different periods or provenances, in order to see whether patterns of difference in diction can also be found. The hit-and-miss nature of this approach is not improved by the form of the resources currently available for investigating repeated phrases, which consist simply of six volumes of line-indexes to the critical edition of the text. This is clearly not very satisfactory, since it permits checking of line-initial and whole-line formulae only. It happens that there is greater metrical freedom at the beginnings than at the ends of epic lines, so that an enormous class of line-final formulae exists to satisfy the metrical demands of the cadence — vocatives like *bharatarṣabha*, 'O bull-like descendant of Bharata', for example — and I have had no chance to take any systematic account of these.

The two commonest metres of the *Mahābhārata* are called *triṣṭubh* and *anuṣṭubh*. Of these, it is the *triṣṭubh* which is generally found in the earliest passages — indeed, Mary Carroll Smith succeeded in demonstrating, again by combining analysis of metre with analysis of content, that if the early *triṣṭubhs* are excerpted from the existing text, through which they are scattered apparently at random, they provide a fairly coherent 'core' narrative. These early *triṣṭubhs* are relatively free-form; indeed, it is their lack of regularity that distinguishes them from 'classical' *triṣṭubhs* or *upajātis*, many of which found their way into the text at a later period. The *anuṣṭubh*, though slightly less venerable as an epic metre, is much more widely used, however, and accounts for 94% of the verses in the critical edition.[27] An important point is that it too has no fixed sequence of longs and shorts in the first half of the line: this results in many line-initial formulae being portable between the two metres, a fact which was probably influential in the development of the text (and, indeed, in the development of the metres themselves).

27 Mary Carroll Smith, *op. cit.*, 3.

Table Showing Percentage Frequency Per Book of Sample Formulae

Book	1	2	3	4	5	6	7	8	9	10	11	12	13	14	15	16	17	18
Expected frequency	11.3	3.6	15.0	3.4	9.9	5.9	8.7	3.5	3.2	0.9	1.4	17.7	7.7	4.8	2.4	0.5	0.2	0.3
atha vā	11.0	6.6	19.0	5.1	6.6	5.1	6.6	2.2	3.0	0.0	1.5	21.2	6.6	5.1	0.7	0.0	0.0	0.0
itahāsaṃ purātanam	1.5	0.8	3.0	0.0	5.3	0.0	0.0	0.0	0.0	0.0	0.0	54.9	28.3	11.3	0.0	0.0	0.0	0.0
ity uktaḥ sa/ity uktā sā	0.0	0.0	10.0	0.0	0.0	0.0	0.0	0.0	1.7	0.0	0.0	3.3	31.7	36.7	11.7	0.0	1.7	3.3
idaṃ vacanam abravīt/abruvan	13.7	6.9	21.6	4.9	9.8	5.9	13.7	4.9	2.0	2.0	2.9	5.9	2.0	3.9	0.0	0.0	0.0	0.0
tato 'bravīt/'bruvan	12.0	2.7	18.7	6.7	6.7	5.3	14.7	6.7	9.3	0.0	0.0	5.3	5.3	2.7	4.0	0.0	0.0	0.0

'Expected frequency' is the length (in chapters) of each book expressed as a percentage of the length of the entire *Mahābhārata*.

All values are rounded to a single significant digit.

Values deviating from the expected frequency by +5% or more are underlined once; those deviating by −5% or more are underlined twice.

Let us start with a statistical analysis of a rather crude sort — estimating the percentage figure of formulaic diction in three samples of text which are of demonstrably different age and type. Chapter 22 of Book 5 (The Book of the Effort) is composed entirely in early *triṣṭubhs*, and is shown by Mary Carroll Smith to be the first of a sequence of ten almost unmodified 'core' chapters. It consists (in the version of the critical edition) of 39 stanzas, all of them comprising the normal four lines except for stanza 31, which contains six lines. Of the total of 158 lines in this chapter, 111 are wholly or partly repeated elsewhere in the *Mahābhārata*: a percentage figure of around 70%. Chapter 29 of Book 6 (the Book of Bhīṣma), by contrast, is a passage from the *Bhagavadgītā* (chapter 7 of that text). I examined only the first 20 of its 30 four-line *anuṣṭubh* stanzas: repeated phrases are found in 24 lines out of 80, or 30%. A late didactic passage, chapter 6 of Book 13 (the *Anuśāsanaparvan* or Book of Instruction) scores slightly higher, with 39 'formulaic' lines in its first 25 *anuṣṭubhs* — i.e. 39%.

To a large extent, this is merely stating the obvious: that epic formulaic diction is more likely where the sense is 'You should ask their health at my behest' (5.22.38c) than where it is 'Practising yoga and resorting to me' (6.29.1b). There is an additional point to be made, though: a significant number of the repeated phrases found in the didactic passages recur only in other similarly didactic passages. If we take out of account those 'formulae' in the *Anuśāsana* passage which are repeated only in other chapters of *Anuśāsana* and *Śānti*, the percentage drops from 39% to 27%. If we perform a similar exercise with the *Bhagavadgītā* passage, ignoring phrases repeated only elsewhere in the *Gītā* itself or in the later didactic books, the percentage falls from 30% to approximately 19%. The point here is not merely that these figures contrast all the more strikingly with the 70% score of the early *triṣṭubh* chapter; just as important, they demonstrate the existence of sub-vocabularies within the overall lexicon of *Mahābhārata* diction, and thus provide another possible statistical test for marginal passages.

This idea can be tested out by applying it to a sequence of specific phrases (see table). We can calculate percentage figures for the occurrence of a given phrase in each book of the epic, and then compare these figures with those which a completely random scatter would have produced. I have tried this out on a number of fairly common phrases, and have found the results interesting, because this time they are not so predictable. As a 'control' we may consider line-initials *atha vā*, 'or else', which, with 137 occurrences, follows almost exactly the expected spread, not deviating from it by more than 4% in any book. At the opposite extreme comes *itihāsaṃ purātanam* (133 occurrences), in fact part of a two-line phrase *atrāpy udāharantīmam itihāsaṃ purātanam,* 'and in this connexion they tell the following ancient story'. This has around three times the predictable frequency in the late didactic Books 12 and 13 (*Śānti* and *Anuśāsana*), where it introduces numerous improving tales; in the (also late) Book 14 it has over twice the predictable frequency; elsewhere it hardly occurs at all, except for near predictable frequency in Book 5. Clearly passages containing this tag are unlikely to be early, wherever they occur.

Various phrases introducing or terminating quotations have define patterns of distribution. *ity uktaḥ sa/ity uktā sā*, 'being thus addressed, he/she . . .' (60 occurrences) hardly appears at all in the first eleven books (except the mainly late Book 3), and is far below predictable frequency in Book 12, but occurs frequently in Books 13-5 — this being the first sign we have had of a distinction between Books 12 and 13 (*Śānti* and *Anusāna*). *idam vacanam abravīt/abruvan*, 'he/they spoke these words' (102 occurrences), by contrast, is at predictable frequency or higher in narrative books, rare in the two major didactic ones. *tato 'bravīt/'bruvan*, 'then he/they spoke' (75 occurrences) is rare in *Śānti*, noticeably common in two of the battle books (the Books of Bhīṣma and Śalya), and at or near predictable frequency elsewhere. Other cases could be quoted, but these should be sufficient to show that there are patterns in the diction of the *Mahābhārata* which may help shed light on the way in which the text developed into its present shape. Unfortunately, more of Hopkins's 'parisaṃkhyā philosophy' is needed to root them out: we could hardly have guessed in advance that 'being thus addressed' would have so different a distribution from 'he/they spoke these words'.

If, as appears to be the case, diction can serve as a 'new' criterion for establishing a satisfactory textual archaeology for the *Mahābhārata*, it is a criterion which requires just as much delicacy in application as those which Hopkins worked with. Not all early *triṣṭubh* passages, for instance, are highly formulaic: the extent to which formulae are used reflects, among other things, the degree of specificity of the 'given essential ideas' in question. If a journey or an encounter is being described, we may expect it to share features and phrases with other journeys and encounters; but if — to take an actual example — the current topic is the defeated Pāṇḍavas donning antelope-skins in readiness to start their forest-exile (2.68.7f.), the uniqueness of the event will inevitably be reflected in more nearly unique phraseology. Again, joint application of different criteria is necessary: metre shows that the passage is probably early, and content shows why diction seems not to show the same thing. A tiny trowelful of information gleaned from the gigantic *Mahābhārata* mound; all we have to do is repeat the exercise for every one of the work's 100,000 stanzas, and the dig will be complete.

'ONCE UPON A KINGDOM . . .':
BENIN IN THE HEROIC TRADITIONS OF BENDEL STATE, NIGERIA

ISIDORE OKPEWHO
(University of Ibadan)

Introductory

The name Benin has commanded the attention of students of history and culture for so long that any newcomer hardly stands a chance of treading on territory not already well explored. Yet, part of the appeal of Benin studies lies in the fact that various pieces of evidence thrown up in this field invite further examination; part also derives from the fact that every once in a while we can see gaps in the territory which the earlier explorers have ignored but which yield exciting challenges.

One notable gap may be seen in the life and programme of the Scheme for the Study of Benin History and Culture (generally known as the 'Benin Scheme') inaugurated by Professor K.O. Dike in 1956. The Scheme had a checkered life, due largely to a basic conflict of interests between the main disciplines supporting it. Although art historians and archaeologists were co-opted into it at one stage, the business was primarily in the hands of scholars trained essentially in history on the one hand and anthropology on the other. At a period in humanistic scholarship when historians and anthropologists debated hotly among themselves as to who was best qualified to study traditional or (more fashionably) 'primitive' societies, Benin was seen as a test field where it was hoped a fruitful collaboration could be achieved. 'The Scheme for the Study of Benin History and Culture', says Bradbury, the anthropologist and principal researcher of the project, 'is an experiment in interdisciplinary cooperation. Its main aim is to discover how much can be learnt of the history of Benin through whatever sources and methods are available and

613

practical, and so to lay a foundation for further historical studies in the central area of southern Nigeria'.[1]

Obviously it was hoped that this collaboration might result in the publication of a 'cultural history' of Benin. But the collaboration never truly materialised. Bradbury devoted himself to turning out a series of independent studies mostly along anthropological lines, later brought together by Peter Morton-Williams under the title *Benin Studies*[2]; under an earlier programme, he had produced a quite informative monograph of *The Benin Kingdom*[3], again basically along anthropological lines and relying considerably on oral evidence. But the historian of the scheme, Alan Ryder, showed little regard for the oral tradition. In his notable book *Benin and the Europeans*[4], he has relied entirely on evidence derived from European documents on the period and in a few places treats the claims of the oral evidence a little patronizingly. Other independent contributions were made by the art historian Philip Dark[5] and the archaeologist Graham Connah.[6] Bradbury returned to England in 1961, and even by the time of his death in 1969 there was little hope that the interdisciplinary history of Benin would take anything like a practical shape.

Although Bradbury, as a professional ethnographer in the tradition of Malinowski and Radcliffe-Brown, did take account of the oral tradition in his studies, his writing reveals a certain underestimation of its usefulness which is only a shade better than Ryder's attitude. The limitations in Bradbury's use of the oral tradition may be put down to the narrow functionalism which characterized various shades of social studies at this

1 R.E. Bradbury, *Benin Studies*, ed. P. Morton-Williams, London 1973, 17.
2 This work was published posthumously.
3 R.E. Bradbury, *The Benin Kingdom and the Edo-speaking Peoples of South-western Nigeria*, London 1957.
4 A.F.C. Ryder, *Benin and the Europeans, 1485-1897*, London 1969.
5 P.C. Dark, *Benin Art*, London 1960.
6 G. Connah, 'Archaeological Research in Benin City, 1961-64' in *Journal of the Historical Society of Nigeria* 2 (1966) and 'New Light on the Benin City Walls' in *Journal of the Historical Society of Nigeria* 3 (1967).

time. The work of the Benin Scheme in particular was geared towards the specifically pragmatic purposes of historical reconstruction from which aesthetic considerations were largely excluded. This may be seen to some degree in Bradbury's study of the Benin 'cult of the hand', *ikegobo*.[7] He begins his study by telling us, in relation to the bronze shrine used in the cult, that he 'shall not be concerned with the technical or aesthetic qualities of the casting'. He recognizes that the events depicted in the figurine are narrative in intent, but goes on to reveal a fairly narrow, functionalist appreciation of the nature of the narrative:

> By narrative I mean simply that they were intended to convey some information about specific events or particular persons. Provided that they can be properly dated and interpreted such bronzes are potential sources of certain kinds of historical information, but dating and interpretation present many difficulties.

Bradbury also collected and published actual narratives[8]; but in both his editorial and analytical treatment of these tales we can see the functionalist biases once again at play and the aestheticist interest eloquently absent.

This paper is by no means an attempt to resuscitate the Benin Scheme. It leans, rather, in the direction of more recent Beninologists like Sidahome[9] and Ben-Amos[10] who have explored oral narrative traditions in and about Benin from an interest not so much in historical reconstruction as in the re-creative culture of the traditional folk. Specifically, the paper seeks to probe how Benin, in establishing a political and cultural hegemony over a variety of peoples, came to loom so large in their mythic imaginations. I will be dealing mostly with heroic narratives, because it was essentially within the context of war and other such confrontations that these peoples formed their images of Benin.

7 Bradbury, *op. cit.* (1973), 251-70.
8 *Ibid.*, 271-82.
9 J.E. Sidahome, *Stories of the Benin Empire*, London 1964.
10 D. Ben-Amos, *Sweet Words: Storytelling Events in Benin*, Philadelphia 1971, and 'Two Benin Storytellers' in *African Folklore*, ed. R. Dorson, Bloomington 1972.

For this study, I am limiting the area of Benin influence to the political boundaries of present-day Bendel State; although Benin was reputed to have controlled an empire that went far beyond this area especially to the west, it is here that its cultural imprint has survived most vividly. Accordingly, I will be making use of a selection of stories recorded from communities in this area by a number of people: by past students of the English Department at the University of Ibadan who did fieldwork, under my supervision, in their villages in the Etsako, Isoko, Kwale and Ijo areas; by the poet-dramatist John Pepper Clark in his classic edition of *The Ozidi Saga* from the Ijo; by Joseph Sidahome in his collection of Ishan tales under the title *Stories of the Benin Empire*; and by me from my own fieldwork among the Bendel Igbo.[11] But first, let us examine the backgrounds of Benin influence over these peoples.

Historical and Cultural Relations

It is convenient to limit this study to the political boundaries of present-day Bendel State because — despite the changing political fortunes of Nigeria and the accompanying boundary adjustments designed both to reduce the areas of inter-ethnic friction and to evolve a manageable administrative framework for the nation — this area has continued to demonstrate a high degree of cultural uniformity which seems to have compelled successive federal administrations to leave it pretty well intact with its various constituent units. One notable aspect of this uniformity may be seen in language. There are twelve major ethnic units in the state which may be conveniently reclassified into four linguistic groupings: Edo, Igbo, Ijo, and Yoruba (for the Itsekiri), all part of the KWA group of the Niger-Congo language family. Alagoa has pointed out that these four language groups are estimated to have parted ways

11 Of the various colleagues who have helped me in this study, I would particularly like to thank Professors Obaro Ikime of the History Department, Onigu Otite of Sociology and Dr Airen Amayo of English. I alone, however, take the blame for whatever shortcomings there are here.

about 5000 years ago;[12] but in the daily speech of the Bendel peoples the overlaps between them so outweigh the cleavages that 'there can be an argument, at least theoretical, that all the peoples of the Bendel State belong to one social stock'.[13]

Although the fortunes of history and political experience have bred in the various peoples of Bendel State certain sensitivities which must be respected, it may safely be said that for a long time Benin established itself and remained the principal member of that social stock. I am, of course, aware of the implications of such an acknowledgement. This paper will be concerned with how the various peoples of the old Benin empire so accepted the prominence of Benin (called *Ado*, *Idu*, *Aka*, etc. in the folk traditions of the area) that they subordinated their mythic imaginations to the overarching image of the imperial power. But the influence is just as noticeable in contemporary cultural scholarship. Although the Ishan, Etsako, Urhoho, Isoko and other peoples have scarcely been in the habit of calling themselves Edo, scholars have continually imposed that identity on them, presumably as an acknowledgement of the high degree of similarity in social institutions revealed between these peoples and the Bini.

The name itself, Edo, is reported by Egharevba to have originally been that of the slave who helped to save the life of Oba Ewuare in the course of his struggle for the kingship of Benin; on the death of the slave the Oba 'caused the country to be known as Edo after his deified friend'.[14] This may be no more than an eponymous claim, and there is even less justification for the same claim being extended by scholars to peoples who have hardly any illusions about what names to call themselves. In an otherwise stimulating paper, Otite firmly states:

Just as the Bini are 'the Edo of the Benin Kingdom' . . .

12 E.J. Alagoa, 'Ijo Origins and Migrations I' in *Nigeria Magazine* No. 91 (1966), 282.
13 O. Otite, 'Historical Aspects of the Sociology of the Bendel State of Nigeria' in *Journal of the Historical Society of Nigeria* 9 (1977), 44.
14 J.U. Egharevba, *A Short History of Benin*, 3rd edn., Ibadan 1960, 16.

so also the Urhobo are the Edo of their various kingdoms/states and the Ishans the Edo of their various chiefdoms etc. Academically it is currently a non-question to say who is the original or genuine Edo and who is not.[15]

Although I recognize the hegemonic menace to which Otite was reacting, I do not consider it particularly urgent that the name Edo should be enthusiastically embraced by people who have perfectly respectable names by which they have been called for as long as anyone can remember.[16]

Still, the power and the position of old Benin within this large social stock can hardly be denied. Whether or not we accept that the visible kinship derives from the impact and imprint of Benin's imperial might, we can at least recognize various shades of cultural similarity between Benin and other groups in this area both Edo and non-Edo. We cannot, of course, expect perfect uniformity across the entire area of the state. However extensive the contacts may have been between Benin and the other groups, the latter have for a long time had historical and other links with communities beyond the present state boundaries — especially across the River Niger to the east and north-east and the creeks of the delta to the south-east — that have inevitably left some imprints on their cultures. But the cultural kinship with Benin is substantial. Perhaps the most noticeable aspect of this is in the pattern of social and political organization. In most areas of the state, it has been found that the basic unit of government is the village

15 O. Otite, 'Who Are the Edo?' in *Edo Language and Its Orthography*, Benin City 1974, 19.
16 There is some gratuitous benevolence in the following statement by Evinma Ogieiriaixi: 'In all my publications, I have consistently maintained that the term *edo* does not exclude the speech-forms of the people of the so-called "*edo* Group of Languages" who live outside the Benin divisions of Midwestern Nigeria (now Bendel State). Accordingly, *edo* for me is not synonymous with *Idu* (Bini). The latter to me, is a variant of *edo*, just as Esan, Ora, Urhobo, Isoko, etc. are variants of *edo*'. See E. Ogieiriaixi, 'Inconsistencies in the Old *edo* Orthographies' in *Edo Language and Its Orthography*, Benin City 1974.

or town;[17] even though Ikime has argued for the clan as the large context of village institutions and traditions among the Urhobo and Isoko, he himself acknowledges the fundamental autonomy of the village in the day-to-day government of the two related peoples.[18]

The control of affairs within this unit also reveals a considerable kinship between Benin and the other communities. Casting a broad comparative glance on evidence assembled by various scholars working in the area, Otite has recognized a general pattern of dual or plural organization in the sociopolitical life of the respective communities, arising partly from the convergence of various streams of migration and partly from the imposition of an alien-derived rulership system on the indigenous village structure.[19] At the bottom of this governmental structure, on the level of indigenous organization, we find that the male population of each village is divided into three age grades — or four, as in the case of the Urhobo-Isoko.[20] On average, the youngest age-set, covering the ages from ten to about twenty-five are responsible for some of the lesser duties needed to keep the environmental, social and cultural life of the community functioning properly: these include the cleaning of the streets of the village, building and maintenance of the premises of the ruler, the digging of graves, and other basic but demanding tasks. The age-set(s) immediately following this represent the main executive class of the society; not only is the first age-set directly answerable to them, but they are generally charged with conducting some of those duties germane to the survival of the community, like (in the past) waging war on other communities with which they may have had scores to settle (boundary disputes, gross assault by citizens of one community on another, refusal to pay mandatory tributes, and so on). The final age-

---

17 Bradbury, *op. cit.* (1957); N. Thomas, *Anthropological Report on Ibo-speaking Peoples of Nigeria, Part 4: Law and Customs of the Ibo of the Asaba District, S. Nigeria*, New York 1969 (1914), 6-10.

18 O. Ikime, *Niger Delta Rivalry*, London 1969, 14-6 and *The Isoko People: A Historical Survey*, Ibadan 1972, 28-42.

19 Otite, *op. cit.* (1977), 43-53.

20 Ikime, *op. cit.* (1969), 15-6.

grade is made up of the elders — aged roughly from fifty upwards, who not only superintend the duties of the median age-set(s) but constitute the ultimate authority on the key issues of the cultural and religious life of the community.

This all-pervading structure might leave the impression that the village political organization in the area is fundamentally gerontocratic in character. But the structure is further complicated, or perhaps enhanced, by a system of titled organizations into which male citizens are qualified to enrole on attainment of various kinds of achievement (e.g. killing dangerous animals or, in the past, claiming human heads in war) or, as frequently nowadays, on the payment of usually high fees. So much more highly are these titles rated than age in the conferment of status in both the social and political life of the village that a man may suffer some humiliation if he does not take any title. Among the Urhobo, for instance, the final age-set are known as the *ekpako* (sg. *okpako*), and the corresponding titled group into which they could enrol is that of the *edio* or *ehonmwonren* (sg. *odio* and *ohonmwonren*); any *okpako* who did not take the title is excluded from the major deliberations relating to the life of the village and is commonly derided as an *okpako igheghe*, ('ordinary elder', or 'worthless elder'). In Asaba, a man of forty who has taken the *alo* title could interrupt and supersede a non-titled man of fifty in the course of his speech simply by dropping his goatskin fan on the ground and standing up; the ensuing scene may be uncomfortable and a few objections raised, but the older man would normally have no choice but to let the titled younger man take precedence.

At the top of the village socio-political structure is the ruler of the community. There is no strict uniformity across the area of Bendel State in the method of choice of such a ruler. In many communities the office is traditionally awarded to the oldest man within the titled group in which the old men are qualified to enrol — in effect, a unification of the principal merits of age and title in the village status-system. In Benin, of course, the office of *Oba* is hereditary. Despite the periodic inter-family strife which the monarchy is known to have undergone throughout its history — due largely to

contests over primogeniture[21] — all available evidence indicates
that the kingship has stayed within the Oranmiyan-descended
line of rulers beginning with Eweka I. Some communities,
especially among the Ishan where the earlier rulers (*Enigie*)
were appointed by the Oba of Benin from among his sons
and top state functionaries, have also observed the hereditary
system of rulership.

Both in Benin and in the other communities in this area,
the relationship of the titled organization to the monarchy is
essentially conciliar. The inherent potential for confrontation
between the king and his advisers is perhaps obvious. Benin
history shows abundantly how far a monarch could go in
satisfying his whims or his emotions — as in the case of Oba
Ewuakpe who, grieving the death of his mother, 'ordered a
wholesale massacre of his people',[22] or of Oba Ewuare earlier
who, lamenting the death of two of his sons by mutual poison-
ing, 'made a strict law forbidding anyone in the land of either
sex to wash and dress up, or to have carnal intercourse for
three years'.[23] Given this likelihood of abuse of power, the
titled organizations have traditionally acted as a counterweight
to the king's prerogatives, an insurance against having all
power concentrated in the hands of one man;[24] indeed in the
case of Benin several conflicts have been recorded between
the king and his titled advisers centring round the desire of
the latter to maintain a balance of power and privilege.[25] In
more recent times, however, the benefits of the conciliar
relationship of the titled class to the ruler have become equally
obvious especially in the more rural communities. Many of
the traditional titles are nowadays taken by middle-aged sons
of the land who are enlightened by 'modern' education and
in the ways of the wider world, and can therefore usefully
counsel the less exposed king in his efforts to bring the benefits
of technological progress to the people.[26]

21 P. Igbafe, *Benin Under British Administration*, London 1979, 2.
22 Egharevba, *op. cit.*, 38.
23 *Ibid.*, 15.
24 Thomas, *op. cit.*, 7, 40; Ikime, *op. cit.* (1969), 25.
25 Ryder, *op. cit.*, 6-9, 15; Bradbury, *op. cit.* (1973), 57.
26 Far less so, of course, in Benin. Since the late fifteenth century,
    when the Europeans first came to Benin for trade and other busi-

From our survey so far it seems clear that Benin shares with most of the present-day Bendel state certain organizational features; at bottom the village or town as the basis of the socio-political structure, marked by a division of the male population into three or four age-sets for the purpose of distribution of labour: superimposed on this is a monarchical system working in studied counterpoise with a network of titled organizations into which men of achievement and of means could enrol. A final point of similarity must be mentioned, and that is a marked agnatic or patrilineal bias in the kingship system[27] as against the tendency towards matrilineage found among some eastern Ijo.[28]

Considering the known power of Benin in most if not all of the period of history of the other groups available for investigation, there is a real temptation to conclude that Benin had something to do with the cultural uniformity hitherto observed. It is entirely possible, of course, that Benin was preceded by some other power that it finally succeeded in crushing. Egharevba mentions the town of Udo as a power that gave the Benin kingdom a good deal of trouble in the latter's infancy.[29] Otite also cites Amaury Talbot as well as Urhobo oral tradition to suggest that Udo preceded Benin as a power and source of migration.[30] And of the Ishan kings, Bradbury tells us:

> Some *enigie* claim descent from chiefs who ruled before the founding of the present Benin dynasty or before the

ness, the monarchy has led the outreach to the world outside Benin. Egharevba reports (*op. cit.*, 27-8) that Oba Esigie sent one of his priests as ambassador to Portugal; he also quotes a letter by a Portuguese missionary to the King of Portugal (dated 20 October 1516) which reports, among other things, that Esigie 'ordered his son and two of his greatest noblemen . . . to become Christians, and built a Church in Benin. They learnt how to read and did it very well.' The present Oba is a Cambridge graduate and has held some of the topmost administrative offices in the country.

27 Bradbury, *op. cit.* (1957), 15.
28 E.J. Alagoa, *The Small Brave City State*, Madison 1964, 23-4.
29 Egharevba, *op. cit.*, 11.
30 Otite, *op. cit.* (1974), 21.

village or chiefdom in question was incorporated in the Benin state.[31]

Despite all this, a good majority of the oral traditions of communities across the present Bendel state invariably make a place for Benin somewhere in the origins of their peoples and various aspects of their culture. Even though most scholars would agree with Alan Ryder that such claims are 'certainly the product of a hankering after prestige, or simply the adoption of the most likely story, given the canons of traditional historiography',[32] there is no doubt that Benin did make such an impact on their lives as to dominate their historical imagination.

Let us quickly survey a few of these historical traditions. Of the Ishan, Okojie tells us that the name derived from the Benin phrase *esan fua*, meaning 'those who fled', a reference to their ancestors who migrated from Benin following the harsh regimen imposed by 'Oba Ewuare the selfish';[33] Egharevba, however, takes the Ishan origins from Benin further back to the *Ogiso* period.[34] Of the Edo group of peoples, the Ishan are perhaps the most influenced by Benin. For not only were some of the earliest *enigie* (sg. *onogie*) or kings actually appointed by Obas of Benin, primarily as guardians of military and ritual outposts, but even later *enigie* independently installed by their own communities had to seek validation of their offices from Benin; besides, there existed a curious vassal relationship whereby each Ishan chiefdom had as its intermediary in Benin one of the major ministers of state (*Ezomo*, *Uwangue*, etc.) through whom they sent tributes (e.g. livestock, food crops, slaves) to the Oba and hoped to maintain good relations with him.[35] Further north of the Ishan, the relationship with Benin was somewhat looser, to

31 Bradbury, *op. cit.* (1957), 33.
32 Ryder, *op. cit.*, 3.
33 C.G. Okojie, *Ishan Native Laws and Customs*, Lagos 1960, 21; P. Ayewoh, 'Tradition and Originality in Ishan Poetry and Weaving' (Honours Essay, English Department, University of Ibadan), Ibadan 1979, 1.
34 Egharevba, *op. cit.*, 5.
35 Bradbury, *op. cit.* (1957), 75-6.

some extent because Benin had to contend with dynastic and
military powers like Nupe and Igalla bearing down from the
more northerly areas beyond the Niger. Yet Benin continues
to be cited as the original homeland. 'All the Etsako tribes',
for instance, as Bradbury again tells us, 'refer to a period of
oppression and civil war in Benin which led to an exodus of
refugees to the North'.[36]

Of the delta peoples, most of the Urhobo and Isoko clans
claim Benin origin,[37] although there were inputs from Igbo
and Ijo sources to the east and south-east. Here again, the hold
of Benin was not so strong due largely to the distance involved
and the hostile terrain (mangrove forests and swamps) which
must have proved an encumbrance to invasion. For instance,
when the Oba of Benin sent a punitive force against one of
the Orhobo communities, Ewu, and had it burnt down because
the people did not seek sanction from Benin on the installation of their king, the Ewu people quietly rebuilt their town
and would still not seek the required sanction; the Oba's forces
never returned to the place.[38] Otherwise, most of these communities felt compelled, out of regard for the political and
ritual power of Benin, to repair to Benin and seek the Oba's
blessing on the appointment of a king *Ovie* (a variant of the
Bini word *ogie*), receiving royal tokens in return.

---

36 *Ibid.*, 101; J. Edemode, 'The Hero in Uzairue Heroic Narratives'
    (Honours Essay, English Department, University of Ibadan), Ibadan
    1972, 187.
37 Ikime, *op. cit.* (1969), 6 and *op. cit.* (1972), 21.
38 Ikime, *op. cit.* (1969), 14.

Of the 'non-Edo' groups in the Niger Delta, most Ijo clans consider themselves indigenous or autochthonous, tracing their dispersals to only a few 'dispersal centres' within their own area.[39] Still, a few Ijo clans point to roots in Benin. The Mein clan, considered by Alagoa as 'obviously influential over all of the Western Delta',[40] is reported by tradition to have been founded by an ancestor of the same name who left Benin 'because of internal wars' and settled first at Aboh and later at Ogbobiri on the Sagbama-Igbedi Creek. From here some of his descendants dispersed to found other settlements like Kiagbodo under the leader Mgbile, and Akugbene under Kalanama. Once established, each leader sought legitimacy (encouraged no doubt by antecedent Urhobo and Isoko practice) by making contact with the Oba of Benin and receiving political sanction of his title (*pere*) as well as material tokens (bronze insignia, etc.) in return for allegiance to Benin especially in matters of trade.[41] The Tarakiri clan — ancestral home of *The Ozidi Saga* — also looks to Benin origins. Although the

39 E.J. Alagoa, *A History of the Niger Delta*, Ibadan 1972, 187.
40 *Ibid.*, 67.
41 *Ibid.*, 52-3, 63-6. On Mgbile's journey to Benin to be ordained as *pere*, see A.O. Edoh, 'The Epic Narrative Tradition in the Torubiri Epic, Kiagbodo Town, Bendel State' (Honours Essay, English Department, University of Ibadan), Ibadan 1979, 2-3. Further on the search for legitimacy, Edoh says: 'Any Ijaw Pere (king) at that time who did not go on a chieftaincy pilgrimage to Benin City was regarded as inferior and generally nicknamed juju priest . . . Conditions to be satisfied before becoming Pere, my father told me, were difficult. Among them was the producing of a child while in Benin by a Benin woman'.

eponymous(?) Tara or Tarakiriowei is said to be related to
the Kolokuma east of the Sagbama-Igbedi Creek, tradition
has it that their father Ondo 'lived at Benin, but left with his
three sons because the Oba seized private lands and levied
heavy taxes'. Wars with the Mein and other clans caused much
dispersal among the Tarakiri, but Orua remains the principal
settlement of this clan.[42] As with the Urhobo-Isoko neighbours, the physical presence of Benin here was negligible.

By far the largest 'non-Edo' group in Bendel State are the
Igbo communities west of the Niger and embracing the
present-day Oshimili, Aniocha, Ndokwa and Ika Local
Government areas. Here the sources of derivation are varied,
but it is clear that Benin exercised an early influence in the
history of the area. In Asaba, for instance, traditions speak
mainly of the foundation of the town by Nnebisi from Nteje
near Awka east of the Niger. But there were confrontations
with Benin, one of which followed an invitation to Benin by
an autochthonous unit (Achala) contending with Nnebisi's
descendants. Some of the communities in the Aniocha area
also trace their origins to the east, like Ogwashi (= Ogwa-
Nri or Ogwa-Nshi, i.e. meeting-place of the Nri) which looks
back to the Igbo civilization of Nri; others claim autochthony,
like some of the area around Isele-Uku. Here again, Benin
made itself felt early enough. Obior is reported by Egharevba[43]
to have been founded by a rich Biniman named Ovio who fell
out of grace with the reigning Ogiso and was forced to
migrate with his followers. Benin is also said to have attacked
and dispersed some elements of the sister communities of
Onicha-Ugbo, Onicha-Ukwuu, and Onicha-Olona and forced
them to flee across the Niger;[44] in fact, the name Asaba is
said to have derived from a Benin statement *A'i sa ba*, meaning
'we cannot cross', made by the pursuing imperial troops.

Unlike the delta country, much of the terrain in this area
was readily accessible to Benin forces. Benin as usual received
regular missions from kings (*obis*) seeking validation of their
offices and in addition demanded annual tributes. Any

42   Alagoa, *op. cit.* (1972), 71.
43   Egharevba, *op. cit.*, 4.
44   Thomas, *op. cit.*, 3.

community that proved in any way recalcitrant to the imperial will was instantly visited with a punitive expedition. One of the interesting but by no means exceptional narratives I recorded from an informant, Mr Ojiudu Okeze of Igbuzo (Ibusa, near Asaba), tells of a curious annual mission from the Oba of Benin demanding a tooth from an old man of the town for a yearly festival in Benin; the Oba and his forces were ultimately destroyed in a confrontation with the man's t h r e e sons, one of whom was then installed as Oba! 'An Igbuzo man', I asked incredulously, 'crowned Oba of Benin?' 'Yes,' he affirmed. 'Don't you see that section over there' — pointing towards one of the town's quarters — 'that was Benin!'[45]

How did Benin come to loom so large in the narrative imagination of these subject peoples that — as in the case of my narrator Ojiudu — it was fabled to be just around the corner? Ikime, discussing Isoko traditions, has stated that 'it is reasonable to expect that those clans which left Benin as refugees would not be anxious to maintain close links'.[46] It might equally be urged that the memory of Benin origins and contacts among these Bendel communities would hardly have been so dramatic and pervasive had that history been a happy one. It is true that some narratives portray the Oba as just and wise (even Solomonic) in his decisions. But a substantial majority of them recall experiences so harsh that the Oba, as Benin in general, frequently emerges as a menace which must be confronted and overcome.

These stories were no doubt inspired by the physical cruelties and generally harsh demands on life in old Benin. It is easy perhaps to dismiss the evidence cited by European scholars as being cobbled together in order to support the larger imperial designs of the European presence there. For instance, one of Vice-Consul Gallwey's official reports on a visit to Benin in 1892 speaks of such a proliferation of human sacrifices and of corpses 'strewn about in the most public places' that

45 For another story of a Benin punitive expedition to Igbuzo, told me by my old teacher Mr Aniemeka, see Okpewho, *Myth in Africa*, Cambridge 1983, 62-3.
46 Ikime, *op. cit.* (1972), 22.

the city 'might well be called "The City of Skulls" '. However, the real aims of the imperial officer emerge clearly enough:

> The rule appears to be one of Terror, and one can only hope that this Treaty may be the foundation of a new order of things throughout the vast territory ruled by the King of Benin.[47]

The oral traditions of various peoples, however, paint such a vivid picture of terror that one could hardly blame those who fled to save life and limb. According to an Abraka tradition, their founding ancestor 'Avbeka was a son of an Oba of Benin whose birth it had been necessary to keep secret in order to save his life, because the then Oba, his father, had given instructions that all male children born to him should be killed so that there would be no obvious heir to the throne who could become the centre of palace plots.'[48]

Other stories point to an equally capricious urge for blood and vengeance on the Oba's part. In the Agboghidi epic from Uzairue, the Oba is shown to have annihilated the people of the town of Iyolulu and enslaved the remainder of the population, and on another occasion to have demanded the head of the new-born child of his adversary Agboghidi.[49] In the Ukwuani (Kwale) narrative of 'Onodi Onye-mma' the Oba, incensed that he is losing the favour of a young girl to the hero Gbodumeh, orders that her womb be 'tied' to prevent her ever getting pregnant.[50] Despite Sidahome's dedication of his collection of Ishan tales 'to the Oba of Benin'[51] and the frequently favourable portraiture of the

47　See Ryder, *op. cit.*, 347.
48　Ikime, *op. cit.* (1969), 7.
49　J. Edemode, 'The Agboghidi Epic' (Project Essay, English Department, University of Ibadan), Ibadan 1977, 10, 12.
50　F.A. Anene-Boyle, 'The Hero in Ukwuani Heroic Narrative' (Honours Essay, English Department, University of Ibadan), Ibadan 1979, 96.
51　Sidahome may indeed be connected to the Benin monarchy: see Egharevba, *op. cit.*, 84. In his Introduction, Sidahome tells us that his tales 'are Benin stories as told in Ishanland'. It is also interesting to note that unlike some tales I have myself collected from the Bendel Igbo — e.g. at Igbuzo (Ilusa) and Onicha-Ugbo — none of the Ishan tales in Sidahome's collection shows a local hero

Oba in these stories, standard references to cruelty emerge
now and then. For instance, on learning that the hero Elonmo
had intruded into the apartment of one of his wives, the Oba
'ordered Elonmo to be executed without delay that very
evening, and ordered the execution to be one of shame. That
meant that Elonmo was to be hacked to pieces, and the
pieces dumped in a special enclosure near the sacred tree
which stood opposite the city market. There the pieces
would be eaten by dogs, vultures, and night-prowling wild
beasts.'[52] In the story of 'Okodan', we are told that 'the
daily prayer of the Oba's subjects was: 'From the anger of
the Oba, O God, deliver us' (p. 26).

Such terrors are echoed by no less an authority than the
Bini historian Egharevba. Lamenting 'the atrocious hearts of
the people'[53] as responsible for the numerous migrations
from Benin, he documents throughout his *Short History of
Benin* the most vivid incidents of horror that had become a
mark of the socio-political life of the city and empire, from
reckless fratricide (pp. 13, 26, etc.) to the whimsical disregard
for the life of the average citizen on the part of the monarchy
(pp. 21, 38, etc.). And if anyone would still dispute Gallwey's
report, perhaps the following epitaph by Egharevba to the
rule of Oba Ovonramwen, who died in Calabar whither the
British had exiled him, will prove convincing:

> That the character of the Benin people had sunk very low
> was shown by the numberless human sacrifices which they
> offered, and oaths such as *Oba o gha gb-ue* (May the Oba
> kill you) showed that they feared the Oba more than God
> or the gods. The old Benin, with its barbarities and horrors,
> had to fall before the new Benin could rise and take its
> place.[54]

destroying the Oba and ascending the throne of Benin.

52 Sidahome, *op. cit.*, 133.
53 Egharevba, *op. cit.*, 5.
54 Egharevba, *op. cit.*, 60. Egharevba may of course have been influ-
    enced somewhat by the numerous European authorities on Benin
    (Ling, Roth, etc.) that he had consulted in compiling his work. But
    as a member of one of the palace organizations (the House of
    Iwebo) he must have had independent access to considerable
    information.

But perhaps the most dramatic element in the memory of the emigrants, the most solid context within which in their stories they have sought to take their revenge on old Benin, is war. Numerous traditions of origin in this area speak of internal or civil wars in the city state of Benin as the primary cause of migration. Not the least of these were the grim fratricidal contests within the rulership, like the one between the sons of Oba Ozolua or the war over primogeniture between the two eldest sons of Obanosa;[55] there were also struggles between the Oba and his dignitaries, like the fight between Oba Ehengbuda and the Iyase.[56] Having left Benin, however, the emigrants and their hosts did not know much peace from it. For war became firmly established as an instrument of Benin policy, ordered by a hierarchy of generals beginning with the Iyase, followed by the Ezomo and then the Ologbosere. Egharevba tells us that 'it usually happened that a king would declare war about three years after his accession to the throne';[57] the period of utmost war-mongering was perhaps the reign of Oba Ozolua, generally regarded as the most avid devotee of battle.[58] The main purpose of these wars appears to have been the anxiety to secure the widest area of economic control, especially in the face of European commercial activities along the Atlantic seaboard; the Obas must have felt an urgent need to keep alive the transit routes as well as sources of supply of articles within the empire.[59] Thus if any vassal community within the empire did not secure validation from the Oba of the installation of a new ruler (Onogie, Obi, Ovie, etc.) or present yearly tributes to Benin, this was usually taken as an act of apostasy or rebellion and visited with a punitive expedition.

But the military machine soon degenerated to a reckless adventure, to such an extent that the Oba would send soldiers to a community simply 'as a matter of routine. They did not interfere with the local government, but it was customary to entertain them lavishly or face condign punishment like the

---

55 Egharevba, *op. cit.*, 26, 43.
56 Ryder, *op. cit.*, 15.
57 J.U. Egharevba, *Benin Law and Custom*, Port Harcourt 1949, 35.
58 Egharevba, *op. cit.* (1960), 23; Ryder, *op. cit.*, 12.
59 Bradbury, *op. cit.* (1973), 47-51; Ryder, *op. cit.*, 15.

burning down of an entire village'.[60] The recklessness and arrogance may best be seen in the careers of the Ezomo, who became so much the centre-piece of the war organization that they rivalled the Oba in riches if not in power. 'They delighted in warfare', Egharevba tells us about them, 'as a hungry man delights in food and if their history could be written it would make a big volume.'[61] Is it any wonder then that the subject communities of the empire, living constantly in fear of attack from Benin, developed such a psychology about war that in their narrative imagination they have repeatedly sought to exorcise the bogey of Benin? Let us now turn to a sample survey of the content of these heroic narratives.

Mythological Relations

In a sense these stories from outside Benin may have been inspired by stories told within Benin; the emigrants may thus be seen to be striving to recall the archetypes (in some instances at least, notably Ishan) but to have only succeeded in twisting the original imagery and symbolism in the warp of time. Ben-Amos gives us an insight into these archetypes:

> The Benin kingdom was one of the main West African empires and its traditional history is abundant with tales of intra and intertribal warfare, conquests, and victories. ... The Oba is certainly the political, religious, and social centre of Benin culture. Yet, throughout its folklore, art, beliefs, and even its political system, there are undertones of tensions between the rural areas and the court.

Ben-Amos goes on later to cite instances of performances by professional Bini storytellers he has himself recorded, having to do with contests between the Oba and his nobility.[62] The outcome of these contests is of course obvious, as Ben-Amos

60 Ikime, *op. cit.*, (1969), 14.
61 Egharevba, *op. cit.* (1960), 81. On the recklessness and arrogance of the Ezomo, see further Okpewho, '*Ezemu*: A Heroic Narrative from Ubulu-Uno, Bendel State' in *Uwa Ndi Igbo: Journal of Igbo Life and Culture*, No. 1 (1984), 70-85.
62 Ben-Amos, *op. cit.* (1972), 106-7, 110-1.

elaborates elsewhere in a discussion of Benin folklore and ethnomusicology:

> Finally, in the expressive dimension, the heroes of the professional storyteller are rural magicians and other powerful rural people, or suffering characters on the margins of Benin society. The Oba himself looms in the background as a threatening figure whom the hero cannot combat . . .[63]

This may well be true of storytellers within Benin, who could not be expected to put the dreaded Oba in an inferior position. Besides, these storytellers are probably the descendants of those who had faith enough in the nation to remain while others left it. But Ben-Amos' observation is far less true of stories told outside Benin, where the image of the Oba (and the Ogiso of the antecedent dynasty) is frequently a negative one. Even the Ishan, who may be considered the closest to the Bini both geographically and culturally, tell stories in which the will if not the personality of the Oba is successfully combated by local heroes.

Despite his courteous bow to the Benin monarchy in the dedication of his book, Sidahome[64] occasionally portrays heroes who set themselves up in counterpoint to the imperial will. For instance, in the first story titled 'Eneka', the action of the hero Eneka in interrupting the Ezomo of Uzebu's obeisance to the Oba and later flooring the Oba's champion wrestler Igbadaken has a subtle undertone of revolt to it. In the story titled 'Elonmo', the hero infiltrates the Oba's palace and abducts one of the harem (an abomination in Benin), overcomes all the grim obstacles put in his way by the imperial machine, and is triumphantly installed Onogie (local king) in place of the incumbent who had aided the Oba against him. 'When the news . . . was reported to the Oba of Benin as required by custom', we are told in the closing lines, 'the Oba accepted the fact and confirmed the appointment. He realized that the feud between himself and Elonmo was directed by fate, and decided to end it with good grace.' The Ishan, it is to be understood, were also victims of the obsessive

63 Ben-Amos, *op. cit.* (1971), 54.
64 Sidahome, *op. cit.*

militancy of old Benin; so that even when they tell 'Benin stories' in their homeland, they cannot help giving vent to some of their repressed feelings about the sad old days. Heroes like Eneka and Elonmo are a reification of that resentment.

Further away from Benin, however, the revolt is stronger. The stories may hark back nostalgically to Benin backgrounds — as in one Ukwuani (Kwale) tale which starts by recalling 'those times, long before we settled here' and the 'great men — men like the Oba of Idu (Benin), men like Izomo the warrior, Igwara of Idu, Ologbo-selem and Akpe'.[65] But there is a progressive reduction of the image of Benin the further we move from the city, such that we can recognize the following general pattern:

First, the principal figures of the imperial organization — the Oba (or Ogiso) and his generals and major warriors — are set up for humiliation if not eventual destruction or at least treated as symbols of the dangers and evils that must be eliminated for the peace and well-being of the community. Secondly, the land of Benin is conjured as a seat of terror that lurks menacingly around the peripheries of the community, attracting other symbols of evil that cannot easily be identified with any known figures in Benin history and society.

Let us make a quick survey of a few of these figures and symbols inspired by the memory of Benin.

Agboghidi

Ben-Amos tells us that the story of Agboghidi 'is one of the corner-stones' of professional storytelling performances in Benin and is frequently the piece that opens these:

> The plot concerns rural chiefs, their conflicts with each other, collisions between father and son, and struggles to gain the favours of women . . . Agboghidi, the rural chief,

65 Anene-Boyle, *op. cit.*, 10. Characteristically, most of these figures were imperial warlords. The Ezomo and Ologbosere were members of the supreme military command. Igwara (Benin 'Aruanran') was the governor of Udo who fought Oba Esigie fiercely for a long time until he was finally subdued. He survives in heroic lore as a fierce giant, to be discussed later in this study.

fights not only against the other country rulers, but also against the chiefs of Benin City, though not against the Oba himself.[66]

Agboghidi is certainly one of the principal figures in Benin oral tradition, and it is arguably from this random source that Egharevba has composed the 'historical' portrait of such a figure. But in Egharevba, Agboghidi is not so much the name of a specific person as a title, a sort of commander or military governor, first appointed by Oba Ehengbuda in the late sixteenth century and stationed at Ugo 'to keep the warlike people of Iyekorhionmwo from attacking Benin City'.[67] The better-known Agboghidi of Ugo comes up, however, in the reign of Oba Akengbuda in the eighteenth century, where his real name is given as Emokpaogbe. Perhaps we should quote the account in full so as to put the personality of the Agboghidi in proper perspective:

> Soon after the accession of Akengbuda, a prince of the house of Oboro-Uku came to Benin City to be invested as Ogie or Obi (king) of Oboro-Uku. While dancing round the city after his investiture, according to custom, he called on the Izomo at Uzebu, who presented kolanuts to him through his beautiful daughter Adesua who had been betrothed to the Oba. When the Obi caught sight of her he wanted to marry her, but she insulted him, calling him 'Bush Ruler' in derision. The Obi was indignant, and when he got home he used charms to bring Adesua to Oboro-Uku. Against the advice of her servant, she asked leave of her parents to go to Oboro-Uku market to demand a debt owed to her for the sale of goats. When the Obi heard she was there he sent for her, and when she again refused his attentions and insulted him he had her murdered.
>
> When the tidings reached Benin City the Ezomo went to the palace to break the news to the Oba, and to tell him of his intention to make war against Oboro-Uku. The Oba however, said that he would avenge his lover's death himself.

66 Ben-Amos, *op. cit.* (1971), 52.
67 Egharevba, *op. cit.* (1960), 33.

Akengbuda sent troops under the command of Imaran Adiagbon, and another contingent under Emokpaogbe the Agboghidi (Onogie) of Ugo. After severe fighting the town of Oboro-Uku was captured and the head of the Obi was sent by Imaran to the Oba. A dispute then arose between the two generals, each endeavouring to convince the Oba that the victory was due to his special valour, though in fact the credit belonged to Emokpaogbe.

Emokpaogbe was very dissatisfied with the rewards given him by the Oba, and when he returned home to Ugo, acting on the advice of his head slave Arasomwan, and a war drummer, he behaved in such an unbecoming manner that a serious report was made to the Oba against him. The Oba sent for him to come to Benin City, but he refused and had the messengers killed. He then declared war against the Oba, who at first refused to engage in conflict with this general who had distinguished himself in the Oboro-Uku campaign, and offered to pardon him. But Emokpaogbe would not desist and began to harrass the city. The Oba was compelled to despatch three companies of warriors, Obakina, Igbizamete, and Agbobo, dressed in red uniforms, under the command of Ologbose and Imaran. They camped at Ugboko-niro, and fought several battles, and Ugboko-nosote, one of the villages allied to Ugo, and a fierce battle was fought about a mile distant from the town. Emopkaogbe was defeated, but he escaped, and before he could be overtaken he drowned himself in the Jamieson (Igbaghon) river. It is said that Emokpaogbe's wife Emokpolo, who was a sorceress, helped her husband greatly.[68]

Sidahome's Ishan version of this story[69] follows essentially the same lines: as mentioned earlier, it is entirely possible that it was from the same general pool of performances — spanning the Benin-Ishan region — that Egharevba drew for his historical reconstruction. In Sidahome, however, we get all those details that the empiricist Egharevba must have felt

68 *Ibid.*, 41-2.
69 Sidahome, *op. cit.*, 45-72.

inclined to eliminate, especially because they were of little interest to his monarchically centred history of Benin.

In Sidahome, then, the following details about Agboghidi — reflecting the general pattern of the folk hero's life — emerge. He is born to the Onogie (king) of Ugo and his wife who, following a succession of daughters, are told they will have a son (Emokpaogbe) who will cause great trouble but will be a great warrior. He emerges from his mother's womb with a complete set of teeth and in six months is a fully-grown, formidable but repulsively ugly adult. In an effort to get rid of him, his father the king charms him with an illness which defies all remedy. In the end his mother takes him to 'Obolo', whose famed magician-king (Ogiobolo) not only cures Emokpaogbe but makes him impervious to all dangers and powers (including those of Ogiobolo himself) as well as weapons; they also enjoin an eternal bond of loyalty on each other. On Emokpaogbe's return, his father makes further plans to kill him, but is killed instead, and Emokpaogbe succeeds him with the name Agboghidi of Ugo.

Fate brings Agboghidi into marriage with the extraordinarily beautiful lady, Emokpolo, born on the same day as him and likewise born with a complete set of teeth. He also acquires a slave from Obolo who plays enchanting music that drives Agboghidi into wild acts of heroism. He gets into all kinds of amorous adventures, acquiring a new wife Udin and falling into a near-fatal love affair with a river-goddess Igbaghon. The rest of Aghoghidi's career echoes essentially Egharevba's account of the confrontation between Benin and Oboro-Uku (Obolo) and Agboghidi's role in it, right down to the treachery of Ima of Ogbelaka (Egharevba's Imaran) and the war between Agboghidi and the forces of the Oba. There are a few interesting twists in Sidahome's version, though. While Egharevba tells us that the Oba sent 'three companies of warriors . . . dressed in red uniforms' against Agboghidi, Sidahome has it that this is an army of little children dressed in r e d, a combination found to be taboo to Aghoghidi. He continues to flee from this army until in the end he turns into a rope 'although it is also believed by many that Agboghidi drowned himself'. His wife Emokpolo, appropriated by the Oba, later joins Agboghidi in the spirit world, where he continues to threaten that he will destroy the world. The story ends on an aetiological note:

> This explains the great thunderstorms. The lightning flashes are the brandishing of Agboghidi's great sword, Ghoma-Gbesin. The thunder is Agboghidi's showing his rage to the world. The dull echoing which follows the thunder is, of course, his dear wife Emokpolo, soothing and calming him down in order to protect the world she loved.

On October 12, 1980, I recorded the story of the war between Benin and Ubuku-Uku from my distinguished informant, Mr Charles Simayi of Ubulu-Uno.[70] Although the figure Agboghidi does not feature at all in this story,[71] the events contained are clearly a variation on those in Egharevba and Sidahome. Whereas in both versions the Ubulu king goes to Benin to secure validation of his title by the Oba, in Mr Simayi's version the leader Ezemu, an expert medicine-man, goes to Benin in response to a general invitation to traditional doctors across the empire to save an incumbent Oba from dying soon after coronation, like successive Obas before him. Having cured the Oba, Ezemu is rewarded with the Oba's first daughter as wife, and her little brother as page. On his way from Benin, he is accosted by the Ezomo who would not let a provincial ruler take a Benin princess away as wife; Ezemu demurs, but on reaching Ubulu draws the princess to him by force of magic. In the ensuing war between Benin and Ubulu, the imperial forces suffer severe losses, losing one contingent after another to a tiny band of seven hunters led by Ezemu! In the end Benin is forced to sue for peace; as a cardinal part of the settlement, a town (Abudu) halfway between Benin and Ubulu is marked as the boundary between the two peoples, with a firm injunction that the Bini should never again kill the Ubulu.

70 Okpewho, *op. cit.* (1984).
71 I have not encountered the Agboghidi figure so far in the oral traditions of the Bendel Igbo. But I understand that the name appears in the traditional titles of the Obi of Onitsha (eastern Igbo), Ofala Okagbue I.

Besides the disappearance of the Agboghidi figure in this
version, there is a significant reduction in the image of Benin:
an imperial power is brought to its knees by a small provincial
community.[72] Particularly remarkable is the treatment of the
Oba of Benin's image. In Egharevba he is shown as being
master of his own decisions and actions. In Sidahome the
'peace-loving Oba' continually advises patience against his
people's urgent pleas for war with the Obolo. But in the Ubulu
version, the Oba is cast alternately as bloodthirsty (he orders
the execution of doctor after doctor who fails the test that
will qualify him to treat the sick Oba) and lacking in firmness
(he does allow himself to be driven into war with Ubulu,
earning the reproof of his soothsayer in the end); in fact, it is
the Oba himself that timorously leads the Bini peace party to
meet Ezemu and his men at Abudu!

The Aghboghidi figure re-emerges in an epic from the
'Edo-speaking' Etsako;[73] here again, in an area sufficiently
far from the seat of the empire, the image of Benin and particularly of the Oba suffers a considerable reduction. In this
story, Agboghidi is used essentially as a symbol of the revolt
of a provincial people against the imperious, high-handed
government of the Oba of Benin. Briefly, the Bini annihilate
the town of Iyolulu and enslave the remainder of the population; the young hero Agboghidi is received into the Oba's
household. But he suffers one humiliation after another (e.g.
being cheated of the game he has killed) purely on the grounds
that he is an outsider, not one of the Oba's children. He continually revolts against this degradation, until one day someone
confronts him in a public gathering with the real facts of his
background — i.e. what happened to his community. This is
the final blow. Agboghidi makes away with a daughter of the
Oba, against the latter's protests, and war is effectively
declared. Agboghidi returns to his annihilated village Iyolulu,
where he is eagerly received by a sorceress Oledo who provides
him with magical aid as well as regular warnings of attack from

72 Ubulu seems to command a certain reputation in the folk traditions
     of this area: an Ukwuani (Kwale) narrative also tells how Benin was
     forced to a compromise with her. See Anene-Boyle, *op. cit.*, 85-9.
73 See Edemode, *op. cit.*

Benin. The Oba sends guards upon guards, and army after army, but Aghboghidi exterminates them one after the other until, as we are told, Benin is 'empty of men . . . There are only women in Edo now' (Edemode, 'The Agboghidi Epic', 24). The Oba tries other schemes, working in consultation now with sorcerers who devise magical antidotes to Agboghidi's mystical power. But the war drags on for some more years. In the end the sorcerers discover Agboghidi's real taboo: on one day all the women left in Benin suddenly become 'pregnant without any sexual intercourse'; on the last day of the ninth month they all give birth to male children, who begin to walk and talk that same day; they are then equipped with red uniforms and sent to destroy Agboghidi. Unable to ward off this last danger, Agboghidi and Oledo decide to take their lives, drowning themselves and the children in the sea.

This Etsako story of Agboghidi reveals its Benin connections in a few places. Apart from the details of red-uniformed warriors and the hero's death by drowning (along with a sorceress) the injustices visited on Agboghidi in the king's household may be seen as a variant on the Benin detail of Agboghidi being cheated of his achievement in the Oboro-Uku war. Besides, Benin and Iyolulu are shown to be so near to each other that the Oba and Agboghidi can see one another from their respective houses (Edemode, *op. cit.*, 12) – an effort, perhaps, to echo the nearness of Benin and Ugo in the 'original' story. However, the revolt against Benin in this provincial tale is just as evident. The Oba is portrayed as powerless and helpless before the humiliating career of the hero; a song which begins 'I threaten, I threaten the king' (*ibid.*, 28) underlines the anti-monarchical spirit of the tale; another song urges the hero 'Agboghidi kill Edo!' (*ibid.*, 24) for, after all, 'It's not brutal, It's no waste/That men killed one another in Edo' (*ibid.*, 31); and all through the story the Oba's blood-lust is emphasized by his constantly calling for the head of adult and child alike.

The figure Agboghidi also appears in the Ijo epic entitled *The Ozidi Saga*, edited and translated by the poet-playwright John Pepper Clark. In Bendel State, the Ijo occupy perhaps the furthest reaches of the old Benin empire; and though, as seen above, some of the clans invoke Benin roots, this is one of those areas where the political and cultural control of Benin could be said to be weakest. It is therefore no surprise that the principal figures of Edo folklore do not enjoy quite the same prominence in the traditions of this non-Edo people.

To be sure, Benin continues to be invoked as a large mythical setting for Ijo stories. In his Introduction to *The Ozidi Saga*, Clark makes the following observation on the attitude of the various narrators he has recorded to the setting of the story:

> In the Okabou text the stress is on Orua, or Oruabou, that is, the city seen as a state set in some remote time and place, although within the present boundaries of Tarakiri Clan. Both Afoluwa and Erivini make no such insistence on the Ijo setting of the story, being content to use Ado, the other name for Benin City, the conventional setting of Ijo tales and fables. This, of course, is no evidence that these stories derive from Benin or that the city is the original home of those who own them. Rather, Ado, to the Ijo imagination, is the embodiment of all that is distant and mysterious, the empire of improbable happenings that together with the world of spirits help to explain the events of their own lives. Okabou in fact was always self-conscious when, prodded on by Madam Yabuku of Inekorogha, leader of the recorded session at Ibadan, he toed the clearly patriotic line of preferring the local name to the foreign one of Ado. Beyond this, he retains all other names that are clearly non-Ijo, principal ones like Ozidi, Oreame, Orea, Temugedege, and Ogueren which in all likelihood are Benin, while Odogu is obviously Ibo.[74]

74 J.P. Clark, ed., *The Ozidi Saga: From the Ijo of Okabou Ojobolo*, Ibadan 1977, xvii. The Benin derivation of Ozidi is dubious. A variant of the name is Azudu: see Clark, 'The Azudu Saga' in *African Notes* I (1963), 8-9. There is a Bini word, *Ozudu*, meaning something like 'stout-hearted', an apt epithet for a hero. Beyond this I have not been able to connect the name Ozidi with any Benin sources. On the problem of the Benin setting of *The Ozidi Saga*, see further Okpewho, 'The Oral Performer and His Audience: A Case Study of *The Ozidi Saga*' in *The Oral Performance in Africa*, ed. I. Okpewho (forthcoming).

This faintness of the image of Benin is no doubt responsible both for the loss of the standard elements in the Agboghidi canon — dying in a body of water, red-uniformed soldiers, etc. — and indeed for the considerably subordinate position which this character occupies in the Ozidi story. For despite its Benin echoes, this story is thoroughly Ijo in both its ecology and its cultural background, and the various characters in it, whatever their derivations, are subordinated to the superior image which the Ijo oral tradition has created for the local hero Ozidi. Thus, although Agboghidi is one of the few 'human' opponents of the hero and is indeed the first assigned to confront him in the series of battles that Ozidi fights, it takes Ozidi the least time of all to dispose of him (Clark, *op. cit.*, 65-70). In this story, then, we have one of the clearest examples of what happens to images and symbols from Benin (a) in an area where Benin political and cultural hemegomy was not so strong, and (b) when the local tradition asserts itself.

Aruanran

A somewhat similar pattern may be seen in the fortunes of the character Aruanran. There is a much larger fabulary shroud covering this figure, it seems, and perhaps for this reason he gets rather short shrift in the empiricist programme of Egharevba. There are basically four references to him in the *Short History*.[75] First, in the war-mongering reign of Oba Ozolua, 'Okhumwu was conquered by Prince Aruanran one of the Oba's sons, who brought a large number of captives to Benin City.' Next, we are told that he was one of the first three sons of Ozolua, the others being Osawe and Ogidogbo; in an effort to find out who was the strongest of the three they were made to pole-vault over a pond in the palace quarter, and while Aruanran and Osawe succeeded, Ogidogbo fell down and was crippled, thus losing the contest for the succession to the obaship. The third reference to Aruanran concerns the contest for the throne between Aruanran and Osawe on the issue of primogeniture. Though he was born first, Aruanran's birth was announced later than Osawe's, and a struggle

75 Egharevba, *op. cit.* (1960), 24, 25-6.

later ensued during which Aruanran 'went to an old woman
at Uroho village who trained him in the art of black magic,
which he used after the death of his father in his struggle
with Osawe.' The final reference deals with Aruanran's fratricidal war with Osawe, now crowned Oba Esigie. According
to Egharevba, Esigie

> ... was greatly worried by his brother Aruanran, chief
> of Udo, a man of giant stature. At last a punitive expedition
> was sent against Udo. Many battles were fought, some-
> times one side being victorious and sometimes the other.
> The fiercest went by the name of *Okuo-Ukpoba* (Battle
> of Blood) in which Oni-oni, the only son of Aruanran,
> was killed. To avoid being taken prisoner, Aruanran
> drowned himself in the lake, Odighi n'Udo.

As we can see, the only concessions Egharevba makes to
the folk imagination in these references are to Aruanran being
'a man of giant stature' and to his being equipped with magical
skill. In Ben-Amos, however, we get a little more insight into
his image in the Benin oral tradition. Ben-Amos sees him as
one of the 'folk anti-heroes, tragic figures who were part of
the king's family but failed to live up to their royal status . . .
a foolhardy giant' who was cheated out of his inheritance and
ended his life by drowning in a lake.[76] More pertinently,
Ben-Amos tells us that in these Bini stories of Aruanran he is
represented as 'a giant who had twenty toes and twenty
fingers, and one who could never tell whether he was coming
or going'.[77]

There is a rather full treatment of the Aruanran story in
Sidahome's anthology of 'Benin stories as told in Ishanland'.[78]
Again as with the Aghoghidi story, there are striking similarities
in detail between Sidahome and Egharevba (although the
latter is a much abbreviated and selective statement); but there
are also striking departures and elaborations. We first meet
Arualan (as he is called in Sidahome) in his proto-life as the
troublesome and hateful spirit Ekatakpi. The Oba of Benin,

76 Ben-Amos, *op. cit.* (1972), 109.
77 Ben-Amos, *op. cit.* (1971), 44.
78 Sidahome, *op. cit.*, 164-96.

Ozolua, and his favourite queen Ohomi are worried about their childlessness and the king sends to the spirit world for a solution; Ekatakpi, after considerable solicitude and violating all injunctions laid on him by the king of the spirit world, is reincarnated in Benin as the child of Ohomi (and named Idubo) but he is born at the same time as another child Esigie (to queen Idia) whose birth is announced first. Robbed of his primogeniture, and hated by the Oba in his early childhood, he withdraws to live with the sorceress queen of Uroho, Iyenuroho, better known as Iyenugholo. Under her this extraordinary child with ten digits on each limb and a mighty head, grows by leaps and bounds to be an overtowering giant. The sorceress renames him Arualan (giant), and equips him with all manner of magical supports to ensure total invincibility, including the power to cause her own destruction. Arualan loses no time in putting his powers to the test: he causes Iyenugholo to be turned into a bee and disappear forever.

Arualan (in his proto-self Ekatakpi) came into the world destined to become a great warrior. His first military feat after leaving Iyenugholo's palace is his victory over Esohen, king of the remote town Amagba; Arualan destroys the town and brings the head of the intractable Esohen to Oba Ozolua, thus winning the love and attachment of a father who once disowned him. Reinstated with pomp and honour in Benin, Arualan goes on to perform his most endearing feat. The town of Okhumu is ruled by a powerful king (who has continually harrassed Benin) and defended by the giant Egbamarhuan who happens to have been fortified with magic by the same Iyenugholo who made Arualan invincible. The war between the Benin and Okhumu forces proves a long and fierce one: but Arualan is able to summon his most infallible tools of sorcery to destroy the enemy and lead a triumphant army and numerous hostages back to Benin.

With the decline in age and wisdom of Oba Ozolua a confrontation between the princes Arualan and Esigie becomes inevitable. By a slip of the tongue and contrary to his own eager intent, Ozolua irrevocably names Arualan the king of Udo (instead of Edo); all attempts by the Oba to rectify the situation fail, and Esigie is finally crowned Oba of Benin on

Ozolua's death. In the end the two brothers are drawn into a
war, which Arualan loses by a tragic error. He orders that his
entire possessions be thrown into the lake Odighi if he does
not return triumphantly from his march against Benin. Meanwhile the Benin citizens, fully aware they cannot withstand
Arualan, withdraw from the city to a man. Arualan returns to
Udo disappointed but hoping to strike again at Benin some
day; however, his subjects at Udo, seeing their king returning
without the usual sounds of triumph, dump all his possessions
into the lake in obedience to his orders. This is the final
despair; Arualan jumps into the lake and is lost for ever. But
he is deified and the point of disappearance 'is regarded as
sacred ground to this day'.

The native Benin versions of the Aruanran story, as represented at least by Egharevba and Ben-Amos, are not particularly positive. Egharevba, a palace historian, is patronising
as ever. Ben-Amos is even less charitable in his treatment of
the giant. Grouping him with the eighteenth-century Oba
Ewuakpe, Ben-Amos says:

> Both were deviant persons within the court, failures
> within a hierarchical society, rejected by the system
> because of their own misdoings.[79]

Both Egharevba and Ben-Amos also talk about Aruanran as
suffering defeat, with Egharevba specifically suggesting
military defeat in which Aruanran took his own life 'to avoid
being taken prisoner'.[80] The picture is, however, not quite so
bleak in Sidahome's Ishan portrait of the hero. Although in
his proto-life in the spirit world he demonstrates considerable
recalcitrance and destructiveness, in the human world he shows
himself to be a hero very much in control of his stupendous
urge for martial action. This is most visibly demonstrated in
his treatment of the *agent-provocateurs* from Okhumu: he
repeatedly sends them back with a warning to their king to
desist from testing the wrath of Benin. On the eve of the
Okhumu war, we are told, Oba Ozolua

---

79 Ben-Amos, *op. cit.* (1971), 44.
80 Egharevba, *op. cit.* (1960), 26.

prayed that Arualan might strike his enemies
hard, but that his enemies should be powerless
to strike him.

Arualan objected to this last prayer:

'This is to be a battle between men, and
it should not be one-sided,' he said.
'Pray that my enemies should be able to
strike me, but that I shall emerge victorious.'[81]

And far from suffering any military defeat, he comes to
grief only as the victim of a tragic flaw in his massive self-
confidence. On the whole, therefore, we could safely consider
Sidahome's Ishan portrait of the hero Aruanran as sympathetic. He emerges as a superior factor in the Benin political
situation; in the Ishan oral tradition his image has been utilized
for the legitimization of revolt against an overbearing imperial
machine.

Much further away from Benin City, in the delta regions
to the South, the image of Aruanran undergoes essentially
two kinds of transformation. First, he is portrayed as a giant
constantly putting his restless energy at the service of the
oppressed. In one of the Ukwuani narratives collected by
Anene-Boyle, this giant of twenty toes defends his father, the
Oba of Idu (Benin), against the men of Atu who have come
on the last of the quinquennial missions to pluck the tooth of
the Oba for their festival; Igwara (as Aruanran is called among
the Ukwuani) kills them all to a man and puts an end to the
obnoxious ritual.[82] In another story, Igwara defends his
brother's wife, Oyibo, against the seducer Okalimadu and kills
the latter in a grim fight, though he goes on later to turn
Oyibo into an ant-hill apparently because he sees her (an
exceptional beauty) as a source of more troubles in the future
(*op. cit.*, 90-3). Although the giant's old grudge against Benin
survives in so far as he sometimes turns around, unprovoked, to
slaughter fellow-citizens of Idu (*ibid.*, 75), in these Ukwuani
stories the emphasis in the portraiture of Igwara seems to be

81   Sidahome, *op. cit.* 186.
82   Anene-Boyle, *op. cit.*, 75 ff.

on his using his stupendous energies for the destruction of those who make themselves into a menace to his people — though he is often more a menace himself and a dangerous individualist.

A second transformation of the Aruanran image puts him in very much the same position in which we saw Agboghidi — in the environment of Ijo folklore, as far away from the seat of the old Benin empire as we could get in this area. Once more, there are clear echoes of the Benin origins of the figure Ogueren or Oguaran, as he is called in *The Ozidi Saga*.[83] He is a giant of unimaginable size, a man 'of twenty hands, twenty feet', uprooting silk cotton and iroko trees as he tramples along (*op. cit.*, 102).[84] As with Agboghidi, however, this legendary figure from Benin is simply a victim of the urge of a local tradition to assert its own heroes; so that, although he gives Ozidi a great deal more trouble than Agboghidi does, Ogueren crashes to his ruin in the face of Ozidi's irrepressible onslaught.

Other Images

Our survey of the major figures in the heroic narratives of communities once dominated by Benin shows that to a large extent these narratives — in so far, that is, as Benin is their point of reference — are used for validating the resentment which the communities felt against that domination.

It will have been observed that, despite their demonstrably rebellious spirit, these narratives featuring the major heroic figures of the Benin oral tradition do make concessions sometimes to Benin, often by way of betraying a certain attachment to the homeland. This is perhaps a manifestation of the nostalgia felt by those emigrants who took the 'Benin' stories to their new places of abode; Bowra made useful observations (albeit in a different context) on this romantic attachment on the part of a people which 'leaves home for some distant land

83 Clark ed., *op. cit.* (1977), 102-26.
84 Cf. Sidahome, *op. cit.*, 178. In his play *Ozidi* (London 1966), Clark pushes the image of the giant a little further by attributing the huge moat around the old city of Benin to Ogueren's simply walking round the city walls (p. 82).

and keeps touch with its past by glorifying it in legends'.[85] Hence we find Igwara in Ukwuani narratives principally defending his father the Oba of Benin and its people. An Isoko narrative entitled 'The story of Odugo and his wife Ibakpolo', which is clearly a variant of the Agboghidi story, also tells of the hero Odugo fighting in defence of the Oba but losing all restraint, until he is brought to grief by an army of red-uniformed children.[86] However, even in such stories it is clear that, however deep the attachment felt for the homeland, there is usually a subtle comment against those who made life impossible whether in that homeland or in the emigrants' new home: usually, the Oba and his generals.

Of the various other images from Old Benin that have received negative treatment in the heroic traditions of subject communities, a particularly interesting one is that of the tooth-plucking Oba, that is, an Oba who every year demands one tooth from the mouth of a prominent man (leader) of a subject community for an annual festival. There is a strange twist to this image among the Ukwuani (Kwale) in 'The Narrative of Oba Nkpeze',[87] for here the Oba is the Oba of Benin who every year must surrender a tooth to envoys from the town Atu for an annual festival, until Igwara (Aruanran) puts an end to the obnoxious order. In other traditions, however, the finger is pointed squarely against Benin. Akegwure discusses one such tale from the Isoko:

> The Omofobhon epic treats the theme of an Oba who would send a band of warriors to 'pluck' the tooth of a particular man to him annually. This tooth he would offer to his personal god as festival offering. This continued for many years until the just God gave this man a hero child Omofobhon who avenged his father's shame by confronting and defeating each successive band of warriors and heroes sent against him by the Oba.[88]

85 C.M. Bowra, *Homer*, London 1972, 80.
86 J.W. Welch, 'The Isoko Clans of the Niger Delta' (Ph.D. Thesis, University of Cambridge), Cambridge 1935, 409-10.
87 Anene-Boyle, *op. cit.*, 75-84.
88. P.O. Akegwure, 'The Hero in Isoko Heroic Narratives' (Honours Essay, English Department, University of Ibadan), Ibadan 1978, 4.

On 13 October, 1980, I collected a very similar story from Mr Ojiudu Okeze at Ibusa; in this case, the ensuing war culminates in the killing of the Oba and the enthronement of the youngest son of the old man (who had annually lost a tooth) as the new Oba of Benin. In the Isoko and Ibusa versions of the tooth-plucking story we have, it would seem, a symbolization of the tributes which Benin exacted annually from these subject communities and the spirit of revolt whereby they sought to throw off for ever the yoke of subordination which had been hanging round their necks.

History and Fantasy

The variety of evidence so far examined seems to indicate that in a good many cases the oral traditions of a subject community — insofar as they recall Benin whether directly or indirectly — have been employed to highlight one aspect or other of their painful past within the empire. In these tales, Benin may not always be directly identified as a culprit and may indeed be treated with sympathy; but even in such cases a careful analysis will show that the accusing finger is being pointed at Benin albeit obliquely, and that the story only holds up for castigation an evil, set well within the time when Benin had a dominant influence over the life of the community. For instance, in the Ukwuani 'Narrative of Oba Mkpeze',[89] it seems clear that we have an inversion — motivated whether by politics or by art, we cannot really tell — of the system whereby Benin annually imposed tributes that hurt her subjects right down to their eye-teeth. Or perhaps the inversion was psychologically motivated: the Ukwuani would like to see Benin visited, even for a limited time, with the sort of cruelties it practised on other communities!

Did the Ukwuani borrow that tale from their neighbours (e.g. the Isoko) or their ethnic kin (e.g. the Igbuzo) before making that inversion? This question touches the very heart of the limitations in our present study of the history and

89 Anene-Boyle, *op. cit.*, 75-84.

culture of this area. In the earlier part of this paper I have done no more than corroborate both oral and documentary evidence in establishing the political dominance of Benin over a spread of communities. I started by identifying, again following both forms of evidence, a wide variety of cultural similarities between Benin and these communities. But until we can establish by other methods 'which peoples are older than which or who drove whom in what direction',[90] it would be difficult, if not pointless, to press any diffusionist claims on these narrative traditions.

In fact, we have to be careful what steps we take in constructing our empiricist histories, and the perspectives from which we assemble our information. I suspect that part of the trouble with the Benin Scheme derived from the fact that the labours of that project were centred to a disproportionate degree on Benin, with the aid no doubt of influential figures like Egharevba. However, a comparison of the evidence of Evharevba and any of the traditions from outside Benin on any historical event — like the Benin-Ubulu war — soon reveals that one man's history is another man's fantasy. In his dynastic history of Benin, Egharevba seems hardly to have left any room for military failure on the part of any of the Obas: there is, however, reason enough to believe that Ehengbuda, who, according to Egharevba,[91] died in a boat accident, may have in fact suffered a military defeat (given the war-mongering fever of that era) and died in the process.

So, too, with the evidence from the oral traditions of the subject communities: none of them would be expected to tell stories which put them in an inferior position to Benin even though we know that, in terms of organisation at least, Benin at that time stood a better chance of winning any military confrontation. And since, given the painful memory of their experiences with Benin, very few of them had reason to love it, the more fantastic the claims they make, the happier they will be to have surmounted, psychologically at least,

90 Alagoa, *op. cit.* (1966), 282.
91 Egharevba, *op. cit.* (1960), 33.

those 'inaccessible barriers' — to borrow Todorov's phrase[92]
— that Benin by its very might and position constituted to
their self-realisation as well as peace. Benin is evoked as a
backdrop even in animal tales that have no human participants,[93] and perhaps there is no greater proof than this of her
pervasive influence. But it is mostly in the heroic narratives,
set against the background of war and other tests of physical
and supernatural strength, that the subject communities
have steadily sought to turn the tables against a bogey that
loomed so large in their lives.

92 T. Todorov, *The Fantastic: A Structural Approach to a Literary
    Genre*, trans. R. Howard, Ithaca 1975, 158. I must point out, how-
    ever, that while I applaud the recognition by writers like Todorov
    and Rabkin of the role of the f a n t a s t i c in all creative literature
    and especially the narrative, I have little sympathy for the sort
    of abstract generic taxonomy that they indulge. Their analyses
    seem to rest entirely on a consideration of the reader of printed
    narratives (including folktales) as well as the characters of the nar-
    rative drama. They cite Propp in their discussion of folktales, and
    consequently suffer from the basic failure of Proppian taxonomy,
    which is a lack of consideration of the sociological basis of the tales.
    For instance, for the Ubulu people to represent themselves as having
    trounced Benin thoroughly and brought her to her knees may be
    seen as a legitimate manipulation of historical truth for the psycho-
    logical comfort of the community; but would anyone either in
    Benin or in Ubulu view the fantastic details of the Ubulu story as
    'a direct reversal of ground rules' (E. Rabkin, *The Fantastic in
    Literature*, Princeton 1976, 14) operating in oral culture, in which
    notions of magic and the supernatural permeate daily life and
    thought as deeply as the tales?
93 See Okpewho, *op. cit.* (1983), 66 and Ben-Amos, *op. cit.* (1971), 15.